Alice Spatz
≠
Paul Spatz

ACTIVE GAMES
and CONTESTS

BY

BERNARD S. MASON, Ph.D.

Author of "*Camping and Education*"
Co-Author of "*The Theory of Play*," "*Social Games for Recreation*"
Editor, "*The Camping Magazine*"

AND

ELMER D. MITCHELL, Ph.D.

Director, Department of Intramural Sports, University of Michigan
Author of "*Intramural Sports*"
Co-Author of "*The Theory of Play*," "*Social Games for Recreation*"

A·S·B&Cº

NEW YORK
A. S. BARNES AND COMPANY

PREFACE

IN view of the rapidly increasing amount of printed material on both
the theoretical and practical aspects of play and recreation, any new
book on the subject must present an original approach. This need has
been uppermost in the minds of the authors in the preparation of this
volume. Realizing the fact that the play leader of today is faced with
new and urgent problems, they have planned to acquaint the reader
with practically all play activities of an active nature so that a selection
can be made to fit almost any occasion that might arise. The completeness
and comprehensiveness of the book, presenting as it does under one cover
the entire scope of active play, is, it is hoped, one of its contributions. In
accomplishing this end, the traditional and well-known forms of play
are presented together with newer, original, and unique approaches. The
book is planned to be of interest to play leaders of all types—physical edu-
cators, playground leaders, camp leaders, social workers, and club leaders
in boys' and girls' work, and so forth.

The book also presents an original classification of games and contests.
This systematic presentation will aid in its use as a text.

The reader should bear in mind that *Active Games and Contests* is a
companion volume to *The Theory of Play* and supplements *Social Games
for Recreation*. It presents only the more active types of play, but used in
conjunction with *Social Games for Recreation,* the games and contests for
all types of play occasions will be available.

The one phase of the physical type of activity that has not been covered
in this new book is the field of rhythmic activities. This is precisely the
field where books abound. Here no duplication would be justified. Furthermore, to do justice to this field would necessitate a series of books in
themselves. For similar reasons the field of gymnastic exercises has not
been treated.

Throughout history, games have grown up rather informally as a tradi-
tion and have had no particular inventor. Recently, however, the un-
precedented growth of physical education, camping, club, and leisure-time
programs, together with the appearance of professional workers and special-
ists in these fields, has resulted in the deliberate invention of a host of new
games and variations. This book, therefore, has been able to utilize a large
amount of newly conceived material.

Although play activities of a related nature have been grouped together,
the idea of progression has been preserved. This is particularly true in the
case of the highly specialized team games where minor games of a less
complicated nature provide the lead-up opportunities for acquainting the

player with the game in its highest form of development. The emphasis in the case of the highly organized sports like football, basketball, tennis, hockey, and so forth, has not been upon the technical aspects of individual skill or team play, but rather upon presenting an understanding of the object of the game and of its rules.

The games and contests have been classified for age use in a general rather than a specific manner. Inasmuch as age likings for play activities shade off rather gradually from one year to the next instead of showing a sharp demarcation and dropping of interest, activities cannot be classified as desirable for one particular grade in school or year of the individual's life. For this reason a general age period has been suggested during which each activity may be used. If a game has outstanding carry-over interest, several age periods have been listed, i.e., junior high school, senior high school, maturity. Furthermore, it is difficult to draw any clear demarcation between activities suitable for boys and girls. As a rule, however, the leader of groups of either sex will have no difficulty in determining whether any particular activity described will be suitable for the groups in question.

Wherever possible credit has been given, but this on the whole has been difficult. The older games have grown up by custom and no one individual can be connected with their origin. Frequently, the authors have accredited a game to some source only to find later upon studying older books, the same activity already described. Wherever similar games have been encountered, the ones found most frequently in the state manuals, showing universal use, have been included.

As always in the authors' experience, the National Recreation Association has been most helpful in suggestions and also in the generous way in which they have permitted the use of play material from their collections. A number of individuals have assisted by suggestions for original games and by comments on the chapters as they were prepared. The members of the Intramural Staff at the University of Michigan have been very generous in making these recommendations and their assistance is fully appreciated. Professor J. H. McCulloch of the Michigan State Normal College read the entire manuscript with painstaking care, and made invaluable suggestions and recommendations. The authors are indebted to Mr. George F. Martin of Cincinnati for his careful and skillful preparation of the diagrams which accompany the text.

BERNARD S. MASON
ELMER D. MITCHELL

SEPTEMBER I, 1935

TABLE OF CONTENTS

PART I

Contests Between Individuals

PART II

Contests Between Groups

PART III

Goal, Tag, and Combat Games

PART IV

Team Games

CONTENTS

PART V

Water, Winter, and Mounted Activities

PART I

CONTESTS BETWEEN INDIVIDUALS

CHAPTER I

CONTESTS OF THE RUNNING TYPE

CONTESTS are simple comparisons of ability along special lines. Any trial of ability may be called a *test* but to have a *contest* there must be opponents. In a test one simply determines his ability for his own satisfaction. The object in the various systems of tests is to present standards whereby one may determine his ability, and then attempt to improve his ability and *defeat his own previous record*. In contests he attempts to defeat opponents. Any of the events described in the following pages on contests may be used either as tests or contests.

Contests differ from *games* in three significant ways: *First,* in a contest there is no interference with the contestant on the part of his opponents, whereas in a game there is constant and deliberate interference with his plans and plays. *Second,* strategy and deception have no place in a contest, while games are full of unexpected situations, strategy, and deception—it is part of a game to outwit one's opponents and confuse them as to what one intends to do. *Third,* a contest presents few if any situations where the player must exercise choice as to his moves, whereas games are filled with opportunities and emergencies calling for choice.

Contests may be held in any of the fundamental physical movements. These involve contests in locomotion such as running, jumping, and climbing, and contests in handling objects such as throwing, catching, striking, kicking, pushing, pulling, and butting. There are also contests in locomotion in which the contestant rides a vehicle of some sort. Furthermore, there are contests in handling objects of a mechanical nature.

Certain of the contests in the fundamental movements have through years of use become very highly standardized. These are spoken of as the track and field events.

There are innumerable minor contests not so well standardized, but which carry a greater appeal for ordinary gymnasium, playground, and club-meeting use. Consequently much more space is devoted to these than to the standard events. Many of these are connected with the skills used in the major games and serve admirably as lead-up activities developing the skills in the fundamental movements.

Contests may be held between groups as well as individuals. The relay race is perhaps the best-known form of group contest. In addition, there are two other methods of group competition in contests: (1) mass competition in which all players compete at once, and (2) group competition in which the individuals compete separately and score points for the team.

Games can be classified in many ways. When classified from the standpoint of the objectives and movements of the players, we find that they fall under the following heads: (1) goal games, (2) tag games, (3) games of personal combat, (4) team games of the baseball type, (5) of the tennis type, (6) of the soccer football type, (7) of the rugby football type, (8) of the hockey type, (9) of the basketball type.

In the chapters which follow, contests and games are described, under the headings of the classification indicated above. There is a type of group play which cannot be classified either as contests or games in that there is no competition. This is imitative play such as we see in story plays, rhythmic plays, and children's plays of simple imitation. The word "plays" is applied to such activities. These activities do not fall within the scope of this book.

A word of explanation is necessary regarding the treatment of water activities, winter activities, and horseback-riding activities. These activities include both contests and games and might be scattered throughout the chapters of the book. However, for the convenience of the practical play leader who may use the book, they have been grouped in chapters by themselves and appear near the end of the book under the titles of "Water Activities," "Winter Activities," and "Horseback-Riding Activities."

In this chapter the individual contests of the running type are described. The other types of contests are presented in the following chapters of Part I and Part II.

TRACK EVENTS

Track Events	Sprints	100-yard dash
		220-yard dash
	Hurdles	120-yard high hurdle
		220-yard low hurdle
	Middle distance runs	440-yard run
		half mile
	Long distance runs	one mile
		two miles

The Sprints

Playground, Gymnasium   *Late Elementary School to Adults*

There are two of these in standard interscholastic and intercollegiate competition: the 100-yard and the 220-yard runs. In the Olympic games the runs are from 100 meters up. The 100-yard run is too long for the standard distance for elementary-school pupils and consequently the following distances are suggested:

	Girls	Boys
Fourth Grade	40 yards	50 yards
Fifth Grade	50 yards	60 yards
Sixth Grade	60 yards	75 yards
Seventh Grade	75 yards	75 yards
Eighth Grade	75 yards	100 yards

To avoid interference between competitors, all sprint events should be run in lanes at least three feet in width and clearly marked with lime. Lane positions are determined by lot.

Present-day sprinters invariably use the crouch start and are favoring more and more the use of starting blocks which not only save time but afford firmer and more exact foot placement. If starting blocks are not available, a small hole is dug for the toe of each foot. No exact measurements for the placing of blocks or holes can be given as they vary with coaches and individuals. However, approximate standard form puts the front foot about eight inches behind the starting line while the knee of the back leg rests on the ground beside the instep of the front foot. The first finger and thumb of each hand are placed on the starting line with elbows locked.

When the starter calls "Get on your marks," the runners take positions similar to that described above. He then calls "Get set," at which each man moves slightly forward and upward. When all are ready and motionless and at least two seconds after the command "Get set," the starter discharges the pistol as the signal to go. If any part of a runner's body is in motion before the shot, it is a false start. The offender is warned and if he breaks again is disqualified.

The Hurdle Races

Playground, Gymnasium   *Senior High School to Adults*

There are two of these: one of 120 yards, with ten hurdles three-and-one-half feet high; and one of 220 yards, with ten hurdles two-and-one-half feet high. The ten hurdles divide the course into eleven parts: in the 120-yard race the two end sections are fifteen yards each and the hurdles ten yards apart; in the 220-yard race the course has eleven equal portions, each twenty yards. The start is made as in a sprint race. All hurdles must be attempted. Stepping out of one's lane does not disqualify but in no way may one interfere with the running of one's opponents. Two hurdles may be knocked over without forfeiting the race, but a record cannot be made unless all the hurdles are left standing.

On indoor tracks shorter hurdle races are used, sometimes forty yards with three hurdles. Hurdle races as long as 440 yards are sometimes run, using ten hurdles three feet high, spaced thirty-five yards apart.

The Distance Runs

Running Track   *Senior High School to Adults*

The distance runs are commonly divided into two groups: The middle distances which include the quarter- and half-mile runs; and the true distance runs, comprising the mile and two-mile. Many authors include the quarter with the sprints because the method of starting and the average speed made in running approaches very near to that of the sprints.

In running longer distances, no lanes are used, except occasionally in the quarter-mile, but no runner may cross in front of another until he is at least two full strides in advance.

Cross-Country Race

Open Country   *Senior High School to Adults*

The cross-country runs take place on courses from a mile and a half to seven miles in length. Extreme care should be exercised not to overtax high-school competitors and the course for such athletes should not be over two-and-one-half miles long. The course is marked by flags as follows:

> Red flag: indicates turn to the left
> White flag: indicates turn to the right
> Blue flag: indicates that the course is straight ahead

These flags are one foot square and are on poles extending not more than four nor less than two feet from the ground.

The team scoring the lowest number of points is the winner. First place counts one point, second place two points, and so on. The number of runners on each team to score is usually five, but may be any number agreed on by the committee. The number must be at least one less than the number allowed to enter. If less than five (or the number determined by the committee) finish, the places of all members of that team are disregarded.

Marathon

Open Country   *Adults*

The marathon race is a run of approximately twenty-five miles. It is too severe for all except mature men with unusual physique, and even then must be preceded by intense training.

Walking Race

Playground, Gymnasium   *Junior High School to Adults*

Walking races were standard events at one time, but owing to the difficulty experienced by judges in determining whether a contestant is walking or running, this event is exceedingly difficult to supervise satisfactorily and declined in popularity. It is still used frequently at picnics and carnivals.

The event is conducted as in the runs except that the contestant walks. In a walk the heel of the advancing foot must be on the ground before the toe of the back foot leaves the ground. The distances used vary from 220 yards to a mile.

MINOR CONTESTS OF THE RUNNING TYPE

Novelty Races

Playground, Gymnasium, Club, Picnic   *Elementary School to Adults*

The novelty races are enjoyed by the average person much more than the standard races. A great many excellent novelties are described as relays in Chapter XIII, "Relays Based Primarily on Locomotion." Since the method of running or locomotion is the same in the individual race as in the relay, there is no need in repeating them here.

These races are listed below, in approximately the same order in which they appear in Chapter XIII under the relays of similar name. The reader will have no trouble in determining how to conduct the event as an individual race after reading the description of the relay.

Meet at the Switch

Schoolroom   *Early Elementary School*

The teacher stands in front of the room, a bean bag in each hand. Two players stand ready and at a signal each takes one of the bags from the teacher's hands and they run around the room in opposite directions, passing at the rear of the room like cars on the switch, each passing to the right. The one returning the bag to the teacher first wins.

This can be made a group contest by having two teams, counting one point for each winner; the team with the highest score wins.

Crossing the Brook

Playground, Gymnasium   *Early Elementary School*

Draw two lines on the floor for the banks of the brook, wider in some spots than in others. The players form in line and take a running jump across the brook. Those who step in the brook must drop out of line to dry their feet. Those who are successful in the jump continue around a course and jump again. Have them jump each time at a wider place than on their previous jump. When all the wide spots have been jumped, have the players jump the narrow sections with a standing broad jump.

Three-Legged Race

Gymnasium, Playground, Picnic   *Late Elementary School to Adult*

The contestants race in pairs. The players of each pair stand side by side facing in the same directions. Their inner legs are strapped or tied together at the ankles and above the knees, and they place their inner arms around each other. Thus fastened together, they race to the finish line. The race is handled as in the ordinary runs. Distances of from 30 to 100 yards may be used.

Sack Race

Playground, Picnic   *Late Elementary School to Adult*

The contestants stand in burlap sacks which are long enough to reach to the hips. Holding the sacks hip high, they jump or run to the finish line. If they fall down, they are permitted to regain their feet and continue. A distance of twenty-five yards is far enough.

Donkey-and-Rider Race

Gymnasium, Picnic, Club   *Late Elementary School to Adult*

The players compete in pairs. One drops to all fours and the other sits on his back. They thus race to the turning line, where they reverse positions and race back to the starting line.

This is an excellent father-and-son contest, with the father acting as donkey the entire distance. It should not be used, however, unless the players have their legs covered.

Wand Race

Gymnasium   *Late Elementary School and Junior High School*

Draw a starting line and finishing line at opposite sides of the playing space. The players stand at the starting line each with a wand or stick balanced on his right forefinger. The stick may be held in balance by the other hand until the starting signal is given, but thereafter may not be touched with the free hand unless it falls. At the signal the players advance balancing the stick. If the wand drops off it must be replaced at the point where it fell before advancing farther. The one wins who reaches the finishing line first.

Variation.—The players line up, each balancing a wand as described above. At the signal they run forward, and the player wins who goes the farthest before his wand falls and hits the floor.

Shoe Scramble

Playground, Gymnasium, Club *Late Elementary and Junior High Schools*

The players remove their shoes and place them in a pile about fifty feet from the starting line. The players should mark their shoes in some way so as to recognize them. The shoes must not be tied together. The players line up behind the starting line and the leader mixes up the shoes. At the signal they dash for the shoes, each player selecting his own. He puts them on, laces them up, and returns to the starting line. The player returning first with shoes completely laced wins.

The players are permitted to throw unwanted shoes as far as they can so that the others cannot find them.

Dressing Race
(*Equipment Race*)

Playground, Picnic, Club   *Late Elementary to Senior High School*

Between the starting line and the turning line mark four lines at regular intervals. At the signal, each player runs to the first line and takes off his shoes, to the second and takes off his stockings, to the third and takes off his belt, to the fourth and takes off his shirt. Each article is left on the line where it was removed. Having crossed the turning line, the runner returns and puts on each article as he reaches it. All buttons must be buttoned and shoe strings tied. The player finishing first wins.

One Out

Playground, Gymnasium, Club   *Late Elementary and Junior High Schools*

Establish a starting line behind which the players stand. About twenty feet distant establish a parallel line, and place stones or sticks on it, numbering one less than the number of players. The objects should not be bunched as is frequently the custom, but spread along the line to avoid collisions and equalize the running distance.

At the signal the players dash for the objects. The player failing to secure one falls out. One object is then discarded and the remainder placed on the line again, and the contest repeated. Continue until only one player remains. This player is the winner.

Circle Race

Playground, Gymnasium   *Late Elementary to Senior High School*

Arrange the players in a circle standing about arms' length apart. Have them face to the right so that they are in single file around the circle. At the signal they all start to run around the circle, each trying to pass the runner in front of him. All passing must be done on the outside. When players are passed they fall into the center of the circle and are out of the race. The last player remaining in the contest wins.

Occasionally the leader may give a signal causing the runners to turn and run in the opposite direction; this reverses the relative positions of the runners.

Champ-Nit Circle Race.—This is similar to the Circle Race but instead of deciding the fastest player it determines the slowest. Arrange the players in a circle and have them start running around the circle as in the Circle Race. Whenever a player touches the back of the runner in front of him, the one doing the touching drops out. Thus the slower runners remain in and the faster ones are eliminated. Continue until only one remains in the circle.

Base-Running Contest

Baseball Diamond   *Late Elementary to College*

A regular baseball diamond is needed. The contestant takes the crouching position with one foot against home base. At the signal he runs the circuit of the bases, touching first, second, third, and home base in order. A stop-watch is used and the time recorded. The contestant with the best time wins.

Run to First Base
(*Bat and Run*)

Baseball Diamond   *Junior High School to College*

A pitcher and catcher take their usual positions and the contestant takes his position and bat. The contestant bats the pitched ball and runs to first. The stop-watch is started at the crack of the bat and is stopped when the runner touches first. The contestant with the best time wins.

Human Top Race

Gymnasium, Club   *Late Elementary to Senior High School*

Give each contestant a barrel hoop. Each lies on his back on the floor, raises both arms and both legs vertically, and thrusts hands and feet through the hoop. At the signal they move to the finish line by rocking, spinning on the back, or any way they can get there except by use of the hands or feet. The hoop must remain on the arms and legs throughout. The one finishing first wins.

Barrel Rolling

Playground, Gymnasium   *Junior and Senior High Schools*

The players take turns in standing on the side of a barrel and attempting to roll it. The winner may be determined in two ways: (1) the person that rolls it the farthest before falling off; (2) the one who stays on the longest from the time he starts to roll the barrel.

Potato Race, Number 1

Playground, Gymnasium   *Late Elementary School to College*

```
*     *     *     *     *     *     *     *
*     *     *     *     *     *     *     *
*     *     *     *     *     *     *     *
*     *     *     *     *     *     *     *
*     *     *     *     *     *     *     *
*     *     *     *     *     *     *     *
*     *     *     *     *     *     *     *

o     o     o     o     o     o     o     o
```

Establish a starting line and draw a one-foot circle on it for each contestant. The circles should be six feet apart. Starting from the center of each circle and on a line at right angles to the starting line, establish eight spots two yards apart. Draw a finish line parallel to the starting line, running through the eighth row of spots. Place a potato, stone, or block of wood on each spot.

The contestants stand behind the circles on the starting line. At the signal, each contestant runs forward, picks up one potato, runs back and puts it in the circle. He then runs forward and picks up another potato, and so on until all the potatoes are in the circle. The potatoes may be picked up in any order but once a potato is picked up it must be put in the circle before another potato is handled. Having put all potatoes in the circle the contestant runs to the finish line.

The number of potatoes used depends upon the needs of the players. The following schedule is suggested:

> Fourth grade—four potatoes
> Fifth to sixth grades—five potatoes
> Seventh to ninth grades—six potatoes
> Tenth grade and over—eight potatoes.

Indian-Club Race.—In the gymnasium, the Indian-Club Race usually takes the place of the Potato Race. The event is conducted in the same way, except that Indian clubs are used.

Potato Race, Number 2.—The potato race required by the athletic badge tests for girls of the National Recreation Association is as follows:

Secure two wooden cubes measuring two and one-half inches. (Potatoes of uniform size or beanbags may be used.) Mark upon the floor or ground five yards in front of the starting line a square measuring twelve inches in outside dimensions. Five yards farther on mark a circle six inches in diameter, and five yards beyond this a second six-inch circle. Distances should be measured to center of square and circles. Place a block in each of the six-inch circles.

At the signal the contestant runs from the starting line, picks up the nearer block and places it in the square, runs and secures the farther block, touches square with it and replaces it in farther circle, then goes back, picks up the other block, places it in the nearer circle and returns to the starting line. The total distance is seventy yards. Blocks may not be dropped or thrown but must be placed in every case. One try only is allowed, but the event must be run over if either of the blocks is placed outside of the circle or the square. It is permissible to have the block on the line if it is more in than out.

All-Up Indian-Club Race [1]

Playground, Gymnasium   *Late Elementary to Senior High School*

Draw two tangent circles, each three feet in diameter. In one of the circles place three Indian clubs. At a point thirty feet distant from a line passed through the centers of the circles and parallel to it, draw a line to be used as a starting line.

On the signal the contestant runs from the starting line, transfers the three clubs, one after the other, to the vacant circle so that they remain standing, and runs back to the starting line. The girl makes three such trips, finishing at the starting line. Only one hand may be used in transferring the clubs. The surface within the circles should be smooth and level. A wide board may be used when the test is made out of doors. Total distance is sixty yards.

STILT CONTESTS

While any type of stilts may be used in these events it is recommended that they be six feet long, and that the footrests be placed twelve inches from the bottom and never more than eighteen inches. Unless the contestants are expert on stilts it is recommended that the foot straps be not used in racing since it is difficult to remove the foot in case of a fall.

Straight Stilt Race

Playground, Council Ring, Yard   Late Elementary and Junior High Schools

The contestants stand behind the starting line and at the signal mount the stilts and race to the finish line. The rules of the ordinary runs apply. Distances of fifteen to fifty yards may be used.

Backward Stilt Race.—The distance is from thirty to fifty yards. The contestants line up with their backs to the starting line and race backward to the finish line.

Obstacle Stilt Race.—Establish a starting line, and fifty yards distant a turning line. Every ten yards down the course stretch a light rope tightly across the course one foot from the ground—there is thus a rope on the ten-, twenty-, thirty-, and forty-yard lines.

The contestants line up at the starting line and at the signal race to the first rope and *step* over it, to the second rope and *jump* over it, to the third rope and *step* over it, to the fourth rope and *jump* over it. They then go to the turning line, and return following the same routine. The player finishing first wins.

[1] From *Athletic Badge Tests for Boys and Girls,* p. 11. Physical Education Series No. 2, 1923. By permission of the United States Bureau of Education, Department of Interior.

Zigzag Stilt Race.—The course is fifty feet long. Every five feet in each lane place an Indian club or stick of wood of similar size and shape. The contestant zigzags down the course, going to the right of the first club, to the left of the second, and so on. When he reaches the last club he circles it to zigzag back to the starting line. The player finishing first wins.

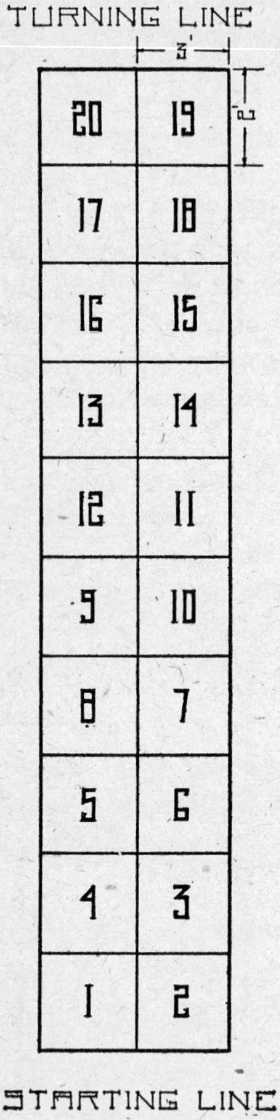

TURNING LINE

|— 3' —|

20	19
17	18
16	15
13	14
12	11
9	10
8	7
5	6
4	3
1	2

STARTING LINE
FIGURE I.

Stilt Events in the Circular Court

Playground, Yard
Late Elementary to Senior High School

Draw an eighteen-inch circle on the ground for each contestant. Each contestant holds his stilts in his hands with the stirrup ends resting in the circle. At the signal he mounts and performs the following series of events in order. When he falls or leaves the circle he is credited with one miss and the contest is to see which contestant can complete the series in the order named with the fewest misses.

The events are as follows:

1. Turn completely around to the right.
2. Turn completely around to the left.
3. Jump up ten times.
4. Raise left stilt and stand on right for five seconds.
5. Raise right stilt and stand on left for five seconds.
6. Walk around the edge of the circle, stepping on the line each step.

Stilt Events in the Rectangular Court

Playground, Yard
Late Elementary to Senior High School

Lay out a court, with lines of lime as illustrated in Figure 1. The court is six feet wide and twenty feet long, divided lengthwise by a center line, and crosswise by lines dividing it into two-foot blocks.

The contestants compete one at a time. The first contestant starts with the first event and if successful continues with the others in order until he fails. The others then compete in turn. When the first player's turn comes again he begins with the event in which he failed previously. The player wins who completes the events in the fewest number of turns.

1. Walk on the stilts through the court without touching the lines. At the turning line dismount and return in the same way.
2. Walk through the court and back straddling the center line.

3. Walk through the court stepping in every block.
4. Walk stepping in the odd-numbered blocks only.

In each event the player dismounts on crossing the turning line, remounts, and returns. The following fouls constitute a miss or failure in the event: (1) touching a line; (2) going outside of the court; (3) dismounting any place between the starting and turning line.

Trick Stilting

Playground   *Late Elementary to Senior High School*

This contest is designed to pick the best stunt or trick performers on stilts. Prepare and announce beforehand a list of tricks on the order of the ones given below. Each contestant is expected to perform these tricks and having completed them, to perform any other tricks he may desire.

The judges pick as the winner the contestant who performs the greatest number of tricks, taking into consideration also the skill and grace with which he performs them.

The following list may be used.

1. Hopping or jumping on two stilts.
2. Balancing on one stilt.
3. Hopping on one stilt.
4. Kick for height.
5. High jump.
6. Dancing.
7. Hand-stand on stirrups of standing stilts.

ICE-SKATE, SKI, AND SNOWSHOE CONTESTS

See Chapter XXVII, "Winter Activities."

RUNNING CONTESTS IN *SOCIAL GAMES FOR RECREATION*

Cigar Race.	Fluffy Race.
Pipe Lighting Race.	Easter Egg Contest.
Rubber Band Contest.	Pueblo Water-Maiden Contest.
Feather Blowing Race.	Peanut Race.
Balloon Blowing Race.	Clothespin Race.
Balloon Sweeping Race.	Prisoner's Race.
Balloon Jumping Contest.	Husband and Wife Race.
Lip Card Contest.	Blind Horse and Jockey Race.

CHAPTER II

RIDING CONTESTS

ROLLER SKATING

ONLY standard four-wheel steel roller skates may be used in these events. Rubber, wooden, or composition wheels are prohibited.

Roller-Skating Straight-Away Race

Pavement   *Elementary to Senior High School*

This event calls for a smooth straight-away and consequently paved streets offer about the only possibility. Distances of 50 to 440 yards may be used depending on the age and capacity of the players. The event is handled as in ordinary runs.

Backward Roller-Skating Race.—The contestants stand behind the starting line with their backs toward it. They skate backward to the finish. For straight-away races, distances of 100 to 220 yards may be used.

Roller-Skate Coast for Distance

Pavement   *Elementary to Senior High School*

Establish a starting line and fifty feet beyond it a coasting line. The contestants line up on the starting line, skate to the coasting line, and from there on coast. On crossing the coasting line the feet must be together and both on the ground; no motion of the arms, legs, or body is permitted. The player coasting the farthest wins.

Single-Skate Coast for Distance.—Each contestant wears one skate only. The conditions are as in the Roller-Skate Coast for Distance. The players run fifty feet, and then coast on the one skate. If any contestant touches his foot to the ground after crossing the coasting line, he is credited with the distance where he touched the ground. The player coasting the farthest wins.

Single Roller-Skate Race

Pavement   *Elementary to Senior High School*

Distances of 50 to 100 yards may be used, depending on the age of the players. Each player wears one skate only, which may be worn on either foot. Motion is applied by pushing with the free foot. Running is not permitted, and the skate must be kept on the ground as much as possible. The player finishing first wins.

Zigzag Roller-Skating Race

Pavement, Skating Rink   *Elementary to Senior High School*

The distance is one-hundred yards. Every ten yards in each player's lane place an Indian club or block of wood of similar dimensions. The skaters zigzag through the Indian clubs, to the right of one, to the left of the next, and so on. On reaching the hundred-yard line, they circle the clubs, and zigzag back to finish at the starting line. The player finishing first wins.

Three-Legged Roller-Skate Race

Pavement, Skating Rink   *Elementary to Senior High School*

The players compete in pairs, each pair having their inside legs tied together at the ankle and above the knee. Skates are worn on the outside legs only. They move by pushing with the inside feet. The distance is one-hundred yards and the pair finishing first wins.

Travelers' Race

Pavement, Skating Rink   *Elementary to Senior High School*

Each contestant holds a suitcase in one hand and an open umbrella in the other, and skates to the finish line. The player finishing first wins. The distance is one-hundred yards.

Roller-Skating Obstacle Race

Pavement   *Elementary to Senior High School*

The distance is 125 yards. Four obstacles are placed every twenty-five yards as follows:

1. Tennis net under which the contestants must crawl.
2. Row of tables over which they must climb.
3. A hurdle not higher than six inches which must be jumped.
4. A row of barrels with top and bottom removed; each contestant must crawl through a barrel.

The player finishing first wins.

Paper-Throwing Contest on Roller Skates

Pavement   *Elementary to Senior High School*

Draw a line down the center of the pavement, and twenty-five feet to one side of it place five barrels with the open end facing the line. The barrels should be at least twenty-five feet apart. The contestants take turns in competing. Each is given ten rolled newspapers which he may carry in a bag if he desires. Each skates on the far side of the line (away from the barrels) and attempts to throw a newspaper in each barrel. He throws first to the left, and after passing the last barrel turns and skates back, throwing to the right. He must be in motion at the time each paper is thrown. One point is scored for each paper thrown in a barrel.

Tandem Roller-Skating Race

Pavement, Skating Rink   *Elementary to Senior High School*

The contestants race in pairs. They stand side by side grasping right hands together and left hands together. In this position they race. Distances of from 100 to 220 yards may be used. Any pair letting go of each other's hands is eliminated.

Variation.—The two players stand one behind the other, the back player placing his hands on the front player's waist.

Roller-Skate Potato Race

Pavement, Skating Rink   *Elementary to Senior High School*

In this event the players wear roller skates but otherwise the rules of the regular Potato Races apply (see page 11). Four or five potatoes are usually sufficient.

Roller-Skate Tug-of-War

Pavement   *Elementary to Senior High School*

Five or more contestants comprise each team, each player wearing one skate only. The event is conducted as in the regular Tug-of-War events (see page 145).

Roller-Skating Lap Race

Large Gymnasium, Skating Rink   *Elementary to Senior High School*

This is an event for a skating rink or a large gymnasium. Establish a corner marker at each corner out from the side wall one-third of the width of the floor and an equal distance from the end wall. The difficulty in turning on roller skates makes it impractical to require sharp turns. The corner markers are made by inserting a small flag in a small block of wood. Establish a starting line in the middle of one of the long sides.

The contestants line up behind the starting line and race the required number of laps, finishing at the starting line. On the average skating rink, distances of from one to eight laps may be used depending on the age and skill of the contestants.

Roller-Skating Carnival

A block of a downtown street may be roped off for a city-wide roller-skating carnival with representatives of all playgrounds competing. Care should be taken to allow space enough beyond the finish lines for the skaters to come to a stop.

The following program is suggested.

Under Twelve Years of Age

Boys	Girls
50-yard Dash	35-yard Dash
50-yard Single-Skate Race	35-yard Single-Skate Race
Coast for Distance	Coast for Distance

Under Fifteen Years of Age

Boys	Girls
75-yard Dash	50-yard Dash
75-yard Single-Skate Race	50-yard Single-Skate Race
Coast for Distance	Coast for Distance
Paper-Throwing Contest	50-yard Tandem Race
Three-legged Race	

Over Fifteen Years of Age

Boys	Girls
100-yard Dash	75-yard Dash
100-yard Single-Skate Race	75-yard Single Skate Race
Coasting for Distance	Coast for Distance
Paper-Throwing Contest	75-yard Zigzag Race
Zigzag Race	75-yard Tandem Race
100-yard Tandem Race	Partner (Boy and Girl) Race
Obstacle Race	

BICYCLE EVENTS

Bicycle events usually take place on a pavement. Care should be taken to see that the road is closed to traffic and that all side roads crossing it are carefully blocked.

Speed Races

Street, Running Track   *Junior High School to Adults*

Bicycle races for speed are popular among boys. The events most commonly used are the quarter, half, mile, two-mile, five-mile, and ten-mile. The quarter and half may be ridden on a quarter-mile running track, but the usual procedure is to close a well-paved road to traffic. The events are conducted as in running races. Care should be exercised to see that young contestants do not race in events calling for too long a distance.

Bicycle Slow Race

Playground, Street   *Late Elementary School to Adults*

The course is fifty yards long and laid out in lanes two-and-one-half to three feet wide. The object is to ride as slowly as possible and be the *last* to cross the finish line. A contestant is immediately eliminated if his bicycle leaves his lane, if he touches a foot to the ground or other object, or if he touches another contestant outside his lane. The player finishing last wins, or if no one finishes, the one wins who goes the farthest.

Bicycle Plank Ride

Playground, Street   *Late Elementary School to Adults*

Enough planks are needed so that when they are lined end to end they will extend 150 feet. The planks should be exactly five inches wide and one inch thick. The planks should be nailed together or staked to the ground with metal stakes.

The contestants take turns in riding the plank. Each may start as far behind the plank as he chooses—a start of at least fifteen feet is advisable. Each attempts to keep his bicycle on the plank the entire distance. If the bicycle leaves the plank, the distance is marked. The one who rides the farthest wins. In case of a tie, the contestants involved ride again.

This is a difficult feat, and those who finish the entire distance will be few indeed.

Paper-Throwing Contest on Bicycles

Playground, Street   *Late Elementary to Senior High School*

Place five barrels in a row not less than twenty-five feet apart. Draw a line twenty-five feet away from the barrel line, and parallel to it. Give each contestant ten rolled newspapers. Each rides his bicycle, staying on the far side of the line (away from the barrels), and attempts to throw a newspaper into each barrel as he passes it. He throws first to the right, and after he has passed the barrels, he turns and goes back, throwing to the left. The papers must be thrown while on the bicycle.

One point is scored for each newspaper thrown in a barrel, and one point is deducted for each time a rider gets off his bicycle for any purpose. In case of a tie the player making the best time wins.

The players may carry a bag to hold the newspapers.

Hill-Climbing Contest

Street   *Junior High School to Adults*

Hill climbing contests with bicycles are extremely strenuous events. When used as a novel event for average groups, a hill should be selected which has a rather steep incline but which is short. If a long steep hill is to be used, the contestants must be in condition, and a physical examination before the race is imperative.

Give the contestants a start of twenty-five feet on the level ground at the foot. The one wins who first reaches the finish line at the top.

Bicycle Potato-Race

Playground, Street   *Late Elementary School to Adults*

Establish a starting line, which also serves as the finish line. Place a barrel hoop on this line for each player; the hoops should be eight feet apart. Ten yards from this line place another row of hoops, each with a potato in it. Similar rows of hoops are placed at twenty yards and thirty yards. There are thus three potatoes in a row for each player.

Each player, on the signal, rides to the first potato, dismounts, picks up the potato, mounts, rides back and puts it in the hoop at the starting line. He then gets the other two potatoes, one at a time, and places them in the hoop. The player wins who has all three potatoes in his hoop on the starting line first.

Variation.—Instead of using potatoes, use a six-inch block of wood with a two-foot broom handle stuck in it. These are set in the hoops, handle up, and the riders pick them up without dismounting. In doing so the rider must circle on the far side of the stick, away from the starting line.

Variation.—In this event potatoes are used and each contestant is given a three-foot stick, pointed at one end. He rides to the first potato and without dismounting attempts to secure it by sticking it with the pointed end of his stick. He may ride past it and attempt to spear it as often as necessary, but is disqualified if he touches the ground with any part of his body. In other respects the event is like the above.

Spearing the Ring

Playground, Street   *Late Elementary School to Adults*

Each rider is equipped with a ten-foot bamboo pole which he must hold within three feet of the end. The course is 250 feet long. Station ten officials along this course at intervals of twenty-five feet, each holding a curtain ring at arm's length out in front, or erect uprights with crossbars from which the rings are suspended by twine. The players ride the course one at a time and attempt to spear the rings with the pole. The end of the pole must enter the ring and is then withdrawn as the player rides on, and the pole put in position to spear the next ring. Each is credited with one point for each ring he spears. To touch a foot to the ground in the course of the event disqualifies the player.

Bicycle Candle Race

Playground, Street   *Late Elementary School to Adults*

Each rider carries a lighted candle and rides as fast as possible without extinguishing the candle. The one wins who first finishes the one-hundred-yard course with the candle lighted.

Bicycle Obstacle Race

Playground, Street   *Late Elementary to Senior High School*

The course is 150 yards long. Twenty-five yards from the starting line lay a barrel on its side in the path of each contestant. The barrels must have both ends removed. At the signal, each rider rides to his barrel, dismounts, and dives through the barrel. Then each mounts and crosses the finish line.

Trick Riding

Playground, Street   *Senior High School to Adults*

Trick riding adds much color to a bicycle carnival. It is limited to those with experience in stunt riding. The competition is judged by a committee of judges. The following events may be used:

1. Steering the bicycle with the feet.
2. Pedaling first on one side, and then on the other.
3. Riding under the crossbar.
4. Standing on the crossbar with one foot and holding on to the handle bars with the hands.
5. Riding on one wheel.
6. Sitting on the handle bars and riding backwards.

Bicycle Carnival

A bicycle carnival featuring races and stunts by representatives from all playgrounds makes an excellent city-wide event for a city recreation department. A block of a downtown street may be roped off for the event. The Jacksonville, Florida, Playground and Recreation Department uses the following program with prizes for each event donated by local merchants:

Decorated Wheel Parade	Paper-Throwing Contest
Tricycle Race	Spearing the Ring
Trick Riding	Scooter Race
Potato Race	Plank Riding
Slow Race	Candle Race

In connection with the above bicycle races, racing championships are held with the following program:

Junior Events	*Senior Events*
(Riders under 16 years)	(Riders over 16 years)
One-half Mile	One-half Mile
One Mile	One Mile
Two Miles	Five Miles
Five Miles	Ten Miles

SCOOTER AND COASTER-WAGON CONTESTS

Scooter Races

Street, Playground   *Elementary and Junior High Schools*

Scooters, commonly thought of as the playthings of small children, are excellent equipment for novelty races for all ages including adults. In playground meets children usually furnish their own scooters.

Scooter races are commonly conducted by city recreation departments on a section of a city street roped off for the occasion. Care should be taken to see that sufficient space is provided beyond the finish lines for the vehicles to come to a stop.

Standing Scooter-Race.—The contestants line up on the starting line, each with his scooter. They place one foot on the scooter, and at the signal propel themselves by pushing with the other foot. Straight-away distances of 50 to 220 yards may be used, depending on the age and capacity of the contestants.

Kneeling Scooter-Race.—This race is performed as in Standing Scooter-Race except that the contestant kneels with one knee on the scooter and pushes with the other foot. Distances of 50 to 220 yards may be used.

Sitting Scooter-Race.—This race is performed as in the Standing Scooter-Race, except that the contestant sits on the scooter with one leg either side and propels the scooter by pushing with the feet on the ground. Distances of twenty-five to fifty yards may be used.

Backward Scooter-Race.—This contest is performed as in the Standing Scooter-Race, except that the contestant stands with his back to the starting line, places one knee on the scooter and propels it by pushing with the other foot. Distances of twenty-five to fifty yards may be used.

Obstacle Scooter-Race.—Erect a tennis net across the street midway between the starting line and the turning line. The contestants race to the net, lift the scooters over, jump the net, and continue. They race to the turning line, return crossing the barrier again, and finish at the starting line.

Pushing Scooter-Race.—The players compete in pairs. One sits on the scooter and the other pushes him to the turning line fifty yards distant. Here they change places and race back.

Zigzag Scooter-Race.—A block of wood or a box is placed every ten yards for a distance of one-hundred yards in the lane of each contestant. The contestant zigzags down the course, to the right of one box, to the left of the next, and so on. On reaching the last box, he circles it and zigzags back to the starting line.

Skipmobile Races

Street, Playground   *Elementary and Junior High Schools*

Skipmobiles are made by attaching the rollers from a roller skate to the ends of a board three feet by six inches by two inches; handle bars are attached by nailing a piece to the front, three feet long and two inches square, to the top of which a short cross piece is nailed.

The following events may be used, each conducted as in the scooter race bearing the similar title:

Standing Skipmobile-Race   Obstacle Skipmobile-Race
Backward Skipmobile-Race   Zigzag Skipmobile-Race

Coaster-Wagon Races

Street, Playground   *Elementary School*

Coaster wagons are ordinary express wagons. The following events may be used.

Straight Coaster-Wagon Race.—Each contestant kneels in his wagon with one knee, or sits sidewise in the wagon, and propels it with his foot. Distances of 100 to 220 yards may be used.

Coaster-Wagon Slow Race.—The distance is fifty yards and the wagon wins that crosses the finish line *last*. Wagons coming to a complete stop are eliminated.

Coaster-Wagon Obstacle Race.—Conducted like the Obstacle Scooter-Race.

Coaster-Wagon Pushing Race.—Conducted like the Pushing Scooter-Race.

Block-Wheel Wagon Races

Street, Playground   *Elementary School*

Wagons of this type have wheels made of solid blocks of wood, six inches or less in diameter. The events are the same as those described for Coaster-Wagon Races.

Chariot-Wagon Race

Street, Playground   *Elementary and Junior High Schools*

Chariots have two wheels only. A soap box is attached to the axle and a tongue provided with which the chariot is drawn. Chariots made with bicycle wheels have a decided advantage over those made with other types of wheels and consequently the chariots should be divided into two classes, those with bicycle wheels and those without.

Two contestants pull the chariot and one rides in it. Distances of 150 to 300 yards may be used.

POGO-STICK CONTESTS

A pogo stick consists of an upright pole with a spring on the bottom; foot rests are attached to each side at right angles to the pole and about a foot from the ground. The contestant holds the pole in his hands, mounts it with both feet, and leaps forward with it; the spring causes a rebound and makes long leaps possible.

Pogo sticks were extremely popular at one time but are seldom used at the present moment and are difficult to obtain. They doubtless will return to popularity and will be available at sporting-goods stores. It is to be hoped that they will, for their use is unusually fascinating, and they are valuable tools for recreational leaders.

Pogo-Stick Race

Playground, Gymnasium, Yard   *Elementary and Junior High Schools*

The contestants stand behind the starting line, each holding his pogo stick. At the signal they mount the sticks and move to the finish line by a series of leaps. If the players fall from the sticks, no forward progress may be made until they remount. Distances of fifteen to fifty yards may be used.

Backward Pogo-Stick Race.—This is conducted like the above except that the contestants race backwards. The distance should be short.

Pogo-Stick Broad Jump

Playground, Yard   *Late Elementary and Junior High Schools*

Establish a jumping line. The contestants jump up to the line on the pogo sticks and then jump forward. The one jumping the farthest wins. The event is conducted like the Running Broad Jump.

Pogo-Stick Lane-Race

Playground   *Late Elementary and Junior High Schools*

Mark a lane with a line on the ground. For a distance of ten feet, it is twelve inches wide; from ten to twenty feet it is eight inches wide; beyond twenty feet it gradually tapers down to a two-inch straight line.

The contestants take turns in jumping down the lane on a pogo stick. The one who goes the farthest before leaving the lane wins.

Pogo-Stick Events in the Rectangular Court

Playground, Yard   *Late Elementary and Junior High Schools*

Lay out a court with lime exactly like that described in Stilt Events in the Rectangular Court (Figure 1, page 14). The contestants perform the same series of stunts described for stilts and the event is conducted in the same way.

ICE-SKATE, SKI, SNOWSHOE, AND SLED CONTESTS

See Chapter XXVII, "Winter Activities."

HORSEBACK-RIDING CONTESTS

See Chapter XXVIII, "Horseback-Riding Activities."

CHAPTER III

JUMPING, VAULTING, AND CLIMBING CONTESTS

JUMPING AND VAULTING CONTESTS

Running High Jump

Playground, Gymnasium   *Late Elementary School to Adults*

THE usual dimensions of the high-jump pit are fourteen feet wide and ten feet in depth. The uprights are placed twelve feet apart. The crossbar may be square with beveled edges, one-and-one-eighth inches thick, or triangular, measuring one-and-three-sixteenth inches on each face. Although standards with pins not over three inches long are commonly used, official equipment is one which permits the crossbar to rest upon a standard the top of which measures one-and-one-half inches wide and two-and-three-eighths inches deep. In informal meets such as on the playground and in camp, a light bamboo pole may be used for the crossbar, but regulation uprights are essential.

Each contestant must clear the bar without displacing it from its supports. The bar is first placed at a height that all can clear; each has three trials if necessary and then the bar is raised. Each contestant is credited with the highest distance at which he clears the bar.

Standing High Jump

Playground, Gymnasium   *Late Elementary School to Adults*

This event is conducted in the same way as the Running High Jump. The contestant may stand with his feet in any position but must leave the ground one foot at a time in jumping. If a foot is lifted from the ground twice, or two springs are made without an attempt to clear the bar, it counts as a trial.

Standing Double High Jump.[1]—The contestant stands on both feet facing the bar and jumps with both feet simultaneously. His body must be kept square to the front throughout and he must land on both feet simultaneously with his back to the bar. Violation of these rules counts as a trial. The bar is raised as in the regular high jump.

[1] The idea for this event was taken from S. C. Staley, *Individual and Mass Athletics*, p. 39. Copyright, 1925. By permission of A. S. Barnes and Company, publishers.

Pole Vault

Playground   *Senior High School to Adults*

The pole-vault pit is fourteen feet wide and twelve feet in length. The uprights are stationed twelve feet apart and the crossbar must not exceed one-half inch in thickness nor extend more than three inches beyond the uprights.

The pole vault is conducted like the high jump. The contestants must not climb the pole; the upper hand may not be raised after the competitor leaves the ground nor may the lower hand be raised above the upper. The bar must be cleared without displacing it. Whenever the competitor leaves the ground in an attempt, or passes under the bar, he is charged with a trial.

Running Broad Jump

Playground, Gymnasium   *Late Elementary School to Adults*

The scratch line for the running broad jump consists of a take-off board two inches thick, eight inches wide, and at least four feet long. It is set firmly in and on the same level as the ground. The ground in front of the scratch line must be flush with the scratch line. The jumping pit should be six feet wide, should begin about five feet in front of the take-off board and should extend twenty-five feet. It should be dug out to a depth of from twelve to eighteen inches and filled with loose sand to the level of the take-off board.

The contestant may run as far as he pleases, but must jump from or behind the scratch line. In order to insure a perfect take-off, two marks are placed on the ground, at approximately sixty and eighty feet from the scratch line. The jumper starts running from the eighty-foot line, and with practice he knows that if he hits the second line exactly, he is practically certain of a good take-off.

If one steps over the plank so as to break ground in front of it, the jump is not measured, but it counts as a trial. The jump is measured with a tape from the front of the plank to the nearest point at which the jumper breaks ground, whether with feet, hands, or body. Each contestant has four trials, and one more than there are places to be scored qualify for the finals. Those who qualify make four more jumps, and all qualifying jumps count in the final tabulation of places.

Running Double Broad Jump

Playground, Gymnasium   *Junior High School to College*

This event is like the Running Broad Jump except that the contestant must make the jump with both feet on the take-off board. He runs forward, jumps on the take-off board with both feet, and then jumps forward, landing on both feet.

Standing Broad Jump

Playground, Gymnasium   *Late Elementary School to Adults*

The event is conducted in the same manner as the Running Broad Jump. The contestant stands with both feet toeing the scratch line. He may sway back and forth at will but is not permitted to lift either foot before the jump. The jump is made from both feet and the jumper lands on both feet.

Standing Backward Broad Jump.—This event is like the Standing Broad Jump except that the contestant jumps backward from the take-off. Measuring is done as in the Standing Broad Jump.

Double Standing Broad Jump

Playground, Gymnasium   *Junior High School to College*

The event is conducted best on level ground or floor without the use of a jumping pit. The contestant toes the scratch line with both feet and makes two successive jumps, the second jump being made immediately after and as a continuation of the first. The distance is measured from the scratch line to the nearest point touched by the jumper on his second jump.

Triple Standing Broad Jump.—Same as the above except that the contestant takes three jumps in succession.

Seven Standing Broad Jump.—Same as the above except that the contestant takes seven jumps in succession.

Standing Broad Hop

Playground, Gymnasium   *Junior High School to College*

Conducted like the Standing Broad Jump, this event consists of hopping from the take-off board and landing on the same foot. The contestant must retain his balance after the jump and not touch the ground with his other foot or hands until the jump is completed.

Double Standing Broad Hop.—The contestant stands on one foot, hops, lands on the same foot, and immediately hops in similar fashion again. He must keep his lifted foot off the ground until the second hop is completed. The distance is measured from the take-off to the nearest point where the ground was broken on the second hop.

Triple Standing Broad Hop.—Same as the above except that three hops are taken.

Seven Standing Broad Hop.—Same as the above except that seven successive hops are taken.

Running Broad Hop

Playground, Gymnasium   *Junior High School to College*

Conducted like the Running Broad Jump, in this event the contestant runs to the scratch line, hops with one foot, and lands on the same foot. He must retain his balance after the jump and not touch the ground with his other foot or hands until the jump is completed.

Hopping Broad Hop.—This event is like the Running Broad Hop except that the contestant hops to the take-off board instead of running.

Standing Hop, Step, and Jump

Playground, Gymnasium   *Junior High School to College*

The contestant stands on one foot on the take-off board, hops forward and lands on the same foot, steps forward on the other foot, and jumps forward landing on both feet. No pauses are permitted in the process. Measuring is done as in the broad jumps.

Running Hop, Step, and Jump.—This event is like the Standing Hop, Step, and Jump except that the contestant runs to the take-off board.

Standing Leap and Jump.[2]—The contestant stands with both feet toeing the scratch line. He jumps, landing on one foot and immediately jumps again landing on both feet. The jump is taken without halt after the leap.

Standing Hop, Skip, and Jump.—The event is conducted like the Standing Broad Jump. The contestant stands on one foot on the take-off board, hops and lands on the same foot, swings the other foot in back of the hopping foot landing on it, then jumps forward landing on both feet. No pauses are permitted between hops and jumps.

Running Hop, Skip, and Jump.—Conducted as in the Standing Hop, Skip, and Jump except that the contestant runs to the take-off board.

Standing Broad Step

Playground, Gymnasium   *Junior High School to College*

The contestant stands on one foot on the take-off board, jumps, and lands on the other foot. Preliminary hops are not permitted. Measuring is done as in the Standing Broad Jump.

Double Standing Broad Step.—Same as the above except that two successive steps are taken.

[2] The idea for this contest was taken from S. C. Staley, *Individual and Mass Athletics*, p. 35. Copyright, 1925. By permission of A. S. Barnes and Company, publishers.

Triple Standing Broad Step.—Same as the above except that three steps are taken.

Seven Steps.—Same as the above except that seven steps are taken.

Standing Whole Hammon [3]

Playground, Gymnasium   *Junior High School to College*

The contestant stands toeing the scratch line. In succession, he takes two hops, two steps, and two jumps. No hesitation between the movements is permitted. Each has three trials and is credited with his best distance.

Pole Vault for Distance

Playground   *High School and College*

Establish a take-off line. A pole-vaulting pole is used. The contestant runs to the take-off line, places his pole on the ground and vaults as far as possible. The measuring is done as in the Running Broad Jump. Each contestant is given three trials.

Bat Vault for Distance.—Similar to the above, except that a baseball bat is used. Holding one end of a baseball bat, the contestant toes the jumping line, places the other end of the bat as far ahead as he desires, and leaps forward as in the Pole Vault for Distance. The player jumping the farthest wins.

Running Broad Jump on Stilts

Playground   *Late Elementary and Junior High Schools*

Establish a jumping line. The contestants run on stilts to the line and jump. The event is conducted like the Running Broad Jump.

Stilt Hop, Step, and Jump.—The contestants run on stilts to the jumping line, hop on one stilt, land on the same stilt, step, and jump. The event is conducted like the Hop, Step, and Jump.

Rope Jumping and Skipping Methods

There are several movements which may be used in jumping and skipping the rope:

Skipping.—Stand on right foot, hop on right foot and pass the rope under it, step on left foot, hop on left foot and pass the rope under, repeat on right foot, and so forth.

Running.—The player runs in place with no hop between the steps. He steps over the rope each time a foot is raised, first with the left and then with the right.

[3] From N. P. Neilson and F. W. Cozens, *Achievement Scales in Physical Education Activities*, p. 37. Copyright, 1934. By permission of A. S. Barnes and Company, publishers.

Single Jump.—Both feet are together and the rope is jumped with no intervening hops.

Double Jump.—Both feet are together and there is an intervening jump; that is, the rope is jumped on every other jump.

Backward Skipping or Jumping.—The rope is held in front and swung backward under the feet. Any of the four skips described above may be used.

Skipping on One Leg.—One leg is held off the floor and the contestant skips on the other leg.

Stiff-Leg Kick Forward.—The player skips or jumps the rope (with or without an intervening hop), first with one foot and then the other, and throws the raised leg forward on each skip, keeping it stiff at the knee.

Stiff-Leg Kick Backward.—Same as the above except that the leg is kicked backward.

Spread Eagle.—Stand with the feet spread and jump the rope with or without an intervening hop.

Crossed-Foot Jump.—The rope is jumped with the feet crossed, alternating the position of the feet on each jump.

Buck and Wing.—Click the heels together between the jumps.

Click Handles.—Click the handles of the jumping rope together each time the rope is jumped.

Rope Skipping—Fifty Skips

Playground, Gymnasium   *Elementary and Junior High Schools*

A rope from seven to nine feet long is used, depending on the size of the player. Three-eighths-inch cotton sash cord is ideal for jumping ropes. A stop-watch is used in timing the event. The jumper starts skipping or jumping with the signal and completes a specified number of jumps. For elementary school children fifty skips are sufficient, and for all above the sixth grade, one-hundred skips. The contestant completing the skips in the shortest time wins. On the start the rope is held behind and touching the legs.

Any of the types of crossing the rope described above may be used.

Rope Skipping—Thirty Seconds.—The player is given thirty seconds to skip or jump the rope and his skips or jumps are counted. The one completing the greatest number during this time wins. Any of the various skips described above may be specified.

Rope Jumping with Long Rope

Playground, Gymnasium, Home   *Elementary School*

In these events a long rope is used with two players (turners) swinging the rope while the others jump it.

Contests may be conducted using one of three plans:

1. Select the event and have each child jump in turn until he or she misses. The one jumping the longest wins.

2. Select five events and have five ropes swinging. Each child goes from one rope to the next and attempts to perform the feat required in each rope. The contest is to see who can complete the series without a miss.

3. Divide the players into teams and conduct as in Number 2. Count the players in each team who complete the series without a miss—this total is the team's score.

The following events are selected from those presented by the National Recreation Association in *88 Successful Play Activities.*[4]

Keep the Kettle Boiling.—"Ropes are placed at suitable intervals around the playground or radiating from the center. The players form in twos, threes, or fours, and at a signal all run round the course, jumping each rope in turn. The object of the game is to keep the jumping continuous; the ropes should therefore be quite low at first. Later they may be raised slightly, but they should be adjusted to the capacity of the weakest jumper."

Over the Swinging Rope.—"The ropes, arranged as in No. 1, are swung slowly from side to side, and the players must judge their jumps accordingly. Later the difficulty may be increased by changing the rate of the swing."

Serpents, or Over the Waves.—"Waves are made in the ropes by one turner at each end moving his arm upward and downward, slowly or quickly at will. Players jump over the ropes, watching carefully, as the height and speed of the waves will probably be different at each rope."

Over and Under.—"The players jump over one rope and crawl under the next."

Steps.—"The ropes are arranged in increasing heights."

Hot Peas.—"Turn the rope as fast as possible. Spell H-O-T-S and at the end of that begin counting 1-2-3, etc., and turn fast at the beginning of the count. The girl jumping most wins."

Red, White and Blue, Stars Over You.—"The rope is turned as the girl jumps three times. For 'Stars over you' the rope is turned high over her head as she stoops. This is then repeated. Other verses may be added instead of repeating, such as 'Red, white and green, you are a queen.' The girl jumping most wins. No one may jump over 50 verses. (This number is allowed as the jumper rests every three jumps.)"

Building a House.—"The participants line up, jumping over the rope one at a time and repeating until one is left. Each time the line begins again, the rope is raised about two inches."

Over the River.—"This involves running through without jumping and without being touched by the rope. That is, jumpers must cross the river without getting wet. Each in turn runs through until only one is left who has not missed."

Double Rope.—"Two ropes are used turning toward each other, one slightly after the other. The jumpers run in jumping as many times as possible. (Not over 50.)"

[4] See National Recreation Association, *88 Successful Play Activities,* pp. 45, 49. Copyright, 1933. By permission of National Recreation Association, publishers.

Rocking the Cradle.—"The rope is swinging about four inches above the ground and the jumper jumps from one side to the other until she misses. (Not over 75.)"

Run Against the Wall.—"The jumper runs in when the rope is being turned away from her and jumps as many times as possible. (Not over 75.)"

Rope Skipping with Long Rope.—These events are conducted like those in Rope Jumping with Long Rope, except that the rope is skipped instead of jumped.

The following events are taken from those suggested by the National Recreation Association in *88 Successful Play Activities.*[5]

All in Together.—"As the name implies, the children enter as quickly as they can and try to continue skipping until all are in. As soon as the last player enters, count is kept of the number of skips that are kept up. (Note: The easiest way to enter is from the side.)"

Running In.—"The children, in groups of five or more, run in from a little distance, and then after a certain number of skips, out again without checking the rope."

Over the Moon.—"Both the preceding games can be taken with the rope turned backward."

Salt, Mustard, Vinegar, Pepper.—"The children run in, and when all are in they say: 'Salt, Mustard, Vinegar, Pepper.' At the word 'Pepper,' the rope is gradually turned faster and faster."

French Almond Rock.—"The players jump over the rope as it swings from side to side, saying the following rhyme: 'Handy-pandy, sugardy candy. French almond rock.' Then the rhyme is repeated while the players skip in the usual way. Then all crouch down while the rope is turned over their heads, to the same rhyme. On the last word, 'rock,' the players rise and the rhyme is repeated for the third time while they skip. The entire process may be repeated, or the first set of skippers may run out and a new set begin."

Higher and Higher.—"The rope is turned so that it does not quite touch the ground and is very gradually raised so that the players must jump or lift their knees higher and higher to clear it."

Double Dutch.—"Two ropes are used. The turners have a rope in each hand; they hold their arms rather far apart and make the ropes touch the ground alternately. The ropes may be turned either inward or outward."

CLIMBING CONTESTS

Rope Climb

Playground, Gymnasium   *Junior High School to College*

A rope an inch and a quarter to two inches in diameter is needed. The smaller size is preferable below the college level. It should hang from

[5] See National Recreation Association, *88 Successful Play Activities,* pp. 46, 47. Copyright, 1933. By permission of National Recreation Association, publishers.

a point at least eighteen feet from the floor and should reach to a point three feet or less from the floor. Tape or ribbon should be fastened to the rope to mark the following distances from the floor: twelve feet, sixteen feet, and eighteen feet. The twelve-foot distance is recommended for junior high school, the sixteen-foot for high school, and the eighteen-foot for college. A stop-watch is used in timing.

At the signal the contestant starts to climb the rope and continues until he touches the height marker. The time is taken from the signal to the time when his hand touches the marker.

Rope Climb—Arms Only.—This event is conducted as in the stand ard Rope Climb except that the contestant must climb with his arms only. He sits on the floor at the start with his hands on the rope and must not touch the floor again once he leaves it after the starting signal.

Greased-Pole Climb

Playground, Camp, Picnic   *Junior High School to Adults*

Remove the bark from a straight smooth pole, tack a half dozen strips of red cloth to the top end, and erect it so that it extends out of the ground about twenty feet. Grease the pole well with axle grease. The contestants take turns in attempting to climb it, and the one wins who succeeds in removing a strip of cloth from the top. Probably not more than one will reach the top, but in case of a tie, have the winning contestants climb again.

The grease on the pole serves two purposes—it makes the climbing difficult, and it prevents leg abrasions in case the players wear only swimming trunks, as is frequently the case in camps. As an added precaution, the contestants should be encouraged to wear an old pair of trousers if possible.

CHAPTER IV

THROWING AND CATCHING CONTESTS

FIELD-MEET THROWING EVENTS

THE standard throwing events used in track and field meets are the Shot Put, Javelin Throw, Discus Throw, and Hammer Throw.

Shot Put

Playground   *Junior High School to Adults*

The shot is a round iron or brass ball, eight pounds in weight for junior-high-school contests, twelve pounds for high-school, and sixteen pounds for college contests. The shot is put from a circle seven feet in diameter, four feet of the circumference of which is a toe board four inches in height. The circumference is marked by an iron, wood, or rope band.

Each contestant is given four trials and one more than there are places to be scored, qualify. Those who qualify are given four more trials and each is credited with his best distance. The measurement is taken from the nearest edge of the first mark made by the shot to the nearest point of the circle.

A foul put is one in which any part of the body touches the top of the stopboard or ground outside of the circle while making an attempt.

Javelin Throw

Playground   *Senior High School to Adults*

The javelin consists of a wooden shaft with a sharp metal point, and weighs not less than 1.765 pounds. It is thrown from behind a scratch line two-and-three-fourths inches wide and twelve feet long. The javelin must be held by the grip at the moment the throw is executed. No throw counts in which the point of the javelin does not strike the ground before any part of the shaft. The thrower must not place his foot upon the board in throwing, nor step across the line, until the throw is marked. The rules for trials and qualifying are the same as for the Shot Put.

Discus Throw

Playground   *Senior High School to Adults*

The discus is a flat disk of metal and wood weighing four-and-one-half pounds. It is thrown from a circle eight feet two-and-one-half inches in diameter, subject to practically the same rules as the Shot Put. All throws to be valid must fall within a ninety-degree sector marked on the ground.

Hammer Throw

Playground   *College*

The hammer consists of a metal sphere called the hammerhead and a wire handle. The complete implement must not be more than four feet in length, and its weight not less than sixteen pounds. It is thrown from a circle seven feet in diameter. The event is handled as in the Shot Put with the added requirement that the hammer must fall within a ninety-degree sector marked on the ground.

MINOR THROWING EVENTS

Beanbag Board Toss

Playground, Gymnasium, Home   *Elementary School*

There are two types of beanbag boards in common use, either of which may be used. The one shown in Figure 2 is about twenty-four inches high and eighteen inches wide. Three round holes are cut in it as

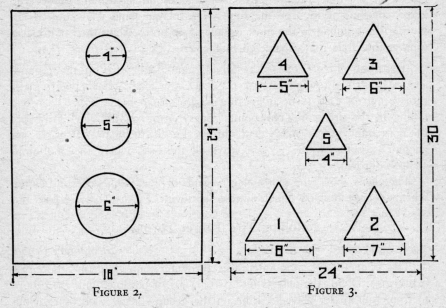

FIGURE 2.   FIGURE 3.

in the diagram, the upper one four inches in diameter, the middle one five inches, and the lower one six inches. The holes count 3, 2, and 1.

The board illustrated in Figure 3 has five triangular holes varying in size from four to eight inches. The board is twenty-four inches wide and thirty inches high. The holes score 5, 4, 3, 2, and 1.

The board is set at a forty-five degree angle. The throwing line is ten feet away. Each contestant throws three bags, one after the other. The contestant who secures twenty-one (or fifty) points first wins.

Beanbag Target Toss.—Draw on the floor three concentric circles one, two, and three feet in diameter, and number the circles, 5, 3, 1 from the center circle outward. The players stand at a line fifteen feet away and toss five beanbags at the target. When one has made his five throws a judge records the score made from the positions of the bags: each lying within the inner circle counts 5, next circle 3, outer 1. A bag lying on a line scores as in the inner space. The next player takes the bags and throws in the same way.

Beanbag Six Circles.—Establish a throwing line, and at right angles to it mark six circles in a row on the floor. The circles should be about one foot in diameter and three feet apart, the nearest one being six feet from the throwing line. Line up the players in file behind the throwing line.

The first player tosses a beanbag attempting to put it in the nearest circle. Whether succeeding or not he goes to the rear of the line, and the other players throw in turn. On the second time around, those who succeeded in the first attempt throw for the second circle, and those who failed continue trying for the first. The player wins who succeeds in putting the beanbag in the most distant circle first. If any part of the bag touches the circle it is considered in.

Beanbag Tire Toss.—Lay an old automobile tire on the ground, and establish a throwing line twenty feet or so away. Each player tosses three beanbags each turn, attempting to drop them in the tire. Each bag falling in the tire scores one point. Bags resting on the rim of the tire do not count unless subsequent throws knock them in. If there are enough bags for all the players, leave all the bags where they fall until all have thrown.

The player wins who scores eleven points or goes farthest beyond eleven when all have had an equal number of throws.

Rolling-Tire Target Throw

Yard, Playground, Picnic, Club   *Elementary School*

This is one of the most interesting throwing contests in that the target is moving. Divide the players into two groups; if possible, limit the groups to from four to six players. Line up the groups facing each other about twenty feet apart. A player from each group is assigned to act as roller; the two rollers stand in the center area, one at each end (see Figure 4). Each player in the group has a beanbag or potato.

At the signal one roller rolls an old automobile tire down the center of the area between the two groups. Each player attempts to toss his beanbag through the tire as it passes. Then the second roller rolls the tire back.

The rollers then join their groups and two other players act as rollers. Continue until each player has acted as roller.

Each beanbag tossed through the tire counts one point. The player or team wins who has the highest score when all have acted as rollers.

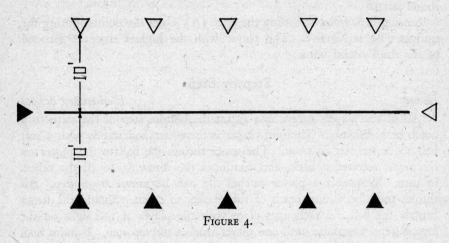

FIGURE 4.

Blackboard Target Throw

Schoolroom   *Early Elementary School*

Draw a target on a blackboard in the playroom consisting of five concentric rings. The center ring is six inches in diameter and each succeeding ring is four inches from the one next smaller. Soft rubber balls are used of the size of tennis balls. Place the balls in a pasteboard box with a little pulverized chalk in the bottom. The balls thus become covered with chalk and leave a mark when they hit the blackboard.

Establish a throwing line twenty to thirty feet away, the distance depending on the age and skill of the players. Each contestant is given ten throws. The circles score from the center out as follows: 5, 4, 3, 2, 1. Balls striking on the line score in the higher circle.

Stoop Target

Steps to a Porch   *Elementary School*

This is a spring-time favorite of children, particularly girls, in many sections. Establish a throwing line about fifteen feet in front of the steps to a porch. The object is to throw a rubber ball with a view to hitting the edge of a step (A, Figure 5) if possible, and failing here, to hit the wall between the steps (B).

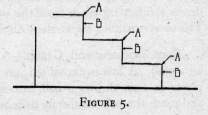

FIGURE 5.

The players throw in turn. The contest consists of three rounds, each round consisting of three throws per player. The first player throws three times, then the second, and so on. When all have thrown, the second round starts.

Scoring is as follows: hitting the edge (A) scores ten points; hitting the upright (B) scores five. The player with the highest score at the end of the third round wins.

Step by Step

Home   *Elementary School*

All of the players except one sit on the bottom step of the steps to a porch or a stairway. The odd player is the tosser and stands with a soft ball about ten feet in front. The tosser throws the ball to the player on the right, receives it back, and continues the throwing to all the others in turn. Whenever a player catches the ball he moves up a step. All throws must be within reach of the players to count. Should the tosser fumble the ball, he exchanges place with the player at the right on the lowest step. Continue until one player reaches the top step. If more than one reach it together the play continues down the steps until one is out in front.

Progressive Throw and Catch

Playground, Gymnasium   *Early Elementary School*

Divide the players into groups of four. Two players in each group throw and catch a softball for two minutes, then the other two players throw and catch. The pair that completed the most catches in the two minutes move up to the next group and change partners.

As described, the contest may be used as a lead-up activity for Baseball. It may be used also in connection with training for Basketball or Football by changing the ball to a basketball or football.

Throw, Bounce, and Catch

Playground, Gymnasium   *Late Elementary and Junior High Schools*

A wall is necessary for this contest. Give the first player a softball or rubber ball. A freely bouncing ball adds much interest, such as a tennis ball or codeball. The player takes any position he chooses, throws the ball against the wall, runs, and attempts to catch it. He is given three trials and marks the farthest catch from the wall. The others then compete in turn. The player making the farthest catch wins.

Spot Bounce and Catch.—A circle two feet in diameter is drawn on a wall. A line is drawn ten feet from the wall and parallel to it. Each player in turn throws a ball, attempting to hit the wall inside the circle and catch the ball on the fly as it rebounds. He continues to throw until he misses the circle or fails to catch the ball. One point is scored for each successful attempt. One-hundred points is the game, and the person scoring it first wins.

Baseball Throw for Distance

Playground, Gymnasium   *Junior High School to College*

In preparing for this event, first establish a throwing line three feet long. Fifty yards away from this line and parallel to it, mark a line on the ground twenty yards long. Similar lines are drawn every ten yards up to 100 yards; there will thus be a line at 50 yards, 60 yards, 70 yards, 80 yards, 90 yards, and 100 yards (see Figure 6). A baseball is used. The contestant stands behind the throwing line and throws the ball with

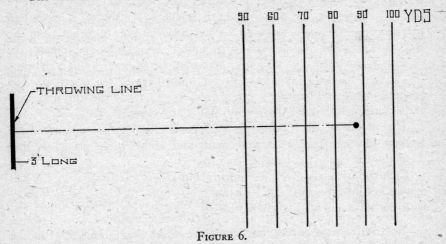

FIGURE 6.

or without a run. The point where the ball first hits the ground is marked. The distance is measured with a tape measure from this point to the nearest distance line. Balls falling outside the ends of the distance lines, or balls thrown by contestants who step over the throwing line, are not measured, but count as trials. Each contestant is given three throws and credited with his best distance.

Softball Throw for Distance.—A twelve-inch softball is used and the event is conducted like the above.

Baseball Throw for Accuracy.—A target must be painted on the wall or on a wooden board constructed for the purpose. The board should be six feet square. The target consists of five concentric circles one, two, three, four, and five feet in diameter. The circles score 5-4-3-2-1 from the center out. The target is placed so that the outside line is six inches above the ground. A throwing line is established forty-five to ninety feet away depending upon the skill and maturity of the contestants.

Each contestant is given ten throws. One foot must be behind or in contact with the throwing line when the ball is released. Throws hitting

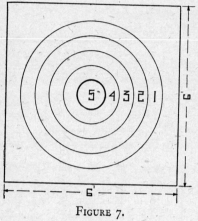

FIGURE 7.

a division line score in the inside circle. The contestant making the highest score wins.

Baseball Pitch for Accuracy.— A pitching target is necessary for this event. It consists of a rectangular area eighteen inches wide and thirty-six inches high. It may be painted on the wall, may be a frame of wood, may be a suspended sheet of canvas, or may be a hole cut in a canvas. The bottom side should be twenty inches from the ground. The target represents the area over home base through which a ball must pass to be a strike. The pitching line should be forty-five feet away for players of the fifth and sixth grades, and sixty feet for the seventh grade and over.

The athletic badge tests of the National Recreation Association call for a target fifteen inches wide and twenty-four inches high, placed so that the bottom is twenty-four inches from the ground.

Each contestant is given ten throws and scores one point for each ball that strikes in or on the outline of the target. One foot must be in contact with the throwing line when the ball is released.

Softball Pitch for Accuracy.—The same target is used as in the Baseball Pitch for Accuracy. A twelve-inch softball is used. The pitching line may be twenty-five, thirty, or thirty-seven feet distant, depending on the age and skill of the contestants. The underhand pitch must be used. In throwing, the contestant may take one step forward but the other foot must be in contact with the line when the ball is released.

Catcher's Throw to Second Base

Baseball Diamond   *Junior High School to College*

This interesting event is staged on a regular baseball diamond. A barrel open at one end is placed on its side on second base, with the open end toward home base. Blocks of wood or stones should be placed by the sides of the barrel to prevent it from rolling and the open end should be elevated three or four inches.

The contestant stands on home base and throws the baseball attempting to put it in the barrel. One foot must be on home base at the moment the ball is released. Each contestant is given five throws. Points are scored as follows: throwing the ball in on the fly—three points; throwing it in on the first bounce—two points; on the second bounce—one point; contestant with the highest total score wins.

Fielder's Throw to Home Base

Baseball Diamond   *Junior High School to College*

A judge and three assistants are needed, each assistant having a stick or small white flag.

The contestants stand in deep center field. The object is to throw the baseball to home base, causing it to strike the ground as near to home base as possible. When the first contestant throws, an assistant sticks his flag in the ground at the point where the ball hit as it fell from the fly, and records the name of the contestant. The other two assistants place their flags in similar fashion when the next two contestants throw. Thereafter, whenever a ball hits nearer to home base than the most distant flag, this flag is moved to the new position and the name of the contestant recorded. Each contestant has three attempts, making one throw each turn. The contestant wins whose flag is nearest to home base.

Baseball Throw and Catch

Baseball Diamond   *Junior and Senior High Schools*

On a regulation baseball diamond place a pitcher and three basemen. The contestant stands on home base. He must catch the ball delivered from the pitcher, throw to first, catch the return, throw to second, catch the return, throw to third, and catch the return. He thus is required to catch four throws and throw to each of the bases, giving a possible seven errors. A throw is considered good if both hands can be placed upon it by stretching with one foot on the base. In case of a bad throw to the contestant, the throw should be repeated.

Softball Throw and Catch.—This is conducted like the Baseball Throw and Catch except that a twelve-inch softball is used and the event takes place on a playground ball diamond.

The athletic badge tests for girls of the National Recreation Association require thirty-six-foot baselines and a thirty-foot pitching distance.

Ball Roll for Accuracy

Picnic, Playground   *All Ages—Girls*

Drive a stick or flag in the ground and mark a throwing line sixty feet away. Each contestant takes turns in rolling a softball at the flag, endeavoring to cause it to come to rest near the flag. Each is given three throws. The one wins whose ball comes to rest nearest the flag.

Forward Pass for Accuracy

Football Field, Playground   *Junior High School to College*

A rugby football goal and a few feet of ordinary rope are required for this event. The target is established by hanging two ropes ten feet long from the crossbar so that they hang six feet inside the two goal posts. This gives three areas ten feet high and six feet wide inside the two goal posts. The contestant, holding a rugby football, stands on the twenty-yard line and attempts to throw the ball through the target. One foot must be in contact with the line when the ball is released. Balls going through the central zone score two; those going through the outer zones score one. Each contestant is given five or ten throws.[1]

Variation.—For more experienced players a discarded automobile tire may be used as a target. Secure the largest tire possible and suspend it by a rope from the crossbar of the football goal so that the center is six feet from the ground. Tie a rope to each side and stretch tightly to the two goal posts to prevent any movement. The contestants stand on the fifteen- or twenty-yard line and pass the ball attempting to put it through the tire. Each is given ten throws and scores one point for each throw that passes through the tire.

Football Center-Pass for Accuracy.—Suspend a large automobile tire from the crossbar of the football goal so that the bottom of the tire is about two and one-half feet from the ground. Stretch ropes tightly from the sides of the tire to the uprights in order to hold it in position. The throwing line may vary for the different age levels. A wooden target may be substituted if preferred.

Each player in turn makes ten (or five) passes from the snapper-back position, scoring one point each time the ball is put through the target.

If players are expert, the following variation should be used.

Variation.—Using the target as a pivot, draw a semicircle on the ground with a ten-yard radius. Mark ten points on this semicircle, equally distant from each other. The players make one pass from each of these points. They are thus caused to pass at difficult angles.

Forward Pass for Distance.—A football field greatly facilitates the measuring because of the presence of the yard lines. The contestant stands behind the goal line and passes the ball with or without a run. Stepping over the goal line is a foul and counts as a trial. The player throwing the greatest distance wins.

[1] The description of this event follows that given in S. C. Staley, *Individual and Mass Athletics,* p. 75. Copyright, 1925. By permission of A. S. Barnes & Company, publishers.

Soccer Throw for Distance

Playground, Gymnasium   *Junior High School to College*

A soccer ball is used. The contestant toes the throwing line, holds the ball in both hands overhead and throws it forward. The distance is measured from the line to the point where the ball first hits. Stepping over the line before the mark has been established is a foul and counts as a trial. Each contestant is given three trials.

Speedball Throw for Distance

Playground, Gymnasium   *Senior High School to College*

A speedball or soccer ball is used and the event is conducted like the Basketball Throw for Distance (page 45).

Speedball Accuracy Pass.—A speedball or soccer ball is used and the event is conducted like the Basketball Accuracy Pass (page 46).

Overhead Dribble for Distance.—Establish a throwing line. Each contestant throws the speedball or soccer ball into the air from behind the line and immediately runs forward and attempts to catch it. The object is to make a catch as far beyond the line as possible. Each is given five (or ten) attempts and is credited with his best distance. The one catching the ball at the greatest distance wins.

Basketball Throw for Distance

Playground, Gymnasium   *Late Elementary School to Adults*

Establish a throwing line on the ground about three feet in length. The contestant stands at stride behind the line at right angles to the throwing direction, with the basketball firmly gripped in one hand, and throws it. The distance is measured from the point on the line nearest which the contestant stood to the point where the ball first touched the ground. Stepping over the line is a foul and counts as a trial. Each contestant is given three throws and is credited with his best distance.

While the above is the standard Basketball Throw for Distance, any of the following throws may be used:

Forward Overhead Throw.—Stand facing the throwing line with the ball held by both hands above head. Throw from the overhead position, with or without a run.

Chest Throw.—Stand facing the throwing line with the ball held by both hands in front of the chest. Throw the ball by snapping the arms forward, with or without a run.

Side Throw with One Arm.—Stand sideways to the throwing line with the ball held with the back hand only at shoulder height. Throw the ball with an overhand push or swing, with or without a run.

Toss.—Stand facing the throwing line with the ball held in both hands between the knees. Toss it forward.

Side Overhand Throw.—Stand sideways to the throwing line with the ball held in both hands above the head. Swing the body toward the throwing line and release the ball, pushing it with the rear arm.

Side Underarm Throw.—Stand sideways to the throwing line, holding the ball in both hands at shoulder height. Bend the forward arm up and throw the ball with both hands under it.

Basketball Accuracy Pass.—Draw a circle on the wall four feet in diameter, the center of the circle four feet from the floor. Establish a throwing line twenty feet away. Each contestant is given ten throws at the circle. Each hit scores one point. As skill develops the type of throw may be specified. For older players the throwing line may be moved back.

Basketball Throw and Catch.—The contestant stands behind a throwing line, throws the basketball, and immediately runs forward and tries to catch it. Each is given three throws. The one wins who catches his throw at the most distant point from the throwing line.

Variation.—Fifteen feet in front of the throwing line place two poles with a rope stretched between them at a height of ten feet. The contestant toes the starting line, holds the ball in both hands, and tosses it over the rope. Immediately upon releasing it he runs forward under the rope and attempts to catch it. Each is given five (ten) attempts, and the one wins who completes the most attempts successfully.

With beginners, it is well to allow the ball to be caught on the first bounce. With older and skilled players, the throwing line may be moved back.

The players should be coached to give the ball a wrist spin toward them in releasing it.

Running and Catching.[2]—At a distance of thirty feet from the starting line and parallel to it stretch a cord ten feet from the ground.

On the signal the girl runs from the starting line, tosses a basketball or a volleyball over the cord, catches it, and runs back to the starting line. Three such trips are made, finishing at the starting line. In case of failure to catch the ball, it must be secured, tossed over the cord (either direction), and caught before running is continued.

The starting line and the cord should both be well away from any

[2] From *Athletic Badge Tests for Boys and Girls*, p. 11. Physical Education Series No. 2, 1923. By permission of the United States Bureau of Education, Department of the Interior.

wall, back stop, or other object, so that neither the contestant nor the ball shall touch any obstruction during the run. Total distance is sixty yards.

Basketball Foul Shoot

Playground, Gymnasium   *Late Elementary School to College*

Foul shooting tournaments are frequently held in connection with basketball tournaments as well as in playground and gymnasium work. Each contestant is given twenty-five throws from behind the free-throw line. Each fair throw going through the basket scores one point. All those who make fifteen successful throws are qualified to throw twenty-five additional throws. The ten highest scorers then throw fifty more. The player wins who makes the highest score out of the hundred throws.

Basketball Goal Shooting

Playground, Gymnasium   *Late Elementary School to College*

There are several types of contests in basket shooting which may be conducted. These events may be varied by specifying the type of shot which must be made.

Long Shots.—The contestant stands behind the circle enclosing the free-throw line and takes ten (or fifteen) throws for the basket. He is allowed one step in shooting and may not step over the circle line. One point is scored for each successful throw.

Goal Throw.—The regulations for the basketball goal throw of the athletic badge tests for girls of the National Recreation Association are as follows:

From a point directly under the center of the goal, semicircles should be drawn with radii of ten, twelve, and fifteen feet, for throwing lines.

The girl may stand at any point outside of, but touching the throwing line for her event. The basketball used shall be of standard size and weight.

The goal may be made either by a clear throw or by bouncing against the back-board.

Five or six throws, as the case may be, shall count as one trial.

Follow-up Shooting, Number 1.—The contestant stands behind the free-throw line and throws for the basket. If he makes it he scores two and takes his next throw. If he misses, he runs for the ball and shoots from the point at which he secures it. If he catches it before it hits the floor and makes the basket he scores two; if he secures it after it touched the floor and makes the basket he scores one. After the follow-up throw the contestant takes his next trial from behind the free-throw line as before. Each contestant is given ten trials and the one with the highest score wins.

Follow-up Shooting, Number 2.—The contestant takes his first throw from behind the free-throw line, follows up the throw, and if it was successful throws again from the point where he recovered the ball. He continues to throw from the point where he recovers each ball, until he fails, scoring one point for each goal made. Having failed, he returns to the free-throw line for his second trial. Each contestant is given from three to five trials and the one with the highest score wins.

Follow-up Shooting, Number 3.—Each contestant is given ten throws. The first throw is taken from behind the free-throw line and the throws thereafter from the point where the ball was recovered. All shots must be made from within three seconds after the ball was recovered, and no steps may be taken. If the ball goes out of bounds it is returned to the free-throw line. One point is scored for each goal made.

Shooting Against Time.—One minute is allowed each contestant. The first throw is made from behind the free-throw line and the remaining throws from the point where the ball is recovered. One point is scored for each basket made within the minute.

Basketball Twenty-One

Playground, Gymnasium   *Junior High School to College*

This is one of the most popular basketball contests. It requires one basketball goal. Draw a line across the floor parallel to the end line, at the back of the circle surrounding the free-throw line. All throwing must start behind this line.

The first player, standing behind the line, throws for the basket and immediately follows up with a short shot. If he makes the long shot he scores two, and the short shot, one. The players take turns in throwing. The one making twenty-one points first wins, and all start from zero in the next contest.

A rule is sometimes used to the effect that the player must score twenty-one even—if he goes over that number, he must start over.

Variation.—If the long shot is made, the player is given another try for a long shot in addition to the short shot.

Variation.—The player throws until he misses from the free-throw line, scoring one for the first basket, two for the second, three for the third, and so on. The player scoring twenty-one first wins.

Variation.—The player throws from the free-throw line until he misses, scoring two points for each goal. When he misses, he throws from the point where the ball is recovered, and if successful, scores one point and has the privilege of starting to throw again from the free-throw line.

Variation.—The players are in line behind the free-throw line. The first player throws and whether successful or not, the second player follows up and must catch the ball before it hits the floor. If unsuccessful, he is eliminated, and if successful, he throws from the point where the ball is recovered. If no player has scored twenty-one when all are eliminated, the last to be eliminated wins.

Partner Twenty-One.—The partners combine their scores to determine the winner. Another way in which this is played is for one man to take the long shot and his partner the follow-up. The next time they reverse the shots.

Team Form.—Any of the above forms may be used on a team basis with the players alternating. See other types under Basketball Twenty-One—Team Form (page 157).

Five, Three, and One

Playground, Gymnasium   *Late Elementary School to College*

The players take turns in throwing a basketball for the basketball goal, each making three throws in succession. The first is made from the free-throw line, the second from the point where the ball is recovered, and the third from the point where the second throw is recovered. The first throw, if successful, scores five, the second, three, and the third, one. The player with the highest score wins.

Basketball Golf

Playground, Gymnasium   *Late Elementary School to College*

Mark nine spots on the floor in a semicircle around the basketball goal. The players throw from spot Number 1, each throwing in turn until he makes the goal, and counting the number of throws required. They then throw from Spot Number 2, and so on. The player wins who completes the course of nine spots with the fewest throws.

Six-Hole Basketball.[3]—Six three-foot circles are made around the basketball goal, as shown in Figure 8. The players line up and take turns in attempting to throw baskets, starting on the left at circle Number 1. Each basket made advances the player one hole, and he continues to progress until he fails to make a basket. Holes 2 and 4 are marked "safety." If a player overtakes another player in a hole not marked safety, the first player must return and start over again. The person wins who first makes the circuit of the holes and returns to the starting point. A player over-

[3] From N. P. Neilson and W. VanHagen. *Physical Education for Elementary Schools,* p. 200. Copyright, 1930. By permission of A. S. Barnes and Company, publishers.

taken on his return goes back to hole Number 6, rather than hole Number 1.

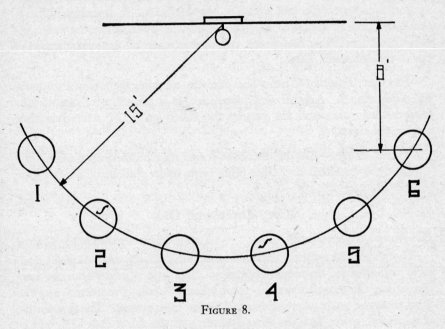

FIGURE 8.

Medicine-Ball Throw for Distance

Gymnasium   *Junior High School to Adults*

A six-pound medicine ball is used. If the event is used below the high-school level, a four-pound ball should be used. A tape measure is needed to measure the distance. The contestant stands on the throwing line and throws the ball in any manner he chooses. The distance is measured from the throwing line to the point where the ball first hits the floor. Stepping over the line is a foul and counts as a trial. Each contestant is given three trials.

Specified Medicine-Ball Throws.—Instead of permitting a free-style throw, one of the following throws may be specified:

Forward Overhead Throw.—The ball is held by both hands over the head and thrown forward.

Backward Overhead Throw.—The ball is held by both hands over the head and thrown backward.

Toss.—The ball is held by both hands between the legs and tossed forward.

Backward Between Legs.—The ball is held by both hands between the spread legs and thrown backward.

Side Overhead Throw.—Standing sideways, the ball is held by one arm and thrown forward with an overhead swing.

Put.—The ball is held on one hand and is put forward as in the Shot Put.

Broomstick Throw for Distance

Playground, Club   *Late Elementary and Junior High School*

This little novelty event uses broomsticks sawed from ordinary house brooms. The contestant holds the broomstick by the end and, standing behind the throwing line, throws it as far as possible. Each is given three throws and is credited with his best distance.

Dart Throwing

Playground, Summer Camp, Clubroom   Late Elementary School to Adults

Dart throwing is an ever-popular activity on playgrounds, in summer camps, and clubrooms.

Equipment.—Excellent darts can be purchased very inexpensively. For outdoor use the target board should be six feet square and for indoor use five feet square. The indoor target may be made of wallboard but the outdoor one should be of wood. To make the outdoor target, build the board six feet square of three-quarter inch clear soft wood. Nail it to two uprights of two-by-four-inch lumber so that the bottom of the board sets off the ground two feet. Paint ten concentric rings on it, the center one six inches in diameter, and each succeeding one three inches from the next smaller. The target is thus five feet over all, with a six-inch space on the sides. Paint the circles black and white alternately.

The indoor target should be thirty inches in diameter having ten concentric rings, the center one three inches in diameter and each succeeding one an inch and one-half from the next smaller.

Number the circles from the center out as follows: 10, 9, 8, 7, 6, 5, 4, 3, 2, 1.

Rules of Ordinary Play.—Establish a throwing line twenty to thirty feet away from the outdoor target, or ten to twenty feet away from the indoor. Two to five players may play at one time. Each contestant has one dart and they throw in turn. When all have thrown they go up and withdraw the darts. Each dart scores the number of points on the ring in which it sticks. Those on the line score in the higher ring. In ordinary recreational play, the contestant scoring one hundred points first wins.

Rules for Tournament Play.—In tournament play each contestant is given thirty-six (or eighteen) throws and is credited with the total score made.

The tournament may be conducted in two ways: (1) all contestants may throw their thirty-six darts, one after the other, each being credited with the total score made, and the one with the highest score being declared winner; (2) the contestants may be paired as in the standard tournament or elimination plan, and each two contestants paired throw against each other.

As in all activities in which pointed instruments are used, the event needs careful supervision.

Dart Baseball

Playground, Club, Summer Camp   *Late Elementary School to Adults*

For outdoor use the diagram shown in Figure 9 is painted on a board four feet square. It should be nailed to pieces of two-by-four-inch boards

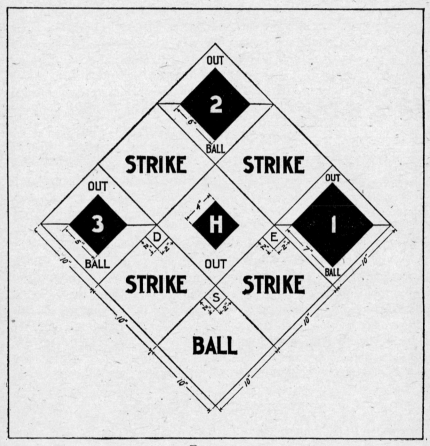

FIGURE 9.

and set up at a convenient height. For indoor or home use, the diagram may be put on a piece of wallboard of similar dimensions.

The throwing line is from fifteen to twenty feet distant. The players choose sides and the procedure follows that of regular Baseball. Square "H" is a home run, "1" is a single, "2" is a two-base hit, and "3" a three-base hit. When a batter makes a hit he leaves his dart in the square and when a succeeding batter hits, he advances his dart an equal number of bases. If a batter hits "E" (error) or "D" (dead ball) he takes his base. "S" stands for a sacrifice hit.

If a dart fails to hit the board it counts as an out. The same is true if a dart fails to stick and falls.

LARIAT-THROWING CONTESTS

Lariat throwing carries a peculiar appeal to boys, and after a little preliminary instruction, lassoing contests are particularly popular. Thirty-five feet of three-eighths-inch manilla rope makes an excellent practice lariat. Lighter rope is not heavy enough to carry when thrown. Double one end of the rope back and wire it, making a three-inch loop or eye—this is the honda. Slip the other end of the rope through the honda. Avoid metal hondas—they are too heavy for ordinary use and are dangerous on lariats used for play.

Roping Stationary Targets

Playground, Club, Summer Camp   Late Elementary to Senior High School

Place a chair or similar object on the floor or ground and establish a throwing line twenty feet from it, or nearer for beginners. Each contestant is given twenty throws, and the one circling the chair with the noose the most times wins.

Either the *wind-up throw* or the *toss* may be used. In the *wind-up throw,* the roper stands about four feet behind the line, lets out a noose about four feet long with his right hand, swings it over his head a few times from right to left, then takes a long step toward the target with his left foot, and throws the noose with an overhand motion. In the *toss,* the roper stands as before, holding a four-foot noose in his right hand, with the right arm at his side, and the noose spread on the floor behind him. He steps toward the target and throws without a wind-up, using much the same arm motion that he would use in throwing a ball at the target.[4]

Roping Running Targets

Playground, Club, Summer Camp   Late Elementary to Senior High School

In this lariat-throwing contest the target is a running boy. Establish a line along which the runner is to run, and parallel to it and ten feet from it, a throwing line. The roper stands behind the throwing line, yells to the runner to run, and attempts to rope him as he passes. As soon as he ropes him, the roper lets out rope or drops his rope, in order not to throw the runner. The runner should station himself so that he runs at least fifty feet before passing the roper.

[4] For complete instructions on how to throw a lariat, see Bernard S. Mason, *How to Spin a Rope.* New York: Boy Scouts of America, 1930.

Contests may be conducted in roping the runner by the feet and by the head. Each roper is given ten throws and the one roping the runner the most times wins.[5]

BOOMERANG THROWING

Boomerang throwing is one of the most delightful of pastimes. There is something particularly intriguing about throwing the stick and watching it circle and come back to one's hand without having to take as much as a step to reach it. There is something fascinating to the spectator also, in watching the gracefully spinning sticks circle and double circle through the air and back to the waiting hands of the thrower.

Unfortunately so little information has been available on the construction and handling of boomerangs that the sport is practically unknown. Most people think of boomerangs merely in terms of the curved sticks thrown by the Australian primitives. This is one type of boomerang, and perhaps the oldest type, but it is the least efficient of the boomerangs as a "come-back stick." It is also so heavy, and must be thrown with such force, that its use carries a decided element of danger when other people are near, particularly when the spectator cannot judge what course the boomerang is going to take.

For use as a sport, the curved or Australian style of boomerang should be replaced by one of the lighter, more efficient, and more colorful types of come-back sticks. Three of these are described below—the *cross-stick boomerang*, the *wheel boomerang*, and the *boomabird*.

Whenever boomerangs are thrown, the spectators should be grouped in one place and not scattered over the field. This place should be to the right of the thrower, since the boomerang circles from right to left. Thus if it reaches the crowd at all, it will be on its return, and its force will have been spent. Expert boomerang throwers can manipulate the boomerangs around the spectators without danger, even to the point of standing on a stage and throwing them out over the audience, but such tactics are for professionals only. When the less experienced are throwing, the sport should be carefully supervised, although the danger is slight if the types of stick described below are used.

Cross-stick Boomerang

Playground, Camp, Club   *Late Elementary School to Adults*

First let us describe how to whittle out the boomerang—the making is as interesting as the throwing, and happily is a very simple process. One's first attempt at making a boomerang should be confined to small sticks. Secure two of the ruler-like sticks used at gasoline stations to measure the

[5] For details and other roping contests, see Bernard S. Mason, *How to Spin a Rope*. New York: Boy Scouts of America, 1930.

amount of gasoline in automobile tanks. These are ideal, but if they cannot be obtained, use sticks of soft wood (basswood, pine) of about the same size and shape—twelve inches long and one or one-and-one-eighth inches wide. Do not try to use heavy wood—it will not make a boomerang.

First mark out a three-inch area in the center of each stick, as shown in Figure 10. Now bevel the sides of the stick beyond these lines, as shown

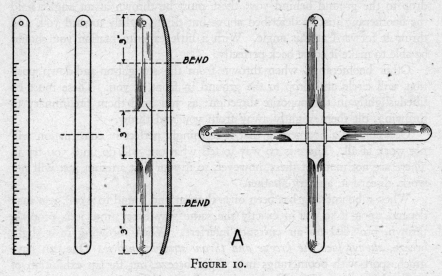

FIGURE 10.

in the illustration. This is done roughly with a jackknife and finished with a wood rasp. Round off both ends of the stick.

Now we must give each end of the sticks a slight curve upward, that is, toward the beveled side. This is accomplished in a moment or two by holding the stick over a candle so that the heat strikes it at a point three inches from the end. When heated, bend the stick upward slightly and hold for a moment until the wood cools—the curve will then be permanent. A very slight bend is all that is needed—not over a quarter of an inch. Bend both ends of each stick in this way.

Now place one stick across the other as in Figure 10, wire together with stove wire, and the boomerang is complete.

The first point to remember in throwing the boomerang is that a perfectly calm day is necessary for the boomerang to work perfectly—the slightest breeze will carry it out of its course. These little boomerangs can be thrown in a gymnasuim.

Grip one of the ends between the thumb and forefinger of the right hand. The beveled side should be toward you as you hold it. Hold up the boomerang at about the level of the head, keeping it straight up and down. Throw it straight forward at head level, using the forearm and wrist only giving it a downward spin with the wrist as you release it to make it whirl as much as possible. Much strength is not necessary. It should cut a perfect circle in the air and come back directly into your hands—provided, of course, that no air currents are taking it out of its course.

No two boomerangs act just alike, and one has to throw each boomerang a few times to figure out just how to throw it to get the best results. Some boomerangs, when held straight up and down and thrown, circle and drop to the ground behind you; these must be thrown at an angle: hold the boomerang just as described above but tilt it slightly toward you, and throw it forward at this angle. With a little experimentation you should be able to make it come back perfectly.

Other boomerangs, when thrown from the straight-up-and-down position, will circle and drop to the ground in front of you. These must be tilted slightly in the opposite direction: as you hold them preliminary to throwing, tilt them slightly away from you and throw.

Occasionally a boomerang that is seemingly perfect in construction will not work at all. There is no way to tell what one will do until you try it. There are not many of these, however, so if your first attempt just will not work, discard it, and try another.

When a boomerang has been once thrown and found to work, you may depend upon it to act in exactly the same way every time it is properly thrown, provided no air currents interfere. When throwing in a slight breeze, *always face the breeze and throw straight into it.* One can have much sport with boomerangs in a slight breeze, but for an exhibition of perfect boomerang throwing, absolute calm is required.

Having made the little boomerang of gasoline sticks, you will want to try a large one. Cross-stick boomerangs may be made of any size. Regardless of size, the method of construction is the same, except that the two sticks are bolted together in the larger types instead of wired. An excellent size uses sticks twenty-four inches long, two inches wide, and three-sixteenths inch thick. For an extra large boomerang, use boards three feet long, two-and-three-eighths inches wide, and one-fourth inch thick. If these big boomerangs are too heavy and do not float well, gouge out some of the wood on the back side with a wood gouge, thus making the back side slightly hollow; care should be taken to remove about the same weight of wood from each of the four sections.

Wheel Boomerangs

School, Camp, Club   *Late Elementary School to Adult*

The wheel style of boomerang has three cross sticks instead of two, as shown in B, Figure 11. These boomerangs are made and thrown exactly as in the case of cross-stick boomerangs. Regardless of size, the sticks are bolted together and are not wired. Use wide washers under the bolts.

Sticks of the following dimensions are recommended:

1. Length, 15 inches; width, 1 to 1 1/16 inches; thickness, ⅛ inch.
2. Length, 24 inches; width, 2 inches; thickness, ⅛ to 3/16 inch.
3. Length, 36 inches; width 2⅜ inches; thickness, ¼ inch.

Paint the boomerang sticks white with two-inch stripes of black across them. As the boomerang whirls through the air, the stripes create circles and add color to the event. With a little study, you can arrange the stripes so that a spiral effect is produced as the boomerang sails through the air.

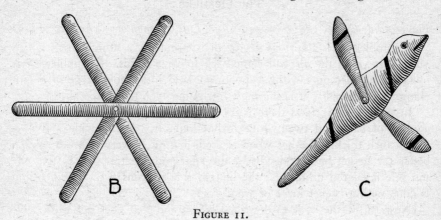

FIGURE 11.

A delightful effect may be produced by attaching lights to each end of the sticks in a big boomerang. Bore a hole about three inches from each end, insert and fasten a flash light bulb, and attach the battery at the intersection of the sticks. Circles of light will thus be produced, and at night the effect is striking.

Boomabirds

School, Camp, Club   *Late Elementary School to Adults*

The boomabird is perhaps the most interesting and colorful type of boomerang. It is made to look like a bird, as illustrated in C, Figure 11. So realistic are these boomabirds in the air that the birds themselves are frequently confused and will swoop down toward the boomabird and come very close to the thrower.

Secure a soft-wood board twenty-two inches long, three-and-one-eighths inches wide, and one-eighth inch thick. Whittle it out roughly in the shape of the bird's body shown in the illustration. The exact shape does not matter. Bevel it on all sides and bend the ends as described above under Cross-stick Boomerangs. With a wood gouge remove some of the wood from the back side, leaving the board slightly hollow—this is to lighten the weight. Now prepare the wings from sticks thirteen inches long and one-and-three-fourths inches wide. Shape them as in the drawing, bevel the sides and ends, and bend the ends upward as in making cross-stick boomerangs. Bolt the wings to the body as illustrated, placing one on top of the body and the other behind the body.

Paint the boomabird a light color and then add stripes in a dark color as illustrated. These stripes create a circular design as the bird whirls through the air.

The boomabird is thrown by exactly the same method used for the cross-stick boomerang.

Tumblesticks

Playground, Camp, Club   *Late Elementary School to Adults*

A tumblestick is a curious device—it is essentially a straight stick which when thrown in the air will come back to your hands. A tumblestick is in fact a boomerang but the most unique and little-known type of boomerang. Consequently it is the most intriguing type to the spectators.

In spite of these facts there is no boomerang so easy to make. Secure a piece of basswood twenty-four inches long, two inches wide and one-fourth inch thick. If other wood is used, it must be very light and soft—better try to get basswood. Bevel the edges on the top side so that the top side is curved uniformly; the bottom side remains flat. The beveling is done with a pocket knife or wood rasp.

Now throw the stick as described below and if it does not work, give each end a very slight bend upward, toward the beveled side, as described under Cross-stick Boomerangs. The tumblestick is now complete.

Now to throw it: Hold one end in the right hand between the thumb and forefinger with the beveled side toward you. Throw it over your head and forward, giving it a spin with your fingers as you release it so that it whirls and hums in the air. As you release it you must also turn your wrist sharply downward so that the stick is given a motion causing it to turn over in the air. Do not use much muscle—it is done with the forearm and wrist.

The tumblestick will hum and whir, go up a few feet, turn over and float back into your hands. Remember that it will not work in a breeze; these delicate sticks are at their best indoors.

Do not be discouraged if the first tumblestick does not work. Make another. You may make several before you get one that can be depended upon to work perfectly on every occasion. When you get a good one, you will have an oddity that few people know how to make and throw.

Boomerang Accuracy Contest

Playground, Camp, Club   *Late Elementary School to Adults*

This contest must take place on a perfectly calm day. There is usually less breeze early in the evening than at any other time.

Mark out a circle one foot in diameter. The contestant stands with one foot in the circle, throws the boomerang, and catches it when it returns. He may turn around to follow the course of the boomerang, but is not permitted to lift the foot from the circle at any time. He throws ten times and is credited with one point for each catch. The one with the highest score wins.

All boomerangs used must be made by the contestant himself. He may change boomerangs any time during the competition.

Boomerang Endurance Contest

Playground, Camp, Club   *Late Elementary School to Adults*

In this contest the boomerang wins which stays in the air the longest time. A stop-watch is used. Each contestant is allowed ten throws and credited with his best time. The time is taken from the moment the boomerang is thrown, to the time when it is caught. If the boomerang is not caught the time is not taken, but it counts as a trial. The conditions of throwing and catching are the same as in the Boomerang Accuracy Contest. All boomerangs must be made by the contestant.

Some boomerangs will float very slowly and make two circles around the thrower before returning. This is the type that is ideal for this contest.

Boomerang With the Most Unique Action

Playground, Camp, Club   *Late Elementary School to Adults*

Some boomerangs circle the thrower two or more times and perform peculiar stunts in the air before returning. The contestant wins this event whose boomerang of his own making performs the most unique stunts in the air or completes the most circles around the thrower. Each thrower continues to throw until the judges are satisfied as to the typical performance of his boomerang.

Most Unique Type of Boomerang

Playground, Camp, Club   *Late Elementary School to Adults*

The contestant wins this event who displays the boomerang which, in the opinions of the judges, is of most unique construction. By experimentation, boomerangs of all sorts of queer shapes may be made, following the principles of construction described above. No boomerang is considered unless it performs perfectly and can be caught without stepping.

AXE THROWING

Boys quite universally find in axe throwing a particularly appealing activity. There is, of course, an element of danger in axe throwing, if the activity is carried on promiscuously and without adequate supervision. The dead tree or log which is used as a target should be fenced off with rails and a leader should always be present to supervise the throwing.

A hand axe may be thrown in several different ways. The type of throw usually used in contests is the Straight Overhand Throw. To cause the axe to stick in the target, one must stand at exactly the right distance from the target. The axe revolves when it is thrown, and unless one is at the right distance, the blade will not be in a position to stick when it hits the target. In the Straight Overhand Throw, the axe will make one revolution and stick at five steps, two revolutions at ten steps, and so forth.

In making the straight overhand throw, stand five steps from the target, grip the axe as near the end of the handle as possible, and hold it straight up and down with the blade toward the target. Step toward the target and throw with a downward jerk of the arm. The wrist should be kept stiff and care should be taken not to slope the axe sidewise in releasing it.

Axe Throwing for Consistency

Camp, Club, Playground   *Junior and Senior High Schools*

Each contestant is given twenty-five throws from the one-revolution distance (five steps from the target). He is credited with one point for each throw in which the axe sticks in the tree or board. The five highest point winners are given twenty-five additional throws, and each is credited with his best record whether thrown in the first or second series of twenty-five throws. The contestant with the highest score wins.

Axe-Throwing Contest for Most Consecutive Hits.—Each contestant continues to throw the axe until he misses, and is credited with the number of consecutive good throws which he makes. The one making the most consecutive throws wins the contest.

Axe Throwing for Distance

Camp, Club, Playground   *Junior and Senior High Schools*

Each contestant is allowed three throws to stick the axe in the tree or board from the one-revolution line. If he sticks it on the first throw, he is allowed to move back to the two-revolution line. If he misses on the first throw, he is allowed two additional throws.

Having stuck the axe from the one-revolution line, he is given three throws to stick it from the two-revolution line, and thus he continues to move back until he fails to stick the axe in three tries. The contestant wins who sticks the axe at the greatest distance from the target.

Other Axe-Throwing Events

A complete description of the various methods of axe throwing, together with additional contests, will be found in Chapter XVI, "Woodcraft Contests," in *Social Games for Recreation*.

THROWING AND CATCHING CONTESTS IN OTHER CHAPTERS

Snowball Tenpins.

Pelting the Snow Man.

Snow Snakes.

Snowball Twenty-One.

Pelting the Pipe.

THROWING AND CATCHING CONTESTS IN *SOCIAL GAMES FOR RECREATION*

Rope Quoits.

Chair Quoits.

Bottle Quoits.

Clothespin Ring Toss.

Washer Pitching.

Disk Quoits.

Beanbag Waste-basket Pitch.

Waste-basket Throw.

Waste-basket Bounce Throw.

Paper Plate Toss.

Peanut Target Throw.

Umbrella Toss.

Muffin Pan Penny Toss.

Calendar Toss.

Hoop Target.

Disk Roll.

Cards in the Hat.

Potato Jab.

Ping-Pong Bounceball.

Feeding the Elephant.

Funnel Ball.

Potato Tossing.

Tin Can Pebble Toss.

Bull-Board.

Exo.

Fruit Jar Ring Toss.

Washer Baseball.

London.

Shooting the Bottles.

Hanker Throw.

Egg Throwing Contest.

Rolling Pin Throwing.

Bag Throwing.

Ping-Pong Ball Roll.

False Alarm.

Rubber Heel Toss.

Bottle Top Toss.

Pointless Dart Throw.

Shuttlecock Target Toss.

Shuttlecock Hoop Toss.

CHAPTER V

STRIKING, SWINGING, AND KICKING CONTESTS

STRIKING AND SWINGING CONTESTS

Fungo Hit for Accuracy

Baseball Diamond   *Junior High School to College*

THIS interesting event is carried on on a regular baseball diamond. A judge and three assistants are needed. Each assistant has a stick or small white flag.

The contestants stand in deep center field. The object is to toss up the ball and bat it so that it will fall as near to home base as possible. When the first contestant bats, one of the assistants sticks his flag in the ground at the point where the ball struck and records the name of the contestant. The other two flags are similarly placed by the other two assistants after the second and third contestants have batted. Thereafter no record is kept of the batted balls until a ball strikes the ground nearer to home base than the most distant flag. Then this flag is removed and placed in the new position, and the assistant records the name of the contestant who batted the ball. Each contestant is given three attempts, making one attempt each time his turn comes. The contestant wins whose flag is nearest home base.

Tennis Serve for Accuracy

Tennis Court   *Late Elementary School to College*

Above the regular tennis net on a tennis court a second net is stretched, leaving a space of thirty inches between the two nets. A rope may be used in place of the upper net. The contestant stands in the usual serving position of tennis and serves one ball into the left service area, the next into the right, and so on. The ball must be driven through the space between the two nets. The object of the upper net is to prevent the contestant from lobbing the ball easily into the service area which is no test of one's serving ability. Each contestant is given ten serves and scores one for each good service.

Variation.[1]—Upon a wall, mark a space thirteen-and-one-half feet long and thirty inches wide, the lower line of the rectangle being thirty-six inches

[1] From *Athletic Badge Tests for Boys and Girls*, p. 12. Physical Education Series No. 2, 1923. By permission of the United States Bureau of Education, Department of Interior.

from the floor or ground. A line is drawn on the floor or ground thirty-eight feet from the wall and parallel to it. Upon this line is marked a thirteen-and-one-half foot space directly opposite the thirteen-and-one-half foot space on the wall. In making the serve the player must stand behind this thirty-eight foot line, but may not be within the thirteen-and-one-half foot space marked on this line. The ball may strike the upper line and be good but must clear the lower line.

Four, five, or six serves, as the case may be, shall count as one trial.

Tennis Stroke for Accuracy

Tennis Court   *Late Elementary to Senior High School*

Extend the center line on one side of the tennis court back to the rear line, thus dividing the side of the court into four parts. These four areas are called right service-court, left service-court, right back-court, and left back-court. The leader or referee stands on this side of the court, and the contestant on the other side.

The leader throws a tennis ball to the contestant and at the same time calls an area of the court, such as "Right service-court" or "Left back-court." The contestant attempts to hit the ball into the area named, and if successful scores one point. The leader throws twenty balls, calling each of the four sections five times. The sections are called at random.

Then the next contestant competes and the one with the highest score wins.

Volleyball Serve for Accuracy [2]

Playground, Gymnasium   *Late Elementary to Senior High School*

A volleyball net or piece of cord shall be stretched at a height of eight feet across the center of the playing space. Twenty-four feet distant a line shall be drawn on the floor or ground parallel to the net. The contestant with volleyball in hand shall stand facing the net and toeing the line with either foot. She tosses the ball with one hand, as in tennis, and strikes it with the other hand over the net so that it will fall within a square ten by ten feet. This square shall be marked on the floor or ground ten feet from the net and at right angles to it. If the contestant steps forward over the line before the ball strikes the ground, no score is allowed, but it counts as one serve.

Five or six serves, as the case may be, shall count as one trial. The serve may be made either underhand or overhand.

[2] From *Athletic Badge Tests for Boys and Girls,* p. 12. Physical Education series No. 2, 1923. By permission of the United States Bureau of Education, Department of the Interior.

Golf-Putting and Driving Events

Playground, Golf Course, Yard   *Junior High School to Adults*

Golf-Putting Contest.—A line is marked on the green six feet from the hole. The object is to putt the ball into the hole from this line. Each contestant makes ten putts in succession and scores one point for each ball that enters the hole. The contestant with the highest score wins.

Golf Approach for Accuracy.[3]—Drive a peg ten inches long in the golf green beside the cup. Tie a string forty feet long to the peg. Tie ribbons on the string at distances of ten, twenty, and thirty feet from the peg. Establish a driving line one-hundred feet from the hole.

The first contestant is given ten golf balls and drives them one after the other from the driving line, attempting to cause them to come to rest as near to the hole as possible. The balls are left on the ground where they stop. When all ten balls are driven, take the string and measure the balls, one at a time. Balls in the hole score ten, those within ten feet of it score five, those between ten and twenty feet score three, those between twenty and thirty feet score one, and those beyond thirty feet score nothing. After all contestants have driven, the one with the highest score wins.

When played on the playground, a tin can may be sunk for the hole, and three concentric circles marked on the ground with radii of ten, twenty, and thirty feet from the hole.

Golf Drive for Distance.—Establish a driving line. One-hundred yards out from this line drive two stakes about fifty yards apart so that an imaginary line drawn between them would be parallel to the driving line. Stakes should be driven in similar fashion every twenty-five yards up to the two-hundred-yard line. These distance stakes are to facilitate measuring. A hundred-foot tape is used in measuring.

The contestant places his ball upon the driving line and drives it as far as possible. The distance is measured to the point where the ball stops. Balls which do not come to rest in the fairway are disregarded, but count as trials. Measuring is done as in the Baseball Throw for Distance (page 41). Each contestant has three trials and is credited with his best distance.

Hockey Striking Events

Playground, Hockey Field   *Late Elementary School to Adults*

Hockey-Goal Golf.—Mark nine spots in a semi-circle around the field-hockey goal. With field-hockey sticks, the players hit the ball from spot Number 1, attempting to put it through the goal. Each continues to

---

[3] Taken from the description in S. C. Staley, *Individual and Mass Athletics,* p. 83. Copyright, 1925. By permission of A. S. Barnes & Company, publishers.

hit in turn from this spot until he makes the goal, counting the hits required. They then hit from spot Number 2, and so on.

The player wins who completes the course of nine spots with the fewest strokes.

Shinney Golf.—Same as the above, using a shinney stick and paddle-tennis ball.

Hockey Drive for Accuracy.—The driving is done from a line thirty-five yards from the goal, although the distance may be varied to suit the capacity of the players. Each player is given ten (or five) drives and scores one point each time the ball is put through the goal.

Hit the Can.—Place a gallon tin can or water bucket on the ground between the goal posts of the hockey goal. The striking line is from the striking circle fifteen yards out. Each player is given ten attempts, one each turn, to drive the hockey ball and hit the can. One point is scored each time the can is hit, and the player with the highest score wins.

Hockey Drive for Distance.—Establish a striking line. The players take turns in driving the hockey ball from the line with the stick, each being given ten (or five) drives. The one driving the ball the farthest wins. The measuring is done as in the Baseball Throw for Distance (page 41).

Hockey-Dribbling Race.—The players line up on the starting line, each with a hockey stick and ball. At the signal they dribble the ball to the turning line, stop it, and dribble back to finish at the starting line. The player finishing first wins. The turning line should be thirty to fifty yards distant.

Variation.—Station a person on the turning line opposite each player. On reaching the turning line, the player dribbles the ball around the person and then back.

Obstacle Hockey-Dribbling Race.—Midway between the starting and turning lines place a low obstacle. The players line up on the starting line with hockey sticks and balls. At the signal they dribble to the obstacle, scoop the ball over it, dribble to the turning line, stop the ball, and dribble back as before to finish at the starting line.

Circle Hockey-Dribbling Race.—Arrange the players in a circle, each with a hockey stick and ball. The ball is placed by the feet. One player, "it," goes around outside the circle carrying her ball. She touches a player with her stick, drops her ball, turns, and dribbles around the circle in the opposite direction. The person tagged dribbles her ball around the circle in the direction opposite to that taken by "it." The one putting the ball through the vacant place first wins, and the other is "it."

In dropping her ball, "it" must drop it so that it falls vertically.

Polo-Driving and Dribbling Events

See Polo Drive for Distance, Polo-Dribbling Race, and Polo Drive for Accuracy in Chapter XXVIII, "Horseback-Riding Activities."

Striking and Swinging Contests in Other Chapters

Polo Drive for Distance.   Polo Drive for Accuracy.
Polo-Dribbling Race.   Hockey Golf.

Striking and Swinging Contests in *Social Games for Recreation*

Tumbler Golf.   Balloon-Batting Race.
Golf Target-Board Putting.   Spike-Driving Contest.
Nail-Driving Contest.   Log-Chopping with Hand Axe.
Log-Chopping Contest.   Cross-cut Sawing Contest.

KICKING CONTESTS

Rugby Football Kicking Events

Football Field, Playground   *Junior High School to College*

Rugby Punt for Distance.—The contestant stands behind the goal line of the football field, drops the ball, and kicks it before it touches the ground. At the time the foot hits the ball, the contestant must be behind the line. The distance is measured as in the Baseball Throw for Distance (page 41).

Rugby Place-Kick for Distance.—The ball is set on end on the goal line of the football field. The contestant runs up and kicks it as far as possible. Having kicked it, he may cross the line. The measuring is done as in the Baseball Throw for Distance (page 41).

Rugby Place-Kick for Accuracy.—The regulation goal is needed. The kicking line may be placed from twenty to thirty yards away depending on the age and skill of the contestants. The contestant stands the ball on the kicking line, runs, and kicks it, attempting to put it over the crossbar. Each goal made scores one point. Each contestant is given ten kicks.

Rugby Drop-Kick for Accuracy.—A regulation goal is needed. The kicking line may be fifteen to twenty-five yards away depending on the age and skill of the contestants. The contestant stands behind the kicking line and drop-kicks the ball, attempting to put it over the crossbar. Each goal kicked scores one point. Each contestant is given ten kicks.

Drop-Kick for Distance.—This event is conducted like the Rugby Punt for Distance, except that when the contestant drops the ball he allows it to touch the ground and kicks it immediately after it rebounds.

Soccer Football Kicking Events

Soccer Field, Rugby Field   *Junior High School to College*

Soccer Place-Kick for Distance.—Conducted in the same way as the Rugby Place-Kick for Distance.

Soccer Punt for Distance.—Conducted in the same way as the Rugby Punt for Distance.

Soccer Place-Kick for Accuracy.—Use a regulation soccer goal and soccer ball, and proceed as in the Rugby Place-Kick for Accuracy, except that the ball is kicked between the goal posts and under the crossbar. Balls going through the goal on the fly score two and those going through on the bounce or rolling score one.

Speedball Kicking Events

Speedball Field, Football Field   *Junior High School to College*

Speedball Punt for Distance.—Use a speedball and conduct like the Rugby Punt for Distance.

Speedball Drop-Kick for Distance.—Use a speedball and conduct like the Rugby Drop-Kick for Distance.

Speedball Drop-Kick for Accuracy.—Use a speedball and conduct like the Rugby Drop-Kick for Accuracy.

Speedball Place-Kick for Distance.—Use a speedball and conduct like the Rugby Place-Kick for Distance.

Speedball Place-Kick for Accuracy.—Use a speedball and conduct like the Rugby Place-Kick for Accuracy except that the ball is kicked between the goal posts and under the crossbar.

Kick and Catch.—A person rolls the speedball or soccer ball on the ground toward the contestant. The contestant kicks it into the air and attempts to catch it. Each contestant is given ten attempts and scores one point each time he succeeds.

Codeball Kick for Distance

Football Field, Playground   *Junior High School to Adults*

An official codeball is laid on or behind the goal line. The contestant kicks it as it rests on the ground, kicking either with or without a run. Each contestant is given three kicks. The one kicking the greatest distance wins. The distance is measured to the point where the ball comes to rest not where it first hits the ground.

Kick, Bounce, and Catch

Playground, Gymnasium   *Late Elementary to Senior High School*

A wall is needed for this event. Give the first player a soccer ball or codeball. The latter is much to be desired because of the ease with which it bounces. The player takes any position he desires and kicks the ball against the wall, runs, and attempts to catch it on the rebound. He is given three attempts and marks his farthest catch. The other players compete in turn and the one making the farthest catch wins.

CHAPTER VI

CONTESTS BASED ON HANDLING MECHANICAL OBJECTS

In the events described in this chapter, the objective centers around the skillful handling or manipulation of some object of a mechanical nature. In some of the events the mechanical feature is strongly evident, as in Riflery and Model-Airplane Flying; in others it is minor, as in Rope Spinning and Kite Flying.

These events are of the following types: (1) Archery, (2) Riflery, (3) Trap Shooting, (4) Blow-Gun Shooting, (5) Bait and Fly Casting, (6) Top Spinning, (7) Kite Flying, (8) Rope Spinning, (9) Model-Airplane and Balloon Flying, (10) Model-Boat Events.

ARCHERY

AT certain periods of history archery has been the most popular of all sports. As a recreational sport today it has a far-flung and ever-increasing following among all ages and sexes. It is an excellent corrective for some posture difficulties and for under-developed individuals.

Archery Tournaments

Playground, Camp   *Late Elementary School to Adults*

Most shooting with bow and arrow is done on a regulation field and at regulation targets. In schools and camps the season usually terminates in archery tournaments and consequently most of the shooting throughout the season is done according to tournament rules as to distance and equipment.

Field.—Sometimes a permanent shooting line is established and the targets moved to the required distance for each event. A much better method, however, is to line up the targets in permanent position and establish a series of shooting lines at the various standard distances from the target line.

As illustrated in Figure 12, the course for men is one-hundred yards long, with other shooting lines drawn at distances of eighty, sixty, fifty, and forty yards from the targets. The course for women is sixty yards long with other lines at fifty, forty, and thirty yards from the target. At least six yards of space should be allowed for each shooting lane.

The grass around and for some distance behind the targets should be mowed very short and raked to prevent losing arrows. The course should be laid out to the north and south if possible to relieve competitors from the necessity of looking into the sun, and there should be a background of trees, hills, or buildings behind the targets to provide points of aim.

Equipment.—For outdoor shooting, targets forty-eight inches in diameter are used. The face of the target consists of a circular piece of oilcloth on which five concentric rings are painted. The diameter of the painted area is forty-eight inches. This target face is attached to a target made of

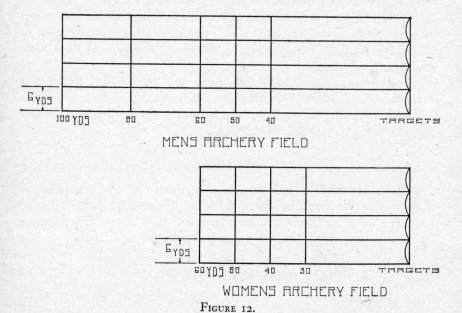

FIGURE 12.

sewn straw. The target is supported by a target stand made of soft pine or cypress, so that the target leans back slightly and the center of the bull's-eye is exactly four feet from the ground.

Standard commercial targets of the best quality are the most serviceable and durable. In camp, a usable target may be made by setting up two bales of straw and attaching the target face to them. Faces may be made at home by coloring the back side of a fifty-four-inch square of oilcloth. The radius of the bull's-eye is four-and-four-fifths inches and each ring is of the same width. The coloring may be done with paint or wax crayon.

Arrows are usually twenty-seven inches in length for men and twenty-six inches for women. Children frequently use arrows twenty-four inches long.

Ground quivers made of wire and stuck in the ground at the shooting line are a decided convenience.

Events and Distances.—There are several standard rounds in use in archery tournaments, the York Round for Men, the National Round for Men and Women, the American Round for Men and Women, the Metropolitan Round for Men, the Metropolitan Round for Women, and the Columbia Round for Women. There are junior rounds in the National, American, and Columbia. A tournament may consist of one or all of these rounds.

The distances for the various rounds are as follows:

York Round for Men
　　Seventy-two arrows at one-hundred yards.
　　Forty-eight arrows at eighty yards.
　　Twenty-four arrows at sixty yards.
National Round for Men and Women
　　Forty-eight arrows at sixty yards.
　　Twenty-four arrows at fifty yards.
Junior National Round for Boys and Girls
　　Forty-eight arrows at fifty yards.
　　Twenty-four arrows at forty yards.
American Round for Men and Women
　　Thirty arrows at sixty yards.
　　Thirty arrows at fifty yards.
　　Thirty arrows at forty yards.
Junior American Round for Boys and Girls
　　Thirty arrows at fifty yards.
　　Thirty arrows at forty yards.
　　Thirty arrows at thirty yards.
Metropolitan Round for Men
　　Thirty arrows at one-hundred yards.
　　Thirty arrows at eighty yards.
　　Thirty arrows at sixty yards.
Metropolitan Round for Women
　　Thirty arrows at sixty yards.
　　Thirty arrows at fifty yards.
　　Thirty arrows at forty yards.
Columbia Round for Women
　　Twenty-four arrows at fifty yards.
　　Twenty-four arrows at forty yards.
　　Twenty-four arrows at thirty yards.
Junior Columbia Round for Girls
　　Twenty-four arrows at forty yards.
　　Twenty-four arrows at thirty yards.
　　Twenty-four arrows at twenty yards.

A double round in any of the above consists of shooting two rounds in succession.

Tournaments frequently feature team rounds, flight shooting, and various novelty events as described below.

Shooting.—Four archers are assigned to each target, and are numbered to designate the order in shooting. Number 1 archer shoots three arrows, then Number 2 shoots three arrows, and so forth. When all four have shot, they all shoot three more arrows in turn. When all have shot six arrows, they all go to the target for the scoring. Archer Number 2 withdraws the arrows of the archers in the order in which they shot and Archer Number 1 records the score. As each arrow is withdrawn the score is called and recorded by the scorer. Each archer should use arrows with markings of different colors to facilitate scoring.

Scoring.—The target has five rings, and arrows piercing these rings count nine, seven, five, three, and one. The score for each arrow is recorded on the score card and then the number of hits and the total score. That is, if six arrows were shot, two of which landed in the outer ring and one each in each of the other rings, the score would appear on the card as follows:

975311 6-26

This indicates that six hits were made which totalled to a score of twenty-six.

An arrow passing through the target, or rebounding from the scoring area of it, scores five points regardless of where it hit. An arrow on the dividing line scores in the higher circle even though it barely touches it. An arrow which jumps off the string counts as a shot unless the archer can touch it with his bow.

In tournaments, the archer wins who has the highest total score for all shots. Hits are not counted in adding the score but only the points made.

In case of a tie, the archer wins who has the highest score at the longest range. If a tie still exists, the competitor wins who has the highest score at the next longest range.

In the national championships for men, the archer wins who has the highest total score in the double York and double American rounds. For women the archer wins who has the highest total score in the double National and double Columbia rounds.

Team Competition.—Although team competition does not fall under the title of this chapter, a description of the team rounds in archery should be included here. A standard team consists of four contestants, but for informal competition, any number may compete provided the teams are equal in size. There are two methods commonly used in informal competition between archery clubs: (1) All members of the competing club comprise the club's team (or as many members as possible to achieve teams of equal size), and the total score made by the team is divided by the number of players on the team. The team with the highest average score wins. (2) All members of the club shoot with the understanding that the four (or other agreed-upon number) who make the highest scores will comprise the team and their scores only will be used in determining the team's score. Either of these informal methods is preferable to the use of the standard four-player team, in that more players have a chance to compete.

The team rounds are as follows:

Men: ninety-six arrows at sixty yards.
Women: ninety-six arrows at fifty yards.
Juniors: ninety-six arrows at forty yards.

Indoor Archery.—Archery ranges may be set up with little expense in gymnasiums, vacant rooms, attics, and basements. Fifteen to twenty yards is ample distance. A backstop behind the targets is needed to prevent breaking arrows; felt curtains, wall board, or bales of straw may be used for this purpose. The size of the target depends upon the length of the range; if the regulation four-foot target is taken as the standard for thirty yards, a two-foot target would be used for fifteen yards.

Archery Golf

Camp, Club, Golf Course   *Junior High School to Adults*

Archery Golf is an excellent sport which can be played the year around, winter and summer, in all kinds of weather. Neither snow, rain, nor

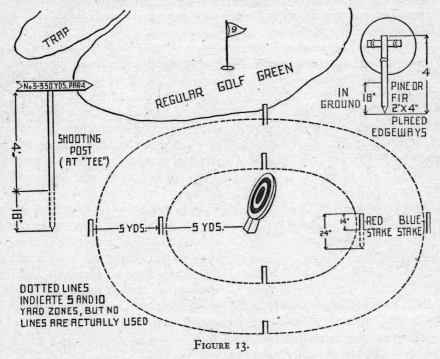

FIGURE 13.

frozen ground necessarily stops it. It takes Archery out of the category of a fair-weather sport only.

Archery Golf is golf played with a bow and arrow. A golf course is frequently used, with the targets placed a few feet to one side of the regular golf holes. However, any open field serves the purpose. Targets are set up on the field at suitable intervals of from one-hundred to three-hundred yards, after the order of the holes in a golf course. A nine-target course can be established in twenty or twenty-four acres, but a five-target

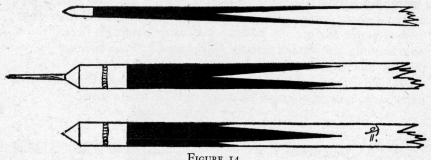

FIGURE 14.

course is very satisfactory, especially when it is possible to shoot first up the course to target Number 5, then back down to target Number 1, thus making nine targets in all.

Targets.—The simplest target is a bale of straw stood on end with a stake driven into the ground to hold it upright. A cardboard disk four-and-one-half inches in diameter is

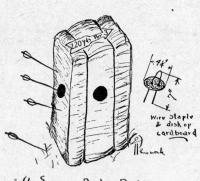

Ye Straw Bale Butts.

attached to each of the four sides of the bale, held in place by a long wire staple. On top of the bale and fastened to it in the same manner is a pointer or arrow of wood or cardboard pointing to the next target and giving the distance in yards.

Bows and Arrows.—Regular Archery Golf calls for three types of arrows: (1) flight arrows for the distance shots; (2) approach arrows; and (3) target arrows. However, flight arrows, even though footed, are fragile and easily broken. For ordinary use by non-expert archers, it is wise to use only one type of arrow—a substantial, footed approach arrow. For winter use, these arrows are equipped with a small spike or nail protruding from the end to prevent skidding on snow and ice.

For summer play, regular target bows may be used. However, for cold weather the best bow is the flat or so-called Indian style. This type is less apt to break in cold weather than the common type of target bow.

The Play.—Standing at any target, each archer shoots one arrow at the next target. Two or three shots may be needed to get within reasonable strkiing distance. Each succeeding shot is taken from the spot where the preceding arrow comes to rest. A score of one is counted for each shot taken. When close enough, the archer attempts to shoot the cardboard disk on any one of the faces of the bale. If he succeeds he has "holed out." If he misses the disk but hits the bale, he is considered as having "holed out" but an extra point is added to his score.

The general procedure and scoring follows that used in Golf.

Clout Shooting

Playground, Camp   *Senior High School to Adults*

A target forty-eight feet in diameter is laid out on the ground and the object is to shoot the arrows so that they will drop into the target. The target may be marked with lime or with tennis tape. The radius of the bull's-eye is four-and-four-fifths feet and each ring is of this same width. A flag is erected in the center of the bull's-eye.

The shooting line for men is 180 yards from the center of the target, and for women, 120 yards. The round consists of thirty-six arrows per archer.

Scoring is as follows: hitting the clout, ten points; arrow nearest the clout, five points; next nearest arrow, three points; third nearest arrow, one point.

Flight Shooting

Open Country   *Senior High School to Adults*

This is shooting for distance. Special bows and arrows are needed. There is danger from stray arrows and the event requires an unobstructed open field and careful supervision.

Roving

Open Country   *Senior High School to Adults*

This ancient sport consists of walking through the woods and fields and shooting at marked natural targets at frequent intervals. The targets, called "rovers," are marked with paint or colored cloth; they may be bushes, colored spots on the ground, spots on hill sides, tree trunks, and so forth. If a regular trail is followed, shooting lines may be established, but the usual procedure is to shoot from the spot where the target is sighted. Each archer is given two shots, and one point is scored by the arrow coming closest to the target. The archer scoring seven points first wins.

This sport is frequently played with no marked targets. The archers agree on a first target, and the winner has the privilege of picking out the next target as they walk along.

Specially prepared roving arrows are available which are not damaged by striking a hard surface such as a tree trunk.

Roving is acceptable only in areas which are not frequented by people. In sections much used for hiking, as is usually the case around summer camps, the danger of people walking into the line of the arrows is too great to justify the activity, unless very careful supervision is provided.

William Tell Archery Contest

Playground, Indoor Archery Range   *Expert Archers*

Draw a picture of a boy on wallboard and cut out the figure. Erect it and place an apple on the head. An archer who hits the boy is eliminated. The first to hit the apple wins. The distance may be fifteen to thirty yards depending on the skill of the archers.

Archery Balloon Shooting

Open Space   *Junior High School to Adults*

Inflate toy balloons with gas and tie them along a line on the ground with string so that they float at varying heights from six to twenty feet from the ground. Each archer is allowed three shots at each balloon, shooting in turn, one arrow each time. The archer breaking the balloon wins.

Variation.—Inflate the balloons with air and suspend them from a horizontal wire so that they hang six or eight feet from the ground.

Rabbit Hunting

Open Country   *Junior High School to Adults*

Toy rabbits of stuffed cloth or papier-maché are purchased from a toy store for a few cents and hidden in the grass along a designated trail. The archers hunt for the rabbits and shoot at them from the spots where the rabbits are sighted. When an archer spies a rabbit he calls "Rabbit" and scores one point. He shoots one arrow from this point and then the other archers shoot one each from the same spot. The shooting continues until the rabbit is hit or until each archer has shot three arrows. An archer hitting the rabbit scores five points. If the rabbit is not hit, the nearest arrow scores three, and the archers search for the next rabbit.

Archery Wand Shooting

Playground   *Expert Archers*

In this event the target consists of a wooden wand or stick. It is made of soft wood, preferably white pine, cypress, or balsam. It is two inches wide and six feet long. Men shoot from a distance of one-hundred yards and women from sixty yards. The round consists of thirty-six arrows and the archer wins who scores the most hits.

Still-Hunting the Buck [1]

Camp, Open Country   *Late Elementary to Senior High School*

This sport was originated by Ernest Thompson Seton for camps and woodcraft circles and has met with wide-spread popularity.

The deer is made of straw and burlap over a wire skeleton. The wire frame is made in the dimensions shown in Figure 15. The straw is

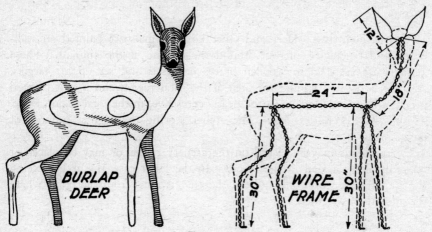

FIGURE 15.

wrapped and tied around the wire until the deer has the desired shape, and then burlap is wrapped around it and sewed. Black and white paint gives it the realistic touch.

On the side of the deer a large oval is marked to indicate the vital regions and a spot marks the heart.

One individual is assigned to hide the deer. With a pocket full of corn and the deer under his arm he starts out, dropping two or three kernels of corn every yard. He hides the deer in any place he chooses except in front of rocks or on top of a ridge.

After ten minutes the hunters start out following the corn trail. The hunter who first spies the deer calls "Deer." This hunter shoots one arrow from this spot and if he misses all the others shoot one arrow. If no kill is made, they take five steps and shoot in turn again. This continues until within ten yards of the deer, or until a hit is made; in the latter case all further shooting must be done from the spot where the hit is made. If

[1] The idea for this contest was taken from E. T. Seton, *The Birch Bark Roll of Woodcraft*, p. 17 ff. Copyright, 1931. By permission of A. S. Barnes & Company, publishers.

the hunter who finds the deer is nearer to it than ten yards all shooting must be done from this spot.

A shot in the heart scores ten and ends the hunt. A shot in the large oval is a body wound and scores five. A shot outside the large oval is a scratch and scores two. If, after all have shot three arrows from a spot ten yards away, the heart has not been struck the contest ends and twenty-five points are awarded the hunter who hid the deer. The hunter with the highest score wins.

This contest requires careful supervision; the players should be kept together behind the shooters to avoid any possibility of being hit by stray arrows.

Game Hunting.—Deer and other large animals are painted on wall-board and the board cut out around the outline of the animals. These animals are attached to wooden braces or easels and set up for targets. A circle is painted around the area of the vital region and a spot painted over the heart. An arrow in the heart scores five, in the vital region three, and in the extremities, one. The archer scoring the highest number of points wins.

The animals may be placed on the archery range, or may be placed at intervals along a trail in the woods. In the latter case, the archer seeing the animal first scores one and the shooting is done from the point where the animal was sighted.

RIFLERY

Riflery is a most popular sport in many organized summer camps and in many schools. On a properly constructed range and with adequate supervision to insure safety, it is a most desirable and worth-while sport.

Range.—The standard distance for target shooting is fifty feet for junior and interscholastic competition, and fifty and seventy-five feet for adults. The range should thus be sufficient in length to establish two firing lines, one fifty feet from the target rack and the other seventy-five feet. A minimum width of four feet is needed for each firing point.

The target rack consists of boards to which the targets are tacked. The boards are replaced when destroyed by the bullets. Behind the target-rack a backstop must be constructed. For outdoor ranges, a steep hill is the best backstop. Gentle slopes may be dug out so that there is a perpendicular surface behind the target rack. Bullets ricochet off rocks and keep going, and consequently all stones should be carefully removed. If a hill is not available, a backstop may be constructed of loose cribbing filled with dry earth and sodded. The cribbing should be at least three feet thick, not less than ten feet high, and extend not less than six feet beyond the ends of the rack.

For backstops for indoor ranges the National Rifle Association recommends the use of three-eighths-inch steel plates hung at an angle of thirty to forty-five degrees. Steel plates should also be placed at the ends of the rack and on the floor.

Rifles.—Any .22 caliber rifle using a rim-fire cartridge may be used. Metallic sights only are permitted.

Targets.—National-Rifle-Association fifty-foot or seventy-five-foot five-bull targets are used. For juniors, the National-Rifle-Association single-bull junior target is used which is of the same dimensions as the fifty-foot five-bull target except that additional scoring rings are added.

When the single-bull junior target is used, five shots are fired at each target; when the five-bull target is used, two shots are fired at each bull.

Scoring.—The rings are scored as follows: 10, 9, 8, 7, 6, 5. On the junior target the additional rings score 4, 3, and 2. Shots which break or touch a line are scored in the higher circle.

Standard Riflery Contests

Camp, School, Club Rifle Range   *Junior High School to Adults*

Scholastic or Junior Rifle Contest.—Each contestant shoots forty shots from the prone position. The shots are fired in four strings of ten record shots each. The contestant with the highest score wins.

Junior Gallery Rifle Contest.—Each contestant shoots ten shots in each of the following positions: prone, sitting, kneeling, standing. The contestant with the best total score wins.

Senior Gallery Rifle Contest.—The National Rifle Association individual gallery-championship regulations[2] call for three stages, each to consist of two strings of ten shots, as follows:

First stage: one string prone, one sitting
Second stage: one string prone, one kneeling
Third stage: one string prone, one standing

There are two sections, section A at fifty feet, and section B at seventy-five feet.

Any small-bore rifle with metallic sights may be used.

Interscholastic Team Rifle Contest.—Teams consist of ten contestants. The meet consists of three stages, each stage consisting of two strings of ten shots each. The stages are as follows:

First stage: two strings in the prone position
Second stage: one string prone, one kneeling
Third stage: one string prone, one standing

[2] See National Rifle Association. *Gallery and Home Range Matches for the Rifle and Pistol*, p. 8. Washington: National Rifle Association, 1933.

In military-school competition the three stages are as follows:

First stage: one string prone, one sitting

Second stage: one string prone, one kneeling

Third stage: one string prone, one standing

Girls' teams should shoot three strings of ten shots each from the prone position.

The team with the highest aggregate score wins. In the National-Rifle-Association competition, the five high aggregate scores count for a record.[3]

String-Shooting Contest

Camp, School, Club   *Junior High School to Adults*

Suspend a box of candy by a cord near the target board. The contestant who can shoot the candy down by cutting the string with the bullet can have it. The contestants shoot in turns, each taking one shot at a time. Should the candy be dropped before all have had one shot it should be suspended again. In case two drop it, declare a tie and have them shoot it off.

Since the candy itself may be hit by the bullet, it is well to wrap a box of sand to resemble a box of candy, and have the real candy at hand to present.

Crayon Rifle Contest

Camp, School, Club Rifle Range   *Junior High School to Adults*

Erect a strip of two-by-two-inch lumber in front of the target board, extending the length of the backstop. In this strip bore five three-eighths-inch holes, one-half inch apart and one-half inch deep. In each hole set a white crayon. Set up as many sets of crayons as there are contestants or as many as the width of the backstop will permit.

Each contestant is given five shots. The one breaking the most crayons wins.

Wand Shooting with Rifle.—Stick a slender stick about three-eighths inch thick in the ground at the target board. Each contestant is given five shots. One point is scored each time the stick is hit.

Candle-Shooting Contest

Camp, School, Club Rifle Range   *Junior High School to Adults*

Set up a row of five candles on a board at the firing line and light them. Each contestant is given five shots to extinguish the candles. He scores one point for each candle extinguished. Shots which hit and knock over a candle score as a miss. The contestant with the highest score wins.

[3] See National Rifle Association, *Rule Book for Junior Marksmen*, p. 16. Washington: National Rifle Association, 1932.

Match-Lighting Contest.—Erect a strip of board parallel to the ground in front of the backstop. The same strips used for the Crayon Shooting Contest may be used. In it erect ten matches by inserting them in small holes bored with an ice pick. Each contestant is given ten shots. First place goes to the one who succeeds in lighting a match. The other places are awarded to those who break the most matches.

Tack-Driving Contest

Camp, School, Club Rifle Range　　　　*Junior High School to Adults*

Set up a board painted white against the backstop in each shooting lane. In each board put five large-headed tacks. The tacks are driven in just far enough to hold them in place. Each contestant is given five shots. The one driving the most tacks wins.

Pendulum Shooting

Camp, School, Club Rifle Range　　　　*Junior High School to Adults*

Suspend a block of wood four inches square by a three-foot cord near the target board. Start the block swinging from side to side in pendulum fashion. Each contestant is given ten shots to hit the swinging pendulum. Each hit scores one point. The contestant with the highest score wins.

Balloon Rifle-Shooting Contest

Outdoor Rifle Range　　　　*Junior High School to Adults*

Erect a bar above the backstop and suspend as many small toy balloons as possible from it on strings. If the wind is blowing this event will be particularly interesting. Each contestant is given five shots. They shoot in turn, one shot at a time. The one who breaks the most balloons in five shots wins. If there is no wind the contest is too simple and the firing line should be moved back.

Balloon Rifle-Shooting Variation.—Balloon shooting becomes decidedly fascinating if gas-filled balloons are available and the background to the backstop is such that they can be tied to long strings so that they float high in the air. Tie the strings to the ground and float the balloons at varying heights of from twenty to one-hundred feet.

Big-Game Hunt

Camp, School, Club Rifle Range　　　　*Junior High School to Adults*

Five animal crackers are tied by strings to the backstop. The crackers represent an elephant, a lion, a tiger, a bear, and a jackass. Place a set of crackers in each shooting lane.

Each contestant is given five shots. Hitting the elephant scores five, the lion three, the tiger two, the bear one, and the player hitting the jackass loses all points. The contestants of course do not know the name of the animal at which they are shooting. Award the winner a box of animal crackers.

Putting the Pupil in the Bull's-Eye

Camp, School, Club, Rifle Range   *Junior High School to Adults*

Make a number of three-inch cardboard disks, colored black, and fasten them to the backstop. Mark the exact center of each with a pin prick. Each contestant is assigned one disk and is given five shots at it. The one who comes the nearest to hitting the exact center is awarded the prize of putting the pupil in the bull's-eye.

Shoot the Bird

Outdoor Rifle Range   *Junior High School to Adults*

Shooting objects which are tossed in the air after the manner of the circus cowboys holds a peculiar appeal to boys. Use a block of wood about four inches square. The tosser stands behind the shooter and tosses the wood up in the air so that at its highest point it is about ten feet in front of the shooter. Each contestant is given ten attempts and scores one each time the block is hit. The player with the highest score wins.

The trick in this event consists of shooting when the block is at its highest point; it comes to rest momentarily there before falling.

Novelty Riflery Meet

Camp, School, Rifle Range, Club   *Junior High School to Adults*

A most interesting novelty riflery meet may be conducted by using some of the contests described in the foregoing pages. In riflery, as in any sport, players like occasional novelty events calling for the skills of the sport instead of constant participation in formal events.

Such a novelty program could include the following:

Wand Shooting.   String (box of candy) Shooting.
Candle Shooting.   Crayon Rifle Contest.
Pendulum Shooting.   Tack-Driving Contest.
Balloon Rifle Shooting.   Match-Lighting Contest.
William Tell Rifle Contest.   Big-Game Hunt.

TRAP SHOOTING

Trap Shooting is a popular sport in which clay targets are thrown into the air by a mechanical device called a trap, and shot with a shot gun. It is an interesting sport in itself and excellent practice for game-bird hunting.

Grounds and Equipment.—For one trap, an area 100 by 250 yards is needed. If more than one trap is to be used, the traps should be at least twenty-five yards apart and preferably thirty. Visibility is usually better at all hours of the day if the targets are thrown to the north. It is necessary to allow 250 yards of free space in front of the target; shot will not carry that far, but in the interests of safety, at least that much space should be allowed. The background should be a level field or water; trees and hills are not satisfactory in that the target is difficult to see.

Many types of traps are on the market. The trap should be sunk in a pit below the level of the ground, or in a small enclosure built of wood.

The firing line should be sixteen yards in back of the trap. Five firing points should be marked on the line, three to five yards apart.

Standard clay pigeons are used.

Twelve-gauge shot guns are considered standard for Trap Shooting. Larger guns are barred in the official rules, and no handicaps are offered those using smaller guns. However, those with smaller guns may compete in informal play at a closer distance, say fourteen yards.

Trap-Shooting Contest

School, Camp, Club   *Junior High School to Adults*

The contestants agree on the number of targets to be shot. The usual numbers are twenty-five and fifty. The contestant stands on the firing line —holding the gun in informal shooting position, with the stock away from his shoulder. He is not permitted to put the gun to his shoulder until the bird is in the air.

When ready, he calls, and the puller releases the bird. To score, the bird must be actually broken; "dusting" a bird does not count.

The player wins who breaks the most birds out of the run of twenty-five or fifty.

Silent Trap Shooting.—The shooter is not permitted to call to the puller. The puller releases the bird whenever he chooses, and the shooter has no warning until he sees the bird in the air.

Handicap Shooting.—With competitors of varying abilities, it is well to classify them and handicap the better shots. The shooting distances may be as follows:

Average .... 16 yards
Good .... 17 to 19 yards
Excellent .... 21 to 23 yards

Bird Shooting

School, Camp, Club   *Senior High School to Adults*

In this novelty form of Trap Shooting, the contestant starts twenty-five yards from the target and works toward it. The puller releases the bird at any time he chooses, and the shooter has no warning. The contest is designed to approximate the conditions encountered in game-bird hunting.

Sniping

School, Camp, Club   *Senior High School to Adults*

In this event the shooter stands twenty-five feet *in front* of the trap, facing away from it. He starts to walk away, and the puller sends birds over his head whenever he chooses. He must take at least one step between shots. He shoots twenty-five shells before returning. The contest works best when the shooter has an automatic gun. When double-barreled guns are used, two shooters take the field at once, alternating in shooting. As a matter of safety, the two shooters should remain in line and several feet apart.

Skeet

School, Camp, Club   *Senior High School to Adults*

Skeet is a form of trap shooting that is particularly interesting to those who have developed proficiency in shooting clay pigeons. It differs from ordinary trap shooting chiefly in the layout of the field.

Two trap houses are placed forty yards apart, so arranged that birds shot from one will fly over the top of the other. Using a point midway between the two trap houses as the center, a semicircle is marked on the ground connecting the two trap houses. On this semicircle seven shooting stations are marked, equidistant from each other; an eighth station is marked midway between the two trap houses.

The contestant shoots first from Station 1, then from Station 2, and so on throughout the ·series of eight stations. Thus when standing in each station the birds fly at a different angle in respect to the position of the shooter, and when standing in Station 8, they fly directly overhead. A particularly interesting aspect of Skeet is the shooting of doubles: two birds are released simultaneously, one from each station, and the shooter attempts to bring them both down, shooting his first shell at the outgoing bird and his second at the incoming one.

The details of the construction of the range and the shooting rules may be obtained from the official rule book.[4]

BLOW-GUN CONTESTS

Blow guns appeal strongly to boys and girls and their use is to be recommended both as recreation and as an exercise for the lungs.

Equipment.—Commercial blow guns may be used when they can be obtained, but failing here, very satisfactory ones may be made in a few minutes from glass tubing. The glass tubes should be five to six feet

[4] See *Official Skeet Average and Rule Book.* Boston: National Skeet Shooting Association, Inc. published annually.

long with an opening one-fourth to three-eights inch in diameter. Wrap the tubes with tape to prevent breaking. Chemistry laboratories usually have tubing of the proper size.

The arrows are made from splints cut from a bamboo pole. They should be ten or eleven inches long. Select a section of a pole where the nodes are ten or eleven inches apart, or as near this as possible, and saw out a section between the nodes. Split the section into splints and shave them down to one-eighth inch in diameter. Sharpen one end and insert the other end into the small end of a cork which is just large enough to slip into the glass tube. Instead of a cork a wad of cotton may be glued to the end. Dip the corks or wads in paint or dye, thus making them with different colors.

Targets should be made of corrugated paper, eighteen inches square. Draw five concentric rings, three, six, nine, twelve, and fifteen inches in diameter. Number them from the center out as follows: 5, 4, 3, 2, 1.

Blow-Gun Contest for Accuracy

Playground, Summer Camp, Club   Late Elementary to Senior High School

Establish a shooting line fifteen to twenty feet from the target. Insert the arrow in the gun with the cork end toward the mouth. Slide the arrow down so that the cork rests about an inch from the mouth of the blow gun. Take the end of the gun in the mouth and give a quick puff.

For informal play, two to five players may shoot at one time, taking turns, each shooting arrows of a different color from the others. When all have shot they go to the target and withdraw the arrows. Arrows score the number of points indicated by the circle in which they strike. Those on the division lines score in the higher circle. The contestant scoring fifty points first wins.

In tournament play each contestant is given thirty-six (or eighteen) shots and is credited with the total score made. The one making the highest score wins.

Blow-Gun Shooting for Distance

Playground, Summer Camp, Club   Junior and Senior High Schools

Standing behind the shooting line, the contestants shoot the arrows as far as possible. Each is given three shots and is credited with his best distance. The one with the greatest distance wins.

Since there is an element of danger from the arrows, an open field is needed and careful supervision should be exercised.

CASTING CONTESTS

Casting contests are interesting even to inexperienced fly and bait casters. Children and beginners, when learning to cast, enjoy them after the fundamentals of the cast have been mastered.

Accuracy Bait-Casting Contest

Camp, Club, School   *Junior High School to Adults*

Any casting rod may be used. The reel must be free-running and the use of clicks and drags is prohibited. In most casting contests, a half-ounce casting weight is used on the end of the line. Contests may also be conducted using one-fourth-ounce weights.

The target consists of a circular board thirty inches in diameter. For informal contests a thirty-inch barrel hoop may be used. Five such targets are needed, placed 60, 70, 80, 90, and 100 feet from the casting line. The contest may be conducted either on land or water. If on water, the targets are anchored at the specified distances.

Each contestant makes ten casts in all—two at each target. He makes one cast at the 60-foot target, then one each in order at the 70-, 80-, 90-, and 100-foot targets; then the order is reversed and he casts from the 100-foot target back to the 60-foot target. Only one hand may be used on the rod in casting.

If the casting weight hits the target, a perfect cast is made. For each foot or fraction thereof away from the target, one demerit is charged against the caster. After the ten casts have been made, these demerits are added and divided by the number of casts. The result is called the "demerit percentage" and is subtracted from one hundred to obtain the "percentage" or score of the caster. No more than ten demerits may be credited for any one cast. In ordinary tournaments on water the judges estimate the distance away from the target that the weight falls; since bait casting is usually quite accurate, the distance is small and easily estimated.

Fisherman's Accuracy Bait-Casting Contest.—This contest is the same as the above except that an official five-eighths-ounce plug is used for the weight, and the five targets are placed at varying distances between forty and eighty yards from the casting line.

Bait-Casting for Distance

Camp, Club, School   *Junior High School to Adults*

This event takes place on a lawn. The conditions regarding equipment are the same as in the Accuracy Bait-Casting Contest.

From a casting line each contestant makes five casts, one each turn. The distance is measured from the casting line to the point where the weight falls. The total distance in feet of the five casts is added and divided by the number of casts. The result is the caster's score.

If the line breaks, the caster scores zero on that cast. If the contestant steps over the casting line before the weight strikes the ground, one foot is deducted from the distance of the cast for each foot or fraction thereof the caster stepped over.

Accuracy Fly-Casting Contest

Camp, Club, School   *Junior High School to Adults*

In official fly-casting contests the rod must not weigh more than five ounces nor exceed eleven feet in length. However, informal contests may be conducted by using rods of any size provided there is not too much variation. There are no restrictions on reels or lines except that the lines must not be weighted. A leader of not less than six nor more than twelve feet in length is used. One fly is attached to the leader, from which the point of the hook has been broken.

The targets are thirty-inch rings. Barrel hoops or old bicycle tires do very nicely. There are three of these, stationed in water at 45, 50, and 55 feet from the casting line. The caster makes five casts at each ring. When he completes the five casts at the nearest ring, he is ordered to cast for the next farthest, and so on.

A fly falling in the ring scores a perfect cast. One demerit is charged against the caster for each foot or fraction thereof between the fly and the ring. After the fifteen casts, the demerits are totalled and divided by the number of casts. The result is the demerit percentage. This is subtracted from one hundred and the result is the caster's score. On still water the fly will float at the spot where it falls and the judges can estimate the distance from the target.

In contests for beginners it is well to use five targets instead of three, placed at varying distances, with the most distant target not more than forty feet from the casting line. Paint each target a different color. The caster makes three casts at each target. Having completed the three casts at one target, the official calls the next target by color.

Variation.—Place hazards or obstructions in the line of the casts, over which the casts must be made. This approximates the conditions encountered in stream fishing.

TOP-SPINNING EVENTS

Top spinning is a spring-time favorite the world around. The use of novelty contests built on this popular activity will have a wide-spread appeal among children.

Endurance Spin

Playground, Club, Home   *Elementary and Junior High Schools*

At the signal all contestants spin their tops. The signal is given by counting "One, two, three, go" and any top that is not on the ground and spinning by the word "Go" is eliminated. The top wins that spins the longest. A top is considered as having stopped spinning when its side hits the ground.

Top-Spinning Accuracy Throw

Playground, Club, Home   *Elementary and Junior High Schools*

Draw a target on the floor or pavement thirty inches in diameter by drawing five concentric circles. The bull's-eye is six inches in diameter and the distance between the circle lines is three inches. Number the rings 5, 4, 3, 2, and 1.

From a line three feet away, each contestant is given five attempts to throw his top at the bull's-eye, and is credited with points according to the ring in which his top lands, provided the top spins after hitting.

Top Spin for Distance

Playground, Club, Home   *Elementary and Junior High Schools*

Establish a throwing line which each contestant must toe or stand behind. Each contestant is given five attempts in turn to spin his top as far beyond the throwing line as possible. Each throw is marked with chalk and the thrower's initials at the point where the top struck the ground. Each contestant is credited with his longest distance and the one wins whose top hit and spun at the greatest distance.

Fifty-Foot Top Dash

Playground, Club, Home   *Elementary and Junior High Schools*

Establish a starting line and fifty feet distant a finish line. The contestants line up on the starting line, each holding his top and a piece of chalk. At the signal each spins his top as far ahead as possible. He immediately runs forward, marks the point with the chalk where the top is spinning, picks up the spinning top, toes the spot, and spins it again as far ahead as possible. Each continues until he spins his top across the finish line. If a player fails to spin the top on a throw, he must return to the mark from which he threw and repeat the throw. The player wins who first crosses the finishing line.

Foot-Spinning Contest

Playground, Club, Home   *Elementary and Junior High Schools*

Wind the top and place it on the ground with the point up. Step on the end of the cord with the left foot, and kick the top with the right foot, thus making it spin.

Each contestant is given five attempts and the one wins who succeeds the most times.

Stunt Top Spinning

Playground, Club, Home   *Elementary and Junior High Schools*

This contest consists of picking up a spinning top on the palm of the hand and then performing certain feats with it. Whatever the feat, the top must *first be picked up on the palm of the hand*.

The contestants take turns in attempting the following feats, each making one spin each turn. Each must continue trying each feat until he performs it, but has only one attempt each turn. The player wins who first completes the series.

1. Pick up the spinning top on the palm of the right hand.
2. Perform Number 1, toss the top up and catch it on the palm of the left hand.
3. Perform Number 1, toss the top up and catch it on the back of the right hand.
4. Perform Number 1, toss the top up and catch it on the back of the left hand.
5. Perform Number 1, and cause the top to spin on the index finger.
6. Same as Number 5, and transfer the top from the index finger back to the palm of the hand.
7. Perform Number 1, toss up the top and catch it on the thigh of the right leg.
8. Perform Number 1, toss up the top, and duck under it and catch it on the back.
9. Perform Number 1, toss up the top, catch it on the top or back of the head.

Top-Spinning Meet

Playground, Club   *Elementary to Junior High School*

A novel meet may be conducted involving top-spinning skills by the use of such events as the following, all of which are described in the preceding pages.

Endurance Spin	Fifty-Foot Top Dash
Top-Spinning Accuracy Throw	Stunt Top Spinning
Top Spin for Distance	

KITE-FLYING EVENTS

The interest in kite flying is perennial, and curiously enough, it has a large following among adults as well as children. The following novelty events are always popular.

Altitude-Flying Contest

Playground   *Elementary to Senior High School*

Each contestant has one hundred yards of string attached to his kite. The contestant wins who flies his kite at the highest altitude. In judging the altitude, the kite is awarded first place which is nearest overhead when the hundred yards of string is all out.

Kite-Looping Contest

Playground   *Elementary to Senior High School*

Each kite has fifty yards of string with a stick attached to the end. The flyers may run as far as they choose in letting out all the string provided they stop on the flying line. After all have reached the flying line, or when a reasonable time has been allowed for all to reach it, the signal is given and the flyers cause the kites to loop by pulling on the string. The loops made by each kite are counted for a period of six minutes. The kite making the most loops in this period wins.

Reeling-In Contest

Playground   *Elementary to Senior High School*

Each kite has fifty yards of string attached to it. When all the string is out and the contestants are standing on the flying line, the signal is given and each reels in his kite on a single stick, winding in figure-of-eight style. The contestant wins who first brings his kite to hand on the flying line with all the string wound on the stick.

Kite-Messenger Contest

Playground   *Elementary to Senior High School*

The kite-messenger is made as follows: Cut out a five-inch disk of cardboard and through the center of it insert a paper tube four-and-one-half inches long. The tube should be five-sixteenths of an inch in diameter. The cardboard disk is glued to the middle of the tube. Fifty yards of string is used, one end of which is attached to the kite and the other end passed through the tube of the messenger. The type of string should be specified and all kites must have the same kind. Varying degrees of smoothness of the string would give some players an unfair advantage.

The contestants put their kites in the air and let out the fifty yards of string. At the signal the messengers are released and allowed to go up the string. The player wins whose messenger first touches the bridle adjustment string of the flying kite.

Novel Kite Contest

Playground, School, Club   *Elementary School to Adults*

This is a contest in the construction and flying of novel types of kites. The judges judge on the following points:

Unusual style of kite.	Decorations—accessories.
Construction—workmanship.	Manner of flying.
Appearance.	Behavior in the air.

Artistic Kite Contest

Playground, School, Club   *Elementary School to Adults*

The contest has to do with the construction and decoration of artistic kites. The judges judge on the following points:

Workmanship and neatness of construction.

Shape and style of kite.

Coloring.

Decoration.

Beauty.

Across-the-Lake Kite Flying

Playground, Club, Camp   *Elementary School to Adults*

This is a scheme for flying a kite across the lake. The greatest sport in the use of these kite rafts is open to those who live near one of the Great Lakes or a big bay of the ocean. Each contestant makes a raft, and puts a return address in a sealed bottle on the raft. The rafts are then sent sailing "out to sea." The winner is the one who receives a reply from

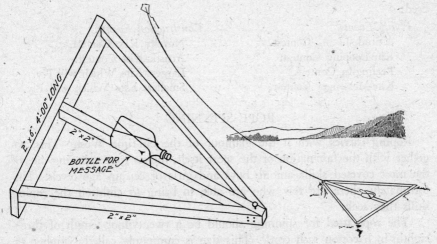

the finder of the raft on the other side of the lake, in the shortest time, or, if you choose, from the greatest distance away.

Make the raft as shown in the drawing. The back board is a piece of two-by-six-inch timber, four feet long. The other pieces are two-by-two-inch stuff, the center piece being four feet long. Put a screw eye at the front end to which the kite string is attached.

Wire a bottle securely to the top side of the raft as illustrated. Insert in it a self-addressed post card, and a note asking the finder to record the time and place of discovery, and mail it. Cork and seal the bottle carefully.

A day must be selected when the wind is blowing away from the shore. Each contestant puts his raft in the water. Then the kites are put in the air in the usual manner, and the strings are attached to the rafts. At the

signal the rafts are all released and the kites drag them on their way
to their unknown ports. If the wind keeps up the kites will stay aloft until
the raft is pulled up on the opposite shore. The weather man might give
some good tips as to the best time to stage the contest.

Any type of kite may be used. A raft of the size described is heavy
enough to keep a kite of average size under control. Note that the back
board extends down into the water and thus acts as a drag.

Variation.—This contest is for a small lake that can be easily crossed
in rowboats or canoes. No message bottles are needed on the rafts. The
kites are released as described above, and the contestants then cross the
lake in the boats. The kite wins that first reaches the opposite shore.

Kite Meet

Playground, Club   *Elementary and Junior High Schools*

An interesting meet for a playground may be built up around kite
flying and construction. The following events described above may be
used:

Flying Events.   *Construction Events.*
   Altitude-Flying Contest.   Novelty Kite Contest.
   Kite-Looping Contest.   Artistic Kite Contest.
   Reeling-In Contest.   Largest Kite Which will Fly.
   Kite-Messenger Contest.   Smallest Kite Which will Fly.

ROPE SPINNING

Roping carries with it the glamour of the old-time West. This, together with the fascination of the sport itself, makes rope spinning one of
the most coveted skills among boys and girls of certain age levels. Unfortunately, there are few who are able to bring to children the roping
skills they seek.

The rope used for spinning should be a twenty-foot length of three-
eighths-inch cotton sash cord. This size is commonly called Number 12.
Without a rope of this type and size, a person cannot hope to learn rope
spinning. The end should be doubled back and wired, forming a three-
inch loop or honda. Excellent spinning ropes already prepared for use are
on the market. There are many tricks calling for shorter and longer
ropes, and for metal hondas, but the beginner's rope should be as specified
above.

The Flat Spin

Club, Camp, Playground, Gymnasium   *Late Elementary School to Adults*

The flat spin consists of spinning a small noose in front of the roper,
parallel to the ground and near to it. It is perhaps the easiest spin to learn
and is the foundation for many more difficult tricks.

Using a twenty-foot spinning rope, arrange the noose as in A, Figure 16. Note that the noose is small—the approximate size can be estimated by studying the relative sizes of the noose and the roper in the picture. Note that the end of the rope extends well beyond the left hand.

Holding the rope as illustrated, throw the noose over with the right hand with a right to left motion, letting go of it with the left hand but not with the right. Allow it to drop to the ground. Do this several times without attempting to spin.

Now, lay the rope over as before, and as you do so, give it a circular

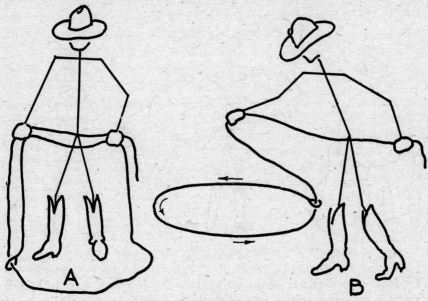

FIGURE 16.

spin with the right hand from right to left, and let go of the noose, keeping hold of the spoke only. Keep it spinning with the spoke, as in B.

Remember that it will not spin unless you give the noose the initial circular motion before you let it go. It is as if a bicycle were lying on the ground and you attempted to take hold of a tire and spin the wheel—your hand would make a circular motion. When you throw the noose over, give it this same circular spin, being careful not to let go too soon. Having released it, keep it going by spinning it with the end held in the hand.

Do not use much muscle—the spinning is all done with the wrist. To use the arm strenuously would break the spin. Do not jerk the rope, but try to spin it gently and evenly. Roping is rhythm, and if you change the rhythm, the change must be made gradually.

To make the spinning noose larger, let out rope gradually. This is done by opening the right hand and letting an inch or two of rope slip out each time the noose spins around.[5]

The Wedding Ring

Playground, Club, Camp   *Late Elementary School to Adults*

To perform the wedding ring or body spin, arrange the rope as in A, Figure 17. Note that the honda rests near the ground—it is important that the spoke or end of the rope be about this length. The end of the rope is in the right hand—the left hand merely holds the noose open. Keeping the left hand at the same level that it is on the start, throw the rope up and down over the head with the right hand, as illustrated in B.

FIGURE 17.

Let it drop to the level of the waist, then give it a hard spin with both hands in a circular motion around the body from right to left. Let go of the noose, raise the right hand over the head, and keep it going, as in C.

Do not hurry and do not use much strength. The rope is spun with a wrist and not an arm motion. The rhythm of the spinning noose should be kept constant, and if changed, the change must be made very gradually.

The wedding ring is the foundation for many other tricks in roping and once it is mastered, the way is open to more difficult and spectacular tricks.[6]

Rope-Spinning Contest

Playground, Club, Camp   *Late Elementary School to Adults*

The rope-spinning contests are possible only when the contestants are able to do several tricks. Prepare a list of tricks such as the following,

[5] For detailed descriptions of this and other rope spinning tricks, see Bernard S. Mason, *How to Spin a Rope*. New York: Boy Scouts of America, 1930.

[6] B. S. Mason, *How to Spin a Rope*. New York: Boy Scouts of America, 1930.

each contestant being required to perform as many as he is able, and then to perform any additional tricks that he can: [7]

Wedding Ring	Flat Spin
Hand Shaking	In and Out
Juggle	Up and Over
Jumping over Spoke	Skip
Hand Shaking around One Leg	Butterfly
Hand Shaking around Alternate Legs	Ocean Wave

The judges judge on the basis of number of tricks performed, smoothness, grace, and rhythm.

MODEL-AIRPLANE AND BALLOON-FLYING EVENTS

The following activities are built upon the use of model airplanes and the flying of toy balloons.

Model-Airplane Endurance-Flight Contest

Playground, Club   *Late Elementary to Senior High School*

In this event, model airplanes, made by the contestants, are flown with the object of determining which plane will stay in the air the longest.

The contestants should be divided into classes, such as juniors from ten to fourteen years of age, and seniors from fifteen to twenty-one years of age. While the airplanes may be of any model, separate events should be staged for each type, such as the Stick Tractor Contest, the R.O.G. Stick Tractor Contest, and the Commercial Plane Contest.

Specifications for Planes.—All planes must be made by the contestants entering them. The Extension Department of the Milwaukee Public Schools, as quoted by the National Recreation Association,[8] lays down the following specifications for contest planes:

Commercial. Maximum wing spread 21"—must be proportioned to the 'Wakefield Formula' as follows:

$$\frac{(\text{Fuselage length})^2}{10} = \text{minimum area of maximum section of fuselage}$$

Example: $\dfrac{(20'')^2}{10} = 4$ sq. in. or a fuselage 2 in. square (or its equal) through the largest section.

Models must rise off of the floor.

Models must be rubber powered only and rubber may be fully enclosed or an opening of 2 sq. in. may be allowed for access to rubber. (Pusher type allowed.)

[7] These tricks are explained in detail in Bernard S. Mason, *How to Spin a Rope.* New York: Boy Scouts of America, 1930.

[8] See National Recreation Association: *88 Successful Play Activities,* p. 59. Copyright, 1933. By permission of National Recreation Association, publishers.

"*Stick Tractor*. Any design; rubber powered; length of motor stick not to exceed 15″ (length to be considered from thrust bearing "head" to rear hook). Tail boom allowed. Model to be hand launched.

"*R. O. G. Stick Tractor*. Any design; rubber powered; must have landing gear with wheels. Length of motor stick not more than 15″ (length to be considered from thrust bearing head to rear hook). Model must rise off of floor. Tail boom allowed.

"*Exhibition*. Any scale model may be entered. Card must accompany each plane, stating the name of the model and scale of reduction. Clubs must enter three or more models."

Trials.—Each contestant may have three official trials in each event in each class in which he is entered. Each contestant may have three planes of each class for the three trials.

All hand-launched planes must be launched not higher than six feet from the ground.

Timing.—The time is recorded from the instant the referee gives the signal, or the instant the plane leaves the floor or the hand, and ends when the plane contacts the floor or strikes an obstruction and remains there for more than three seconds.

Scoring.—The best time made by a contestant in his three trials is credited to him. The contestant wins the event whose plane remains in the air the longest.

Officials.—The *referee* observes the launching of the planes, signals the timers at the start of a flight, and enforces the rules.

The *three timers* record the time of each flight and report it to the clerk.

The *clerk* checks the entries and records the records of flights.

The *inspector* inspects all planes to see if they conform to regulations.

Glider Contest

Playground, Club   *Late Elementary to Senior High School*

A glider is a heavier-than-air craft that has no inherent power to move but is dependent upon air currents. The contestants launch the gliders from hand, not over six feet above the ground, using no slings or accessories of any kind to give them momentum. The time is recorded from the time the glider leaves the hand, and the glider wins that stays in the air the longest provided the flight terminates at least twenty feet from the starting point.

Model-Airplane Construction Contest

Playground, School, Club   *Junior and Senior High Schools*

The classes of contestants and types of planes are the same as stated in the Model-Airplane Endurance-Flight Contest. All planes must be made entirely by the contestants entering them. The workmanship of the planes is judged by two or three expert judges on the basis of 100 as follows: fuselage, 20; wings, 20; tails, 15; landing gear, 15; color, 10; general neatness, 20.

Balloon-Sailing Race

Playground, Picnic   *Elementary and Junior High School*

For a colorful event for a special playground celebration, or for a large picnic or fiesta, this event is unexcelled in the interest the children take in it. It should be publicized for several days in advance.

Give each contestant a large gas-filled toy balloon to which a brightly colored sealed envelope is attached. Hydrogen should be used to fill the balloons. On the envelope is printed "Finder—Please Open." In the envelope is inserted a stamped postcard addressed to the playground director. The card explains to the finder that the balloon is entered in a contest and asks him to write on the card the location where it was picked up and mail it.

Each card contains a number and when the balloon is given to the player his name and balloon number are recorded. At the signal all release their balloons. Allow two weeks to elapse and then award a small prize to the player whose balloon was reported as being picked up at the greatest distance from the playground.

Interest in this contest will extend over a two- or three-weeks period. Balloons frequently float for great distances, being carried by the wind. Large toy balloons often stay in the air several days when filled with hydrogen. It is said to be on record that a toy balloon floated from England to America.

MODEL-BOAT EVENTS

These contests involve the use of model sailboats and model motorboats.

Model-Sailboat Race

Playground, Club, Summer Camp   *Late Elementary School to Adults*

Young children enjoy sailing model boats very much. Competitive races with model sailboats, however, are events which also appeal strongly to older children and even adults, provided the sailboats are made by the entrants themselves. Any style or size of model sailboat may be entered provided the contestant made it himself.

The contestants line up on the starting line in shallow water and on the signal release their boats and allow them to take wind. The boat wins that first crosses the finish line.

Sailboat Construction Contest

Playground, School, Club, Camp   *Junior High School to Adults*

No boat may be entered unless it has been constructed entirely by the contestant. The following events are suggested:

Best Constructed Boat.—Judged for design, construction, and workmanship. Action in the water is not included.

Best Show Boat.—Judged for attractiveness of decorations and design.

Best Sailing Boat.—Judged for speed and action in the water.

Largest Boat.

Smallest Boat.

Model-Motorboat Contest

Playground, Club, Summer Camp   *Junior High School to Adults*

The conditions are the same as in the Model-Sailboat Contest. The boats must be constructed by the contestants entering them. They must move under their own power. The event should take place on calm water and the distance should be short enough to be within the capacity of the type of boats used. The boat finishing first wins.

BOOMERANG THROWING

The methods of making and throwing boomerangs are described in Chapter IV, "Throwing and Catching Contests," pages 54-59.

CHAPTER VII

PUSHING, PULLING, AND BUTTING CONTESTS

PUSHING AND PULLING CONTESTS

Chinning
(Pull-Up)

Playground, Gymnasium   *Late Elementary School to College*

A HORIZONTAL bar is needed for this event. An acceptable substitute may be found in the rungs of a ladder which is set at an angle against a building. The bar must be high enough so that the contestants' feet clear the floor.

The contestant begins with his hands on the bar, palms forward and thumbs under the bar. Then, with his arms straightened at full length, he pulls himself up without a kick, snap, jerk, or swing, until his chin touches the bar. Lowering himself again until his arms are straight, he repeats the pull-up, and continues until forced to stop. He is credited with one point for each time his chin touches the bar.

Push-Up

Playground, Gymnasium   *Late Elementary School to Adults*

The contestant lies on the floor, face downward, hands open and placed close to the shoulders. He straightens his arms supporting his weight on hands and toes with back stiff, and then lowers his body again until his chin and only his chin touches the floor. He continues as long as possible, each push-up counting one point. Touching the floor with any part of the body except the chin, hands, and toes, or failure to straighten the arms or keep the back stiff, or failure to touch the chin, are fouls and the push-up does not count.

Sit-Up

Gymnasium   *Late Elementary to Senior High School*

The contestant lies on his back, head resting on the floor, feet together, arms extended with palms of hands resting on the thighs. He raises the trunk of his body to a sitting position, keeping his heels on the floor, knees and elbows straight, sliding his hands down his legs. Having reached the sitting position he immediately lies down and when his head touches the floor he at once raises the trunk again. He continues until forced to stop. Each erect position counts one point.

Chinese Pull-Up

Playground, Gymnasium, Club   Late Elementary to Senior High School

Two opponents sit on the floor facing each other and with soles of feet touching. A three-foot stick such as a broom handle is needed. Both grasp the stick with both hands. At the signal each tries to pull the other off the floor or make him break his hold, using a straight and steady pull.

Badger Pull

Playground, Gymnasium, Club   Elementary and Junior High Schools

Draw a line on the ground about three feet long. Tie two towels together at both ends, forming a collar. The opponents kneel either side of the line facing each other. The collar is placed behind their necks and they back up until the collar is stretched tight and they are equidistant from the line. At the signal they attempt to pull each other entirely over the line. A player loses when (1) he is pulled over the line, (2) when he allows the collar to slip off his head.

Collar Pull

Playground, Gymnasium, Club   Elementary to Senior High School

This is on the order of the Badger Pull, except the players are facing in opposite directions. A twelve-foot rope is needed, in each end of which a two-foot loop is tied with a knot that will not slip. The players kneel, facing opposite directions, and the rope is looped around the back of the neck and under the armpits. A towel may be placed across the back of the neck for protection from the rope. They move away until the rope is tight. Draw a line midway between them. At the signal they attempt to pull each other over the line. The knees may be raised or not.

Variation.—Like the above except that the players take a hands-and-feet position and are not permitted to drop their knees to the floor.

Tractor Pull

Playground, Gymnasium, Club   Elementary to Senior High School

Two pairs compete at one time. One player of each pair is the horse and the other the rider. Draw a three-foot line on the floor. The two horses take positions on hands and knees, facing in opposite directions and with feet touching on the line. The riders mount the horses' backs facing in the same direction as the horses with legs wrapped around the horses' bodies. They reach back with both hands and grasp each other's wrists with the wrist grip. At the signal each pair attempts to pull the other over the line. The pair wins that pulls the other pair across the line or that succeeds in dislodging the opposing rider.

Leg Tug-of-War

Playground, Gymnasium, Club   *Elementary to Senior High School*

A five-foot length of three-eighths-inch rope and two towels are needed. Two players compete at once. Wrap a towel around the right ankle of each of the contestants to prevent the rope from hurting and then tie one end of the rope tightly over the towel. The two players face in opposite directions and stretch the rope tight. Mark the ground under the middle of the rope. At the signal they pull. The one wins who first pulls his opponent over the line.

Peg Pick-Up

Playground, Gymnasium, Club   *Junior and Senior High Schools*

Tie the ends of a six-foot rope together. The two players take hold of the loop and stretch it tight. Four feet beyond each player place a handkerchief or a peg of wood on the ground. At the signal they pull, each trying to reach and pick up the handkerchief or peg. The player wins who picks up the object or causes the other to drop the rope.

Four-Way Tug (Circular Tug-of-War).—An endless rope is needed, large enough so that when it is spread out it is about five feet in diameter. Four men grasp the rope in one hand at different points and stretch it, thus stretching the rope into a square. Four feet beyond the reach of each player a handkerchief is placed on the ground.

At the signal all pull in an effort to reach and pick up the handkerchief. The player picking up his handkerchief first wins.

Variation.—Use a slightly larger rope and have the players stand inside it. The rope is placed behind the neck and under the arms of each player.

Three-Way Tug.—Same as the above with three players pulling.

Squat-Tug

Playground, Gymnasium, Club   *Elementary to Senior High School*

An eight-foot rope is needed. The two contestants squat in a full knee bend each holding one end of the rope with both hands. At the signal they try to cause each other to fall by pulling. The player wins who causes the other to fall and at the same time retains his own balance.

Partner Squat-Tug.—The second player of each pair squats behind the first and holds him by the waist.

Hopping Tug

Playground, Gymnasium, Club   *Elementary and Junior High Schools*

The two contestants stand on one foot, each holding the end of a six-foot rope. By jerking, pulling, and maneuvering they try to upset each other. The one wins who causes the other to fall, drop the raised foot, or drop the rope.

Pull Over

Playground, Gymnasium, Club   *Elementary to Senior High School*

Establish two lines ten feet apart. The two contestants stand midway between the lines, back to back, and grasp each other's wrists with a wrist grip. Each attempts to pull the other over the line. The player wins who first pulls the other completely over the line.

BUTTING CONTESTS

Soccer Head-Butt for Distance

Football Field, Playground   *Junior High School to College*

This event is conducted best on a rugby football field. Standing behind the line, the contestant tosses the ball in the air and butts it with his head as far as possible. He may throw it as high as he chooses and run as far as he chooses, but must be behind the goal line when the ball is butted. The measuring is done as in the Baseball Throw for Distance.

Speedball Head-Butt for Distance.—This is conducted like the Soccer Head-Butt for Distance, using a speedball or a socccer ball.

Goat-Butting Race

Playground, Gymnasium, Club   *Elementary to Senior High School*

A ball is needed for each contestant; volleyballs or soccer balls are preferable but basketballs or softballs may be used. Each contestant places his ball on the starting line and stands behind it. On the signal he bends over and butts the ball with his head toward the finish line. He follows the ball and continues butting it by diving at it or dropping to hands and knees and butting it. Hitting the ball with any part of the body but the head eliminates the player. The contestant wins whose ball crosses the finish line first; it is the ball which determines the winner, not the runner. A finish line should be drawn of sufficient width so that all runners could cross it running abreast; the ball must be butted so that it actually crosses this line and does not cross an imaginary extension of it at either end. Distances of thirty to fifty yards may be used.

CHAPTER VIII

TRACK MEETS AND SPORT MEETS

YEARS of use have standardized track and field meets both in respect to the events used and the methods of conducting the events.

With the perfection of coaching technique in the major games such as Baseball, Basketball, and Football, a number of contests have been developed involving the elements of these games. Many of these have been described in the foregoing chapters on contests between individuals. They are valuable as practice for the game from which they are derived and are interesting as events in themselves.

Interesting meets may be staged with contests derived from any one of the major sports. These are not play days featuring a variety of games and play events, but are meets concentrating on contests derived from some particular major sport. A number of suggestions for such meets are presented in this chapter together with the lists of events used in standard track and field meets.

Regardless of the type of events used, the method of conducting the meet should follow in general that used in a regular track meet.

Officials.—The number of officials necessary to conduct a meet varies according to the importance of the meet, the number of teams competing, and the events held. Dual meets do not require as many officials as the larger meets. The following list of officials is for a large track meet; in small meets, some of these may be eliminated or the duties combined:

One Referee
Four Inspectors
One Clerk of the Course
Five Assistant Clerks
One Scorer
One Announcer
One Marshal and two Assistants
One Surveyor
One Physician
One Head Track Judge and other Judges (there should be twice as many Judges as places to score)
Three Timers
One Starter
One Head Field Judge and eight other Field Judges or Measurers.

No such array of officials is necessary in the novelty meets described later in this chapter. However, the following will usually be indispensable:

referee, starter, clerk, scorer, finish judges for the races, timers, and judges for the field events. It is often possible to combine the duties of the referee and starter, and of the clerk and scorer.

The referee has general charge of the meet, enforces the rules, and decides all questions regarding the conduct of the meet.

The clerk of the course holds the names of the competitors and assigns them to heats and gives them positions on the track according to the drawings. He sees that all contestants are in position before the time for their event to start.

The starter has control of the runners at the starting mark and gives the starting commands and signals. He is the judge as to whether any competitor goes over his mark too soon. He recalls the competitors in case of an unfair start. He signals with a pistol shot the beginning of the last lap in the distance runs.

The judges of the finish record the place winners in the races. Each judge is assigned the place he is to pick. One judge picks the first-place winner, one the second-place winner, and so on. One more place winner should be picked than the number to score. In large track meets, two judges are assigned to pick each place winner.

The timekeepers are equipped with stop-watches. They start the watches at the flash of the pistol and stop them when the first runner reaches the finish. If two watches agree and the third disagrees, the time marked by the two is accepted. If all disagree, the time marked by the watch giving the middle time is accepted.

The head field judge sees that the field events start and continue without delay. The other judges measure, judge, and record each trial of each competitor in all events in which the record is one of distance or height.

Scoring.—In meets where two places are counted, first place scores five and second place three. When three places are counted, the scoring is five, three, and one. When four places are counted, it is five, three, two, and one. When five places are counted, it is five, four, three, two, and one. When six places are counted, it is ten, eight, six, four, two, and one.

In case two or more competitors tie in an event, the points are divided equally between the competitors, and the prizes are awarded by lot.

Track and Field Meets

Running Track, Playground   *Junior High School to Adults*

The following are the events commonly used for interscholastic and intercollegiate track and field meets, in the order in which they are usually scheduled:

Interscholastic Meets

1. 2:00 P.M.	120-Yard Hurdles		2:00 P.M.	{ Shot Put
2. 2:15 P.M.	100-Yard Dash			{ Pole Vault
3. 2:25 P.M.	1 Mile Run			

4. 2:40 P.M.	Half-Mile Relay	
5. 2:55 P.M.	440-Yard Dash	
6. 3:10 P.M.	220-Yard Hurdles	

2:30 P.M. { Discus / High Jump

7. 3:25 P.M.	880-Yard Run	
8. 3:35 P.M.	220-Yard Dash	
9. 3:45 P.M.	1 Mile Relay	

3:00 P.M. { Javelin / Broad Jump

Intercollegiate Meets

1. 2:30 P.M.	1 Mile Run	
2. 2:40 P.M.	440-Yard Run	
3. 2:50 P.M.	100-Yard Dash	
4. 3:00 P.M.	120-Yard Hurdles	
5. 3:10 P.M.	880-Yard Run	

2:30 P.M. { Pole Vault / High Jump / Shot Put / Javelin

6. 3:20 P.M.	220-Yard Run	
7. 3:30 P.M.	2 Mile Run	
8. 3:45 P.M.	220-Yard Hurdles	
9. 3:55 P.M.	1 Mile Relay	

3:10 P.M. { Discus / Broad Jump / Hammer

Baseball Meet

Baseball Diamond   *Junior High School to College*

A baseball "track and field meet" is excellent as a novelty meet for playground and summer-camp use. It also adds much color as a preliminary to a baseball game. Professional baseball teams frequently use it as an added attraction, staging it during the intermission between doubleheaders.

The following events, described in the foregoing chapters, constitute an interesting program:

1. Fielder's Throw to Home Base.   4. Catcher's Throw to Second Base.
2. Fungo Hit for Accuracy.   5. Run to First Base (Bat and Run).
3. Base-Running Contest.

In professional baseball circles the last event is frequently eliminated in favor of a regulation one-hundred-yard dash.

Basketball Meet

Basketball Court   *Junior High School to College*

A meet involving basketball skills makes an interesting competition for gymnasium and playground. The following program of events described in preceding chapters may be used:

1. Foul Shoot.   4. Accuracy Pass.
2. Shooting Against Time.   5. Basketball Twenty-One.
3. Long Shots.

One of the dribbling relays described in Chapter XVI, "Throwing Relays," may be added if the program needs it.

Football Meet

Football Field   *Junior High School to College*

A meet involving rugby football skills may consist of the following events, described in foregoing chapters:

1. Punt for Distance.
2. Forward Pass for Accuracy.
3. Drop-Kick for Distance.
4. Place-Kick for Accuracy.
5. Forward Pass for Distance.
6. Drop-Kick for Accuracy.
7. Place-Kick for Distance.
8. Football Center-Pass for Accuracy.

Soccer Meet

Rugby Football Field, Playground   *Junior High School to College*

Soccer players enjoy an occasional meet involving the various types of soccer skills. A program may be made up of the following events, all of which are described in preceding chapters.

1. Punt for Distance.
2. Throw-in for Distance.
3. Goal-Kick for Accuracy.
4. Head-Butt for Distance.
5. Place-Kick for Distance.

Other events may be added involving dribbling, corner-kicking, and bounce kicking.

Speedball Meet

Rugby Football Field, Playground   *Senior High School to College*

The following events may be used in a Speedball meet. They are all described in the preceding chapters.

1. Punt for Distance.
2. Drop-Kick for Accuracy.
3. Place-Kick for Distance.
4. Throw for Distance.
5. Head-Butt for Distance.
6. Drop-Kick for Distance.
7. Kick and Catch.
8. Overhead Dribble for Distance.

Golf Meet

Golf Course   *Junior High School to Adults*

An interesting meet for a playground or a golf club can be developed using contests in golf skills. Expert golfers enjoy this type of competition and even inexperienced players and children on the playground participate in them with enthusiasm. The program may include the following:

1. Approach for Accuracy.
2. Golf Putting.
3. Drive for Distance.
4. Clock Golf.
5. Golf Target Board Putting.[1]

[1] Described in *Social Games for Recreation*.

Field-Hockey Meet

Hockey Field   *Junior High School to College*

The following hockey events may be used in a hockey meet:

1. Hockey Dribbling Race.
2. Hockey Obstacle Race.
3. Hockey Drive for Accuracy.
4. Hit the Can.
5. Hockey Drive for Distance.
6. Zigzag Hockey-Driving Relay.
7. Hockey-Driving Shuttle Relay.
8. Hockey Golf.

Tennis-Type Events for Meets

Tennis Court, Gymnasium, Playground   *Elementary School to Adults*

Games of the tennis type do not lend themselves to contests involving their skills as readily as the other types of games. There is, therefore, less opportunity to build an interesting program featuring these skills exclusively. The following events may be included in the other meets described above:

Tennis Serve for Accuracy   Volleyball Serve for Accuracy
Tennis Stroke for Accuracy

Novelty Track and Field Meet

Playground, Gymnasium, Club, Camp

Late Elementary and Junior High Schools

An occasional "track and field" meet made up of novelty events is an excellent feature. *There are enough events described in the preceding chapters to make up different programs for dozens of such meets.* The following example of a program serves to illustrate the type of events to use. Events such as these which will meet the needs of all types of groups will be found in the foregoing chapters.

Running Races
  Backward Race
  Broom-Riding Race
  Siamese-Twins Race
  Three-Legged Race
  Barrel-Obstacle Race
Jumps
  Standing Backward Broad Jump
  Seven Standing Broad Jumps

Throws
  Basketball Throw and Catch
  Broomstick Throw for Distance

Bicycle Races
  Bicycle Speed Race
  Bicycle Slow Race
  Bicycle Plank Race

CHAPTER IX

CONTESTS RESEMBLING GAMES

IT will be recalled that a contest is a fair comparison of abilities—there is no interference by one's opponents; the conditions are fixed and situations do not arise calling for choice or strategy. In a game, on the other hand, there is constant interference by one's opponents, the situation is constantly changing, and is constantly calling for strategy and choice.

The events described in this chapter, although commonly thought of as games, are essentially contests. The elements of games, however, do appear in them to a limited degree.

These events are classified according to the prominence of the game element: (1) contests in which the game element is minor; (2) contests in which the game element is prominent.

CONTESTS IN WHICH THE GAME ELEMENT IS MINOR

The events in this section come very close to being pure contests. There is no opportunity for interference by one's opponents, but varied situations do arise which call for choice. These varied situations are created by the contestant himself, rather than by his opponents, but nevertheless he must make the choice, and since the changing conditions do arise, the events are scarcely comparable to a pure contest, such as the Broad Jump, in which the entire situation is fixed beforehand and the contestant knows exactly what it is.

An example is found in Bowling. One's opponents cannot interfere with him and he is free to bowl the balls as best he can. However, if he knocks down seven pins, and three scattered pins remain standing, he must decide between the various possibilities in rolling his next ball to knock down all or as many pins as possible. The situation is different than if six or five pins had been knocked down.

In such an event as Mumblety-Peg, the contest element seems predominant, but when one considers the wide variety of situations which the rules create, all of which must be met in order, the event takes on somewhat of the aspect of a game, and certainly the event could scarcely be classified with the contests of the throwing type.

Bowling

Bowling Alleys   *Junior High School to Adults*

Bowling takes place on specially constructed, smooth, wooden alleys. The play consists of rolling the bowling balls down the alley with the object of knocking over ten wooden pins standing at the farther end.

Equipment.—The alleys are forty-one to forty-two inches wide and measure sixty feet from the foul line to the number-one pin. Official bowling pins are used measuring fifteen inches in height. Balls must not exceed twenty-seven inches in circumference nor sixteen pounds in weight.

The Play.—The bowler stands any distance he chooses behind the foul line, takes any number of steps he chooses, and rolls the ball. If his foot or any part of his body comes in contact with the alleys beyond the foul line the ball is declared foul. This counts as a ball bowled by the player but no score is made by it and all pins knocked down are immediately replaced. The players take turns, each being allowed to bowl two balls unless he knocks down all the pins with one.

Scoring.—One score is made for each pin knocked down, and an additional score is given as follows:

If all the pins are knocked down by the first ball, it is called a "strike," and the score made with the first two balls in the next turn is added to the first score as well as being counted in the second. If all the pins are knocked down with the first two balls, it is called a "spare," and the score made with the first ball of the next turn is added to the preceding turn as well as being counted in its own place. Each player begins each turn with his pins all up and the alley clear of balls. Ten rounds make a "frame." If in a certain frame player A.B. scored in his ten rounds 6, strike, spare, 7, spare, 6, strike, spare, 9, and 8, while his opponent, C.D., scored 9, 8, strike, spare, 8, strike, spare, spare, 4, and 7, the scoreboard would be filled out as follows. It will be noticed that only the totals are entered, so that the score written in each space is the total score up to that time. X means a strike; /, a spare. A spare in the tenth round gives a player another throw; a strike, two more throws.

		X	/		/		X	/		
A.B.	6	26	43	50	66	72	92	111	120	128
		X	/		X	/		/		
C.D.	9	17	37	55	63	83	100	114	118	125

Team Form.—In team bowling, teams usually consist of five bowlers, but may consist of any number agreed upon. Competing teams bowl on adjoining alleys, one team to an alley, alternating alleys after each frame. The players of each team take turns in bowling and the team score is arrived at by adding the individual scores of its members.

There are two methods of determining match winners: (1) the team wins that wins two out of three games, or three out of five games; (2) the scores of the three (or five) games are added and the team wins that has the highest total score.

Duck Pins

Bowling Alleys　　　　　　　　　　*Junior and Senior High Schools*

The Duck-Pins game is very similar to Bowling. The pins are much smaller, nine inches in height, and the balls must not exceed four-and-one-half inches in diameter.

Each player rolls three balls in each frame and two frames at a time. A line is drawn ten feet beyond the regular foul line and any ball delivered beyond this line is declared foul.

The scoring follows the method used in regular Bowling. If the bowler knocks down all ten pins with his first ball, a strike is credited and he does not bowl his next two balls in that frame, but the score of the next two balls in the following frame or frames is added to the score for this frame, as in Bowling. If all pins are knocked down by the first two balls bowled, a spare is credited and the third ball is not bowled, but the score made by the first ball in the next frame is added to the score for this frame. If all three balls are bowled, the player is credited with the number of pins knocked down as his score for the frame.

Tenpins

Schoolroom, Home　　　　　　　　　　*Elementary School*

Ten wooden pins nine inches high, resembling bowling pins in shape but very much smaller, are set up in the same formation used in setting bowling pins, with the apex toward the bowler. The pins in each row are ten inches apart—it is a great help to place chalk marks on the floor to indicate the positions of the pins. Twenty to forty feet away establish a foul line. The bowler stands behind this line and rolls a wooden ball or a softball at the pins.

The bowlers bowl in turn, each being entitled to roll three balls each turn. If pins are still standing after the second bowl, the player rolls his third ball and is credited with the total number of pins knocked down by the three bowls. However, if all pins are knocked down by two bowls, he scores a spare and does not roll his third ball, but the pins knocked down by the first ball of the next frame are added to his score for this frame, as in Bowling. Likewise, if all pins are knocked down by his first ball, he is credited with a strike and does not bowl the other two balls, but the pins knocked down by the first two balls of the next frame are added to the score of this frame. The method of scoring described under Bowling should be read.

Each turn constitutes a frame, and ten frames constitute a string. Three strings is a match.

Ball Bowling.—Set up ten Indian clubs or sticks of wood of similar size in the arrangement used in placing bowling pins. Bowl at them with a basketball, volleyball, soccer ball, softball, or croquet ball. Score as in Bowling.

A gym mat or an old rug thrown over a chair may be placed behind the pins for a back stop.

Soccer Bowling

Club, Picnic, Playground, Gymnasium   *Elementary School to Adults*

Using Indian clubs or sticks of wood of similar size for pins, kick a soccer ball at them. The procedure and scoring is as in Bowling.

Skittles

Club, Playground, Camp   *Elementary School to Adults*

Skittles is similar to Tenpins but a wooden disk is used instead of a ball. It has an advantage over Tenpins in that it does not require a smooth floor and can be played almost any place.

Use regular tenpins or sticks of wood about nine inches high and two inches in diameter. The disks are four-and-one-half inches in diameter and about one-and-one-half inches thick. Three disks are needed for each player.

Arrange the pins and play as in Tenpins. There are two methods of propelling the disks: they may be thrown at the pins with a flat toss as in Horseshoe Pitching, or one may slide them along the floor.

Skiddles

Playground, Camp   *Elementary School to Adults*

Skiddles is an outdoor game which is rapidly regaining a much-deserved popularity for camp and playground use.

Five pins or round sticks are needed, four-and-one-half inches long and an inch-and-one-half to two inches thick. In addition, three throwing sticks are needed, fourteen inches long and two inches thick. Both of these types of sticks may be made from tree branches or saplings.

Mark a throwing line, and sixty feet distant draw a thirty-inch square on the ground, placed cornerwise to the throwing line. Place a pin on each of the four corners of the square and the fifth pin in the center. The pin nearest the throwing line scores one point, the one to the right two points, the one to the left three points, and the farthest one four points. The center pin scores ten points.

The players take turns in throwing the throwing sticks, each throwing all three sticks each turn. Each scores the value of the pins he upsets.

As traditionally played, the game is one-hundred points and if one goes over one hundred, he must start over. A better game results if this rule is eliminated, however, and the one declared the winner who first reaches one hundred or goes farthest beyond it when all have thrown an equal number of sticks.

Tire Bowling

Yard, Playground, Picnics   *Late Elementary to Adults*

This is an interesting form of bowling which uses discarded automobile tires in place of balls. For bowling pins, use quart milk bottles or sticks of wood fifteen inches high and three inches in diameter. Ten are needed, which are arranged on the ground as in Bowling. Establish a bowling line thirty feet distant.

Each bowler bowls two tires each turn. The scoring is as in Bowling. If all are knocked over by one tire, it scores a strike; by two tires, a spare. If less than ten are knocked over by the two tires, the player scores one for each pin he upsets.

The player with the highest score in ten frames or turns, wins.

Tin-Can Bowling

Yard, Playground   *Elementary School*

Six one-quart tin cans are needed. Punch holes in the bottom for drainage and sink them in the ground level with the surface in the following positions: sink one can in the center and then sink the remaining five in a circle around it, the circle having a radius of eighteen inches. About twenty feet distant establish a bowling line. Ordinary croquet balls are used.

The players take turns, bowling two balls each turn. If a ball rolls into the center can five points are scored; the other cans score one point. Twenty-one points constitute the game.

Arch Bowls

Yard, Playground   *Late Elementary to Adults*

This contest uses the arches and balls of Croquet. Set up ten croquet arches side by side, just far enough apart to allow a ball to go between them easily. These arches are numbered from left to right, one to ten— actually numbering the arches is not necessary. Establish a bowling line parallel to the arches, at a distance of fifteen feet or more, the distance depending on the smoothness of the lawn and the skill of the players.

Each player bowls one ball each turn, attempting to put it through each arch in order—the first arch must be made before the second, and so on. The player wins who first completes the sequence of the arches.

Variation.—Use croquet mallets and strike the balls.

Bowling on the Green
(*Lawn Bowls*)

Playground, Lawn   *Junior High School to Adults*

This is a form of play bearing a close resemblance to Curling. It is played on a smooth lawn called a bowling green surrounded on all sides by a six-inch trough. Wooden balls called "bowls" are used which are not round but have one side turned with a less curvature than the other. Each player has two of these bowls. A smaller ball, white in color, is called the "jack."

The first player bowls the jack out on the lawn as a mark for the bowling. The bowls are bowled at it in turn, and the score is counted as in Quoits by noting the nearness of the balls to the jack. The jack, as well as the other bowls may be moved by being hit by a bowl in play. This makes it more like a true game to that extent. Bowls which roll into the trough are out of play and do not count.

The players bowl from a small rubber mat, and when a turn (called end) is completed, the mat is carried to the opposite end of the green, and the bowling is repeated from that end.[1]

Bowl Spot-Ball

Lawn, Playground   *Junior High School to Adults*

This is a variation of Bowling on the Green, which is excellent for home and playground use in that it uses any kind of balls that happen to be available and needs no other equipment. Croquet balls are ideal. One ball, known as the "spot ball," should be painted white or marked in some way. Each player has one ball. Establish a foul line near one side of the lawn.

The players draw lots for the privilege of rolling the spot ball. The winner stands behind the foul line and rolls the spot ball out on to the lawn, and then rolls his own ball attempting to make it come to rest as near the spot ball as possible. Each of the other players then roll their balls in turn.

The score is counted according to the number of players; if there are four players the nearest ball scores four, the next three, and so on. If a player's ball hits the spot ball and moves it, he does not score anything. If two or more balls are tied for distance the scores of the balls in question are added and averaged.

On the second frame, the winner of the preceding frame rolls the spot ball and then his own ball. The others follow in the order of their scores in the preceding game.

Fifty points constitute the game.

[1] Detailed rules may be found in *Quoits and Horseshoe Pitching, Lawn Bowls and Boccie,* a handbook of the Spalding Athletic Library.

Bowling Contests in *Social Games for Recreation*

Golf Tee Tenpins.   Swing Ball Tenpins.

Mumblety-Peg

Lawn, Playground   *Elementary and Junior High Schools*

Mumblety-Peg is an old pastime, consisting of tossing a pocket-knife from various positions so that the blade will stick in the ground.

Equipment.—While any pocket knife may be used, the Boy-Scout knife is official for tournament play. The leather punch which this type of knife carries is used instead of the blade—this reduces the danger of players cutting themselves.

Matches.—A match consists of three long games or seven short games. The best two out of three long games or four out of seven short games determines the winner.

Playing Rules.—Players may either sit or kneel on the ground. All throws are made with the right hand unless otherwise specified below. The knife when thrown must stick in the ground so that the referee can place at least two fingers between the ground and the handle of the knife.

Each contestant performs the following series of stunts in order. The long game is for boys and the short game for girls.

The following series of stunts is that considered as official by the National Recreation Association.

Penknife Rules (Long Game):

Front.—Knife on palm of right hand with blade toward finger tips, toss knife upward and inward causing blade to stick in ground.

Back.—Place knife on back of right hand and toss as for front.

Punch.—Make a fist with right hand. Place knife handle across the finger-nails with blade toward thumb; twist hand quickly toward the left sticking blade into the ground.

Snaps.—Hold blade between thumb and forefinger of left hand with handle pointing toward the right. Strike the handle downward sharply with right hand, causing blade to stick into the ground.

Seven Pennies.—Hold blade between thumb and first finger of right hand with handle away from contestant and snap knife away from tosser, sticking it into the ground. This must be done seven times in succession.

Around the Horn.—Hold blade of knife between the index finger and thumb of right hand, as for *Pennies,* and swing the knife, with handle toward the ground, around the head from left to right; then snap away from tosser as in *Seven Pennies.*

Shave the Peg.—Place blade between the first and second fingers and hold with thumb, have handle pointing away from body and point of blade toward person tossing; snap knife away from tosser.

Cut Left.—Hold knife as for Pennies and snap downward across left arm striking left wrist with the right.

Cut Right.—Opposite to *Cut Left.*

Headings.—Same as for *Seven Pennies* except the handle of knife is touched against the forehead before snapping.

Chinnings.—Same as Headings except that chin is touched with handle.

Snaps.—See Rule 4; must be done three times in succession.

Drop In and Pull Out.—Hold knife handle between thumb and forefinger of right hand and drop the knife through a hole made by touching the tips of the forefinger and thumb of the left hand. After blade sticks in ground, pull knife back through the hole by the blade with the handle touching ground and the index finger and thumb holding blade; snap as in *Seven Pennies.*

Shave the Barber.—Hold left hand with palm in and little finger toward the ground. Place knife flat against the palm of left hand with cutting edge toward tosser and handle toward the ground. With the fingers of the right hand pull blade of knife toward the contestant, giving a downward snap.

Lady Dives.—Hold right hand vertical with back of it toward the players; place point of knife against the heel of the hand and the handle against the finger-tips; push upward and forward, giving a loop effect to the knife.

Pinwheel.—With the handle at right angles to the right hand and the arm at right angles to the body, hold the point of the blade loosely between thumb and first finger; flip the knife toward the left with a downward push of the thumb.

Kick 'Em Out.—Place handle of knife flat on palm of left hand with the blade protruding over the little finger side; strike blade downward with right hand.

Cop's Club.—Hold knife as for Seven Pennies, but flip toward tosser. Immediately strike upward with same hand causing knife to spin in opposite direction.

Tony Chestnut.—Starting at toe place point of blade on end of shoe and snap away from player. Repeat same at knee, again at the chest, and then from front part of the head. The toe may be elevated and the point of the knife may be placed against thumb when snapping from chest.

Fingers.—Same as *Pennies* except that the blade is held between the thumb and each finger consecutively and two snaps are made with the first finger and thumb and one with the second, third and little fingers.

Johnny Jump the Fence.—Stick knife into ground at an angle and about one foot away place left hand with palm toward the knife and little finger touching the ground; with the right hand strike the knife up and forward, causing it to go over the left hand or fence and stick into the ground.

O-U-T Period.—Place point of knife on left wrist and with right thumb and forefinger on top of knife snap to ground; at the same time say "O," repeat at elbow and say "U," repeat at shoulder and say "T." Make a fist as in "Punch" and place knife along finger-nails with blade toward little finger side; twist wrist inward quickly and say "period." These last four stunts must be performed consecutively in order to complete the game.

Penknife Rules (Short Game):

Front.—Same as *Long Game.*

Back.—Same as *Long Game.*

Punch.—Same as *Long Game.*

Rabbit's Ears.—Extend index and little fingers; hold the second and third fingers closed with thumb; rest knife on extended fingers with blade toward thumb side; stick knife into ground with inward twist of wrist.

Snaps.—Same as *Long Game.*

Five Pennies.—Same as *Long Game* except five flips are made in succession instead of seven.

Slice the Ham.—With the left palm toward the player place point of knife against the thick of the hand near the little finger side, handle of knife toward the thumb side of hand. With right forefinger and thumb end of the handle pull the knife toward the contestant.

Lady Dives.—Same as *Long Game.*

Shave the Peg.—Same as *Long Game.*

Cut Right.—Same as *Long Game.*

Cut Left.—Same as *Long Game.*

O-U-T Period.—Same as *Long Game.*[2]

Mumblety-Peg Baseball [3]

Playground, Home   *Elementary and Junior High Schools*

Equipment.—While the ground may be used for the playing surface it is much better to use a soft wood board.

Any pocket knife may be used but a knife of the size and shape of a Scout knife is recommended. Open the large blade of the knife half way and the small blade to its full extent.

Players.—The contest is best played between two players. If more, each plays independently and keeps his own score.

Length of Contest.—A certain number of innings may be agreed upon. Each player plays until he makes three outs before the next player plays. Or eleven or twenty-one points may be agreed upon as the limit. In this case each player makes one out and then the next player plays.

Rules.—The large blade of the knife, which is open half way, is stuck in the surface so that the tip of the small blade, open to its full extent, rests on the surface. The player then places a finger under the handle of the knife near its end and lifts it so that the knife flips end over end.

The result of each play is determined by the position of the knife when it rests:

Home run: small blade sticking in the surface.
Three-base hit: large blade sticking in the surface.
Two-base hit: both blades sticking in the surface.
One-base hit: large blade sticking in with small blade resting on surface.

[2] From National Recreation Association, *88 Successful Play Activities,* p. 23 ff. Copyright, 1933. By permission of National Recreation Association, publishers.

[3] The idea for this contest was taken from National Recreation Association *88 Successful Play Activities,* p. 26. Copyright, 1933. By permission of National Recreation Association, publishers.

Strike: knife resting on back of handle.

Out: knife resting on side of handle, or three strikes.

Men on bases advance only the number of bases scored on succeeding plays.

Jackstones

Playground, Yard   *Late Elementary School to Adults*

Jackstones is an ancient contest played with small stones. It develops dexterity, accurate judgment of space and distance, and calls for considerable coordination of hand and sight.

Equipment.—Six jacks and one ball are needed. The jacks are three quarters of an inch in diameter. Modern metal jacks have replaced the stones of the ancient game. The ball is about the size of a golf ball and made of semi-hard rubber.

Any smooth level surface may be used for the playing area.

Order of Playing.—The players take turns in competing. The order of playing is determined by the lag. To lag, the players toe a pitching line and throw a jack to the lag line ten feet distant. The player whose jack comes closest to the line, on either side of it, wins the right to lead. The others follow in the order that their jacks come nearest to the lag line.

The Game.—The winner is the player who goes through the following series with the fewest misses:

1. *Baby Game,* played through sixes.
2. *Downs and Ups.*
3. *Eggs in the Basket,* played through sixes.
4. *Crack the Eggs,* played through sixes.
5. *Upcast,* played through sixes.
6. *Downcast,* played through sixes.
7. *Pigs in the Pen,* played through sixes.
8. *Pigs Over the Fence,* played through sixes.
9. *Sweeps,* played through sixes.
10. *Scrubs,* played through sixes.
11. *Double Bounce,* played through sixes.
12. *Bounce, No Bounce.*

The following are the official rules adopted by the National Recreation Association:

1. **Baby Game.**—Toss the ball up, and while ball bounces once pick up jack or jacks, then catch the ball. This is all done with the right hand. After the ball is caught, jacks are transferred to the other hand.

Ones.—Scatter all jacks upon the playing surface by a single movement of the right hand. Toss the ball, pick up one jack and after ball has bounced once, catch the ball in the right hand. Transfer the jack to the left hand and proceed as before until all six jacks are in the left hand.

Twos.—Jacks are picked up by twos; otherwise proceed as in ones.

Threes.—Jacks are picked up by threes, in the same manner as before.

Fours.—Pick up four jacks and then two jacks, or vice versa, two jacks and then four jacks, depending upon the grouping on the playing surface.

Fives.—Pick up one jack and take the remainder on the next play. Or if it is easier, the five jacks may be picked up first and then the one remaining jack.

Sixes.—Pick up all jacks at one time.

2. **Downs and Ups.**—All jacks and ball in right hand. Toss ball upward, lay down all jacks and catch ball in right hand. Throw ball up again, pick up all jacks and catch ball in right hand.

3. **Eggs in Basket.**—Scatter jacks, toss ball, pick up one jack, right hand only used, and while ball bounces once, transfer jacks to the left hand, then catch ball with the right hand. When all jacks have been picked up and transferred to the left hand, the jacks are all put in the right hand and scattered again. Proceed through twos, threes, fours, fives and sixes.

4. **Crack the Eggs.**—Scatter jacks with right hand. Toss ball with right hand, and while ball bounces once, pick up one jack with right hand, crack it on the playing surface, and catch ball in right hand which is still holding the jack. Transfer the jack to the left hand and proceed as before until all jacks are picked up. Scatter again and proceed by twos. Scatter again and proceed by threes, etc., through sixes.

5. **Upcast.**—Scatter jacks with right hand. Toss ball with right, pick up one jack with right hand and catch the ball in the right hand after it has bounced once, same as in *Baby Game*. Toss the ball up again with the right hand and while it bounces transfer the jack to the left hand, and then catch the ball in the right hand. Continue until all jacks are in the left hand. Scatter again from the right hand and proceed by twos, then threes, etc., through sixes.

6. **Downcast.**—Scatter jacks with right hand. Toss ball with right hand, pick up one jack with right hand and catch the ball in the right hand after it has bounced once, same as in *Baby Game*. Bounce the ball downward and transfer the jack to the left hand, then catch the ball with the right hand. (This differs from *Upcast* in that the ball is started on the bounce by turning the palm of the hand toward the ground and then letting go of the ball.) Proceed through sixes.

7. **Pigs in the Pen.**—Place left hand on the playing surface, finger tips and wrist touching the surface and forming the pen. Toss the ball upward and while it bounces once, pick up one jack with right hand and push it into the pen, then catch the ball in the right hand. Thumb and forefinger are lifted from the playing surface when jack is pushed in, but any jack or jacks left outside the thumb constitute a "miss." Scatter again with the right hand and proceed as before, putting jacks into the pen by twos, then by threes, etc., through sixes.

8. **Pigs Over the Fence.**—Place left hand at right angles to the playing area, little finger resting on the playing surface. This forms the wall or fence. Scatter the jacks, toss the ball upward with the right hand and pick up one jack with the right hand. While ball bounces once, place the jack on the far side of the left hand (over the fence). When all six jacks are picked up, re-scatter with the right hand and proceed by twos, then threes, etc., through sixes.

9. **Sweeps.**—Scatter jacks, toss ball and while ball bounces once, place fingers on one jack and without lifting it from the playing surface, sweep it across the

surface with the right hand until it is close to the body. Then pick it up and catch the ball with the same hand. Sweep all jacks singly, then re-scatter and proceed sweeping by twos, then by threes, etc., through sixes.

10. **Scrubs.**—Scatter jacks, toss ball, pick-up one jack and scrub it across the playing surface with a backward and forward movement. Keep jack in right hand and after ball has bounced once, catch the ball in the same hand. Transfer jack to the left hand and proceed until all six jacks have been "scrubbed." Re-scatter and scrub by twos, and then threes, etc., through sixes.

11. **Double Bounce.**—This is played the same as the *Baby Game,* but ball must bounce *twice* before it is caught. Play through sixes.

12. **Bounce, No Bounce.**—Scatter jacks with right hand. Toss ball upward, pick up one jack while ball bounces once and catch the ball in the right hand. With jack still in right hand, toss the ball upward with the right hand, transfer the jack to the left hand and catch the ball in the right hand *without allowing it to bounce.* Continue until all jacks have been transferred to the left hand, then re-scatter and proceed by twos, threes, etc.

Fouls or Misses.—The following are fouls:

1. Using wrong hand to catch the ball.
2. Failure to pick up the proper number of jacks required by ones, twos, etc., that is, picking up three jacks while playing twos, or four jacks while playing fives, etc.
3. Clothesburn. Allowing the ball or jacks to touch the body or clothing while catching the ball, except the hand used to catch the ball.
4. Two hands. Catching the ball with both hands.
5. Drop jack and drop ball. Failure to hold the ball or jacks until movement is completed.
6. Touching any other jack while attempting to pick up a jack or group of jacks.
7. Double grab. Trying twice for the same jack or group of jacks.
8. Double bounce in any game except double bounce.
9. Changing sitting or standing position after jacks have been scattered. Plays must be made from original position.
10. Failure to begin a turn with the proper stunt. (This should always be the one on which the player missed on his last turn.)
11. Failure to comply with the instructions for all games after the Baby Game. For instance, allowing only one bounce in the *Double Bounce Game.*[4]

Hop-Scotch

Playground, Pavement   *Elementary and Junior High Schools*

Hop-Scotch is a very old contest, known to many countries with local variations. It requires very little space and the equipment costs nothing.

Court.—The court is laid out on a smooth level cement surface. It is

[4] From National Recreation Association, *88 Successful Play Activities,* p. 20 ff. Copyright, 1933. By permission of National Recreation Association, publishers.

outlined as shown in Figure 18, with lines approximately five-eighths of an inch wide. The lines may be chalked or painted, and should be of uniform width.

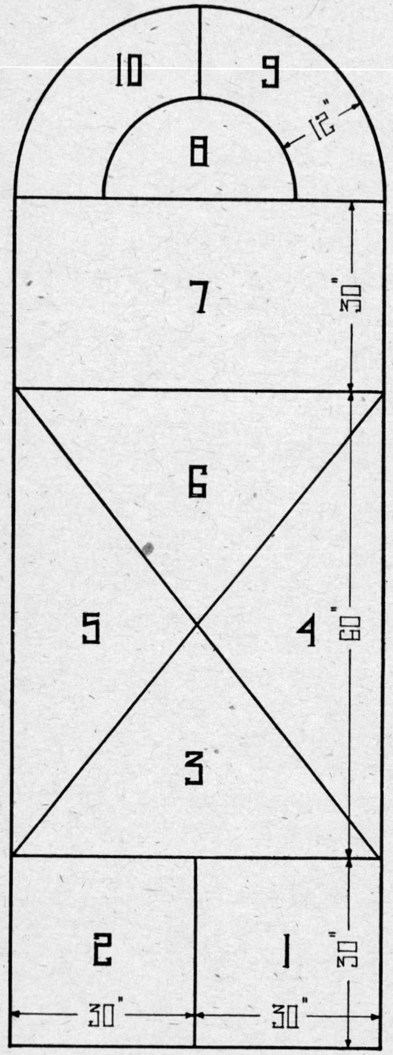

Puck.—The puck may be of any material and of any dimensions provided it does not exceed three-and-one-half inches in length, width, or other dimensions. The players usually provide their own.

Object.—The object is to perform the stunts listed below in the fewest trials. The play consists of tossing the puck into the areas of the court, following a definite order or progression. The puck is then retrieved by kicking it beyond the baseline, while performing a series of hops, jumps, or steps.

Starting Position.—The contestants stand on one foot in hopping position behind the baseline of the court, holding the puck in one hand.

Stunts.—The following stunts are taken from the official rules as adopted by the National Recreation Association:

FIGURE 18.

Stunt No. 1.

a. Toss or drop puck into square No. 1.

b. Hop into square No. 1.

c. Take any number of hops in square without touching any line with hopping foot or any other part of body before, during or after touching puck in square with hopping foot only.

d. Kick puck out of square over and beyond baseline.

e. Finally, hop out of square over and beyond baseline. Don't step out. If no error has been made, proceed to Stunt No. 2.

Stunt No. 2.

a. From starting position, toss puck into square No. 2.

b. Hop into square No. 1 and then into square No. 2.

c. Take any number of hops and kick puck in square or directly out beyond baseline.

d. Finally, retrace course outward by hopping to square No. 1, then hopping beyond baseline. If no error has been made, proceed to Stunt No. 3.

Stunt No. 3.

a. From starting position, toss puck into triangle No. 3.

b. From this position, standing on one foot, leap into squares landing with right foot in No. 1 and left foot in No. 2 at the same instant.

c. Jump from both feet and land on either foot in triangle.

d. When ready, after pushing or sliding puck with hopping foot, kick puck toward or beyond baseline. If it stops in a square of smaller number without resting on a line it must be retrieved as follows:

e. Return by leaping into squares 1 and 2 with right foot in No. 2 and left foot in No. 1 at the same time. If puck has only reached one of these squares raise either foot and, while hopping, kick puck out. Then hop beyond baseline. If no error has been made, proceed to

Stunt No. 4.

a. From starting position, toss puck into triangle No. 4.

b. Advance as in Stunt 3 to triangle 3 and hop into triangle No. 4.

c. Retrieve puck as in Stunt 3.

d. Hop into 3 and return as in Stunt 3. If no error has been made, proceed to

Stunt No. 5.

a. From starting position toss puck into triangle No. 5.

b. Advance as in Stunt 4 and hop into triangle No. 5.

c. Retrieve puck and return as before. If no error has been made, proceed to

Stunt No. 6.

a. From starting position, toss puck into triangle No. 6.

b. Advance as in Stunt 3 to No. 3.

c. Leap to alight with right foot in triangle 4 and left foot in 5, at same time, and jump from both feet to land on one foot in triangle 6.

d. Retrieve puck as before.

e. Return by leaping to alight with right foot in 5 and left foot in 4 at the same time, jump into 3 with one foot only, leap into 2 and 1 with right foot in 2 and left foot in 1 at the same time, and jump out beyond baseline to land on one foot. If no error has been made, proceed to

Stunt No. 7.

a. From starting position, toss puck into rectangle No. 7.

b. Advance as in Stunt No. 6 and leap to land on both feet at same time in rectangle 7.

c. Walk about in 7, moving puck with foot or feet alone until in position to retrieve it by kicking it out over baseline or into a space of smaller number.

d. Return by raising one foot and hopping into triangle 6, and continue out as before. If no error has been made, proceed to

Stunt No. 8.

a. From starting position, toss puck into semicircle No. 8.

b. Advance as before to 7 and when ready to progress to space 8, raise either foot and hop out of rectangle into semicircle, landing on one foot.

c. Retrieve puck as before.

d. Return by leaping to land both feet at the same time in rectangle 7 and when ready continue as in Stunt 7. If no error has been made, proceed to

Stunt No. 9.

a. From starting position toss puck into arc No. 9.

b. Advance as in Stunt No. 8.

c. Retrieve while in hopping position in semicircle by picking up the puck by hand from arc No. 9.

d. Return as in Stunt No. 8 carrying puck in hand.

Stunt No. 10.

a. From starting position, toss puck into arc No. 10.

b. Advance as in Stunt No. 9 and hop into arc No. 10.

c. Retrieve as in Stunt No. 9.

d. Hop into semicircle 8 and return as before, stopping for a few seconds' rest in No. 7 if desired.

Stunt No. 11.

a. From starting position, without tossing or carrying puck, advance as in Stunt 8 to semicircle.

b. Leap to land on both feet at the same time with right in arc 9 and left in arc 10.

c. About face and reverse position of feet by a leaping half turn.

d. Return by jumping to land on one foot in semicircle and continue out according to Stunt No. 8.

Fouls, Errors or Misses.—A player loses his turn under the following conditions:

1. If he tosses the puck while not in proper hopping position behind the baseline. Leaning over the baseline is permitted.

2. If the puck, on throw, does not come to rest entirely within the designated space so that a vertical line dropped from any edge of the puck intersects one of the court lines.

3. If the puck, on kick, comes to rest so that a vertical line dropped through any part of it touches a court line.

4. If the puck, on kick, passes out of the court over a side line, not the baseline.

5. If the player touches any court line with footwear or coming to rest on a foot so that a vertical line dropped through the footwear would touch a line.

6. If a player commits any irregularity in progression, as judged by the umpire.[5]

[5] See National Recreation Association, *88 Successful Play Activities*, p. 6 ff. Copyright, 1933. By permission of National Recreation Association, publishers.

Hop-Scotch Golf

Yard, Playground   *Elementary and Junior High Schools*

Lay out a circle twenty-five feet in diameter and at equal distances around it sink nine tin cans flush with the surface. The cans should have holes punched in the bottom for drainage. If desired the Clock Golf Course (Figure 18), with its twelve holes may be used. For a temporary course, four-inch holes may be dug in the ground in place of the cans. Indicate one can for the Number 1 hole, and number the others consecutively. Each player has a small wood block or chip two or three inches in diameter.

The first player, hopping on one foot, tries to put the block in the first hole in the fewest possible kicks. Then the other players try. When all have made the first hole, they proceed to the second. The player wins who completes the circuit of nine holes in the fewest kicks.

O'Leary

Playground, Home   *Elementary and Junior High Schools*

One, two, three, O'Leary,
Four, five, six, O'Leary,
Seven, eight, nine, O'Leary,
Ten, O'Leary, Postman.
(Tune—One little, two little, three little Indians)

Any small rubber ball is used. Bat the ball to the ground with the palm of the hand to "One, two, three" and perform the prescribed movement each time on the word "O'Leary." On the third count, the ball is hit harder so that it will bounce higher. On "Ten, O'Leary, Postman" give the ball one bounce and catch it on "Postman."

The following movements are to be performed:

1. One, two, three, O'Leary: swing the right leg outward over the ball.
   Four, five, six, O'Leary: swing the right leg outward over the ball.
   Seven, eight, nine, O'Leary: swing the right leg outward over the ball.
   Ten, O'Leary, Postman: Bounce the ball once and catch it.
2. Swing the left leg outward over the ball on "O'Leary."
3. Swing the right leg inward over the ball on "O'Leary."
4. Swing the left leg inward over the ball on "O'Leary."
5. Grasp the edge of the skirt with the left hand and make the ball pass upward between the arm and the skirt on saying "O'Leary."
6. Same as Number 5, except that the ball drops through from above.
7. Grasp the right toe with the left hand and make the ball pass upward in the circle thus formed.
8. Same as Number 7, except that the ball drops through from above.
9. Grasp the right wrist with the left hand, forming a circle with the arms, and make the ball pass up through it.

10. Same as Number 9, except that the ball drops through from above.

11. Touch the forefingers and thumbs together and let the ball drop down through the circle thus formed.

12. To the words "One, O'Leary," "Two, O'Leary," "Three, O'Leary" and so on, bounce the ball alternately to the right and left of the right foot, moving the foot from side to side.

13. Same as Number 12, except that the foot is kept in place.

14. To the words of Number 12, pass the right leg outward over the ball on every bounce.

15. Same as Number 14, except that the left leg is passed outward over the ball.

16. Same as Number 14, except that the right leg is passed inward over the ball each bounce.

17. Same as Number 14, except that the left leg is passed inward over the ball.

18. To the words, "Jack, Jack, pump the water, Jack, Jack, pump the water, Jack, Jack, pump the water, So early in the morning," bounce the ball as in Number 1, making a complete turn to the right on the word "morning."

19. Same as Number 18, turning to the left.

20. Same as Number 1, except that the right leg is swung twice outward over the ball.

21. Same as Number 1, except that the left leg is swung twice outward over the ball.

22. Same as Number 5, except that the ball is passed twice through the circle of the arm and skirt, upward.

23. Same as Number 1, except that the right leg is swung outward over the ball on each bounce.

24. Same as Number 1, except that the right leg is swung inward over the ball on each bounce.

25. Same as Number 5, except that the ball is made to go through the circle of the arm and skirt on every bounce.

26. On the word "O'Leary" perform a scissors jump over the ball.

27. On the word "O'Leary" swing the right leg inward and the left leg outward over the ball.

28. Same as Number 27, passing the legs over the ball on each bounce.

CONTESTS IN WHICH THE GAME ELEMENT IS PROMINENT

The events in this section are a cross between games and contests. Although the contestant is free from interference by his opponents most of the time, yet interference with his play occasionally takes place. A familiar example is seen in Croquet. The rules permit your opponent to place his ball against yours and strike it with his mallet, sending your ball out of position for the next play. This is a decided game element. But even though his ball may have been knocked out of position by his opponents, one is free *when his own turn comes,* to play without interference. In a true game, such as Tennis for example, there is constant interference from the opponent during the course of play—the opponent is at liberty to strive constantly to prevent the play from meeting with success.

Golf

Golf Course   *Junior High School to Adults*

The origin of golf is said to go back many centuries to a primitive game played by shepherds in which a small stone was driven with the shepherd's crook a given distance, the object being to reach the goal with the fewest drives. In its present form the game is of Scotch origin. In numbers of participants golf would probably be one of the three most popular games in the United States. It would have many more adherents were it not for the fact that the equipment is relatively expensive, and free or low-priced courses are not sufficient in number to meet the demand.

A full course of eighteen holes requires a space of about one-hundred acres, preferably of rolling ground. A nine-hole course would require half the space. In this case for a full "game" one must play twice around.

Course.—The course is called a "golf links," and consists of eighteen different links or, as they are generally called, holes. Each hole consists of a "tee," a "fairway," and a "putting green." The "tee" consists of a section of a well-clipped turf, level and from ten to twenty feet square, as a starting point. The "fairway" is a strip 150 to 200 feet wide of well-mowed meadow land, stretching away approximately 400 yards to the flag at the hole which marks the end of that link. There are usually some "hazards" along the sides and sometimes across the fairway to catch poorly played balls, either natural hazards, as trees, brooks, or ponds, or artificial hazards, as "bunkers" (a mound of earth) or sand traps. The "putting green" is a space from sixty to seventy feet wide, of closely-clipped turf, level or slightly undulating. Near the center of this putting green is a four-inch cup set in level with the ground. In the center of the cup is a slender standard a few feet high with a flag at the top to indicate to the player the exact location of the hole for which he is playing.

The links or holes vary in length from 75 yards to 600 yards. The average length is from 300 to 400 yards. The distance around the course of eighteen holes is from 6,000 to 6,400 yards, or a little more than three miles and a half.

Equipment.—Several golf sticks or clubs are necessary in order to play a good game. The most important of these are as follows: a driver, a brassie, a mid-iron, a mashie, a niblick, and a putter. The driver and the brassie are clubs with wooden heads and are used for distances of 160 to 250 yards. The other clubs have iron heads and have more loft or pitch to them progressively, except the putter, which has nearly a straight face. The mid-iron is used for distances of 150 to 180 yards, the mashie for pitching balls 75 to 150 yards, the niblick for getting out of sandpits or bunkers or high grass, or for pitching balls high for distances of 25 to 75 yards, and dropping them on the putting green near the flag. The putter is used only on the putting green to drive the ball into the cup. The club used depends on the distance desired and on the position of the ball, whether it lies well or poorly on the turf. The ball used is a white hard rubber ball 1.68 inches in diameter and 1.62 ounces in weight.

The Play.—The object of play is to drive this ball around the links in the fewest strokes possible, in competition with another player, who plays his own ball. In "medal play" the one who secures the lowest number of strokes is the winner; in "match play" the one who wins the majority of holes is first. Each link or hole is played as a unit from the tee to the cup. When the ball has been "holed," that is, driven into the cup, it is lifted by the hand, and the player goes a few rods away to the tee of the next link or hole of the course; and so on until he has completed the full eighteen holes. This ends the game unless there is a tie. In match play, in case of a tie, the players start around the course again and play until one of the competitors wins a hole; in medal play, to break a tie, it is usual to play at least nine more holes.

"Par" means the number of strokes that an extra-good player should use in playing around, seventy-two strokes being about right for the average course. The term is used as referring to perfect golf. The term "two-some" is applied to a game in which there is only one player on each side. A "foursome" is a match in which there are four players, two on each side, each playing his own ball. A "two-ball foursome" is a match in which there are two players on each side, the partners using but one ball and playing the strokes alternately.

In the regular foursome, the customary practice in scoring is to count both low ball and low total; that is, the low ball for a particular hole counts one point for the pair whose player made it, and the low total of the two paired players counts one point for this side. If one team has low ball and the other side has low total (as for example, Team A has scores of 4 and 7 and Team B has scores of 5 and 5, then the results are nullified and neither side gains an advantage. In professional foursomes, the practice of counting only the low ball is often found.

Team Competition.—A match between two teams usually consists of four twosomes and two foursomes. Each team may, therefore, have four players in the singles and four players in the doubles, but the better players usually play in both the twosomes and the foursomes.

Eighteen points are allowed for the match, distributed as follows:

Four twosomes ....3 points each............ 12 points
Two foursomes ....3 points each............ 6 points

In the twosomes points are earned as follows:

The winner of the first nine holes................................... 1
The winner of the second nine holes............................... 1
The winner of the eighteen holes................................... 1

In the foursomes, the points are awarded as in the twosomes.

When golf clubs meet in competition, the Nassau System is frequently used. Any number of players from the clubs may compete and the points are awarded as described above. To determine the winning club, the scores of the individual competitors are added.

Clock Golf
(Round-the-Clock Golf)

Playground   *Junior High School to Adults*

This modification of golf is of recent origin and is designed to provide golf play on a limited space. It is excellent as a recreational game and provides splendid practice in putting. It can be played in the yards of homes or on any level lawn twenty-five feet square.

Course and Equipment.—Draw a circle on the ground twenty to twenty-four feet in diameter. Mow the grass closely. Around the circle place

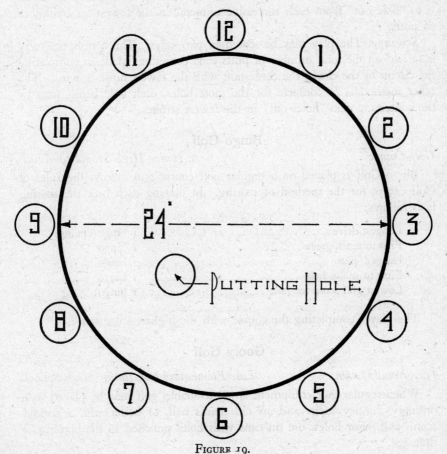

FIGURE 19.

twelve markers at regular intervals representing the twelve numerals on the face of a clock. The markers may be purchased from sporting goods stores or the numerals may be painted on the bottoms of tin cans set in the ground so that they are flush with the surface. The putting hole is placed somewhere within the circle, in such a position that the distance from the hole to the different numerals varies. A tin can with holes punched in the bottom for drainage is very satisfactory for the putting hole.

Only one type of club is used—the putter. Each player needs one putter and a golf ball.

Players.—Two to four players may play, each competing independently. Or a foursome may be formed with two players on each side, each playing his own ball. Or a two-ball foursome may be played with two players on each side, the partners using but one ball and playing the strokes alternately.

The Play.—The putting stroke of golf is the only stroke used. Each contestant in turn putts the ball from the one-o'clock marker, then from the two-o'clock marker, and so on around the face of the clock. The object is to "hole out" from each successive numeral in the fewest total number of putts.

Scoring.—The play may be scored in two ways. The commonest way is to add up the total number of putts each contestant made in completing the circuit of the clock; the contestant with the fewest number wins. The other method is to compete for the most holes, each hole being won by the contestant who "holes out" in the fewest strokes.

Bingo Golf

Golf Course   *Junior High School to Adults*

Bingo Golf is played on a regular golf course and follows the rules of Golf except for the method of scoring. In playing each hole the scoring is as follows:

Longest drive	1 bingo (point)
First to reach green	1 bingo
Longest putt	1 bingo
First to make hole	1 bingo
Lowest golf score for hole	1 bingo

The player completing the course with the highest score wins.

Goofy Golf

Playground, Lawn   *Late Elementary and Junior High Schools*

When regular golf equipment is not available, golf may be played with ordinary shinney sticks and an old tennis ball, or better still, a paddle-tennis ball. For holes, use tin cans with holes punched in the bottom for drainage.

Croquet Golf

Playground, Lawn   *Late Elementary to Adults*

This is a very satisfactory and interesting game of the golf type which can be played on any playground or large lawn, and since nothing more than tin cans and croquet equipment is needed, the expense is insignificant.

Course.—With careful planning a nine-hole course may be laid out on a section of lawn no larger than 150 by 200 feet, or smaller if need be. Tin cans six inches in diameter and six inches deep are used for holes—punch holes in the bottom for drainage and sink them flush with the surface.

The distances for the holes may vary from thirty to ninety feet. The greens are fifteen feet in diameter and the tees five feet wide. The fairways should be about four feet in width. Hazards should be constructed and the children will add others of every description from their own materials. Home-made markers can be easily made.

Equipment.—Croquet mallets and balls are used.

Rules.—Except on the greens, the ball must be hit with the mallet held between the legs. When the side stroke is allowed, the desire for distance leads to hitting so hard that mallets are broken.

In other respects the general rules of Golf apply.

Par.—In general it will be found that the following figures will approximate par for the various distances:

35 feet and under .... Par 2
36 to 70 feet .... Par 3
71 to 100 feet .... Par 4

Sidewalk Golf [6]

Pavement   *Late Elementary and Junior High Schools*

This game was originated by Sydney Strong in 1930. The course is laid out with chalk on a paved area and a checker is snapped with the finger from hole to hole.

Course.—A section of pavement or floor thirty feet square is needed for a simple course. At each corner draw a six-inch square to serve as a "hole" as in Figure 20. These squares should be about thirty feet apart. More squares may be added if desired, distributed so that they are approximately thirty feet apart. Beside each square mark a tee. Hazards and bunkers may be added.

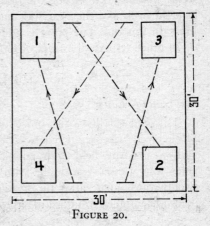

FIGURE 20.

[6] Contributed by Sydney Strong, New York.

Equipment.—Ordinary checkers are used. Bottle tops may be substituted.

The Play.—The checker is snapped with the middle finger, not tossed or thrown. The players in turn snap for square Number 1, each counting the number of snaps required to make it. Then they snap for Number 2. The player wins who completes the course in the fewest snaps. Each square must be completed by all before proceeding to the rest.

Marble Golf

Playground, Lawn   *Late Elementary and Junior High Schools*

This ingenious contest combines Marbles and Golf. It is immensely popular among boys who know it in the spring of the year. It adds to marbles a colorful aspect and brings a new type of competition into this time-honored game.

Course.—Any clay or hard-packed corner of a playground or lawn may be used. The holes vary in length from twenty to sixty feet. Each should contain at least one hazard and the boys display amazing ingenuity in adding clever hazards of their own make out of almost any old thing.

The fairways should be marked with lime lines and should be from sixteen to twenty-four inches wide. Tees consist of small mounds of earth. The holes are made of the smallest-size baking-powder cans, with holes in the bottom for drainage and sunk flush with the ground. They should contain enough sand so that the marbles can be easily withdrawn with the fingers.

Equipment.—Each player needs one ordinary marble.

The Play.—All shots must be made from the "knuckles-down" position. If the marble goes outside the line marking the edge of the fairway, it is brought back and the next shot made from the point where it crossed the line. In this case, one point is added to the score.

In other respects the rules of Golf apply.

Hockey Golf [7]

Playground, Lawn   *Junior High School to Adults*

This event follows the procedure of Golf but uses the skills of Field Hockey. It was originated by Bertha Kellar, Monterey, California.

Course.—Any field with reasonably smooth turf may be used. Nine poles four to six feet high, with flags, are needed. These are set up twenty yards apart after the fashion of the poles in a golf course. The poles are numbered, indicating the order in which they must be played.

[7] The idea for this game was taken from the University of Michigan, Staff of Physical Education for Women, *Physical Education Activities for High School Girls,* p. 110. Copyright, 1928. By permission of Lea and Febiger, publishers.

Equipment.—Field-hockey sticks and balls are used.

The Play.—The procedure and scoring is as in Golf. A player holes out when his ball hits the pole. In case a player swings his club over his shoulder in striking the ball, five points are added to his score. The player wins who completes the course with the fewest number of strokes.

Codeball on the Green

Open Field, Golf Course   *Junior High School to Adults*

Codeball on the Green was invented in 1929 by Dr. William E. Code. It is an outdoor adaptation of Dr. Code's original game of Codeball in the Court. It is a combination of Golf and Soccer. It resembles Golf in that the playing field consists of a series of "holes" of various lengths up to three-hundred yards, with a cup at the end of each. It resembles Soccer in that an inflated rubber ball is kicked by the player.

Codeball on the Green is growing rapidly in popularity. The cost of equipment to the individual player is negligible; it offers all of the outdoor advantages of Golf, is slightly more strenuous than Golf, and gives the player a satisfactory work-out in less time than Golf.

The Course.—A field, preferably grass-covered, of at least ten acres is needed for a good course. Fourteen official bowls are needed; these are aluminum basins forty-one inches wide at the base, rising cone-shaped seven inches from the turf to an opening eighteen inches wide.

These bowls are distributed across the course, the distance between them varying from 50 to 300 yards. Fourteen kick-offs are needed, each consisting of two arrow markers fourteen feet apart and pointing in the direction of the bowl. The distance from the bowl to the next kick-off should be at least thirty-five feet.

The course should be so laid out that it is broken by hazards and skirted by the rough.

Ball.—An official codeball is used. This is an inflated rubber ball six inches in diameter and twelve ounces in weight. It rebounds very freely.

Object.—The object is to foot the ball in the fewest number of kicks over the fairways, bowling out in each of the fourteen bowls.

Contestants.—Matches may be played in twosomes or foursomes. Threesomes may also be played.

The Start.—Priority of play at the start is determined by lot. Thereafter, the player who wins the bowl kicks first at the next kick-off.

At the kick-off the ball is placed between the kick-off markers and kicked as it lies on the ground. If it is kicked from a point ahead of the markers, it may be recalled by an opponent and is then kicked over again without penalty.

The Play.—A player may not touch the ball with his hands except to remove it from a bowl or an unplayable hazard. If the ball must be removed from an unplayable hazard, it must be placed at a point not nearer the bowl and a penalty of one kick is charged against the player. If a player's ball hits another ball, the latter must be replaced and the former shall be played where it lies.

Each attempt to kick is counted as one kick. If a player casually moves his ball in play the penalty is one kick. If a player kicks his ball while it is moving there is a penalty of two kicks in medal play and the loss of the bowl in match play.

The ball farthest away from the bowl usually is played first, except when the play is around the bowl, when a near ball may be played first when the player hopes to halve the low ball of his opponents who have already bowled out, and thus permit his partner who is away to strive to win.

Bowling Out.—Near the bowl it is advantageous to foot the ball with the sole of the foot rather than the toe, sweeping the foot over the top of the ball, thus giving it an overspin which keeps its straight in its ascent of the bowl and steady when it drops. If the ball rebounds out of the bowl it must be played until it rests in the bowl. When a player bowls out he must remove his ball from the bowl immediately.

Twenty-four inches constitutes a stymie. If an obstructing ball is less than twenty-four inches from the ball to be played it must be removed and the place marked so that the player who is away may have a clear kick to the bowl.

Scoring.—The scoring is as in Golf (page 125).

Par.—Pars are as follows:

100 yards or less	3
101 to 200 yards	4
201 to 350 yards	5
351 to 500 yards	6

Other Contests in this Book Which Follow Golf Procedure

Basketball Golf.   Shinney Golf.
Hockey Golf.   Hop-Scotch Golf.

Contests of the Golf Type in *Social Games for Recreation*

Party Golf.   Tire Golf.
Table Golf.   Pebble Golf.

Horseshoe Pitching
(*Barnyard Golf*)

Playground, Yard, Picnic   *Late Elementary School to Adults*

Horseshoe Pitching is an ancient and much loved type of informal play. It is essentially a contest but has one characteristic of a game in that a player may interfere with his opponent to the extent that he may knock his opponent's shoe away from the stake by hitting it with his own shoe, and may nullify his opponent's ringer by placing a ringer on top of it.

In informal play the stakes are from thirty to forty feet apart and discarded horseshoes are frequently used. The game consists of twenty-one points.

In tournament play, however, more definite rules are in vogue, which differ from those in common use.[8]

Court.—The stakes are placed in the center of a *pitcher's box* which consists of a wooden frame six feet square. The frame is made of two-by-four-inch material and is placed in the ground so that it extends not more than one inch above the surface. For a distance of at least eighteen inches around the stake the box should be filled with potter's clay or similar material to a depth of at least six inches. The clay should be moistened to a putty-like consistency.

The *stakes* should be of iron, one inch in diameter, perpendicularly inclined one inch toward the opposite stake and extending eight inches above the ground.

The regulation distance between stakes is forty feet, measured from where the stake enters the ground. For women and boys in contests and tournaments, the distance should be thirty feet.

Horseshoes.—The horseshoes must not exceed seven-and-one-half inches in length, seven inches in width, and two-and-one-half pounds in weight with toe or heel calks extending out not more than three-quarters of an inch. The openings between the calks must not exceed three-and-one-half inches, inside measurements.

Game.—A regulation game consists of fifty points, and the contestant first scoring this number wins. Match contests between two players consist of three games of fifty points each.

First Pitch.—At the beginning of a game the contestants toss for the choice of first pitch or follow. At the beginning of the second game the loser of the preceding game has the first pitch. During the games, the contestant scoring has the lead.

Pitching Rules.—The contestants pitch both shoes, one after the other, from the pitching box into the opposite pitching box. A contestant is not permitted to walk across to the opposite stake and examine the position of his opponent's shoes before pitching.

When a contestant has the first pitch he must, after delivering both shoes, stand back of a line even with the stake and out of the pitcher's box, or forfeit the value of the shoes pitched.

[8] The rules here given follow the regulations of the National Horseshoe Pitching Association for New Jersey and Pennsylvania State Championships. See National Recreation Association, *88 Successful Play Activities,* p. 42 ff. Copyright, 1933. By permission of National Recreation Association, publishers.

The front of the pitcher's box (three feet in front of the stake) is the foul line and any pitcher stepping over this line in delivering his shoe loses the value of his pitch.

If a shoe strikes the frame of the pitcher's box or other object it is called a *foul shoe* and does not score.

Ringers.—Any shoe to be scored as a ringer must encircle the stake far enough to permit a straight-edge to touch both heel calks and clear the stake.

Scoring.—The shoes score as follows:

If a shoe when thrown moves another shoe both shoes are measured from their new position.

The closest shoe to the stake scores *one* point. If both shoes are closer than the opponent's they score *two* points.

A ringer scores *three* points.

A ringer and a closest shoe scores *four* points.

A double ringer scores *six* points and is the highest score a contestant can make.

In case each contestant has a ringer, the next closest shoe scores and all such ringers are credited as ringers pitched but not counted as a score.

If each contestant has a double ringer, both double ringers are cancelled and no points scored.

If a contestant has two ringers and his opponent one, the pitcher having two ringers scores *three* points.

In case of a tie of all four shoes, such as four ringers or all four shoes an equal distance from the stake, no score is recorded and the contestant who pitched last is awarded the lead.

A shoe leaning against the stake has no advantage over a shoe lying on the ground and against the stake; all such shoes are ties. If a contestant has a shoe leaning against the stake, it counts only as a closest shoe. (In informal play such shoes are called "leaners" or "hobbers" and score two points.)

Measurements.—All measurements should be made by the use of calipers and a straight edge.

Quoits

Playground, Yard, Picnic   *Late Elementary School to Adults*

As popularly played, quoits is the same as Horseshoe Pitching with the exception that circular metal rings are used in place of horseshoes. While the game may be played according to Horseshoe-Pitching rules, there are certain differences in the official quoits regulations. The principal difference is that the pin or stake is driven in the ground until the "mott" (head of the pin) is level with the surface of the ground.

Court.—The distance from pin to pin in the English and Caledonian rules is eighteen yards. For playground use the distance is thirty feet for seniors and twenty feet for juniors. The latter distances are recommended.

The pins should be surrounded by an area of stiff clay to a depth of at least six inches and not less than four feet in diameter.

The pins should be from twelve to eighteen inches in length and from five-eighths to three-fourths of an inch wide at the top. They should have a hole punched in the center of the top for measuring. They are driven in the clay until the mott or head of the pin is level with the surface of the bed.

Quoits.—Official quoits consist of a circular metal ring with a hole four inches in diameter in the center. The rim is two-and-one-half inches wide. For senior contest the quoits should not weigh less than three pounds.

First Pitch.—The first pitch is decided by a toss of a coin. Thereafter the winner of the immediately preceding game has the lead and throws both of his quoits consecutively.

Pitching Rules.—The pitcher is not allowed to step ahead of the pin in pitching. He may stand astride of the pin providing his feet are back of the center of the pin. He may stand at any distance back of the pin and step forward, provided he does not step in front of the pin.

The quoits must be delivered with the convex surface uppermost, but a quoit turned in the act of delivering or by being struck by another quoit counts.

Ringers.—A pitched quoit which encircles the pin is a ringer.

Hobbers.—A pitched quoit resting on the pin is a hobber.

Scoring.—The quoits score as follows:

1. A ringer counts *three* points.
2. A double ringer counts *six* points.
3. A ringer topped by an opponent counts *six* points for the person pitching the last ringer.
4. A triple ringer scores *nine* points for the person pitching the last ringer.
5. A ringer topped by two hobbers, both of which touch the pin, counts *seven* points for the person pitching the hobbers.
6. A pitcher pitching a ringer and a hobber that is topped with a hobber by an opponent scores *three* points for his ringer.
7. A ringer and a hobber count *five* points.
8. A ringer topped by a hobber pitched by an opponent counts *three* points for the player pitching the ringer.
9. If a double ringer is topped by a hobber, *six* points are scored by the person pitching the second ringer.
10. If a ringer is topped by a ringer and then a hobber by an opponent, *eight* points are scored by the person pitching the last ringer and hobber.
11. A hobber counts *two* points.
12. A hobber topped by another quoit counts *two* points for the quoit nearest or resting on the pin.
13. In case of two opposing quoits resting on the pin, they are removed and the nearest of the remaining two quoits count *one* point.

14. Two hobbers score *four* points in case both touch the pin.

15. In case neither a ringer or a hobber is made, the nearest quoit to the pin counts *one* point.

16. If two quoits pitched by the same player are nearest the pin, *two* points are scored, one for each nearest quoit.

17. In case of a tie between two opposing quoits, they are removed and the remaining two quoits measured and *one* point scored for the nearest quoit.

18. If three quoits are in contact with the pin, two are considered as tied, and the remaining quoit scores *one* point for its owner.

Measuring.—All measuring is done by calipers from the center of the pin to the nearest part of the quoit.

Game.—The game consists of twenty-one points. The player or pair scoring twenty-one points first wins. Matches consist of the best two out of three games.

Tire Quoits

Playground, Yard, Picnics   *Late Elementary School to Adults*

This is a most interesting type of Quoits using old automobile tires for quoits. Drive two poles in the ground thirty feet apart—the poles should be sturdy and extend above the ground eighteen inches.

Two or four players may play; if there are four, they play in teams of two and one player of each pair stands at each post. Each player at one end has two tires.

The first player rolls the tire with a single shove attempting to make it roll to the peg at the other end and fall over it. He then rolls his second tire, and then his opponent rolls his two.

The scoring is as in Horseshoe Pitching. If a tire actually circles the stake, it scores three. If no tires circle the post, the nearest tires score one each as in Horseshoe Pitching. See the detailed statement of scoring under Horseshoe Pitching.

The two players at the other end then roll the tires back. The player winning the immediately preceding throws has the privilege of throwing first in the next round.

A player may not step beyond the peg in rolling his tire, but may stand as far behind it as he chooses and run as far as he likes provided he does not go beyond the peg.

Twenty-one points constitute the game.

Quoit Contests in *Social Games for Recreation*

Rope Quoits.   Clothespin Ring Toss.
Chair Quoits.   Washer Pitching.
Bottle Quoits.   Disk Quoits.

Fruit Jar Ring Quoits.

Curling

The game is described in Chapter XXVII, "Winter Activities."

Shuffleboard

Club, Pavement
Late Elementary School to Adults

Court.—The court is laid out on a floor or pavement. Figure 21 shows the layout. Both ends are alike and the distance from point to point is fifteen feet.

Disks and Cues.—Eight circular disks are needed, six inches in diameter and one inch thick. These may be purchased or made at a mill. Four are painted red and four blue.

The cues are likewise easily made. They consist of a five-foot handle with a head three-and-one-half inches wide and curved to fit the disks. The maximum length must not exceed six feet three inches.

Players.—Teams of one or two may play. In singles, both play from the same end of the court and change when all disks are shot. In doubles, the two partners play from opposite ends of the court, one team using disks of one color and the other team the other color.

Object.—The object is to shove the disks with the cue so that they come to rest in the scoring areas at the opposite ends of the court.

The Play.—The first play is made from the right side of the court followed by a play from the other side. The players thus alternate. In subsequent games, the winner of the preceding game starts.

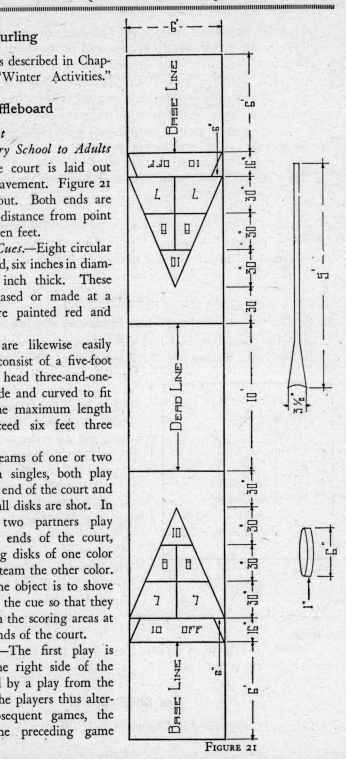

FIGURE 21

In doubles play, the two opponents at one end play all eight disks, and then the other two play from their end of the court.

The players place their disks in their half of the 10-off space and play the four disks from this area—the penalty for violation is five points off the score. Players are not allowed to step on or over the first line of the court—violation results in a penalty of five points off.

If a player's disk stops in a scoring area, it may be knocked out of the court or into the "10-off" area by his opponent.

Scoring.—A disk scores in the area in which it rests after all eight disks have been played. Disks resting on a division line do not score. Disks that stop nearer to the players' end than the farthest dead line are dead and removed at once.

The game is fifty points. If both sides have fifty or more points the side having the most points wins. In case of a tie, the eighth disk is shot twice from each end and the side having the highest score wins.

Kick Shuffle

Home, Club   *Late Elementary and Junior High Schools*

Draw the court illustrated in Figure 22 on the sidewalk, pavement, or floor. Establish a kicking line fifteen feet distant. Three wooden disks are

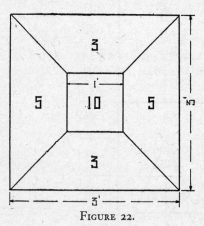

needed, four inches in diameter and two inches thick. Square blocks of wood four inches square and two inches thick may be used instead of disks, and are easier to make. For informal play, children use any block of wood not exceeding four inches.

The first player stands on one foot on the kicking line and kicks a disk with the other foot, attempting to put it in one of the spaces in the court. He then kicks the other two disks. The player is credited with the total of the points allowed for the spaces in which his disks rest. Disks on a line score the lower space number; those touching an outside line score nothing.

FIGURE 22.

The players take turns kicking three disks each turn. The one wins who scores fifty points first.

Ice Shuffleboard

This game is described in Chapter XXVII, "Winter Activities."

Shuffleboard Contests in *Social Games for Recreation*

Shanty Shuffleboard.   Parlor Shuffleboard.

Target Shuffleboard.

Croquet

Playground, Lawns   *Elementary School to Adults*

Court.—The court may be of any size depending on the space available. It should be level with the grass mowed short. Two wooden stakes are located, one at each end of the court; they are one-and-one-quarter inches in diameter and extend above the ground one-and-one-half inches. The position of the wickets is shown in the following diagram, O representing a stake and X a wicket:

```
            X                    X

 O      XX           X           XX      O

            X                    X
```

Occasionally two wickets are placed in the center instead of one.

The wickets should extend above the ground ten inches but the width is optional. For beginners they should spread not less than five inches, but may be narrowed for expert play. If the arches are too narrow for the skill of the players, interest will be destroyed.

Balls and Mallets.—Wooden or hard rubber balls, three-and-three-eighths inches in diameter, are used. These are colored red, white, blue, and black.

Mallets may be of any size and style, and may be changed as often as desired in the course of the play.

The Play.—The object is to drive the ball by hitting it with the face of the mallet through the series of arches, following the specified course. The stake at which the play starts is called the home stake. The ball is placed in front of the home stake, and hit through the first two arches, to the right-wing arch, to the center arch, to the lower right-wing arch, to the two lower center arches, and to the lower stake. The ball is then played back to the home stake by hitting it through the lower center arches, to the lower left-wing arch, to the center arch, to the upper left-wing arch, to the upper center arches, and to the home stake.

Each player making an arch or stake may have a trial at the next one in order, and continues until he misses. Instead of making an arch, a player may, with any stroke, hit the ball of a partner or an opponent, and then may lay his ball beside the one that was hit and strike it so as to move the other ball as well as his own; a partner's ball thus may be sent forward to a better position and an opponent's ball is driven to a place from which it will be more difficult or impossible to make an arch. The player or team first to finish a round of the arches and stakes is the winner.

Roque.—Roque is a game similar to croquet, but is played on a more accurate course and with more specific rules. These rules may be found in *Lawn Sports,* a handbook of the Spalding Athletic Library.

Modern Croquet.—Modern croquet is a much more accurate game than ordinary croquet and played according to different rules. These rules may be found in *Lawn Games,* a handbook in Spalding's Athletic Library.

Disk Croquet

This indoor form of Croquet is described in *Social Games for Recreation,* Chapter IX, "Small Equipment Games for Club Room and Home.'

Marbles [9]
(*Ringer*)

Playground, Home   *Elementary and Junior High Schools*

Of the various types of Marble play, Ringer is the best known, most standardized, and most commonly used contest for tournament play. It is played in a ring ten feet in diameter, with thirteen marbles arranged in the center on a cross, the object being to shoot these marbles out of the ring, the player shooting out the largest number being the winner.

Ring.—On a smooth level area of hard clay, or other suitable substance, inscribe a ring ten feet in diameter, inside measurement. The outline of the ring should be approximately one-half inch wide and one-half inch deep.

With the center of the ring as a point of intersection, mark or paint two lines at right angles to each other to form a cross on which to place the playing marbles. Place one marble at the center and three each on the four branches of the cross, each marble three inches away from the next one.

Establish a lag line by drawing a straight line tangent to the ring and touching it at one point. Directly across the ring and parallel to the lag line, draw another straight line tangent to the ring to serve as the pitch line.

Marbles.—The marbles must be round, made of glass, and of uniform size measuring not more than five-eighths of an inch in diameter.

The shooters may be made of any substance except metal, must be round and not less than one-half inch nor more than three-fourths inch in diameter by exact measurement.

Players.—From two to six players may play in a game, except in championship matches when two only play.

[9] These rules follow those adopted by the recreation executives of New Jersey and Pennsylvania as quoted by National Recreation Association, *88 Successful Play Activities,* pp. 37 to 42. Copyright, 1933. By permission of National Recreation Association, publishers.

Tournament play is open to boys and girls fourteen years of age and under.

The Lag.—Before the game the players lag to determine the order of shooting. To lag, they stand toeing the pitch line or knuckling down upon it, and toss or shoot their shooters to the lag line across the ring. The player whose shooter comes nearest the lag line, on either side, wins the lag and the privilege of shooting first. The others follow in order accordingly as their shooters were next nearest the lag line. The same shooter that is used in the lag must be used in the game following the lag. Starting succeeding games, the winner of previous games shoots first but the other players lag for order.

Playing Rules.—Each player in turn knuckles down just outside the ring line, at any point he chooses, and shoots into the ring to knock one or more marbles out of the ring. A player must knuckle down on all shots so that at least one knuckle is in contact with the ground, and he must maintain this position until the shooter has left his hand.

Marbles knocked out of the ring are credited to the player knocking them out and the player continues to shoot from the spot where his shooter comes to rest. If a shooter goes outside of the ring, after shooting a marble out, the player recovers it and continues by shooting from the ring line, taking "roundsters" if desired, that is, shooting from any point around the ring.

After a miss, a player picks up his shooter and holds it until his next turn and then takes roundsters and shoots from any point of the ring line.

Whenever a marble or shooter comes to rest in the groove marking the ring, it is considered out of the ring. If its center is inside the ring it is considered inside the ring.

If a shooter slips from a player's hand and the player calls "slips," the referee may order "no play" and permit the player to shoot again, provided the shooter does not travel more than ten inches and the referee is convinced it was an actual slip.

Marbles knocked out of the ring are picked up by the player who knocks them out.

Scoring.—The player first obtaining seven marbles is the winner of the game, providing that on obtaining the seventh marble the shooter also goes out of the ring. If the shooter remains in the ring on this shot, the marble or marbles knocked out on this shot are respotted on the cross line, the shooter picked up, and the shot counted as a miss.

A match may consist of one, three, or five games. It is not the total high score, but the games won that determine the winner.

Ties.—In games where more than two players are engaged, if two or more players lead with the same score, those in the tie play a new game to break the tie.

Fouls and Penalties.—It is a foul if a player

1. Raises his hand before the shooter has left his hand.

2. Moves his hand forward before the shooter has left his hand.

3. Smooths or otherwise rearranges the ground or removes any obstacles. He may request the referee to clear obstructions. Penalty: the player loses his shot.

4. Changes shooter during the course of any game. Penalty: disqualification.

5. Communicates in any way with his coach during the course of the game. Penalty: forfeiture of all marbles he has knocked out of the ring, said marbles being respotted on the cross.

6. Walks through the ring. Penalty: forfeiture of one marble, which is respotted.

Officials.—The officials shall be a referee and a scorer; if a scorer is not available the referee shall keep score.

Bridgeboard [10]

Playground, Club, Home   *Elementary and Junior High Schools*

The object is to roll marbles through arches in a board. To make the board, secure a hardwood board eight inches wide, three feet long, and one inch thick. With a two-inch auger, bore nine holes down the center of the board, an inch and a half apart. Then saw the board in two on a line with the center of the holes. This will make two bridgeboards. From the left, number the arches 1, 3, 5, 7, and 9, and from the right, number them 2, 4, 6, and 8. The highest numbers are thus in the center.

When the bridgeboard is placed on the floor or ground, nine arches are available through which the marbles may be rolled. Each marble scores the number of the arch through which it passes. The players roll in turn, and fifty points is the game.

Variation.—Make the holes larger and roll tennis balls.

[10] The idea for this event was taken from the University of Michigan, Staff of Physical Education for Women, *Physical Education Activities for High School Girls*, p. 7ᴸ. Copyright, 1928. By permission of Lea and Febiger, publishers.

PART II

CONTESTS BETWEEN GROUPS

CHAPTER X

MASS CONTESTS

CONTESTS between individuals tend to draw into competition those of better-than-average ability, rather than the rank and file of players. Contests between groups, on the other hand, have the advantage of arousing keen interest among players of less ability as well as the better few.

Contests between groups fall under three headings: (1) mass contests; (2) individual competition with points scored for team; (3) relay races. Mass contests are considered in this chapter, and the other types in the following chapters.

In mass contests, each team takes part as a whole, with all members competing at the same time.

Tug-of-War

Playground, Gymnasium, Picnics　　　　*Junior High School to Adults*

There are several methods of conducting the time-honored and ever-popular tug-of-war. From the following methods, the one should be selected which best suits the age of the players and the nature of the occasion.

Tug-of-War—Distance Method.—A long rope is stretched out on a level surface; the members of one team grasp one end, those of the other team the other end. A handkerchief is tied around the rope to mark its middle, and two lines are marked on the ground four yards apart and at right angles to the rope. The rope is stretched so as to bring the handkerchief midway between the two lines. At the signal, the teams pull. The team wins which pulls the handkerchief past the line first.

Tug-of-War—Time Method.—This event is conducted like the above except that a single line is drawn under the handkerchief marking the middle of the rope, and the teams pull for thirty seconds. The team wins which has pulled the handkerchief on its side of the line at the end of the period.

Rush Tug-of-War.—Stretch the rope on the ground, tie a handkerchief on it to mark the middle, and mark two finish lines on the ground at right angles to the rope, each ten feet from the handkerchief. Establish a starting line fifty feet from each end of the rope. The teams line up behind the starting lines and at the signal, rush for the rope and start pulling. The team wins which pulls the handkerchief across its finish line first.

Mounted Tug-of-War.—Arrange the rope as in the Tug-of-War—Distance Method. The players of each team pair up as horses and riders. The riders mount the horses, wrapping their legs around the horses' backs. The riders hold the rope, and at the signal the teams pull. Any rider falling must let go of the rope until he is mounted again.

The contest may be conducted by either the distance or time method described above.

Circle Tug-of-War.—The players form in a circle holding a rope, the ends of which have been tied together. A line is drawn across the circle—all on one side of it compose one team, and those on the other side the other team. At the signal the teams pull, and the one pulling the other over the line first wins.

Touch
(*Touch Iron*)

Playground, Gymnasium, Club   Late Elementary to Senior High School

This excellent contest is unsurpassed in recreational value and is played enthusiastically by all ages. It can be played any place, however large or small the space may be.

Divide the group into two teams and line them up facing each other about six feet apart. The leader, standing at one end, calls the name of some object near at hand, and instantly all players run to that object, touch it, and return to their positions in line. The team with all its members in line and at attention first wins.

Such objects as the following may be called: wood, metal, paint, plaster, glass, radiator, door, grass, stone, tree, and so forth. The leader may keep a ball near him and occasionally kick it and call "Ball" or "Leather." Often the leader calls "Me" and runs.

Players are not permitted to touch any object or article of clothing on their own person or on the person of any other player unless such an article be specifically named. That is, if "Metal" were called the players would not be permitted to touch their own belt buckles or jackknives, or those which any other player carried on his person. The only condition under which such an article may be touched is when the leader gives an order such as "Touch Bill Jones' new shoes."

File Race

Playground, Gymnasium, Club   Late Elementary to Senior High School

Divide the group into teams of from six to twelve players. Line the teams up in file formation behind a common starting line. Establish a turning line forty to sixty feet distant. At the signal all the players of each team, keeping their original positions, run to the turning line, where the file swings around and returns to the starting line. The players are not permitted to pass those in front of them and must keep in file. The team finishing first wins.

Chinaman's Race

Playground, Gymnasium, Club   Late Elementary to Senior High School

Arrange the teams in parallel files. Have each player reach back between his legs with his right hand and grasp the left hand of the player immediately in back of him.

At the signal the teams, thus joined together, race to the turning line, swing around, and race back to the starting line. The team finishing first with the file unbroken, wins.

Quartet Race

Playground, Gymnasium   Late Elementary to Senior High School

Each team consists of four players. The teams line up behind the starting line with all the players of each team standing abreast facing the line and with hands joined. At the signal they race to the finish line. Any team failing to keep hands clasped throughout is eliminated. Distances of 50 to 100 yards may be used.

This race may also be conducted by having the players link arms instead of holding hands.

Variation.—Give each team a stick six or eight feet long. They hold the stick in front of their chests with both hands on it.

Backward Line-Race

Playground, Gymnasium, Club   Late Elementary to Senior High School

Three players constitute a team. The two end players on each team have their backs to the starting line and the middle player faces the starting line. They lock elbows, and at the signal run to the finish line, with the center player steering. The first team finishing intact wins.

Rodeo Race

Playground, Gymnasium, Club   Elementary and Junior High Schools

The players compete in threes. Number 1 stands on the starting line. Number 2 stands behind him, bends down and grasps him around the waist. At the signal, Number 3 jumps on Number 2's back and the three race to the finish line.

Centipede Race

Playground, Gymnasium   Late Elementary to Senior High School

Divide the group into teams of eight or ten players each. The members of each team line up in file, one behind the other, with the leader standing just behind the starting line. Each player locks his arms around the waist of the player in front of him. At the signal the teams run in this locked file formation to the finish line. If any player loses his hold his team is disqualified. Much sport is added if the teams are caused to cross a turning line, swing around and return to the starting line for the finish.

Variation.—Same as the above except that the players clasp the belts or hips of the player in front.

Centipede Overtake Race.—Arrange a circular course by setting a number of jumping standards or chairs in a circle around which the teams run. The circle should not be more than forty feet in diameter. Divide the group into two teams and arrange each team as in the Centipede Race, stationed on opposite sides of the circle. At the signal they run, attempting to catch the other team so that the first player may tag the last player of team in front. If the line breaks the team must stop at once and rejoin its parts. The team wins which tags the other.

Rail-Riding Race

Playground, Gymnasium   *Late Elementary to Senior High School*

Divide the group into teams of eight. A ten-foot pole, preferably bamboo, is needed for each team. The players straddle the pole, all facing front, and grasping the pole with the hands. Throughout the race, the front man must keep at least one hand on the end of the pole in front of him, and the rear man must keep one hand on the end of the pole behind him. At the signal, the teams run while straddling the poles.

Much sport is added if the teams are caused to cross a turning line, swing around, and return to the starting line for the finish.

Crew Race.—This contest is on the order of Rail-Riding Race. The players straddle the pole all facing backward except the last player who faces forward. The last player acts as coxswain and steers and gives directions to the crew. The "boat" moves as formed to the finish line, swings around and moves back to the starting line for the finish.

The end players at each end of the pole must keep one hand on the pole behind them throughout the race.

Caterpillar Race

Playground, Gymnasium   *Junior and Senior High Schools*

Arrange the players of each team in file, one behind the other, facing the starting line. Establish a turning line twenty-five to forty feet distant. Each player bends down and grasps the ankles of the man in front; the front man places his hands on the floor. At the signal the lines move forward to the turning line, swing around, and return to the starting line.

The front man must walk on hands and feet throughout. The team wins that finishes first with the entire team intact as at the start.

Chain Crab-Race

Playground, Gymnasium, Clubs   *Junior and Senior High Schools*

Divide the group into two teams and arrange the players of each team in file formation, facing the starting line. Establish a turning line thirty to forty feet distant. Have the players sit on the floor with feet pulled well up against the thighs. Each player leans back and grasps the ankles of the man behind him. At the signal they raise their buttocks from the floor and the line moves forward toward the turning line. They cross the turning line, swing around, and move back across the starting line. The team wins which completely crosses the starting line first with the team intact as at the start.

Reverse Chain Crab-Race.—The teams face in the opposite direction and race backward.

Combined Chain Crab-Race.—This race combines the two races described above. The two teams move to the turning line as in the Chain Crab-Race, and without turning around, return as in the Reverse Chain Crab-Race.

Under the Arch

Playground, Gymnasium, Club   *Elementary and Junior High Schools*

Divide the group into two or more teams and arrange them in parallel files about six feet apart. Number the players of each team from the front back. The leader calls two *consecutive* numbers, for example, "Four and Five." Immediately Numbers 4 and 5 of each team turn sideways facing each other and form an arch by joining their hands overhead. The players behind them run in file under the arch, and swing around outside the arch and back into position again; at the same time the players in front of the arch run to the rear, join onto the end of the file, follow it through the arch, and take their original positions. When all are through the arch the players forming the arch fall in their original position in the line. The team with all players in position and at attention first wins.

The leader should call the numbers at random, thus keeping the players in suspense.

Roman Chariot-Race

Playground, Gymnasium   *Late Elementary and Junior High Schools*

Divide the players into groups of three. Two are designated as horses and join hands while the third acts as driver. With reins of cord the driver drives his horses to the turning line and back to the starting line.

The team that finishes first wins. The turning line should be from 50 to 100 yards distant.

When used on play days, the reins may be of colored streamers and the driver may wear a colored head band with streamers flowing behind.

Blind-Man's Race

Playground, Gymnasium   *Late Elementary to Senior High School*

The contestants compete in threes. Two are blindfolded, stand side by side, and hold inside hands. The third who is not blindfolded stands behind them and holds their outside hands. An upright such as a jumping standard is placed twenty yards in front of each team. On the signal they run forward with the back man guiding by pulling on their hands and shouting commands. Reaching the post they circle it and race back to the starting line.

Keep-It-Up

Playground, Gymnasium   *Late Elementary School*

Divide the group into two teams and have each scatter over separate sections of the playing space. Give each team a volleyball. At the signal the players of each team volley the ball among themselves attempting to complete as many volleys as possible. Each time the ball is volleyed the players count "One" for the first volley, "Two" for the second, and so on.

When the ball touches the floor or wall, or is caught by a player, it is dead and the team is credited with the number of volleys it completed. The team completing the most volleys scores one point. The next game is then started. The team wins that scores eleven points first.

Another method of conducting the contest is to count consecutive volleys until one team reaches one hundred. This team is the winner.

When inexperienced players are playing, it is well to allow a player to volley the ball more than once in succession. Later the rule should be made that a player cannot touch the ball until it has been touched by another.

Line Keep-It-Up.—Arrange each team in a line. The ball is volleyed down the line and back until it is declared dead.

Double-line Keep-It-Up.—Arrange each team in two lines facing each other, the two halves being a few feet apart. The ball is volleyed in zig-zag fashion; the first player of one line volleys it to the first player of the other line, who volleys it to the second player of the first line, and so forth.

Circle Keep-It-Up.—Arrange each team in a circle. The ball is volleyed from player to player around the circle. *Variation.*—The ball is volleyed at random across the circle.

Skin the Snake

Playground, Gymnasium   *Junior and Senior High Schools*

Divide the players into two teams of any number and place them in parallel files. Have the players stand at stride with feet well apart. Each player reaches between his legs with his right hand and with it grasps the left hand of the player behind him. At the signal the line moves backward, the rear player lying on his back, still holding the hand of the player in front. Each player lies down as his turn comes. Players lying on the floor should keep their legs close to the body of the player in front. When the entire file is on the floor, the rear man rises, moves forward, and the others in turn do likewise. The team wins which first has all of its players on their feet with all hands still clasped.

MASS CONTESTS IN OTHER CHAPTERS

Water Tug-of-War.   Water Touch.

MASS CONTESTS IN *SOCIAL GAMES FOR RECREATION*

Signalling Touch.   Signalling Execute.   Form A.

CHAPTER XI

INDIVIDUAL COMPETITION WITH POINTS SCORED FOR TEAM

IN the group contests considered in this chapter, all members of the team do not compete at the same time as in mass contests, but rather they compete singly, each individual meeting in competition one representative of the opposing team. When the team member wins in his competition, he scores points for his team.

The usual plan is to number the individuals and call out the numbers at random, thus bringing individual competitors from opposing teams together; or the players may line up and compete when their turn comes. When the individual wins, one point is scored for the team.

In some types, each team selects a number of individual contestants to represent it in each event. Each team is credited with the points won by the contestants—five for first place, four for second, three for third, two for fourth, and one for fifth. Sometimes only three places are selected, scoring five, three, and one.

Attention

Playground, Gymnasium   *Late Elementary to Senior High School*

This delightful contest is best played by two teams of from eight to twelve players each. If there are more players two contests should be started.

Line up the two teams eight feet apart, each in single rank and facing the other. Have the players of each team number off so that the holders of each number stand opposite each other (Figure 23). The leader stands between the lines at one end. Use the end walls of the gymnasium as turning lines or if outdoors, establish a line at each end, twenty feet from the players.

The leader calls a number, for instance "Three." The two players holding this number run to one end wall or line, then to the other end wall or line, and then back to their positions in the lines. The player who comes to attention in his position first scores one point for his team. The team that scores eleven points first wins.

The leader should call the numbers at random to keep all the players alert. The captains keep their own team's score and call it out loud after each run.

Plus-and-Minus Attention.—This is a most fascinating variation of Attention, calling for computing numbers as well as running. Arrange the teams as in Attention.

Designate one team as "plus" and the other team as "minus." The leader calls two numbers, such as "Six and three." The two players desig-

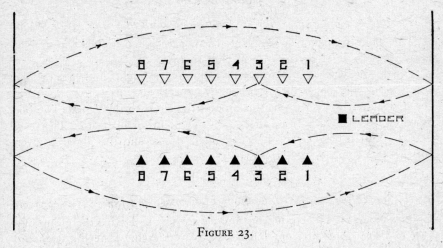

FIGURE 23.

nated run as in Attention. The players to run in this case will be Number 9 of the plus team (6+3) and Number 3 of the minus team (6−3).

Circle Attention.—This is an adaptation of Attention usable when there is not enough space for the line form. Arrange the players in a circle. Divide the circle in half making two teams. Number the players on each team consecutively so that opposing players with the same numbers stand directly opposite each other. The leader calls a number and the two players holding this number run around the outside of the circle to the right and back to their positions again. The player coming to attention first scores one point for his team. The team scoring eleven points wins.

Like Numbers Touch

Playground, Gymnasium, Club   Late Elementary to Senior High School

This is a combination of Touch and Attention. Divide the group into two teams and line them up in ranks facing each other, about eight feet apart. Number the players of each team so that the opponents holding the same number are opposite each other. The leader calls the object to be touched and a number—for instance, "Touch door—Three." Whereupon the two players holding this number run, touch the door, and return to position. The player first coming to attention in his position scores one point for his team. The team scoring eleven first wins.

The numbers should be called at random so that all will be kept alert. Name such objects as the following: plaster, metal, paint, glass, the end wall, stone, tree, ball (kick the ball so that they must chase it), Bill Jones (he runs).

Spoke Race

Playground, Gymnasium, Club   *Late Elementary to Senior High School*

The spoke formation is excellent when space is too limited for straight away races, as is often the case in club rooms.

Divide the players into teams of from five to eight, and arrange the teams as in the spokes of a wheel (Figure 27, page 164). At the signal the first player of each team runs around the circle to the right. The one reaching his original position first scores one point for his team. The players who ran then go to the hub end of the spoke and the signal is given for the next runners.

Grab Ball

Playground, Gymnasium, Club   *Late Elementary and Junior High Schools*

This contest is suitable when numbers are small. Divide the group into two or three teams of from four to six players each. Line the teams up in a single rank with all the players facing a common starting line. Leave a little space between the teams. Number the players of each team. About twenty feet out mark a line parallel to the starting line, and on it scatter balls, stones, or sticks numbering one less than the number of teams. If there are three teams use two balls; with two teams use one.

The leader calls a number, for instance, "Two." The Number Two's dash forward and try to secure a ball. The player failing scores one point against his team. The team wins which has the lowest scores when the play ceases.

Change the Club

Playground, Gymnasium, Club   *Late Elementary to Senior High School*

This interesting contest is on the order of Snatch-Ball. Mark two lines on the floor parallel to each other and about forty feet apart; mark three circles midway between them, two feet in diameter, one in the center and the other two at the ends, as in Figure 24. The center circle is common to both teams but the end circles belong one to each team. In the center circle place two balls, handkerchiefs, sticks, or Indian clubs.

Divide the group into two teams and place the players of each team behind one of the lines and facing it. Number the players of each team from opposite ends of the line so that the two players holding the same number stand diagonally opposite each other. (See diagram.)

The leader calls a number, for instance 'Two." Each Number 2 dashes to the center circle, picks up a club (or whatever object is there), places it in his team's end circle, and returns to his position. The player coming to attention first scores one point for his team. The team scoring eleven points first wins. When the next number is called, the runners transfer the clubs from the end circles back to the center.

Call the numbers at random so that all are kept in a constant state of expectancy. Announce the score frequently.

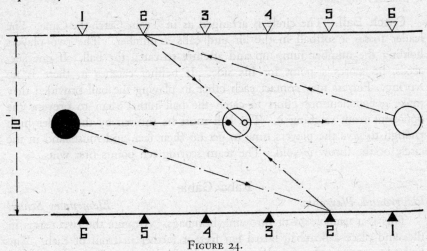

FIGURE 24.

Variation.—Seat the players on the ground. The player wins, who, after running, seats himself in position first.

Variation.—Seat the players on the floor. When a number is called, the holders of that number crawl on hands and knees, transfer the club, and crawl back to position. The one seating himself first wins.

Team Catch-the-Cane

Playground, Gymnasium, Club   Late Elementary and Junior High Schools

This game is on the order of Circle Snatch-Ball. Arrange the players in a circle not more than fifteen feet in diameter, facing in. Divide the circle into two teams and number the players so that the players of the two teams holding the same numbers are directly across the circle from each other. The leader holds a three-foot stick or baseball bat vertically on the floor in the center by steadying it with his finger. He calls one of the numbers, and the players holding that number dash for the stick and attempt to catch it before it falls to the floor and snatch it away so that the opponent cannot grasp it. A player securing possession of the stick scores one point for his team. If both fail to secure it before it touches the floor, or if both catch it simultaneously, no points are scored. The numbers should be called at random to keep up a high state of expectancy. The team scoring ten points first wins.

Team Spin-the-Platter.—Same as the above except that a kettle cover is spun on the floor instead of using the stick.

Team Catch-the-Balloon.—Same as the above except that the leader drops a toy balloon as he calls the number instead of holding the stick. The player wins who secures the balloon first provided he gets it before it touches the floor.

Catch Ball.—The circle is arranged as in Team Catch-the-Cane. The leader tosses a softball in the air and calls a number. The two players holding the number jump up and attempt to catch the ball. If one succeeds, he scores a point for his side. If neither catches it, there is no scoring. Players may contact each other in playing the ball provided they make a conscientious effort to catch the ball rather than to prevent the opponent from catching it. The ball must be thrown by the leader high enough to give the players time to get on their feet, and must land in the circle or the throw is void. The team scoring ten points first wins.

Faba Gaba

Playground, Playroom   *Elementary School*

This is a team form of throwing beanbags. Arrange the two teams in files and place a beanbag board ten feet or farther in front of each. The first players of each team throw three beanbags at the board, and then the next player throws, and so on. The holes count three, two, and one points and the team wins that scores fifty points first.

Serve and Sit

Gymnasium, Playground   *Late Elementary to Senior High School*

This is a contest designed to develop ability in serving a volleyball. A volleyball court and ball are used. Divide the players into two teams and line up each team behind the serving line.

The first player of one team serves the ball into the opposing court. If the serve is good he sits down and the first player of the opposing team serves. If the serve is not good the player goes to the other end of the line to await his next turn and the next player of the opposing side serves.

The team wins that has all its players seated first.

Baseball Overtake Contest

Baseball Diamond   *Later Elementary to Senior High School*

All positions of the infield are occupied except shortstop. The pitcher holds a softball. The runner stands on home base and at the signal runs the circuit of the bases. At the same time, the pitcher throws the ball to the catcher on home base and from there the ball is thrown around the circuit of the bases. One point is scored for each base the runner reaches ahead of the ball.

After all the running team have run, the teams change positions.

Variation.—Same as the above except that all fielding positions are occupied, and the runner throws the ball into the diamond before running. If it is fielded in the infield, it is thrown to home base and then around the circuit of the bases. If it is fielded in the outfield, it is thrown to first base and then around the circuit.

Basketball Toss-Up

Playground, Gymnasium   *Late Elementary to Senior High School*

Arrange the players on the teams according to height and line up the two teams facing the center circle of the basketball court. The first player of each team enters the circle and the leader tosses up the ball between them. They jump and try to hit the ball. The one succeeding scores one point for his team. Then the next two compete. The team wins that has the highest score when all have jumped.

Basketball Twenty-one—Team Form

Playground, Gymnasium   *Junior High School to College*

Two basketball goals are needed. Divide the group into two teams and line each up behind the free-throw line in front of its basket. Give the first player of each team a basketball. Appoint a scorer for each team.

At the signal, the first player of each team throws for the basket, and whether he makes it or not, immediately runs to the rear of the line. The second player secures the ball and throws from the point where he secures it, then the third player, and so on. No bouncing or dribbling is permitted. Each time a goal is made one point is scored and the scorer calls the score out loud. When all have thrown, the first player throws again. The team making twenty-one baskets first wins.

Variation.—Any of the individual forms of Basketball Twenty-one (Chapter IV) may be used on a team basis by having the players of the two teams alternate in throwing.

Arch Goal-Ball

Playground, Gymnasium   *Junior and Senior High Schools*

Divide the players into two teams and line one up behind each free-throw line facing the basket. A waste-paper basket may be used if a basketball goal is not available. Give the last player of each team a basketball.

At the signal the ball is passed forward over the heads of the players until it reaches the front player, who throws for the goal. Whether he makes it or not, the first player gets the ball, runs to the rear of the line, and starts the play again. Each goal made scores one point. Play for a period of three or five minutes and the team wins that has the highest score.

Variation.—Use any of the methods of passing described in the chapter on "Object-Passing Relays."

Variation.—Have each thrower continue to throw until he makes the goal.

Football Target Punt

Football Field   *Junior High School to College*

For this group contest, establish two targets by marking out areas ten yards square, touching the side lines and between the thirty-five and twenty-five yard lines, diagonally opposite each other. The two teams line up behind the thirty-five yard lines. The teams are thus thirty yards apart.

The players of each team take turns in punting the ball, trying to cause it to fall into the opposite target. Three points are scored by each ball that falls into the target on the fly, and one by each ball that rolls into the target. No blocking of the kicks by opponents is permitted.

Football Snatch-Ball

Playground, Gymnasium   *Late Elementary to Senior High School*

Mark two parallel lines on the ground four feet apart. Divide the players into two teams and stand them behind the lines facing each other. A player stands at each end to act as snapper-back. One snapper-back passes the football back between his legs so that the ball goes down the lane between the lines. Without stepping over the lines, the players of both teams reach out and attempt to catch the ball. The player that catches it scores one point for his team. If it is fumbled by one player and is caught by another before it touches the ground, it counts. If a player steps over the line in catching the ball, it does not count. The ball is then snapped from the other end of the line.

Archery and Riflery Team Competition

The team events in Archery and Riflery would normally fall within the classification of this chapter, in that the individual members of the team compete and score points for the team. For the convenience of the reader and recreational leader who may use the book, however, it was thought advisable to group all the Archery material together, and all the Riflery events together. The team events in these sports will therefore be found with the individual events, the Archery on page 72, and the Riflery on page 79.

Bowling Team Events

Team competition in Bowling is described in the section dealing with the Bowling events between individuals. See page 109.

Golf Team Events

For the convenience of the reader, all Golf events are grouped together. The team events will be found with the Golf events between individuals, on page 126.

CONTESTS IN *SOCIAL GAMES FOR RECREATION* BASED ON INDIVIDUAL COMPETITION WITH POINTS SCORED FOR TEAM

Nature Symbolism Race.	Card Compass Race.
Nature Old-Sayings Race.	Old-Sayings Race.
Signalling Attention.	Affinities Race.
Arithmetic Attention.	Auditory Scouting for Words.

CHAPTER XII

METHODS OF CONDUCTING RELAYS

IN THE relay races all players of a team compete in turn, each starting as the preceding player finishes.

TRACK RELAYS

The standard relay races used in track meets are the half-mile, mile, two-mile, and four-mile distances. Occasionally a quarter-mile and medley relay are used.

Relay teams usually consist of four runners, no one of whom may run more than one relay. Only those contestants may compete in the final heat who competed in the trials.

Each runner carries in his hand a baton which he passes to the team mate succeeding him, within a twenty yard zone marked by lines drawn ten yards on each side of the exchange line. Within this twenty yard zone the baton must be handed, not thrown—failure to pass it disqualifies the team.

The teams draw for their positions at the starting line and the batons must be exchanged in these same positions. However, in the mile, two-mile, four-mile, and medley relays, the starting lanes of the contestants are reversed from inside to outside at each exchange of the baton. That is, if there are seven lanes the team starting in lane 1 exchanges the baton in lane 7 the next time, and the time following in lane 1 again. The team starting in the middle lane exchanges in the same lane throughout.

SUGGESTIONS ON CONDUCTING MINOR RELAYS

When a group meets regularly, as in a gymnasium class, playground group, or club, it is desirable to have permanent relay teams which are comparatively equal in ability. The time-consuming process of organizing teams each period is thus eliminated. The organization is still further simplified by the use of a permanent starting line each time. The teams can then be given a permanent position on the line, and all that is needed is to announce relays and the teams can organize themselves in their regular positions on the line. This is speeded up greatly by making a contest out of lining up for the relays and awarding points to the teams getting in position first, these points to be added to the total points made by the teams in the relays which follow.

Forming Teams.—There are four common methods of breaking a group into relay teams:

1. Have the captains choose teams. This is usually unsatisfactory because it consumes too much time. Furthermore, there is the possibility of an undesirable effect upon the personalities of those who are always left until last when teams are chosen.

2. Line the group up in one rank, according to height, with the largest players at the right end. Have the players count off by four's if four teams are wanted, or by the number of teams desired. On command, have the Number 1's stay in place, the Number 2's take two steps forward, the Number 3's four steps, and the Number 4's six steps, and so on. Close the ranks and march them to the starting line. Such formal methods of marching usually detract from the spirit of play and as a rule should be avoided.

3. Line up the players, count off and march them forward as before. Instead of marching them to the starting line, appoint a captain for each team and instruct him to take his team informally to the starting line and line them up in file.

4. Line up the players in rank. Select as many captains as there are to be teams and station them on the starting line. Have the players count off by the number of teams desired, that is, if three teams are desired have them count off by three's. Tell the Number 1's to run and line up behind the first captain, the 2's behind the second captain, and so on.

Uneven Teams.—When some teams are short a player it is not wise to cause players from the other teams to sit out in order to even up the teams. Have one player on the short teams run twice. In the passing relays this is impossible of course, and it may be necessary here to ask players from other teams to drop out. These players should be asked to assist in the officiating. After each relay have them join their teams again and have other players fall out.

Starting and Turning Lines.—Establish a common starting line for all the teams. From forty to sixty feet distant establish another line parallel to it. This is the turning line. Indoors, a wall is to be preferred as the turning line in most relays, the runners merely touching the wall and running back to the starting line. It is usually desirable to establish a permanent starting line at the desired distance away from a wall, and then to mark a permanent turning line six feet out from the wall for use in those relays in which a wall is not usable.

Starting Succeeding Runners.—When succeeding runners are merely touched off there is a tendency to steal at the transfer. Consequently it is recommended that an object be passed by the runner to the succeeding player. This may be a handkerchief, stick, or stone. Groups meeting regularly will want regular objects to use for this purpose. The official baton of the track relays may be used, and the practice in handling it is a good preparation for track, but in recreational relays with all types of players participating, the baton is so small that it is easily dropped at the transfer, and consequently slows up the running. It will be found that three-foot wands made from broomsticks will not only be excellent convenient objects to pass but will find many other uses in relays.

A method which may be used at times to prevent stealing at the transfer is to have the runner run to the rear of the line, and hand the stick to the last player; it is then passed up to the front player who runs when he gets it.

Another method excellent from the standpoint of preventing stealing at the transfer follows: Place the starting line about fifteen feet out from a wall and arrange the teams in parallel files behind it and facing it. The teams thus stand between the starting line and the back wall. At the signal player Number 1 of each team runs to the turning line and back, touches the wall behind his team, then runs up and gives the stick or handkerchief to Number 2, who repeats. Instead of crossing the starting line too soon, the tendency is for Number 2 to run back to meet Number 1. In case no wall is available, a line may be marked a few feet behind the teams.

Still another method which accomplishes the same end is as follows: Player Number 1, as he returns from the turning line, runs past his team to the right, goes around the end of his team and comes up the other side, and gives the stick to Number 2. Number 1 then takes his original place. Number 2 runs to the turning line and back, goes around the end of his team and comes up the left side, giving the stick to Number 3, and so on. This method is frequently used by having the last player run first, which makes a particularly effective method of running events of the type of the Somersault Relay, and the Crawl-Under Relay, described later.

Marking the Last Runner.—It is a great help in picking winners to mark the last runner in each team conspicuously. Players, too, like to know when the last players of the other teams are running. This can be done by tying a handkerchief around the last player's arm, having him take his shirt off, wear a hat, or roll a stocking down. Groups meeting regularly may find it desirable to provide permanent colored sashes; these can be transferred quickly when necessary, as would be the case when the rear man runs last in one relay and the front player last in the following relay.

Throwing up Arms at the Finish.—The custom of having all members of a team throw up their arms and yell when their last runner finishes is strongly recommended. This not only facilitates judging but the yelling adds greatly to the spirit and enthusiasm.

Penalties.—It is usually much too severe a penalty to a relay team to disqualify it for the infraction of a rule by one of its players. The foul may have been inadvertently committed in the excitement or may be due to misunderstanding as to what was expected of him. The other players on the team are not at fault. When younger players are competing considerable leniency should be shown.

With players who have reached the team stage, however, the rules should be definitely enforced and the following method of penalizing is recommended: award one point for finishing first, two for second place, and three for third place. Add one point for each foul committed. The team with the lowest score wins.

Recording Scores.—When several relays are to be run in succession, the score should be kept and if possible recorded conspicuously on a blackboard after each relay. Determine the score as described in the preceding paragraph and record it. The team with the lowest score wins. When a group meets regularly and uses relays at most meetings, it is well to keep a permanent score and add each meeting's score to the total of the preceding meetings.

METHODS OF CONDUCTING RELAYS

Simple File-Relay Method

Arrange the teams in parallel files facing the starting line as in Figure 25. Sixty feet in front (more or less to meet conditions), mark a turning

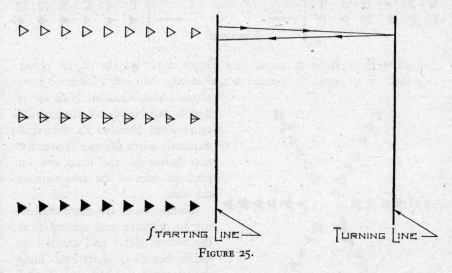

FIGURE 25.

line. Give the first player of each team an object to pass—stick, baton, handkerchief, ball.

At the signal, the first player of each team runs to the turning line, returns, and touches off the second player by handing him the object. The second player runs and touches off the third player. Continue until all have run. The team finishing first wins.

Having completed his run, Number 1 starts a new file to the left of his team. Each player after running joins this new file. Thus when the relay is over the team is already arranged in file formation for the next relay.

When the last runner of each team finishes, all members of his team throw their arms over head and yell.

One of the methods of preventing stealing at the transfer, described on page 161, may be used.

Shuttle-Relay Method

The shuttle race is a form of relay in which the team is divided into two halves, each half being placed in file opposite the other half with

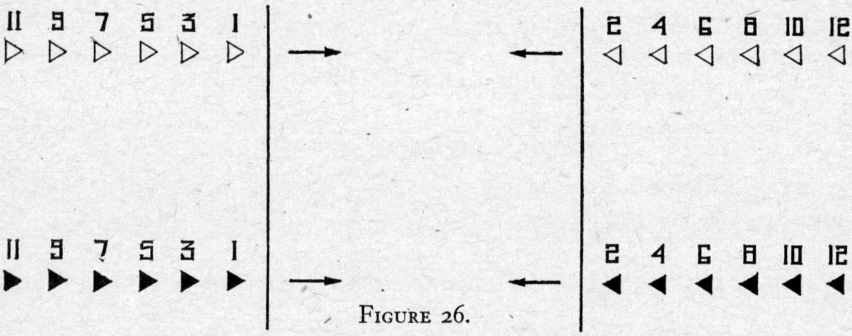

FIGURE 26.

the racing area between them (see Figure 26). At the signal player Number 1 runs across to Number 2 and touches him off; Number 2 runs across and touches off Number 3; and so on. Number 1, having run, remains on Number 2's side; consequently when the race is over the two halves of the team are on opposite sides of the area than at the start.

Shuttle races are more confusing to organize and operate than the Simple Relay and are not so satisfactory for ordinary use. They do, however, make a fast race and are well adapted to large teams and a limited space.

FIGURE 27.

The great majority of the relays described in the following chapters can be adapted to the shuttle method. The play leader will have no difficulty in determining how most of the relays described can be conducted in shuttle fashion.

Spoke-Relay Method

This is a good type of relay when space is too limited for straight-away races. Arrange the teams like the spokes in a wheel, radiating from a hub as in Figure 27. At the signal the last player of each spoke runs around the circle to the right and touches off the second player who repeats. The first player then takes his place at the hub end of the spoke. Continue until all have run. The team finishing first wins.

Circle-Relay Method

Arrange each team in a separate circle. Mark a circle on the floor in front of the players inside of which they must not step.

At the signal the first player of each circle runs around the circle and back to his position, touching off the player to his right. This player then runs around the circle and touches off the third player. Continue until all have run. The circle finishing first wins.

This method is less satisfactory than the File-Relay and Shuttle-Relay methods above because of the difficulty in judging and the difficulty the players encounter in telling where their team stands in relation to the other teams as the race progresses.

Relay Methods for Small Spaces

These methods are described in *Social Games for Recreation,* Chapter VI, "Social Relays and Group Contests."

CHAPTER XIII

RELAYS BASED PRIMARILY ON LOCOMOTION

THE outstanding feature of the relays in this chapter is locomotion. Some of them involve handling objects but such handling is usually incidental to the locomotion and is added to supply variety and interest.

These relays fall under the following headings: (1) standard relays, (2) novelty running relays, (3) impeded-progress relays, (4) novelty tandem relays, (5) riding relays, and (6) miscellaneous relays.

STANDARD RELAYS

The standard relays are straight running relays with nothing of the novelty involved. There are five formations used in conducting such relays, all of which have been described in the preceding chapter. For ordinary use in informal relays as they are used in gymnasium, playground, and club work, the Simple File-Relay Method will be found the most advantageous.

The methods are as follows:

Simple File Relay (page 163)

Shuttle Relay (page 164)

Spoke Relay (page 165)

Circle Relay (page 165)

Track Relay (page 160)

NOVELTY RUNNING RELAYS

These relays all involve a novelty element of some type, either in the method of locomotion, or the handling of some object, or performing some stunt while running.

These relays may be conducted from the file formation used in the Simple File Relay (page 163), or from the Shuttle Formation (page 164). The file method will be found most advantageous under ordinary circumstances. Chapter XII, "Methods of Conducting Relays," should be read for the details of the methods which will lead to the greatest success.

Unless shorter distances are specified, the turning line should be between forty and sixty-five feet from the starting line—it is better to use a short distance, making a fast race. Several short relays are much better than one or two long ones.

In the relays which call for crawling on the floor, there is danger of knee abrasions. If the players are in gym clothes these should be used with discretion. They are excellent for clubroom and picnic use where the boys are usually fully dressed but are wearing play clothes.

One of the methods of preventing stealing at the transfer, described on page 161, may be used.

Sore-Toe Relay

Gymnasium, Club, Playground   *Elementary School to Adults*

Establish a starting line, and from forty to fifty feet from it and parallel to it, establish a turning line. If possible use the wall of the gymnasium for the turning line. Arrange the players of each team in file, one behind the other, behind the starting line as in Figure 25.

At the signal the first player of each team raises one foot forward, grasps the toe with both hands, and hops on one leg to the turning line. Here he raises the other foot, grasps the toe as before, and hops back to the starting line. He touches off the second player who then repeats. Having run the first player starts a second file just to the right of the first. The race continues until the last player crosses the starting line, whereupon all players of the team throw their hands over their head and yell. The team finishing first wins.

Hopping Relay.—The players hop on one foot to the turning line, and return hopping on the other foot.

One-Leg Relay.—The player raises one leg behind and grasps it with both hands. He hops in this position to the turning line, then raises the other foot, grasps it as before and hops back.

Skipping Relay.—The players skip to the turning line and back. In skipping the player steps on his right foot, hops on his right foot, steps on his left foot, hops on his left foot, and so forth.

Crawling Relay.—The players crawl on hands and knees. They are not permitted to rise to the toe as a means of propelling themselves. The turning line should be thirty feet distant.

Foot-to-foot Relay.—The players advance by placing the heel of the advancing foot against the toe of the back foot on each step. The turning line should be twenty feet distant.

Eskimo Relay.—With feet together and knees stiff, the contestant moves by means of a rapid series of toe springs. The turning line should be thirty feet distant.

Heel Relay.—The runner runs on his heels, keeping his toes off the floor throughout.

Stiff-Knee Relay.—Keeping his knees stiff the contestant runs to the turning point and back.

Toe-Hold Relay.—Bending forward and grasping his right toe with his right hand and his left toe with his left hand, the runner travels to the turning line and back.

Crisscross Toe-Hold Relay.—Bending forward and grasping his right toe with his left hand, and his left toe with his right hand, the contestant travels to the turning line and back.

Heel-Hold Relay.—The runner bends forward, grasps his left heel with his left hand and his right heel with his right hand. In this position he travels.

All-Fours Relay.—On hands and feet the contestant runs to the turning line and back.

Rolling Relay.—Lying on the floor parallel to the starting line, each player in turn rolls to the turning line and back. The turning line should be about thirty feet distant.

Backward All-Fours Relay.—The players take the ordinary hands-and-feet position but race backward.

Animal-Imitation Relays

Gymnasium, Club, Playground　　　*Late Elementary to Senior High School*

These relays involve an element of imitation which adds much interest. They are conducted in the same way as the Sore-Toe Relay described above.

Kangaroo-Jumping Relay.—The runner places a cardboard between his ankles, and holding it by means of his legs only, jumps to the turning line and back. The turning line should be about thirty-five feet distant. If the card is dropped, it must be replaced before further progress is made.

Variation.—Instead of using the cardboard, place a basketball between the legs.

Gallop Relay.—The runner places one foot in front of the other, and keeping the feet in the same relative position, gallops to the turning line and back.

Crab Relay.—Each player supports himself on hands and feet, back toward the floor, and feet toward the starting line. In this position he travels.

Reverse-Crab Relay.—Same as the Crab Relay, except that the player travels with his hands to the front instead of his feet.

Elephant Relay.—Each runner runs on hands and feet with knees and elbows stiff. Legs and arms must be kept absolutely rigid.

Bear-Walk Relay.—On hands and feet each runner travels by stepping with the right hand and left foot simultaneously and then stepping with the left hand and right foot simultaneously.

Frog-Jumping Relay.—Each runner in turn takes a position on hands and feet, hands close together, feet slightly spread with knees outside of the arms. He advances by a series of frog-like jumps, leaping forward, landing on hands, and then bringing the feet up to the original position.

Lame-Dog Relay.—On two hands and one foot and holding the other foot out behind, each player in turn travels to the turning line and back.

Snake-Walk Relay.—Each player in turn advances as follows: step on the left foot, swing the right foot around behind the left and at the same time rock forward on toe of the left so that the right foot is in advance of the left when it touches the floor; then swing the left foot in back of the right in similar fashion. The turning line should be twenty feet distant.

Seal Relay.—Each player in turn lies on the floor, face downward, places his hands on the floor pointing outward, and walks on his hands, dragging his legs behind. The legs should be kept straight and the toes pointed.

Pass-the-Buck Relay

Gymnasium, Club, Playground   *Elementary School to Senior High School*

The players stand at stride, bend, and thrust the right hand back between the legs. At the signal the rear man slaps the hand of the player in front of him, who immediately slaps the hand of the man in front of him, and so the "buck" is passed to the front player. When the front player is slapped, he runs to the turning line, returns to the rear, slaps the hand of the rear man and then takes his position at the rear of the line. This continues until the original leading man is back at the head of the line.

Run-and-Sit Relay

Gymnasium, Club, Playground   *Late Elementary School to Adults*

The first player runs to the turning line, sits on the floor, raises his feet, and taps them together three times, rises, and returns, touching off the second player who repeats. Continue until all have run.

Zigzag Relay

Gymnasium, Club, Playground   Late Elementary to Senior High School

Directly in front of each team and near the turning line, set up a row of five Indian clubs three feet apart. At the signal the first player runs forward, zigzags between the clubs, crosses the turning line, zigzags back between the clubs and then runs to the starting line, touching off the second player who repeats. To compute the score, count one point for each club knocked over, subtract three for finishing first, two for finishing second, and one for finishing third; the team with the lowest score wins.

Loop-the-Loop Relay

Gymnasium, Club, Playground   Late Elementary School to Adults

At the signal the first player of each team runs back and around the rear end of his team and then to the turning line. He returns and touches off the second player, who runs around the rear end of the team and then to the turning line, and so on. Continue until all have run.

Circle-the-Post Relay

Gymnasium, Club, Playground   Late Elementary School to Adults

Directly opposite each team on the turning line, station a man to serve as the "post," or set up a jumping standard or an Indian club. At the signal, the first player runs to the "post," completely circles it once without touching it, and returns to touch off the second player who repeats.

Dizzy-Izzy Relay

Gymnasium, Club, Playground   Late Elementary School to Adults

The hilarious event is much enjoyed by both contestants and spectators, but it needs careful supervision.

Give the front player of each team a baseball bat. Station an official at the front of each team. At the signal, the first player holds the bat vertically, placing the *end of the bat on the floor* and placing his forehead *on* the upper end. He then runs around the bat five times. The official beside him counts out loud each time a circuit is made and at the end of the fifth circuit, slaps him on the back as the signal to run. The player then drops the bat and runs to the turning line, returns and touches off the second player, who repeats. Care must be taken to see that the bat is not lifted from the floor and that the player keeps his forehead on it.

The interest in this contest centers around the struggle of the dizzy runners to get to the turning line and back. When played indoors, it is well to station a man or two near the side walls, for the dizzy runner invariably runs somewhat off his course instead of straight toward the turning line, and occasionally falls forcefully against the wall. When a runner is heading toward the wall, the man stationed there should shove him off and prevent him from colliding with the hard surface.

Match-Box Relay

Gymnasium, Club, Playground   *Late Elementary School to Adults*

The humorous element in this contest makes it popular as a sociable event for parties and club meetings as well as for playground and gymnasium use.

The turning line should be from thirty to forty feet distant. Place a match-box cover on the nose of the first player of each team. At the signal he runs to the turning line, returns, and pushes the match-box cover on the nose of the second player without the use of the hands. The second player then repeats.

If the box falls off the nose, the runner may set it on end with his hand, but from then on it must be pushed on the nose with the aid of the nose only. The usual custom of not allowing the player to touch the box cover at all when it falls off, slows up the contest too much. If the cover falls to the floor in the process of transferring it to another player, the first player must put it back on his own nose and then attempt the transfer again. Continue until all have run.

Tunnel Relay

Gymnasium, Club, Playground   *Late Elementary to Senior High School*

Place a player, preferably a larger one, in front of each team, at a point half-way down to the turning line. Have these players spread their legs widely. At the signal, the first player runs, dives between the legs of the stationed player, runs to the turning line, returns, dives between the legs again, and then runs to the starting line and touches off the second player who repeats.

Chair-Arch Relay.—Same as the Tunnel Relay except that chairs are used to form the arch. Midway between the starting and turning lines place two chairs in front of each team, lying on the front side so that the backs overlap, thus forming an arch.

Jump-Ditch Relay

Gymnasium, Club, Playground   *Late Elementary to Senior High School*

Midway between the starting line and the turning line, draw two lines across the floor of such distance apart that the players can jump over them. The space between these lines is known as the ditch. At the signal the first player runs forward, leaps over the ditch, runs to the turning line, returns, leaps the ditch, and touches off the second player, who repeats.

Crawl-Under Relay, Number 1

Gymnasium, Club, Playground   *Late Elementary to Senior High School*

The players stand at stride with feet well apart. At the signal, the first player in each team turns, drops to his hands and knees and crawls back between the legs of the team. Having reached the rear, he rises, and runs to the turning line, returns and touches off the second player who repeats. The first player then goes immediately to the rear of the line.

Variation.—Have the rear player run first. He crawls forward between the legs, runs to the turning line, returns, touches off the player at the end of the line, and then takes his place at the front of the line.

Variation for Small Space.—When there is not sufficient space for the run to the turning line, it may be eliminated. The first player in each team crawls back between the legs, runs to the head of the line, touches off the second player, and then takes his place at the rear of the line.

Crawl-Under Relay, Number 2.—This relay is suitable for limited space. At the signal the first player takes one long step forward, and spreads his legs. The second player crawls under the first player's legs, rises and stands in front of him spreading his legs; the third player crawls through the legs of the first two and stands in front with his legs spread. Continue until the original leading player is back at the head of the line.

Weaving Crawl-Under Relay.—Arrange the teams in parallel files, then have them face to the side with legs at a wide stride and feet touching those at either side. At the signal the first player of each team crawls through the legs, going in and out down the line, through the second player's legs from the front, the third player's legs from the rear, and so on. On reaching the end of the line he runs to the turning line and back and touches off the second player who repeats. Number 1 then goes to the end of the line and spreads his legs.

In-and-Out Relay

Gymnasium, Club, Playground   *Late Elementary School to Adults*

Space the players so that they are four feet apart. At the signal the rear player zigzags in and out between the players, to the left of one, to the right of the next, and so forth. When he reaches the front of the line he sprints to the turning line and back, touches off the last player in the line, and then takes his place at the head of the line. The player touched off runs in the same way.

Variation.—The rear player zigzags in and out between the players as above until he reaches the front of the line. He then runs back to his original position and touches off the player ahead of him. This player zigzags to the front of the line, then runs around the rear of the line and back to his position, touching off the player in front of him, who repeats.

Obstacle Relay

Gymnasium, Club, Playground   *Late Elementary to Senior High School*

Between the starting line and the turning line, place a series of obstacles in the path of each team, such as chairs, jumping standards laid on the side, rolled mats, and so forth. At the signal the first player runs to the turning line, jumping or hurdling the obstacles as he goes; having crossed the turning line he returns, rejumps the obstacles, and touches off the second man who repeats.

Human-Obstacle Relay.—Station four men in line with each file between the starting and turning lines, ten yards apart. The first stands erect, the second at stride with feet well spread, the third in leapfrog position, and the fourth erect. At the signal the first player of each team runs around the first man, dives through the legs of the second, vaults over the third, runs completely around the fourth, and returns direct to the starting line, touching off the second player who repeats.

Barrel-Obstacle Relay.—A barrel with both ends removed is placed in the path of each team half way down to the turning line. The first player dives through the barrel, runs to the turning line, returns, dives through the barrel again, and finishes, touching off the second player who repeats.

All-Up Relay
(*Set 'em Up Relay*)

Gymnasium, Club, Playground   *Late Elementary to Senior High School*

Directly opposite each team at the turning line, draw two tangent circles on the floor, two feet in diameter, and place three Indian clubs in one. Books set on end, bottles, or blocks of wood may be substituted for the Indian clubs. At the signal the first player of each team runs to the clubs, picks them up using one hand only, and sets them up in the other circle. He then returns and touches off the second player, who runs to the clubs and places them back in the original circle. The third player sets them in the other circle again, and so on. If a club falls down before a runner reaches the starting line, he must return and set it up again.

Variation.—Using one circle only, the runner upon reaching the clubs, knocks them over with his foot and then sets them up again in the circle.

Variation.—The runner picks up one club at a time and strikes the top of the club on the floor, then sets it up in the circle again.

All-Up-and-All-Down Relay.—Opposite each team on the turning line, set up three Indian clubs, bottles, books, or sticks of stove wood. At the signal the first player runs forward, knocks the clubs down, returns and touches off the second player, who runs forward and sets the clubs up again. The third player knocks them down, and so on.

Feet and Club Relay.[1]—Opposite each team on the turning line, set up one Indian club. At the signal the first player of each team runs forward to the club, sits on the ground, kicks the club over, and sets it up using only his feet. He then returns and touches off the second player who repeats.

Ball-and-Bottle Relay

Gymnasium, Club, Playground   *Late Elementary to Senior High School*

Half way down to the turning line place three pop bottles in the path of each team and on the top of each bottle place a golf ball; at the turning line place three more bottles without balls. At the signal, the first player of each team runs to the bottles, removes the balls and places them on the bottles at the turning line. He then touches off the second player who brings the balls back to the original bottles, and so on.

Jump-the-Stick Relay

Gymnasium, Club, Playground   *Late Elementary to Senior High School*

Give the first player of each team a wand or broomstick. At the signal player Number 1 turns, gives one end of the stick to Number 2 and holds on to the other end. They both bend down holding the stick between them about six inches from the floor and parallel to it, and run back to the end of the line of players, one on each side of the line. Each player jumps over the stick as it reaches him. When the stick has reached the end, the first player remains there; the second runs with the stick to the turning line, returns, gives one end of the stick to the third player, and repeats. Continue until all have run and the first player is back at the head of the line.

Variation for Small Space.—When space is limited the runs to the turning line may be eliminated.

Head-Balancing Relay

Gymnasium, Club, Playground   *Late Elementary School to Adults*

A book is placed on the head of the first player of each team. At the signal the first player runs to the turning line and back and places the book

---

[1] The idea for this relay was taken from S. C. Staley, *Games, Contests, and Relays,* p. 259. Copyright, 1934. By permission of A. S. Barnes & Company, publishers.

on the head of the second player who repeats. The runner is not permitted to touch the book with his hands unless it falls off, in which case he must stop, replace the book, and take his hands off it before making further progress.

William Tell Relay.—Same as the Head-Balancing Relay except that an apple is used instead of the book.

Message Relay

Gymnasium, Club, Playground   *Late Elementary School to Adults*

This ever-popular relay calls for mental alertness more than physical ability. Place the captains on the turning line opposite their teams. Give each captain a folded card on which a brief message of not more than ten words is written. All cards contain the same message. At the signal the captains open the cards and read the messages. When a captain is sure he knows it, he drops the card on the floor, runs and gets the first player in his file and returns with him, whispering the message to him on the way. When they reach the turning line, the captain stays there and the first player goes back to get the second. Continue until all have run. When the last player of a team gets the message he runs to the leader who is stationed near the starting line, and states the message to him. Since the messages as stated are invariably far from correct, the team turning in the nearest correct statement is declared the winner.

The captains should be cautioned to read the message deliberately before running. When the captains drop their cards the leader should immediately pick them up. The players should be warned to run slowly and pay attention to the message.

Potato-and-Spoon Relay

Gymnasium, Club, Playground   *Late Elementary School to Adults*

Six feet in front of each team there is a circle with a potato in it; at the turning line there is another circle, empty. Give the first player of each team a spoon. At the signal he runs to the potato, picks it up in the spoon without the use of the other hand, runs to the second circle, deposits the potato in it, returns to the starting line, and gives the spoon to the second player. This player runs to the potato, picks it up, and brings it back to the first circle, and so on.

Stab-the-Spud Relay.—Six feet in front of each team draw a circle eighteen inches in diameter; draw a second circle of the same size opposite each team on the turning line. In this second circle place a potato for each player on the team. The first player of each team has a pointed stick.

At the signal the first player of each team runs to the far circle, stabs a potato with his stick and returns to the rear circle and deposits the potato in it, then gives the stick to the second player who repeats.

Potato Relay.—This relay follows the arrangements used in the Potato Race (page 11). The teams are lined up at the starting line and each player handles the potatoes in turn. The first player places the potatoes in the circle, and the second returns them to their original places, the third places them in the circle, and so on.

Potato-Carrier's Relay.—In front of each team's position is a row of eight circles with a potato in each, as in the Potato Race (page 11). The first player of each team has a small basket or box. At the signal the first player runs down the course, picks up all the potatoes and puts them in the basket, then returns and gives the basket to the second player, who replaces the potatoes. Continue until all have run.

Coat-and-Hat Relay

Gymnasium, Club, Playground   *Late Elementary School to Adults*

Give an old hat and a rain coat to the first player in each team. At the signal he runs to the turning line, putting on the coat and hat as he goes, returns, takes them off and gives them to the second player, who repeats. The coat and hat may be put on while the player is running, but must be entirely on when he returns to the starting line; he is not permitted to start to take them off before crossing the starting line.

Barrel-Rolling Relay

Gymnasium, Club, Playground   *Late Elementary School to Adults*

Place an empty barrel on its side on the starting line in front of each team. At the signal, the first runner rolls the barrel to the turning line, turns it around and rolls it back to the starting line. The second player then repeats, and so on.

Variation.—The players must roll the barrel by kicking it with the feet and are not permitted to touch it with any other part of the body.

Trundle-Wheel Relay

Gymnasium, Club, Playground Late Elementary and Junior High Schools

This relay is based on the use of the perennially popular trundle wheel. It is particularly seasonable in the spring. To make the trundle wheel, secure an old tricycle wheel or other similar metal wheel. In the hub insert a hardwood stick which will protrude four to six inches on one side. One wheel is needed for each team. For indoor use, wheels which do not have a hard rubber tire are difficult to handle.

Give the first player of each team the wheel and a three-foot stick. At the signal the player sets up the wheel, places his stick under the hub stick, and rolls the wheel to the turning line and back, giving it to the second player who repeats. Continue until all have run.

Tire-Rolling Relay

Gymnasium, Club, Playground   Late Elementary to Senior High School

Give the first player of each team an old automobile tire. Place an Indian club opposite each team on the turning line. At the signal the first player rolls the tire to the turning line, rolls it around the Indian club and back, and gives it to the second player who repeats.

Tire-Jumping Relay.—Establish a rolling line ten feet in front of the files. Place the first player of each team on the rolling line and give him an old automobile tire.

At the signal the roller of each team rolls his tire toward his team by giving it one shove. The players in turn stride-jump the tire. If the roller did not steer the tire exactly straight the line must shift enough to be in line with the tire. If a player knocks down the tire in attempting to jump it he must recover the tire and give it to the preceding player who rolls it back again. As soon as the roller rolls the tire he runs to the front of the line. When the last man jumps the tire, he rolls it to the rolling line and then rolls it at his team again. Continue until the original roller rolls the tire across the rolling line.

Through-the-Tire Relay.—Have all the players drop to hands and knees. Give the first player of each team an old automobile tire. At the signal the first player goes through the tire head first; the second player takes the tire and repeats and so on to the end man. When the end man has gone through the tire he runs to the head of the line, rolling the tire, goes through it again and thus starts it back down the line. Continue until the original leader of the line is back at the front.

Hoop-Rolling Relay

Gymnasium, Club, Playground   Late Elementary to Senior High School

Place an Indian club on the turning line opposite each team. At the signal the first player rolls the hoop with his hand down the course and around the club and back to the starting line, handing the hoop to the second player who repeats. The hoop must be rolled all the way and not carried. If the club is knocked down it must be replaced before the runner continues.

Hoop-and-Stick Relay.—Give the first player a wand or two-foot stick with which to propel the hoop. He starts the hoop by holding it with his hand and striking the side with the stick and thereafter propels it by batting it with the stick only. He rolls it across the turning line, then back to the second player who repeats. If the hoop falls the hand may be used in starting it again.

Through-the-Hoop Relay

Gymnasium, Club, Playground   Late Elementary to Senior High School

At the signal the first player of each team runs forward and passes the hoop down over his head and jumps out of it. He does this once between the starting line and the turning line, and once on the return to the starting line. He then gives the hoop to the second player who repeats.

Through-the-Hoop Relay—Feet First.—At the signal the first player runs forward, steps in the hoop and raises it over head once on the way to the turning line and once on the way back. He then touches off the second player who repeats.

Hoop-Diving Relay

Gymnasium, Club, Playground   Late Elementary to Senior High School

Station a man with a hoop in front of each team, half way between the starting and turning line. He holds the hoop with the edge touching the floor and the opening toward the team. At the signal the first player runs forward, dives or crawls through the hoop, runs to the turning line, returns, dives through the hoop again, and touches off the second player who repeats.

Big-Hoop Relay.—Withdraw the nails from three wooden barrel hoops and, using these as sections, nail them together thus making a large hoop three to five feet in diameter. One of these large hoops is needed for each team. At the signal the first player of each team runs back, holding the hoop vertically with the bottom near the floor. All the players jump through the hoop in turn. The first player then runs to the turning line, returns, hands the hoop to the second player, and takes his place at the rear of the line. The second player repeats.

Rope-Skipping Relay, Number 1

Gymnasium, Club, Playground   Late Elementary to Senior High School

Opposite each team on the turning line place an eight-foot skipping rope. At the signal the first player in each team runs to the turning line, picks up the rope and skips or jumps it any style four times; he then drops the rope and returns to the starting line, touching off the second player who repeats.

Variation.—Skip or jump the rope backward four times.

Variation.—Specify the style of skipping or jumping: single jump, double jump, skip, running in place, jumping with one leg, and so forth.

Rope-Skipping Relay, Number 2.—Give the first player of each team an eight-foot skipping rope. At the signal he runs to the turning line, running over the rope three times as he goes; he returns running over the rope three times, and gives it to the second player who repeats.

When the players are experienced at rope skipping, they may be required to step over the rope every other step.

Variation.—Have the players run backward running over the rope as before.

Leapfrog Relay, Number 1

Gymnasium, Club, Playground   Late Elementary to Senior High School

Each player leans forward placing his hands on his knees in leapfrog position; spread the files sufficiently to give room. At the signal the rear player vaults over all the players in turn and when he reaches the head of the line, he leans forward and takes his position there; as soon as the rear player has passed the next to the rear player, this player starts vaulting also. Continue until the players are in the same position in the file as at the start.

Leapfrog Relay, Number 2.—At the signal the rear player of each team vaults over all the players in turn until he reaches the head of the line. He then runs to the rear, takes his original place, and touches the player in front of him. This player vaults over all the players ahead of him, and when he reaches the front of the line, runs to the rear, leaps over the end man to his original place, and touches off the player in front of him. . Continue until all have run. This method is perhaps the least confusing of the various leapfrog relays.

Leapfrog Relay, Number 3.—Send player Number 1 midway between the starting and turning lines and have him lean forward in the leapfrog fashion. Player Number 2 runs forward at the signal, vaults over Number 1, stops and leans forward, and Number 1 vaults over him. Number 2 then remains in place and Number 1 runs to the turning line, returns and touches off Number 3. Number 3 vaults Number 2 and leans forward; Number 2 vaults Number 3, runs and touches off Number 4. Continue until all have run.

Leapfrog Relay, Number 4.—Station the Number 1 player of each team about five yards in front of his team and have him lean forward in the leapfrog position. At the signal, Number 2 runs forward, vaults over him and runs to the turning line, returns and touches off Number 1 who in turn touches off Number 3. In the meantime Number 2 leans forward in leapfrog position. Number 3 then repeats. Continue until all have run.

Leapfrog Spoke Relay.—Arrange the teams as described under the Spoke-Relay Method (Figure 27, page 164), having the players spaced at arm's length apart.

At the signal the end player of each team runs around the circle, returns to his spoke, and leaps over the back of the player now on the end as in leapfrog. This player then runs around the circle. The first player continues to leap over the backs of all players on his team until he reaches the hub end of the spoke. Continue until all have run.

Automobile Relay [2]

Playground, Gymnasium, Club   *Elementary and Junior High Schools*

Arrange the teams in parallel files and number the players of each team. Give each number specific instructions which he is to follow when his turn to run comes: All Number 1's represent a car with a flat tire going to the garage (hop on one foot to the turning line and run back). Number 2's represent a car with carburetor trouble (take three steps forward and two backward to the turning line and run back). Number 3's have a wheel off (go on two hands and one foot to the turning line and run back). Number 4's have a battery burned out (pushed by Number 5 to the turning line; both run back). Number 6's represent a car that is all right but an old car (run on all fours both ways). Number 7's represent a car that will run in reverse only (run backwards to the turning line and back). Number 8's represent a good car (run fast both ways). If there are more players, other situations can be easily added. Award five, three, and one points for finishing first, second, and third, and deduct one point for each runner that fails to follow instructions all the way.

Somersault Relay

Gymnasium, Playground   *Late Elementary to Senior High School*

At the signal the first player of each team progresses to the turning line and back by a series of somersaults. No progress may be made with the feet—each somersault is followed directly by the next. On returning, the first player touches off the second who repeats. The turning line should not be over thirty to forty feet distant.

Stunt Relays

Gymnasium, Club, Playground   *Late Elementary to Senior High School*

Place a mat in front of each team, midway between the starting and turning lines. Specify some gymnastic stunt or feat which is to be done. The first player of each team runs to the mat, does the stunt, runs to the

[2] The idea for this relay was taken from the *Content Committee Report*, Marjorie Hillas, chairman.

turning line, returns to the mat and repeats the stunt, and then touches off the second player who repeats.

Such stunts as the following may be used:

1. Forward roll.
2. Run backward and do a backward roll.

3. Cart wheel.
4. Headstand.

Medley Relay

Gymnasium, Club, Playground   *Late Elementary School to Adults*

Number the players and instruct them how each is to move when his turn comes. The same method of locomotion is not assigned to more than one player of a team. The Number 1's may be instructed to hop on one foot down to the turning line and run back; the Number 2's to go on all fours, the Number 3's to run backward, and so forth. Any of the methods of locomotion in the above relays may be used.

IMPEDED-PROGRESS RELAYS

In these relays the runners are impeded or restricted in some way, usually by some object or appliance on the feet. Handicapped in this way, free locomotion is impossible.

Most of the novelty relays described in the preceding chapters involve the manipulation of some object or the performance of some stunt that in a sense impedes free progress. However, only those relays are classified in the following section in which the free movement of the legs is definitely impeded, usually by some object on which the contestant stands. The Tin-Can Stilt Race is an example.

Paper-Walking Relay

Gymnasium, Club, Playground   *Late Elementary School to Adults*

The turning line should not be more than fifteen feet distant. Place two newspapers folded twice, or two pieces of cardboard, on the floor in front of each team. At the signal the first player steps on the paper, bends down and grasps one of the papers in each hand. He places one of the papers forward, steps on it, then places the other forward and steps on it. In this manner he makes progress to the turning line and back, touching off the next player who repeats.

Fan-Walking Relay.—Same as the Paper-Walking Relay except that large palm-leaf fans are used. The first player of each team stands on the fans with the handles extending forward. He bends down, grasps the handles, and runs forward on the fans by pulling them forward.

Brick-Walking Relay.—Same as the Paper-Walking Relay except that bricks are substituted for the papers.

Pail-Running Relay

Gymnasium, Club, Playground   *Late Elementary School to Adults*

In this interesting relay two buckets of the large size are needed for each team. Standing with one foot in each pail and holding on to the handles, the first player of each team runs to the turning line and back. He then gives the pails to the second player who repeats. Continue until all have run. The turning line should not be more than twenty-five feet distant.

Dishpan Relay

Gymnasium, Club, Playground   *Late Elementary School to Adults*

A large dishpan is needed for each team. At the signal the first player of each team sits in the pan, and with his hands and feet on the floor slides the pan forward to the turning line and back. He then gives the pan to the second player who repeats. The turning line should not be more than twenty feet distant.

Variation.—Same as the above except that the players turn their backs to the starting line, sit in the dishpan and move backwards.

Chair-Walking Relay

Gymnasium, Club, Playground   *Late Elementary to Senior High School*

Two substantial straight-back chairs are needed for each team. The first player places the chairs side by side with backs turned toward the starting line. He stands with one foot on each chair and clasps the backs of the chairs with his hands. At the signal he walks to the turning line and back by lifting the chairs forward by the hand, and stepping on them. On returning to the starting line he gives the chairs to the second player who repeats. Continue until all have run.

The turning line should not be more than thirty feet distant.

Chair-Stubbing Relay.—A sturdy straight-back chair is placed in front of each team with its back toward the starting line. At the signal the first player stands on the seat of the chair, grasps the back with his hands, and by jerking the chair moves forward to the turning line. Here he jumps off, picks the chair up and runs back, giving it to the second player who repeats. The turning line should not be over fifteen feet distant.

Slipper Relay

Gymnasium, Club, Playground   *Late Elementary School to Adults*

A large pair of house slippers or rubbers is needed for each team; they must be larger than required by the largest player so that they will be kept on with difficulty. At the signal the first player puts the slippers on, runs to the turning line, returns, takes the slippers off and gives them to the second player who repeats. If the slippers fall off they must be replaced before continuing.

Shoe Relay.—Halfway between the starting line and the turning line, mark a line across the floor. The first player of each team runs to this line, takes off his shoes and leaves them, runs to the turning line, returns, puts on his shoes, and runs to the starting line, touching off the second player. The shoes must be completely laced. Continue until all have run.

Tin-Can Stilt Relay

Gymnasium, Club, Playground   Late Elementary to Senior High School

The tin cans are prepared by running a three-foot length of light rope through small holes on opposite sides of the can near the top. The ends of the rope are tied together so that when a player stands on the cans, the ropes reach to his knees. Tomato-juice cans or soup cans from which the contents have been removed by holes punched in the top are ideal, in that both top and bottom still remain. Two cans are needed for each team.

At the signal the first player of each team mounts the cans and runs on them to the turning line and back, giving the cans to the second player who repeats. The turning line should be about forty feet distant. Continue until all have run.

Plank Relay

Gymnasium, Club, Playground   Junior and Senior High Schools

Two hardwood planks fifteen inches square and one inch thick are needed for each team. To the middle of one edge of each plank a six-foot rope is attached. The first player of each team stands with one foot on each plank, with the rope side to the front, and holds one of the ropes in each hand. At the signal he travels to the turning point and back by lifting the planks with the ropes and setting them forward. He then gives the planks to the second player. Continue until all have run. The turning line should be twenty to thirty feet distant.

Summer-Snowshoe Relay

Gymnasium, Club, Playground   Junior and Senior High Schools

The "snowshoes" are made of barrel tops. Nail a cross strip five inches wide across the top of the barrel top, and to it nail a toe strap of leather, or better still of tin from a tin can. For gymnasium use, care should be taken to remove the rough edges and to see that there are no nails protruding from the bottom.

At the signal the first player mounts the "snowshoes" and runs to the turning point and back, giving the "snowshoes" to the next player who repeats. Continue until all have run.

Barrel-Stave Ski Relay on Land.—For each team, two barrel staves are needed, made into skis by nailing on foot straps of tin from a tin can, or of leather. Select wide barrel staves. The first player of each team mounts the skis and at the signal moves to the turning line and back with a sort of skating motion. He gives the skis to the second player who repeats.

Circus-Sandal Relay

Gymnasium, Club, Playground   *Junior and Senior High Schools*

From a piece of four-by-four-inch wood construct high "sandals" similar to those used by circus performers on rainy days. These are quickly made by simply sawing off two pieces of the four-by-four, twelve inches long, and nailing on foot straps. The foot straps may be of heavy canvas, leather, or tin cut from a tin can. Two "sandals" are needed for each team. At the signal the first player of each team puts on the blocks of wood and runs to the turning line and back, giving the sandals to the second player who repeats. Continue until all have run. The team finishing first wins.

Hoop-Hobble Relay

Gymnasium, Club, Playground   *Junior and Senior High Schools*

The first player of each team places his feet in the hoop and spreads his legs so that the hoop is held parallel to the floor at ankle height. At the signal he runs forward to the turning line and back with the hoop around his legs, then gives the hoop to the second player who repeats. The runner must not allow the hoop to rise higher on his legs than half way to his knees, and he is not allowed to touch it with his hands. Continue until all have run. The turning line should be twenty to thirty feet distant.

Hoop-Running Relay.—At the signal the first player makes progress to the turning line and back in the following manner: Holding the hoop in the right hand he bends forward so that the hoop is nearly parallel to the floor and close to it; he steps in it with the right foot and then with the left, transfers the hoop to the left hand, steps out with the right foot and the left, swings the hoop behind him and takes it in his right hand, and repeats the steps. On returning to the starting line he touches off the second player who repeats. The turning line should be fifteen to twenty-five feet distant.

Crisscross Hoop-Running Relay.—At the signal the first player of each team moves to the turning line and back in the following manner: With his legs close together he inserts the hoop between them perpendicular to the floor and touching it; he steps through it with his right foot, crosses his left foot over in front of the right, crosses his right foot in front of the left and so on. Each step is made through the hoop. On returning to the starting line, he gives the hoop to the second player who repeats. The turning line should be fifteen to twenty-five feet distant.

Sit-in-Hoop Relay

Gymnasium, Club, Playground   Late Elementary to Senior High School

At the signal the first player of each team sits in the hoop, pushes the top of it up over his shoulders against his neck, and pushes it against the back of his knees. He may then stand as erect as possible provided he keeps the hoop against the back of the knees. In this position he runs to the turning line and back, giving his hoop to the second player who repeats. The turning line should be twenty to thirty feet distant.

Stilt Relay

Gymnasium, Club, Playground   Late Elementary to Senior High School

This contest is interesting for all ages, even though the players have had but very little experience with stilts. The turning line should be thirty feet distant. Give the first player of each team a pair of low stilts. At the signal he mounts the stilts, moves to the turning line and back, giving the stilts to the second player, who repeats. Continue until all have run.

Pogo-Stick Relay

Gymnasium, Club, Playground   Late Elementary to Senior High School

Pogo sticks are an interesting addition to the equipment for supervised play. They form the basis of a most interesting and hilarious relay provided the players are familiar enough with them to stay on them at all successfully. One stick is needed for each team.

At the signal the first player of each team mounts and, with the aid of the spring in the end of the stick, jumps to the turning line and returns, giving the stick to the second player who repeats. If a player falls off he must remount the stick at the point where his foot first touched the floor before making further progress. Continue until all have competed.

NOVELTY TANDEM RELAYS

In these relays two players from each team run at once. In other respects the procedure is as in the Simple File Relay (page 163). These are among the most interesting of the relays.

Since the players compete in pairs, there should be an even number of players on each team. If uneven, designate one player to run twice.

Back-to-Back Relay

Gymnasium, Club, Playground   Late Elementary to Senior High School

The first two players stand back to back and link elbows. At the signal the front player leans forward, lifts the back player off the floor, and thus carries him to the turning line. At this line he lowers the back player to the floor and that player immediately leans forward, lifts the first player and carries him back to the starting line. They touch off the next pair who repeat.

Siamese-Twins Relay

Gymnasium, Club, Playground   Late Elementary to Senior High School

The turning line should be from thirty-five to fifty feet away. The players run in pairs. Give the first two players of each team a four-foot stick, such as a broomstick. They stand back to back and straddle the stick, grasping it with both hands in front. At the signal, they move toward the turning line, one running forward and the other backward. Upon reaching the turning line, they stop and without turning around, return to the starting line, where they give the stick to the next pair who repeat. Continue until all have run.

Swing-Around Relay

Gymnasium, Club, Playground   Late Elementary School to Adults

The players race in pairs. At the signal, the first two players of each team join hands and run to the turning line, at which point they swing completely around, swinging each other around in a circle with joined arms. They then return to the starting line and touch off the next pair of runners who repeat.

Broom-Riding Relay

Gymnasium, Club, Playground   Late Elementary to Senior High School

Give the first player of each team an old house broom. The players run in pairs. The first player holds the end of the broom handle with both hands. The second player sits on the brush part of the broom as near the end as possible, places his feet on the broom stick and holds the stick with his hands. In this position they race to the turning line and back; then the second player pulls the third. Continue until the last player has ridden the broom.

Bicycle-Tire Relay

Gymnasium, Club, Playground   Late Elementary to Senior High School

An old bicycle tire is needed for each team. At the signal the first and second players, before crossing the starting line, stand close together and slip the tire down over their heads and around their waists. In this position they run to the turning line and back. They then remove the tire and give it to the third and fourth players who repeat. Continue until all have run.

Over-the-Border Relay

Gymnasium, Club, Playground   *Late Elementary to Senior High School*

Station the captain of each team behind the turning line, facing his team. At the signal, the captain runs forward, grasps the hand of the first player on his team and both run back to the captain's original place. The captain then stays there, but the one whom he took over goes back and gets the next player, and so the race continues until all have been brought over and a new line formed behind the captain.

Wheelbarrow Relay

Gymnasium, Club, Playground   *Junior and Senior High Schools*

This is a thrilling and spectacular event both to spectators and contestants. Old tricycle wheels at least a foot in diameter are used. Through the hub a sixteen-inch iron rod is inserted, just large enough to fit the hub. The wheel thus revolves on the rod.

At the signal the first player of each team places his hands on the bar of the wheel as near the ends as possible, and the second player grasps his ankles and lifts his legs. He pushes him to the turning line and back. Then the second player takes the wheel and the third player pushes him and so on.

Human Wheelbarrow Relay.—The turning line should be twenty feet distant. The contestants compete in pairs. At the signal, the first player places his hands on the floor, the second player grasps his ankles and lifts his legs. In this position they travel to the turning line, the front player traveling on his hands. On reaching the turning line they reverse their positions and return, touching off the second pair who repeat.

Ditch-Diggers Relay.—Give the first player of each team a wheelbarrow. At the signal player Number 2 sits in the wheelbarrow and is wheeled by Number 1 to the turning line and back. Then Number 2 wheels Number 3, and so on.

Plank-Sled Relay [3]

Gymnasium, Club, Playground   *Junior and Senior High Schools*

A plank is needed for each team, fifteen inches wide and two feet long. Two six-foot ropes are attached to the plank, one at each end of one of

[3] The idea for the use of these planks was taken from A. B. Wegener, *Play Games*, p. 11. Copyright, 1930. By permission of the Abingdon Press, publishers.

the long sides. These are worth-while articles of equipment for supervised play.

The first player of each team takes the ropes of the plank and the second player stands on the plank, reaching forward and holding a rope in each hand. At the signal the first player pulls the second to the turning line and back. The second player then pulls the third, while the first player goes to the rear of the line. Continue until all have ridden the plank.

Variation.—The rider stands on the plank but does not hold the rope. If he falls off, the plank must be returned to the spot where he first touches the floor in order to allow him to mount again.

Tandem Hopping Relay, Number 1

Gymnasium, Club, Playground   *Junior and Senior High Schools*

The turning line should not be more than thirty feet distant. The two players face each other and raise their left legs toward each other. Each grasps the other's raised leg at the ankle and in this position they hop to the turning line and back, touching off the second couple.

Tandem Hopping Relay, Number 2.—The first two players stand one behind the other. The front player raises his left leg behind and the back player grasps the leg by the ankle in one hand. The back player also raises one leg, and in this position they hop.

Tandem Hopping Relay, Number 3.—The two partners stand side by side, lifting their inside legs, and placing their inside arms around each other's shoulders. In this position they hop to the turning line and back, touching off the second couple.

Centipede Relay

Gymnasium, Club, Playground   *Late Elementary to Senior High School*

This is a relay adaptation of the Centipede Race. At the signal the second player of each team wraps his arms completely around the waist of the first player in front of him, and in this position they run to the turning line and return, touching off the next pair, who repeat. Continue until all have run.

Caterpillar Relay

Gymnasium, Club, Playground   *Late Elementary to Senior High School*

The first player in each team bends down and places his hands on the floor; the second player bends down and grasps the first player by the ankles. In this position they move to the turning line and return, touching off the next pair who repeat. The distances should be short. The turning line should be twenty to forty feet distant.

Chain-Crab Relay.—The first two players of each team sit on the floor, one behind the other, with feet pulled well up against the thighs. The front player leans back and grasps the ankles of the back player; the rear player places his hands on the floor behind him. In this position they move across the turning line, return and touch off the second pair of players who repeat. Continue until all have run.

Reverse Chain-Crab Relay.—Same as the above except that the players face in the opposite direction and race backward.

Pony-Express Relay

Gymnasium, Club, Playground   *Junior and Senior High Schools*

Have each team select its lightest and smallest player to act as rider. At the signal the rider mounts the back of the first player who carries him to the turning line and back. The rider then transfers himself to the back of the second pony *without touching the floor*. The second pony then repeats. Continue until all have run. The team finishing first wins.

Horse-and-Rider Relay.—Have the players arrange themselves according to height with the largest players in front. At the signal the second player mounts the first player's back, and is carried by him to the turning line where he dismounts. The horse stays at the turning line, and the rider returns, picks up the third player, and repeats. Continue until all are behind the turning line.

Carrying-the-Injured Relays

Gymnasium, Playground, Club   *Junior and Senior High Schools*

These relays involve the use of various first-aid methods of carrying the injured.

Arm-Carry Relay.—The players of each team are stationed according to size, the largest players in front. At the signal the first player of each team picks the second player up by the first-aid carry known as the arm carry: he holds him in his arms with one arm under his thighs and the other behind his back, while the man being carried puts one arm around his carrier's neck. He carries him to the turning line and back, then the second player carries the third, and so on.

Dead-Man's-Carry Relay.—At the signal, the second player of each team places his arms over the first player's shoulders; the first player grasps his waist, leans forward lifting him off the floor and runs with him to the turning line and back. The second player then carries the third, and so on.

Fireman's-Lift Relay.—At the signal the first player picks the second up by the first-aid carry known as the fireman's-lift: the first player faces the second, bends forward and puts his right arm under the second player's crotch; the second player lies over the first player's shoulders; the first player takes the second player's right wrist in his right hand and straightens up. He runs to the turning line and back. The second player then carries the third, and so forth.

When the players have become expert, they may be required to lift the rider from the floor where he is lying in prone position.

Waist-Carry Relay.—At the signal the second player places his arms around the waist of the first player, picks him up and carries him to the turning line and back. The third player then carries the second, and the first player goes to the end of the file.

Chair-Carry Relay.—Two players carry a third by the first-aid carry known as the chair carry. At the signal the first two players of each team form the chair as follows: they face each other, each grasping his own left forearm with his right hand, midway between the wrist and elbow; each then grasps the other's right forearm with the left hand. The third player sits in the chair, putting his arms around his supporters' necks, and is carried to the turning line and back. The second and third players carry the fourth.

RIDING RELAYS

In the following relays, the contestants propel and ride a vehicle of some sort.

Roller-Skating Relays

Playground, Gymnasium, Rink　　　　*Elementary to Senior High School*

Roller-skating relays follow the same method used in running relays. The following methods of skating may be used:

Straight Relay.—The skaters race to the turning line and back, touching off the second skater.

Backward Relay.—The skaters start backward.

Tandem Relay, Number 1.—The skaters skate in pairs standing side by side and grasping right hands together and left hands together.

Tandem Relay, Number 2.—One skater stands behind the other and holds him by the belt or shoulder.

One-Skate Relay.—The skaters use one skate only, riding on it and pushing with the other foot on the floor.

Scooter Relays

Playground, Gymnasium, Club, Picnic　　　　*Elementary School to Adults*

Scooters are the basis of several relays which are most interesting to all ages. Adults enjoy them as novelties as well as children. One scooter is needed for each team. Arrange the teams in parallel files. The first contestant races to the turning line and back, then gives the scooter to the second player who repeats. The following methods of travelling may be used:

Standing.—The player places one foot on the scooter and propels by pushing with the other foot on the ground.

Kneeling.—The player kneels with one knee on the scooter and pushes with the other leg.

Sitting.—The player straddles the scooter and sits on it with one leg on each side. He propels himself by pushing with the feet on the floor.

Backward.—The player, facing backward, places one foot on the scooter and propels himself by pushing with the other foot on the ground.

Tandem Relay.—The first player sits on the scooter and places his feet on it near the tongue. The second player holds him and pushes him by placing his hands on his shoulders. On their return to the starting line, the second player rides and the third pushes.

Skipmobile Relay

Playground, Gymnasium   *Late Elementary and Junior High Schools*

Skipmobiles are home-made scooters using wheels taken from a roller skate. The construction of these is described under Skipmobile Races (page 24).

The first player of each team is given a skipmobile. He places one foot on it and propels it by pushing with the other foot. He races to the turning line and back, giving it to the second player who repeats.

Horseback-Riding Relays

The mounted relays are described in Chapter XXVIII, "Horseback-Riding Activities."

MISCELLANEOUS RELAYS

These relays are of an unusual nature and cannot be classified with the other relays described in this chapter.

Standing Broad-Jump Relay

Playground, Gymnasium, Club   *Late Elementary to Senior High School*

Arrange the teams in file formation, with the front players facing a common line. Place the most experienced and reliable player of each team at the front to act as captain. At the signal the captains toe the line and jump. The second player places his toes at the point where the first player's heels touched or at the nearest point where his body touched, and jumps as before. Continue until all have jumped. The team jumping the greatest distance from the starting line wins.

When there are not enough officials for each team, have the captains determine where each successive jumper is to stand before jumping. After the captains jump they exchange places so that no captain is officiating for his own team.

Human Croquet Relay

Gymnasium, Playground, Picnic, Club   Late Elementary School to Adults

Two teams of nine players each are needed. Since one team must form the arches while the other team runs, the event must be against time.

The players of team Number 2 form the arches and arrange themselves as in croquet:

```
                        2                  2
IIIIIIII   0   22              2                22   0
                        2                  2
```

The Number 2 players bend down and place their hands on the ground, thus forming an arch; or, if preferred, they stand with legs at stride, forming an arch. Team Number 1 lines up at one end as illustrated. Place some object on the ground at the opposite end to represent the stake.

At the signal the first player of team Number 1 crawls through the first two arches, runs to the right-wing arch and crawls through it, then to the center arch, to the lower right-wing arch, to the two lower center arches, and touches the stake. He then returns through the two lower center arches, to the lower left-wing arch, to the center arch, to the upper left-wing arch, and to the two upper center arches. He then touches off the second player, who repeats. Continue until all have run. The teams then change positions and team Number 2 runs. The team making the best time wins.

Variation.—Have nine players form the arches as described above. Divide the remaining players into two teams and station one team in line behind each stake. At the signal the first player of each team runs through the arches following the course described above—they are of course running in opposite directions. On returning, the first player of each team touches off the second who repeats. Continue until all have run. The team finishing first wins.

The sport in this event centers around the fact that the opposing players, running in opposite directions, frequently reach an arch at about the same time. The scramble that results adds a humorous touch and the contest is excellent for such situations as picnics.

Human-Hurdle Relay [4]

Playground, Gymnasium   *Junior and Senior High Schools*

Arrange the teams in circles, facing outward. The players seat themselves with legs extended and close together, feet pointing away from the center of the circle. A space of at least one foot should exist between each player. Each circle counts off from left to right. At the signal Number 1 stands, faces right, and runs or jumps over the legs of all players until he is back to his position, then sits down and touches off Number 2, who then repeats. The team wins whose last player is first to reach his original sitting position with hands raised over head, provided no fouls have been committed. The following are fouls: (1) failure to jump or step over the legs; (2) jumping over more than one player's legs at a time; (3) touching off a player before being seated.

Variation.—As soon as Number 1 has jumped over the legs of Number 2, the latter immediately stands and follows. Similarly, Numbers 3, 4, and so forth, follow. When each player reaches his original position he must sit down immediately in order that the players following may step over his legs. The last player after returning to his position, remains standing.

RUNNING RELAYS IN *SOCIAL GAMES FOR RECREATION*

See Chapter VI, "Social Relays and Group Contests," and Chapter XVIII, "Picnic and Outing Activities."

[4] The idea for this contest was taken from N. P. Neilson and W. Van Hagen, *Physical Education for Elementary Schools,* p. 348. Copyright, 1929. By permission of A. S. Barnes and Company, publishers.

CHAPTER XIV

STRIKING, KICKING, AND BUTTING RELAYS

THE chief characteristic of the relays in this chapter is striking, kicking, or butting an object. A few of them involve striking, kicking, or butting only, but most of them combine running with striking, kicking, or butting.

RELAYS INVOLVING STRIKING ONLY

Zigzag Hockey-Driving Relay

Playground   *Junior High School to College*

Arrange the teams in zigzag formation as diagrammed in Method B, Figure 29, Zigzag Ball-Passing Relay. The first player of each team drives the hockey ball with the hockey stick to the second player, who stops it and drives it to the third, and so on. When the last player gets it, it is driven back as before to the first player. The team finishing first wins.

Hockey-Driving Shuttle Relay

Playground   *Junior High School to College*

Arrange the teams as in the Shuttle Relay (Figure 26). Player Number 1 of each team drives the hockey ball to Number 2 with a hockey stick; Number 2 drives it to Number 3; and so on. The team finishing first wins.

Circle Hockey-Driving Relay

Playground   *Junior High School to College*

Arrange each team in a circle with one of its members in the center. Draw a three-foot circle in which the center player must stand. All have a hockey stick and the center player also has a ball.

At the signal the center player of each team drives the ball to one of the circle players who stops it and drives it back. The center player then drives to the next circle player and so on around the circle. The team finishing first wins.

RELAYS COMBINING LOCOMOTION WITH STRIKING, KICKING, OR BUTTING

Driving the Pig to Market

Playground, Gymnasium, Club   *Elementary and Junior High Schools*

The teams are arranged in parallel files. Give the first player of each team a wand or three-foot stick cut from a broomstick, and a "pig" in the form of a pop bottle or milk bottle.

At the signal the first player of each team drives the pig to the turning line and back by pushing and batting it with the wand. The wand and pig are then turned over to the second player who repeats. Continue until all have run. The team finishing first wins.

Stick-and-Ball Relay.—Give the first player of each team a straight three-foot stick, such as a broomstick, and a softball. At the signal the first player runs to the turning line and returns, knocking the ball along the ground with the stick as he goes.

Dumb-bell Pushing Relay.—Place a dumb-bell or Indian club on the floor in front of each team and give the first player of each team a wand or short stick. At the signal the first player pushes the dumb-bell to the turning line, then pushes it back to the starting line and gives the stick to the second player, who repeats. The dumb-bell must be rolled and not batted or tossed with the stick.

Croquet-Mallet Relay.—Place the mallet heads on the floor or ground, the handle being separated and in the hands of the leading players. The object is to roll the mallet head to a turning line and return, whereupon the second player races. Since the mallet head will not roll straight forward, but will swerve in any number of directions, considerable uncertainty is provided. The steering must be done with the handles held perpendicular to the ground.

Hockey-Dribbling Relays

Playground, Gymnasium   *Junior High School to College*

The relays involve the dribbling of a ball with a field-hockey stick. They are useful in lead-up and practice events for Field Hockey.

Hockey-Dribbling Relay.—Arrange the teams in parallel files. Give the first player of each team a field-hockey club and ball. At the signal the first player dribbles the ball to the turning line, stops it, dribbles back, and gives the second player the stick. The second player then repeats. Continue until all have run. The team finishing first wins.

Hockey-Dribbling Shuttle Relay.—Arrange the teams as in the Shuttle Relay (Figure 26). Player Number 1 of each team dribbles the hockey ball with a hockey stick to Number 2, who dribbles it back to Number 3, and so on.

Zigzag Hockey-Dribbling Relay.—Arrange the teams in parallel files and spread the players so that they stand ten feet apart. Mark the spots where the end players stand—the players at the end of the line must remain on these spots in order to prevent the teams from closing in toward the center. Player Number 1 holds a hockey stick and ball.

At the signal Number 1 dribbles the ball in and out between the players, to the right of one, to the left of the next, and so on. On reaching the end of the line, he circles the last player and dribbles back as before. When Number 1 reaches the starting line, all players move one space toward the starting line and Number 2 takes the stick and repeats, while Number 1 runs down and takes the end position at the far end. Continue until all have run.

Obstacle Hockey Shuttle Relay.—Arrange the teams as in the Shuttle Relay (Figure 26) and place a low obstacle between them. At the signal, player Number 1 dribbles the hockey ball with the hockey stick to the obstacle, scoops it over, and then dribbles it to Number 2, who dribbles back to Number 3, and so on.

Circle Hockey-Dribbling Relay.—Arrange each team in a circle and mark the circle on the ground in front of the players. Player Number 1 of each circle has a hockey stick and ball. At the signal Number 1 dribbles to the right around the circle and when he reaches his original position, hands the stick to Number 2 who repeats. Continue until all have run.

Pepper-Batting Relay

Playground, Gymnasium   *Junior High School to College*

Arrange each team in a semicircle. Station one player in front of each team with a bat and give the end player at the right of the semicircle a softball or baseball. At the signal the player with the ball tosses the ball to the batter who taps it with the bat back to him. The player secures the ball and tosses it to the next player, who repeats by tossing it to the batter. Continue until the last player at the left has received the ball from the batter. This player runs and takes the bat, and the batter runs to the right of the semicircle and tosses the ball to the new batter. The play continues until all have batted and the teams are in the position they held at the beginning of the contest. The team finishing first wins.

In case the batter misses the ball, he must secure it and throw it back to the thrower, who tosses it to him again.

Foot-Dribble Relay

Playground, Gymnasium   *Junior High School to College*

The teams are arranged in parallel files. Place a soccer football on the floor in front of the first player of each team. At the signal the first player of each team dribbles the ball with his foot across the turning line and then dribbles back to the second player who repeats. The first player, however, must *place the ball directly in front of the second player so that he can kick it without moving.* The first player must direct the ball and move it only with his feet and the second player is not permitted to move from his position to reach the ball. Continue until all have run. The team finishing first wins.

Goat-Butting Relay

Playground, Gymnasium, Club   *Late Elementary to Senior High School*

The teams are arranged in parallel files. Place a basketball, volleyball, soccer ball, eodeball, or even a softball on the floor in front of each team. At the signal the first player drops to hands and knees and butts the ball toward the turning line with his head. He may run or crawl in following the ball, may dive at it in butting it, but may not strike it with any part of the body except the head. Having put the ball across the turning line, he butts it back to the second player who repeats. Continue until all have run. The team finishing first wins.

Crawling events such as this should not be used unless the players have their legs covered.

Tunnel Goat-Butting Relay.—This relay is suitable for a small space. The players of each team stand in file with feet at stride and well apart. Give the first player of each team a volleyball, soccer ball, or basketball. At the signal the first player rolls the ball back between the rows of legs. The last player drops to his knees, stops the ball with his head and crawls forward through the tunnel of legs, butting the ball forward with his head but not touching it with his hands. When he reaches the front he stands and rolls the ball back between the legs again. Continue until the player who headed the line at the start is back in that position.

CHAPTER XV

OBJECT-PASSING RELAYS

THE competition in these relays is based primarily upon passing an object from player to player.

The object-passing relays are of two types: (1) those involving passing and no running; (2) those involving both passing and running.

In conducting relays involving the passing of objects, lines should always be marked on the floor on which the front and rear players are to stand. This keeps the players spread properly and equalizes the lengths of all the teams.

RELAYS INVOLVING PASSING ONLY

These relays are particularly well adapted for use in situations where space is limited. Since there is no running, they can be used in any space sufficient to allow the teams to stand in line. They are also excellent for use in groups of adults who do not care for much running.

Passing Relay

Playground, Gymnasium, Club, Schoolroom   Elementary School to Adults

Divide the group into two teams and place them facing each other about ten feet apart. Give the first player of each team a ball or other object. At the signal the object is handed from player to player until it reaches the end, then it is passed back to the first player again. The team finishing first wins.

When the players are familiar with the contest, it will be well to make each contest consist of passing the ball down and back three times without stopping.

Two-Object-Passing Relay.—Same as the above except that two objects are passed. Both objects are on the floor at the feet of the first player. At the signal he picks up one and passes, then picks up the other and passes it.

Behind-the-Back Passing Relay.—Same as the above except that the ball is passed behind the back from player to player.

Combination Passing Relay.—The ball is passed down the line as in the Passing Relay, and back as in the Behind-the-Back Passing Relay.

Spin-Around Relay

Playground, Gymnasium, Club　　　*Late Elementary School to Adults*

Arrange the teams in parallel lines, facing sideways. The first player of each team has a ball or other object. At the signal, the first player spins around and passes the ball to the second, who spins and passes it to the third, and so on. When the last player gets it he starts it back to the front. The team finishing first wins.

Two-Object Spin-Around Relay.—Same as the above except that two objects are passed one after the other, and each player spins around twice before passing each object.

Overhead-Passing Relay

Playground, Gymnasium, Club　　　*Late Elementary School to Adults*

Arrange the teams in parallel files, and give the first player of each team a ball. Have the players spread so that each can just touch the man in front of him, then mark the floor by the feet of the front player and the rear player—these two players must keep their feet on these lines.

At the signal the ball is passed over the head to the rear of the line. When the last player gets it he calls "About face" whereupon the players turn around and the ball is passed back.

Two-Object Overhead-Passing Relay.—Same as the above except that two objects are passed one after the other. When the last man gets the first object he lays it on the floor until he gets the second, and then calls "About face," and the balls are passed back.

Between-the-Legs Passing Relay.—Same as above except the ball is passed between the legs.

Over-and-Under Passing Relay.—Same as the above except that the first player passes the ball over his head to the second player, and the second player passes it between his legs to the third. It thus goes over and under until the last player gets it. He calls "About face" and starts it back by passing it over his head.

Pass-and-Turn Relay.—At the signal the first player passes the ball back overhead to the second player and immediately turns around facing the rear; the second player passes the ball and turns, and so on. When the last player gets the ball, he turns and passes it back, turning again and facing front. When the front man gets it he places it on the floor and throws his hands overhead. The team finishing first wins.

The contest is usually conducted by passing the ball back and forward three times in succession without stopping.

Military Relay

Playground, Gymnasium, Club   *Late Elementary School to Adults*

This is a combination of the methods of passing listed under the Passing Relay and the Overhead-Passing Relay above. Arrange the teams in the same way.

The first player of each team passes the ball *overhead* to the second player and it is thus passed back to the rear player. When he gets it he commands "About face" and the ball is passed back *between the legs* to the head of the line. When the front player gets it he commands "Right face" and the ball is passed *sideways* down the line. When the rear man gets it he commands "About face" and the ball is passed *behind the back* to the front man to finish. The team finishing first wins.

Beanbag Sidewise-Passing Relay

Schoolroom   *Elementary School*

Place a beanbag or eraser on each desk of the row on one side of the room. If vacant places exist, move the players to the front or back so that all vacant seats are in one transverse row. When the signal is given each player in the rows having the bags passes his bag to the player across the aisle, and this continues until the bags are held by the players in the row at the opposite side of the room. This may be repeated, passing in alternate directions, and keeping score to show how many times each transverse row wins.

Variation.—Place the beanbags on the floor beside the seats on one side of the room. At the signal each player sitting beside a beanbag picks it up with the near hand, transfers it to the other hand overhead, and places it on the floor on the other side of the desk. The next player then picks it up and repeats the process.

Circle-Passing Relay

Playground, Gymnasium, Club   *Elementary School to Adults*

Divide the group into two teams of from eight to sixteen players each. Arrange each team in a circle and designate a captain. Give the captain a ball, wand, or bat. At the signal, the captain passes the ball to the player on his right and the passing is continued around the circle. The ball is passed around the circle five times. The first time it passes the captain he calls "One," the second time "Two," and so forth. When it reaches the captain after the fifth time he holds the ball overhead and calls "Five." The team finishing first wins.

The relay may be played as a social game with the players seated.

Circle Spin-Around Relay.—Same as the above except that each player spins around once after he receives the ball and before passing it.

Circle Bounce-Pass Relay.—The ball is passed to the player on the right by bouncing it on the floor.

Circle Overhead-Pass Relay.—Face the players in the same direction. The ball is held overhead by both hands and passed forward from player to player.

Single-Circle Passing Relay

Playground, Gymnasium, Club　　　　*Late Elementary School to Adults*

Arrange the players in a single circle and have them count off by two's. The Number 1's constitute one team and the Number 2's the other. The two captains stand side by side, each with a ball. At the signal the Number 1 captain passes the ball to the right to the next Number 1 player, and the Number 2 captain passes to the left to the next Number 2 player. The ball is thus passed around the circle and the team wins which gets it back so that the captain can lay it on the floor first.

If desired, the ball may be passed around the circle three or four times instead of once.

Variation.—Use a bounce pass.

Variation.—Each player spins around once before passing the ball.

Variation.—Use two balls for each team, passed one after the other.

Variation.—Use two balls with each player spinning around twice before passing each ball.

Circle Overtake Relay

Playground, Club　　　　*Late Elementary School to Adults*

Stand the players in a circle and have them count off by two's, thus dividing the group into two teams, each team consisting of every other man around the circle. Designate as captains two opposing players who stand directly opposite each other, and give each a ball. The balls are passed by hand from player to player in the same direction, the object being to pass the other team's ball. If the ball is dropped, the player who dropped it must get it, return to his position, and pass it again.

RELAYS COMBINING PASSING OBJECTS AND LOCOMOTION

These relays combine the passing of objects from player to player and locomotion of some type.

Schoolroom Overhead Relay

Schoolroom　　　　*Elementary School*

Place an eraser on the front desk of each row. At a signal to start, the first child in each row takes the eraser with both hands and passes it overhead to the child behind him. This continues till the last child receives it. The last child runs forward with it on the right side of his row and sits in the front seat; at the same time all players in the row move back a seat. The child in the front seat passes the eraser back as before and the play continues until the player who was in the front seat at the beginning is back in it again. The row wins which accomplishes this first.

Beanbag Backward-Passing Relay.—Stand the players of alternate rows at the right side of their seats. The other rows remain seated and compete in the second race. The front player of each row holds a beanbag in both hands. At the signal the player raises the beanbag overhead with both hands and drops it to the floor; the second player picks it up and repeats. When the last player gets the bag he runs down the aisle to the left of the seats and takes his place at the head of the line and repeats the passing. The other players move back to make room. The team wins which first brings the original first player of each row back to the head of the line.

Hurly-Burly Beanbag Relay.—The players are seated in their seats. A beanbag is placed on each front seat. At the signal each front player takes the bag and tosses it up and back over his head. The player behind him must clap his hand after the bag is thrown and then catch it or pick it up and do the same with it. The rear player, on getting it, hops down the aisle to the front of the room and there executes some movement previously agreed upon; while he is doing this all the other players move back one seat. When he has finished the movement the player from the rear takes the front seat and begins as at first. This continues until the player who was in the front seat reaches it again and puts the bag on the desk as in the beginning. The row doing this first wins.

Overhead Relay

Playground, Gymnasium, Club   *Late Elementary School to Adults*

This relay is adapted to a small space. Divide the players into teams of from six to twelve players each and arrange them in parallel files, facing front. Draw lines on the floor marking the position of the front and rear players. Give the front player of each team a ball. At a signal the ball is passed back over the heads of the players; the rear player on getting it runs forward on the right side of his team, takes his place at the front, and at once begins the same play. This continues until the player who was in front at first comes to the same place again and holds the ball up. The team doing this first wins. It is a foul if any player fails to handle the ball in his turn, if any player who drops the ball does not himself get it and pass it on from his place in the row, or if end players do not stand on the floor lines.

Variation.—Arrange the players so that the starting line is thirty to fifty feet from a wall, or, if outdoors, draw a turning line thirty feet in front of the starting line. When the ball has been passed back to the end man, he runs to the wall or line, then back to his position at the front of the line, and starts the ball back again.

Over-and-Under Relay, Number 1.—Arrange the teams as in the Overhead Relay and space the players at arm's length apart. At the signal the first player of each team passes the ball back over his head to the second player, who passes it back between his legs to the third, the third player over his head to the fourth, and so on. When the last man gets the ball he runs to the head of the line and starts the ball back again. The team wins that first returns the original player to the head of the line.

When possible establish a turning line and use the longer run as described in the preceding variation.

Over-and-Under Relay, Number 2.—At the signal the ball is passed backward over the head until the last player receives it; the last player then runs to the front of the line and starts the ball back by passing it between the legs. The method of passing thus alternates between overhead and between the legs. The team wins which first brings the original front player back to the front again.

Stride Ball-Rolling Relay

Playground, Gymnasium, Club   Late Elementary School to Adults

Arrange the teams in parallel files and have the players stand at stride with the legs widely spread. Give the first player of each team a ball. A wand or baseball bat may be substituted for the ball. At the signal the first player rolls the ball or slides the bat back between the row of legs. The last player takes the ball or bat, runs to the turning line and returns, taking his position at the head of the line. He then rolls the ball back between his legs and those of the others of the team. Continue until all have run and the original player at the head of the line is back in that position. The team finishing first wins.

Stride Ball-Passing Relay.—Same as above, except that the ball or bat is passed back between the legs from player to player. Each player must handle the ball or bat, and not allow it to touch the floor.

Variation for Small Space.—If there is not enough space for the distance run, it may be eliminated. The last player, upon obtaining the ball or bat, runs to the head of the line and rolls the ball or slides the bat back. Played in this way, the relay may be used in a small room.

Pass-and-Run Relay

Playground, Gymnasium, Club   *Late Elementary School to Adults*

Divide the group into two teams and line them up in two ranks facing each other about twenty feet apart. The players stand abreast with about two feet of space between them. Definitely mark the spots where the end players must stand; the end players must keep one foot on this spot.

Give a ball or stick to one of the end players of each team. At the signal this player passes the ball or stick to the next player and the passing is continued until the player at the other end gets it. This player then runs entirely around the opposing team and back to the head of his line, where the passing is started again. The play continues until the players are back in their original positions again. The team that finishes first wins.

Chair-Passing Relay

Gymnasium, Club   *Late Elementary School to Adults*

This contest is suitable when space is limited and is excellent also for sociable occasions.

Divide the group into two teams and arrange them in two ranks facing each other. Give the end player of each team a chair. At the signal the chair is passed from player to player down the line; when the last player receives it he sits on it, raises his feet and knocks them together three times, picks the chair up and runs with it to the other end, sits down again and knocks his feet together three times, and then passes the chair down the line again. When the last player in the line gets it, he repeats. Continue until the players are in their original positions again. The team finishing first wins.

Variation.—As the chair is handed to each player, he sits on it and knocks his feet together three times, then stands and hands it to the next player. The relay is over when the chair reaches the end of the line.

Tadpole

Playground, Gymnasium, Club   *Late Elementary to Senior High School*

Arrange one team in a circle and the other in a file with the first player of the file within three feet of the circle as in Figure 28. Give a ball to the player in the circle who stands nearest the file. At the signal the ball is passed from player to player around the circle—it must make as many trips around the circle as there are players on the team. At the same time the first player in the file runs around the circle and back and touches off the second player, who repeats. Continue until all in the file have run. The players in the file are thus racing the ball as it is passed around the circle. The team wins which finishes first.

Since the ball can normally be passed more rapidly than the runner can run, it is well to specify a type of pass which will slow up the passing,

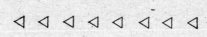

FIGURE 28.

such as a bounce pass. If a player fumbles the ball, he must secure it and return to position before passing it on. After a game or two the teams should be reversed.

OBJECT-PASSING RELAYS IN *SOCIAL GAMES FOR RECREATION*

See Chapter VI, "Social Relays and Group Contests," and Chapter XVIII, "Picnic and Outing Activities."

CHAPTER XVI

THROWING RELAYS

THESE relays are based upon throwing objects from player to player. Relays of this type are not only interesting and popular in themselves but provide excellent practice in handling a football or basketball and are thus valuable as lead-up and practice events for Football and Basketball.

The throwing relays are of two types: (1) those involving throwing only; (2) those involving both throwing and running.

RELAYS INVOLVING THROWING ONLY

In this group of relays, the competition centers around throwing and nothing else—there is no running.

Zigzag Ball-Passing Relay

Playground, Gymnasium, Club   Late Elementary to Senior High School

Arrange the players in zigzag formation; any one of the three methods illustrated in Figure 29 may be used, but if space permits, Method B will probably be found most acceptable. Give the first player a basketball or football. At the signal the ball is passed from player to player; when the end player gets it he immediately starts it back. The team wins which first gets the ball to the first player. If a player fails to catch the ball, he must recover it and return with it to position before throwing.

Variation.—The ball must be bounced once in passing it to the next player.

Variation.—The ball is rolled instead of thrown.

Variation.—The ball is passed by use of the center-pass of Football.

Variation.—Specify any of the specific passes of Basketball.

Throwing Shuttle Relay

Playground, Gymnasium, Club   Late Elementary to Senior High School

Arrange the teams as in the Shuttle Relay (Figure 26), with the sections fifty to sixty feet apart.

A softball, basketball, or football may be used, depending on the skill to be developed. Player Number 1 throws the ball to Number 2, who

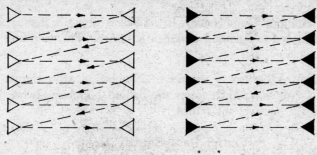

METHOD "A"

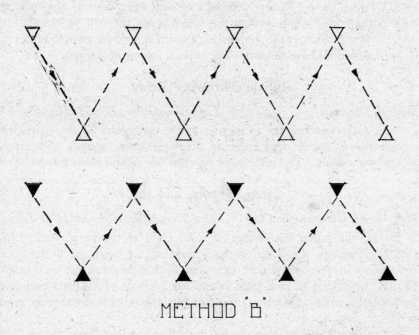

METHOD "B"

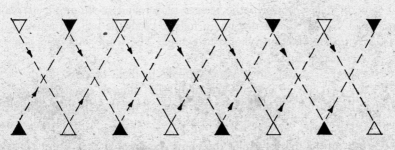

METHOD "C"

FIGURE 29.

throws to Number 3, and so on. If the ball is dropped, it must be recovered and returned to position before being thrown. The team finishing first wins.

Variation.—Number 1 throws to Number 2, who throws back to Number 1, Number 1 then tosses the ball to Number 3 who throws to Number 4 and receives the return.

Center-Pass Shuttle Relay

Playground   *Late Elementary to Senior High School*

Arrange the teams as in the Shuttle Relay (Figure 26), with about ten yards between them. Player Number 1 of each team assumes the snapper-back position of football and at the signal snaps the ball to Number 2, who catches it, assumes the snapper-back position, and passes to Number 3. Continue until all have thrown. The team finishing first wins.

Infield Throwing Relay

Baseball Diamond   *Late Elementary to Senior High School*

Four players occupy the four bases of the diamond. At the signal the catcher throws to the first baseman, who throws to second, and so on around the circuit. The time is taken, then the second team throws.

Catch, Throw, and Sit

Playground, Gymnasium, Club   *Late Elementary to Senior High School*

Divide the group into teams of from eight to twelve players. Line each team against the walls of the gymnasium or room, or if outdoors, form them in a hollow square facing in so that they can see each other. Station the captain of each team fifteen feet in front of his team and give each captain a ball. Mark a three-foot circle in which the captain must keep one foot.

At the signal each captain throws his ball to the first player to the right of the line, who catches it, throws it back, and then sits down on the floor; the captain then throws to the second player and so on until all players are seated. If any player or captain fails to catch the ball, he must recover it and return to position before throwing. The team wins which has all its players seated first.

Use the ball that is in season—softball, football, or basketball.

When the players are familiar with the contest, specify the type of throw: the various basketball passes, bounce throws, football center-pass, and so forth.

Catch and Throw.—Like the above except that the sitting feature is eliminated.

Catch, Throw, and Squat.—Arrange the teams in parallel files. Station the captain of each team fifteen or twenty feet in front of his team, and facing it. Mark a three-foot circle in which the captain must keep one foot. At the signal the captain throws the ball to the first player who catches it, throws it back to the captain and sits down; the captain then throws over the head of the sitting first player to the second player, who repeats. Continue until all are sitting. The team finishing first wins.

Variation for Schoolroom.—The players stand in the aisles beside their seats with the captains standing ten to fifteen feet in front of their rows. When each player receives and returns the ball, he sits down in his seat.

Ten Trips

Playground, Gymnasium, Club   Late Elementary to Senior High School

Three players constitute a team. A basketball, volleyball, or softball may be used. Station the three players on each team in line, each player thirty to forty feet from the next. The players stand in this order: 1—2—3. Give the ball to Number 2, who acts as captain. At the signal the ball is thrown in this order: 2—1—3—1—2. This constitutes one trip and upon receiving the ball at the end of the trip, the captain calls "One." Continue until the ball has made ten trips. The throwing is continuous—there is no intermission or hesitation between the trips. The team wins that completes the ten trips first.

Overtake Relay

Playground, Gymnasium, Club   Late Elementary to Senior High School

This relay is well adapted to a small playing space. Arrange the players in a circle and have them count off by two's. The one's play against the two's. One team should be marked by a colored sash, a handkerchief around arm, or some other way that will make players easily distinguishable. Select a captain for each team and station him near the center of the circle. Give each captain a ball. Designate a player of Captain Number 1's team for him to pass the ball to, and directly opposite this player, designate a player of Captain Number 2's team for him to throw to. At the signal each captain tosses the ball to the designated player who immediately passes it back. The captain then throws to the next player of his team to the left, who passes it back. The ball is thus passed to each member of the team in turn, and tossed back, going around the circle clockwise. The throwing continues until one team's ball passes the other—this team is the winner.

Variation.—Instead of designating players on opposite sides of the circle to start the game, designate two opposing players standing side by side. One captain passes the ball around the circle as described above, going clockwise, while the other captain passes going counterclockwise. The team wins that gets the ball back to the starting player first.

RELAYS COMBINING THROWING AND LOCOMOTION

In these relays the throwing of balls or other objects is combined with running or some other type of locomotion.

Run-and-Throw Relay

Playground, Gymnasium   *Late Elementary to Senior High School*

Arrange the teams behind the starting line in parallel files. Thirty to sixty feet in front of the starting line establish a finish line. Give the first player of each team a basketball, volleyball, or softball. At the signal Number 1 runs to the finish line, turns, and throws the ball to player Number 2, who runs to the finish line and throws to Number 3. Having thrown, Number 2 lines up behind Number 1. This continues until the last player crosses the finish line. If a player fumbles the ball, he must recover it and return to the starting line before beginning his run to the finish line. The team wins which finishes first.

Variation.—Line the teams in file behind the end line of the basketball court, with player Number 1 of each team standing on the center line of the court. Number 1 throws the ball to Number 2, turns, and runs to the far end of the court. Number 2, after receiving the ball, throws it to Number 1 at the far end, and then runs to the center line. Number 1 then throws the ball to Number 2 and remains at the far end. Number 2, on receiving the ball, throws to Number 3 to repeat. Continue until all are lined up behind Number 1 at the far end.

Beanbag Run-and-Throw Relay.—The turning line should be twenty to forty feet distant. Give the first player of each team three beanbags. At the signal the first player runs to the turning line and throws the beanbags, one after the other, to the second player, who catches them and repeats. If the catcher has to run to catch or pick up the bags, he must return to the starting line before beginning to run. The team with all across the turning line first, wins.

Beanbag Target Relay

Playground, Gymnasium, Club   *Elementary School*

Arrange the players of each team in file formation, one behind the other. Ten feet in front of each team draw a twelve-inch circle on the floor. Give the first player of each team three beanbags. At the signal, the first player tosses the bags, one after the other, attempting to put them in the circle. The team is credited with one point for each bag resting in the circle or on the line. Immediately after the last bag is thrown the first player runs forward, gathers the bags and gives them to the second player, and then goes to the end of the line. When all have thrown the team is declared the winner which has the highest score, determined by adding the individual scores of each player plus three, two, or one for finishing first, second, or third.

Pass-and-Toss Relay

Playground, Gymnasium   *Late Elementary to Senior High School*

Divide the group into teams of ten to twenty players each. Then divide each team into two halves and place the two halves in lines facing each other and ten feet apart. The first player of one line has a ball. At the signal, the ball is passed as rapidly as possible from player to player of that line. When the last player gets it, he tosses it across to the opposite player of the other line and immediately crosses over and stands beside that player. The ball is passed up the second line and when the end player gets it he throws it across to the opposite player and crosses over after passing. The lines keep moving to make room for the players who cross. Continue until the player who had the ball at first gets it again after he has moved entirely around and back to his original place. The team completing the relay first wins. The ball must be handled by every player, or a foul should be called.

Variation.—Use two balls, starting the second ball at the rear end of the second line at the same time the first ball leaves the front end of the first line.

Corner Spry

Playground, Gymnasium, Club   *Elementary and Junior High Schools*

Divide the group into four teams and place one team in each corner, players in file, and facing the center. The four team captains stand in the center of the floor facing their groups, each having a ball or beanbag. At the signal each captain tosses the ball to the first player of his team, who returns it to the captain, and steps to one side. The captain then throws to the second player who throws back and then steps behind the first player. It is passed in this way to all the players, and when it reaches the last one, the captain calls "Corner Spry," at which the first player runs out and becomes captain, all the players move up one place, and the former captain takes the last place. Each player thus is captain in turn, and each tosses the bag to all the players before calling "Corner Spry." The team whose original captain comes to the captain's position and receives the ball first, after all the members of his team have served as captain, wins the contest.

Over-the-Top Relay

Playground, Gymnasium, Club   *Late Elementary to Senior High School*

Arrange the teams in parallel files. Midway between the starting line and turning line stretch a volleyball net or rope across the floor, about eight feet high. Give the first player on each team a basketball or volleyball. At the signal he runs to the net, throws the ball over it, runs under the net, catches the ball, runs to the turning line, returns, throwing the ball over the net again, and gives the ball to the second player who repeats. If the runner fails to catch the ball, he must return to the side of the net from which the ball was thrown and throw again. Continue until all have run. The team finishing first wins.

Bowling Relay

Gymnasium, Club   *Late Elementary and Junior High Schools*

Arrange the teams in parallel files. The turning line should be about forty feet from the starting line. Opposite each team, place three Indian clubs on the turning line, arranged in a row at right angles to the teams, the clubs being one foot apart. The first player rolls a basketball or volleyball, attempting to knock down the clubs. He immediately runs and gets the ball and carries it back to the second person on his team, who has moved up to the starting line. The game continues until one team has bowled down all their clubs. The first team to bowl down the clubs scores one point. All the clubs are then set up and the contest starts again, with the next player in order bowling first.

Tunnel-Rolling Relay

Playground, Gymnasium, Club   *Late Elementary and Junior High Schools*

The teams are arranged in parallel files. Station one player on the turning line directly opposite each team; have him stand at stride with feet widely spread. Fifteen to twenty feet out from the turning line mark a line on the floor. Give the first player of each team a basketball or volleyball.

At the signal the first player runs to the line, stops and rolls the ball, attempting to put it through the legs of the player at stride. Whether he succeeds or not, he runs to the turning line, recovers the ball, returns to starting line and hands it to the second player, who repeats. To determine the winner, one point is awarded a team for each time the ball was rolled through the legs of the player at stride, plus three points for finishing first, two for finishing second, and one for finishing third. The team with the highest score wins.

Center Run

Playground, Gymnasium   *Late Elementary to Senior High School*

Divide the groups into two teams and arrange each in a circle. Number the players around the circle. Preferably there should be an odd number of players. Give player Number 1 of each team a basketball. At the signal Number 2 runs into the center of the circle and catches a pass from Number 1. Number 2 then immediately throws the ball to Number 3. As soon as Number 3 gets the ball, Number 4 runs into the center, receives the ball, and passes it to Number 5, and so on. In this way the ball is passed around the circle, and play continues until it has made four complete circuits. When the ball reaches player Number 1 after making the first circuit, Number 1 calls "One"; when it reaches him the second time, he calls "Two," and so on. The team wins that completes the four circuits first.

Basketball Pass-and-Shoot Relay

Playground, Gymnasium   *Junior High School to College*

A basketball goal is needed. At the opposite end of the court from the goal, line up the teams in file formation with the players one behind the other. Give the first player in each team a basketball. The players run in pairs. At the signal the first two players of each team run toward the goal, passing the ball back and forth between themselves, following all the rules of making progress in Basketball. A player must not run with the ball in his possession. Reaching the vicinity of the basket, each player is given one attempt to throw for it, then they return as before to the starting line, and hand the ball to the next two players. A team scores one point for each goal made and one point for finishing first; one point is subtracted for each progress foul made. The team with the highest score wins.

Basketball Dribble Relay

Playground, Gymnasium   *Junior High School to College*

A basketball goal is needed. The teams are lined up in file formation at the opposite end of the court from the goal. Give the first player in each line a basketball. At the signal the first player advances by dribbling the ball, following all the rules governing dribbling in Basketball. Nearing the goal, he makes one attempt to make it, then dribbles back to the starting line, and hands the ball to the next player who repeats. One point is scored for each goal made and one point for finishing first; one point is deducted for each dribbling foul made. The team with the highest score wins.

Variation.—Same as the above except that each contestant continues to shoot for the basket until he makes it, before returning to touch off the next runner.

Basketball Run-and-Shoot Relay

Playground, Gymnasium   *Junior High School to College*

Arrange two teams in parallel files behind the end line of the basketball court and under the basket, with one player of each team (thrower) stationed behind the center line. At the signal, the thrower of each team throws to the first player, who runs out to receive the throw, and immediately turns and shoots for the basket. He then recovers the ball and throws it to the thrower, who passes it to the second player. Continue until all have thrown. Score one point for each basket made plus one for finishing first.

This relay may be varied by placing the teams at various positions in relation to the basket.

The contest may also be conducted by having player Number 1 of each team run out, receive the pass from the thrower and shoot, retrieve the ball, and then take the position of the thrower. The thrower then goes to the end of the team. After Number 2 shoots for the basket he becomes the thrower.

PART III

GOAL, TAG, AND COMBAT GAMES

CHAPTER XVII

GOAL GAMES

IN these games competition centers around getting possession of, or reaching a goal or base. In some games there are many goals but always at least one less than the number of players. In others there is a common goal. The goal games are divided into three groups, varying much in the degree of activity.

GROUP I

In this group of goal games only two or three players are active at a time, while the others stand and look on.

Skip Away

(Filling the Gap)

Playground, Gymnasium   •   *Elementary School*

Arrange all the players except one in a circle, close together and facing in. The extra player, "it," is outside the circle. "It" runs around the circle and tags some player on the back. "It" immediately turns around and runs in the opposite direction around the circle. The player touched runs around the circle in the direction opposite to that taken by "it." The player who first reaches the gap steps into it and wins. The other player becomes "it" for the next play. Players should be cautioned to avoid collisions as they pass each other. The passing should always be to the right.

Swing Around.—When the running players meet on the opposite side of the circle from the gap they hook elbows, swing each other around, and then continue in their original direction to the gap. This is a more satisfactory game than the preceding, in that it avoids the danger of collision.

Good Morning.—This variation is suitable for younger players. When the runners meet on the opposite side of the circle from the gap, they stop, shake hands, bow and say "Good Morning," repeating these courtesies three times, and then continue in their original directions to the gap.

Hop Away.—Played exactly like Skip Away, except that the runners hop on one foot.

Run for Your Supper.—The players are arranged in a circle. One player who is chosen by the teacher goes around inside, holds out his hands between two players and says, "Run for your supper." The two run around the outside of the circle in opposite directions; the one who first returns to the vacant place wins, and may start the next runners. The game may be varied by skipping, walking, galloping, flying, and so forth, instead of running.

Partner Skip Away (Flying Dutchman).—All players except two stand in a circle, facing in, arranged in pairs, each pair holding hands. The odd pair is "it." "It" runs around the circle and tags the joined hands of one of the pairs in the circle. "It" immediately turns around and runs around the circle in the opposite direction. The pair tagged runs around the circle in the direction opposite to that taken by "it." The pair reaching the vacant space first wins. The other pair becomes "it."

Three Around.—Arrange all but one player in a double circle, facing in, the rear players directly behind the front players and four feet back. The odd player, "it," runs around the outer circle to the right and tags a player, then turns and runs around the circle in the opposite direction. The tagged player immediately tags the player in front of him and the two run around the circle between the two lines, the rear man to the right and the front man to the left. The last of the three runners to reach the vacant space is "it" for the next game.

Four Around.—Arrange a triple circle, thus causing four to run at once.

Circle-Zigzag
(*Circle Weaving Race*)

Playground, Gymnasium   *Late Elementary and Junior High Schools*

Arrange all but one player in a circle, three feet apart and facing in. The extra player, "it," stands outside the circle. "It" runs around the circle to the right, and slaps a player on the back. "It" then darts inside the circle and starts back around the circle in the reverse direction, weaving in and out, passing in front of the first player, in back of the second, in front of the third, and so forth. The man tagged weaves around the circle in a similar fashion in the direction opposite to that taken by "it." When they meet they stop, step inside, grasp hands and spin each other around once, then continue weaving around the circle. The runner reaching the gap first wins. The loser becomes "it."

Team Circle-Zigzag.—Divide the players into two teams and arrange them alternately in a circle, facing in and three feet apart. Designate two opposing players who are standing side by side to start the game. On a signal they run in opposite directions, weaving in and out around the circle. When they meet they join hands and spin each other around once as in Circle-Zigzag. They then continue weaving around the circle until they reach the vacant gap. The player reaching it first scores one point for his team. Then the next two players run. The game continues until all have run. The team with the most points wins.

Spoke Tag

Playground, Gymnasium, Club   *Elementary School*

This game is acceptable when space is limited as is often the case in a clubroom.

Divide the players into groups of five to eight and arrange them as in the spokes of a wheel (Figure 27, page 164). There is one extra player who is "it." "It" goes around the circle and slaps one of the end men on the back. The end man then hits the man in front of him and so the slap is passed until the end man at the hub end is hit. He calls "Hip" and all the players of the group then run around the circle to the right outside of the players, and attempt to get back into their original positions. "It" also attempts to get into one of the positions, and the player left without a place is "it" for the next game. No player in the line may start until the word "Hip" is called.

The Beater Goes Round

Playground, Gymnasium   *Late Elementary School to Adults*

Arrange all the players except one in a circle, facing in with their hands behind their backs. Give the extra player a knotted handkerchief or small knotted hand towel. He goes around the circle and places the handkerchief in a player's hand. The player immediately swats the player on his right and chases him around the circle, beating him as often as possible until he gets back to his starting place. The player holding the swatter then gives it to someone else. When the extra player hands the swatter to a player, he steps into the place the player vacates.

Variation for Schoolroom.—The players are seated in their seats with eyes closed and hands held behind the back. A player with a knotted handkerchief goes up and down the aisles on tiptoe and drops the handkerchief in some player's hand. The player receiving the handkerchief at once begins to beat the player in front of him between the shoulders with it. The one hit jumps up and runs around the room to escape and the beater chases him and hits him as often as he can until the runner has regained his own seat. The beater then goes around on tiptoe, puts the handkerchief in another player's hands, and the game goes on.

Bulldog and Master

Playground, Gymnasium   *Early Elementary School*

Designate one player as "bulldog" and one as "master." The others stand in a row facing the master. The bulldog chooses a color, which he whispers to the master, so the others cannot hear. The master then gives the children turns in guessing the color. When a child guesses it, the master says, "Chase the bulldog," and the child who guessed the color chases the bulldog. When he catches him, he must get back and touch the master's hand before the bulldog does. If successful he is the new master and the master is the new bulldog and the game goes on as before. If the bulldog gets back to the master without being caught, he is the new master and the master is the new bulldog.

Mailman [1]

Gymnasium, Club, Party   *Elementary School to Adults*

The players are standing or seated in a circle. Each chooses the name of a post office, which may be that of any city. One player stands in the center and is the mailman. He asks each one in order what post office he represents, and they must answer. He then calls the name of two or three post offices and the players having those names must change places. If the mailman can get a place during the exchange the one left out must be the mailman. If the players do not change places promptly the mailman may count ten, and any player who has not then left his place forfeits it, and must change places with the mailman.

Hopping Numbers-Change

Playground, Gymnasium   *Late Elementary and Junior High Schools*

This is a more strenuous variation of the social games of Numbers-Change. Arrange the players in a circle and number them. Select an "it," and have him stand in the center of the circle. "It" calls the numbers of three of the players and the players holding the numbers change places by hopping on one foot. "It," hopping on one foot, attempts to get to one of the vacant places. If he succeeds the player without a place becomes "it"; if he fails, he remains "it."

Catch-the-Cane

Playground, Gymnasium, Club   *Elementary School to Adults*

Arrange the players in a compact circle not more than fifteen feet in diameter. Number the players. Select an "it," give him a three-foot stick or baseball bat, and place him in the center. "It" sets the stick upright on the floor and steadies it by placing his finger on top. He calls a number and the player holding that number darts for the stick attempting to catch it before it hits the floor. In the meantime "it" takes the player's position

---

[1] There are a number of social games usable for all ages which are very similar to this, such as Numbers Change, Postman, and Fruit Basket. These are described in *Social Games for Recreation.*

in the circle. If the player succeeds, he returns to his position and "it" holds the stick again. If he fails, he becomes "it."

Variation.—If the player whose number is called, fails to catch the stick he has one point scored against him. Whether he succeeds or fails he holds the stick next time. A player having three points scored against him must pay a forfeit.

Mathematical Catch-the-Cane.—Have the players number off. "It" calls a simple problem to indicate the number such as "Six plus three" or "Three times three." The player indicated (Number 9 in this case) runs for the cane.

Spin-the-Platter.—Same as the above except that a kettle cover is spun on the floor instead of using the stick.

Catch-the-Balloon.—Same as the above except that "it" drops a toy balloon as he calls the number instead of holding the stick. The player must catch the balloon before it touches the floor.

GROUP II

All players are active in this group of goal games.

Hunter

Schoolroom   *Early Elementary School*

The players are seated in their seats. A leader is selected who walks around the room and says, "Who would like to hunt rabbits with me?" (The leader names any animal he chooses.) The players fall in line behind him and follow him. When all are marching, the leader calls "Bang" and all rush for their own seats. The first one in his seat may be the leader for the next game.

Squirrels in Trees

Playground, Gymnasium   *Early Elementary School*

Have three players stand so as to represent a hollow tree, facing center with hands on each other's shoulders; have a fourth player stand within to represent a squirrel. Have the other players notice how this is done and then have them all form groups of four in the same way. There must be one extra player who is a squirrel without a tree. On the signal, all the squirrels must change trees and the homeless squirrel tries to get to a tree. This leaves another squirrel out and the game is repeated. After a few plays, have each squirrel choose one of the players of the tree to change places with him, so as to give all a chance to be squirrels. When the numbers are small, circles or other marks on the floor may represent trees.

Puss-in-the-Corner

Playground, Gymnasium   *Early Elementary School*

Each player except one has a goal. It may be a mark, chair, stick, other object, or a corner. The one who has no goal goes up to another player and says, "Pussy wants a corner." The answer is "Ask the next door neighbor." During this time the others, by sly beckonings, change goals, and the odd player tries to get one. When he has tried several times without success he may go to the center of the space and call, "All change," and all must change goals, giving him a better chance. The one left out is "it" and the game begins as before.

Ball Puss-in-the-Corner.—"It" is provided with a soft ball. He may secure a corner either by running to one as above, or by hitting a player with the ball as he is changing goals. In the latter case, "it" takes the hit player's goal.

The First of May

(*Moving Day*)

Schoolroom   *Early Elementary School*

Two adjacent rows play the game together. The first of May is moving time, and the seats are houses. The houses not occupied are haunted and are marked by placing a book on them; they thus become permanently unoccupied. There must at all times be one more player than houses. The player without a house is "it." He walks up and down the street between the two rows. The residents along the street change houses before and behind him and he tries to get a house while it is vacated. Whenever he chooses "it" may call "The first of May," whereupon all players must change houses immediately.

Poison Seat.—The players are seated at their desks. Place a book on each unoccupied desk and on one occupied desk. The book marks the desk as poisoned and it cannot be occupied. At the signal all players change seats and the one failing to obtain a seat goes to the front of the room. A book is placed on another occupied seat and the game is repeated. Continue until all but two are eliminated. These are winners.

Music Rush

Playground, Gymnasium   *Elementary School*

Mark as many places on the floor as there are players, less one, these marks being in four groups in different parts of the floor or play area. If there is a piano it may be used. When the music begins all the players follow the odd player in a march about the center of the room; when the music stops, all rush for the marked places. The one left out is leader next time. Chairs may be used in place of floor marks if they are available.

The leader may give the signals when music is not to be had, or the players may sing as they march, rushing for the goals when the last word is sung.

Variation for Schoolroom.—The leader leads the marching line up and down the aisles. When the music stops all rush for a seat. Mark the seats which are not to be used by placing books on them.

Snatch a Club.—Give all players but one an Indian club and arrange the players in a circle. The odd man, "it," stands in the center. The players set their clubs on the floor in front of them. They then march around the circle to music, the clapping of hands, or the beating of a stick on the floor. When the music stops, all players including "it" try to snatch a club. The one who fails becomes "it" for the next game.

The Ocean is Stormy.—All players except two are arranged in pairs, holding hands, and scattered about the playing area. Each pair draws a three-foot circle around its position. Each pair secretly selects the name of a fish. The odd players, known as sharks, hold hands and walk around the area calling the names of fish. When the name of a fish which has been adopted by a pair is called, that pair falls in behind the sharks and marches after them. When the sharks have called all the fish they can think of, they say, "The ocean is stormy," at which all run for the empty circles. The pair failing to secure a circle become the sharks for the next game.

Change All.—Arrange all the players except one in a circle, facing in and four feet apart. Each player marks his position by drawing a circle or digging a hole. Draw a small circle in the exact center of the playing circle to be occupied by the odd player who is "it." "It" calls "Change all," whereupon all players exchange goals. Players are not allowed to take a position immediately to their right or left. During the exchange, "it" tries to get possession of one of the positions. The player left without a position not only becomes "it" but has one point scored against him. The game continues until some player has three points scored against him, when he must pay a forfeit.

Come With Me

(Come Along)

Playground, Gymnasium   *Elementary School*

Arrange all players except one in a circle, facing in, about three feet apart. Each player marks his spot with a chalk mark on the floor, or by a stone or hole. The players sit behind their marks. The odd player, "it," has a stick and walks around inside the circle. He taps his stick in front of a player and says, "Come along," whereupon the player falls in behind "it" and places his hands on "its" shoulders. This continues until "it" has as many following him as he desires. He then calls "Going home" and all dash for a vacant place. The player failing to secure a place is "it" for the next game.

Variation.—Arrange the circle of players as before but have them face to the right and hold their right arm out to the side. "It" goes around outside the circle and grabs a player by the arm, saying "Come along." The player falls in behind the leader and grabs a third player. When several are in line, the leader says "Go home" and all dash for the vacant places.

The Boiler Burst—Goal Form [2]

Schoolroom, Club, Party   *Elementary School*

All players except one are seated, there being one less seat than the number of players. The odd man, "it," stands in front and tells a story. At the most exciting moment he says, "And then the boiler burst," whereupon all players change seats and "it" attempts to secure a seat for himself. The player left without a seat tells the next story.

Grab a Partner

Gymnasium, Club, Party   *Early Elementary School*

All players, except one, pair up in couples and form a circle, facing right, with three or four feet between the couples. The extra player, "it," stands in the center. The music starts and the players march around the circle. When the music stops, every player on the inner side must move forward and join the outside player of the next couple ahead. The one who is "it," tries to get a place. He must not leave the center till the music stops. The one left out must go in the center for the next play. When no music is available, the leader may clap his hands.

Merry-Go-Round.—Arrange all players except one in a double circle, the inside line facing to the right, and the outside line to the left. The two lines then march in opposite directions. The odd player stands in the center. On a signal or when music stops, all stop marching and with right hand grasp the right hand of a partner; the odd player tries to get a partner. The one left out goes in the center the next time.

Forest Lookout.—Arrange all the players except one in a double circle, facing in. The inside players are trees and the outside players stand directly behind the trees. The odd man is the fire warden and takes his place in the circles. The fire warden says, "Fire in the mountain, Run, Run, Run," and claps his hands. The players in the outside circle begin

[2] There are many social games usable for all ages which are very similar to this game, such as Fumble, Stage Coach, and Going to Jerusalem. These are described in *Social Games for Recreation.*

running to the left. Suddenly the fire warden stops clapping and dashes *in front* of a tree, and the runners do likewise. The runner who fails to find a tree becomes fire warden and the trees are now runners.

Vis-a-Vis.—Divide all the players except one into two teams. The odd player is "it." Members of Team A choose partners from Team B, and the couples scatter. "It" calls out instructions which the others execute, such as, "Face to face," "Back to back," "Join hands," "Kneel on knees," and so forth. When he calls "Vis-a-Vis," the Team B men remain stationary and the Team A players run for a new partner. The player failing to secure a partner becomes "it." After a few exchanges, have the Team B men do the exchanging while the Team A players remain stationary.

Back-to-Back.—All players except one are arranged in couples, standing back to back with elbows locked, and scattered at random over the playing area. The odd player, "it," calls "All change," at which each player must seek a new partner and hook elbows with him, back to back. The player failing to secure a partner is "it" for the next game.

Goal Duck-on-the-Rock

Playground, Gymnasium   *Late Elementary and Junior High Schools*

This is a goal variation of the tag games of Duck-on-the-Rock and Circle Duck-on-the-Rock.

Each player is provided with a beanbag. As traditionally played by the boys, each player uses a stone, but in the circle arrangement there is an element of danger in using stones. Arrange all the players except one in a forty-foot circle and have each player mark his position, either with chalk or by digging a hole in the ground. In the center of the circle a stool or large stone is placed. The odd player, "it," places his beanbag (duck) on the large center stone or stool and takes a position just outside the circle. Each player in turn tosses or throws his beanbag at the duck, attempting to knock it off. When the duck is dislodged, all the players who have thrown, together with "it," rush to get a beanbag and return to one of the marked positions. They may pick up any beanbag and return to any position. The player failing to obtain a position becomes "it" for the next game.

Pig in the Hole

(*Kettle Drive*)

Playground   *Late Elementary and Junior High Schools*

The game is played with a small ball or other object known as the "pig." Each player is provided with a stick of the size of a cane. A hole is dug in the ground having about twice the diameter of the pig. All the players except one form a circle around the hole, the players being about ten feet from the hole. Each player in the circle digs a small hole in the ground in front of him (Figure 30).

The pig is placed in the center hole and all the players put the end of their sticks under it. At the signal, they throw the ball out, run, and put the ends of their sticks in the holes in the circle. The player failing to get a hole is the driver. He immediately attempts to knock the ball into the center hole with his stick. The other players attempt to prevent this by knocking the ball away with their sticks. The driver may attempt, when he sees the opportunity, to put the end of his stick in one of the holes in the circle, and if he succeeds, the owner of that hole becomes driver. The players may leave their holes at will to knock the ball away from the center hole, but are liable to lose possession of their circle hole in so doing. A vacant hole may be taken by any player. The pig may not be kicked or played in any way except with the stick. If the driver succeeds in putting the pig in the hole, the game starts over again.

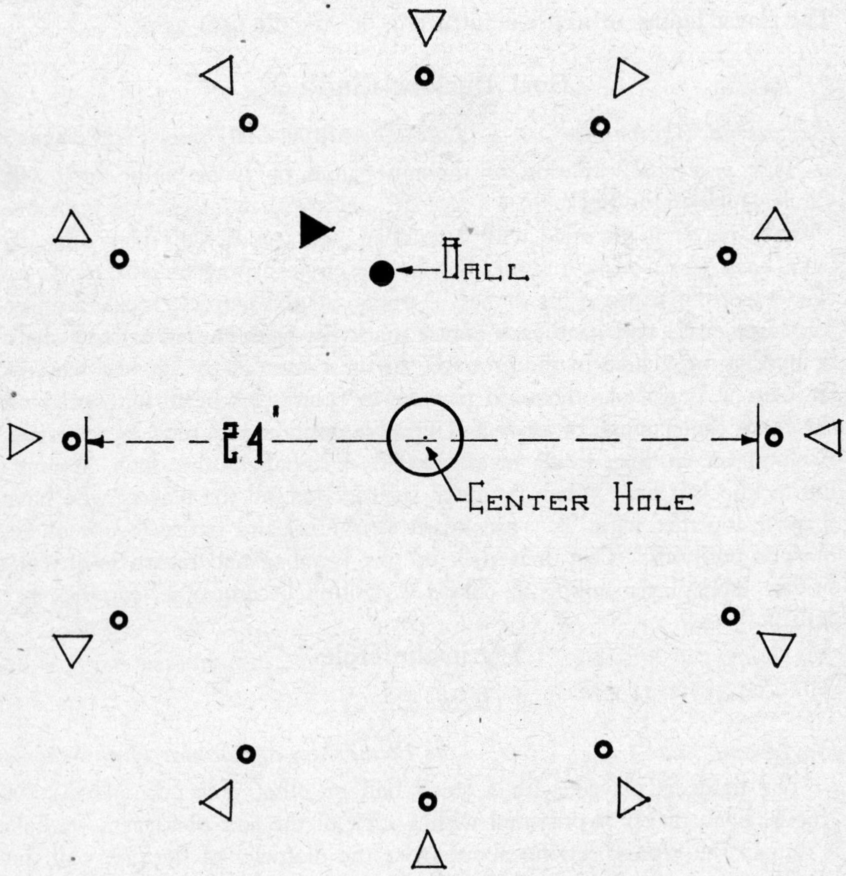

FIGURE 30.

Goal Circle-Ball

Playground, Gymnasium   *Late Elementary and Junior High Schools*

Select one player as "it" and arrange the remaining players in a double circle, the rear players standing directly behind the front. "It" stands in the center. Give the inner circle a basketball. The players of the inner circle pass the ball among themselves, and as soon as a player passes it he immediately changes places with the player behind him. While this exchange is taking place, "it" attempts to get into one of the places. If he succeeds the player left without a position becomes "it." Also, if a player is responsible for the ball hitting the floor, he exchanges places with "it."

Club Rush

Playground, Gymnasium   *Late Elementary and Junior High Schools*

Place a row of Indian clubs or dumbbells near one end of the gymnasium and line the players up in a single rank at the opposite end. There should be one less club than players.

At the signal the players dash for the clubs and attempt to secure one. The player failing is out of the game. Remove one club and repeat. Continue until only one player is left. This one is the winner.

Cap Rush.—Boys like to play this in the yard using caps instead of clubs.

GROUP III

These are games with a common goal. For the most part they are all games of hiding and seeking. A goal or home is chosen; one player is usually "it," and the others are given opportunity to hide in different ways. Most of the games are dramatic to a considerable degree. Counting-out rhymes are used to decide who shall be "it" the first time.

Gypsy

Playground, Woodland, Yard   *Early Elementary School*

A playing area with hiding places is necessary. Designate one spot as a goal and place all the players in it except two, one of whom is "gypsy" and the other the "mother." The gypsy hides and the mother says to her children, pointing to each in turn:

> I charge my children everyone
> To keep good house while I am gone;
> You and you, but especially you,
> Or else I'll beat you black and blue.

The mother goes a short distance away and blinds. The gypsy comes in, takes the children away, and hides each. The mother returns, finds her children gone, and goes in search of them. When all have been found and returned to the goal, all choose the gypsy for the next game.

I Spy

Playground, Yard   *Early Elementary School*

An area providing hiding places is needed. The one who is "it" covers his eyes while he counts one hundred or some other number agreed upon. Then he seeks the players who have hidden. To catch a player the one who is "it" must see him, call "I Spy ——," and tag the goal. If one can reach the goal before "it" can do so, he is free.

As frequently played by children, the games do not start over until all are captured. The captured ones assist "it" in finding the rest. The first one caught, however, becomes "it" for the next game.

Go-Stop.—This game differs from the above only in the manner of blinding. The game starts with all the players touching the goal; the one who is "it" says "Go," shuts his eyes while counting ten aloud, then calls "Stop," and opens his eyes. Anyone seen moving must come back to the goal. This is repeated until all have gotten out of sight, then the search begins and proceeds as in "I Spy."

Animal Hunt.—Establish a circular goal six feet in diameter in the center of the play area, preferably around a tree or post. Select one of the players to be "hunter"; the remaining players are "animals." The hunter blinds, counts one hundred, and calls "Coming." In the meantime the animals hide. When the hunter sees an animal he calls "I spy," and both run for the goal. If the hunter reaches the goal first, or tags the animal, the animal becomes prisoner and remains in the goal. If the animal reaches the goal first, he is free to hide again. The game continues until all but one animal is caught; this one is winner.

Run, Sheep, Run

Playground, Woodland   *Late Elementary and Junior High Schools*

This is a team game of hide and seek. Two teams are chosen, one hiding and the other blinding. The captain of each team is the shepherd and does not hide, but he hides the others. When the captain of the hiding team has his players hidden he returns to the goal and accompanies the searching team. He calls warning to the sheep as the others search, either directly or through the use of code words, previously agreed upon. When a member of the searching team sees one of the hiding team he tells his captain, who calls "Run, sheep, run," whereupon all players of both teams run for the goal.

If the hiding players are not detected and the captain of the hiding team thinks the searchers are far enough away from the goal to enable his team to reach the goal first, he calls "Run, sheep, run." The player reaching the goal first wins the game for his side. Then the other side hides, and so on.

Wolf.—This game involves tagging, but it is so much like this group of games that it is best described here. Mark out a goal six feet in diameter around a tree or post, if possible. The player who is "it" is called the "wolf," and he hides while the others all blind at the goal and count one hundred. Then they all go to hunt for him. When one sees the wolf, he shouts "Wolf," and all race for the goal. If the wolf can tag any before they reach the goal, those tagged become wolves, and go and hide along with him. The game continues until all are captured.

Bear Hunt.—This game is like the above except that "it" is called the "bear" and when a player sees "it" he cries "Bear," whereupon all, including the bear, run for the goal. All who reach it after the bear are eliminated. The game continues until all are eliminated. The last player to be eliminated wins.

Kick, Hide, and Seek

Playground, Woodland   *Late Elementary and Junior High Schools*

This game is most successful in wooded areas where hiding places are many and near at hand. Mark out a goal three feet in circumference and place a soccer ball in it. Select an "it" and assemble the players around the ball. One of the players kicks the ball as far as possible and all run and hide. "It" recovers the ball, places it in the goal, and goes in search of the players. When he sees one he calls "I spy ———," and both run for the ball. The one reaching it first kicks it and runs for a hiding place. The other player is then "it" and must return the ball and search.

While "it" is hunting the players, any player may steal into the goal and kick the ball which necessitates its return by "it" before further searching is possible. If "it" observes the player running for the ball, he may call his name and then no one but the player named or "it" himself may kick the ball.

Green Wolf (Throw the Stick, Yards Off).—Make a goal on the ground six feet in diameter, preferably around a tree or out from a wall. Lean a stick up against the tree or wall. Select one player to be "it." One of the players throws the stick as far as possible and all run and hide. "It" recovers the stick, sets it up on the goal, and sets out in search. When he sees a player he calls "I spy ———," and both "it" and the runner dash for the goal. If "it" reaches it first the player is a prisoner and must remain in the goal. If the runner reaches the goal first he throws the stick and "it" must recover the stick before further searching.

When there are prisoners in the goal, and a player is able to steal in and throw the stick, he and any one of the prisoners he may select are free to hide again. "It" replaces the stick and continues to search. The game continues until all the players are prisoners, or if time is limited "it" is considered the winner if he has half of the players in prison when the allotted time ends.

Kick the Can.—Instead of using a stick, place a tin can in the center of the goal. "It" counts one hundred while the others hide. When he spots a hider, the two rush to kick the can. In other respects the game is like the above.

Last Man Across

Playground, Gymnasium   *Late Elementary and Junior High Schools*

Mark out two goal lines about fifty feet apart. Arrange all the players behind one line. At the starting signal all the players run for the opposite goal. Players may trip, hold, or block the other players in order to retard them. The last man over the goal is eliminated. They then line up and run back. The game continues until all have been eliminated but one. This man is the winner.

Swatter Pin-Guard

Playground, Gymnasium   *Late Elementary and Junior High Schools*

In this game the goal to be reached is an Indian club. Stand the Indian club on the floor, appoint one of the players to guard it, and give him a swatter made from a knotted towel or handkerchief. The players attempt to knock the pin down with hand or foot. The guard tries to swat any player coming near the pin. Those who are hit withdraw temporarily and have one point scored against them. When a player knocks over the pin, he becomes the guard for the next game, and all eliminated players re-enter the play. A player having three points scored against him must pay a forfeit.

Team Form.—Divide the players into two groups and arrange each in twenty-five-foot circles. Stand an Indian club in the center of each circle. Have each team select a guard, giving him a swatter, and place him inside the opposing team's circle. Through strategy and decoying, the players attempt to knock down the pin with hands and feet, while the guard defends it by hitting all comers with the swatter. Those hit are eliminated. The team upsetting its pin before the opposing team upsets theirs scores one point. Play immediately stops in both circles, the guards return to their teams, and two new guards are selected. The team scoring ten points first wins. The game may be varied by giving the guard two swatters.

Hot Butter and Blue Beans

Playground, Yard   *Late Elementary and Junior High Schools*

Instead of the players hiding in this game a light wooden paddle is hidden while the players blind. "It" hides the paddle and calls "Hot butter and blue beans." The players then hunt for the paddle. When they are far away from it, "it" calls "Cold," "Colder," or "Freezing." When they get close he calls "Warm," "Warmer," or "Hot."

When a player finds the paddle he yells "Roasted," and all players run for the goal with the player with the paddle chasing and paddling all he can catch. He then hides the paddle for the next game.

GOAL GAMES IN OTHER CHAPTERS

Mounted Musical-Chairs   Mounted Hide-and-Seek

GOAL GAMES IN *SOCIAL GAMES FOR RECREATION*

Fumble   Musical-Chairs
Stage Coach   Going to Jerusalem
Blow-Out   Tire Change
Numbers Change   Compass Point Change
Scoot   Tracking the Deer
Fruit Basket   Hare and Hound Race
Flower Garden   Escaped Convict
Toy Shop   Hunting the Foxes

How Do You Like Your Neighbors?

CHAPTER XVIII

TAG GAMES

HUNTING and warfare are symbolized by tag games, the main activities being chasing and flight, ending in capture or escape. Capture is usually indicated by "tagging," which means touching with the hand; sometimes one is captured by hitting him with a thrown object, or it may be required that a runner be actually held, at least long enough to tag him three times. Most of these games are entirely individualistic, but a few involve simple cooperation.

Tagging is a characteristic feature of many games, even games of high organization such as Baseball or Football. In the games classified in this chapter as tag games, tagging and escape from being tagged is either the sole or at least the primary object of the game.

The tag games fall into six groupings according to type, organization, and complicacy. The groups are discussed and the games described below.

In most tag games the mythical "it" is something to be avoided and the players run from "it" to prevent his tagging them. In other games the mythical "it" is something to be coveted, and "it" runs away while the others attempt to tag him and thus become "it." These two types are illustrated below in Simple Tag and I Have It.

Simple Tag

Playground, Gymnasium, Home   *Elementary School*

One player is selected as "it" and chases the others who run to escape being tagged. When "it" tags one of them, that player becomes "it."

I Have It

Playground, Gymnasium, Home   *Elementary School*

This is the opposite of tag—instead of "it" chasing the others and attempting to tag one of them, he runs with the others in pursuit and attempts to keep "it" as long as possible. The player tagging him becomes "it."

GROUP I

In the games of this group, only a few players are active at once, usually only two or three who are selected by the leader. If the other players are active, it is for the purpose of helping or hindering the chaser in his efforts to capture the runner.

Fox and Farmer

Playground, Gymnasium   *Early Elementary School*

The players stand in a circle, hands at sides. The teacher appoints a farmer and a fox. The farmer tries to tag the fox. The fox runs in a zigzag manner among the players, and the farmer must follow in exactly the same path. When the farmer catches the fox, the teacher appoints two other players to be fox and farmer.

In this game a runner and a catcher are both chosen by the teacher; the catcher must go in the exact path of the runner, and the other players have only to stand and look on while the chase goes on. It is suitable for special cases where there is liability to overdo and where the teacher should control every detail of exertion.

Cat and Rat

Playground, Gymnasium   *Early Elementary School*

Arrange the players in a circle, grasping hands. One player is outside and is the cat; another is within the circle and is the rat. The cat says, "I am the cat." The rat replies, "I am the rat." The cat says, "I will catch you." The rat says, "Come, pray do." The cat then tries to tag the rat. The players assist the rat by letting him pass under arms and prevent the cat from doing so.

If it proves too difficult for the cat to tag the rat, have two cats chase the same rat. If there are forty or more players, it will be better to have two games. When the rat is caught, let those who have been running go in the circle, and choose other runners. When older children are playing the dialogue may be omitted.

Fox's Tail

(*Fox and Geese*)

Playground, Gymnasium, Club   Late Elementary and Junior High Schools

Select one player to be the fox ("it") and another to be the gander. The remaining players (geese) line up in file behind the gander, firmly grasping the shoulders of the man in front. Only the last goose in the file is eligible to be tagged. The gander attempts to keep the fox in front of him and thus protect his geese. When "it" succeeds in tagging the last man, the goose tagged becomes "it" and the fox takes the head position as gander.

The last player in the line may be required to tuck a handkerchief under his belt. He is not tagged until the handkerchief is removed.

Broncho Tag (Hook-on Tag).—This game, very similar to the above, is more suitable for older boys. Choose one player to act as "it" and divide the remaining players into groups of three. The players of each group of three stand in file, one behind the other, with arms around the waist of the one in front, thus forming a unit called the broncho. "It" tries to hook on the tail of any broncho while the bronchos try to prevent this by running and whipping around. When "it" succeeds, the head of that broncho becomes "it" for the next game.

Four-Man Circle-Chase

Small Playing Space *Elementary and Junior High Schools*

Arrange the players in a circle, facing in. Count off by fours. The leader calls a number from one to four. All players bearing the number run around outside the circle, attempting to tag the runner ahead. Runners who are tagged are eliminated from the game. Runners who tag players continue to run, attempting to tag others. Those who are not tagged before reaching their original place in the circle, step into it. Call another number and proceed as before. When all numbers have been called renumber those who remain in the circle and start over. Continue in this way until only four are left who are the winners.

The number of runners may be adjusted to the number of players— instead of using four, count off by threes, fives, or even sixes if conditions demand.

Variation.—Have the players run two or three times around the circle instead of once.

Maze Tag

Gymnasium *Late Elementary and Junior High Schools*

Arrange the players in parallel ranks, spread so that there is at least four feet of space between them. Each player stands about four feet directly behind the player in the line in front of him. A runner and a chaser are chosen. The players all face the same direction and grasp hands with those on each side. The chaser tries to tag the runner, going up and down the rows but not breaking through or going under arms. The leader aids the runner by commanding "Right face" or "Left face" at the proper time. At this command the players drop hands, face, grasp hands in the new direction, thus blocking the passage for the chaser.

If the runner is not captured in a period of one minute, the leader may assist the chaser by giving commands for turns which will make it difficult for the runner to escape. Two chasers may be used to pursue the same runner if tagging still proves difficult. Choose new runners at frequent intervals.

GROUP II

Tag games of the second type usually have but two or three players active at once, but the play is made continuous by a rule that the winner or loser of the first round shall start the next round. This furnishes added incentive to make each player do his best.

Whether the winner or loser should be "it" for the next round depends in part on the game and in part on the temper of the players. If they look upon the chance to be "it" as a privilege, and all would like to be "it," then the winner should have it, but if the position appeals to the players as a task, it should be assigned to the loser. It will be noticed that in the description of the games it is sometimes the winner and sometimes the loser who is said to be "it" for the next round, but it will often be desirable to reverse this rule to fit the inclination of the players. To make the winner "it" brings in the best players all the time, while the other plan calls out the slower and more indifferent ones. To make this group of games successful the teacher must study the problem and decide this point wisely.

Circle Chase Tag
(Slap Jack)

Playground, Gymnasium   *Elementary School*

Arrange the players in a circle with one outside who is "it." "It" runs around the circle and tags a player on the back, then turns in the opposite direction and runs around the circle. The tagged player becomes "it" and pursues the runner around the circle. If "it" tags him before he gets back to the vacant place the runner becomes "it"; if he succeeds in reaching the vacant place, he is free.

Skip Tag.—Have the players skip instead of run.

High Windows.—Arrange the players in a circle holding hands. If "it" does not succeed in tagging the runner before he makes two circuits around the circle, the players call "High windows" and raise their arms. The runner runs under arms and is safe. "It" then tags another player.

Drop the Handkerchief

Playground, Gymnasium, Yard   *Early Elementary School*

All the players except one stand in a circle facing in. The extra player is the runner. He runs around the outside of the circle and drops a handkerchief on the floor behind some player, who then becomes chaser. The chaser tries to tag the runner before he can reach the vacant place the chaser has left. Both may run around, across, or through the circle. If the chaser tags the runner, the latter is runner again; if not, the chaser becomes runner for the next game, dropping the handkerchief behind another player.

The Night Before Christmas

Schoolroom, Home, Party   *Early Elementary School*

Arrange the players in a circle. Give each player the name of something connected with the story of Santa Claus, such as sled, reindeer, snow, fur coat, chimney, Christmas tree, stocking, candy, pop corn, horn, drum, and so forth. One chosen to be "it" must stand in the center and tell a Christmas story. Whenever he mentions the name of any of these things, the one who has that name must turn around; if the name of Santa Claus is mentioned all must turn around. Any player who can be tagged by the one who is "it" before he has turned completely around, must be "it" and go on with the story. The circle must be of the right size to make this game successful.

Since the odds are against "it," the game is often more successful when played with the players seated on chairs in a circle. In this case, they stand, turn around, and sit down again.

Exchange Tag

Schoolroom   *Elementary School*

The players are seated in their seats. The one chosen to be "it" stands in front of the rows of seats. The teacher calls the names of two players who must try to exchange seats before the one who is "it" can tag either of them. The one tagged becomes "it." If neither is tagged, two other names are called with the same one "it."

Variation.—Play standing in a circle formation spread out at arm's length apart. "It" must stand in the center of the circle and not at one side when calling.

Line Tag.—Arrange the players in two lines about fifty feet apart, with "it" standing midway between them. "It" names a player in one line who immediately names a player in the opposite line. The two run for each other's places and "it" attempts to tag one of them. A player tagged becomes "it."

Have You Seen My Sheep?

Playground, Party   *Early Elementary School*

Arrange the players in a circle. One player is chosen to act as the shepherd. He goes around the outside, taps a player on the back, and asks, "Have you seen my sheep?" The player asks, "How is he dressed?" The shepherd then tells something of the dress of one of the players in the circle, such as, "He wears a blue sweater and low shoes." The player questioned tries to guess, as details are added to the description. When he guesses correctly the shepherd says "Yes" and the guesser chases the one described. Both must run on the outside of the circle. If the chaser catches the runner before the latter has returned to his place, the chaser becomes shepherd; if he does not, the runner becomes shepherd. Notice that the shepherd does not run.

This is a good game for a hot day, when something is wanted to slow up the activity.

Garden Scamp
(*Fox and Gardener*)

Playground, Gymnasium   *Elementary School*

The players form a circle, holding hands. Select one player for the "scamp" who stands inside the circle, and another for the "gardener" ("it") who goes outside the circle. The gardener walks around the circle, suddenly looks up and sees the scamp inside the circle and says, "Who let you in my garden?" whereupon the scamp replies "No one," and the chase starts. The scamp runs across the circle in and out among the players, between their legs and performs any feats he chooses, with the gardener hot on his heels, following the exact path and antics of the scamp. When he catches the scamp, the gardener joins the circle and the scamp becomes the new gardener. If the gardener fails to follow the exact course and copy the antics, the leader stops the game, and the scamp selects a new gardener.

Circle Weave-Tag.—This variation is suitable for older children. Arrange the players in a circle, facing in the same direction with their hands on the shoulders of the one in front. "It" names the player he chooses to chase. The runner weaves in and out among the players with "it" following the *exact* course of the runner. "It" is permitted to skip players only when the runner skips. When the runner is tagged he becomes "it" and names the next runner. Since slow runners will select slow runners to chase, it is wise to start the game with the faster players; otherwise they may not get a chance to play.

Variation.—The runner has the advantage in the above game and it is often difficult for "it" to catch him. It helps the game if the leader gives a signal after a moment of chasing, at which time the players in the circle may hinder the runner by obstructing his passage between them, and assist "it" by opening convenient passageways.

Variation.—Use a double circle instead of a single one. The runner weaves in and out among the players of both circles.

Animal Tag
(*Animal Chase, Zoo*)

Playground, Gymnasium   *Elementary School*

Mark out two goals about fifty feet apart. Select one player as the hunter and station him behind one goal. The opposite goal is known as the zoo—the remaining players are lined up behind it. Each player is secretly given a name of an animal. The hunter calls the name of an animal. If no one holds this name, he calls another, and so on until he hits upon one that some player has. This player runs to the opposite goal and returns. The hunter immediately runs to the zoo, turns, and attempts to tag the runner on his return trip. If the animal is tagged he becomes the hunter. Whenever a runner successfully returns to the zoo after his name was called, he is given a new animal name.

Center Base

Playground, Gymnasium   *Elementary School*

Arrange the players in a circle and place a ball or other object in the center. Choose one player to be "it." This player takes the ball and throws it to another player. The player receiving it must replace the ball in the center of the circle and then try to tag the one who is "it" before the latter can touch the ball. Either player may run around or through the circle in any direction. If the one who is "it" can touch the ball before he is caught, he may be "it" again. If he is caught, he goes in the circle and the chaser is "it."

Pass and Change

Playground, Gymnasium   *Late Elementary and Junior High Schools*

The players stand in a wide-spread circle with "it" in the center. "It" calls the names or numbers of two players and at the same time passes the ball to a third. The players named immediately dash to each other's places. The player in the circle who catches the ball throws it back quickly to "it." "It" then throws the ball at one of the players who are exchanging places. If he hits him before he reaches his new position in the circle, the running player is "it." Failing to hit the player, he remains "it."

Use a soft rubber ball, used softball, volleyball, or soccer ball, and arrange the size of the circle accordingly—small balls which can be thrown swiftly call for a larger circle than a large ball.

Bull-in-the-Ring

Playground, Gymnasium   *Late Elementary and Junior High Schools*

From ten to sixteen players stand in a circle with hands firmly grasped, forming a closed ring. One player who is the "bull," stands within. It is his object to break through the line and get away; it is their object to keep him inside. He walks about and examines the arms and hands and asks of what these parts of the ring are made. They reply, "Iron," "Wood," "Leather," "Steel," inventing something as best they can to suggest the difficulty of breaking through. He then tries to break through; and, when he succeeds, he runs and the others give chase. The one who is first to tag him can be the bull next time.

Bull-and-His-Keeper.—This variation of Bull-in-the-Ring is popular among older boys, even among young men. The "bull" stands inside the ring and chooses a "keeper" who stations himself outside the ring. The keeper assists the bull in his efforts to get out of the ring by pulling up or shoving down arms, pulling the bull through, or shoving players aside. Once the bull is free, both bull and keeper run, and the players who can manage to tag them take their places as bull and keeper for the next game.

Bear-in-the-Pit.—The players are arranged in a circle with hands firmly clasped. The "bear" is stationed inside and attempts to get out by diving under or over the arms, between legs, or by breaking through. Once free, all give chase—the one who tags him becomes the bear. It is less rough than Bull-in-the-Ring in that the option of crawling under or climbing over is usually selected in preference to smashing through.

Last Couple Out

Playground, Gymnasium   *Late Elementary School to Adults*

This game is popular with both sexes from the sixth grade to adulthood. It is suitable for groups of from seven to thirteen players—if there are more, two games should be started.

The players stand in couples and the odd player is "it." The couples stand in a column, one behind the other, with the odd player on a line three feet in front, his back toward the players. The odd player calls, "Last couple out," and the rear couple must separate, run forward, and try to join hands with one another in front of the column before the odd player can tag either of them. The odd player may not look around and so cannot see the players till they have passed him. If they succeed, the odd player

FIGURE 31.

is "it" again. If he tags one, that one is "it" and the catcher has the other one of the couple for a partner.

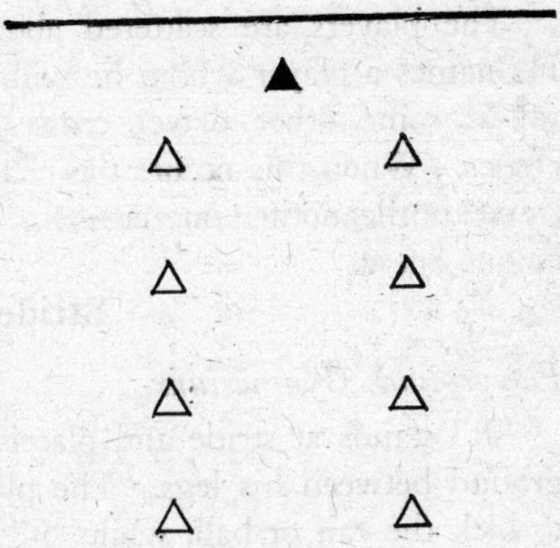

GROUP III

In the games of this type all the players are kept on the alert by a rule to the effect that the runner may shift his liability to be tagged to another player by some device, which varies with the different games. In one or two cases other players may take his place if they wish to do so. The rule that any player tagged instantly becomes the chaser and the one who caught him becomes the runner, prevents any lag in the speed of the play.

Cap Tag

Playground, Gymnasium, Yard   *Elementary School*

Players scatter about the playing space. By use of a counting rhyme, select one player to be "it"; also select a runner and give him an old cap. Only the one holding the cap may be tagged. "It" tries to tag the runner, who runs or passes the cap to some other player who must not refuse it. When a player holding the cap is tagged, he becomes "it." If the cap is dropped, the chaser may grab it, and the one who touched it last is "it." The cap must be passed by handing it, not throwing it.

Variations.—Instead of a cap, use a dumbbell, ball, handkerchief, or other object. The game goes by various names depending on the object, such as Dumbbell Tag, Handkerchief Tag, and so forth.

Posture Tag.—The runner and chaser carry a beanbag on the head without using hands to keep it in place. When the runner puts the bean-bag on any other player's head, that player becomes runner.

Cross Tag

Playground, Gymnasium, Yard   *Elementary School*

The players are scattered about the area. One is chosen to be "it." He names a player whom he will chase, and chases him until he tags him, unless some other player crosses the line between the runner and the chaser. When this occurs the chaser chases the one who crossed and continues until another one crosses. Whoever is tagged is "it" and the game begins anew.

Stride-Ball Tag [1]

Playground, Gymnasium   *Late Elementary to Senior High School*

"It" stands at stride and places a tin can, soccer ball, or softball on the ground between his legs. The players maneuver around "it" in an effort to kick the can or ball, while "it" tries to defend it. When a player kicks the can or ball, "it" chases him. However, if another player kicks the can again before "it" tags the runner, "it" must chase that player rather than the original runner. When "it" tags the runner, the runner becomes "it," and stands at stride over the ball.

Chair Tag

Gymnasium, Playroom, Schoolroom   *Elementary School*

The players are seated on chairs in a wide circle. Choose a chaser and a runner. The runner may become free by taking a seat with another player, or touching his chair; this player must then jump up and be

---

[1] Contributed by J. H. McCulloch.

runner. If the chaser tags the runner, the latter at once becomes chaser and attempts to tag the one who caught him.

In the schoolroom the game is played with the players seated in rows in the regular school seats.

Three-Deep

Playground, Gymnasium   *Late Elementary School to Adults*

Three-Deep is probably the best known and most commonly played circle game. Its popularity is doubtless deserved but some of its variations described below possess greater playing values.

First choose a player for chaser ("it") and another for a runner. Arrange the remaining players in a circle, count off by twos and have each number one step behind the player at his right. This quickly gives a double circle.

"It" chases the runner and attempts to tag him. The runner may become safe by going in front of any group of two and remaining there, thus forming one group that is "three deep." The chaser can tag the rear one of any group that is three deep. The player who finds himself at the rear of a group of three, should hasten to go in front of a group before the chaser can tag him. One who is tagged at once becomes chaser, and should tag the one who caught him if possible.

The rules for chasing vary as follows:

(1) Neither runner nor chaser are permitted to cut across the circle.
(2) The runner may cut across the circle at will but the chaser is not permitted to do so.
(3) Both runner and chaser may cut across the circle at will.

Nothing is gained by the first method. The second method places the odds in favor of the runner and slows up the game. A much faster and more satisfying game with more frequent changes, is achieved by using the third method and permitting both to run across the circle as they choose. Running away from the circle should be prohibited by restricting the play to a zone close up to the sides of the circle.

By frequent suggestions, the leader can discourage long runs and encourage frequent changes.

Two-Deep.—This is similar to Three-Deep except that players are in a single circle. When the runner steps in front of a player, that player becomes the runner.

This is a better game than Three-Deep in that the latter game keeps too many players inactive. When there are enough players for Three-Deep it is usually better to start two games of Two-Deep.

Three-Wide.—This is probably the most popular of the games of the Three-Deep type among boys and girls. The partners stand in a circle with arms locked. "It" chases the runner, following the rules of Three-Deep, who hooks on the outside arm of one of the pairs, thus releasing the third player.

Two-Deep Leap Frog.—Among boys, this is a very popular and vigorous variation of Three-Deep. Arrange the players in a single circle as in Two-Deep. They all stoop and grasp their ankles with their hands, or put their hands on the floor. The runner who is being chased leaps over the back of a player as in Leap Frog, thus shifting the responsibility to the player over whom he jumped. In other respects the rules of Three-Deep apply. If players put their hands on their knees instead of their ankles, the game is slowed up by the difficulty some players will encounter in leaping over.

Underneath Three-Deep.—Arrange the players as in Three-Deep and have them stand with legs widely spread. To become safe the runner must crawl from behind under the legs of the two players and stand in front. The back player then runs. In other respects the play is as in Three-Deep.

Underneath Two-Deep.—Arrange the players as in Two-Deep and play as in Underneath Three-Deep.

Partner Tag.—This is essentially Three-Wide without the circle formation. Select a runner and a chaser. All other players pair up, and join hands, and scatter around the playing field. If a runner hooks onto the arm of one of the members of a pair, the third man becomes runner. If the chaser tags the runner, the runner becomes chaser, and the chaser becomes runner.

Fox and Squirrel.—Arrange the players in groups of three. Two players in each group face each other with hands on shoulders, thus forming a hollow tree and the third player (squirrel) stands inside the hollow tree. There must be an odd squirrel and also another player who is the fox. The fox chases the odd squirrel, who can escape the danger by going in a tree, since foxes cannot go there. But a tree will hold only one squirrel, hence the squirrel in a tree must run out as soon as a second one enters, and the fox has one squirrel to chase all the time. Any squirrel tagged by a fox, when out of a tree, instantly becomes a fox, and the fox then instantly becomes a squirrel and must run away and get in a tree to avoid being caught. Stop the game at frequent intervals and have the squirrels become trees and the trees squirrels.

This game can be played by using circles or marks on the floor instead of trees—this is more satisfactory than the traditional form in that fewer players are kept idle.

Animal Cage (Basket Three-Deep, Third Man).—This is a very similar game to Three-Deep except that the partners face each other and put their hands on each other's shoulders as in Fox and Squirrel. "It" chases the runner as in Three-Deep who may become free from being tagged by stepping inside the arms of the two players of any couple. The chaser must chase the one of this couple toward whom the runner turns his back.

When players are unfamiliar with the game, it often prevents confusion if the runner, as he steps between the players of a couple, names the player to be chased; otherwise both may think they are to run.

Circle Broncho-Tag.—This is another game of the Three-Deep type. Select a runner and a chaser. Arrange a double circle as in Three-Deep. The rear man in each couple grasps the front man around the waist, thus forming a "broncho," the front man being the head and the rear man the tail. "It" chases the runner following the rules of Three-Deep. The runner tries to grab onto the tail of the broncho and if successful he becomes the tail of the broncho and the former head becomes the runner. The broncho tries to prevent the runner from catching on by twisting, turning, and bucking, but the head of the broncho must not use his hands to hinder the runner. If the chaser tags the runner when he is loose, the runner becomes the chaser, and the chaser, runner.

The circle may be abandoned and the couples allowed to scatter and move at random over the playing area.

Last Man "It."—In all the above games of Three-Deep type, the same "it" continues until he tags the runner, and when a player seeks safety by joining the players in the circle, the released player is chased by "it." In Last Man "It," when a player seeks safety by joining the players in the circle, the released player becomes "it" and chases the original "it." All of the above games of the Three-Deep type may be played in this way.

Circle-Ball
(Center Catch, Touch Ball, Ring Ball)

Playground, Gymnasium   *Late Elementary School to Adults*

This excellent game is popular with all from about the fifth grade to maturity. An alert vivacious leader can develop much sociability and fun with it. Business men like to play it with a medicine ball instead of a basketball.

Arrange the players in a circle and spread at arm's length; the one who is "it" stands within. The players in the circle have a basketball which they pass from one to another to keep it away from "it," who tries to touch it or to catch it. If he touches it, the last player who touched it is "it."

The game is sometimes played with a rule to the effect that if a player makes a wild throw over the heads of those in the circle, he becomes "it," but boys in the gymnasium prefer to allow "it" and the nearest players in the circle to scramble for the ball; in case a player gets it first he immediately throws it back to the circle. The roughness and strenuousness of this appeals to the boys and adds excitement to the game, and the hazard of "it" touching it first is sufficient to prevent intentional wild throws.

This game is at its best with not more than twenty-four players; more than that would call for two games.

In football season, a football may be substituted for the basketball.

Variation.—Instead of passing straight to another man in the circle, the ball must bound once on the floor as it crosses the circle.

Variation.—The ball must be tossed to the man next to the player in either direction, instead of across the circle at random.

Soccer Center-Ball.—Arrange the players in a circle with "it" in the center. The players kick a soccer ball back and forth in any direction across the circle while "it" attempts to touch it. When "it" touches the ball, the last person kicking it becomes "it." The circle players may not touch the ball with their hands. If the ball is kicked over the heads of the circle players, the person kicking it is "it."

If the ball goes out of the circle between two players it is still in play and the nearest player runs for it, and "it" may pursue if he chooses. In returning the ball to the circle the player must use his feet only.

Channel-Ball.—Select an "it" and arrange the players in a circle, legs at stride, facing around the circle. "It" is in the center. The players pass a ball backward and forward between their legs while "it" tries to touch it. If he succeeds, the last person touching it is "it."

GROUP IV

In the games of this group all players are equally liable to be tagged, but there is often some way to become exempt, either by going into a space where the chaser may not come, or by assuming some position agreed upon as making one free from liability to be tagged. In several cases it lies within the player's choice to be active or comparatively quiet. Any player tagged when not exempt at once becomes "it" and the game goes on without delay.

Scat

Schoolroom, Playroom   *Early Elementary School*

The players form a line facing front. One is the "teacher" and stands a few feet away. She goes through certain exercises, the class following. Suddenly she cries "Scat," and all run to the "home," a place marked off at the one end of the room, the "teacher" chasing them. If one is caught, he becomes "teacher." If no one is caught, the same teacher acts again.

The Shepherd and the Wolf
(*Wolf, Wolf, and Sheep*)

Playground, Gymnasium, Yard   *Early Elementary School*

Select one player to act as the wolf ("it") and another as the shepherd. The remainder are sheep. Mark out a sheepfold. The shepherd assembles the sheep in the fold and the wolf finds a hiding place. When the wolf is hidden, he howls and the shepherd leads his sheep cautiously in the direction of the noise. When he sees the wolf he cries, "I spy a wolf." The sheep bleat and run frantically back to the field, with the wolf in pursuit. If the wolf tags a sheep, the sheep becomes wolf.

Frog in the Sea

Schoolroom, Playroom, Home   *Early Elementary School*

Mark a two-foot circle on the floor in which the frog sits with legs crossed. The other players mill around just out of reach saying:

> "Frog in the sea
> Frog in the sea
> Frog catch a firefly
> But can't catch me."

The frog must remain in the squatting position while he tries to tag the teasing players. When tagged, a player becomes frog.

Old Mother Witch

Playground, Gymnasium, Yard   *Early Elementary School*

All the players chase after the witch, poking, pulling, and teasing her in every possible way as she walks along. As they follow after her they call

> "Old Mother Witch fell in the ditch,
> Picked up a penny, and thought she was rich."

The witch then turns and asks, "Whose children are you?" Any name may be given and the witch goes on, but if they should say, "Yours," the witch gives chase and the first one caught takes her place.

The children are not so apt to want to be caught in this game because of the teasing the witch has to endure.

Tommy Tiddler's Ground.—Played exactly like Old Mother Witch except with the use of the following rhyme:

> "I'm on Tommy Tiddler's ground,
> Picking up silver by the pound."

It is more suitable for boys than Old Mother Witch.

King's Land

Playground, Gymnasium, Yard   *Early Elementary School*

Mark a space for the king's land and select a player to be king. The other players try to tease and annoy the king by stepping on his land; then he tries to tag them. One who is tagged becomes king and the game continues.

Variation.—Have the players join hands and march up toward the king, who is seated on his throne, keeping step with the words:

> "I'm on the King's Land, the King's not at home,
> The King cannot catch me till I say 'Come!'"

At the word "come," the king gives chase.

His Royal Highness.—Select one player for His Royal Highness and appoint two royal guards. The remaining players are rebels. His Royal Highness stands on his throne, a small circle in the center of the area, with his royal guards beside him. The three then stroll around the kingdom (play area) and as soon as they leave the throne the rebels annoy the king and attempt to spank him. As soon as the king is struck, he names the player who hit him and the royal guards give chase. The king runs for the throne, being spanked by any rebels who can catch up with him. Once on the throne, he is safe. The guard who tags the rebel who struck the king is free, the rebel becomes the king, and the king becomes a royal guard.

King's Bodyguard.—The king and his guards are selected and stationed just as in His Royal Highness. The three venture forth with the guards in the lead who have their hands clasped. The players attempt to tag the king while the guards prevent them by blocking, tackling, and holding. The king protects himself by moving around the guards. When the king is tagged he loses his position, the player who tagged him becomes the second guard, and the first guard becomes king.

Charley Over the Water
(*Sally Over the Water*)

Playground, Gymnasium   *Early Elementary School*

This old game is always popular among small children. Arrange the players in a circle with "it" in the center. The players march around the circle singing:

> "Charley over the water
> Charley over the sea
> Charley catch a blackbird
> But can't catch me."

When the last word is sung, all stop and attempt to place a hand on the floor before "it" can tag them. Anyone tagged becomes "it."

Pincho

Playground, Gymnasium   *Elementary School*

Establish a line, the area behind which is the safety zone. All the players except "it" line up on the line and hold hands. "It" stands five paces in front with his back to the line and walks forward with the players advancing behind him.

The player on the left end of the line pinches the next player's hand when he chooses, and the second player passes on the pinch at any time he desires. When the last player's hand is pinched he yells "Ouch" and the players release hands and run back to the safety zone with "it" in pursuit. If "it" tags a player before he reaches the line, that player becomes "it."

Hand-Slapping Tag

Playground, Playroom, Home   *Elementary School*

This quiet game is a tag variation of the dual combat, Hand Slapping. Arrange the players in a circle, elbows at sides, holding hands in front with palms up. "It" goes around inside the circle and unexpectedly slaps some player on the hands. The player may avoid being slapped by withdrawing his hands or turning them over. A player when slapped becomes "it." Players may not withdraw or turn their hands until "it" slaps at them; if they do so they become "it."

Squat Tag

Playground, Gymnasium, Yard   *Elementary School*

Choose one player to be "it." The players scatter about the area and "it" tries to tag them. The players may become safe from being tagged by assuming a squatting position. When "it" is not near they stand up and run again. Each player may use this method of escape three times, and then may escape only by running. If "it" retreats five steps from a player who has escaped by assuming the squatting position, and then returns, the player must run or is liable to be tagged. Anyone who is tagged becomes "it" and the game continues.

Turtle Tag.—Same as Squat Tag except that the players to become exempt must be on their backs with hands and feet up in the air.

Hindoo Tag (Mohammedan Tag).—Same as Squat Tag except that safety is achieved by dropping to hands and knees and putting the forehead on the ground.

Skunk Tag.—Same as Squat Tag except that safety is obtained by grabbing the toe with one hand and the nose with the other, thus standing on one foot. *Variation:* The safety position is with the arm under one knee and the hand of the same arm grasping the nose.

Floor Tag.—Same as Squat Tag except that the safety position is with one hand on the floor.

Hang Tag.—Same as Squat Tag except that freedom from being tagged is secured by hanging from some support by the arms and lifting the feet from the floor. Desks and seats can serve as supports in the schoolroom, but the game is more satisfactory in a gymnasium where there are bars, rings, and other apparatus, or in the open where there are trees.

Sole-Mate Tag.—Same as Squat Tag except that all the players except "it" pair up in couples and achieve safety by sitting on the ground with the soles of their feet touching those of their partners.

Statue Tag.—Same as Squat Tag except that "it" demonstrates a comic position or statue which is to be used as the safety position. The players do not attempt to run but tantalize "it" by assuming first a natural and then the demonstrated position. Each new "it" demonstrates a new position.

Ankle Tag.—In order to avoid being tagged, a player must catch and hold another player by the ankle. The player being held is eligible to be tagged and must break away and run or get hold of another player's ankle.

Wood Tag

Playground, Yard   *Elementary School*

Select one player to serve as "it." He chases the other players who are safe only when touching wood. A player may not touch wood for safety more than three times, however, and thereafter must run to escape. A tagged player becomes "it."

Variations.—Tree Tag, Iron Tag, Plaster Tag, Paint Tag, Grass Tag, Leaf Tag, Stone Tag.

Fence Tag

Playground   *Elementary School*

This is a good game when there is a low fence or obstruction easily leaped over.

"It" is on one side and the players on the other. They jump the fence to "it's" side and are eligible to be tagged, and must leap back to gain safety. "It" may not tag anyone whose feet are in the air as he is jumping the fence. A player tagged becomes "it" and may tag back immediately.

Straddle the Pole

Playground, Gymnasium, Yard   *Elementary School*

Lay a long pole on the ground, or draw a line to represent the stick. Children playing in the streets frequently use a crack in the pavement.

Select one player to serve as "it." At the start all the other players straddle the line. When straddling the line they are safe but when off it they are liable to be tagged. "It" may not step over the line or reach over it, but must always run around the ends to tag a player. When a player is tagged he becomes "it."

Tire Tag

Playground, Yard   *Elementary School*

Each player has an old automobile tire which he rolls as he runs. "It" must roll his tire with him as he attempts to tag players. A player is safe if he stands astride his tire with both feet on it. This of course is an uncertain position to hold and upsets are many. When a player is tagged he becomes "it."

Steps

Playground, Gymnasium, Club   *Elementary and Junior High Schools*

Select an "It" and have him blind against a wall or post. Line the players behind a starting line about sixty feet distant. "It" calls "Go" and counts ten out loud rapidly, and then turns so that he can see the players. On the word "Go" the players immediately start toward "it" but must not be seen moving by "it" when he turns. All who are seen moving are sent back to the starting line. Continue until some player advances close enough to touch "it." This player wins.

Statues.—Line the players in a single rank. "It" stands about twenty feet in front. The players demonstrate the statue or pose they will assume. "It" turns his back to the players, counts ten, and turns to observe the players. Any player whom he sees moving or whose pose is not like that demonstrated, exchanges places with "it."

Advancing Statues.—This is a combination of Steps and Statues. Arrange the players in single rank on the starting line. Select an "it." Each player demonstrates the statues or pose he will assume. "It" closes his eyes against a wall or post about sixty feet in front of the starting line. He calls "Go" and counts ten out loud rapidly. While he is counting the players advance toward him, but when he ceases counting they stop and assume the pose. "It" turns at the count of ten and orders back to the starting line all those whom he sees moving or whose pose is not as demonstrated. Continue until some player reaches and touches "it." This player is the winner.

Shadow Tag

Playground, Yard   *Elementary School*

The game requires a sunshiny day. "It" tags the players not by touching them but by stepping on their shadows and calling the names of the player making the shadows. A tagged player immediately becomes "it."

Sore-Spot Tag
(*Japanese Tag*)

Playground, Gymnasium, Yard   *Elementary School*

The players are scattered about and "it" attempts to tag. When a player is tagged he must place his hand on the spot where he was tagged and in this position try to tag someone else.

The game is often slowed up considerably because of the inability of "it" to run rapidly when holding his hand in the spot where he was hit. To eliminate this, the game is often played by requiring him to have his hand in the spot only when in the act of tagging another player.

Couple Tag

Playground, Gymnasium   *Elementary School*

The players pair up in couples, each couple with *right* hands clasped. One couple is "it." "It" attempts to tag the other couples and, if successful, the tagged couple becomes "it." All couples including "it" must keep hands clasped throughout. If a running couple breaks their handclasp they become "it." If "it" breaks hands while tagging, the tagging does not count.

Couple Change-Tag

Playground, Gymnasium   *Elementary School*

Arrange the players in couples, holding hands, with one extra player who is "it." Designate one player in each couple as Number 1 and the other as Number 2. Each couple marks its base on the ground or floor. "It," standing in the center of the area, calls "One's change," "Two's change," or "All change." In the first case the One's run and pair up with another partner; in the second case, the Two's run, and in the third case all pairs run with hands joined and exchange bases. Any player tagged by "it" while not standing on a base with hands joined with his partner becomes "it."

Goal Tag.—Mark as many three-foot circles (goals) on the floor or ground as there are players. Designate one player to be "it." When "it" leaves his goal, all players must leave theirs and seek a new goal. They cannot return to the goal just left, nor can two players occupy the same goal. "It" tries to tag a player during the exchange and if successful, that player takes his place as "it." A player is safe if any part of his body is in the goal.

Circle Spot-Tag (On the Spot).—Arrange the players in a widely spread double circle with "it" in the center. Each player marks his position on the floor or ground. Supply "it" with a basketball, volleyball, soccer ball, or softball. The players exchange positions with each other at will. "It" attempts to hit them with the ball when they are not standing on a marked position. "It" may run with the ball if he chooses. A player hit while off a post becomes "it."

Blind Hop-Tag

Playground, Gymnasium, Yard   *Elementary School*

Select an "it" and blindfold him. The remaining players hop about on one foot. "It," however, may run and attempts to tag someone while blindfolded. If a player touches both feet to the ground he must stand on the spot until "it" tags someone. A player tagged while hopping or standing still becomes "it."

Blindman's Swat-Tag.—Select an "it," blindfold him, and give him a swatter. Appoint a partner for him. The remaining players scatter over a limited area thirty to forty feet square, depending on the number of players. The players must hop on one foot when moving, but "it" and his partner may run. "Its" movements in attempting to tag the players with the swatter are determined by his partner who directs him. When a player is tagged he becomes "it" and the former "it" becomes his partner.

Blindman's Buff

Playground, Gymnasium, Yard   *Elementary School*

Arrange the players in a circle, holding hands and facing in. "It" is in the center, blindfolded and carrying a stick the size of a cane. The circle walks to the right and whenever "it" chooses he halts it by rapping the floor with his stick. He then points toward the circle with the stick and if he points between two players the circle continues to move. If he points at a player, that player enters the circle and "it" attempts to tag him. If he has trouble locating him, as he doubtless will, the leader calls "One step in," whereupon every player in the circle takes one step inward and thus reduces the size of the circle. This is repeated as often as necessary. When tagged, the player becomes "it" and the former "it" joins the circle.

Question Blindman's Buff.—When pointed out, the player goes up to "it" and is asked three questions which he answers in any way he chooses. He will, of course, disguise his voice. If "it" guesses his name, they exchange places.

Feeling Blindman's Buff.—When "it" tags the player in the center, he runs his hands over him and attempts to identify him. If he fails, he continues to be "it." This variation is only possible when the players all know each other.

Animal Blindman's Buff.—When "it" points at a player in the circle he does not have to catch the player but rather names a bird or beast; the player goes up to "it" and imitates the call of the creature named three times. If "it" guesses the player's name, the player becomes "it."

Singing Blindman's Buff.—Instead of being asked to imitate a bird or beast, the player, when pointed out, sings the scale, up and down. If "it" guesses his name they exchange places.

Still Water, Stop.—Blindfold "it" and station him in the center of the play area, with the remaining players gathered around him. "It" spins around three times and calls "Still Water, Stop"; while he is spinning, the others scatter and stop on the command. "It" then attempts to locate and tag the players who can take one step only to avoid him and thereafter must remain stationary. When "it" locates a player he runs his hands over him and has two guesses as to his identity. If the guess is correct, the player becomes "it," otherwise "it" continues until successful.

Blindman's Ten-Steps.—Same as the above except that after calling "Still water, stop," "it" takes ten steps, long or short as he chooses, in an effort to tag a player. If successful the tagged player becomes "it." Otherwise, "it" spins again and repeats the process.

Circle Blindman's Tag.—Arrange the players in a circle, facing in and holding hands. "It" is in the center, blindfolded. "It" attempts to tag a player in the circle, while the circle moves about attempting to keep its players away from "it." Hands must remain clasped throughout. When "it" tags a player he runs his hands over him and has two guesses as to who he is. If he guesses correctly, the two exchange places; if he fails, he continues as "it."

Such variations may be used as described in Feeling Blindman's Buff,

Animal Blindman's Buff, Singing Blindman's Buff, Question Blindman's Buff.

Circle Blindman's Swat-Tag.—Same as Circle Blindman's Tag except that "it" carries a swatter made from a towel or loosely rolled newspaper. He tags with the swatter.

Blindman's Numbers Change.—Number the players in the circle and put the highest number in the center as "it," and blindfold him. Give "it" a swatter. "It" calls three numbers and the players holding these numbers exchange places. "It" tries to hit one with the swatter while they are doing so. If successful the hit man becomes "it." If unsuccessful "it" continues.

Barley Break

Playground, Gymnasium   Late Elementary and Junior High Schools

For this very old game, a rectangular strip of ground or the gymnasium is divided into three equal spaces as in Figure 32. The center area is known as the barley field. The players pair up in couples, an equal number in

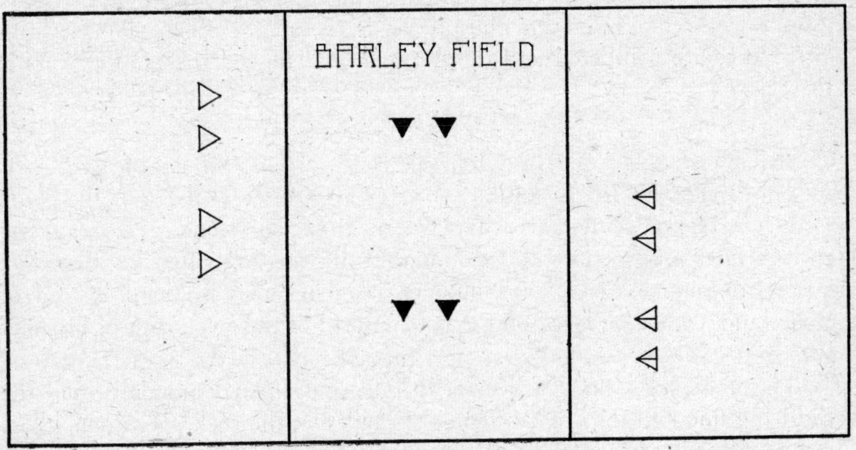

FIGURE 32.

each area. Players in the center area must keep their arms locked, while the others do not need to do so.

The couples in the end zones venture into the barley field, tramping down the barley and taunting the couples who have their arms linked by saying "Barley Break!" When one is caught he remains inactive in the barley field until his partner is captured. When the two are caught they become "it" (custodians of the barley field) and the others return to the end zones. The custodians of the barley field cannot go outside the field, nor can the other players take refuge in the field opposite to their own.

Help Tag

Playground, Gymnasium   *Elementary School*

A player is selected for "it" and is given a beater, such as a knotted rag, or rolled newspaper. He secures his first helper by tagging him three times with the swatter. The helper catches and holds another player and calls "Help," whereupon "it" rushes over, and if the player has not escaped before he gets there, swats him three times with the swatter. All swatted players become helpers. The game continues until all are caught. The first one caught becomes "it" for the next game.

Tagging Champion

Playground and Gymnasium   *Elementary and Junior High Schools*

Establish two goals about forty feet apart. Line up the players behind one goal and number them. Number 1 takes his place midway between the goals as "it." The leader gives the signal, whereupon all run to the opposite goal. "It" tags as many as possible, calling "one," "two," and so forth, as he tags each player. When all have reached the opposite goal, Number 2 becomes "it" and the process is repeated. When all have been "it," scores are compared and the one who has tagged the most players is the champion.

Duck-on-the-Rock

Playground, Gymnasium, Yard   *Late Elementary School to Adults*

When played outdoors each player has a small stone. Place a large rock or block of wood on the ground and draw a throwing line thirty feet away from it. When played indoors, beanbags may be used instead of stones and a stool is placed on the floor instead of the large rock or block of wood.

The first play is to decide who is "it." Each player stands behind the throwing line and throws his stone or beanbag at the rock, The one whose stone or bag is farthest from the rock is "it."

"It" places his stone or bag, known as the duck, on the rock and stands by to guard it. The others stand behind the throwing line and in turn throw their stones or bags in an effort to knock the duck off. If a player fails, he may stand back of the line and wait until someone succeeds, or if he chooses, he may run out, pick up his rock, and try to get back to the throwing line before "it" tags him. He may gain safety by putting his foot on his stone, but once he picks it up, he is not permitted to put it back on the ground for safety. If he returns safely he may throw again.

When someone knocks the duck off, all who have thrown run out, pick up their stones, and run back to the line. Before "it" may attempt to tag them he must replace his duck on the rock. Anyone tagged becomes "it." If two stones or bags lie touching each other, the owners may get them without being tagged.

If any player, while throwing, steps over the line he becomes "it."

Variation.—Draw a twelve-foot square and place the rock in its center. The throwing line is thirty feet away as before. A player who fails to knock the duck off may venture up to the twelve-foot square with safety and is liable to be tagged only when inside the square.

Spud

(Ball Stand, Stone Ball, Call Ball)

Playground, Gymnasium   *Late Elementary to Senior High School*

This is a very popular game among boys, who always seem to derive particular joy in throwing to hit each other. Girls of high-school age also enjoy it.

A used softball or a soft rubber ball of the size of a softball is needed. The player starting the game stands with the ball in the center of the gymnasium, with the other players gathered around him. He tosses the ball in the air and at the same time calls the name or number of a player. The player named dashes for the ball and all others scatter. As soon as he gets it he calls "Halt," whereupon everybody stops instantly. Then without moving from the spot where he picked the ball up, he throws it at one of the players, who may dodge in any way he chooses, provided he keeps one foot in place. If the thrower misses, one "spud" is scored against him and all gather around while he throws the ball up again and calls another name. If he hits the player, however, one "spud" is scored against the player hit and he immediately picks up the ball, calls "Halt," and attempts to hit someone else. This goes on until someone misses his mark.

The real fun of the game comes when a player has three "spuds" scored against him. He must then stand up against the wall, back toward the players and hands on his knees. The players line up behind a throwing line twenty feet away and each gets a free throw at him.

Additional sport may be added to the game by allowing the man against the wall to throw back at every player who misses him. In this case the man who misses turns around on the firing line and takes the same position as the man took against the wall.

To speed the game up, two "spuds" instead of three may be used to cause a man to become the target of the firing squad. The game is sometimes played by counting a "spud" against a man only when he misses in throwing and not when he is hit; this is undesirable, however, in that fewer players face the firing squad which is the angle of the play to which the players look forward.

For smaller children, or groups varying greatly in age, the ball may be rolled at the players instead of being thrown. In this case, no dodging whatever is permitted.

When played outdoors, mark off limits beyond which players cannot run.

Buddy Spud.—In this interesting version of Spud, each player has a partner (buddy). The game proceeds just as in Spud except that the player whose name is called has the option of throwing to hit a player, or throwing to his buddy who may be in a more favorable position to hit someone. The ball may not be passed more than once, however. If the partner fails to catch the ball, or fails to hit a player, one "spud" is counted against the pair. When a pair has three "spuds" (or two if desired) counted against it, both partners stand up in turn before the firing squad.

Wall Spud (Stand Wall Ball).—This popular adaptation of Spud requires a wall or high board fence. A soft rubber ball or playgroundball is used. The player selected for the thrower throws the ball against the fence or wall and calls the name of a player. This player secures the ball while the others scatter, calls "Halt," and from then on the procedure is exactly as in Spud.

Blocking Wall Spud.—This rough variation is very popular among older boys. It is played as described above except that when the ball is thrown against the wall and a player's name is called, everyone tries to block the player and prevent him from catching the ball, which he must catch either on the fly or first bound. They must not touch the ball, however. If he succeeds in catching it, he throws it against the wall and calls another name. If he fails to catch it, all scatter, and when he secures it he calls "Halt" and from then on the rules of Spud apply.

Days of the Week.—This version of Wall Spud is suitable for younger boys. It is usually played with a group of not more than six or seven. The players are named by the days of the week—Monday, Tuesday, and so forth. One starts the game by throwing the ball against the wall and calling the name of a day in the week as he does so. The player, holding this name, tries to catch the ball and the others run away. If he fails to catch it he can make up for the failure by hitting a player with the ball. He must throw from the place where he picked it up, calling "Halt" when he secures it. If he fails to make the hit, a point is scored against him. The player whose name was called makes the next throw against the wall. In other respects the procedure is as in Spud.

Mounted Spud.—This is a team form of Spud, and is more properly classified under Group V of the tag games, but for convenience it is listed here with the other types of Spud.

Divide the players into two teams and decide which team is to act as bronchos and which as riders. The bronchos form in a circle and the riders pick their bronchos and mount their backs. The riders pass a soft-ball among themselves and the bronchos attempt to cause the riders to fumble by rearing and bucking, but cannot leave the circle. When a rider misses, all riders dismount and scramble for the ball, while the bronchos scatter. The rider getting the ball attempts to hit a broncho; if he fails one spud is scored against his team. If he succeeds, the broncho who is hit tries to hit a rider and if he fails a spud is scored against his team. After each failure the riders and bronchos change positions and the former bronchos mount the former riders. The team getting three spuds scored against it must line up its players as a team against the wall, and the members of the other team get one throw each at them as in Spud.

Roly Poly
(*Nigger Baby*)

Playground, Gymnasium   *Elementary and Junior High Schools*

Establish a line at one end of the playing area. Each player then digs a hole in front of this line about eight inches in diameter and three or four inches deep. Indoors a circle of chalk may be drawn instead. Ten feet in front of this line establish a throwing line behind which the players stand.

One player starts the game by rolling a soft playgroundball from behind the throwing line endeavoring to cause it to enter one of the holes. When it enters a hole the owner of that hole runs forward and secures the ball, then calls "Stop." In the meantime all others have scattered. When "Stop" is called they must all stop and not move a foot thereafter. The player with the ball then throws it at one of the players. If he hits him one point is scored against the hit player. If he misses, one point is scored against the thrower. When a player has three points scored against him he must stand before a wall and all are given a throw at him from a line twenty feet distant.

Variation.—When played indoors with chalked circles instead of holes, the player starting the game walks along in front of the circles then suddenly places the ball in a circle and runs.

Ball in Cap.—The players lay their caps in a straight row on the ground. About ten feet in front the players stand. The first player tosses a tennis ball or small rubber ball at the caps, attempting to have it lodge in one of the caps. He continues throwing until he succeeds. The owner of the cap runs and the tosser chases him. The owner tries to touch his cap before he is tagged by the tosser. If he succeeds he becomes the tosser for the next game. If he fails the original tosser continues to toss in the next game.

Poison Circle

Gymnasium, Playground   *Late Elementary to Senior High School*

Arrange the players in a circle with hands firmly clasped, spread as wide as possible. About four feet inside draw a circle on the floor or ground. In the center place a softball.

At the signal everyone pulls and pushes in an effort to force one another into the poison circle. When a player steps in, everyone calls "Poison" and runs away, while he gets the ball and tries to hit one of them. If more than one is pulled into the circle they scramble for the ball and the one getting it throws. After the throw, the circle is formed again.

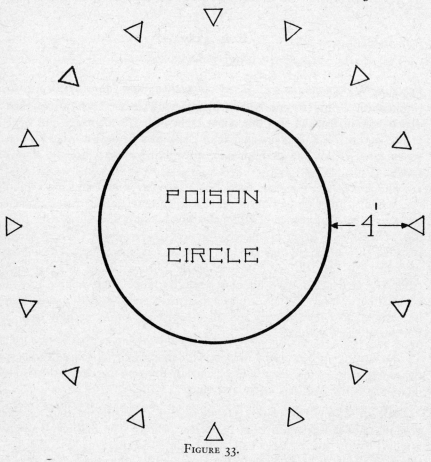

FIGURE 33.

Poison Spot.—This game is better suited for older boys than the above. Use a three- or four-foot poison circle—the center circle of the basketball court is ideal. In it place a piano stool or a box of similar size. The circle forms around it and the game proceeds as before. Anyone stepping in the circle or touching the stool in an effort to jump over it, is out of the game. Also, when two players break their grip both are out. When the circle gets down to three players, they form a circle beside the poison circle and attempt to force each other in. The last man to remain in the game wins.

Poison Snake.—This game is much used by children for informal play. Instead of using a poison circle, place a rope such as the clothesline on the ground, circling and twisting it around. The players join hands in a circle around the rope, and attempt to pull each other into the snake. Anyone touching the snake is poisoned and out of the game. Continue until one is left.

Soccer Tag

Playground, Gymnasium   *Late Elementary to Senior High School*

The players are scattered about in a limited area. "It" has a soccer ball or a codeball which he kicks at the players. Anyone touched by it becomes "it" and has one point scored against him. If "it" touches the ball with his hands or kicks it so that it goes higher than the chest, he has a point scored against him.

When a player has three points scored against him he must stand facing the wall with his hands on his knees, and the players each get one chance to kick the ball at him from a line fifteen feet away. The ball is placed on the line and kicked from the floor.

Jump the Shot

Playground, Gymnasium   *Late Elementary to Senior High School*

This exciting, active, and very popular game calls for a rope about fifteen feet long at the end of which a weight is tied. An old tennis shoe is ideal, or a bag of beans may be used.

Arrange the players in a circle with plenty of room for jumping between them. The leader or other experienced person stands in the center with the rope and begins swinging the weight around the circle, gradually letting out more rope until it reaches the players and is moving close to the floor. The players jump the rope as it passes. If the rope or weight touches a player he is out of the game. The last man standing wins. When only a few players are left, much fun can be added by changing the speed of the rope—this calls for constant alertness on the part of the players.

Considerable skill is required in swinging the rope satisfactorily. It may be swung standing, the swinger turning with the rope, but is best handled by sitting or lying flat on the back—this facilitates a swing of even height from the floor.

Variation.—The players face to the left and run around the circle toward the on-coming rope.

Variation.—The players stand on one foot and hop the rope. They change feet only when the leader so orders.

Variation.—The players face to the left and hop around the circle on one foot toward the on-coming rope.

Variation.—When a player is hit, count one point against him and let him continue to play. When three points are checked up against him, have him stand up against the wall and face the firing squad as in Spud.

Variation.—Instead of eliminating a player when he is hit, have him exchange places with the swinger. This is possible only with older players because of the skill required in swinging.

Jump the Stick.—This is very similar to Jump the Shot but is a faster and more exciting game. A slender bamboo pole fifteen or more feet in length is used instead of a rope and weight. Arrange the players in a circle, facing in. The leader stands in the center and swings the pole around so that the end passes a few inches above the floor. The players jump it as in Jump the Shot. Those who touch the pole are eliminated. The last player remaining in wins.

Dare Base

Playground and Gymnasium　　　*Late Elementary to Senior High School*

Goal lines are marked off at each end of the field as in Pom-Pom-Pull-Away, and another line is marked directly across the center of the field which is called the "dare base." On the dare base two catchers stand. The players run from one goal to the other with the catchers running out and trying to tag them. They may stop for safety on the dare base, but must continue in the same direction when they run again; that is, they cannot return to the goal from which they came. Players caught are out of the game. The last player caught becomes the catcher for the next game and chooses his assistant.

This game must be rated as inferior to Pom-Pom-Pull-Away, owing to the fact that the players are eliminated and out of the game as soon as they are caught.

GROUP V

We now have, for the first time, games involving simple co-operation in place of the complete individualism of the previous games. These games differ a little on account of the playing space, but mostly in the dramatic features of the play.

Giant's Cave

Playground　　　　　　　　　　　　　*Early Elementary School*

Select one player for the mother. She assembles her children on a goal. Select another player for the giant and have him hide; his hiding place is known as the giant's cave.

Children: "Mother, may we go out to play?"

Mother: "Yes, but don't go near the giant's cave."

The children run out and play around until mother calls, "Children, come home or the giant will catch you."

They all run for the goal and the giant runs out and catches as many as he can. Those caught are giants and aid him in capturing the others as the game continues.

Run, Rabbit, Run.—Divide the players into two groups, one designated as foxes and the other rabbits. The rabbits are safe in their home, a goal at one end of the play area. The foxes scatter through the forest. The old mother rabbit takes her children out for a walk. They tiptoe gently for the fox may be near. Suddenly the leader of the foxes calls out "Run, rabbit, run," whereupon all the rabbits dash for their home while the foxes try to tag them. All who are caught become foxes and help catch the remaining rabbits in the next game. The game continues until all rabbits are caught.

Twelve O'Clock at Night.—Mark off a fox's den in one corner and a chicken yard in another. Choose a player to be the fox and another to be the mother hen. The rest of the players are chickens. The mother hen arranges the chickens in a compact group and then leads them up close to the fox's den and inquires: "If you please, Mr. Fox, what time is it?" If he replies any hour except midnight, they are safe and may play about; the hen lets them play a moment and then gets them together again and, moving a little closer to the fox's den, asks the time once more. When he replies "Twelve o'clock at night," they must run to the chicken yard, and the fox tries to tag them. Those who are caught must go into the fox's den and help him catch the chickens the next time.

Bring out the dramatic features of the game. Have the hen cluck to her brood and the chickens peep and otherwise mimic little chicks.

Sheep, Sheep, Come Home.—One player is the wolf and has a den at one side of the field. The mother sheep is in the middle of the field and the sheep are at one end.

The game begins by the mother sheep calling, "Sheep, sheep, come home." They answer, "We're afraid."

Mother: "Of what?"

Sheep: "The wolf."

Mother: "The wolf has gone to Dixieland and won't be back for seven days, so sheep, sheep, come home."

The sheep then run to the opposite end of the field, while the wolf runs out and catches as many as possible. Those caught go to the den to help catch the others and the game is repeated.

Brownies and Fairies.—Establish two goals thirty to forty feet apart; divide the players in two equal groups and station one at each goal. One group (fairies) turn their backs while the others' (brownies) creep up as quietly as possible. One fairy is watching and when they are ·near, calls, "Look out for the brownies." The fairies then chase the brownies to their goal and tag as many as they can. All who are caught are fairies. Then the brownies turn their backs and the fairies come up quietly, and so on. The side wins that has the greatest number when play ceases.

The Flowers and the Wind

Playground, Gymnasium   *Early Elementary School*

Divide the players into two equal groups and the playing space into three equal parts. One side represents the flowers and the other side the wind. The flowers meet at their end and choose a flower they will represent. Then they play about in the middle or neutral space until the players representing the wind guess the right flower; then all the flowers run to their goals and the wind tries to tag them. The flowers caught are put in a vase (section of the floor). Repeat until all the flowers have been caught.

Spider and Fly

Playground, Gymnasium, Yard   *Early Elementary School*

Establish two goals at each end of the playing area with a circle drawn in the center equally distant from them. The "spider" ("it") sits motionless in the circle. The "flies" mill around the circle buzzing as they go; they circle closer and closer, buzzing more loudly the nearer they get. Suddenly the spider jumps up and chases them to either goal. Those who are tagged join the spider and sit down in the circle to assist in tagging when the original spider gives the signal to chase again. The last fly caught wins and becomes the spider for a new game.

Oyster Supper

Playground, Gymnasium   *Early Elementary School*

The two teams line up facing each other at least thirty feet apart. The players of Team A extend one hand. A player chosen from Team B crosses over to Team A and goes down the line touching each hand. When this player decides which member of Team A shall be the chaser, that hand is slapped and the player runs back to his own line. If the player from Team B reaches his line without being tagged, he is safe. If the runner is tagged, he then becomes a member of the opposite team. The chaser from Team A then taps the hands of Team B and the game continues until time is called. The team having the largest number wins.

Circle Squat-Tag

Playground, Gymnasium   *Early Elementary School*

The players are arranged in a circle with "it" inside in a squatting position. About twenty feet out from the circle of players, a circle is drawn on the ground. The players tantalize "it" with remarks and suddenly "it" jumps up and chases the players who are safe only when they reach the outer circle. All who are tagged become "it" and join the original "it" in the squatting position. When the original "it" gives the signal they all give chase. The game continues until all are caught. The last player caught is "it" for the next game.

Injun Tom
(*Nigger Tom*)

Playground, Gymnasium   *Early Elementary School*

Establish two base lines about twenty-five feet apart. "It" stands on one line and the other players on the other. The following dialogue takes place;

> "It": Did you ever?
> Players: No I never!
> "It": See an Injun?
> Players: Injun who?
> "It": Injun Tom.
> Players: Tom who?
> "It": Tom Chase.
> Players: Chase who?
> "It": Chase ———!

"It" then names a player who must run to the other goal while "it" runs out and attempts to tag him. If he is tagged he becomes "it" and assists in tagging the others. The dialogue is then repeated.

Fox in the Morning

Playground, Gymnasium   *Early Elementary School*

This game is similar to Pom-Pom-Pull-Away but is more suitable for small children because of the dramatic angle.

The goals should be about forty feet apart. "It" is called the fox and stands midway between the goals. The players are called geese and stand behind one goal.

> Fox: Fox in the morning.
> Geese: Goose and gander.
> Fox: How many of you?
> Geese: More than you can handle.
> Fox: I'll see.

At this signal the geese run to the opposite goal and the fox attempts to tag them. All who are tagged become the fox's helpers. The play is then repeated. The last one caught is the fox for the next game.

Dodgeball

Playground, Gymnasium   *Late Elementary to Adults*

Divide the players into two groups. One side forms a circle and the other scatters inside it. The circle men throw a volleyball, soccer ball, codeball, or sport ball at the inside men, endeavoring to hit them. The center men dodge in any way they choose but must not leave the circle. Those hit withdraw from the circle. In the case of girls, a player hit above the hips is not considered hit.

Instead of throwing directly at the center men, a circle man may pass to someone else in the circle in an effort to confuse those in the center. The last man remaining in the center is declared the winner. When all have been eliminated the sides reverse and the center men form the circle.

The practice of using two balls is not recommended. It eliminates the opportunity to use one's skill in dodging, for one cannot hope to watch and dodge successfully more than one ball at a time. If the numbers are large, start two games instead of using two balls in one circle.

Instead of eliminating the center men who are hit, the game may be played by having them join the players in the circle until the center is cleaned. Another method is to have the center men, when hit drop dead inside the circle and remain there until all have been dropped.

Bombing the Enemy.—This form of Dodgeball is popular among boys for informal play. Draw a circle on the ground fifteen or twenty feet in diameter. All the players except one stand in the circle. The single player stands outside the circle with a volleyball, small rubber ball, or used softball. He throws the ball at the players in the circle who run around and dodge in any way they choose. When a player is hit below the shoulders he leaves the circle and joins the thrower in bombing the players. Continue until only one is left in the circle. This player wins the game and becomes the bomber to start the next game.

Soccer Dodgeball.—Arrange the teams as in Dodgeball. A soccer ball, codeball, or sport ball is given to the outside team. The outside team kicks and butts the ball, attempting to hit the inside players with it. The ball may not be touched with the hands. If the ball stops inside the circle, one of the outside players may recover it by kicking it or dribbling it with the feet, but it may not be kicked at the inside team until the player is outside the circle. When a player is hit he is eliminated. When all are eliminated, the sides change. The team eliminating the other in the shortest time wins.

Chain Dodgeball.—Select five players and arrange them in file, each firmly grasping the player ahead around the waist—this is the horse. The remaining players form a circle around the horse. The circle players attempt to hit the horse on the tail (last player). The horse avoids this by keeping his head toward the ball. The first man in the file may use his hands to knock the ball back to the circle. When the tail is hit, the player drops off and goes into the circle, and the player who hit him becomes the head. When the circle is large, use two horses.

Locomotive Dodgeball.—This is exactly like the above except in the dramatic features. The chain of players is known as the train and the circle players attempt to hit the caboose.

Snow Dodgeball.—See Snow Dodgeball in Chapter XXVII, "Winter Activities."

Team Dodgeball.—The various team forms of Dodgeball are classified in Group VI of this chapter, under the team tag games. See Dodgeball—Team Form, Three-Team Dodgeball, Progressive Dodgeball, Field Dodgeball.

New Orleans

Playground, Gymnasium, Club   *Elementary School*

Two goal lines about sixty feet apart are needed. Divide the group into two teams and place them behind the opposite lines. Team Number 1 secretly decides upon some trade it will represent and then approaches Team Number 2 with the following dialogue:

> Number 1: Here we come.
> Number 2: Where from?
> Number 1: New Orleans.
> Number 2: What's your trade?
> Number 1: Lemonade.
> Number 2: How's it made?

Team Number 1 then acts out the motions of the trade selected. Team Number 2 tries to guess the trade. When a member of Team Number 2 guesses it correctly, Team Number 1 runs for its goal with Team Number 2 in pursuit. All who are tagged before they reach their goal join Team Number 2. Team Number 2 then selects a trade.

Austin-Boston.—Establish two goals about sixty feet apart. One team lines up behind each goal. One team is known as the folks from Austin and the other is known as the folks from Boston.

The Austin folks decide on some trade and approach within six feet of Boston's goal. The Boston players say "Who are you?" to which the others answer "We're the folks from Austin." The Boston folks then ask "What's your trade?" The Austin players then give the initials of the trade they selected such as T S for teaching school, and go through the motions of teaching school.

When a Boston player guesses the trade the Austin players run for their goal and the Boston folks chase them. All who are tagged join the Boston side. Then the Boston players select a trade.

Black-and-White
(*Oyster Shell*)

Playground, Gymnasium, Club   Late Elementary to Senior High School

Divide the players into two teams of equal number and name them "Black" and "White." Draw two parallel lines three feet apart across the middle of the playing space—this is neutral territory. At each end of the gymnasium, or thirty to forty feet away, draw a goal line. The players line up beside the neutral zone, toeing the lines, the blacks on one side and the whites on the other, as in Figure 34. A disk, one side of which has

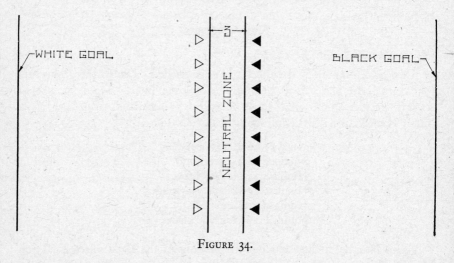

FIGURE 34.

been colored black and the other white, is tossed up so that it falls in the neutral zone. If the black side comes up, the blacks run back to their own goal with the whites in pursuit. All who are tagged join the white side. If the white side of the disk comes up, the whites are chased by the blacks. A player may tag as many of the opposition as possible. The game is won by the side which secures all the opponents or which has the largest number when play ceases. If there is no leader the captains take turns in tossing up the disk.

In order to avoid confusion and argument, the taggers round up the players they tag and lead them back to their own side.

Variation.—A particularly interesting variation is obtained by using a large die or cube of wood instead of the disk. It is painted black on three sides and white on three sides. Make the cube by sawing four inches off the end of a piece of four-by-four.

The cube is rolled between the two lines of players as in rolling lawn dice. The color that is up when the cube comes to rest indicates the team which is to run back to its goal.

Heads-and-Tails.—Instead of a black and white disk a coin is tossed and the teams are named "Heads" and "Tails." The leader examines the coin and calls out which side comes up.

Oyster Shell.—An oyster shell is frequently used in place of the disk, the dark side representing black and the light side, white. Hence the name Oyster Shell, which in some localities is given to the game.

Crows-and-Cranes

Playground, Gymnasium, Club   Late Elementary to Senior High School

This is a game similar in nature to Black-and-White, but more popular among those familiar with both games.

Establish two goals sixty to eighty feet apart and line up one team behind each goal. One team is known as "Crows" and the other as "Cranes." The leader stands in the middle and gives the command, "Forward March," whereupon the teams march forward. Just after he gives the command, the leader calls, "Cr-r-r-rows" or "Cr-r-r-ranes," holding the word until the teams are close together. If the call terminates in "Crows" the crows dash back to their goal with the cranes in pursuit, or if the call is "Cranes" the cranes run back. All who are tagged join the other side.

Much of the fun element in the game depends upon the cleverness of the leader. The calls should be drawn out as long as possible, thus adding to the suspense and uncertainty of the players. Occasionally after starting the call the leader terminates it with either "Crackers" or "Crawfish," which confuses the players momentarily; he then immediately calls the proper word.

In order to satisfy the players that the teams are being called by chance, the leader often tosses a coin just as he gives the command, "Forward, March," examines it quickly and if it shows heads, he immediately starts to call "Crows."

Black-and-Blue.—Use the names "Bl-l-l-lack" and "Bl-l-lue" instead of "Crows" and "Cranes." The deceiving words then are "Blank," "Blast," and "Blubber."

Tale of the Crows and Cranes.—Line the players up toeing the neutral zone instead of the goals. The leader tells a brief story involving many words starting with "Cr-r-r-r," trailing out each of these words. As soon as "crows" or "cranes" is mentioned the chase is on. For example, he might say, "The room was cr-r-r-rowded with cr-r-r-abbed cr-r-r-reatures cr-r-r-rawling around eating cr-r-r-rackers. One cr-r-racked individual said 'Cr-r-rackers make me cr-r-razy, I prefer to cr-r-runch on *Cr-r-r-rows.*' "

Crows, Cranes, and Crabs.—This is exactly like Crows and Cranes except that the leader may call "Crows," "Cranes" or "Crabs." When "Crabs" is called no player may move. Those who do move, go to the other team.

Signal Chase.—Establish two goals sixty to eighty feet apart, and line up one team on each goal, both teams facing in the same direction. On command the rear team marches forward until it is five or six feet behind the front team. At this point the leader blows a whistle and the rear team runs back to its goal with the front team in pursuit. All players tagged join the other team. The teams then line up as before but facing in the opposite direction and the game is repeated with the positions of the teams reversed. The team wins which has the most players when play ceases.

Pom-Pom-Pull-Away
(*Pull Away, Rushing Bases*)

Playground, Street   *Elementary and Junior High Schools*

Establish a goal line at each end of the playing space. The one who is "it" stands in the middle ground and calls,

> "Pom-Pom-Pull-Away
> Come away or I'll fetch you away."

At this all of the players, who have taken places behind one of the goals, must run across to the other goal. All those tagged join the original tagger and help to tag the rest, who must run across again when the call is repeated. All the taggers yell the call in unison under the leadership of the original "it." The game continues till all are caught. The first one tagged is "it" for the next game.

Hill Dill.—This game is played exactly like Pom-Pom-Pull-Away except for the call:

> "Hill Dill, come over the hill
> Or else I'll catch you standing still."

Ham, Chicken, Bacon.—Played exactly like Pom-Pom-Pull-Away except for the call: "Ham, ham, chicken, ham, bacon." On the word "bacon," all must leave the goal.

Red Rover.—This version of Pom-Pom-Pull-Away is commonly played between the curbs of the city streets. The call is "Red Rover, come over, or I'll pull you over."

One Step Off and All the Way Across.—This variation, familiar in many sections, is played just like Pom-Pom-Pull-Away, except for the call: "One step off and all the way across."

Come Blackey.—This is played the same as Pom-Pom-Pull-Away except that the starting phrase is "Come Blackey" and a player must be slapped on the back three times or held for a count of three to be tagged.

Chinese Wall.—This is similar to Pom-Pom-Pull-Away, except that the area in which "it" can tag is limited. Two lines ten feet apart are drawn across the center of the area—the ground between these lines is the wall and "it" stands on it to guard it. The players run across the wall at will while "it" tries to tag them. All who are tagged assist "it."

Tackling Pom-Pom-Pull-Away.—This is like Pom-Pom-Pull-Away except that the tagging is done by tackling the runners so as to bring them to the ground. Consequently, the game calls for old clothes. Mark out an area that is thirty yards long and ten yards wide, and in the center mark out a ten-yard area equally distant from the two end lines. "It" stands in the center area and must do his tackling within this area.

The players line up behind one end line and at the signal run for the other end. "It" attempts to tackle them as they go through the center area. All who are tackled becomes "it's" helpers. A runner is considered tackled if he runs out of bounds across the side lines. The last player tackled is "it" for the next game.

Black Tom.—This is very similar to Pom-Pom-Pull-Away. Mark two lines on the floor, dividing the playing space into three equal parts. One player is "it," and stands in the middle space and the other players stand in one end. When "it" calls "Black Tom" three times all the other players must run through the middle space to the other end, and he tags as many as he can. If they do not start promptly he may go after them and tag them at any time until they reach the other end space. All who are tagged go in the middle space and help catch the others.

Only the one who was "it" at first can call the players legally, and if any of them run into the middle space when anyone else calls or when any call is given other than "Black Tom," they are considered as caught without being tagged. Likewise, any player who leaves the goal before the original "it" calls "Black Tom" three times is considered caught, and to trick them into starting too soon "it" may call "Black Tom, Black Tom, Blue Tom" or "Black Tom, Red Tom, Black Tom." When all are caught another game begins with the first one caught as "it."

Black Man.—Exactly like Black Tom except for the call, "Who's afraid of the Black Man?"

Wheel Away.—In some sections the above game is played with the call "Wheel Away, Wheel Away, Wheel Away."

Stingo.—Stingo proceeds like Pom-Pom-Pull-Away except for the climax of the game. When all but one have been caught, instead of this player becoming "it" for the next game he cries "Stingo" and runs in any direction he chooses with the others in pursuit. He tries to keep "it" as long as possible and the person tagging him automatically takes "it" and attempts to escape the others.

This game is particularly effective on ice skates.

Bears and Cattle

Playground, Gymnasium, Street   Elementary and Junior High Schools

Mark off a goal at each end of the playing area and a bear's den at one side opposite the center. Select one player to be the bear who takes his place in the den, and divide the remaining players (cattle) into two sides, one behind each goal. The cattle run across to the opposite goals and the bear gives chase. All whom he tags become bears and join hands with him in the den. The original bear is at one end of the line and the first player tagged is at the other end throughout the game. The end players only may tag. If the line breaks, the cattle may chase the bears back to the den and all who are tagged become cattle. The last player to be tagged is the bear for the next game.

Red Lion.—This is a more complicated form of the above game. Select a player to serve as the "red lion" and have him take his place in the lion's den, a large circle drawn at one end of the area. The players gather around the den, taunting the lion with the rhyme:

> "Red lion, red lion, come out of your den
> Whoever you catch will help you then."

The lion rushes out and attempts to capture a player by holding him long enough to call "Red lion" three times. The lion then takes the player back to the den to assist him capture the rest. As they go back to the den the players may spank them with the open hand below the waist.

The players gather and call the rhyme again, but this time the lion and his helper come out with hands joined. To capture a player they must hold him encircled in their arms while they call "Red lion" three times. They then rush back to avoid being spanked.

From now on the way in which the lions come out depends upon the directions given by the leader. If he calls "Doubles" the lions come out in pairs as before. If he calls "Cow catcher" they come out in a chain and a player is captured whenever any two of the lions in the chain pass their clasped arms over his head. If the call is "Tight" the chain comes out and captures the player by surrounding him; they go back to the den with the prisoner inside the circle.

Whenever the lions are out, players may try to break apart their hands. If this is done, the lions must scramble back to avoid being spanked.

The game ends when all players are captured. The last caught becomes the red lion for the next game.

If the players seem too old for the use of the rhyme, it may be eliminated.

Tiddle-de-Winks

Gymnasium, Club   *Late Elementary and Junior High Schools*

This is a game much loved by boys. It is played at night in a gymnasium or clubroom. Divide the group into two teams and station them at opposite ends of the gymnasium or room. If the players do not know each other well, mark one team in some conspicuous way.

At the signal the teams advance toward each other attempting to capture opposing players and take them back to their own goal. As the teams near each other the leader turns out the lights and thereafter flashes them on and off about every ten seconds. The players thus get merely a glimpse of the opponents for a second and must proceed in darkness most of the time.

A captured player may resist as he is being taken to the goal, but once there he becomes a member of the team capturing him. He must remain at that goal until time is called. Time is called at the end of each minute of play and the lights are turned on to allow all to determine who have been captured and how the personnel of the two teams stands. The team having the most men at the end of the game wins.

Chain Tag

Playground, Gymnasium   *Elementary School*

Place limitations on the play area so that the players cannot scatter too widely. Select an "it" who picks another player to assist him and the two join hands. When a third player is tagged he takes his place between the two, and so the chain grows. The first two "its" remain at the end of the line throughout. Only the end players may tag. When the chain closes on a player it is permissible for him to break through the line or crowd under the hands. When the chain breaks, it must be reunited before tagging is legal. When girls are playing it is wise to prohibit breaking through. The game ends when the chain is complete. The last two players caught start the next game.

London Loo.—This game is more suitable than the above for girls and players who are liable to become injured. If players try to break through the line or crowd under the hands they may be tagged with the clasped hands of the chain players. This rule tends to eliminate roughness.

Chickidy Hand.—Select an "it" and assemble the players around him. All clasp their own hands. "It" counts ten and the players scatter, each with his hands still clasped, with "it" in pursuit. When a player is tagged he unclasps his hands and joins hands with "it." From then on the game proceeds as in Chain Tag except for the rule that untagged players must keep their own hands clasped.

Catch of Fish
(Fish Net)

Playground, Gymnasium   *Elementary School*

Mark off a goal at each end of the playing area and establish side lines. Divide the players into two teams, one behind each goal. The players at one goal join hands to form the fish net; those behind the other goal are the fish. At the starting signal all the players run for the opposite goal, and the fish net tries to catch as many fish as possible by encircling them. The fish cannot break through the net or go under the hands, but can escape only through the opening at the ends. When the net is closed all who have been captured join that side. The players go back to their goals and the other side forms the net for the next game. The game continues with each side alternating as fish and net until all the players on one side have been captured.

Variation.—After each catch of fish, count the fish and allow them to remain with their own team. After each team has had a given number of turns as the fish net, count up the score to determine the winning team.

Variation.—When older players are playing allow them to charge the line in an effort to break through. Charging is not permitted after the net closes. This rough element appeals to the boys.

Ante Over

Playground, Gymnasium, Yard   *Elementary and Junior High Schools*

This old and popular boys' game requires a building over which the ball is thrown. In the gymnasium a curtain is often stretched across the center.

The two teams take their places on opposite sides of the building. A player of Team A calls "Ante Over" and throws a softball over the building. The Team B players attempt to catch it. If someone succeeds, he and his team mates dash around the building and the player holding the ball attempts to hit one of the Team A players, who may take refuge by running around the building. If he succeeds, the hit player joins Team B and the ball goes to Team A. If no one catches the ball when it is thrown over the building, the side doing the catching calls "Ante Over" and the ball is thrown back. The side wins which has the most players when play ceases.

In some sections the boys call "Pigs tail" if the ball hits the building and bounds back. It is then thrown over again.

GROUP VI

These are team games. A player remains loyal to his team, and if caught remains a prisoner until released.

Snatch-Ball

(*Club Snatch, Snatch the Hat, Steal the Bacon*)

Playground, Gymnasium, Club   Late Elementary to Senior High Schools

This game is always popular among both sexes and is widely played.

Divide the players into two teams and line them up facing each other about thirty feet apart. Midway between the two lines, place a hand-

FIGURE 35.

kerchief, cap, or used softball. Number the players of each team from opposite ends of the line as in Figure 35. The leader calls a number, and the two players holding that number dart up to the handkerchief, each attempting to grab it and get back to his position before the other player can tag him. If he succeeds he scores one point for his team; if he fails, the player tagging him scores one point. The team scoring ten points first wins.

The tendency is for the players to rush for the handkerchief and grab it immediately. This usually leads to defeat. Experienced players pause beside the handkerchief and feint until their opponent is nervous and uncertain.

Calling the numbers at random rather than in rotation keeps all players alert and in a state of expectancy. Care should be taken to see that all numbers are called with equal frequency.

Snatch the Bone.—Players familiar with Snatch-Ball will enjoy this more strenuous and difficult variation. Place two or three benches in a row midway between the two lines and parallel to them. The benches extend the length of the teams if possible, and should never be less than twelve feet in length. Place the ball or handkerchief on the center of the benches. When a number is called, the two holders of this number run forward and leap the bench into the enemy's territory, or straddle the bench with one foot across the line, and from this position attempt to snatch the ball and return to their position without being tagged. The ball may not be snatched unless at least one foot is in the opponent's territory. Having snatched the ball, the player must return to his place in line without being tagged to score the point. No player may run around the ends of the benches—the barrier must be leaped or stepped over.

Plus-and-Minus Snatch-Ball.—Designate one of the teams as "plus" and the other as "minus." The leader calls two numbers such as "Six and two." The player in the plus team to run for the ball would be Number 8 (6+2). In the minus column it would be Number 4 (6−2).

Bottle-Change Snatch-Ball.—Place three circles in a row midway between the teams, one in the center and one at each end (see Figure 24, page 155). One end circle is designated as belonging to one team and the other to the other team. Place two bottles and a handkerchief or ball in the center circle. When a number is called each of the two players holding the number runs to the center circle, secures a bottle, runs to his end circle and places the bottle in it, then runs back to the center circle and attempts to secure the handkerchief and get back to his place without being tagged. In other respects the play is as in Snatch-Ball.

Champion Snatch-Ball.—Arrange all the players except one in a straight line and about forty feet in front station the odd player, known as champion. Midway between place the ball or handkerchief. The champion challenges one of the players and the two run out and proceed as in Snatch-Ball. If the champion wins he remains champion; otherwise he exchanges places with the player he challenged.

Prisoner's Base

Playground, Gymnasium   *Late Elementary and Junior High Schools*

This game, centuries old, is played in various ways in different localities. It is a daring, fighting game which deserves the widespread popularity it enjoys. The varying forms differ in detail only, mostly in regard to the layout of the play area. Two forms are suggested here.[2]

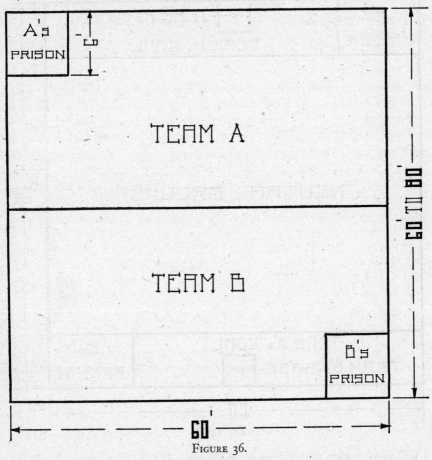

FIGURE 36.

Form Number 1.—The play area is laid out as in the accompanying diagram. Too large an area is defeating to the game. An area sixty feet wide and sixty to eighty feet long depending on the number of players, is recommended. Two prisons are marked out in diagonal corners, each six feet square, as in Figure 36.

[2] For other forms of Prisoner's Base see J. H. Bancroft *Games for the Playground, Home, School, and Gymnasium*, p. 156 ff. New York: The Macmillan Company, 1909.

Teams A and B occupy their respective territories. They venture into each other's territory and when there are liable to be tagged. If tagged, they are taken to prison. A prisoner may be freed from prison when a free member of his own side goes to the prison and tags him. Only one prisoner may be freed at a time by a player. Both prisoner and rescuer are eligible to be tagged while running back to their own territory. A

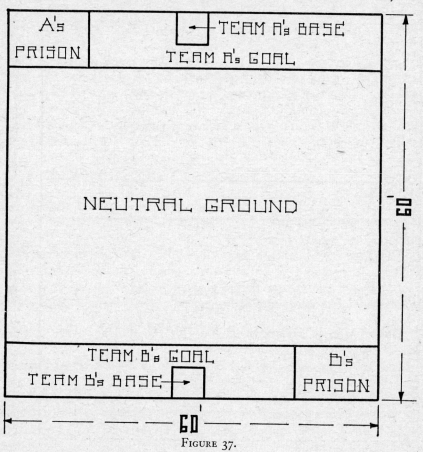

FIGURE 37.

team wins under the following conditions: (1) if it captures all of the opposing players; (2) if it has more prisoners than the other team in a given length of time; (3) if one of its players enters the opponent's prison when there are no prisoners there.

Form Number 2.—This is quite generally regarded as the best and most characteristic form of Prisoner's Base. Arrange the play area as in Figure 37—sixty by sixty feet is ideal for a fast game, but may be increased slightly for a large number of players.

Teams A and B are behind their respective goals. The play starts when a member of Team A ventures into neutral ground. As soon as he does this, a member of B enters in pursuit. The Team A man retreats and may reenter his goal if he chooses. As soon as the B man crosses into the neutral zone a second Team A man goes out to chase him. A second B man may then go after the second A man. A player may tag any opponent provided that opponent left his goal before the player did. That is, a player may capture any opponent who preceded him into the neutral zone. When a player captures an opponent he leads him to the prison and cannot be captured while doing so.

Once in the prison, the prisoner must remain there until freed by some free member of his own team who comes to the prison and tags him. Only one prisoner may be freed at a time by one player. Both prisoner and rescuer may return to their goal without being tagged. When more than one prisoner occupies the prison, they may join hands, and extend the line out into the neutral zone, provided the rear man has one foot in the prison. A rescuer then frees the end man of the line. The first prisoner captured is at the end of the line and new prisoners fall in at the rear of the line.

Prisoner's Base makes possible considerable strategy and team work. Once prisoners occupy the prison, the game centers more around freeing prisoners than tagging opponents.

The game is won when a team (1) captures all of the opponents, (2) succeeds in sending a player into the enemy's goal and touching their base located at the far side of the goal (Figure 37), (3) possesses more prisoners than the other team at the end of a given length of time.

Every Man in His Own Den.—This is a simplified form of Prisoner's Base, suitable for younger players.

Each player marks for himself a den two or three feet in diameter, these dens being scattered as far apart as possible over the playing space. Trees, rocks, or sticks may be used to indicate the dens. They start on the plan of Prisoner's Base, the players trying to make prisoners of one another, but if one is captured he must join his captor in the game instead of being a prisoner. The main rule of "Prisoner's Base" applies: for example, if players 1, 2, 3, 4, 5, and 6 leave their dens in the order of their numbers, player 1 can be caught by any of the others and player 6 can tag any or all of the others he can reach; but as soon as player 1 touches his own den again, that makes him able to tag any of the others.

The play begins by the players "making dares" to induce their opponents from their dens; as they are captured they form fewer and stronger groups, until finally there are two groups of about equal strength or one group that rapidly captures all the rest. That player wins who, with his captives, finally captures all the rest or who has the greatest number of prisoners when the game ends.

Stealing Sticks

Playground, Gymnasium   *Late Elementary and Junior High Schools*

This is a game similar to Prisoner's Base, requiring team work, strategy, daring, chase, and capture.

Arrange the play area as in Figure 38, and place three or four sticks in each stick base. The game proceeds just as in Prisoner's Base with all

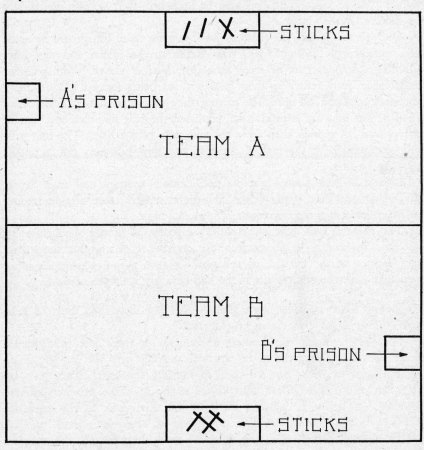

FIGURE 38.

the rules of Prisoner's Base applying in regard to capturing and freeing prisoners. It presents the additional objective of stealing the opponents' stick. When a player succeeds in reaching the enemy's stick base and touching a stick without being tagged, he is permitted to take one stick back to his own territory without being tagged. Teams should organize and elect a captain and a stick guard. The stick guard stands in front of the stick base but cannot enter it until an opponent enters it. The winner is determined by the number of sticks stolen. The rules of Prisoner's Base, Form 2, should be studied carefully before using this game.

Flag Raid.—Mark out an area approximately fifty by one hundred feet and draw a line across the center dividing it into two fifty-foot courts. On each of the back lines, set up six sticks in the ground and tie white rags or handkerchiefs on them. Team A occupies one of the courts and Team B the other. Each team has a six-foot "prison" marked out at the rear corner of its court.

Each team attempts to enter the other's court and secure its flags. If a player secures a flag without being caught he may return with it without being molested. If a player is caught and held while his captor counts five he is placed in his captor's prison. A team may rescue a prisoner by entering the opponents' prison and tagging the prisoner. Both then go back unmolested. Only one prisoner may be rescued at a time and no flag may be captured by a player as he frees a prisoner.

The team securing all of the opponents' flags first wins.

Relievo
(*Ring-a-Lievo*)

Playground, Woodland   *Late Elementary and Junior High Schools*

Mark out a six-foot circle on the ground, known as the prison. Divide the players into two teams. One team enters the prison, blinds, and counts one hundred. In the meantime the other team hides. When through counting, the team in the prison calls "Coming" and starts the search. Two or three players of the searching team should be left to guard the prison, but must not enter it. When a player is sighted he is chased and if captured brought back to the prison. Although boys like to play the game by allowing captured men to fight all the way to the prison, it is better to consider a player captured when he is thrown to the ground. If a member of the hiding team is able to evade the searchers and reach the prison, he may enter it and tag one of the prisoners, calling "Relievo," thus releasing him. Both are then free to hide again. The game continues until all of the hiding team are captured.

Boys familiar with this game enjoy it particularly at night.

Robbers and Soldiers.—This rough and strenuous old game, when properly played, calls for considerable strategy and clever maneuvering. Establish a goal ten feet square. Divide the players into two groups, one group known as soldiers and the other as robbers. There should be five times as many soldiers as robbers. Have the soldiers select a general and the robbers a chief. The soldiers occupy the goal while the robbers hide. More time should be given for hiding than in the average hiding game —at least five minutes. The soldiers then set out in search. Captured robbers are brought back to the goal and may fight all the way. The soldiers may gang up to bring one robber back. Robbers may break out of the prison at any time they are able to fight their way past the guards. The game continues until all robbers are captured.

Holding the Line

Playground, Gymnasium　　　*Late Elementary and Junior High Schools*

Establish two goals 80 to 100 feet apart. One team lines up behind one goal and the other lines up across the center of the field. On the signal to start, the goal-line team runs to the other goal in an effort to rush it within thirty seconds. The center team tries to prevent them by catching and holding them. At the end of thirty seconds, those reaching the goal are counted, and the teams change places. After an equal number of tries, the scores are added and the team with the highest score wins. A time-keeper and score keeper are needed. The game is hard on clothes.

Tail Snatching

Playground, Camp, Club　　　*Late Elementary and Junior High Schools*

Divide the group into two teams and place them behind lines fifty feet apart. Give each team strips of colored cloth an inch wide, each team having a different color. Each player sticks the tails under his belt behind and is not permitted to tie it, twist it around the belt, or conceal the ends.

At the signal the two teams run toward each other and attempt to snatch off each other's tails. Personal contact in the form of holding, shoving, or fighting for the tails is not permitted. One minute is allowed and the team that has the most of the opponents' tails at the end of this time wins.

Tail Fight.—The rough element of this game appeals to older boys more than the above. The event is conducted in the same way except that the players attack each other and attempt to take away each other's tails. The players may or may not be allowed to gang up on one opponent—the leader should use his judgment and consider the nature and temper of the players. Three to five minutes are allowed and the team wins that has the most tails at the end.

Dodgeball—Team Form

Playground, Gymnasium　　　*Late Elementary to Senior High School*

Dodgeball as described under Section V is designed to determine an individual winner. The team forms here described are equally as popular.

Arrange the players and proceed just as described under Dodgeball. When a player is legally hit he leaves the game temporarily. When all the center players are eliminated, the sides reverse, and the circle players go to the center. The team wins which clears the center in the shortest time. This calls for a timekeeper. Two methods of timing are used: (1) The time taken by each team to eliminate the other side may be recorded and the time compared, or (2) each team may be allotted one minute and the team eliminating the most players in this time wins.

Instead of having the center men who are hit leave the game, the game may be played by having them drop dead inside the circle and remain there until all have been dropped.

Block-House Dodgeball.[3]—This is a particularly interesting form of Dodgeball for girls and young players. Arrange one team in a forty-foot circle and place the other team inside. Scatter a dozen child's building blocks inside the circle. A volleyball is used. A timekeeper should be appointed.

At the signal the inside players collect the blocks and attempt to build a three-story block house. The outside players throw the ball at them and as soon as a player is hit, he drops the blocks he is holding and leaves the circle. When one player only is left, however, he must stay in the circle no matter how often he is hit and continue building the house until it is completed, while the outside players continue to throw the ball attempting to knock down the blocks with the ball.

When the block house is completed, the time is recorded and the teams change positions. The team completing the house in the shortest time wins.

Square Dodgeball.—Mark two adjacent squares on the floor, about thirty feet in size. One team scatters in each square. The ball is put in play by tossing it up on the division line between two opposing players, as in Basketball. The players attempt to secure it without leaving their squares. A player is entitled to throw the ball at the opposing team if it has hit the floor or another player before he secures it. When a player is hit he is eliminated. The team clearing the other square first wins. The eliminated players gather around the sides of their team's square and return the ball when it goes out.

This game may also be played by having eliminated players join the other team, or by allowing them to stay in the play and counting the hits made in a given length of time.

[3] The idea for this game is taken from E. M. Bowers, *Recreation for Girls and Women,* p. 46. Copyright, 1934. By permission of A. S. Barnes & Company, publishers.

Three-Team Dodgeball.—The area is divided into three courts as illustrated in Figure 39, each twenty by thirty feet in size. Players are divided into three teams: Team 1 occupies one end court; Team 2 the opposite end court; and Team 3 the middle court. The ball is given to one of the end teams. Appoint a timekeeper to record the time. Teams 1 and 2 throw to hit members of Team 3 in the center court. Any member of Team 3 hit by a fly ball on any part of his body except his head leaves the court. If a player is hit by one of the end court men who has one or both feet over the line, he is not counted out. When the center

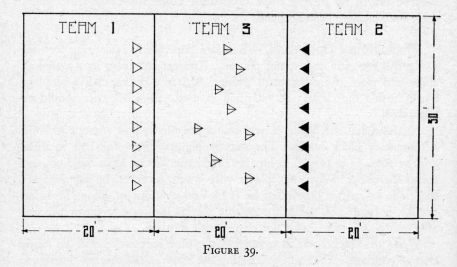

FIGURE 39.

court has been cleared the teams change courts and Team No. 2 occupies the center court. When all teams have occupied the center court, the times are compared and the team wins who occupied the center court the longest.

Use a basketball when boys or girls are playing alone; in mixed groups a volleyball or sport ball should be used. When girls are playing, hitting above the hips is prohibited.

Progressive Dodgeball.—The court and the teams are arranged exactly as in Three-Team Dodgeball. A referee and a scorer are needed, the latter being equipped with a large score board. The scorer also keeps time.

The game is started with the ball in the possession of the center team. It is thrown at either of the end teams in an effort to hit the players. When an end team has possession of the ball, it attempts to hit the players in the center court or opposite end court. Whenever a player is hit by a fly ball on any part of his body except his head, the whistle sounds and a point is scored against his team. The whistle then sounds again to start the play, the ball remaining in the possession of the team scored against. When a player steps over the boundary lines, a point is scored against his team and any points he makes by hitting players on the play do not count. When the ball strikes the floor, players in that court try to get it before it rolls into another court.

The game is played in three five-minute periods. At the end of the first and second periods the teams change courts. Thus each court occupies the center court once. The team with the lowest score at the end of the game wins.

The ball may be thrown directly at the opposition or may be passed to another player who may be in more strategic positions to make the throw. In order to prevent stalling for time on the part of a team which is in the lead, the ball may not be passed more than once to members of the same team and the referee begins to count slowly when a player has possession of the ball; if he does not throw before the count of three, a point is scored against him.

The game may also be played by using two teams instead of three. Team 1 is divided between the two end zones, and Team 2 occupies the center zone. Proceed as before, playing in two five-minute halves.

Field Dodgeball.—A starting line about twenty-five feet long is drawn on the floor or ground. Sixty feet out from the middle of this line a base is placed. Divide the players into two teams. The team in the field scatters between the starting line and the base, and the running team lines up behind the starting line. The leader throws a soccer ball or basketball into the field and immediately starts two players of the running team who run around the base and back to the starting line.

The fielding team attempts to hit the runners with the ball. The fielders may run for the ball but once a player holds it he must stand still to throw it, and may throw either directly at the runner or to another fielder who is in a better position to hit the runners. As soon as a runner is hit or as soon as a runner crosses the starting line another player is started. A score is counted for each runner reaching home safely. After all the players have run the sides change and the game goes on for any number of innings.

Variation.—This is the same as the above game except that one runner instead of two is started at the beginning of the game. The ball is given to this runner and he throws it into the field, then runs around the base and back. In case the runner is hit by the ball and thus retired, he throws up his hands as a signal for the next runner to start. The ball is not returned to the starting line each time a new runner starts, but remains in the possession of the fielding team.

Variation.—This is the same as Field Dodgeball except for the arrangement of the field. The starting line is thirty feet long, and from fifty to sixty feet from it a baseline of equal length is drawn, parallel to the starting line. At each end of this baseline an Indian club or similar object is placed. The runner must run around both of these Indian clubs before returning to the starting line.

WATER TAG GAMES

The following tag games are described in Chapter XXVI, "Water Activities":

Simple Water Tag Games	Water Black-and-White
Water Poison	Water Crows-and-Cranes
Cross the Pool	Water Dodgeball
Duck in the Pool	Water Spud
Water Fish-Net	Water Center-Ball
Log	

WINTER TAG GAMES

The following tag games are described in Chapter XXVII, "Winter Activities":

Fox and Geese	Snowball Tag
Snow Dodgeball	Relievo in the Snow
Snowball Pom-Pom-Pull-Away	

TAG GAMES IN OTHER CHAPTERS

Soccer Snatch-Ball	Champion Hockey Snatch-Ball
Champion Soccer Snatch-Ball	Mounted Tag
Hockey Snatch-Ball	Mounted Pom-Pom-Pull-Away

TAG GAMES IN *SOCIAL GAMES FOR RECREATION*

Hot Potato	Plus-and-Minus Snatch the Handkerchief
Our House is Falling Down	
Snatch the Handkerchief	Champion Snatch the Handkerchief

CHAPTER XIX

GAMES OF PERSONAL COMBAT

BOXING and wrestling are familiar examples of a group of games in which personal combat is the main feature. Fencing is a less familiar example. All three of these are relics of ancient warfare. Other games of the combat type have been devised to satisfy the fighting desire of boys.

The fact that these activities are games is often overlooked, since people think of team games as the type and forget that tennis singles, checkers, and chess are games, although there is but one contestant on a side. The essential features of a game, including strategy, deception, and free choice of the manner of attack, are conspicuous in combats, making them games rather than simple contests.

Both wrestling and boxing demand quick thinking and are excellent for developmental purposes, as they bring almost all the muscles into play. Boxing also requires speed and footwork. Many adults find these sports useful in a recreative sense. They are strenuous, however, and only those who are in training should be allowed to enter tournaments.

The major combats, boxing and wrestling, will be discussed first and the minor combats later.

Wrestling

Playground, Gymnasium   *Junior High School to Adults*

Wrestling is a sport practically as old as civilization, and is popular with people of all lands. There are many distinctive types, the most important of which are the Greco-Roman or European; the catch-as-catch-can, prevalent in America; and jiu-jitsu, a novel form used by the Japanese.

In the catch-as-can style there are two positions from which holds are obtained: standing and kneeling. In actual wrestling matches both types of holds are used. The competitors stand, facing each other on the mat, and after the signal is given, each tries to get a hold that will be to his advantage. The winner must force his opponent on his back so as to make the two shoulders touch the mat at the same time, called a *pin* fall. This means that the opponents may lose their standing position and fall to the mat without a *pin* fall being secured. Then the kneeling holds are employed to win the match.

The competitors are allowed to use any legal hold, the term legal being used because there are several dangerous holds that are barred in amateur bouts.

A few of the fundamental principles of holds, first standing, then kneeling, will be explained, together with the defense that may be used against them.

Wrestling Holds

Standing Holds.—First of all, a strong standing position is necessary, one that will allow the person to be well braced, and yet permit him to move quickly when an opening is presented. This is called the "on guard" position. It is a crouching one, with knees slightly bent and the body inclined forward from the waist up. The feet are set well apart, pointed outward, and the left in advance of the other. The arms are somewhat extended, the left more so.

From this "on guard" position the two rivals will usually grasp each other in the so-called *Referee's Hold.* This hold is a fair one to each opponent, and is the one the referee arbitrarily uses to bring both of them together in case there has been needless delay in seeking openings. In this hold, each boy places one hand over the back of the opponent's neck, at the same time grasping with his other hand his opponent's arm near the elbow. The feet are well spread and back out of reach.

There are any number of good methods of taking an opponent off his feet. A few of the simpler ones follow:

Arm Drag.—Grasp opponent's right elbow with your left hand, turn to the left, placing right foot outside of his right foot, and slide right arm over his right arm, clamping it above the elbow between your arm and side. Continue turning to the left and drop to the mat as opponent loses his balance, forcing him to land squarely on his back or right shoulder. (*Break*—step outside aggressor's tripping leg or grasp him under the thigh with your free hand.)

Head Lock.—Grasp his elbow and turn, as in the preceding hold, but clamp his head between your arm and side instead of his arm; fall to mat as before. (*Break*—as above, jerking the head backward at the same time.)

Tackle or Double Leg Lock.—Stoop suddenly and, rushing under opponent's arms, grasp him around the knees as in making a football tackle. Stand erect, lifting him on your shoulder. Assuming his body is over your right shoulder, swing his legs to the left and drop forward and to the right, whipping him forcibly to the mat on his back. (*Break*—extend legs backward and spread them, throwing your weight on aggressor to force him to the mat under you. A still better way is to lean over opponent's shoulder and grasp him around the waist with both arms.)

Front Waist Lock.—Push upward on opponent's elbow with one hand, and at the same time place other hand under jaw and push head back. This makes an opening to grasp him around the waist, your shoulders against his chest and forearms across the small of his back. Continue advancing with your shoulder, at the same time drawing the lower part of his body under you, and force him backward to the mat. After practice, combine this with a leg trip. (*Break*—jump quickly backward and throw weight forward; place open hand against aggressor's chin and push his head upward and backward.)

Rear Waist Lock—The opening may be made in the same way as for the front waist lock. Another way is as follows: With your left hand push opponent's right elbow forcibly across his chest, turning his body toward the left. Step in rapidly to a position behind him and grasp him around the waist. From this position you can raise him, and swinging his legs to the side as in the double leg lock, whip him to the mat. A method requiring less effort is to turn sideward and drop to the mat, pulling him backward over your extended leg. The rear lock is not so apt to end in a fall, but is useful only to bring opponent to the mat. (*Break*—grasp aggressor's fingers and force his arms apart, stepping forward away from him. If he attempts to lift you twine your leg around his leg.)

Mat Holds.—On the mat, the defensive man is usually upon his hands and knees. It is advisable to turn the feet inward and flex the legs sufficiently so that you are practically sitting upon your feet, with the knees spread rather far apart. The elbows are bent and kept fairly close to the sides, but the hands are placed wider than the shoulders. The head should not be allowed to droop. This insures a low substantial position, from which you will not be easily dislodged, and which in itself protects you from the more dangerous holds. The aggressor may assume a variety of positions dependent upon the hold he is seeking, but space will not permit a detailed description here.

Nelsons.—The holds most commonly used on the neck are the nelsons, and chiefly the half nelson on the near side. Assuming the aggressor is to the opponent's right side and facing in the same direction, the near half nelson is secured by passing the right arm under his right arm, the forearm passing upward in front of his shoulder so that the hand may be placed on the back of the under-man's head. By raising slightly and straightening the arm the opponent's right shoulder is forced upward and his head downward, so that he is thrown over onto his left shoulder or back. The half nelson is always used in combinations with some other hold, for example, reaching beneath the chest with the left arm, grasping his crotch or farther leg at the knee, and so forth. The quarter or bar, three-quarter, and full nelsons are modifications of this fundamental hold. (*Break*—depress the shoulder, bring the arm close to the side and push the head backward; keep low and extend the opposite arm and leg sideward to afford a wider base. Also, a good way is to roll left shoulder backward, grasping for a backhanded hold with the left arm; at the same time clamp his right arm tight to your side to keep him from releasing it.)

Scissors.—Probably next in importance to the nelsons are the scissor holds, in which some part of the opponent is imprisoned between the thighs of the aggressor, the feet being crossed to assist in applying pressure. When applied to the head or body, this can be made a very painful hold and may force the opponent to yield even when his shoulders are not touching the mat. One of the best methods of securing the body scissors is to first obtain a half nelson on the near arm of the opponent, then straddle him and throw your weight in the direction your half nelson is forcing him. As he turns over, lock your legs tightly around his body and, encircling his head with your free arm, hold it firmly against your chest. Keep his arm and head locked and apply pressure with the scissors. (*Break*—the safest and simplest break is to force the aggressor's legs apart with your arm or leg.)

This should give a general idea of a few of the fundamental positions and holds of wrestling. In case the beginner desires to practice other holds, it is highly advisable to do so under the direction of a capable instructor, as serious injuries are quite liable to result from unsupervised wrestling by inexperienced men.

Wrestling Rules

Equipment.—The standard area of the mat is twenty feet square when ropes are used and twenty-four feet square when ropes are not used. When ropes are used they should be one inch in diameter, wrapped and stretched two, three, and four feet, respectively, above the mat. These ropes are stretched from turnbuckles attached to the four corner posts. The posts must be placed at least eighteen inches from the corner. The ropes are kept from spreading by vertical ropes, three-eighths inch thick, three of which are placed equidistant on each side of the ring.

Full-length tights, sleeveless shirts, and heelless gymnasium shoes laced by means of eyelets are recommended. Colored anklets should be worn to distinguish the legs of the wrestlers.

Weight Classification.—Competition is divided into the following weight classifications:

	College	Secondary School
		95 lbs. and under
Flyweight	118 lbs. and under	105 lbs. and under
Bantam	126 lbs. and under	115 lbs. and under
Feather	135 lbs. and under	125 lbs. and under
Light	145 lbs. and under	135 lbs. and under
Welter	155 lbs. and under	145 lbs. and under
Middle	165 lbs. and under	155 lbs. and under
Light-heavy	175 lbs. and under	165 lbs. and under
Heavy	Over 175 lbs.	185 lbs. and under

In secondary school competition the 95 pound class and the 185 pound class are optional.

Legal and Illegal Holds.—In college circles, any hold, lock, or grip is allowed except the following:

1. Hammerlock above the right angle.
2. Twisting hammerlock.
3. Over-scissors.
4. Strangle holds.
5. Full (double) nelson.
6. Toe hold.
7. Body slams, unless the attacker's knee touches the mat before the upper part of his opponent's body hits the mat.
8. Holds over mouth, nose, or eyes.
9. Interlocking of fingers, hands, or arms around body or legs while contestants are on the mat.
10. Bending or twisting of fingers for punishment or to break holds.
11. Any hold used for punishment alone.
12. No striking, kicking, gouging, hair pulling, butting, elbowing, strangling, or anything that endangers life or limb shall be allowed.

In secondary school competition, all the above holds and tactics are illegal and in addition the following are barred:

1. All slams from the standing position.
2. The fall-back (falling backward when opponent is on the contestant's back).

Falls.—Any part of both shoulders held in contact with the mat for a two-second count constitutes a fall. No fall is allowed if the head or one or both shoulders of the defensive contestant are off the mat.

Off the Mat.—If the contestants are interlocked off or on the edge of the mat, they should be brought to the center of the mat. If neither had the advantage just before leaving the mat, they resume by taking a standing position. If one held the advantage, he is given the position of advantage in the referee's position on the mat. If a fall was imminent and the defensive wrestler intentionally left the mat, the contestants are given as nearly as possible the same positions which they held when the bout was stopped. If a contestant persists in going off the mat intentionally, the referee may award the match to the opponent.

Stalling.—While on their feet, the contestants must wrestle; they must make an honest effort to gain a position of advantage, and having gained it, to secure a fall. If a contestant in a position of advantage on the mat is stalling, the referee should order both men to their feet in a neutral position. If a contestant in a neutral position on the mat is stalling, both are ordered to the floor in the referee's position, with the offender underneath.

Injuries.—If a contestant is injured he is allowed a three-minute rest, after which the bout continues as if he had gone off the mat. If he is unable to continue and the injury was accidental, his opponent is awarded the match by fall. If the injury resulted from an illegal hold, the bout is forfeited to the injured player and scored as a fall.

Decisions.—If no fall has resulted after the expiration of the regular period of wrestling, the referee awards the bout to the contestant who shows the greater wrestling ability and aggressiveness, provided the contestant has a time advantage of at least one minute. The time advantage begins when he brings his opponent to the mat and continues as long as he has clearly a position of advantage, even though his opponent may regain his feet temporarily.

Scoring.—In dual meets, when only one of the two contestants in a match secures a fall, five points are awarded to the contestant securing the fall; if both contestants secure falls, the contestant securing the fall in the shortest time wins the bout and is credited with five points, and his opponent is credited with three points for his fall. A decision counts three points. If a contestant secures more than one fall he is credited with points only for one fall. The team securing the highest total of points is declared winner.

Length of Bouts.—College bouts are ten minutes in length unless a fall occurs. If no fall occurs and the referee does not award the bout, two extra periods of three minutes each are wrestled.

If a contestant brings his opponent to the mat and secures a position of advantage within two minutes the bout becomes a continuous bout for the remainder of the period or until a fall terminates it. If neither contestant secures a position of advantage within two minutes, the referee stops the bout and the remaining eight minutes are divided into two four-minute periods. A coin is tossed and the winner chooses between the underneath and behind positions in the referee's position on the mat. At the beginning of the second four-minute period, the positions are reversed. If a fall is obtained in the first four minutes, this terminates only the first four-minute period, and the second four-minute period must be wrestled as if no fall had been made.

In championship meets, in case both contestants secure falls in four-minute or extra-period bouts, the one securing the fall in the shorter time is awarded the points for the fall.

After the main bout and between the extra-period bouts, an intermission of one minute is allowed. Between the periods of the regular bout no more time is taken than is necessary.

Secondary school bouts are seven or eight minutes in length. If neither contestant secures an advantage within two minutes, the remainder of the match is divided into two three-minute bouts and conducted as in college matches.

Officials.—The match is in charge of a referee who starts the bouts, enforces the rules, determines when falls are made, and awards decisions. Three timekeepers keep the time of the bout; one is assigned to each contestant to keep a record of his time advantage.

Boxing

Playground, Gymnasium　　　　　　　*Junior High School to Adults*

Boxing is too intricate a sport to be described in more than a general way. It takes long experience to master the more scientific details of offense and defense, and the beginner should concentrate on perfecting the fundamental principles that are taught him. A correct start is all important.

The most fundamental technique to learn is the method of striking properly. With this advantage, beginners will avoid injuries to the hands. It is important, when striking a blow, to have the thumb bent against the front of the clenched fingers; also to hit with the hand making a continuous line with the forearm as it strikes.

Next it is important to learn the proper boxing position. This is one in which the left foot is extended and pointed almost straight ahead. The right foot is also pointed forward, but to the right at the same time, and the heel is raised so that the weight is on the ball of the foot. The two feet are from a foot to a foot and a half apart, giving the person a well braced position.

Most boxers assume a slightly crouching attitude. The position of the arms is as follows: The right arm is bent, with the fist brought past the center of the chest, and in a position to protect either heart or chin; the elbow is low and kept close to the body, ready to block many of the body blows. The left arm is extended forward toward the opponent's chin, with the forearm inclined slightly upwards. Both palms face downward. The body is bent at the waist so that the head and right shoulder drop slightly and the latter slants slightly away from the opponent.

From this position many blows can be made, but the two that are most fundamental and which every beginner should learn first, are the *straight left jab* and the *right cross.*

The *straight left jab* is a very important blow in boxing. It is carried both to the opponent's face and body. A step forward is made with the left foot, a push being made off the ball of the right foot. If the blow is carried through effectively, the right foot will drag forward although holding to the floor; if not carried through, the boxer may step back with the left foot so that the position is the same as that from which the movement started. As the straight left is made, the right hand is maintaining a defensive position. This permits a block for your opponent, who may strike either over or under your extended left arm; and also a chance for a follow-up blow with the right hand if there is an opening.

This blow is parried by a block with the protecting right hand, again by slipping the head to the side, or by stepping back with the right foot, inclining the head and the body back, thereby causing the opponent's blow to fall short.

The blow just described is useful in winning bouts on points, as the opponent may be reached often, even though not for a hard blow. The second blow mentioned above, the *right cross,* is a dangerous one that carries much force behind it. It is usually successful when the opponent has made a left jab to the body. The right cross is made over the opponent's left arm and driven against his chin. This blow is often used to follow up a feint with the straight left, after the opponent has countered. Beginners are first taught to use the right cross to the opponent's head. There is, however, another blow frequently made with the right hand, which is called the *straight right.* The difference is that this blow goes under the opponent's left arm instead of over it as does the right cross, and is delivered straight-away to the body or chin.

The most successful defense to the right cross blow is to duck the head, keeping the chin low, and raising the left shoulder at the same time to ward off the blow or change it into a glancing one.

Another blow frequently employed is the *uppercut.* This is usually delivered at close quarters. It is started lower than usual and the force is carried upward, usually to the opponent's chin or solar plexus.

The blows commonly known as *hooks* are delivered with either hand, but from a sidewise position with the arm curved considerably.

There is one defensive safeguard that applies to all situations, and that is, always keep the chin down when advancing.

When the two men get hold of each other, as in wrestling, what is known as a "clinch" results. No striking is allowed during a clinch. The referee orders the two men to fall apart. As they do so, each man tries, as a protective measure, to keep his arms outside of the opponent; holding the latter's forearms together, so as to prevent a blow being struck while at close quarters.

An inflated striking bag is helpful in practicing the blows of boxing by oneself. This is suspended from a low ceiling. The bag allows the boxer to practice all the blows that are used, dodging when the bag rebounds. Hitting a heavy bag is also useful in developing striking ability.

Another way in which the boxer practices alone is by the method of "shadow boxing," in which he practices against an imaginary opponent, following him around the ring, leading, feinting, countering, and dodging, as the case may be. This is very vigorous, but an excellent developer of footwork.

Boxing Rules

Ring.—The ring should not be less than sixteen or more than twenty feet square. The floor shall extend beyond the ropes for a distance of at least two feet. The ring is enclosed by at least three rope rails with cloth wrappings. The posts should be properly padded. The floor should be padded at least one inch thick with corrugated paper, matting, felt, or other soft material. For an outdoor ring, a good padding is dampened sawdust covered with tight canvas.

During a match the ring must be cleared of all buckets, chairs, and so forth.

Equipment.—Gloves are to be of the recognized pattern, weighing not less than ten ounces. (Professional boxers often use six- and eight-ounce gloves; twelve-ounce gloves are excellent for practice.) Boxing shoes having spikes or cleats are barred. Sleeveless shirts and trunks reaching to within six inches of the knees are worn.

Weight Classification.—Same as in Wrestling.

Seconds.—Each contestant may be assisted by two seconds. The seconds must not speak, signal, or coach the contestants during the round; must remain seated and enter the ring only at the termination of the contest. They may not enter the ring between rounds.

Fouls.—The following are fouls:

1. Hitting below the belt.
2. Hitting an opponent who is down or who is getting up after going down.
3. Holding an opponent or deliberately maintaining a clinch.
4. Holding an opponent with one hand and hitting with the other.
5. Pushing, or butting, with head or shoulder or using the knee.
6. Hitting with inside or butt of the hand, wrist, or elbow.
7. Hitting with open glove.
8. Wrestling or roughing at the ropes.
9. Going down without being hit.
10. Striking deliberately at that part of the body over the kidneys.
11. Using abusive or insulting language.
12. Any physical action that may injure a contestant except by fair, sportsmanlike boxing.
13. Failure to obey the referee.
14. Coaching or advice from spectators or applause when in the opinion of the referee and judges the occasion warrants.

Penalties.—It is recommended that the referee immediately disqualify a contestant who commits a deliberate foul and award the decision to his opponent. The referee should not give more than one warning for a foul which, although unintentional, may incapacitate the opponent. In the case of minor fouls the referee has the option of awarding the decision to the opponent. The judges penalize contestants in points for all fouls, both major and minor.

Down.—A contestant is considered down under the following conditions:

1. When any part of his body other than his feet is on the floor.
2. When he is hanging helplessly on the ropes.
3. When he is rising from a down position.

When a contestant is down, his opponent must retire out of striking distance and not resume boxing until ordered by the referee.

Scoring.—A maximum of twenty points is awarded to a contestant in each round. Fourteen of these points are for attack and defense. Attack involves clean hits, aggressive action, and well-delivered partial hits. Defense covers blocking, making the opponent miss, balance, and readiness for counter attack. Four points is awarded for generalship, and two for aggressiveness.

Points are deducted for all fouls, and for stalling, covering up with hands, clinching, and hitting while holding opponents.

Number of Rounds.—A contest consists of three rounds. A round is two minutes long in college competition and may be reduced for secondary schools. The intermission between rounds is one minute. If the judges disagree, a fourth round may be ordered.

A bout is terminated if a contestant who is down fails to take his feet in ten seconds.

Officials.—The officials consist of a referee, two judges, two timekeepers, and a medical officer. The referee has general charge of the match. The judges are stationed at opposite sides of the ring, and record points, rounds, and pick the winner. If they disagree, the referee casts the deciding vote. The timekeepers indicate the beginning and end of each round.[1]

FENCING

Fencing is a sport of major interest in Europe and has been gaining popularity steadily in this country. Fencing is done with three types of weapons: foils, sabres, and epees.

Fencing Events

Gymnasium   *Senior High School to Adults*

The Foil.—The foil is a thrusting weapon and the object is to thrust it at the opponent so that the point contacts him some place on the target. The target consists of a vest covering the fencer from the neck to the hip bones and then tapering down to the crotch.

Fencing takes place on a mat forty feet long and three feet six inches wide. The two contestants stand at the center facing each other. They cross swords, step back one step, and the referee calls "Fence."

[1] See "National Collegiate Athletic Association Rules for Boxing," *Art of Self Defense.* New York: American Sports Publishing Company.

There are eight standard thrusts, with parries for each, which are used by fencers. Each of these thrusts is designed to hit a different section of the target on the opponent. There are of course a great many variations of these standard thrusts.

Each time a fencer contacts the target with the point of his foil, he scores one point. That is, he scores one point if the end of his foil touches his opponent any place below the neck and above the crotch and hip bones, including the back. The arms are not part of the target.

The player wins who first scores five points, except that when the score is four all, one player must score two points in succession to win.

The Sabre.—The sabre is a cutting and thrusting weapon and is heavier than the foil.

The rules for sabre fencing are the same as those used for foils with the following exceptions: (1) the target includes the entire body except the legs—trunk, head, and arms are all within the target; (2) a fencer may score by hitting the target with the point of the sabre, with the front cutting edge, and with the upper third of the back edge.

The foils and parries are the same as in fencing with foils, with some adaptation for the protection of the head.

The Epee.—The epee is a dueling sword and is heavier than either the foil or the sabre.

The rules are the same as in foil fencing with the following exceptions: (1) the entire body is the target; (2) the player wins who makes the first three hits; (3) at the start, instead of crossing swords, the points of the weapons are touched. The thrusts and parries are about the same.

Team Competition in Fencing.—A fencing team may consist of either seven or three players. When seven-man teams are used, three fence with the foil, two with the sabre, and two with the epee.

Each of the three foil fencers must meet all of the three opposing foil fencers. Likewise, each of the two sabre fencers must meet both of the opposing sabre fencers; the same applies to the two epee fencers. Thus there are a total of seventeen matches. The winner of each scores one point for his team and the team with the highest score wins.

When three-man teams are used, one player uses the foil, one the sabre, and one the epee. There are three matches, and the team wins that wins two out of the three.

MINOR COMBATS

Tilting

Playground, Camp, Club   *Late Elementary to Senior High School*

This game, originated by Ernest Seton Thompson, is unexcelled in popularity in camp, boys' clubs, and scout troops. It has excellent possibilities when properly handled, and is thrilling both to participants and spectators.

Equipment.—The equipment, being homemade, is frequently faulty in dimensions and consequently the game falls short of its possibilities. The spears should be of bamboo—no other material is usable—and should be about two inches thick at the heavy end. The bamboo poles on which rugs are shipped are the best source. The length of the spears should be not less than six nor more than seven feet—the game is usually played with poles much too long. A hardwood disk is pegged on the end as shown in the illustration, this disk being three-and-one-half-inches in diam-

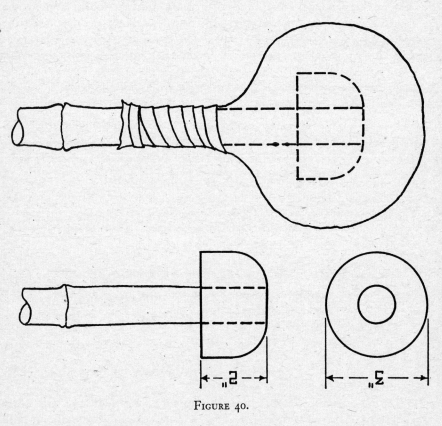

FIGURE 40.

eter and two inches thick. Pad the end tightly with hair stuffing—excelsior soon pulverizes and should be avoided. Cover the padding tightly with canvas and hold by tying it to the pole and then wrapping adhesive tape, as in Figure 40.

The contestants stand on stools. Barrels are frequently used but are too high and dangerous. Small wooden tubs are usable but it is difficult to dislodge good tilters from them. It is better to make stools with a fifteen-inch top and widely spread, strong legs. Place the tops of the stools exactly spear's length apart.

Object.—The object is to dislodge the opponent from the stool by pushing and punching him with the spear.

Start.—The contestants mount the stools and place the ends of the spears on the ground, touching each other, until the starting signal.

Seconds.—Each contestant has one second who stands behind him and catches him in case of a fall.

The Play.—The contestants push, shove, and punch each other above the knees and below the head. It is permissible to place the spear on the back of the opponent's neck and push down, but not to strike above the neck. The pole may not be used as a club in striking the opponent—the blows must be of the punching type. The spear may be swung, however, to strike the opponent's pole in an attempt to cause him to drop it. Defense is accomplished by manipulating one's own spear, batting off the attacking spear with the hand, and wriggling the hips and body.

Fouls.—The following are fouls:

1. Deliberately striking the opponent above the neck (punching straight at the head).

2. Deliberately striking below the knees (punching straight at the legs below the knees).

3. Striking the stool in an effort to dislodge the opponent.

4. Swinging the spear as a club at the opponent.

5. Deliberately rapping the opponent's hand as it holds the spear.

6. Grasping the opponent's spear with the hand. (The hand can be used to ward off the spear but must not close on it.)

Scoring.—A contestant wins under the following conditions:

1. When his opponent touches the floor with any part of his body.

2. When his opponent commits a foul.

3. When his opponent drops his pole.

4. When he is awarded a judge's decision.

If no fall occurs the judges select the winner on the basis of blows struck, defense, and aggressiveness.

Length of Bouts.—The rounds are a minute and a half long with thirty seconds rest between them. A bout consists of three rounds, or until terminated by the fall. If no fall takes place, the judges award the bout at the end of the third round. Championship matches consist of winning two out of three bouts.

Officials.—The officials are a referee, two judges, and a timekeeper. The referee starts the bout and calls fouls. The judges select the winner in case there is no fall. If the judges disagree, the referee casts the deciding vote.

Canoe Tilting.—See Canoe Tilting in Chapter XXVI, "Water Activities."

Pillow Fighting

Camp   *Late Elementary to Senior High School*

This perennial favorite of the summer camp is a strong fighting game when properly handled.

Equipment.—A pole five inches in diameter and about eighteen feet long, free from bark and knots, is needed. It is erected parallel to the ground, just high enough so that when the larger contestants hang by their legs from it their heads will clear the ground by about six inches. It may be supported by lashing it to trees, but it is better to build two movable tripods to hold it. Mats or mattresses should be placed under it. Each contestant needs a pillow.

The Play.—At the signal the contestants strike each other with the pillows in an effort to dislodge each other from the pole. A contestant may use his free hand to steady himself on the pole or to ward off his opponent's pillow but may not grasp his opponent's pillow or touch his opponent's body. When a contestant loses his balance and swings under the pole he is not defeated unless he actually falls to the ground. When hanging from the pole he may continue to fight or may attempt to climb back on top; his opponent may prevent him from climbing back by striking him with the pillow. Each contestant should have a second to hand him his pillow if he drops it.

Fouls.—The following are fouls: (1) grasping the opponent's pillow, (2) striking the opponent with the free hand.

Length of Bout.—Each bout consists of three rounds of a minute and a half, with a thirty-second intermission. The bout is terminated immediately if a fall takes place. Contestants are not permitted to leave the pole during the intermission. If a contestant is hanging from the pole at the end of a round his second assists him back on top of the pole without allowing him to touch the ground.

Scoring.—A contestant wins when his opponent falls from the pole or commits a foul, or when he is awarded the judges' decision.

If no fall occurs before the end of the bout, the judges select the winner on the basis of blows struck, defense, and aggressiveness.

Officials.—The officials consist of a referee, a timekeeper, and two judges.

Pole Boxing.—This game is similar to Pillow Fighting. Instead of using pillows, each player wears one boxing glove. The rules differ from Pillow Fighting in that a player is defeated if he falls under the pole, even though he still clings to it.

Swing Ball [2]

This game was originated by Max Breidenbach of Mainz, Germany. It is a form of combat using an inflated ball of the punching bag type which is suspended from the middle of a rope, the ends of which are held by the two contestants.

Court.—The court is eight meters long and one meter wide, divided into two equal halves by a center line. Each player is limited to one-half of this court and may not step over the center line.

The Play.—Each player holds one end of the string and cooperates in swinging the ball in a horizontal circular motion. When the ball is moving in this fashion they lunge at will in an effort to strike the opponent with the ball. The opponent runs, dodges, ducks, and leans to defend himself. There are several thrusts used to throw the ball at particular parts of the opponent's body.

Fouls.—The following are fouls:

1. Stepping over the boundary lines or center line.
2. Faulty swinging.
3. Allowing the ball to touch the floor.
4. Stalling or delaying the game.

The game starts anew after a foul. In case of repeated violations the referee may penalize by awarding points to the offended player.

Scoring.—The scoring is done according to form and technique displayed by the player and the hits registered. The hits score as follows:

A partial hit, touching the body only slightly—one point.
A full hit noticeable on the break of the swing—two points.
A hit on the wrist of the playing hand does not score.

Length of Game.—The game may consist either of a previously agreed upon number of rounds, or an agreed upon number of points.

Wrestling-Hold Combats

In these little wrestling events a specified hold is taken and the players endeavor to throw each other or cause the other to lose the hold.

Advantage Wrestling.—The players stand facing each other until the signal. The object is to get behind the opponent's back and grasp him around the waist with the arms from behind. When so grasped a player is defeated.

[2] This description is condensed from rules contributed by W. K. Streit, Cincinnati, Ohio.

Square Hold.—In the Square Hold each contestant grasps his opponent's arms, one near the shoulder and the other near the elbow, and the two wrestle facing each other. The contestant wins who makes the other lose his feet or lose his hold.

Collar-and-Elbow Wrestling.—The object is to make the opponent touch the ground with any part of the body other than the feet. The left hand is placed back of the opponent's neck and the right hand grasps the opponent's left elbow. The opponent takes the same hold. The feet may be used to trip up the opponent and make him lose his balance.

Cumberland Wrestling.—Each contestant puts the right arm over the opponent's left shoulder and grasps hands behind his back. The object is to lift the opponent clear of the ground.

Side Hold.—In the Side Hold the two players stand side by side, each grasping the other around the body with one arm. The taller player puts his arm over the shorter player's shoulder and, reaching across his back, grasps his opposite arm. The shorter player takes hold in the same way, except that his arm goes back under the taller player's arm. They grasp the free hands toward the front and try by bending, lifting, and tripping, to throw one another.

Tire Wrestling

Playground, Gymnasium, Club   *Late Elementary to Senior High School*
Place two old automobile tires on the ground so they touch each other. The two players stand one in each tire. At the signal they wrestle to throw each other out of the tire. The one wins who first causes the other to fall or step out of the tire provided he himself remains on his feet in his tire. Any tactics are fair except unnecessary roughness or striking.

Ring Wrestle

Playground, Gymnasium, Club   *Late Elementary to Senior High School*
Draw a ten-foot circle on the floor. Two contestants, standing in the circle, attempt to throw each other out. Any tactics are fair except striking blows and unnecessary roughness. When any part of the body crosses the line, the player is out.

Shoulder Shove.—This is an event particularly well adapted for girls. Establish a circle six feet in diameter. Two contestants enter the circle, fold arms and raise the left foot. The contest is to shove the other out of the circle or cause her to drop her foot.

Master-of-the-Ring.—This is a mass form of Ring Wrestle. Establish a circle fifteen feet in diameter. In the gymnasium the circle around the free-throw line may be used. Twelve or fifteen players stand in the circle. At the signal they all attempt to throw each other out. All tactics are fair except unnecessary roughness. When any part of the body touches the floor across the line the player is out and leaves the circle at once. The player who remains in the circle when all others are out is the Master of the Ring. Two or three officials scattered around the circle are needed to spot those who cross the line.

Cock Fight

Playground, Gymnasium, Club   *Elementary and Junior High Schools*

The two contestants raise the left foot to the rear and grasp it with the left hand. The right arm is free but must be kept in close to the side with fist closed and not used to strike, shove, or pull. At the signal they try to upset each other by charging and shouldering, or to cause each other to drop the left foot to the ground.

Free-for-all Cock Fight.—Have ten or a dozen assume the position described and go after one another. The player who remains standing longest wins. Two referees are needed. With large numbers have them play in groups of ten and then put the winners against each other.

Cock Fight on Stilts

Playground, Yard, Club   *Junior High School*

Lay out a circle six feet in diameter. The contestants compete in pairs. The two opponents lay the stirrup end of their stilts in the circle at opposite sides of the ring.

At the signal they both mount the stilts and endeavor to force each other from the circle or off the stilts. The player loses who first is forced to the ground or outside the circle.

Hop Fight

Playground, Gymnasium, Club   *Late Elementary to Senior High School*

Establish a circle of about eight feet in diameter. The two players stand inside the circle facing each other, fold their arms, and lift one leg in front. At the signal they try to upset each other or force each other from the circle *by use of the lifted leg only.* They may push, hook, or lift with the leg, but must not contact the opponent with any other part of the body.

Cane Fight

Playground, Gymnasium, Club   *Junior and Senior High Schools*

This rough game is much enjoyed by boys, but it needs careful supervision. A strong stick, such as a broom handle, three feet long is needed.

The two players grasp the stick and attempt to take it away from each other. To be defeated, a player must release both hands from the stick.

Wand Wrestling.—Wand Wrestling begins with the two opponents facing each other and both grasping a wand with both hands, the hands being from a foot to eighteen inches apart. At the signal each tries to cause the other to move a foot. The one is defeated who first moves a foot or releases the wand.

Double-Peg Fight

Playground, Gymnasium, Club   *Junior and Senior High Schools*

This is on the order of the Cane Fight, but is less rough and dangerous. Two sticks, one foot long, cut from a broomstick, are needed. The players hold the sticks one in each hand, grasped at opposite ends. At the signal they try to take the sticks away from each other. When one stick is lost, the free hand must not be used to help retain the other stick. If each player wins one stick, the tie is played off by the use of one stick only.

Single-Peg Fight.—Same as the above except that only one peg twelve inches long is used.

Cane Push or Pull.—Draw two lines on the floor six feet apart. The two contestants stand between them. Two two-foot sticks of the size of a broom handle are needed. The players grasp the sticks, one in each hand, holding opposite ends. At the signal they try to put the other over either one of the lines by pushing or pulling. Jerking or twisting in an effort to cause the opponent to release a stick is not permitted. If a stick is released by legitimate pushing and pulling the player loses.

Ball Fight

Playground, Gymnasium, Club   *Junior and Senior High Schools*

Two contestants stand facing each other. They place both hands on a basketball or soccer ball held chest high between them. At the signal they try to take the ball away from each other. All tactics are fair except unnecessary roughness. The one wins who removes the ball from contact with the opponent.

Hand Wrestle

Playground, Gymnasium, Club   *Late Elementary to Senior High School*

The opponents grasp right hands and stand with their right feet braced against each other, outer edges touching. The left foot is well to the rear to give a firm stance. The object is to throw the opponent. The first to move the left foot, or touch the ground with any part of the body except the feet loses.

One-Legged Hand Wrestle.—Each contestant raises his left leg behind and grasps the instep with his left hand. The two players then grasp each other's right hands. At the signal they try to upset each other. A player is defeated if he touches the floor with any part of the body except the standing foot, or if he lets go of the lifted leg.

Indian Wrestle
(*Leg Wrestle*)

Playground, Gymnasium, Club   Late Elementary to Senior High School

The two opponents lie on their backs on the floor with heads in opposite directions, trunks close, and near arms locked at the elbows. Three counts are given; on the first each player lifts his leg nearest the opponent to a vertical position; on the second he brings it back to the floor; on the third he lifts it again, hooks his opponent's leg near the foot with his heel, and attempts to roll him over backward.

Hog Tying

Playground, Gymnasium, Club   Junior and Senior High Schools

Give each of the two contestants a four-foot rope. At the signal they attempt to tie each other's feet together. This is apt to be a strenuous and long-drawn-out fight—it moves more swiftly and is more interesting to spectators if the players merely tie the rope with a solid knot around any part of the opponent's body.

Hanker Fight

Playground, Gymnasium, Club   Late Elementary and Junior High Schools

This is typical of the informal play of boys, but is excellent when conducted on a challenge basis. The opposing players stick a handkerchief in the hip pocket so that it sticks out about two inches, or in the top of the shorts or trousers. The object is to secure the other's handkerchief and protect your own. All tactics are fair except unnecessary roughness.

Kangaroo Fight

Playground, Gymnasium, Club   Late Elementary to Senior High School

The two opponents each places a cardboard about a foot square or a paper between his ankles and holds it there by pressure of his legs. At the signal they approach each other with folded arms and attempt to shove or shoulder each other over or cause each other to allow the cardboard to fall from between the legs.

Crab Fight

Gymnasium, Club   *Junior High School*

The two contestants sit on the floor facing opposite directions and place their hands on the floor behind them. At the signal they raise their buttocks from the floor and each bucks the other with his shoulders, attempting to cause him to drop his buttocks to the floor. The one whose buttocks first touch the floor loses.

Bench Push-Off

Gymnasium, Club   *Junior and Senior High Schools*

Two players stand on a bench, each holding onto a two-foot section of a broomstick with one hand on each end, the stick being crosswise of the bench. At the signal they attempt to push each other off with the stick. The player wins who is still on the bench when the other touches the floor. Mats or mattresses should be placed around the bench.

Stool Cane-Fight.—The two contestants each stand on a stool and take hold of one end of a broomstick. At the signal each tries to pull or push the other off the stool. A player wins if he is still on his stool when his opponent touches the floor or lets go of the stick.

Catch-and-Pull Tug-of-War

Gymnasium, Playground, Club   *Junior and Senior High Schools*

Draw a line across the floor. The two contestants stand one on each side of the line. At the signal they reach over and attempt to grasp the other on any part of the body and pull him over the line. The one loses who is pulled completely across the line first.

Chinese Tug

Gymnasium, Club   *Junior High School*

Draw a line on the floor and place the two contestants one on each side of it, back to back. Each bends down and thrusts his right hand back between his legs and grasps the other's right hand. At the signal they attempt to pull each other over the line.

Dragon's Mouth

Playground, Gymnasium, Club   *Late Elementary and Junior High Schools*

Draw a five-foot circle on the floor known as the "dragon's mouth." The two contestants stand three feet to one side of it. The object is to put the other into the "dragon's mouth." Any tactics may be used, barring unnecessary roughness. One does well to push and throw the other, however, rather than pull him, since a player is captured by the dragon when any part of his body crosses the line of the dragon's mouth.

Arm-Lock Wrestle

Gymnasium, Club   *Late Elementary to Senior High School*

Since this is a strength test, the two opponents should be of approximately the same size and strength. They sit on the floor, back to back, spread their legs widely, and lock arms at the elbows. The idea is to lean to the left, endeavoring to pull the other over so that his right arm or hand will touch the floor. The one accomplishing this first wins.

Neck Pull

Gymnasium, Club   *Junior and Senior High Schools*

The two contestants stand facing each other, bend well forward with heads up, and clasp each other around the neck with both hands. At the signal they pull, attempting to pull the other a distance of five feet back.

Cane-Fight for Handkerchief

Playground, Gymnasium, Club   *Junior and Senior High Schools*

Each of the two players grasps one end of a three-foot broomstick. A few feet to one side a handkerchief is placed on the ground. At the signal each tries to pick up the handkerchief and prevent the other from doing so. The one wins who secures the handkerchief or causes the other to lose his grip on the stick.

Hoop Tug

Playground, Gymnasium, Club   *Junior and Senior High Schools*

A rope hoop two feet in diameter is needed. Two contestants stand back to back midway between two lines twelve feet apart. They slip the hoop down over their heads to the level of the waist. At the signal each pulls, endeavoring to pull the other over the line. The one wins who first pulls the other completely over the line.

Hat-Boxing

Playground, Gymnasium, Club   *Late Elementary to Senior High School*

This is one of the best of the dual combats, equally popular among boys and girls.

Each of the two boxers is given a large straw hat of the type farmers wear. The hat must not be pulled down on the head so as to make it difficult to knock off. The boxers, boxing with open hands, attempt to knock the hat off the other's head. A boxer is not permitted to touch his own hat in order to hold it on or restore it to a more secure position.

Chef's Hat-Boxing.—Place a paper bag on each of the two players' heads, extending down to the ears. At the signal they attempt to box each other's hat off. They are not permitted to touch their own hats with their hands.

Free-for-all Chef's Hat-Boxing.—Put several in the ring at once with bags on their heads. The survivor wins.

Chef's Hat-Swatting.—Each boxer holds a swatter made of a rolled newspaper. They attempt to knock each other's bag off with the newspaper.

Balloon Busting

Playground, Gymnasium, Club   *Late Elementary to Senior High School*

This is one of the most exciting and interesting of the dual combats. Tie a large toy balloon tightly to the left ankle of each of the contestants. At the signal they attack each other with view to breaking the other's balloon. All tactics are fair except unnecessary roughness.

Before two contestants start to fight, ask for a challenger to take on the winner. While the two are fighting, have someone tie the balloon on the challenger's ankle.

Wrist Balloon Busting.—In this variation, the balloon is tied tightly to the left wrist of each contestant. In other respects the event is handled like the above.

Balloon Battle-Royal.—Tie a toy balloon to the waist of each of several contestants. The balloon must be kept in front of the contestant. At the signal they all start to burst the others' balloons and protect their own. The one wins whose balloon is intact when all others are destroyed.

Balloon Boxing

Stunt Night, Picnic, Club   *Junior and Senior High Schools*

For this novel and colorful event, thirty small round balloons are needed. Inflate the balloons and tie each with the end of a twelve-inch string. Two pieces of twine forty inches long are now needed. Tie fifteen balloons to the middle of each of these twines in such a way that they will hang down about twelve inches. Tie the twines around the waists of the two boxers, thus covering them in front with balloons. The boxers wear boxing gloves.

At the signal they box to break the other's balloons. Since this is a show event and used as a novelty on a program, the boxers should be coached to refrain from clinching (in that such tactics break the balloons very quickly) and to be careful to defend their own balloons. The balloons should be punched out.

Variation.—Tie one balloon to the waist of each opponent in front. This leads to more careful boxing.

Cats-on-the-Fence [8]

Playground, Gymnasium, Club   *Late Elementary School to Adults*

A piece of two-by-four-inch timber six or eight feet long is placed broad side up with ends resting on two chairs. The two contestants stand facing each other with feet lengthwise to the board and with the toe of the back foot touching the heel of the front foot. With the right hand they attempt to put off each other by slapping any place on the rival's right arm from the hand to the shoulder. A player wins when his opponent goes off or when his opponent commits a foul by striking on the head or body.

Slap Hand.—Same as the above except that the players stand on a crack or line on the floor instead of the two-by-four.

Sparrow Fight

Playground, Gymnasium, Club   *Late Elementary to Senior High School*

Establish a six-foot circle. Standing in the circle, each contestant bends forward and grasps his ankles with his hands. The object is to upset the opponent or shoulder him from the circle.

Duck Fight.—Establish a six-foot circle. Each contestant squats in the circle and a wand or three-foot stick is placed behind their knees. Each reaches under the stick with his arms and clasps his hands in front of his legs. The object is to upset the opponent or force him from the circle.

Stepping on Toes

Gymnasium, Club   *Late Elementary to Senior High School*

Two players stand facing each other and at the signal attempt to step on each other's toes. The one wins who first steps on the other's toes. The hands may not be used on the opponent.

Face Slapping

Gymnasium, Playground, Club   *Junior and Senior High Schools*

The two contestants stand in boxing stance with left toes touching. Number 1 guards his face with his hands while Number 2 attempts to slap his face with open hand. Neither may move the feet. Number 2 may feint, but when he touches Number 1, a blow has been struck. If

[8] From E. T. Seton. *The Birch Bark Roll of Woodcraft*, p. 32. Copyright, 1931. By permission of A. S. Barnes & Company, publishers.

Number 2 hits Number 1 any place except his face, no credit is given; if he hits him on the face, he scores one point.

As soon as a blow has been struck, Number 1 has his turn to slap Number 2. The player wins who scores five points first.

Heave Ahoy Boxing

Club   *Junior High School to Adults*

Two players, each holding a pillow or swatter, are blindfolded. A rope is tied around the waist of each so that there is at least ten feet of rope between them. At the signal each pulls on the rope to haul the other to him, and pulls whenever he cannot find the other. When the two are close enough, they strike each other with the pillows or swatters. When each round is over they retreat until the rope is taut.

The common practice of playing this game with boxing gloves should be discouraged—blindfold boxing is an exceedingly dangerous practice.

Swatter Boxing

Playground, Gymnasium, Club   *Junior and Senior High Schools*

Each contestant holds a swatter in each hand, made from a rolled newspaper. They box by swatting each other with the newspaper. Two or three one-minute rounds constitute a bout and judges pick the winners on the basis of aggressiveness and blows struck.

Box and Swat.—Each of the two contestants puts a boxing glove on the left hand and holds a swatter in the right. A rolled-up newspaper serves as the swatter. At the signal they box and swat each other. The bout lasts two minutes. The judges render their decision taking into consideration aggressiveness and blows struck.

Are You There, Mike?

Gymnasium, Playground, Club   *Late Elementary to Senior High School*

The two blindfolded players get on their knees facing each other and join their left hands. Each holds a rolled newspaper in his right hand. One of them says, "Are you there, Mike?" and the other answers, "Yes." Whereupon Number 1 swings his swatter in the direction from which the answer came, while Number 2 ducks his head. Then Number 2 asks the question.

This is a great fun-maker for the spectators. After it has been going on awhile, the leader may quietly slip off the blindfold of one of the players and allow the stunt to go on.

Barrel Boxing

Playground, Gymnasium, Picnic, Club   *Junior and Senior High Schools*

Two barrels with bottoms but no tops are placed side by side on the floor, open ends up. The two opponents stand in the barrels, wearing boxing gloves, and attempt to upset each other. Mats or mattresses should be stationed behind the barrels. Each boxer should have a second who holds a stick with which to push the barrel back into range should it jiggle away. The stick may be applied to the barrel only at the base—otherwise it may serve to protect the boxer from a fall.

Variation.— Use barrels with neither top nor bottom. The barrels are pulled up high enough so that the boxers can move about somewhat.

Sack Boxing.—This is the same as Barrel Boxing except that the boxers stand in large burlap sacks which are pulled up to the waist and tied.

Smudge Boxing

Camp, Club   *Junior and Senior High Schools*

This humorous affair is used for entertainment at campfires, stunt nights, and so forth. An old pair of boxing gloves are well blacked with lampblack or soot. The contestants, stripped to the waist, box to blacken each other's faces. The contestant who has the blacker face in three minutes loses.

Knights
(*Horse and Rider*)

Playground, Club   *Junior and Senior High Schools*

This event should not be played on a hard floor in that there is a large element of danger from falls. On soft grass-covered ground it is reasonably safe and very popular.

The players pair up according to approximate weight. Two pairs compete at once. One of each pair is the horse and the other the rider. The riders mount the horses' shoulders. At the signal the pairs try to upset each other. The rider may use his hands to push and pull, and the horses may charge.

This game is frequently played with several pairs competing at once. The pair wins that remains standing when all others are down.

Boxing Knights —Like the game of Knights this contest should never be played on a hard surface, but on mats or soft grass. Two pairs of players compete. One player, the rider, mounts the shoulders of the other, the horse, with his legs wrapped firmly around the horse's body. The riders put on boxing gloves. At the signal the riders box. The function of the horses is merely to hold the riders and keep them in boxing distance. The pair wins which first unhorses the opposing rider or upsets the opposing pair.

Milling the Man

Playground and Gymnasium Game   *Junior and Senior High Schools*

This game is limited to twelve or fifteen players. Select one man to be "it" and have the remaining players form a compact circle, sitting on the floor. "It" stands in the center, folds his arms, makes himself rigid, and falls, keeping his feet in the center of the circle. The players in the circle prevent his hitting the floor by catching him, and push him back and forth around the circle. Anyone responsible for "it" falling to the floor exchanges places with him. "It" must keep himself rigid for the best results.

Broncho Busting

Playground, Gymnasium, Club   *Junior and Senior High Schools*

This event must be practiced awhile before the players will be familiar enough with the technique required to stay on the broncho.

Two players of approximately the same weight compete. The broncho bends down and places his hands on his knees. The rider sits on the broncho's back with legs clamped behind his thighs (not around his body) and hands on his shoulders. The broncho tries to buck the rider off and wins if he succeeds. However, if the broncho falls, he loses. The broncho is not permitted to remove his hands from his knees.

The players alternate as broncho and rider and the one wins who stays on the longest. If one stays on one minute, the bout is stopped and positions reversed. If both stay on one minute, they compete again.

Riding the Broncho

Playground, Gymnasium   *Junior and Senior High Schools*

A "broncho" is formed in the following manner: One player is placed with his back to the wall. This player is known as the broncho's head; all the remaining players except one are arranged in file extending from the broncho's head, each bending well forward and grasping the player in front around the waist. This forms a continuous row of backs.

The odd player mounts the tail of the broncho and starts to crawl to the head. The "bronc" bucks, wiggles, swings his tail, and otherwise attempts to dislodge the rider. The players forming the broncho must not rise, drop to their knees, or release their holds on the waists of the players in front. When a rider touches any part of his body to the ground he is considered bucked off. He then counts the number of players he succeeded in crawling over, this number constituting his score. He then joins on the tail of the broncho and the broncho's head goes to the tail and attempts to ride. When all have tried, the player with the largest score wins.

Variation.—Divide the players into two teams. One team forms the broncho as described above. The other team (riders) form in a column behind the bronchos. At the signal, the first rider mounts the tail and starts to crawl to the head; as soon as he moves forward far enough to give room the second rider mounts, then the third, and so forth. Whenever a rider touches the floor with any part of his body, he withdraws. The number of players who reach the broncho's head is counted and the number constitutes the riding team's score. The two teams then exchange places. The team making the highest score wins.

Line Wrestling

Playground, Gymnasium, Club   Late Elementary to Senior High School

Although this game is hard on clothes, it is exceptionally popular among boys.

Draw a line across the floor and divide the players into two teams. One team lines up on each side of the line. At the signal the players try to grab opposing players and pull them across the line. When both feet are pulled across the line, the player is captured and withdraws behind the line of the team capturing him. Several players may gang up to pull one opponent over. The team that captures the most players in two minutes wins. The best two out of three games determine the best team.

Variation.—Same as the above except that when a player is pulled across the line, he joins the team capturing him and continues to play. The team with the most players in two minutes wins.

Do or Die

Club, Gymnasium   Junior and Senior High Schools

This is a fighting game that boys love and call for repeatedly. Divide the players into two groups and bunch them about fifteen feet apart. Give the captain of each team a folded slip with instructions written on it. At the signal the captain opens his slip and reads it to his team, and they immediately attempt to carry out the orders. For example, one slip might read "Leave the room" and the other team's slip, "Don't let anybody leave the room."

The following orders may be suggestive:

Team 1—Climb on the platform.
Team 2—Don't let anybody climb on the platform.
Team 1—Move the gym mat across the gym.
Team 2—Don't let anyone move the mat.
Team 1—Sit on the floor.
Team 2—Don't let anybody sit on the floor.

Mat Tug-of-War

Gymnasium   *Junior and Senior High Schools*

Place an old gymnasium mat in the center of the gymnasium. Divide the group into two teams and line up one team on each side of the gymnasium. At the signal both teams rush for the mat and attempt to carry it back to their side of the gymnasium. It is permissible for players to throw or pull opponents off the mat and to guard the mat to prevent opponents from touching it. All tactics except unnecessary roughness are permissible.

Four-Mat Tug-of-War.—Divide the group into four teams and place four small gymnasium mats in the center of the gymnasium. Instruct each team to take one mat and place it in a specified corner of the gymnasium, the team winning which places its mat there first. It is permissible to prevent opposing teams from moving their mats by blocking and holding and by using any tactics except unnecessary roughness.

King of the Mountain

Gymnasium, Club   *Junior and Senior High Schools*

This game is similar to Master of the Ring. A large gymnasium mat represents the mountain and is laid on the floor. A player is selected for king and stands on the mountain. The players mount the mountain and attempt to throw the king off. Once the king is displaced, the others fight it out for possession of the mat and the title of king of the mountain. Whenever any part of a player's body goes off the mat he is considered off. The one remaining last is king for the next game.

Team Variation.—The players choose teams and each selects a king. One team mounts the mountain, forming a circle of players around its king. The other team attacks and attempts to displace the king and put its own king on. The attacking king may not mount the mountain until the old king is thrown off. As soon as the old king is displaced and the new king gets on, the game ends, and the new king takes his place surrounded by his army for the next game.

Storming the Fort

Playground, Gymnasium   *Junior and Senior High Schools*

This rough game is much liked by boys in the junior high school and above. Mark out an area ten feet square known as the "fort." A gymnasium mat or slightly elevated wooden platform is ideal. Divide the players into two teams and line them up on opposing sides of the fort and a few feet from it. On the signal the players rush in the fort, attempting to stay in it and throw out the opposing players. All tactics are fair except unnecessary roughness. Time is called at the end of two minutes and all struggle ceases. The team having the most men in the fort wins. If any part of a player's body touches the floor outside the fort he is considered out.

Rush the Stick

Playground, Gymnasium   *Junior and Senior High Schools*

Mark off two lines thirty or forty feet apart and throw a six-foot stick or rope in the center of the area between them. The leader serves as timekeeper. At the signal, both teams rush for the stick and try to get as many hands on it as possible, at the same time trying to prevent the opposing team from getting hands on it. All unnecessary roughness is barred. At the end of one minute the whistle blows and all struggle ceases immediately. The team having the most hands on the stick wins. A player with two hands on it scores for each hand.

COMBATS IN OTHER CHAPTERS

Water Pillow-Fighting.   Tilting on Skis.
Canoe Tilting.   Mounted Hat-Boxing.
                Water Knights.

COMBATS IN *SOCIAL GAMES AND CONTESTS*

Potato Fight.   Are You There, Mike?
Snatching the Hat.   Where Are You, Mike?
Pillow War.   Rattlesnake.
Parlor Tilting.   Settlers and Indians.

PART IV

TEAM GAMES

CHAPTER XX

GAMES OF THE BASEBALL TYPE

THIS group of games includes the American game of Baseball, the English game of Cricket, and a number of minor games based on these two, but suited to younger players, to smaller space, and to varying numbers.

Origin of the Games.—Modern games of bat and ball have been developed by combining an ancient ball play, much like Golf, with the use of bases or goals and the practice of tagging; both of these are prominent features of the games of children. An old game of English children called Four Corners suggests what may have been the starting point in the evolution of these games. Four Corners is nothing more or less than the ancient game of Pussy Wants a Corner, with one addition: the out-player has a small, soft ball, which he tosses to any one of the players on the bases; the player to whom it is tossed strikes at the ball with the open hand, and then, whether he hits or not, each player must run to the next base. The out-player picks up the ball as quickly as possible and tries to hit a runner with it before he reaches a base. Hitting a player with a thrown ball is a form of tag common in many simple games.

A century ago English boys were playing an outdoor game much like this, which they called Feeder. There were several bases in a circular course and the batsman sometimes used a small club. A singular feature of the game was the fact that all the players were "in" but one, which makes it much like the individual tag games.

Next came the regular use of the bat. American boys at the time of the Revolution often played a game similar to One Old Cat, using a soft ball and tagging the runner either by touching him with the ball in hand or by throwing it at him and hitting him with it. This developed into the game of Rotation with three, four, and sometimes five bases. About 1830, players began to form permanent teams and play match games under the name of Baseball. In the seventies the improvement in the manufacture of balls resulted in the making of a ball so hard that the earlier method of hitting a player to tag him had to be dropped. Up to this time the pitcher was allowed only to toss the ball to the batsman, but after 1875 throwing was permitted. This soon led to the use of masks, gloves, and breast protectors, and caused the pitcher's box to be moved farther away from the batsman.

Cricket is believed to have arisen from an ancient game called Stool Ball, played in England in the Middle Ages. In Stool Ball one player, who was said to be "in," stood by a three-legged stool, which he tried to protect while the other players threw the ball at it. The in-player made a score every time he hit the ball with his hand. If an out-player hit the stool or caught a hit ball, he went in, in place of the other. Later the in-player used a bat, and still later the stool was replaced by a crude form of wicket, which has gone through several stages before reaching the modern form.

Cricket matches were played with permanent teams early in the seventeenth century, and it became a common school game early in the nineteenth century.

We see from this historical sketch that while the games of bat and ball arose from the combining of elements that are very old, the games as such are distinctly modern; in fact, they are more recent than tennis, hockey, or football.

Baseball

Playground   *Late Elementary School to Adults*

The game of Baseball is played by two teams of nine men, one of which, called the side at bat, attempts to score runs by batting a pitched ball safely beyond the reach of the opponents, called the fielding side. The person who reaches a base, of which there are four, placed in diamond shape, can advance when a succeeding team mate hits the ball, or by other means later described. A score is made when a runner, going counterclockwise, has succeeded in touching all four bases. The side in the field attempts to get the batter or base runner out by various means. There are rules governing the changing of the two teams so that the one at bat takes the field, and vice versa.

The players of a side must all bat in turn, and then they start from the beginning again. The players in the field station themselves so as to have one man pitch the ball to the batter, and another man to catch the balls that the batter does not hit; also to have four men to protect the bases, and to have the remainder protect against long hits that go past the bases.

The Field.—Baseball needs a level field 325 feet square, but it is often played on a smaller space. A square, whose sides are ninety feet, is marked out (Figure 41). Opposite one corner of the diamond and ninety feet (or less) from it, a backstop is placed, which consists of a wide frame covered with wire netting. At the corner of the diamond, nearest the backstop, home plate is placed—this is a slab of wood or rubber set even with the top of the ground, the shape and dimensions of which are shown in Figure 42.

The other corners of the diamond are called first, second, and third bases, starting to the right from the home plate; and each of these is marked by a canvas bag fifteen inches square, fastened by an iron stake that is entirely under ground. In the middle of the diamond, sixty-and-one-half feet from home plate, is the pitcher's plate, a slab of rubber six inches wide and two feet long.

Scoring.—A "run" is a complete circuit of bases, whether made all at once or in stages. The score is the number of runs made by each team. The team making the largest score in nine "innings" wins the game. When

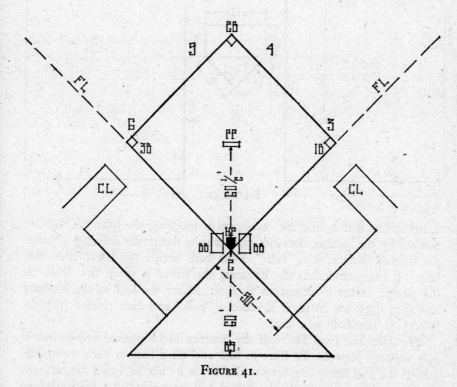

FIGURE 41.

each team has had a turn at bat, it is called one inning; a side remains at bat until three men have been put out. If the score at the end of nine innings is a tie, play continues until one team has a greater score than the other in equal innings. When weather or any other cause stops the game before nine innings are played, the score at the end of the last complete inning is taken as the final score, provided that at least five innings have been played.

The Batsman.—It is the duty of the batsman to bat the ball thrown by the pitcher and then to run to first base as fast as possible. If the batsman strikes at the pitched ball and misses it, or if it passes over the home plate at a height between the batsman's knee and shoulder, the umpire declares a "strike." If this occurs three times the batsman is out, provided the catcher catches the ball on the third strike. If he fails to catch it after the third strike the batsman may run to first base, and is safe if he reaches

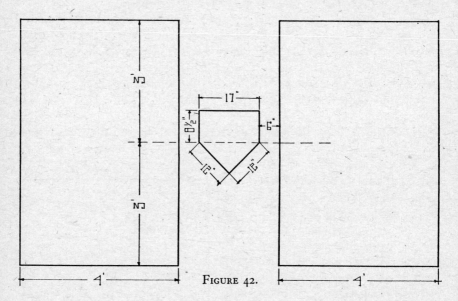

FIGURE 42.

it before the ball is held by an opponent touching the base. If the ball thrown by the pitcher does not pass within the limits defining a strike, the umpire declares it a "ball." Four balls entitle the batsman to first base. If the pitcher hits the batsman, the batter is given first base. If the pitcher makes a movement as if to deliver the ball to the batsman and then does not do so, it is called a "balk" and each runner (not the batter) is advanced one base.

Fair Hits and Foul Balls.—If the batsman hits a pitched ball so that it goes forward between the lines to first and third base or their extensions (called the foul lines), the umpire declares it a "fair hit," and the batsman becomes a base runner. If the batted ball is caught by a fielder before it hits the ground the batsman is out. If it strikes the ground and is afterward thrown to first base and caught there before the runner reaches it he is out; he may be tagged out before reaching first base if it is more convenient to do so.

If the batsman hits the ball so that it goes anywhere outside of the limits of a fair hit, the umpire declares a "foul ball." Fouls count as strikes until two strikes have been called, but are not counted afterward unless caught by the catcher. A ball is foul if it strikes in the diamond and then rolls out between home plate and first or third; it is fair if it strikes out and rolls in.

If a man makes an entire circuit of the bases on one hit, it is called a "home run." There is a hit where the batter does not swing at the ball hard, but instead pushes the bat forward and allows the bat to hit it so that the ball drops dead. Such a play is called a "bunt."

Base Runners.—A base runner, occupying any base, may run to the next base whenever he thinks that he has time to do so before the opponents can throw the ball there to intercept him. If a batsman makes a fair hit while a runner is occupying first base, such runner must go to second to make room for the batsman. This is called a "forced run." Such a runner need not be tagged, but is out if the ball is caught by an opponent on the base before he reaches it.

If the ball is hit in the air and is caught, then the base runner is forced back to the base from which he came, and may be put out if the ball reaches the base before he can touch it. Except in the above instances, the base runner must be tagged with the ball to be put out. In tagging a runner, the fielder must not drop the ball. There are a few special cases to be noted: sometimes the base runner is permitted to advance to the next base without being put out, as for instance, where the umpire calls a balk, where a fielder interferes with the runner, or where the batsman is given first base, thus forcing the other base runners forward; he is required to return to the base from which he came, but without liability of being put out, however, in the instance of a foul hit ball that is not caught.

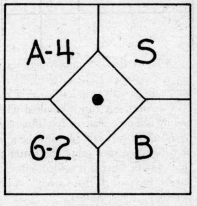

FIGURE 43.

Scoring Record.—Scoring is keeping a record of the game, including the number of runs, how such runs are made, and the record of each individual player. This is done by means of the diagram shown in Figure 43. Symbols are used to show how the player reached first base and how he advanced around the bases. If a run is scored, it is indicated in the center space. For the purposes of scoring, each player is numbered as in the diagram of the field of play.

Scorers differ in the use of symbols. The plan above uses B to indicate that the runner went to first on four balls; S, that he stole second; A-4 that he reached third when second baseman (4) assisted (A) in retiring a batter; 6-2, that he reached home when shortstop (6) threw to catcher (2) too late to stop the score. When the runner scores, a dot is placed in the center of the diamond. If the runner is retired, the number 1, 2, or 3, is placed in the diamond, depending on whether the player is the first, second or third player retired in the inning.

This plan uses the following symbols:

— — Single	S — Stolen base	BK — Balk
+ — Double	B — Base on balls	. — Run
+ + — Triple	H — Hit by pitcher	FC — Fielder's Choice
+ + + — Home Run	W — Wild pitch	E — Error
K — Strikeout	P — Passed ball	

For the purposes of final tabulation, such as appears in the newspapers and is known as the "box score," there are columns after each player's name as in the accompanying diagram.

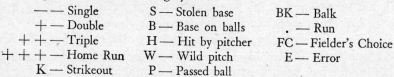

Player	AB	R	H	SH	SB	PO	A	E

AB—At Bat.—Number of times a player came to bat. Whenever a batter is given a base on balls, or is hit by a pitched ball, or makes a sacrifice hit, he is not charged with a time at bat.

R—Runs.—A run is counted whenever a player legally touches all the bases, ending at home plate, before three men of his side are put out.

H—Hits.—A safe hit must be a fair hit ball, which is not caught by a fielder, or which does not cause the batter to get put out at first base, or cause a base runner to be forced; provided, however, that the fielder is not at fault in allowing anyone to reach the base safely. A hit is also given when a batted ball strikes the umpire or a base runner.

SH—Sacrifice Hits.—A sacrifice hit is a play in which the batter voluntarily permits himself to be put out in order that a team mate may advance a base. The most common way to sacrifice is to bunt the ball.

SB—Stolen Bases.—Where a runner advances a base without any assistance from the batter or through any fault of the opponents.

PO—Put Out.—This is credited to the fielder who completes a play which retires an opposing player; *i.e.,* catching a fly ball, tagging a runner, and so forth.

A—Assist.—An assist is given a fielder when he handles the ball in aiding to put out a player.

E—Error.—An error is charged against a fielder when he makes a misplay, like a fumble, or dropping a fly ball.

Percentages.—The percentage is ascertained by dividing the games won by the total number of games played.

Averages.—Batting averages are determined by dividing the total number of hits by the total number of times at bat.

Fielding Averages.—Fielding averages are figured by dividing the total number of put outs and assists by the number of chances the player had to field the ball; *i.e.*, the total of put outs, assists, and errors.

The idea in figuring out any average is to divide the number of successful tries by the total number of tries.

Officials.—The officials of the game are two umpires and a scorer, although it is customary to use only one umpire in informal games. One umpire, stationed behind the catcher, makes decisions including the following; whether the ball is properly delivered by the pitcher; whether a batted ball is fair or foul; whether a batter is out; whether a run shall be scored; whether a pitched ball not hit by the batter is a ball or strike. The other umpire is located on the diamond and decides whether base runners are safe or out at all points except at home base.

Playgroundball
(*Softball, Recreation Ball*)

Playground, Gymnasium   *Late Elementary to Adults*

Playgroundball resembles regular Baseball but is played on a smaller diamond and with a softball. In recent years it has spread into tremendous popularity owing to the fact that it takes less space than Baseball and is better suited for recreational purposes, being less strenuous and violent, less dangerous, and requiring less skill. It is a faster game, if anything, than Baseball. The player of average ability has come to look upon this as his national game, leaving regular Baseball to the highly skilled varsity and professional teams. It is excellent for girls' use and is much enjoyed by adults who are past the point where they can play regular Baseball.

Playgroundball differs from regulation Baseball in the following respects:

Size of diamond.—Playgroundball has not yet been standardized to the point where there is a general agreement in respect to length of baselines and pitching distance. The pitching distance of course varies with the length of the baselines. The following distances are recommended:

Baselines sixty feet—Pitching distance thirty-seven feet, eight-and-one-half inches.

Baselines forty-five feet.—Pitching distance same as above.

Baselines thirty-five feet.—Pitching distance thirty feet.

Baselines twenty-seven feet.—Pitching distance twenty-four feet.

A baseline of sixty feet is quite universally recommended for older boys and adults in recreational leagues—this distance is rapidly becoming regarded as standard. For a diamond of this size the pitching distance commonly used is thirty-seven feet eight-and-one-half inches, but some leagues with unusually efficient pitchers use a pitching distance of forty feet, owing to the fact that the shorter distance throws the odds too heavily in favor of the pitcher. Under average conditions a distance of thirty-seven feet eight-and-one-half inches is recommended.

For girls and junior boys, thirty-five foot baselines and a thirty-foot

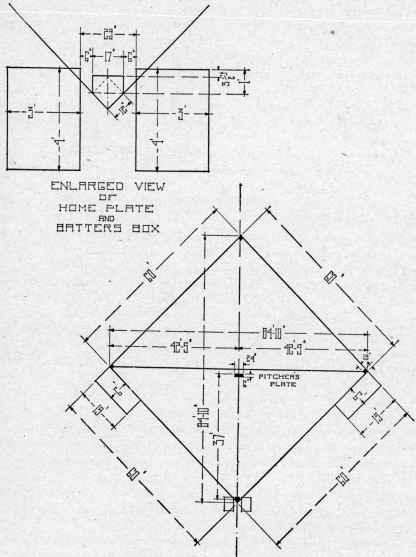

FIGURE 44.—Playgroundball Diamond *

* The above diagram gives the pitching distance at thirty-seven feet. A pitching distance of thirty-seven feet eight-and-one-half inches is frequently used. For other dimensions sometimes used in Playgroundball, see the description in the text.

pitching distance are to be recommended. A twenty-seven foot diamond is seldom used except in a gymnasium.

Equipment.—A twelve-inch softball, either outseam or inseam, is used on the sixty-foot diamond. The same ball is commonly used on the forty-five-foot diamond, although there are some who prefer a thirteen-inch ball on a diamond of this size. For girls' use on the thirty-five-foot diamond, the twelve-inch ball is satisfactory. The twenty-seven-foot diamond calls for the use of a fourteen-inch ball when men are playing.

Equipment.—A twelve-inch softball, either outseam or inseam is used. The nature of the seam is a matter of preference but the tendency is toward accepting the inseam ball for fast leagues. Official softball bats are used— these are smaller both as to length and thickness. The use of spiked shoes is prohibited.

Length of Game.—Seven innings rather than nine constitute a game. In case of a called game, five innings must have been completed for the game to count.

Method of Pitching.—Preliminary to pitching the pitcher must come to rest with both feet on the pitcher's plate and facing the batter. An underhand pitch only is permissible, the arm passing parallel to the body and with the ball not more than six inches from the body. The ball must be thrown with a full arm swing, following through with the arm parallel to the body, and the hand below the hip as it passes the body. A snap or jerky release of the ball at the hip is prohibited. A final wrist motion is permissible however.

In the act of pitching the pitcher may take one step but must keep one foot in contact with the plate until the ball has actually left the hand. After releasing the ball he may advance.

A quick return pitch is illegal.

An illegal pitch is called a ball unless struck at, in which case the ball is in play if hit, and is called a strike if missed.

Balks.—No balks are called, except in the case where there are runners on the bases and a pitcher in the act of pitching drops the ball intentionally or accidentally. Such a throw is called a ball and the runners may not advance.

Bunting.—No bunting is allowed, and a batter who bunts or attempts to bunt is out. A bunt is a ball not swung at but met with the bat or tapped slowly within the infield.

Dead Ball.—A pitched ball hitting the batter while standing in his box is a dead ball, provided the batter does not strike at it nor intentionally permit it to hit him. The batter does not take his base nor may a runner advance. Such a dead ball is called a ball.

Running on Third Strike.—The batter is out immediately after three strikes and is not permitted to run to first base.

Stealing Bases.—Stealing is not allowed while the pitcher holding the ball is in position to pitch with one or both feet on the plate, nor until after the pitched ball has reached or passed the batter. A base runner taking his foot from the base before this time is out.

Fouls.—A batted ball is a foul if it settles on foul territory between home and first base, or home and third base, or which passes first or third base on foul territory, or which strikes on foul territory outside the foul lines in the outfield. A foul is a foul fly if it goes higher than the batter's head. and the batter is out if such a foul fly is caught.

Infield Fly.—The rule is the same as in Baseball: A batter is out and no base runner may advance, nor can a play be made on a base runner, if the batter hits a fly to the infield before two are out with first and second bases, or first, second, and third bases occupied.

The Batter Is Out.—The rules of Baseball apply with the following exceptions: The batter is out (1) if he bunts or attempts to bunt, (2) on the third strike whether the ball is caught or not.

Overthrows.—On an overthrow at first, third, or home base into foul territory, a base runner is entitled to advance one base only provided the throw strikes an obstruction or spectator. If it does not strike such an obstruction he is entitled to advance to the base to which he is running and one additional base provided he can make it. The advance of the runner is determined by the base which he occupied when the pitch started.

Teams.—The rules call for the use of a ten-man team, the extra player being called a short fielder. The players with the exception of the pitcher and catcher may be stationed at any place on the diamond that is deemed most advantageous.

Indoor Baseball.—Indoor Baseball is the same game as Playgroundball, played indoors. The size of the diamond is of course regulated by the size of the floor space, and the length of the pitching distance is regulated by the length of the baselines as described under Playgroundball.

MINOR GAMES OF THE BASEBALL TYPE

The rules of Baseball have been developed by the professional baseball leagues, and are too technical and complicated for children. American boys and girls play a large number of simpler forms of the national game. Typical games of this sort follow.

One Old Cat

Playground, Gymnasium   *Late Elementary School to Adults*

This informal type of Baseball or Playgroundball is acceptable when there are only a few players. It is played with only one base besides the home base, this base being in the position of first base.

There is only one batter. The remaining players occupy the positions of catcher, pitcher, and fielders. The batter is out when he makes three strikes or when any pitched ball is struck at and caught by the catcher on the fly or first bounce, or when a fly or foul is caught. When a hit is made, the runner must run to first base and back to home base before the ball is returned to the catcher who must touch home base to put the runner out.

When the batter is out, the players all move up in rotation, that is, the catcher becomes batter, the pitcher becomes catcher, the first fielder becomes pitcher, and so forth. The batter becomes the right fielder. A player catching a fly exchanges places with the batter.

Two Old Cat.—When there are enough players, two batters may be used. In this case, a batter making a hit and reaching first base may remain there until the other batter hits, thus enabling him to return.

Three Old Cat.—When the number of player permits, three batters may be used. In this case, all the bases of the diamond are used.

Rotation
(*Scrub, Work Up, Rounders*)

Playground, Gymnasium   *Late Elementary School to Adults*

A playgroundball or baseball diamond is used, with softballs and bats, or regular baseballs and bats, depending on the diamond. Select one, two, or three players for batters and have the remaining players occupy the regular field positions of Baseball. The regular rules of Baseball covering fielding and base running apply. When a batter or baserunner is retired, the fielders all move up one position nearer the batter.

The order of rotation is as follows: The retired batter goes to right field; the right fielder to center; center fielder to left field; left fielder to shortstop; shortstop to third base; third baseman to second; second baseman to first, first baseman becomes the pitcher; pitcher to catcher, and the catcher becomes batter.

When a fielder catches a fly ball he becomes batter immediately and the retired batter goes to right field. When all the batters are on the bases and there is none at bat, the base runner nearest home base must reach home before the ball is thrown there; otherwise he is out. The object of the game is to stay at bat as long as possible.

Three Grounders or a Fly

Playground, Gymnasium   *Late Elementary School to Adults*

Softballs and bats or regular baseballs and bats are used. The players agree on one player as batter. The remaining players scatter across the playing area. The batter tosses the ball up and bats it to the players who attempt to field it. The fielder who catches one fly ball or three "grounders" (bouncing or rolling balls) exchanges places with the batter. Once the ball has been touched by a fielder, no other fielder can score on it. With each new batter, all fielders lose the points previously made.

Hot Rice.—This game is exactly like the above except in respect to playing grounders. If the ball is caught off the ground, the fielder, standing on the spot where he caught it, throws it at the batter. The batter must keep one foot on home base, but may try to avoid the ball by dodging, or may use the bat to hit or ward it off. If he is hit by the ball, the player who hit him becomes batter.

Cross-out Baseball

Playground, Gymnasium   *Late Elementary to Adults*

This game is exactly like Playgroundball except that in addition to the usual methods of retiring a runner, he may be put out by throwing the ball across his path ahead of him.

Donkey Baseball

Baseball Diamond   *All Ages*

This hilarious affair has few equals for entertainment. The players ride donkeys and proceed in general as in Baseball. Since the burros are stubborn and move only when they feel inclined, a player may hit what would easily be a home run and fail to reach first base, or an infield hit may go for a home run.

The game was originated in the southwest section of the United States where burros are plentiful, but has recently spread to all parts of the country, being used for the most part by organizations for money-raising purposes.

The game is played on a plapgroundball diamond, except that first, second, and third bases consist of circles about six feet in diameter. Softballs and bats are used.

All players are mounted on burros except the pitcher, catcher, and batter. The batter's burro is held by an attendant on the other side of home base. There are no balls and strikes, so the batter stays in bat until he gets a fair hit. He then mounts and attempts to ride to first base.

The pitcher and catcher are not allowed to leave their boxes to field the ball. A mounted player must field it and throw it to the pitcher, who throws for the out. A fielder or baseman must ride up to the ball and then may get off his donkey to get the ball, but must remount to make the throw. If a baseman gets off his donkey and makes a catch, it does not count as an out, and the runner may keep going.

When there is more than one runner on bases, a fielder may use fielder's choice in throwing for an out. In all other cases, he must throw to the pitcher who throws for the out.

Pegging First

Playground, Gymnasium　　　　*Late Elementary to Senior High School*

This game is played on a playgroundball diamond or baseball diamond. One team is at bat and the other team on the field. The batter attempts to bat the pitched ball and run to first base. If he succeeds, one point is scored. The players of the fielding team attempt to field the ball and throw it to first base in time to retire the runner, and if they succeed, one point is scored for the fielding team.

The players of the batting team bat in order until all have been at bat. Then the teams reverse their positions and the fielding team goes to bat. The team wins that has the most points when an agreed-upon number of innings have been completed.

Beatball

Playground, Gymnasium　　　　　　　　　　*Elementary School*

The game is played on a playgroundball diamond. A volleyball or sport ball is usually used.

The "batter" throws the ball into the field and runs the bases, keeping going until he reaches home or is put out. The fielders field the ball and throw it to first base; the first baseman throws it to second, and it is thus thrown around the circuit of the bases. If the runner reaches home before the ball does, he scores one point; otherwise, he is out.

Many interesting variations may be used by specifying the type of throw which the "batter" must use, such as standing sideways and throwing behind the back, facing backwards and throwing between the legs, raising one leg and throwing under it, and so on.

Hand Beatball.—Same as the above except that the pitcher pitches the ball and the batter bats it with his open hand.

Bowl Beatball.—Same as the above except that the pitcher rolls the ball and the batter kicks it.

Baseball Twenty-one [1]

Playground, Gymnasium　　　*Late Elementary and Junior High Schools*

Twenty-one is played on the regulation playgroundball diamond. The game differs from Playgroundball mainly in the way in which the score is counted. The batter hits the ball and runs the bases as in Playgroundball and continues around until he is put out. If the batter is put out .at first base, he scores no point, but if he passes first base and is put out at second base, he scores one point for having reached first base. If he reaches second

[1] From D. K. Brace, "Games of the Baseball Type." *The Journal of Health and Physical Education,* May, 1932.

base safely he scores two points, if he reaches third base safely he scores three points, and if he reaches home base safely he scores four points. A team continues at bat until it makes three outs, when its members become fielders. The first team reaching twenty-one points wins.

Tomball

Playground, Gymnasium   *Late Elementary and Junior High Schools*

This game is played on a playgroundball diamond and according to Playgroundball rules with the following exceptions:

1. There are no foul balls and the batter becomes a base runner the moment his bat touches the ball regardless of where the ball goes. The fielders must station themselves in such a way as to enable them to field any ball hit.

2. In addition to the methods of retiring runners used in Playgroundball, a runner is out (a) if a batted ball is caught on the first bounce; (b) if the ball is held on any base ahead of him; (c) if the ball is thrown across the path of a runner between bases.

Townball

Playground, Gymnasium   *Elementary School*

In this variation of Baseball, the rules of Playgroundball apply with the following exceptions:

1. The pitchers and catchers occupy the usual positions but the other players scatter any place about the field.

2. A batter is out on three strikes or if any strike is caught by the catcher. The runner is out if a fly is caught or if the ball is thrown between him and the base to which he is running.

3. A team remains in bat until all members have been put out. When all but one have retired and this one scores three runs, he may call in to bat any member of his team that he chooses.

Lineball [2]

Playground   *Late Elementary School*

The field consists of two parallel lines drawn forty-five feet apart. One team lines up behind one line and the other team lines up behind the other line. Each team has a bat. The player at one end of one line bats the ball across the field in such a way as to make the other team have difficulty in fielding the ball. If he succeeds in batting the ball across the opponents' line his team scores one point. One player of the opponents then bats the ball back. Play continues in this way until each player has

[2] From D. K. Brace, "Games of the Baseball Type," *The Journal of Health and Physical Education*, May, 1932.

had an opportunity to bat. In order to count a point the batted ball must be batted on the ground or at least below the opponent's head. When all players have batted, the team with the highest number of points wins.

Speedball (Baseball Type) [3]

Playground   *Late Elementary and Junior High Schools*

Speedball is a variation of Baseball and Playgroundball used by the Department of Physical Education of the state of Maryland. The game is designed to make possible the completion of five innings in a short time.

Only four batters may face the pitcher in any inning. The inning ends when three men are out, or when the fourth batter makes a run, makes a forced out, or is put out by the ball reaching any base ahead of him. Runs hit in by the fourth batter count unless he is put out at first base, as in regular Baseball.

Bases may be stolen starting with the motion of the pitcher's arm. Base runners may steal home, and may score on a throw back to the pitcher. Balks are called. Bunting is allowed. A runner may go either to first or third base, if bases are empty. When a player is awarded base on balls, his team is not charged with having a player at bat.

In other respects, the rules of Playgroundball apply.

Hitball.[3]—This game follows the rules of Speedball (Baseball Type) as given above, except that an inflated sport ball nineteen-and-one-half inches in circumference or soccer ball is used, which is batted with the hand. The game is played on a forty-five-foot baseball diamond.

Hand Baseball

Playground, Gymnasium   *Late Elementary to Senior High School*

This simple form of Baseball is popular among mixed groups of older boys and girls as a social or recreational game, as well as among younger children. A baseball diamond with base lines not exceeding thirty-five feet and a pitching distance of about fifteen feet is needed. A sport ball, soccer ball, or basketball may be used.

Divide the players into two teams as in Baseball. The pitcher tosses the ball with an underhand motion and the batter bats it with his fist or open hand. All the other rules of Baseball apply with the following ex-ceptions:

1. The runner may be put out by hitting him with a thrown ball.
2. Stealing bases is not allowed.
3. Bunting is not allowed.

[3] See *Maryland School Bulletin*, March, 1934, pp. 13, 14.

Variation.—Use a small, soft, rubber ball. The pitcher, standing about twenty-five feet away, throws the ball overhand so that it bounces once and passes the batter between the knees and the shoulder. The batter bats it with his hand. No catcher is needed—if the batter does not want to attempt to bat the ball, he catches it and returns it to the pitcher. One strike or two fouls put the batter out.

Variation.—Use an old softball. There is no catcher, the pitcher serving as both pitcher and catcher. The pitcher stands about six feet to one side of the batter and tosses the ball so that the batter can hit it, making no effort to strike him out.

Punch Ball (Baseball Type).—This is a very popular game among girls. The ball and diamond are the same as for Hand Baseball, except that there is no pitcher's box and home base is three feet wide. The batter stands on home base and the catcher of the fielding team, standing about six feet to one side, tosses the ball to the batter. The batter hits the ball into the field with the fist, and runs bases as in Baseball. To retire the runner, the fielders throw the ball to the catcher instead of to the base to which the runner is advancing.

The runner is out under the following conditions:

1. If the catcher, holding the ball, touches home base before he reaches first base.

2. When he is off base and the catcher, holding the ball, touches home base and calls his name.

3. If a fly ball (fair or foul) hit by him is caught.

In other respects the rules of Playgroundball apply.

Kick Baseball

Playground, Gymnasium   *Lower Elementary to Senior High School*

Like Hand Baseball, this game is popular as a social and recreational game for girls, mixed groups of boys and girls, and for young children.

The diamond should have forty-foot baselines and a pitching distance of thirty feet. A sport ball, codeball, or soccer ball is used. The pitcher rolls the ball to the batter who kicks it with his foot. The rules of Playgroundball apply with the following exceptions:

1. The kicker stands directly in back of home plate.

2. A pitched ball is considered good and may be called a strike if it passes directly over home plate not higher than the kicker's knees.

3. A pitched ball hitting the kicker above the knees is a dead ball, and is counted as a ball unless the kicker makes no effort to avoid it, in which case it is called a strike. Base runners may not advance on the play.

4. Base runners may be put out by hitting them with a thrown ball (boys only).

Soccer Baseball, Number 1 [4]

Playground, Gymnasium   *Late Elementary to Senior High School*

This game holds a particular appeal for elementary school boys and is also frequently used by both sexes as recreational play.

Diamond.—A forty-five-foot playgroundball diamond is used. Second base (called the center base) is placed three feet nearer to home base than the regular position of second base. First base and third base are not used. Points are marked twenty-five feet from home base on the first and third baselines and connected with a line—this is known as the foul line.

Ball.—A soccer ball is used. In informal play, a sport ball or codeball may be substituted.

Teams.—Same as in Baseball.

Length of Game.—Same as in Baseball.

The Play.—The kicker (batter) may punt, drop-kick, or place-kick the ball from home base or either side of it, provided he does not step in front of a line prolonged on either side of the front edge of home base until the ball is kicked.

The ball is held and kicked by the kicker and is not pitched.

The ball must cross the foul line to be a fair kick.

Having kicked fairly, the runner runs to the center base and returns to home base.

The fielders field the ball and attempt to hit or touch the runner with it. The ball must be passed three times before the runner may be hit or touched. The runner may stop at his own risk.

Fair Ball.—A kick is fair if it goes beyond the foul line and inside the side boundary lines (first and third baselines) until it passes first or third base. All boundary lines are considered fair.

Fielding Fouls.—A fielder commits a foul when he—

1. Holds or trips a runner.
2. Enters the foul zone before or after a kick except to retrieve the ball.
3. Plays in foul territory before a kick.
4. Runs (takes more than two steps) while holding the ball.

Penalty: one run is scored.

In all fouls favoring the runner, the runner must complete his run.

Foul Zone Play.—A player may enter the foul zone to retrieve a slow kick. If he does not touch it and it comes to rest in the foul zone, it is a foul kick. If it rolls into fair territory, it is a fair kick.

Running Fouls.—A runner commits a foul when he—

1. Runs into a fielder.
2. Runs outside the forty-five foot diamond.
3. Purposely kicks the ball after becoming a runner.

Penalty: the runner is out.

[4] These rules follow those used by the Cincinnati Public Schools.

Two Fouls in Succession.—When two fouls occur in immediate succession, the first takes preference.

The Kicker is Out.—The kicker is out if he kicks two fouls, that is, balls which fail to cross the foul line or go outside of the right or left boundary lines.

The Runner is out—The runner is out—

1. If a fair or foul ball kicked by him is caught.

2. If hit by a fairly thrown ball or touched by the ball before touching home base after the completion of his run. The fielders must pass the ball three times before hitting the runner. Each pass must be a clear catch. The runner is not out unless these three passes are completed before he is hit.

3. If a player of the kicking team is on the fielding area or diamond.

4. If he fails to touch center base or home base.

5. If, when a fielder holds the ball on center base ahead of the runner after making three complete passes, the runner fails to touch center base within a period of ten seconds.

6. If he commits a running foul.

Scoring.—One point is scored each time a runner touches home base safely after making a fair run.

Officials.—A referee and score keeper are in charge of the game.

Soccer Baseball, Number 2.—This game was submitted by B. E. Wiggins, Columbus, Ohio. It is played on a playgroundball diamond or baseball diamond, and uses a soccer ball. The kicker (batter) place-kicks the ball from home base and then runs the bases as in Baseball. The general rules of Playgroundball apply with the following exceptions: (1) A base runner is out if a fielder possessing the ball touches the base before the runner reaches it—it is not necessary to touch the runner with the ball. (2) Base stealing is permitted at all times except when the ball is in the possession of the kicker at home base preparatory to kicking.

Washburn Ball.—This game is played on a diamond similar to that used in Soccer Baseball. The batter may throw, drop-kick, or place-kick the ball. Each batter must use a method different from the one just preceding him. Fielding and base running are as in Playgroundball.

Triangle Ball

Playground, Gymnasium   *Lower Elementary to Senior High School*

This variation of Baseball is acceptable when there are only a few players. Establish a home plate consisting of a triangle with the apex toward the pitcher's box measuring three feet on each side. First base is placed in the usual position, twenty feet from home base. The pitcher's box is twenty-five feet from the home plate. A softball is used.

A pitcher and catcher are needed for the fielding team, but the catcher functions as a backstop only; the remaining fielders scatter at random about the diamond. The batter hits the pitched ball, runs to first base, and immediately returns to home base as in One Old Cat. The fielders field the ball and throw it to the pitcher who tries to throw it into the triangle before the runner reaches home. The ball may be thrown so that it drops into the triangle, or so that it rolls across it; if rolled it must touch the ground inside the triangle. If the pitcher succeeds, the runner is out; otherwise a run is scored.

After three outs the teams change sides. The game may also be played by the rotation method.

Variation.—Use a sport ball, codeball, or soccer ball and have the batter strike it with his open hand.

Variation.—Use a sport ball, codeball, or soccer ball and have the pitcher roll it to the batter who attempts to kick it.

Kicking Home Runs

Playground   *Late Elementary to Senior High School*

A sport ball, codeball, or soccer ball is needed. The game is played on a playgroundball diamond with baselines of thirty-five feet or forty-five feet. Divide the players into two teams and line them up on opposite sides of the home base. Number the players of each team.

The first player of one team takes his place at home base as the kicker and the first player of the other or fielding team stations himself any place in the field he chooses. The kicker places the ball on the ground, and kicks it, and starts to run the circuit of the bases. The fielder secures the ball and runs to home base with it. The runner scores one point for each base he reaches before the fielder reaches home base. That is, he secures one point for having reached first base, two for second base, and four if he reaches home base. If the fielder catches the ball on the fly, no points are scored.

A runner is considered as retired unless he reaches home base before the ball. The players of one team take turns in kicking until three have been retired, then the opposing team kicks. With each new kicker, the player of the opposing team holding the same number takes the field and fields the ball.

Kick-the-Bar Baseball [5]

Playground   *Late Elementary and Junior High Schools*

This game combines the principles of Baseball with kicking.

Field.—A playgroundball diamond is used with baselines of forty-five

[5] The rules for this game were taken from "Kick-the-Bar Baseball," *Recreation*, March, 1931. By permission of National Recreation Association, publishers.

to sixty-five feet depending on the ability of the players. Draw a line from first base to third base, known as the bunt line.

Equipment.—Instead of a ball, a "bar" is used, consisting of one-foot section cut from an old bicycle tire. No bats are needed.

Teams.—Teams consist of seven players. Six of the players scatter beyond the bunt line and the seventh, the bartender, is stationed at home base.

The Play.—The player at "bat" stands at home base, drops the bar and kicks it into the diamond. He may kick at it any number of times provided he does not touch it. If he kicks it into foul territory or fails to kick it beyond the bunt line, he is out.

Having made a fair kick, he runs the bases as in Baseball. The bases are not played, however, but the fielders throw the bar to the bar tender who touches it to home base. If the bar is touched to home base before the runner reaches the base toward which he is moving, the runner is out. The bartender calls out the base toward which the runner is running as he touches the bar to home base.

In other respects the general rules of Baseball apply.

Scoring.—As in Baseball.

Length of Game.—Seven innings constitute a game.

Long Ball
(*Long Base*)

Playground, Gymnasium   *Late Elementary to Senior High School*

Establish a playing field with a home base (H), pitcher's box (PB) and long base (LB), as in Figure 45.

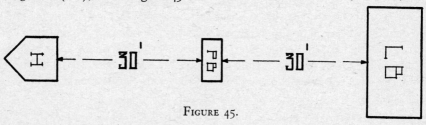

FIGURE 45.

The long base may be a gymnasium mat, or a marked-out area three by six feet. Two teams of three to ten players may play. Every hit is a fair hit, even though it may be nothing more than a foul tip. When the batter hits the ball he must run to the long base, and may either remain there or return to home base. Several players may occupy the long base at once, provided there is one player at bat. When there is more than one player on the base, all may return to the home base on a hit. A run is scored for each base runner who reaches home base safely. Once a base runner leaves the long base he cannot return unless a fly ball is caught.

A batter remains in bat until he hits the ball. A runner is out (1) when a fly ball hit by him is caught, (2) when the ball is thrown to the baseman and held by him with one foot on the base (either home base or long base) before the runner reaches the base, (3) when he is tagged off base by the ball held by an opposing player, (4) when he is hit when off base by a ball thrown by an opposing player. After three outs, the teams change place.

Sprintball

Gymnasium, Playground   *Junior and Senior High School*

Sprintball is an adaptation of Long Ball. The following rules follow those developed by the Baltimore, Maryland, Playground Athletic League.

Court.—The court is forty feet wide and sixty to eighty feet long. A center line runs lengthwise of the court, dividing it into two equal courts. One end line is known as the baseline and the opposite end line as the sprint line. At the baseline, three feet to the right of the center line, home base is placed—it is twelve inches square, placed diamond shape, with the front corner six inches behind the baseline. Batter's boxes are marked out either side of it as in Baseball, these being three by four feet in size. The pitcher's box is twenty-five to thirty feet out from home plate.

Ball.—A sport ball nineteen inches in circumference is used.

The Play.—The fielding team scatters across the court, one of them acting as pitcher and one as catcher. The batter stands in the batter's box and hits the pitched ball with the hand. The pitching is done with the underhand motion used in Playgroundball. After a hit, or on a third strike which is not caught, or after four balls, the batter runs to the sprint line. Except on the third strike, a foul ball not caught is a strike.

The object of the runner is to run to the sprint line and back to the baseline without being hit by the ball. He may stay behind the sprint line without returning as long as he chooses, and any number of runners may be behind the sprint line at one time; however, a batter must always be ready to bat when his turn comes or he is out. After leaving the baseline or sprint line, the runner cannot return unless a fly ball is caught, in which case he must return at the risk of being put out.

After batting, the runner must run to the sprint line *on the right side of the center line, and return on the left side.*

Outs.—A batter is out when:

1. A fly ball is caught.
2. A third strike is caught.
3. He hits the ball while outside the batter's box.

A runner is out when:

1. The ball reaches the sprint line and is held there before the runner arrives.
2. He is touched or hit by the ball in the fielding area.

3. After leaving the sprint line, the ball is held by the catcher or other player on the baseline before he reaches it.

4. If he runs across the center line in either direction.

Innings.—Three outs constitute an inning. Four innings is a game.
Officials.—An umpire and a scorer are in charge.

German Batball

Playground, Gymnasium   *Late Elementary to Senior High School*

This game combines some of the features of Baseball, Tennis, and Basketball. Establish a home plate two feet square and place a post or jumping standard forty feet from it. A soccer ball or sport ball is used. Divide the players into two teams; designate one team as batters and the other as fielders. Scatter the fielding team over the area.

The first batter stands by home base, tosses the ball up and bats it with his fist or open hand, then immediately runs to the jumping standard, around it and back to the home base. The fielders secure the ball and attempt to hit the runner with it. Fielders are not allowed to run with the ball but must pass it to other players in position to hit the runner. A player taking more than one step while holding the ball is considered as running with the ball. Fielders are not allowed to hold the ball longer than five seconds, and any two players may not pass the ball back and forth between themselves more than twice before passing it to another player. Breaking these fielding rules awards a run to the runner.

A batter is allowed three attempts to bat the ball; if unsuccessful on the third attempt, he is out. The runner is out if a fly ball batted by him is caught, or if he is hit with the ball before reaching home base. After three outs, the sides change. A point is scored for each runner who reaches home base safely.

For gymnasium use it is recommended that the more modern form of this game, described below under Batball, be used.

Batball [6]

Playground, Gymnasium   *Late Elementary to Senior High School*

This is a more highly organized and standardized form of German Batball. A volleyball is used.

The Court.—Establish a playing area forty by seventy-two feet as illustrated in Figure 46. One end is known as the serving line and the opposite end as the baseline. Ten feet from the serving line a scratch line is drawn across the court. In the center of the baseline a goal post is placed.

[6] The rules for this game follow in general the rules laid down by N. P. Neilson and W. Van Hagen, *Physical Education for Elementary Schools*, p. 151, Copyright, 1930. By permission of A. S. Barnes & Co., publishers.

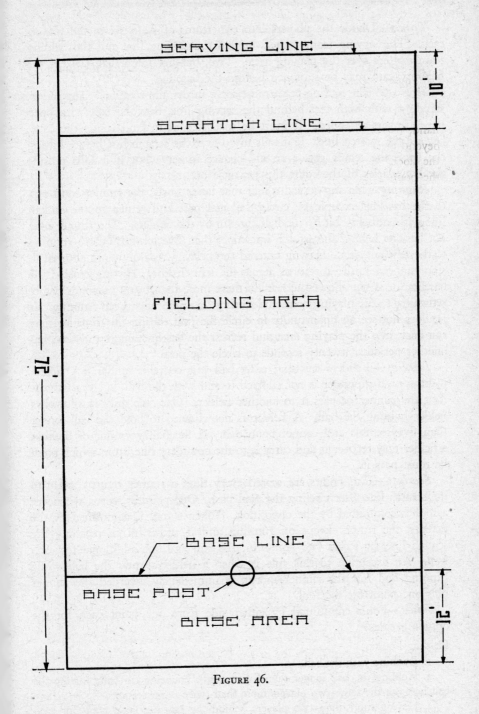

FIGURE 46.

Teams.—Divide the players into two teams of from six to ten players each. The serving team gathers behind the serving line and the fielding team scatters over the playing area. Two, but not more than two, of the fielding team may be stationed behind the baseline.

Serving.—The serving team must serve in definite rotation. The server, standing with both feet behind the serving line, bats the ball with open hand, fingers extended. It must be so batted as to land inside the court beyond the scratch line. If it fails to go over the scratch line before hitting the floor, the server gets a second chance to serve but if it falls outside the boundaries of the court the server is out.

Running.—Having served a ball that lands fairly, the runner must run to the baseline, completely circle the goal post and return to the scratch line without being hit by the ball thrown by the fielders. The runner may not hesitate behind the scratch line more than five seconds before running to the fielding area. Having entered the fielding area he is not allowed to stop running until he returns across the scratch line. Having crossed the baseline he is not allowed to remain there more than twenty seconds before returning to the playing area, and during this time must keep running. If he does not see an opportunity to circle the post during this time he may run back into the playing area and recross the baseline again and then has another period of twenty seconds to circle the post.

Fielding.—Fielders catching a fly ball put out the runner. A fielder picking up a grounder is not allowed to run with the ball, but must throw it at the runner or pass it to another fielder. One step only is allowed a fielder holding the ball. A fielder is not allowed to hold the ball longer than five seconds and cannot bounce it. If the ball goes out of bounds, a fielder may recover it and carry it to the boundary line, from which point he must pass it.

Scoring.—Two points are scored every time a runner returns safely to the scratch line after circling the goal post. One point is scored whenever a foul is committed by the opposition. When a foul is committed by the fielders, the runner keeps on running and if successful in reaching the scratch line, he scores two points for the run and one additional for each foul. An exception to this rule is when a fielder throws the ball while running and hits the runner—a run is immediately awarded the runner plus one point for the foul.

Fouls.—Fouls committed by either side score one point each for the opposing side.

Fielding Fouls:

1. Running with the ball.

2. Holding the ball longer than five seconds; bouncing the ball; passing the ball between the same two players more than twice in succession.

3. Having more than two players behind the baseline (one point for each player over two.)

4. Running across the scratch line.

5. Hitting the runner before he crosses the scratch line.

Running Fouls:

1. Failure to keep running after entering the fielding area. Two fouls of this type in one run retires the runner.

Retiring Runners.—The server or runner is out when:

1. A fly ball batted by him is caught.
2. He is hit by the ball fairly thrown by a fielder.
3. He runs outside the boundary lines.
4. He remains behind the baseline longer than twenty seconds.
5. He fails to cross the scratch line within five seconds after serving.
6. He stops running more than once after crossing the scratch line.
7. He serves outside the boundary lines.
8. He fails to serve the ball fairly as specified above.
9. He fails to serve the ball across the scratch line in two tries.

Game.—Three outs retires a side. Seven innings constitutes a game.

Flash Ball.[7]—This game is essentially the same as Batball. It differs in the following respects:

The ball is batted with the fist instead of being served as in Batball. The batter stands on a batting line drawn in the middle of the serving line. The pitcher stands on a pitching line drawn on the serving line six to eight feet from the batting line.

The pitcher is a member of the batting team. The ball is tossed to the batter who attempts to hit it with his fist into the playing area. A strike is called if he misses the ball, if he fails to strike a ball within batting range, if he hits a foul ball, or if he hits the ball so far out of bounds that it cannot be put into play immediately. A foul is a hit ball falling short of the scratch line. The batter is out when three strikes are called, when a fly ball hit by him is caught, and when he bats out of turn.

The batter becomes a runner when he makes a safe hit, and from then on the procedure is essentially the same as in Batball. There is no post on the baseline and the runner merely has to cross the baseline and return. He is not permitted to stay behind the baseline longer than three seconds.

Bounce Dodgeball.—This game is exactly the same as Batball except that in serving the server drops the ball to the ground and bats it on the rebound.

[7] For a detailed statement of Flash Ball rules see A. B. Crozier *Official Flash Ball Rules.* Reprint from *American Physical Education Review,* January, 1928. Ann Arbor: American Physical Education Association.

Schlagball

Playground, Gymnasium   *Late Elementary to Senior High School*

This variation of German batball is popular in the fall of the year.

Establish a home base two feet square, and place a post or jumping standard forty feet away from it. A soccer ball, codeball, or sport ball is used. Divide the players into two teams one of which scatters about the area as fielders and the other is at bat. One fielder stands behind home base. The first kicker (batter) stands at the home base, drops the ball and punts it into the field (he does not kick it from the ground). Having kicked it he runs around the jumping standard and returns to home base.

The fielders secure the ball and attempt to hit the runner with it or to throw it to the catcher on home base before the runner reaches home. They may not run with it, being permitted to take only one step. Fielders are not permitted to hold the ball longer than five seconds before passing it to another player, and the ball may not be passed back and forth between two players more than twice before being thrown to another player. Breaking these rules gives the run to the runner.

The kicker is allowed three attempts to kick the ball and if he fails on the third attempt he is out. The runner is out (1) if a fly ball kicked by him is caught, (2) if he is hit by the ball, (3) if the ball is held by an opposing player on home base before he reaches home.

After three outs the sides change. A point is scored for each runner reaching home base safely.

Kick Dodgeball (German Kickball).—This game is exactly the same as Batball except that in serving the ball is kicked instead of batted.

Pick-up Kickball.—This is the same as Kick Dodgeball except in respect to the handling of ground balls. A fly ball may be caught and thrown at the runner, but if it is kicked on the ground, it may not be picked up. It may be kicked by a fielder to another fielder or kicked into the air and caught by the fielder who kicked it. Only balls that are caught from the air may be thrown at the runner.

Soccer Batball.—See Soccer Batball in Chapter XXII, "Games of the Soccer Football Type."

Hit-Pin Baseball [8]

Playground, Gymnasium   *Late Elementary to Senior High School*

Equipment.—A soccer ball is used. The game is played on a playgroundball diamond with forty-five-foot baselines. In the gymnasium make the baselines as large as possible up to forty-five feet. A circle six feet in

[8] The rules for this game follow in general those presented in D. LaSalle, *Play Activities for Elementary Schools*, p. 154 ff. Copyright, 1926. By permission of A. S. Barnes and Company, publishers.

diameter is drawn around home base and no batting boxes are used (see Figure 47). The other three bases are one foot square. The pitcher's box is a rectangle four by twelve feet, the front line of which is twenty feet from the home plate. An Indian club is set up on each base, including home base. For outdoor use, the clubs stand up more satisfactorily if screwed to a block of wood five inches square and one-and-a-half inches thick.

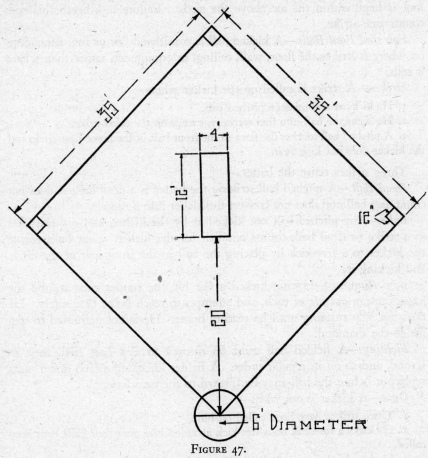

FIGURE 47.

Teams.—Two teams of nine players each are used, stationed as in Baseball.

Object.—The object is to score runs: The kicker (batter) stands in the home circle and kicks the ball as it is tossed to him by the pitcher. Having kicked it fairly, he runs the circuit of the bases without stopping, attempting to reach home base without being put out. To put the runner out the fielders must throw the ball to each base in regular sequence, endeavoring to get it to a base in time to enable the baseman to knock the club down with it before the runner reaches the base. When three outs are made the sides change places.

Pitching.—The pitcher must have both feet in the box when pitching and must roll or toss the ball with an underhand motion.

Kicking.—The kicker stands within the home base circle and at the time his kicking foot touches the ball, the other foot must be within the circumference of the circle. Both feet may be off the floor provided one foot is kept within the air above the circle. Failure to observe this rule counts one strike.

Fair and Foul Balls.—A kicked ball is considered fair or foul depending on where it strikes the floor, wall, ceiling, or equipment, rather than where it rolls.

Strikes.—A strike is called on the kicker when—

1. He kicks at and misses a pitched ball.
2. He kicks the ball into foul territory, except on the third strike.
3. A pitched ball touches the floor in the front half of the home base circle and the kicker does not kick at it.

Three strikes retire the batter.

Dead Ball.—A pitched ball striking the batter is a dead ball; it does not count as a ball and does not convert the kicker into a runner.

Balls.—Any pitched ball not kicked at by the kicker, and not classified as a strike or dead ball, counts one ball for the kicker. Four balls entitle the kicker to a free-kick by placing the ball in the front half of the circle and kicking it.

Base Running.—Having kicked a fair hit, the runner runs around the bases, cutting *outside* of each, and attempts to reach home base safely. He does not stop running until he reaches home. He is not permitted to step inside the diamond.

Fielding.—A fielded ball must be thrown to first base first, then to second, and so on in regular order. A fielder knocking a club down must replace it before the ball may be thrown to the next base.

Outs.—A kicker is out when—

1. Three strikes have been called on him.
2. He kicks a foul ball on a free-kick awarded him after four balls have been called.
3. He knocks down the Indian club on home base.
4. The pitcher knocks down the club on home base with a pitched ball.
5. A foul ball hit by him is caught, provided it rises in the air above his head.

The runner is out when—

1. A fly ball kicked by him is caught.
2. A fair ball kicked by him hits him before it hits the floor, wall, or an opposing player.
3. A fair ball kicked by him knocks down one of the Indian clubs before it touches any object other than the floor or ground.

4. In running he knocks down an Indian club.

5. The opposing team knocks down a club on a base with the ball before he reaches the base.

6. He steps inside the diamond at any point.

7. He interferes with a player inside the diamond.

Interference with Kicker and Runner.—The catcher is not permitted to interfere with the kicker. The penalty for this offence is a free-kick for the kicker.

Fielders are not permitted to interfere with the runner provided the runner stays outside the diamond. The penalty is a run awarded to the runner.

Scoring.—A run is scored when—

1. A runner touches the home base circle without having been put out.

2. A runner is interfered with by a fielder outside the diamond.

Bull's-Eye Baseball

Playground, Gymnasium   *Late Elementary and Junior High Schools*

A wall is needed for this game. Mark out on the wall a series of rectangles as in Figure 48, representing one-base hits, two-base hits, three-base

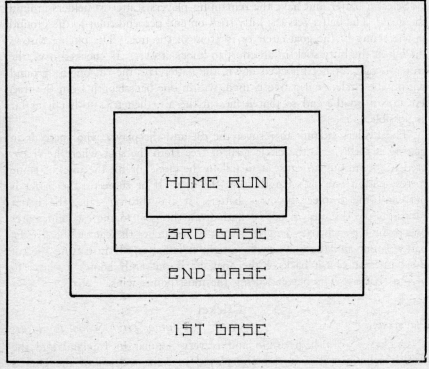

FIGURE 48.

hits, and a home run. Twenty-five to thirty-five feet out from the wall and directly opposite the middle of it, establish a home base. Use a softball and bat. Not more than six players, three on each team, may play the game with interest.

The pitcher stands with his back to the wall and pitches to the batter at the home plate. The batter attempts to bat the ball so that it hits the wall. In case he succeeds he is credited with a hit of the number of bases designated by the spot on the wall hit by the ball. No actual base running is done. If he misses the wall or if the ball is stopped by a fielder, he is out. After three batters are out the sides change.

Tip Cat

Playground, Yard, Woods   *Late Elementary and Junior High Schools*

This is a game of the American pioneer days.

The "cat" (often called kitty or piggy) is made from a stick four inches long and one inch thick by whittling it down to a point at each end. A four-foot stick of the size of a broomstick is used for a bat. A "kitty stick" is also needed consisting of a two-foot length of broomstick. A three-foot circle is drawn for the goal, or if played in the woods, a tree may be used. About thirty feet from it, a pitcher's line is drawn.

Select a batter and have the remaining players scatter as fielders around the goal. The batter sets the kitty stick on end perpendicular to the ground in the center of the goal circle or in front of the tree. The pitcher throws the bat at the kitty stick in an effort to knock it over. If knocked over, the batter is out. If not knocked down, the batter lays the cat on the ground within the circle, or if a tree is used, within one bat's length from the tree. He taps it on the end so that it flies in the air, then tries to bat it as far as possible.

The fielders attempt to recover the cat and the player who succeeds in getting it tosses it to the circle goal or tree from the spot where he recovered it, attempting to cause it to fall in the circle, or hit the tree, or come to rest within one bat's length from the tree. If he succeeds, the batter is out, and the thrower becomes batter. If the thrower fails, the batter measures the distance in bat's length from the goal to the cat, and scores one point for each bat's length. If a player catches the cat on the fly, the batter is out and the player who caught it is batter. If in batting the cat the batter knocks it back of the goal, he is out and chooses a player to become batter. The player scoring the most points wins.

Cricket

Playground   *Junior High School to Adults*

Cricket is of British origin and is very popular in England and the British colonies. It is now being played in some sections of the United States.

Field.—The field is commonly called a bowl and requires a space approximately 150 by 100 yards. In the center of this space two wickets are placed sixty-six feet apart. Each wicket consists of three stumps (posts) twenty-seven inches high and eight inches apart (W in Figure 49). On the top of each stump two small sticks called bails are placed. The ground in front of each wicket should be carefully smoothed or a matting on a firm base used to give a smooth surface.

A line (BB) eight feet eight inches long is drawn, with the wicket in the center, known as the bowling crease. This marks the position of the bowler (pitcher).

A line (PP) is drawn parallel to the wicket and four feet in front of it, called the popping crease. This defines the area for the batter.

Equipment.—The ball measures not less than nine nor more than nine-and-one-fourth inches in circumference. It weighs five-and-three-fourths ounces.

The bat is flat and approximately three feet long. The handle is twelve inches long. The blade is five inches wide, three-and-one-half inches thick at the end, and tapering down to a thickness of two inches at the handle. The handle is wrapped with twine or corked.

Teams.—Eleven players constitute a team. The positions of the fielding players vary with the nature of the bowling and ability of the batter, but the approximate positions are indicated in Figure 49. The diagram illustrates the positions for a right-handed batter. If the batter bats left handed, the fielders would shift so that there would be two fielders on the other side of the bowl in the positions now occupied by Numbers 5 and 11. The circles on the diagram are not actually drawn on the field—they are merely to indicate the relative positions of the fielders.

First Bat.—The captains toss to determine which team will bat first.

The Play.—The bowler (pitcher) stands at one wicket. The batter stands at the other wicket behind the popping crease and another member of the batting team stands at the opposite wicket, beside the bowler. The bowler pitches the ball so that it will come to the batter on the first bounce.

The batter attempts to hit the ball and as soon as he does so, he runs to the opposite wicket and his team mate stationed at the other wicket runs to the wicket at which the batter stood. This exchange constitutes a run and scores one run. If the hit was a long one and the runners have time, they continue to run back and forth between the wickets, scoring a run each time. Six runs are possible on one hit and such a hit corresponds to a home run in Baseball.

Any hit is a fair hit and consequently the fielders must cover the field in all directions from the batter. The bowler attempts not only to cause the batter to miss the ball, but to hit the wicket with the ball and displace the bails on top, thus putting the runner out. It is thus the business of the batter to defend the wicket with his bat. The bowler uses the same

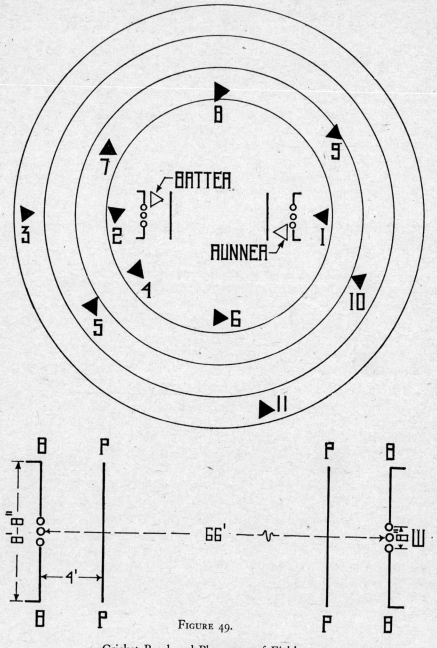

FIGURE 49.

Cricket Bowl and Placement of Fielders

1. Bowler	2. Wicket Keeper	3. Long Stop
4. First Slip	5. Second Slip	6. Point
7. Long Leg	8. Short Leg	9. Mid Wicket On
10. Mid Wicket Off	11. Cover Point	

types of skill displayed by a pitcher in Baseball—speed, change of pace, curves, and drops.

The fielders attempt to catch the ball on the fly and thus put the batter out, or to field it and throw it to the wicket keeper who puts the runner out, not by tagging him with the ball, but by knocking the bails off the wicket with the ball.

The Batter is Out.—The batter is out when (1) a bowled ball knocks a bail off the wicket, (2) he carelessly slips over the popping crease and the wicket keeper knocks the bail off the wicket while he is out.

The Runner is Out.—The runner is out when (1) a fly ball hit by him is caught, (2) when the wicket keeper knocks off a bail with the ball before he reaches the wicket.

Runs.—A run is scored each time the two runners exchange positions. Since the distance is short, the score runs much higher than in Baseball, frequently going into the hundreds.

Length of Game.—An inning continues until the entire team bats in turn. This makes the game slower than Baseball. Two innings usually constitute a game, and it often takes three or four days to complete the game.

Cricket Baseball

Playground, Gymnasium   *Elementary School*

The field consists of a home base and a first base, with a pitcher's box in the usual position twenty-five feet from home base. The distance from home base to first base is thirty-five feet. A soccer ball is used. Just in front of home base three Indian clubs are set up side by side.

One team is at bat end and the other is in the field. The batter stands in front of the Indian clubs, holding a light baseball bat. The pitcher rolls the ball towards the batter who tries to hit it with the bat and then runs to first base and back. The fielders try to secure the ball and throw it to home base and knock down one of the Indian clubs before the runner returns. The batter or runner is out (1) if he has three strikes, (2) if a pitched ball knocks down a club, (3) if a fly ball is caught, (4) if he is touched by the ball in the hands of a fielder, (5) if the fielding side returns the ball to home base and knocks down one of the pins before he returns. After three outs the sides change.

Bucket Cricket

Playground   *Late Elementary and Junior High Schools*

Draw a circle on the ground forty feet in diameter and in the center place a bucket upside down. The fielding team scatters outside the circle and the first batter stands on top of the bucket with bat in hand. A tennis ball or softball is used.

The fielding team tries to hit the bucket with the ball and any member of the fielding team may throw at it, provided he is outside the circle. The batter tries to defend the bucket by hitting the ball. The batter is out (1) when the bucket is hit, (2) when a fly ball hit by him is caught, (3) when he falls off the bucket. The batter continues to bat until he is out and the side continues at bat until all have batted.

Two runs are scored each time the batter hits a ball that is not caught, and one run is scored each time the ball is thrown at the bucket and misses it or is not batted.

Can Cricket

Playground   *Late Elementary and Junior High Schools*

Place two cans on the ground sixty or less feet apart. The pitcher stands by one can, the batter by the other and the runner by the can beside the pitcher. The other players scatter as fielders. The pitcher pitches the ball to knock the can over and the batter attempts to hit the ball. If the can is knocked over, the batter is out.

When the ball is hit, the batter runs to the other can and at the same time the runner stationed at the other can runs to the batter's can. They continue to run back and forth as long as they think they can make the other can without being put out. A runner is out when a fly batted by him is caught or when a fielder knocks the can over with the ball before he reaches it.

When a batter is out, all fielders move up and the catcher becomes batter.

GAMES OF THE BASEBALL TYPE IN OTHER CHAPTERS

Baseball on Skates.   Water Baseball.
Water Batball.

GAMES OF THE BASEBALL TYPE IN *SOCIAL GAMES FOR RECREATION*

Nature Baseball.   Signalling Baseball.
First Aid Baseball.   Mathematical Baseball.
Dramatized First Aid Baseball.

BASEBALL LEAD-UP CONTESTS

Many of the minor games of the Baseball type described in this chapter may be used in developing skills for Baseball. The following contests, described in the chapters on contests, may be used for this purpose also.

Catch, Throw, and Sit.

Catch, Throw, and Squat.

Ten Trips.

Run-and-Throw Relay.

Pass-and-Toss Relay.

Zigzag Ball-Passing Relay.

Throwing Shuttle Relay.

Pepper-Batting Relay.

Base Running.

Run to First Base.

Baseball Throw for Distance.

Baseball Throw for Accuracy.

Baseball Pitch for Accuracy.

Catcher's Throw to Second Base.

Fielder's Throw to Home Base.

Baseball Throw and Catch.

Throw, Bounce, and Catch.

Fungo Hit for Accuracy.

Baseball Overtake Contest.

Ante Over.

Progressive Throw and Catch.

CHAPTER XXI

GAMES OF THE TENNIS TYPE

UNLIKE the games of bat and ball, the tennis games seem to have little or no resemblance to the elementary games of children. They have probably descended from the games of ball played by the ancient Greeks and Romans. The oldest tennis games of which we know were played in Europe in the Middle Ages, and in much the same form as the games are played now. The two oldest tennis games are known as Court Tennis and Racquets, and the tennis games of today are derived from these two, falling with one or two exceptions into two groups, known as the *net games* and the *wall games*.

Court Tennis

Court Tennis, the oldest known tennis game, is played in a special court having walls of stone, a roof, and galleries for spectators on two sides of the playing space. It is the most complex game known; and this, in addition to the great expense of building the court, keeps it from general use. There are probably twenty of these courts in existence, mostly in continental Europe.

THE NET GAMES

The essential characteristics of the net games are the use of a net stretched across the middle of the court, with the opposing players on opposite sides of it, and the batting of the balls back and forth across the top of the net.

Lawn Tennis

Playground, Gymnasium   *Late Elementary School to Adults*

Lawn Tennis is the most popular of all the tennis games. It was devised by Major Wingate, an English army officer, in the early seventies. Some of the best elements of Court Tennis were retained and the game was simplified and adapted to outdoor play. It rapidly gained favor, and is now played in all civilized countries.

Lawn Tennis is played with a small ball and a racket on a level court. One or two players make a team. The object of the game is to bat the ball over a net with the racket, so that it will fall in the opponent's half of the court, and if possible, so that the opponent cannot return it.

The Court.—As shown in Figure 50, the court is divided across its middle by a net and includes four service courts, two back courts, and two alleys. The alleys are used in playing doubles game (two on a side) but not in playing the singles game (one on a side).

The Net.—The net is attached to the posts at a height of three-and-one-half feet and should be three feet high at its center. The full length of one racket (twenty-seven inches) plus the breadth of the head of another (nine inches), gives the exact height for the center. To form right habits of play it is important to keep the net just at this height.

Choice of Side or Serve.—Sun and wind often make one side preferable,

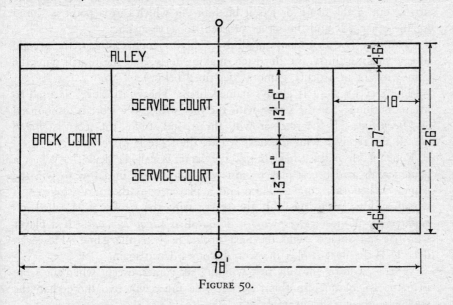

FIGURE 50.

and it is usually an advantage to serve. Before starting to play one player tosses up his racket with a whirling motion and an opponent calls "Rough" or "Smooth" while it is in the air. (Notice the small thread of colored gut woven into the racket near its upper end, so as to be rough on one side and smooth on the other.) The person winning the toss has his choice and may elect either to serve or to take a preferred side of the court.

Serving.—To begin a game one player tosses up a ball and bats it over the net with his racket. This is called serving. He must serve first from the right-hand side of the court, standing with both feet back of the baseline, and must bat the ball so that it will fall in the service court diagonally opposite him; if he fails to do this it is called a "fault" and he immediately tries again; if he serves a fault twice in succession a point is forfeited to the opponents. When the first point has been won or lost the same player serves again, this time from the left side, and he continues to serve alternately from right and left sides until the game is finished.

Returning the Ball.—When a ball has been correctly served the player to whom it is served must hit it with his racket on the first bound and drive it back across the net; in doubles it may fall anywhere in the court across the net; in singles it is not good if it falls in an alley. Any player to whom a ball is returned must return it in like manner, except that returned balls, unlike served balls, may be hit before they strike the ground if the player so desires. This is called "volleying." The ball must not be played until it has passed the net; a player touching the net with his body or racket loses the point. Play continues after each service until some player fails to return the ball—that is, misses it entirely, bats it into the net, or out of the court, or lets it hit him—in which case a point is scored for the other side and the server proceeds to serve again.

Scoring.—The first point made by a player counts fifteen, the second fifteen, making thirty, the third ten, making forty, and the fourth wins the game (except in a deuce game as described below).

The server's score is always named first. The word "love" is used to mean "nothing." If the server wins the first stroke, the score is announced as *fifteen love.* If the receiver wins the second stroke, the score is *fifteen all.* If the receiver wins the next stroke, the score is *fifteen-thirty.*

When both players have forty, the score is called "deuce." When a game stands at deuce, a player must win two strokes in a row to win the game. When the score is deuce and a player wins the next stroke, it is scored as his "advantage." If the server wins the stroke, it is called *advantage in;* if the receiver wins it, it is called *advantage out.* If a player who has "advantage" wins the next stroke, he wins the game. However, if he loses the next stroke, the score becomes deuce again.

A set is won by the side first winning six games, except when the score in game is *five all.* In this case one side must win two more than the opponents to win, for example, 7-5, 8-6.

Let.—This is an old tennis term meaning that the play counts for nothing and is to be played over as if it had not occurred. There are three cases:

1. A ball served before the opponents are ready. This cannot be claimed if the opponent strikes at the ball as if to return it.

2. A served ball that touches the top of the net and then goes on over and into the proper service court. This is called a "net ball" and applies only to served balls. A returned ball doing the same thing is good and play goes on.

3. When a player is prevented from making a play by interference from outside, as when a visitor runs across the court, a dog seizes a ball, and so forth.

Out of Bounds.—A ball is out of bounds only when it has struck the ground (or some permanent fixture) outside the court. If it falls on a line it is good. A player stopping a ball and claiming that it was going out, loses the point; the same thing is true if he allows a ball in play to hit him or his clothing.

Order of Serving.—In playing singles, players serve alternately. In playing doubles, each team may choose which of the two players shall serve first, but when this is once begun the same order must be kept throughout the set. In a three-handed game the single player serves every other game and does not cover the alleys, while his two opponents serve alternately and play the whole court.

Points.—A point is won in any of the following cases:

1. When an opponent fails to return a ball.
2. When an opponent volleys a served ball.
3. When an opponent serves a double fault.
4. When an opponent allows a ball in play to hit him.
5. When an opponent touches the net during play.
6. When an opponent strikes a ball before it has passed the net.

Matches.—Usually the team winning two sets out of three wins the match. Sometimes, in important cases, as in the finals of a tournament, three out of five must be won.

Team Competition.—In tennis matches between two schools or clubs, there are two plans in common use: (1) four singles matches and two doubles matches are played; (2) six singles matches and two doubles matches are played. The latter plan is usually used when the schools are close together and traveling expense is not an important item.

When several teams are competing, the players of all of the teams are arranged in an elimination tournament. The winner of each match in any round of the tournament scores one point for his team. Thus an individual as well as a team championship is determined. The doubles matches are handled in the same way.

Table Tennis
(*Ping-Pong*)

Play Room, Home, Club   *Junior High School to Adults*

Table Tennis or Ping-Pong is a miniature type of Tennis played on a table with a small celluloid ball. It is the outgrowth of a number of forms of miniature tennis developed late in the last century, these games being played with web-covered balls on the floor. The present form of Table Tennis, under the name of Ping-Pong, developed into a craze at the beginning of the present century, and then waned in popularity for several years, being played for the most part by experts. In recent years it has won back the popularity it deserves and is being played today with a strenuousness and skill unknown in the "gay nineties." Table Tennis involves considerable exercise and a large element of skill.

The following rules are for official tournament play:

Table.—The table is nine feet long and five feet wide, painted dark green with a three-quarter inch white line around the outside edges and lengthwise down the center. It sets thirty inches above the floor. For home play tables eight feet long and four feet wide may be used.

The net is of dark green material bound with white tape and is stretched crosswise across the center of the table so that the top is six-and-three-fourths inches above the table.

Balls and Rackets.—Official celluloid ping-pong balls are used. The rackets are of wood and may be surfaced with sandpaper, leather, cork, or rubber to suit the preference of the player. The blade is five-and-one-fourth inches wide, and six-and-one-half inches long, attached to a five-inch handle.

Choice of Service or Court.—The right to serve or receive in the first game of each match is determined by toss. If the toss winner chooses to be server or receiver, his opponent has the choice of court, or vice versa.

The player who serves first at the beginning of the first game, receives at the beginning of the second game. At the end of each game the players change ends of the table.

Service.—Throughout the game except when the score is *twenty all,* the server becomes the receiver and the receiver becomes the server after each five points. When the score is *twenty all,* the server becomes the receiver and the receiver becomes the server after each point.

The server stands behind his end of the table and strikes the ball with his racket so that it bounces from the table on his (the server's) side of the net and passes over the net and bounces upon any portion of the table on the receiver's side.

The server's racket and the ball must be behind the end line of the server's court and between the imaginary extensions of the side lines when he first strikes the ball; should he miss the ball entirely he loses the point to his opponent.

The Play.—The server having made a good service, the receiver attempts to make a good return, and thereafter the server and receiver alternately make a good return until a point is scored. In making a good return, the player strikes the ball in one stroke upon its first bounce, so that it passes directly over or past the end of the net and touches the playing surface of his opponent's side of the table. Striking the ball more than once is prohibited.

Scoring.—A player loses one point:

1. If he fails to make a good service.
2. If he fails to return a good service or good return by his opponent.
3. If he or his paddle touches the net while the ball is in play.
4. If he moves the table while the ball is in play.
5. If his free hand touches the playing surface while the ball is in play.
6. If the ball in play comes in contact with him before it has passed over the end lines or side lines of the table and has not yet touched the playing surface since being struck by his opponent.

7. If a player volleys the ball, that is, strikes or is struck by a ball within his court before it has dropped on the table.

Let.—It is a let and another ball is served under the following conditions:

1. If a served ball touches the net or its supports in passing over the net, provided the serve is otherwise good.

2. If the ball is served when the receiver is not ready. If the receiver strikes the ball, he cannot be considered as being unready.

3. If either player loses the point because of an accident not under his control.

Faults.—Violation of the service rules is a fault and scores one point for the receiver.

Game and Match.—The player first winning twenty-one points wins the game, except that when the score is *twenty all,* the player wins who first makes two more points than his opponent.

A match consists of the best two out of three games. In tournaments, if the players so elect, the final match may consist of the best three out of five games.

Table Tennis Doubles.

—In doubles, four players compete, two on each side. The regular rules for singles apply except that the minor courts of the table, established by the lengthwise center line are used in service.

The pair who are to start the game by serving decide between themselves which one will serve the first five balls, and their opponents decide which will receive. The selected partner delivers the first five services which are received by the selected partner of the receiving pair. Then the player who received delivers the next five services which are received by the player who started the serving. The third five services are delivered by the partner of the server of the first five services, and are received by the partner of the receiver of the first five services. The fourth five services are delivered by the partner of the receiver of the first five services, and are received by the partner of the server of the first five services. The fifth five services are delivered by the server who started the game, and so on until the game is won or until the score is *twenty all.* In the latter case each server in order delivers one service each turn until the game is won.

The service is made diagonally across the table, first right to left, then left to right, and so on. The server's position must be at the right of the center line when he makes a right-to-left service, and to the left of the line when he makes a left-to-right service.

Variation—Tennis Service.

—The service described above is standard. The service known as the "tennis service," however, has been official until recently and is still preferred by some players and used in some tournaments.

In this, the minor courts, established by the lengthwise lines are used. The server stands behind the end of the table, drops or tosses the ball, and hits it with the paddle so that it touches first within the receiver's right minor court. The service is made diagonally from right to left, then left to right, and so on alternately as in Lawn Tennis. Only one ball is served —there is no second service as in tennis.

At the point of impact of racket on ball, both must be behind the end line of the server's court and between an imaginary extension of the side lines. The ball when struck must be below the level of the waist. The service must be strictly underhand—no part of the racket except the handle may be above the waist when the ball is struck. Should the server miss the ball entirely the stroke does not count, but should he touch the ball, however slightly, it is a service.

The order of play after the service is as follows: (1) the server serves, (2) the receiver makes a good return, (3) the partner of the server makes a good return, (4) the partner of the receiver makes a good return, (5) the server makes a good return, and so on.

If a player serves or receives out of turn, the mistake must be corrected as soon as discovered, unless five consecutive serves have been completed, in which case the service and receiving continues in regular order and no penalty is inflicted.[1]

Variation—Tennis Scoring.—While the method of scoring that is described above is official for tournament play, the lawn tennis count is sometimes used for informal play. The play is the same as in the game described under Table Tennis above, but the scoring is as in Lawn Tennis.

Paddle Tennis

Playground, Gymnasium   *Late Elementary and Junior High Schools*

Paddle Tennis was originated by F. P. Beal years ago but was not perfected and standardized by him until about 1920.

Paddle Tennis is a game similar to Lawn Tennis but played on a small court. The smallness of the space needed and inexpensiveness of construction and upkeep, together with the appeal of the game itself, have made it widely used for playground and recreational purposes.

Court.—The lay out of the court is exactly the same as in Lawn Tennis, except that it is one-fourth the size of that used in Lawn Tennis. In laying it out, all dimensions of the Lawn Tennis court should be cut in half (see Figure 51). For outdoor use the lines can be marked out with lime or tape. The height of the net at the posts is two feet and four inches; a sag of two inches is permitted at the center.

[1] See C. G. Schaad, *Ping-Pong*. New York: Houghton Mifflin Co., 1930. Also W. R. Stewart, *Table Tennis Tactics*. Chicago: Martin Publishing Company, 1933.

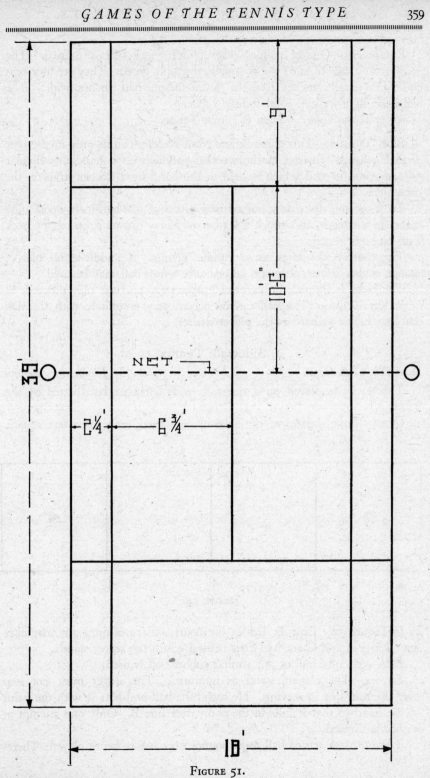

FIGURE 51.

Equipment.—Official paddle-tennis paddles and balls are used. The paddles are made of hard wood, usually three-ply glued. They are fourteen-and-three-quarters inches long by seven-and-one-half inches wide. The ball is of light-weight, solid sponge rubber.

Rules of the Game.—Same as Lawn Tennis.

Slab Tennis.—This game differs from Paddle Tennis only in the type of paddle used. Instead of the wooden paddle with a handle, a circular disk of wood is used which is held to the hand by a leather strap on the back side.

To make the disks, saw out circular pieces of one-half-inch wood, nine inches in diameter, and attach a leather or heavy canvas strap on the back with tacks or screws.

The court is the same as in Paddle Tennis. A paddle-tennis ball of sponge rubber is best, although an ordinary tennis ball may be used.

The hand is slipped through the leather strap and the play proceeds as in Paddle Tennis. The ball can be played very accurately with the slab and may be hit as hard as the player desires.

Sidewalk Tennis

Sidewalk, Club Room   *Elementary School*

This game is played on a sidewalk with a rubber ball batted by the hand.

Court.—Four squares of the sidewalk are used, each three feet square,

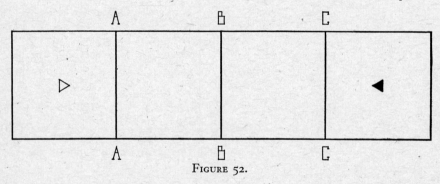

FIGURE 52.

as in Figure 52. Line B divides the court and constitutes an imaginary net. Lines A and C are foul lines behind which the server stands.

Ball.—A tennis ball or any similar rubber ball is used.

Service.—The players stand as indicated. The server must not step over the foul line in serving. He tosses the ball and bats it with the palm of the hand so that it falls in the court over line B. Only one attempt at service is allowed.

The Play.—A served ball must bounce once before being played. Thereafter it may be volleyed or played on the first bounce. The hand must be kept open and the ball "palmed."

Scoring.—Only the server scores. He continues to serve as long as he wins. He scores one point each time the opponent fails to return the ball fairly. He loses the serve when he (1) fails to serve into the opposing court, (2) steps over the foul line in serving, (3) fails to return the ball fairly into the opposing court.

The game consists of eleven points, except when the score is tied at *ten all*. In this case the server must win two points in succession to win.

Hand Tennis

Playground, Gymnasium   *Late Elementary and Junior High Schools*

Court.—A paddle-tennis court and net are used. The court is eighteen by thirty-nine feet in size and the net two feet four inches high. On each side of the net and three feet from it, a line is drawn across the court parallel to the net, known as the foul line. The service-court lines used in Tennis are not needed.

Ball.—Any soft rubber ball which bounds freely may be used.

Teams.—One or two players on a side.

Object of the Game.—The object is to keep the ball in play by batting it with either hand across the net, striking it either on the fly or first bounce.

Serving.—The ball is served from behind the rear line by dropping it to the ground and batting it on the first bounce over the net with an underhand swing. To be considered an underhand serve, the ball must be below the waist when struck. Only one attempt is permitted. In case the served ball hits the top of the net and goes over, it is a "let," and the ball is served over. The server continues to serve as long as he scores points; when he fails to score the point, he loses the serve.

In the doubles game, the side serving at the start of the game has only one hand; when the first server is out the ball goes to the opponents to be served. After this first inning, both players on each side serve in succession before the ball goes to the opponents; that is, when one is out, his partner serves.

Returning the Ball.—The procedure is as in Lawn Tennis. Players are not permitted to step across the foul line during play.

Scoring.—Points are scored only by the serving side. The serving side scores one point (1) when the opponents fail to return the ball over the net so that it strikes the ground within the opposing court; (2) when the opponents step over the foul line during play.

Failure of the serving side to return the ball, or stepping over the foul line, puts the server out.

The game consists of fifteen points.

Net Hand Ball.—The court is thirty by sixty feet in size and four or more players play on a side. The rules of Hand Tennis apply.

Whittennis

Playground, Gymnasium   *Junior High School to Adults*

Whittennis is a game closely resembling Tennis but has the distinctive feature of having a basket two feet in diameter attached to the middle of the net. This basket is a hazard in service and should the ball be served into it, it is a fault and the point is lost. In the course of play, however, hitting the ball into the basket scores one point. In other respects, points are scored as in Tennis. The court is forty feet long and fifteen feet wide, The net is three feet high.[2]

Badminton

Playground, Gymnasium   *Junior High School to Adults*

Badminton was originated in India and had its chief development in England. It is an older game than Lawn Tennis. The game is played extensively in England and Canada, and in recent years has gained a decided foothold in the United States. Its popularity has grown constantly. It is less strenuous than Tennis and thus is better suited for general recreational use. The shuttlecock does not bounce and consequently a smooth surface for the court is not needed as in Tennis; the court can be constructed quickly on any level piece of ground.

Court.—The court is twenty feet wide and forty-four feet long, laid out as in Figure 53. The two alleys down each side of the court, measuring eighteen inches in width, are out of bounds in singles play and are used only in doubles play.

The net is stretched at a height of five feet to the top.

Equipment.—Instead of a ball an official shuttlecock is used, consisting of a piece of cork with feathers attached. The rackets are much smaller and lighter than tennis rackets.

Object of Game.—The object is to bat the shuttle back and forth across the net with the racket without permitting it to touch the ground, endeavoring to so bat it into the opposing court that the opponents cannot return it.

Serving.—Only an underhand swing of the racket is permitted in serving. The service is considered overhand and illegal if the shuttle, at the instant of being struck, is higher than the server's waist.

The server starting the play stands in the right-hand half of the court and serves to the opposite right-hand half-court. If the server wins the point he serves the next time from the left-hand half of the court and into

[2] For complete rules, see *Rules of Whittennis*. Amesbury, Massachusetts: The Whittier Craftsmen, Inc.

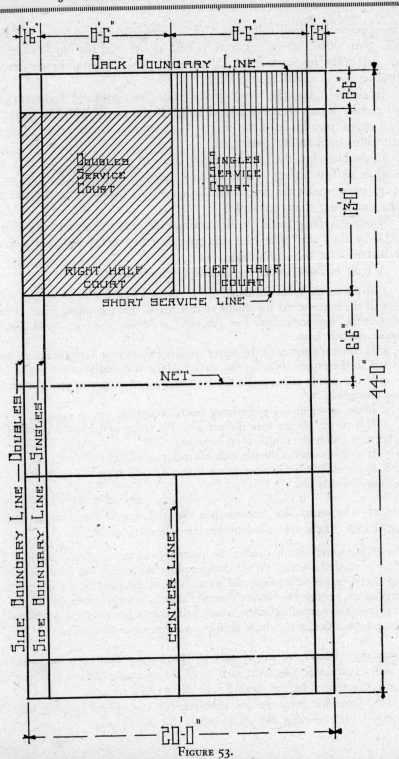

FIGURE 53.

the opposite left-hand half-court. Thus the service is always in the right half-court when the server's score is zero or an even number, and in the left half when his score is an odd number. The server continues to serve until an ace is scored against him.

In doubles play, the server serves from the right-hand half-court and his partner stands in the left-hand half. If the server wins the point, he then serves from his left-hand court. He continues to serve from alternate half courts until an out is declared.

In doubles play, the side serving at the start of the game has only one hand in its first inning. After the first server is out, the opponents serve. In all innings after the first, both players of one side serve in succession— after one is out the other serves.

Faults.—A fault made by the serving side puts the server out; if it is made by the "out" side (the side receiving the serve) it scores a point (called ace) for the serving side.

A fault is made under the following conditions:

1. If the server serves overhand.

2. If the server serves the shuttle so that it falls into the wrong court, or falls short of the short-service line (see diagram) or beyond the long-service line, or outside the side lines.

3. If either the server or the player receiving the service is not standing with his feet in the proper court for the service which is in order.

4. If the shuttle falls outside the boundary lines, or fails to pass the net, or goes through it.

5. If the server makes preliminary feints in serving.

6. If a player reaches over the net with his racket and hits the shuttle (his racket may follow the shuttle over, however).

7. If a player touches the net with his racket or person.

8. If the shuttle is hit twice in succession by players on the same side, or if it is not distinctly hit.

Let.—The word "let" means that the play counts for nothing and is played over. Lets are called under the following conditions:

1. If the served shuttle touches the top of the net in going over, provided the service is otherwise good. (If this happens after the service, the stroke is good.)

2. If the server serves from the wrong side of the court or out of turn and scores an ace, provided the let is claimed or allowed before the next service.

3. If a player standing in the wrong half-court, takes a service and wins the rally, provided the let is claimed or allowed before the next service.

Scoring.—Points are scored only by the serving side. An ace is scored by the serving side whenever the "out" side commits a fault. When the fault is committed by the serving side, the server is out.

The game for men consists of fifteen or twenty-one aces, as may be arranged. For women, the game consists of eleven aces.

In a game of fifteen aces, when the score is *thirteen all,* the side which first reached thirteen has the privilege of "setting" the game to five, and when the game is *fourteen all,* the side which first reached fourteen has the privilege of "setting" the game to three. When the game has been "set" the side that wins the five or three, according as the game has been "set," wins the game.

In the game of twenty-one aces the same method of scoring is used, substituting nineteen and twenty for thirteen and fourteen. In the game of eleven aces, nine and ten are substituted for thirteen and fourteen.

Sponge Badminton

Playground, Gymnasium, Camp   *Late Elementary School to Adults*

This game substitutes an ordinary sponge for the fragile and short-lived shuttlecock used in Badminton. Otherwise, the game is exactly like Badminton.

The sponge ball is almost equally as light as a shuttle, and while its action is slightly different, it is almost equally as fast. One sponge will last a whole season, whereas shuttlecocks often do not stand up for more than a day of constant use. The use of the sponge makes Badminton possible for those playgrounds and summer camps which otherwise might not be able to afford to supply shuttlecocks. The game may be played with either Badminton rackets or paddles as described under Paddle Badminton.

To make the sponge ball, secure a large sponge (not sponge rubber) and cut it down with scissors to a round ball measuring three-and-one-half inches in diameter.

Paddle Badminton

Playground, Gymnasium, Camp   *Late Elementary School to Adults*

Badminton can be played very successfully with paddles instead of rackets. Badminton rackets are light and fragile, and consequently the expense caused by breakage has militated against the general use of the game on playgrounds and in summer camps. The use of paddles will be found much more economical and almost equally as satisfactory. The size of the court remains the same.

Regular paddle-tennis paddles may be used, but it will be more satisfactory to have smaller paddles made resembling Badminton rackets in size and shape. These are made of one-fourth-inch material, sixteen inches long; the striking surface is a six-by-six-inch oval and the handle ten inches long, tapering in width from one-and-one-half inches at the end to one inch at the blade.

The game may be played either with shuttlecocks or a sponge ball as described under Sponge Badminton.

Team Form.—Paddle Badminton may be played on a team basis by increasing the width of the court—regardless of the number of players, the length remains the same. For six-man teams the width should be forty feet, and for eight-man teams, fifty feet. The game is played with paddles and shuttlecocks or sponges, and follows the rules of Volleyball.

Aerial Darts

Playground, Gymnasium, Camp   *Junior High School to Adults*

The court is twenty by fifty feet in size. Teams may consist of two or more players. Regular shuttlecocks are used and the players are equipped with paddles, tennis rackets, or badminton rackets. The rules follow those of Volleyball.

Feather Ball
(*Hand Badminton*)

Playground, Gymnasium   *Late Elementary and Junior High Schools*

While this game is not played with a net, it is similar in principle to the net games and is included here.

A feather ball or shuttlecock is used. The court is twenty feet wide and thirty feet long with a line (imaginary net) drawn across the center dividing it into two courts twenty by fifteen feet in size. Teams may consist of from two to six players, each occupying one-half of the court. The server bats the shuttle with his open hand to the opposite court and it is returned in similar manner. The object is to keep the shuttle from touching the floor. The rules of Volleyball apply to serving, line ball, volleying, relaying the ball, and scoring. Fifteen points constitute a game.

Volleyball

Playground, Gymnasium   *Junior High School to Adults*

Volleyball was invented in 1895 by William G. Morgan, then the director of a Y.M.C.A. gymnasium at Holyoke, Massachusetts. His object was to find a game that would keep more players busy on a small space than could Basketball, and at the same time be less violent and involve less personal encounter. The name is taken from Tennis and means to hit the ball before it strikes the ground; this is the idea of the game—to keep the ball in the air all the time by striking it forward and upward by one or both hands.

Ball.—The game is played with a regulation volleyball which is one inch less in diameter than a basketball and is much lighter, weighing between one-third and one-half as much. For informal play by children, a sport ball is often used.

Court.—The size of the regulation court for men is thirty by sixty feet, divided by the net into two areas, each thirty feet square. For girls and younger players it is wise to reduce the size of the court to twenty-five by fifty feet.

The net is thirty-two feet long and is stretched tightly across the court midway between the end lines and parallel to them, attached to posts outside the court. The height of the net for official men's play is eight feet from the ground to the top of the net, but for general school use and for young players it is recommended that the height be lowered to seven feet six inches. If the size of the players demand, it may even be dropped to six feet six inches.

Teams.—In official match play six players constitute a team, arranged

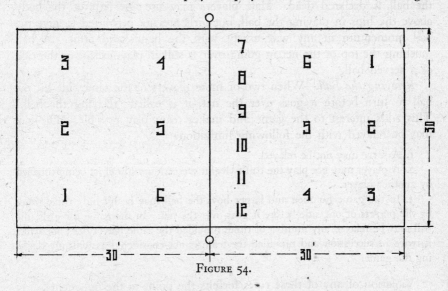

FIGURE 54.

as in the left half of the diagram. The game may be played, however, by as many as twelve on a team, in which case the players are arranged as shown in the right half of Figure 54. For match play for women, eight players constitute a team.

Rotation.—It is not customary in Volleyball, as it is in most games, to have the players hold the same positions throughout the game; they rotate, shifting to each position in turn, moving forward one place every time their side gets a turn at serving. When a player has reached the place indicated on the diagram by the highest number, he shifts next time back to the rear position indicated by number 1, and becomes server.

Serving.—The player occupying the right back position (number 1 in the diagram), standing with both feet behind his own backline, tosses the ball up and then bats it with his hand forward over the net. The hand may be either open or closed in serving. The served ball must not touch the net or any player of the serving side, must go over the top of the net and fall in the opponents' court. Otherwise the serve is lost and the ball goes to the opponents. For men, only one attempt is permitted in serving, but the rules for women permit two attempts. When inexperienced boys are playing it is wise to permit two attempts. A player serves only so long as his side wins; when it fails to win it is out and the opposing side serves. The players serve in turn as they get successive innings, rotating as soon as they get possession of the ball for service.

Returning the Ball.—When the ball is fairly served, the players of the opposing side try to keep it in the air, and to bat it back over the net. Play continues in this manner until the ball strikes the floor, strikes the person of a player below the hips, goes out of bounds, or until, for some reason, the ball is declared dead. Male players may use any part of the body above the hips in playing the ball, but girls are not permitted to give the ball momentum in any way except with the hands and arms. A ball touching the top of the net in going over is still in play, except in the case of a served ball.

Relaying the Ball.—When two or more players of the same side hit the ball in turn before it goes over the net, it is called "relaying the ball." This adds interest to the game and makes team play possible. The ball may be relayed with the following limitations:

1. A serve may not be relayed.
2. A player may not play the ball twice in succession without its being touched by another player.
3. In the game for men and larger boys the ball may be hit only three times by the players of one side before it goes over the net. In the game for girls, the ball may be relayed any number of times provided the same player does not strike it twice in succession and provided the team is not considered as willfully delaying the game.

Violation of any of these rules forfeits the point to the opponents.

Out of Bounds.—The ball is out of bounds whenever it strikes the floor, wall, or any person or object outside the playing field. When the ball hits an object suspended from the ceiling within the field, the ball should be served again unless the opposing side, by playing the ball, tacitly agrees that play should go on.

When the ball strikes outside, the point is lost by the side that last touched it. When a player in trying to return the ball bats it out of the field on his own side of the net, it may be recovered by any player of that side before it strikes. When a ball goes in the net it may be recovered in like manner if this can be done without the player's touching the net.

Illegal Plays.—A player may not—

1. Strike the ball while he is supported by an object or another player.
2. Bat the ball twice in succession.

3. Catch or hold the ball.
4. Reach over the net to strike the ball.
5. Serve out of regular order or step on or over back line in serving.
6. Touch the net while the ball is in play.
7. Interfere with the opponents by entering their court while play is in progress.
8. Delay the game unnecessarily.

Any of the above illegal plays either forfeits the point, or the ball goes to the opponents.

Scoring.—When the serving side wins the point, it counts one for that side. Only the serving side scores.[3] If the serving side loses the point the service goes to the other side. The serving side scores a point whenever—

1. A legally served ball is not returned.
2. An opponent makes an illegal play.

The serving side is out whenever—

1. The server fails to make a legal serve.
2. They fail to return a ball.
3. Any player of that side makes an illegal play.

In the men's game, the side having a two point lead at fifteen or more points wins the game, that is, if a team reaches fifteen points and its opponents have thirteen, it wins because it has a two point lead. If the score is fifteen to fourteen, however, the game has not terminated. The play must continue until one team scores two points more than its opponents.

In the girls' game the team wins which scores the most points in a playing period of thirty minutes (two fifteen-minute halves).

Changing Courts.—The teams change courts at the end of each game. If the sun and wind is a factor affecting the play, the captain of the team with the lesser score may request a change of courts as soon as the opposing team has scored eight points. Only one such change is permitted during a game.

Officials.—The officials for match games are a referee, a scorer and two linesmen, one of whom stands at the left end of each base line.

Giant Volleyball

Gymnasium, Playground   *Junior High School to Adults*

Giant Volleyball is played on a regular Volleyball court but uses a cage ball thirty inches in diameter. The teams may consist of as many as fifteen

---

[3] Schools and other organizations operating on a definite schedule often find that this method of scoring causes the games to last longer than the limit allowed for the play. Under these conditions, the game may be shortened by allowing the receiving side to score one point each time it retires the serving side.

players. It follows the rules of Volleyball except that a served ball may be relayed by two players.

Playing the ball with the head is much used in this game.

Balloon Volleyball

Club, Party, Schoolroom　　　　　　　*Late Elementary School to Adults*

This is an excellent recreational game for clubroom or social gathering. It is played enthusiastically by mixed groups. The game is more strenuous than one would imagine, owing to the fact that the balloon falls so slowly that there is much jumping and stretching to reach it; it also must be hit forcefully to make it carry.

An ordinary toy balloon is used. Stretch a rope across the room six feet six inches from the ground to serve as a net. Establish side lines but it is not necessary to establish a back line. Draw a serving line on each side six feet from the net. The rules of Volleyball apply with the following exceptions:

1. Two attempts are permitted in serving the balloon.
2. The served balloon may be relayed once in order to get it over the rope.
3. When in play, the balloon may be relayed five times before it is batted over the rope, provided that no player bats it twice in succession.

Clubroom Volleyball.—The game is played with a volleyball bladder protected by a covering of thin cloth. In place of the net, a rope is stretched across the room seven feet from the floor. The game is governed by all the rules of Volleyball.

Toss Ball

Yard, Playground　　　　　　　　　　*Elementary School*

Wherever deck-tennis and badminton courts are found, children will be seen tossing balls over the net. Toss Ball is played on such a court and is intended as nothing more than informal play for small children. A light volleyball is used and two or three children constitute a team. The ball is either tossed and caught, or volleyed over the net. In other respects the rules of Volleyball apply.

Doubles Volleyball

Playground, Gymnasium　　　　　　　　*Elementary School*

This is played on a badminton court or court of similar size. Two players play on a side and the regular rules of Volleyball apply.

A variation of this game allows the ball to be bounced once in passing it between two players before it is batted over the net.

Singles Volleyball.—This is played on a badminton or deck-tennis court with one player on each side, following the general procedure of Volleyball.

Water Volleyball

See Water Volleyball in Chapter XXVI, "Water Activities."

Newcomb

Newcomb is described in Chapter XXV, "Games of the Basketball Type." While the game uses a net, court, and ball similar to those used in Volleyball, the ball is caught and thrown rather than batted, and the object of the game is to develop throwing and catching ability. It is a throwing rather than a batting game and therefore conforms to the basketball type rather than the tennis type.

Cabinet Ball

Cabinet Ball is described in Chapter XXV, "Games of the Basketball Type." It is a game played with a light medicine ball following the general plan of Volleyball except that the ball is caught and thrown, which causes it to be classified as a game of the basketball type.

Volley Bounceball [4]

Playground, Gymnasium   *Junior High School to Adults*

Of the many variations of Volleyball in which the ball is permitted to bounce on the floor, this is probably the best for male players. It is a fast game and many who know it prefer it to Volleyball.

Court and Ball.—Same as in Volleyball except that the net is four feet high.

Serve.—Same as in Volleyball.

Returning the Ball.—The ball may be played either on the fly or first bounce. The players may play the ball with the hands or any part of the body above the hips. If the ball hits a player below the hips, it is dead and the point is lost by the team whose player was hit. Since the net is low, the ball may be hit with great force, and much of the play consists of attempting to hit opposing players on the legs, inasmuch as the point is won thereby; whereas if the ball hits the floor, it is still in play and may be returned on the first bounce.

The ball may be relayed following the rules of relaying in Volleyball except that it may be either volleyed or bounced. The ball must cross the net directly from the body of the player and may not be bounced over.

Scoring.—As in Volleyball.

[4] Contributed by Richard Bosse and Max Grob, North Cincinnati Gymnasium, Cincinnati.

Bounce Volleyball

Playground, Gymnasium   *Late Elementary and Junior High Schools*

Court.—Same as for Volleyball.

Equipment.—Same as for Volleyball.

Teams.—Six to twelve players may constitute a team.

Serving.—Same as for Volleyball.

Playing the Ball.—After the service, the receiving team must let the ball strike the ground once before returning it, hitting it over the net on the rebound from the floor. A team may relay the ball by volleying it among its own players as many times as it chooses before allowing the ball to hit the floor, provided the same player does not hit it twice in succession and provided the team is not considered to be willfully delaying the game. Once the ball hits the floor, however, it must be knocked across the net on the first bounce.

Scoring.—Only the serving team scores. It scores one point when—

1. The opposing team fails to return the ball so that it falls in the court.
2. The opposing team allows the ball to hit the floor more than once.
3. A member of the opposing team hits the ball twice in succession.
4. The opposing team hits the ball more than once after it strikes the floor.
5. The opposing team fails to let the ball hit the floor.
6. A member of the opposing team catches the ball.
7. A member of the opposing team touches the net.

When the serving side commits any of the above fouls, it loses the service and the ball goes to the opponents for service. The serving team also loses the service when it fails to score fairly as described under Volleyball.

The game is won by the team which has a two point lead at fifteen or more points as in Volleyball.

Fist Ball.—This game is practically the same as Bounce Volleyball. It differs in the following respects:

1. The ball must be struck with the closed fist, both on service and in play.
2. The server is allowed two attempts to serve the ball and players of the server's side may assist the ball over the net. In the case of such an assist on the first serve, the server is out if the ball does not land in the opposing court. If there is no assist and the serve is not good, the server has a second attempt.

Bounce Netball

Playground, Gymnasium   *Elementary and Junior High Schools*

Court.—The game is played with a volleyball on a volleyball court with the net lowered to a height of five feet. It follows all the rules of Volleyball with the following exceptions:

Serving.—The server stands behind the back line and throws the ball so that it bounces on his own side of the court and goes over the net, landing in the opposing court. Only one attempt is allowed. If the served ball hits the top of the net and goes over, it is a "let" and is served over.

Returning the Ball.—The receiving players bat the ball with the hands so that it will bounce and go over the net. Volleying is not permitted; the ball must always be bounced on the floor. The ball may be bounced between team mates any number of times before it is bounced over the net, provided the same player does not hit it twice in succession and provided the team is not considered as willfully delaying the game.

Spongeball

Playground, Gymnasium   *Late Elementary School to Adults*

This is a delightful, inexpensive, and not-too-strenuous recreational game which was originated by A. B. Wegener. It uses a ball made from an ordinary sponge. The action of the sponge is different from that of any other ball.

Court.—A volleyball court and net are used.

Equipment.—The ball is made from a large sponge and is cut out round to measure approximately three-and-one-half inches in diameter; it is slightly smaller than the twelve-inch softball.

Paddle-tennis rackets or regular tennis rackets may be used.

Teams.—The teams consist of six players. Larger teams lead to confusion and the hitting of players with the paddles.

Object of the Game.—The object is to bat the ball over the net into the opponents' court.

The Play.—The play follows the general plan of Volleyball, except that the ball is batted with the paddles. The players are stationed and rotate as in Volleyball.

Service.—The server stands behind the back line and serves by batting the ball either with an overhand or underhand swing. A second attempt is permitted if the first attempt is not good. No volleying is permitted on the service.

Fouls.—The following are fouls:

1. Crossing the service line in serving.
2. A player hitting the ball twice in succession.
3. More than three players hitting the ball before it is hit across the net.
4. Touching the net with paddle or body.
5. Playing the ball in any way except with the paddle.
6. Striking another player's paddle.

Scoring.—Only the serving side scores. It scores one point each time the opponents commit a foul or fail to return the ball fairly into the server's court.

The team wins that has a two-point lead when fifteen or more points have been scored.

Tennis Volleyball.—In this game the players use tennis rackets or paddle-tennis rackets, and a tennis or paddle-tennis ball. It is played on a volleyball court with six-men teams. The rules are exactly the same as those used in Spongeball.

Leeball [5]

Playground, Gymnasium   *Late Elementary School to Adults*

This game combines the fundamentals of Volleyball and Paddle Tennis.

Court.—A regulation volleyball court may be used, although a court six feet shorter than a volleyball court in length is preferable.

Equipment.—A volleyball net five feet in height is stretched across the floor dividing the playing space into two equal sections. The game is played with paddle-tennis paddles and a sport ball five inches in diameter.

Players.—The teams consist of six players if the court is of the size recommended—more than this cannot be accommodated without danger of the players being hit with the paddles. If a larger playing area is used, more players may be added. The players are lined up in two rows of three each.

Object of the Game.—The object of the game is for each team to keep the ball in play toward its opponents' court as in Volleyball by batting it with the paddle.

Serving.—The players rotate as in Volleyball. A player continues to serve until the ball is lost by her team's failure to legally return the ball. The ball may be served or batted with either an over- or under-arm stroke. Two serves are permitted provided the first serve is not good.

Fouls.—The following are fouls:

1. Contacting the net with body or paddle.
2. Crossing the service line in serving.
3. A player making more than two hits in succession, or more than three players playing the ball before it is volleyed across the net.
4. Batting the ball out of bounds.
5. Striking another player's paddle.

Scoring.—Only the serving side scores. It scores one point whenever the opposing side commits a foul. When the serving side commits a foul, the ball goes to the opposing side for service.

Length of Game.—The game is played in two halves of fifteen minutes each, with the teams changing courts at half time. The team wins that has the highest score at the expiration of the playing time.

[5] This game was originated recently by the girls of Taylor Allderdice High School of Pittsburgh, Pennsylvania, and was contributed by Jeanne E. Muter.

Officials.—There are two officials needed, a referee and a combined timer and scorer.

Bounceball [6]
(*Volley-Tennis*)

Playground, Gymnasium.   *Late Elementary School to Adults—Women*

This game was originated by Carolyn Shaw. It resembles Volleyball in type but is played with the net at the height used in Tennis.

Court.—A court thirty-six by fifty feet is used. If the teams number more than twelve players, the size should be increased slightly. A tennis net is stretched across the court, measuring three feet high at the center. Eighteen feet back from the center of the net on each side, establish a serving line. A volleyball is used.

Teams.—From six to fifteen players may play on a team. The players are numbered and rotate as in Volleyball.

Serving.—The server stands on the serving line midway between the side lines and serves by tossing up the ball and hitting it with the flat of the hand, serving it over the net before it hits the floor. The server has two chances to make a good serve.

If the served ball goes short of the net, another player may assist it over provided it has not touched the floor or any person. The assisting player must hit the ball with the flat of the hand and not more than twice. If the assisted service fails, a second chance to serve is forfeited.

If a served ball touches the top of the net and goes over, the service is repeated.

Returning the Ball.—The receiving side returns the ball by batting it either before it hits the floor or after one bounce, and play continues in this way. The ball may bounce once between each time it is hit by a player, but not more than once. The ball may be hit from player to player on the same team but must be hit with the flat of the hand and not bounced off his body. A player may hit the ball twice in succession but thereafter may not touch it until it has been played by another player. Dribbling downward is not permitted—the ball must be hit up in an effort to put it over the net or to another player. The ball must go over the net directly off a player's hands, not bounced over. Reaching over the net is not permitted.

Scoring.—Only the serving side scores. It scores one point each time the opponents fail to return the ball fairly. When the serving side fails, the service goes to the opponents.

Length of Game.—The game is played in two halves of fourteen minutes each with a two-minute intermission. The teams change courts between

---

[6] These rules are condensed from C. Shaw, "Bounceball," *American Physical Education Review,* May, 1923.

halves, and the side serving at the end of the first half continues at the beginning of the second half.

Deck Tennis

Playground, Gymnasium, Camp　　　*Late Elementary School to Adults*

This game was originated by Cleve F. Schaffer, as a game for a restricted playing space. Its first popularity was attained as a shipboard game and later it became widely used as a land sport. As a recreational game for playground, gymnasium, camp, and back yard, it has a far-flung following. It requires but little space, the equipment is inexpensive, and the game can be enjoyed the first time it is played.

Deck Tennis is not a true game of the tennis type in that the ring is

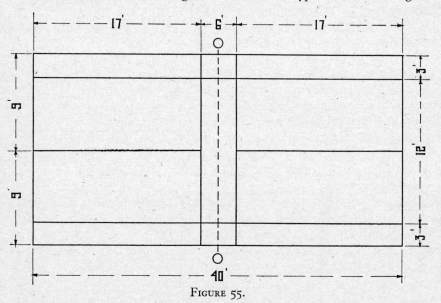

FIGURE 55.

caught and thrown rather than batted, but it resembles the tennis type in other respects.

Court.—The court is eighteen feet wide and forty feet long as illustrated in Figure 55. Three feet in from each side line and parallel to it, a line is drawn, thus creating an alley on each side of the court. This alley is used only in doubles play. Midway between the side lines and parallel to them a center line is drawn. A foul line is drawn on each side of the net, parallel to it and three feet from it. The net is stretched tightly across the court, and is four feet eight inches high at the posts.

In singles play, the area inside the side alleys is used and the center lengthwise line is disregarded. In doubles play, the entire court is used with the center line dividing it into right and left service courts.

Equipment.—The game is played with a ring or quoit six inches in diameter. It may be made of manila rope, one-half inch thick, with the ends spliced together, or the official ring of sponge rubber or inflated rubber may be used.

Teams.—One or two players may play on a side.

Object of Game.—The object is to toss the ring back and forth across the net without letting it hit the ground.

Serving.—The server stands behind the rear line and tosses the ring with an underhand motion into the opposing court. Feinting is not permitted and the ring must be delivered with a minimum upward flight of six inches. The server has only one attempt to make a good service. If the served ring hits the top of the net and falls over into the "dead" area, it counts as a bad service and the ring goes to the opponents for service. However, if a served ring after hitting the top of the net falls into the opposite court, it is a "let" and is served over unless the receiver chooses to play it.

In doubles play, the center line dividing the court into right and left service courts is used. The first server stands behind his right-hand court and serves diagonally into the opponents' right-hand court. If the point is won, the next service is from behind the left-hand court into the opponents' left-hand court, with the server's partner standing in the other court. When the service changes hands, the player who has been serving stands in the right-hand court and becomes the receiver. When it changes hands again, the service is delivered by the player who has been occupying the left-hand court.

The Play.—After the service, the ring is tossed back and forth across the net. The players must use one hand only, the ring being caught with this hand and immediately tossed back over the net. It is permissible to catch the ring against the body but in no case may the other hand be used. The ring must always be tossed, using an underhand or horizontal movement of the arm or wrist. The elbow may not be raised above the level of the shoulder in tossing unless the ring is caught above the shoulder, in which case it may be thrown at the elevation at which it was caught, provided the wrist is turned down and the ring propelled with a tossing motion of the wrist.

The ring must be thrown immediately after it is caught and from the spot where it was caught—holding it, stepping with it, feinting, or making false motions of throwing are prohibited. The ring must be firmly caught on one attempt, not juggled, and must be tossed, not batted.

Scoring.—Only the server scores and he continues serving as long as he wins. The server scores one point when the opponent fails to catch and return the ring fairly within the server's court. If the ring falls into the "dead" area, the point is lost. Rings falling on the lines are considered in. When the server fails at service or fails to return the ring fairly in play, he loses his service.

The game consists of fifteen points, unless a "long set" is agreed upon before play starts. In this case, if the game reaches *fourteen all,* it is necessary for a player to secure two points in succession to win.

Matches consist of the best two out of three games. The players change courts after each game. If at the start of the third game, one player scores eight points before his opponent scores any, the players change courts.

Variation.—The game may be scored like Tennis instead of like Volleyball. Many prefer this method. In this case, the center lengthwise line is used in singles play as well as doubles. The procedure in service and scoring is as described in Lawn Tennis.

Quoitennis (Tenikoit).—This game is very similar to Deck Tennis and differs from it only in the following details:

Court.—The court is smaller than in Deck Tennis, the court proper being nineteen feet long and sixteen feet wide. A line is drawn lengthwise of the court midway between the two side lines. Two-and-one-half feet behind each end line a serving line is drawn, this line being used in service only. There is no "dead" area. The top of the net should be four feet eight inches from the ground.

Equipment.—A hollow, air-vented, rubber ring is used, called a tenikoit.

Serving.—The server stands with toes touching the service line behind his own right-hand court and tosses the tenikoit diagonally into the receiver's right-hand court. On the next serve, he stands behind his left-hand court and serves into the receiver's left court.

The order of serving is as in Lawn Tennis.

Receiving.—The receiver stands toeing the back line of the court (not the serving line) and is not permitted to cross the line until the tenikoit has left the receiver's hand. Then he runs forward to play the tenikoit. In doubles play, however, the partners of the server and receiver may take any position they choose in their own courts.

Scoring.—The Lawn Tennis system of scoring is used. A match consists of the best two out of three sets.[7]

Ring Volleyball

Playground, Gymnasium, Camp   *Late Elementary School to Adults*

This game is played on a deck-tennis court with deck-tennis rings. Four to six play on a side. The game is played according to the rules of Volleyball except that the ring is caught and thrown as in Deck Tennis.

---

[7] These rules have been taken from Parker Brothers, Inc., *How to Play Quoitennis.* Copyright, 1933. By permission of Parker Brothers, Inc., publishers.

Sword Tennis

Playground, Gymnasium, Yard   *Junior High School to Adults*

This is the best development of the number of ancient games in which a ring is caught and thrown by a cane. It is played on a regular deck-tennis court, twenty by forty feet in size except that the dead line is six feet from the net. The net should be six feet high. The ring is a hoop six inches in diameter. While a deck-tennis ring may be used, an embroidery hoop is much to be preferred. Each player holds a walking stick or other stick of similar dimensions.

The game is better when played by two players than by four. The procedure is similar to Deck Tennis. The server stands behind the end line of the court, holding the hoop on the end of his stick, the stick being stuck through the hoop. He tosses it over the net and his opponent catches it on his stick and tosses it back. If the hoop is allowed to slide down the stick until it hits the player's hand he loses the point—this is the most difficult angle of the game. No player may step over the dead line, nor toss the hoop so that it falls in front of the opponent's dead line.

In other respects the game and the scoring is as in Deck Tennis.

THE WALL GAMES

In the wall games there is no net, and the court corresponds to one side of the lawn-tennis court; the ball is batted against the front wall and is played by the opponents when it rebounds. Both sides must use the same court, but each side has exclusive right to it in alternation, the side not in play being obliged to keep out of the way.

Handball—Four-Wall Game

Gymnasium   *Late Elementary School to Adults*

Ireland claims the honor of originating this game. The original Irish game was played in a court with four walls—front, sides, and rear—and this type of court is widely used in America today, although the single-wall court has recently become popular.

Handball is played by all nations today, but it has reached the height of popularity among Latin peoples. It comes close to being the French national game. In Canada, most French denominational schools are equipped with cement or wooden courts to play this game. In America, it is popular in the recreational sense. For that reason, it is found in Y.M.C.A.'s and business men's clubs as well as in college gymnasiums.

Court.—The court consists of a room with four walls and a ceiling. It is twenty-two feet wide, twenty-two feet high, and forty-six feet long. The back wall is frequently only ten feet high, leaving a space seven feet in height behind which a spectators' gallery is built.

Directly across the middle of the court a line is drawn on the floor parallel to the front wall, known as the short-line; this line divides the court into two halves of equal size (Figure 56). Five feet in front of this line another line is drawn, known as the service-line. Eighteen inches from each side wall and parallel to it, a line is drawn connecting the short-line and the service-line, thus forming two service boxes, one at each side of the court.

Ball.—The standard handball is used. It is a black rubber ball one-and-seven-eighths inches thick. In informal play, a tennis ball may be used. Players are permitted to protect their hands with gloves of soft material. In official play, gloves with the thumb and fingers webbed together are prohibited.

Players.—One or two players constitute a team.

Serving.—To serve, the player must stand in the serving space between the short-line and the service-line. He must bounce the ball on the floor and then bat it on the first bounce against the front wall. If he misses the ball he is out. He may bounce it three times before swinging at it, but if he fails to swing on the third attempt he is out. To be in play, the ball must hit the front wall and rebound across the short-line before striking the floor.

If the server's first serve is declared a "short ball" he is given a second service. Failing on the second attempt, he is out. A serve is declared a short ball under the following conditions:

1. If the ball does not rebound beyond the short-line before touching the floor.

2. If the ball rebounds from the front wall and touches the back wall or ceiling before touching the floor.

3. If the ball rebounds from the front wall and touches *both* side walls before touching the floor.

4. If the ball rebounds from the front wall over the back wall and out of the court.

5. If the server steps over the service-line or behind the short-line in the act of serving.

6. In the doubles game, if the server's partner fails to stand in the opposite box with his back to the wall while the ball is being served or leaves it before the ball crosses the short line. If the ball hits the partner, the serve is played over.

Order of Serving in Doubles.—The two teams agree as to which team shall start serving. When the first server of this team is out, he is followed by both his opponents who serve one after the other. Then both members of the first team serve in order. Each player must serve his own hand—to serve out of order puts the serving side out.

Returning the Ball.—After the ball is served one of the opponents must return the ball to the front wall. The ball may be played on the fly or first bounce, but must strike the front wall after it is returned before hitting the floor. The ball may not be played by a player after it has been

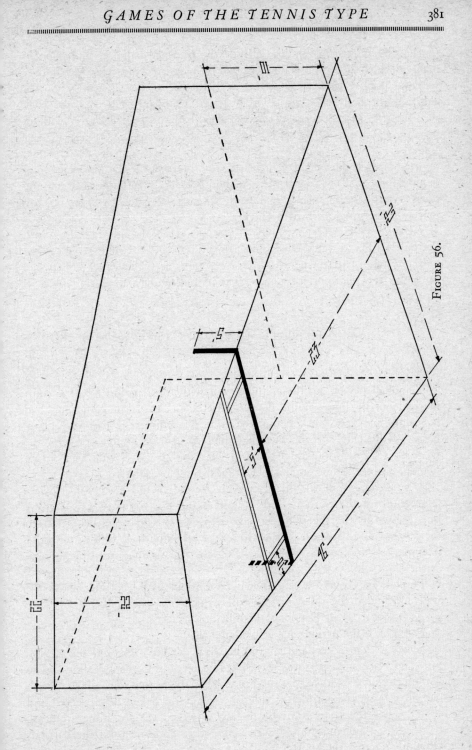

FIGURE 56.

touched by his partner or himself. If the returned ball hits an opponent before it hits the front wall it is out of play and must be served over without penalty. Hitting a partner with the ball counts as a miss for that side. If the ball rebounds from the front wall and goes over the back wall into the spectators' gallery, it is a dead ball and is played over without penalty.

Hinders.—When a player is blocked or interfered with by an opponent in attempting to play the ball it is called a "hinder." If the hinder is unintentional the ball is served over without penalty. Intentional hindering causes the offending player to lose the point. It is not a hinder when a player is interfered with by a partner.

Scoring.—The server wins a point if the receiving side fails to return the ball fairly. Twenty-one points constitute a game. The server is the only one who scores; when he loses he is put out. The server loses when he serves two short or long balls, fails to return the ball during play, or serves out of order.

Handball—One-Wall Game

Playground, Gymnasium　　　　　　　　*Late Elementary School to Adults*

Handball played against a single wall with the remainder of the court marked out by lines on the floor is strictly an American game and had its origin in New York about 1900. It has enjoyed widespread popularity, owing partly to the fact that many organizations do not have the facilities to build four-wall courts. The use of the single wall made Handball possible on outdoor playgrounds and in camps.

Court.—The wall should be sixteen feet high and twenty feet wide. The length of the court is thirty-four feet and the width twenty feet. A line, known as the short-line, is painted across the floor sixteen feet from the front wall and parallel to it (Figure 57). Nine feet behind the short-line, markers are painted on the floor to designate an imaginary line, known as the service-line (see diagram).

For outdoor courts, a six-foot wire extension should be built above the wall and out to the sides, to stop balls which miss the wall.

Ball.—Same as in Four-wall Handball.

Players.—Same as in Four-wall Handball.

Serving.—The server must stand between the short-line and the service-line, and must not step over the short-line or outside the side lines while serving. Doing so twice in succession puts the server out. The server's partner must stand outside the side lines while the ball is being served and cannot enter the court until the ball has crossed the short-line. During service, the opponents must stand behind the short-line until the ball has rebounded across the short-line.

In serving, the ball must be bounced on the floor and struck on the first bounce so that it will strike the wall and rebound across the short-line into the court. The server is allowed three preliminary bounces before striking the ball; more than that puts him out.

A ball served outside the side lines puts the server out. If the served ball is a short ball (fails to rebound across the short-line), or if it is a long

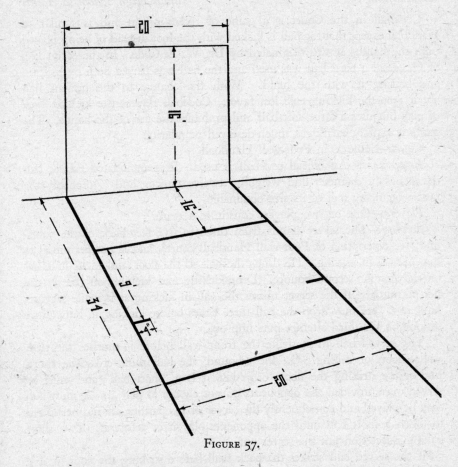

FIGURE 57.

ball (strikes the floor behind the back line), the server is given a second attempt. Failing in both attempts, he is out.

Order of Serving in Doubles.—Same as in Four-wall Handball.

Returning the Ball.—Following a good service, one of the opponents must return the ball to the wall. It may be played on the fly or first bounce, but must strike the front wall after it is returned before hitting the floor, and must rebound into the court. If the returned ball rebounds outside of the court, the side that returned it loses the point. In other respects the rules of Four-wall Handball apply.

Hinders.—Same as in Four-wall Handball.
Scoring.—Same as in Four-wall Handball.

Codeball in the Court

Gymnasium   *Junior High School to Adults*

Codeball in the Court is a game of recent origin and is similar to Handball except that the ball is kicked with the foot instead of being played with the hand. It was originated by Dr. W. E. Code. In the early days of Handball a hard ball was used and the ball was played both by kicking and batting it with the hand. With the change to the present ball about 1900 the kicking rule lost favor. Codeball revives the kicking type of play but uses a large soft ball and prohibits the use of the hands. The game is rapidly earning a much-deserved popularity.

Court.—Same as in Four-wall Handball.

Equipment.—An official codeball is used. It is an inflated rubber ball six inches in diameter and weighing twelve ounces, and is probably the fastest bouncing ball of its size obtainable.

Players.—One or two players constitute a team.

Serving.—The server stands from three to five feet back of the short-line (see description of Four-wall Handball court), and is not permitted to step over it in serving. He drops the ball to the floor and kicks it either on the first or second bounce. Drop-kicking and kicking on the fly are not permitted. If the server misses the ball in kicking at it while serving, he is out. He may drop the ball three times before kicking it, but failure to kick on the third attempt puts him out.

The served ball must strike the front wall before it touches the side-walls, floor, or ceiling. On the rebound, the ball must cross the short-line before striking the floor; otherwise it is a "short ball" and must be served over provided the opponents do not choose to play it. A short ball may be played and consequently the server or his partner are not permitted to touch a short ball until the opponents play it or refuse it. Two short balls in succession put the server out.

If the served ball strikes the back wall before striking the floor, it is a good service and the ball is in play. If the served ball goes into the gallery it is a dead ball and is played over without penalty.

It is a "foot out" and the server loses his service when (1) the served ball fails to strike the front wall before striking some other part of the court; (2) a short ball is touched or interfered with by the server or his partner; (3) two short balls are served in succession.

In doubles play, when the first server of the side serving at the start of the game is out, the service goes to the opponents. Thereafter, both partners serve in succession before the opponents have their inning at service.

The Play.—After the ball is served the opponents must return it to the front wall. In returning it, the ball may be kicked on the fly, first or second bounce. If it touches the floor before hitting the front wall it is a foot out. The ball can be played only by footing it.

If a player in attempting to foot the ball misses it entirely, he may still play it provided it has not bounced more than twice.

If a player foots the ball without sufficient force to carry it to the front wall he or his partner may again foot it provided in the interval it has not touched the ceiling, floor, or wall.

Hinders.—Same as in Four-wall Handball.

If a server has one short ball and a hinder occurs during the second service, the short ceases to be counted against him when he resumes the serve.

Scoring.—The server continues to serve as long as he scores points. He scores one point each time the opponents fail to return a fairly played ball. The receiving side scores one point for putting out the server. In the doubles game, the receiving side scores only one point for putting out both servers.

Fifteen points constitute a game. At *thirteen all* the outplayer or receiver may set to five if he so desires, and at *fourteen all* to three, provided this is done before another ball is served.

Matches consist of the best two out of three games.

Racquets

This is an old game played in castles in Europe in the Middle Ages and still played in a few places.

The playing floor is about forty by sixty feet and is surrounded by smooth walls of concrete about twenty-five feet high. Light is admitted through the roof. Doors are made to shut flush, so as to leave each wall perfectly smooth. The front wall has a metal base thirty inches high called the "telltale"; the ball in play must strike above it or the point is lost.

The ball is of solid rubber and is hit by a light racquet with a small circular head. The play is very fast.

The plan of play and scoring is like Handball.

Squash Racquets

Gymnasium   *Junior High School to Adults*

Squash Racquets is a game closely resembling "Racquets," but played in a court that is much smaller and built of wood instead of stone. This makes it less expensive, so that squash courts are sometimes built in fine residences, and often in modern gymnasium buildings. It is one of the most popular of the wall games.

Court.—Squash Racquets is played in a four-wall court thirty-two feet long, eighteen feet six inches wide, and sixteen feet high. Across the front wall parallel to the floor, a service line is painted six feet six inches from the floor. A metal plate called the "tell-tale" is placed along the bottom of the front wall and measures seventeen inches in height. It is made of sheet metal and protrudes one-and-one-half inches from the wall. The doubles court is forty-five by twenty-five by twenty.

One line is painted across the back wall parallel to the floor, six feet six inches from the floor.

A service-court line is painted across the floor parallel to the back wall and ten feet from it. Two arcs are drawn, one on each side of the court, connecting the service line and the side wall. The arcs extend toward the rear of the court and have a radius of four feet six inches. A line is drawn from the service line to the back wall midway between the side lines.

Equipment.—The official squash racquet is used. It resembles that used in Tennis but has a much smaller head and a longer handle.

Ball.—The official squash ball is used. It is smaller and less firm than a handball and is not as lively.

Service.—The first service is determined by a spin of the racquet. Thereafter, the service changes whenever the server loses a point.

The server may serve from whichever service box he chooses but thereafter he alternates between the boxes until he loses the point. There is no penalty for serving from the wrong box but the receiver may refuse the serve if he desires and demand that it be served over.

The server stands with at least one foot in the service box, and serves the ball by tossing it up and hitting it so that it hits the front wall above the service line before hitting any of the other walls or ceiling, and rebounds so that it falls in the opposite service court either before or after hitting any other wall. Otherwise it is a fault. If the served ball rebounds and hits the back wall on the volley on or above the six-foot-six-inch line, or rebounds and hits the ceiling, it is a fault. Missing the ball in attempting to serve it is also a fault.

After one fault, the server serves again. In case of two consecutive faults the server loses the service.

The Play.—To make a good return the ball must be hit on the volley or on the first bounce off the floor, and must reach the front wall on the fly above the "tell-tale." It may touch any of the walls in the court before or after touching the front wall. The ball may be struck at any number of times before it has hit the floor twice, provided it has not been previously touched.

If, on the first bounce from the floor, the ball hits on or above the six-foot-six-inch line on the back wall, the point is played over.

Keeping Out of Opponent's Way.—Having hit the ball, a player must get out of the opponent's way to give him a fair view of the ball, and avoid interfering with him.

Let.—It is a let and the play repeated—

1. If a player is inadvertently prevented by an opponent from playing the ball.
2. If a player cannot avoid being hit by a ball because of the position of his opponent.
3. If a person, because of fear of hitting his opponent, refrains from striking at the ball.
4. If a player in the act of striking touches his opponent with the racquet.

No let is allowed, however, on any strike made by a player—

1. When he actually touches or is touched by his opponent.
2. When the striker could have made a good return.
3. If the interference is merely with his vision.

Ball Touching Players.—If a fair ball touches either player before hitting the front wall, or before hitting the floor twice on the rebound from the front wall, the touched player loses the point.

If a struck ball hits an opponent before reaching the front wall, the striker wins the point provided, in the opinion of the referee, the ball would have reached the front wall before touching any other wall. If it would have reached the front wall but hit one of the other walls first, it is a let. If the return would not have been good, the striker loses the point.

Balks.—If, in the opinion of the referee, the interference with the striker is deliberate, it is a balk, and a point is scored by the player offended. Unnecessary crowding is a balk.

Scoring.—Each point by a player adds one to his score.

Game.—The player scoring fifteen points first wins the game, except that when the score is *thirteen all* or *fourteen all* the game may be "set" by the receiver if he so chooses. When the score is *thirteen all,* it may be set to five points or to three points, as the receiver prefers. At *fourteen all,* provided the score has not stood at *thirteen all,* it may be set to three.

Match.—A match consists of three out of five games.

Continuity of Play.—Play is continuous until the match is over, except that between the third and fourth games either player may request a rest of not more than five minutes.

Team Competition.—In squash matches between two clubs, the teams consist of five players. The opposing players are paired, and each pair plays a match consisting of the best three out of five games. Each player winning his match scores one point for his team.

When several teams are competing, the teams are arranged in an elimination tournament. Two teams paired together play, following the procedure described above, and the surviving team continues in the next succeeding round.

Squash Tennis.—Squash Tennis is essentially the same as Squash Racquets and is now played on the same court. For detailed rules, see the official rules of the National Squash Tennis Association.

Squash Handball

Gymnasium   *Junior High School to Adults*

Squash Handball was invented in 1922 by W. S. Slater. As the name implies, it is a combination of Squash and Handball. It is played in a four-wall handball court. The game follows the rules of Handball but the ball is hit by a squash racquet. Both singles and doubles may be played. The ball used is the official squash handball.[8]

Paddle Ball

Gymnasium   *Junior High School to Adults*

This is an excellent handball game played with a paddle-tennis ball and paddle. It is played in a four-wall handball court according to Handball rules, except that the system of scoring is that used in Squash Racquets. The server scores one point each time he wins a rally; the outplayer or receiver scores one point when he puts the server out. The game is fifteen points.

Wall Tennis

Playground, Gymnasium, Yard   *Junior High School to Adults*

On the end of a building or on a wall, paint the outline of a tennis net, three feet high and twenty-seven feet long, as in the diagram. Out from the wall mark lines on the ground as illustrated in Figure 58—this constitutes one-half of a regular tennis court. The length of the court may be shortened to the service line if space does not permit the full size.

The play is as in Lawn Tennis. The server stands behind the back line on the A side and serves the ball so that it will strike above the "net" and bounce back into the B court, where the receiver plays it. On the next serve, the players change sides of the court and the server serves into the A court.

Battle-Board Tennis [9]

Gymnasium   *Junior High School to Adults*

This game was conceived by Mary K. Browne to make Tennis practice more interesting and popular, and has proven to be popular as a winter indoor competitive sport.

[8] For detailed description and rules, see W. S. Slater, *The Game of Squash Hand Ball.* Copyright, 1931. Glendale, California: The Glendale Printers.

[9] From M. K. Browne, *Battle Board Tennis.* By permission of Lake Erie College, publishers.

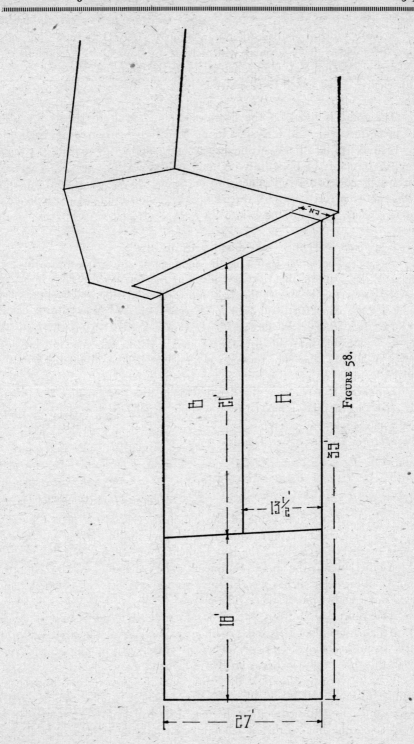

FIGURE 58.

Court.—A board is made of rough lumber, twelve feet high and eighteen feet wide. It is covered with celotex to slow up the rebound and deaden the sound. A tennis net is hung five feet out from the board, attached to gates which can be swung back when not in use. The net is three feet high.

The court is lined on the floor, extending out from the wall. It is eighteen feet wide and forty feet long. Ten feet in front of the back line and parallel to it, a line is painted; a second parallel line is painted twenty feet in front of the back line. A line connecting these two lines is then drawn parallel to the side lines, thus creating two service courts nine feet wide and ten feet deep. A three-foot service box is marked behind each service court, extending back into the back court and adjacent to the side line.

Equipment.—Tennis rackets and balls are used.

Service.—The server stands in the right service box and serves the ball against the wall so that it rebounds into the left service court. When served from the left side, the ball must rebound into the right service court. Only one ball is allowed for each service.

The Play.—After the service, the ball may be played anywhere in the court. Balls hit into the net either directly or on the rebound are lost points. The players take turns in playing the ball as in Handball. If a player is hit by a ball, the point is lost by the player hit.

Hinders.—If a player is interfered with in his effort to play the ball, it is a let and the play is played over without penalty. Obscuring the vision of a player is not interference.

Scoring.—As in Lawn Tennis.

Fives

Gymnasium   *Junior High School to Adults*

Fives is an English game of the handball type. It is played by two or four players in a court with three or four walls. There are several types of Fives in England, the best known being Rugby, Winchester, and Eton—the latter is the more prominent. The ball is one-and-three-fourths inches in diameter; it has a cork center around which twine is wound, and is covered with white leather. The players usually wear gloves.

The court has a front and two side walls, but no back wall as in Handball. The floor is paved. A line is painted across the front wall four feet six inches above the floor. There is also a vertical line on the front wall three feet eight inches from the right hand corner.

Four players usually play the game and the procedure is in general similar to Four-wall Handball. The server's object is not to send a service that cannot be returned; rather, he tosses the ball gently against the front wall above the line so that it rebounds and hits the right wall, and then drops onto the floor. The receiver may refuse any service he does not like, and if he fails to return the ball above the line, no stroke is counted. After the service has been returned, the play proceeds as in Handball. The scoring is as in Handball; fifteen points is the game; at *thirteen all* the game may be set at three or five; at *fourteen all,* at three.

Jai-alai
(*Pelota*)

Gymnasium   *Adults*

Pelota is a form of wall tennis played in Basque countries, Mexico, and South America. The regulation court is much longer than a handball court, having a front and back wall only, but the game can be played successfully on a handball court. The bat is a peculiar structure of basket work strapped to the hand and hollow on one side, so that the ball may be scooped up with it. This bat extends from the elbow to a point eight or ten inches beyond the finger tips. The ball is slightly larger than a handball and very fast.

The play resembles Handball in type but is much faster. The ball may be hit with terrific speed, and is played so that it hits low on the wall and rebounds close to the floor. There is no play off the back wall and this together with the speed with which the ball moves, makes the object of the game one of hitting the ball so that it will rebound past the opponents.

Pallone

Pallone Court   *Adults*

Pallone is the national game of Italy. It was first played at Tuscany in the fourteenth century.

The court is one-hundred yards long and seventeen yards wide. There is a high wall along one of the long sides. The spectators sit on the other three sides, protected by nets. A white line is drawn across the middle of the court. One end of the court is called the *battula,* the other end the *ribattuta.* At the *battula* end is placed a spring board upon which the player stands who is to receive the service.

The *pallone* is an inflated ball covered with leather, four-and-three-eighths inches in diameter. The players wear an oak gauntlet or bat called the *brocciale,* tubular in shape and covered with long protuberances. It weighs five or six pounds, and is provided with a grip for the hand.

Two teams of three players each play the game. There is a seventh player, the *mandario,* who serves the ball and does duty for both teams. The three players on a team consist of the *battiore* (batter), *spalla* (back), and *terzino* (third).

At the start the batter stands on the spring board, and receives the ball thrown to him on the bound by the *mandario.* The batter may ignore the ball until it comes to him to his liking. He runs down the spring board and strikes it with his bat over the center line toward the opponents. The game then proceeds until a player fails to return the ball correctly, or hits it out of bounds, or touches it with his person. This counts a point for his opponents. Four points is the game, counting fifteen, thirty, forty, and fifty.

MISCELLANEOUS GAMES OF THE TENNIS TYPE

The following games, while conforming to the tennis type, cannot be classified under either the net or wall games.

Tetherball

Playground, Camp   *Junior High School to Adults*

Tetherball is an excellent playground and summer-camp game. It was originated in England in 1896 to provide an active game for a small space.

Equipment.—An upright pole standing ten feet out of the ground is needed. It should be planted three feet in the ground and solidly packed so that it does not vibrate. The pole is seven-and-one-half inches in circum-

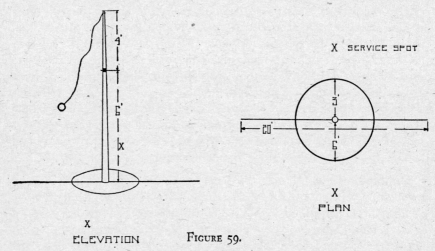

FIGURE 59.

ference at the ground and may taper toward the top. In camps a sapling may be cut and shaped to serve as the pole. A two-inch line is painted on the pole six feet from the ground.

A circle is drawn on the ground around the pole, having a three-foot radius. A line twenty feet long is drawn passing across the circle, dividing it into two equal halves. Two spots are marked on the ground six feet from the pole, one either side of the twenty-foot line and at right angles to it; these are the service spots.

The ball is attached to a cord seven-and-one-half feet long, which is tied to the top of the pole. There are two types of tetherballs in use. One is a tennis ball enclosed in a net casing. The other is a ball with a soft padded center, resembling a baseball in appearance, having a tape sewed to it to hold the rope. The latter type often proves a little the more satisfactory for general playground use, owing to the fact that it stands more battering and is more durable.

The ball is batted with tennis rackets, paddle-tennis paddles, or wooden paddles. Paddle-tennis paddles are the most satisfactory. They are more easily handled in the game, and are durable under the strain of the play. Tetherball is quite destructive to tennis rackets.

Object of the Game.—The object is to wind the cord around the pole by hitting it with the paddle so that the ball will be above the mark on the pole when the cord is completely wound. The opposing player attempts to wind the cord in the opposite direction.

Players.—The game is played with one player on a side.

Serving.—Players toss for the service and the server has his choice of direction. The server stands on the serving spot and bats the ball. If he misses the ball on the service or fails to knock it out of his territory, the service goes to the opponent.

The Play.—After the service, the other player tries to bat the ball in the opposite direction. Thereafter each player hits the ball as often as he can, each hitting it in the opposite direction. Players must keep on their own side of the twenty-foot line, and outside of the circle; breaking this rule gives a free-hit to the opponent, holding the ball as in service. A player must not allow the cord to wind around the racket; to do so gives a free-hit to the opponent. If the cord winds around the pole below the mark on the pole, a free-hit is given to the player in whose direction the ball is winding.

Scoring.—The game is won by the player who winds the cord around the pole so that the ball is above the mark on the pole.

Doubles.—Tetherball may be played with two players on a side by the addition of another circle on the ground around the pole. This circle is larger, having a six-foot radius. The partners alternate in service as in Lawn Tennis. Before service both partners of the serving side must stand outside the larger circle. One player serves and immediately enters the outer circle to play the ball as the cord becomes shortened. His partner must remain outside the outer circle during the play.

Zel-Ball.—Zel-ball is a game similar to Tetherball and played according to the same rules. The pole is movable and is set up on the lawn by inserting it in a metal pipe which has been driven into the ground. For indoor use a metal base is provided into which the upright pole fits.[10]

[10] See *Zel-ball* (leaflet). Mount Holly, New Jersey: Zel-ball Company.

Spotball

Pavement, Home, Playground   *Elementary and Junior High Schools*

This is a game for two players. It is particularly enjoyed as informal play. Draw a circle three feet in diameter on the pavement or floor and draw a line across the center of it extending several feet either side of the circle. A tennis ball or similar rubber ball is used.

The players stand one on either side of the line and outside the circle. Player Number 1 serves by throwing the ball into the circle so that it will bounce into Number 2's court. Number 2 attempts to return it by batting it with the palm of his hand so that it will strike in the circle and bounce in Number 1's court; Number 1 attempts to return it in the same manner. Thus the play proceeds until someone misses.

The server serves as long as he wins; when he loses, the service goes to his opponent. The server only scores, making one point each time his opponent misses. When the server misses no point is scored but the service goes to the opponent.

The following are fouls: (1) stepping into the circle or over the line, (2) failure to bounce the ball from the circle into the opponent's court; (3) catching the ball. Fouls by the server result in the loss of the service, and by the receiver score one point for the server.

The game is twenty-one points. If the score is *twenty all* a player must score two points in succession to win. Two out of three games wins a set.

Variation—Ping-Pong Spotball.—For indoor use, as in a home, draw the circle on the floor and use a ping-pong ball.

Crab Volleyball

Gymnasium, Club   *Late Elementary to Senior High School*

Mark out a court twenty-five by fifty feet in size. Establish a neutral area by making two parallel lines across the floor, six feet apart. Divide the group into two teams and assign one team to each half of the court. The players of each team scatter over their half of the court and sit on the floor.

Standing in the neutral area, the referee tosses a soccer ball or cage ball in the air so that it falls in the court of one of the teams. The players, while sitting on the floor, attempt to kick it over the neutral zone into the opposite team's court. It can be volleyed any number of times before being kicked across the neutral area. When kicked into the other court, the opposing players attempt to kick it back. In moving about the floor, the players may not rise to a standing position but may make progress only by the crab method: on hands and feet with backs toward the floor. The ball must not be touched with the hands.

A team scores one point when the opposing team (1) fails to kick the ball over the neutral zone into its court; (2) commits a foul by moving by other than the crab method, or by touching the ball with the hands.

After each point the referee tosses the ball to the team that won the point.

The team scoring fifteen points first wins.

Hand Batball [11]

Playground, Gymnasium   *Junior High School to Adults*

Establish two goal lines 150 feet apart. Fifty feet out from each goal line draw a six-foot line parallel to the goal line—this is the serving line. Divide the players into two teams and scatter them at random in opposite halves of the field facing each other. Give the black team a volleyball, soccer ball, or sport ball. One of the black players stands on the serving line and with

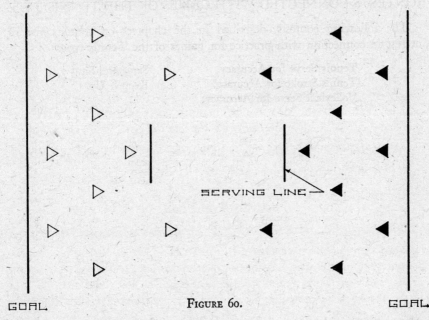

FIGURE 60.

GOAL   GOAL

his fist or open hand bats the ball over into the white team's territory. The white team attempts to catch the ball. The player securing it bats it back into the black's territory from which it is again batted back. The ball is always batted from the deepest point it reaches. The team wins which first bats the ball over the opposing team's goal.

[11] The description of this game follows in general that given in S. C. Staley, *Games, Contests and Relays*, p. 160. Copyright, 1924. By permission of A. S. Barnes and Company, publishers.

Ten Volleys

Playground, Gymnasium   *Late Elementary and Junior High Schools*

Divide the group into two teams and give one team a volleyball. At the signal the player with the ball bats it to a team mate who bats it to another, and so on, the object being to volley it ten times before the other team can touch it and without letting it touch the floor.

The first player who volleys it calls "One," the second player "Two," and so forth. The players of the other team attempt to break up the run by securing the ball and starting a run of ten volleys themselves. Whenever the ball touches the floor, the count stops and must start from one again. A player having volleyed the ball may not touch it again until it touches another player or object. The team wins which first completes ten volleys.

CONTESTS CONNECTED WITH GAMES OF THE TENNIS TYPE

The following contests, described in the chapters on contests, are of interest in connection with practice for games of the Tennis type.

Tennis Serve for Accuracy.   Serve and Sit.
Tennis Stroke for Accuracy.   Keep It Up.
Volleyball Serve for Accuracy.

CHAPTER XXII

GAMES OF THE SOCCER FOOTBALL TYPE

IN football games there is a large round or oval ball, which is advanced either by kicking, passing, or running. Several forms of kicking are employed. "Punting" consists in dropping the ball from the hands and striking it with the instep and side of the foot before it reaches the ground; in the "drop-kick" the ball is allowed to strike the ground and is kicked with the toe of the shoe at the moment it leaves the ground; in the "place-kick" the ball is placed upon the ground, and a player runs forward and kicks it (when the oval football is being place-kicked, it may be kept upright on its long axis by the assistance of a fellow player who holds a finger against the top end of it, but may not be raised above the surface of the ground by artificial tees or mounds of earth); "dribbling" consists of the player running forward and controlling the ball just ahead of himself by short kicks; "passing the ball" is either throwing it to one another and catching it with the hands, or it may mean kicking it from one to another, as in the soccer game. The oval football is thrown from the palm of the hand, and whirled so as to give it a spiral motion in the air.

The two main types of football are the Association game and Rugby. In Association football, usually called "Soccer," a round ball is used, which is handled mostly with the feet, dribbling, passing with the feet, and place-kicking being the usual means of advancing it. Occasionally it is struck with the head or the body, but the use of the hands and arms is barred.

In the Rugby games, the ball may be kicked, passed, or carried in the arms, and a player carrying the ball may be stopped by "tackling." In the Association game there is a resemblance to Hockey in that the ball is driven through the goal under the bar and this is the only method of scoring; in Rugby, however, the ball must be kicked over the bar or directly over one of the goal posts in order to count, and there are other ways of making scores. These two styles of football arose from the fact that the playing field at Rugby was soft, while at Eton and other schools it was hard and stony.

The goals used in all football and hockey games, consisting of two upright posts and a crossbar, represent in a dramatic sense the gates or fortresses of walled cities. In the early days when these games were first played, the teams represented castles or walled towns, and the playing space was often the entire territory between the towns, with the town gates, left open for the period of the game, as the goals.   To drive or carry the ball through one of these goals symbolized the capture of the gate or fortress.   Each team defended its own gate, and thus arose the custom of considering a goal in these games as belonging to the team defending it.

Soccer Football

Playground   *Junior High School to Adults*

The official rules of Soccer as used in college and general adult competition are acceptable for use in the junior and senior high schools with minor variations as noted in the description which follows.   A simplified form of soccer is needed for use in the elementary school grades and the rules for Modified Soccer and other minor soccer games which meet this need are described later in the chapter.

Ball.—The game is played with an official soccer ball, a round ball slightly smaller than a basketball.

The Field.—The field should be level and rectangular in shape.   The maximum field is 130 by 100 yards in extent, the minimum, 100 by 50 yards.   Two posts with a crossbar on top are placed in the middle of the goal lines, these posts being eight yards apart, and the crossbar eight feet above the ground.   The goal is said to belong to the team defending it. Lines are marked six yards outside of each goal post at right angles with the goal line for a distance of six yards and these lines are connected with a line parallel with the goal line.   The space within the lines is known as the "goal area."

Lines are marked twelve yards outside of each goal post at right angles with the goal line for a distance of eighteen yards and these lines are connected with a line parallel with the goal line.   The space within the lines is known as the "penalty area."   (See Figure 61.)

For junior-high-school use, it is recommended that the size of the field be cut down to 200 by 140 feet.   In this case the goal area should be 30 by 18 feet, and the penalty area 108 by 45 feet.

Players.—A regulation team is composed of eleven players, but any number may play the game.   The positions of the players are shown in Figure 62.   The goalkeeper tries to prevent the ball from going between the goal posts.   He may use any part of his body to do so as long as he does not pass outside his goal area.   The two fullbacks act as extra guards to the goal and remain in the vicinity of the goal during the progress of the game.   The three halfbacks keep some distance behind the forwards, advancing or retreating with the ball as the game progresses.   The five forwards advance the ball and score goals whenever possible.   The two outside forwards are called right and left wings.

Length of Game.—The professional game consists of two forty-five-minute halves with a five-minute intermission.   The playing time should be

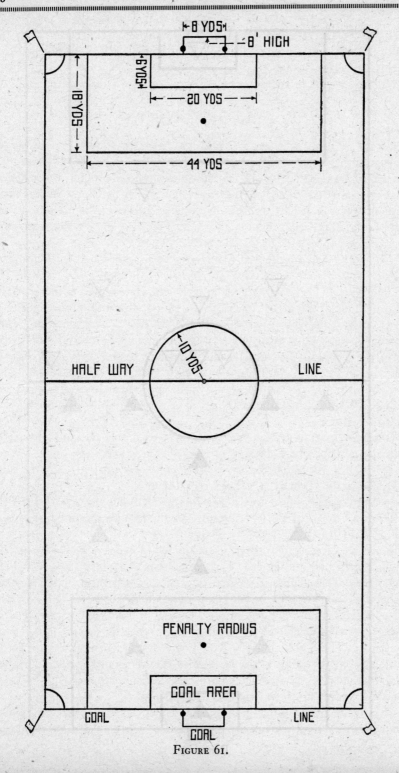

FIGURE 61.

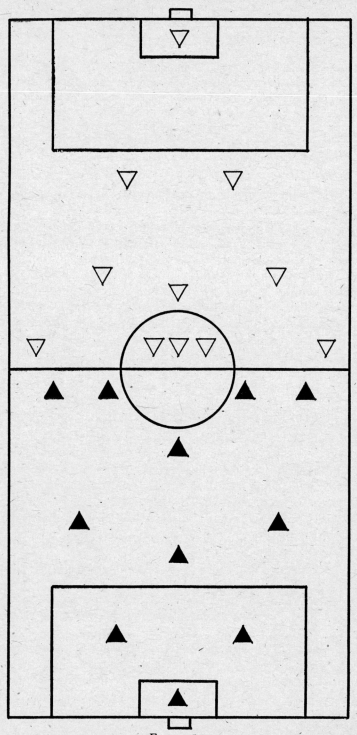

FIGURE 62.

cut down for secondary-school boys and for all girls. The following recommendations are made:

Senior-high-school boys: Ten-minute quarters with a one-minute rest after the first and third quarters, and ten minutes after the second quarter.

Junior-high-school boys: Eight-minute quarters with a two-minute rest after the first and third quarter, and ten minutes after the second quarter.

Girls of all grades: Eight-minute quarters with a two-minute rest between the first and second quarters, ten minutes between the second and third quarters, and four minutes between the third and fourth quarters.

Kick-Off.—The winner of the toss has the option of kicking off or choice of goals.

The game begins by a place-kick from the center of the field in the direction of the opponents' goal. The ball must travel forward the length of its circumference. The opponents must not approach within the circle until the ball has been kicked off; no player may pass beyond the center of the field until the ball has been kicked off.

After the kick-off the ball is kicked about the field until a goal is scored, or the ball goes outside the end line or side lines, or until the referee blows his whistle for some other reason. After the scoring of a goal the losing team kicks off from the center of the field.

The teams change goals at the end of each playing period. After the change of goals the ball is kicked off by the side opposite to the team that originally kicked off.

The Throw-In.—When the ball has passed beyond the side lines, either on the ground or in the air, it is a "touch" and is out of play. It is thrown in by a player on the side opposite to the one that put it out. The player (wing or halfback) must throw the ball in by standing with both feet on the side line and holding the ball with both hands completely over his head. A goal may not be scored from the throw-in, and the thrower may not play the ball again until it has been played by another player. Infringement of this rule gives the ball to the opponents for a free-kick at the place where the act occurred.

Goal-Kick.—When the ball is passed beyond the goal line by a player of the opposite side, it is returned to play by the goalkeeper or a fullback, kicking it into the field from the half of the goal area nearest which it passed over the line. No opposing player may be within ten yards of the ball until it is kicked.

Corner-Kick.—If the ball is played, accidentally or otherwise, behind the goal line by a player defending the goal, then a corner-kick is awarded to the attacking side. A corner-kick is taken from within one yard of the corner flag nearest which the ball was put out. A goal may be scored directly from a corner-kick. The kicker may not play the ball again until it has been played by another player. On all such kicks no opposing player may be within ten yards of the ball.

Suspension of Play.—In case of time out, substitution, or injury to a player, the ball is put in play again by being thrown down by the official at the place where it was when time was called, and it is in play when it touches the ground.

Fouls.—The following are fouls:

1. When the ball is touched intentionally by any part of the hands or arms of any player except the goalkeeper. The referee is the judge of this.

2. When a player violently or dangerously charges an opponent from behind, pushes, holds, trips, or jumps at an opponent. The referee is allowed much discretion in his interpretation as to what is hard play and what is intentionally rough or dangerous.

3. When a player makes a technical evasion of the rules, such as playing the ball a second time before it has been played by another player after a throw-in, free-kick, or penalty-kick; being off-side; carrying the ball by a goalkeeper (this means taking more than two steps while holding the ball); playing the ball before it has touched the ground after being thrown down by the referee; improper throw-in from touch; not kicking the ball forward from a penalty-kick; charging the goalkeeper at the wrong time (the goalkeeper may be charged while holding the ball or obstructing an opponent, or when he has passed outside the goal area, but the charging must not be intentionally rough).

Free-Kick.—A free-kick is awarded for any foul committed outside the penalty area. Opponents must stay ten yards away from the ball until it is kicked. The kicker may not play the ball a second time until it has been played by another player. A goal may be scored direct from a free-kick provided the free-kick is awarded for the committing of fouls listed under number 1 and number 2 above, but not otherwise.

Penalty-Kick.—When a foul of the type described under number 1 and number 2 above is committed by a defensive man within the penalty area, a penalty-kick is awarded the side. The ball is kicked from a point twelve yards in front of the goal (ten yards for junior-high-school players). The penalty area must be cleared of all players except the kicker and the goalkeeper. The goalkeeper may not advance beyond his goal line until the ball is kicked. The ball must be kicked forward and a goal may be scored direct from it. The ball is in play as soon as kicked, but the player who kicked it may not play it again until another player has played it.

Scores.—The side scoring the greatest number of goals is the winner. Each goal counts one point. A goal is scored when the ball has passed between the goal posts and under the bar, provided it is not thrown in, knocked in (struck or propelled with the hands or arms), or carried by any player of the attacking side. A goal may be scored from a penalty-kick or as the result of a free-kick awarded for a foul mentioned under Number 1 and Number 2. A goal may not be scored direct from a kick-off, or goal-kick, or from free-kicks resulting from breaks of the laws included under Number 3.

Change of Players.—The professional rules do not allow the substitution of a player. However, when played by schools and playgrounds, it is recommended that this rule be modified to allow unlimited substitutions with no resubstitution in the same period. A goalkeeper may change with another player by notifying the referee.

Off-side.—The official rules place certain restrictions on when a player is eligible to play the ball. This is called the off-side rule. Because it is quite complicated, it is recommended that it be omitted in junior-high-school games and in intramural games in senior high school. It should not be omitted in the interscholastic games in the senior high school, however.

A player cannot be off-side when he is in his own half of the field, when the opponents have last played the ball, while a goal-kick or corner-kick is being made, or when he is behind the ball. The restriction comes when he is ahead of the ball and it has last been played by a team mate. In this case the rule states that the player ahead of the ball is off-side and may not touch the ball himself or interfere with an opponent unless, at the time the ball was played, there are at least two of his opponents between him and their own goal line. In other words, he must wait until he is again put on side before he is eligible to get into the play.

The Officials.—A referee and two linesmen are in charge.

Soccer for Women.—Soccer as played by women is essentially the same as that played by men. The field is much smaller and the playing period shorter. A player may block the ball with any part of her body but if the blocking is done at chest height, the custom is for the player to fold her arms across her chest or meet the ball with the shoulder. A field-goal counts two points and a penalty-kick one point.

MINOR GAMES OF THE SOCCER TYPE

There are a number of elementary games designed to develop Soccer skills, and games using modifications and simplifications of Soccer rules. These are described in this section. There are also a number of games which combine some of the techniques of Soccer with those of other games such as Basketball and Hockey. While these are not, strictly speaking, games of the Soccer type, they resemble Soccer more than other games and are described here.

Line Soccer

Playground, Gymnasium   *Elementary School*

This simple introduction to kicking games of the Soccer type is played with a soccer ball.

Field.—An area approximately thirty feet square is used.

Teams.—Seven to ten players constitute a team. The two teams line up on the end lines facing each other. One or two players of each team may be stationed on the side lines near their own goal to keep the ball in bounds and defend their goal.

Object of Game.—The object is to kick the ball over the opponents' goal line.

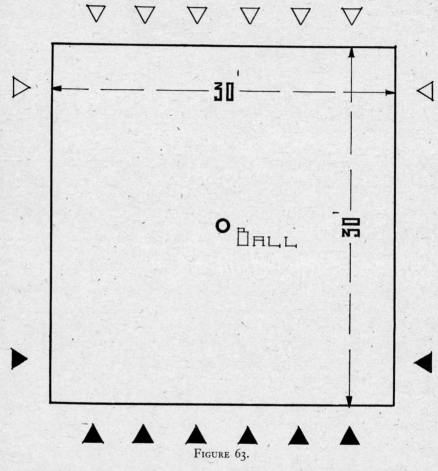

FIGURE 63.

The Play.—The game is played in relays. The referee stands in the center of the field holding the ball. At the signal two players—the one from each team who occupies the extreme right-end position—run toward the center. The referee then drops the ball to the floor so that it bounces, and each of the two players attempts to kick it over the opponents' goal. They continue to play until one puts the ball over the opponents' goal. The ball may be advanced by kicking only; the linesmen may use their hands to stop it, but are not permitted to throw it.

When one of the first two players has scored, the two return to their lines, taking the position at the extreme left end of their team. The line shifts to the right to make room. At the next signal the two players now at the right end compete.

Fouls.—Fouls are called under the following conditions:

1. If the runner touches the ball with the hands.
2. If the linesmen bat or throw the ball forward with the hands.
3. If a runner pushes, holds, shoves, or blocks the opposing runner.
4. If the ball is kicked over the heads of the opposing line.
5. If the ball is kicked over the side line.
6. If a linesman or guard enters the center territory.

Penalty for Fouls.—The runner of the opposing side is given a free-kick from the center of the field. No interference is allowed by the opposing runner.

Scoring.—Two points are scored each time a runner kicks the ball through the opposing line during play. A ball kicked through by a player other than the runner does not count, and the ball is put in play at the center as at the start of the game and with the same runners competing.

One point is scored each time a successful free-kick is made.[1]

Variation.—When numbers are large, have two or three players come out from the right end. The one who was at the extreme right is forward and the other two are backs. When the goal is made, all three join the line at the left.

Triangle Soccer.—Establish a court thirty-five feet square and draw a diagonal line connecting two corners, thus making two triangular courts. One team lines up just in back of the lines along the two sides of one triangle and the other team along the two sides of the other. Place a soccer ball at the middle of the diagonal line.

At the signal the player on the right end of each team runs out and attempts to kick the ball through the other team and across the line. Each kicker may move freely in his own half of the court, but may not cross the center line.

The rules are the same as for Line Soccer.

After the goal is made, the kickers go to the extreme left of their teams and all move over one place. At the next signal the players now on the right compete.

Corner Kick-Ball.—The court is forty by seventy feet in size, larger or smaller to meet the conditions. Six feet in from each end line and

---

[1] The idea for the game was taken from L. Andersen, *An Athletic Program for Elementary Schools,* p. 13. By permission of A. S. Barnes and Company, publishers.

parallel to it, a line is drawn creating an end zone. A team lines up in each of these end zones. A soccer ball is placed on the floor in the center of the court. At the signal two players from each team—one from each end of each team's line of players—run into the court and attempt to kick the ball through the opposite end zone. The players in the end zones attempt to block the ball with any part of the body except the hands, and kick it back so that the center players may play it. Pushing, tripping, holding, and touching the ball with two hands, are fouls.

Two points are scored each time the ball is kicked through the end zone. A foul scores one point for the opponents. After each goal the center players return to their lines, taking the center positions, and the players now occupying the end positions become the center players. The game consists of two ten-minute halves.

Soccer Keep-Ball

Playground, Gymnasium   *Junior and Senior High Schools*

Divide into two teams and mark each team so that they are clearly designated. The game starts when the leader throws the ball on the floor, and thereafter each team attempts to get possession of the ball and kick, butt, or dribble it to team mates and not let the opposing team get it.

Soccer Ten-Kicks.—Divide the players into two teams and mark each in some conspicuous way. The leader throws the ball on the floor and each team attempts to get possession of it. The object is to kick the ball to team mates ten consecutive times.

When a player gets it, he kicks it to a team mate, and this team mate calls "One" and kicks it to another who calls "Two," and so on. The opposing team attempts to break up the run of ten kicks by touching the ball and then making a run of ten kicks itself. All use of the hands is barred. The team making ten consecutive kicks first wins.

Square Soccer

Playground, Gymnasium   *Late Elementary School*

Establish a court thirty-five feet square. One team is lined up on two adjacent sides, and the other team on the other two sides. A soccer ball is given to one team. The object is to kick the ball from the floor through the opposing line not higher than the players' heads. It may be blocked with any part of the body except the hands. The players may enter the court to secure the ball, but must return to their places in line before kicking and at no time touch the ball with their hands. The ball is thus kicked back and forth, the players kicking it whenever it comes their way. One point is scored each time the ball is forced through the opposing line. The game consists of ten points, or a time limit may be set.

Circle Soccer [2]

Playground, Gymnasium   *Late Elementary School*

Establish a double circle, the outer circle twenty to twenty-five feet in diameter and the inner circle four feet smaller in diameter. This leaves a space two feet wide between the circles. Draw a diameter line through both circles (Figure 64). A soccer ball is used.

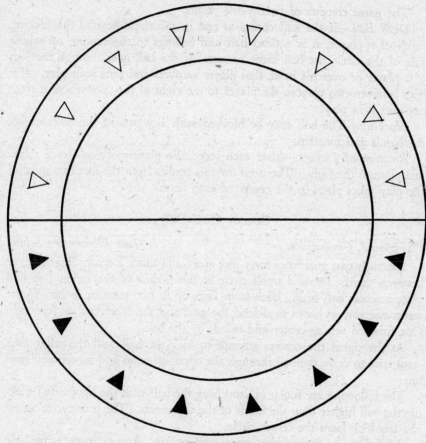

FIGURE 64.

Teams.—The players are divided into two teams which line around the outer circle, one team on each side of the diameter line.

Object.—The object is to kick the ball past the opponents lower than their shoulders.

[2] The description of this game follows that given by N. P. Neilson and W. Van Hagen, *Physical Education for Elementary Schools,* p. 194. Copyright, 1932. By permission of A. S. Barnes and Company, publishers.

Scoring.—One point is scored for the opponents under the following conditions:

1. If the ball is touched with the hands.
2. If a player steps over the inner circle when kicking.
3. If a team lets the ball go over the outer circle.
4. If the ball is kicked higher than the shoulders of the smaller of the two players between whom the ball passed.

The game consists of twenty-one points.

Dead Ball.—If the ball comes to rest in the circle beyond the kicking reach of a player, it is a dead ball and belongs to the captain on whose side of the circle the ball came to rest. If the ball goes through the legs of a player or over his head, that player recovers and puts it in play. If it goes between two players, the player to the right of the spot where it went out puts it in play.

Blocking.—The ball may be blocked with any part of the body except the hands and forearm.

Rotation of Players.—After each score, the players of each team rotate one place to the right. The need for this results from the fact that most of the play takes place in the center of each team.

Soccer Goal-Ball

Playground, Gymnasium   *Late Elementary School*

Establish two goal lines forty feet apart and mark a center line midway between them. Draw a small circle at the middle of the center line and place a soccer ball in it. Each team lines up in two rows in its half of the court, one row as backs to defend the goal and the other row as forwards. One forward acts as center and stands by the ball.

At the signal the centers attempt to kick the ball, and thereafter each team tries to drive the ball through the opposing team and across their goal line.

The following are fouls: (1) touching the ball with the hands; (2) kicking the ball higher than the heads of the opponents. The penalty for a foul is a free-kick from the center circle.

A goal made during play scores two points. A goal from a free-kick scores one point.

After each goal, the forwards and backs should exchange places.

Soccer Snatch-Ball

Playground, Gymnasium, Club   Late Elementary and Junior High Schools

Divide the group into two teams and line them up facing each other forty feet apart. Number the players of each team so that the two opponents holding the same number stand diagonally opposite each other as in Snatch-Ball (page 273). Place a soccer ball midway between the two teams.

The leader calls a number and the two opponents holding this number run out to the ball. Watching his chance, each player attempts to kick the ball and dribble it back to his team's line. If his opponent tags him before reaching the line, no point is scored. If he reaches the line with the ball successfully, he scores one point.

The leader should call the numbers at random.

Variation.—Instead of trying to tag an opponent when he secures the ball, the player continues to play for the ball and attempts to take it away from the opponent and return it to his own team. The player dribbles the ball to his team's line.

Variation.—Instead of returning the ball to his own team, each player attempts to drive it through the opposing team. The player scores one point who kicks the ball through the opposing team not higher than their heads.

The game may be played with or without the line players being permitted to block the ball. In either case the players may not leave their positions in the line.

Variation.—Instead of placing the ball between the two teams, the leader holds it, standing midway between the two teams at one end. He rolls the ball between the two teams and at the same instant calls the number.

Champion Soccer Snatch.—Place one player (the champion) on one line and line up all the other players on the other line. The champion challenges a player and the two run out and proceed as above. The champion holds his position as long as he wins, but when he loses, he exchanges places with the winner.

Soccer Circle Stride-Ball

Playground, Gymnasium   *Late Elementary to Senior High School*

This is a variation of Circle Stride-Ball. Arrange all the players except one in a circle, legs at stride, facing center. The circle should be just large enough so that the feet of the players touch those on either side when the legs are spread widely. The odd player, "it," stands in the center with a soccer ball. He attempts to kick the ball between the legs of the players, who must keep their hands on their knees until the ball has been kicked and then may use their hands to block the ball. When the ball goes through the legs of a player, that player and "it" exchange places.

If the players tend to kick vigorously enough to cause possible injury if the ball rises, have them kick with the side of the foot. If necessary, move the circle back and cause a player to become "it" if the ball goes between his legs or between him and the player to his right.

Pin Soccer [3]

Playground, Gymnasium   *Late Elementary and Junior High Schools*

Pin Soccer is a Soccer type of game which can be played in a small space and with a few players.

Equipment.—A soccer ball and four Indian clubs or sticks of wood of similar size are needed. For outdoor use the clubs or pieces of wood should be attached to blocks of wood four inches square.

Court.—The court is thirty feet wide and forty feet long. The goal areas are sixteen feet long and four feet wide, extending into the court

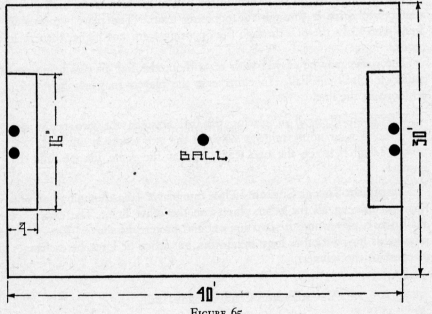

FIGURE 65.

from the end lines, as in Figure 65. Two Indian clubs are set up sixteen inches apart on the goal line midway between the side lines.

Object of the Game.—The object is to knock down the clubs of the opposing team.

The Play.—The game is played in two halves of ten minutes each. To start the game, the ball is placed on the ground in the center of the field. Two opposing players stand with their left sides toward the ball. Each

[3] This game was taken from the description in L. Andersen, *An Athletic Program for Elementary Schools,* p. 23 ff. Copyright, 1927. By permission of A. S. Barnes and Company, publishers.

taps the ground with his right foot, then taps his opponent's right foot above the ball. This is done three times after which each tries to get the ball away from his opponent. In playing the ball, it may be kicked, dribbled, or passed with the feet, but may not be touched with the hands. Players are not permitted to enter the goal area except to retrieve the ball.

Out of Bounds.—When the ball goes over the side line, the end line, or into the goal area, it is kicked in from the spot at which it left the field, by a member of the team opposing the one that last touched it. No point may be scored on the kick-in, and at least one other player must play the ball before a point can be scored.

Fouls.—Fouls are called (1) if a player touches the ball with the hands, (2) if a player pushes, holds, or shoves an opponent, (3) if a player enters the goal area, except to recover the ball.

Penalty for Fouls.—The opposing side is given a free-kick from the center of the field. No obstruction or interference may be offered to a free-kick.

Scoring.—Two points are scored each time a club is knocked down during play. One point is scored each time a club is knocked down by a free-kick.

Rotation Soccer [4]

Playground, Gymnasium   *Late Elementary and Junior High Schools*

This game is designed to safeguard against over-exertion.

Field.—The playing area is forty-five feet wide by seventy-five feet long. Lanes and cross lines are laid out as in Figure 66.

Teams.—Teams usually consist of twelve players, although the game may be played with from nine to eighteen on a side.

Each team is divided into three equal groups and the players are arranged as shown in the diagram.

Object of the Game.—The object is to kick the ball over the opponents' goal line.

Length of the Game.—The game is divided into two halves of eight minutes each.

The Play.—The ball is placed in the center of the field and is put in play by a kick-off. The kick-off is a place-kick in the direction of the opponents' goal. The opponents may not approach within a distance of six yards of the ball until after the kick-off. No member of either side may cross the center line in the direction of the opponents' goal until after the kick-off.

The forwards take the ball down the field by kicking, dribbling, or

[4] This game was taken from the description in L. Andersen, *An Athletic Program for Elementary Schools,* p. 28 ff. Copyright, 1927. By permission of A. S. Barnes & Company, publishers.

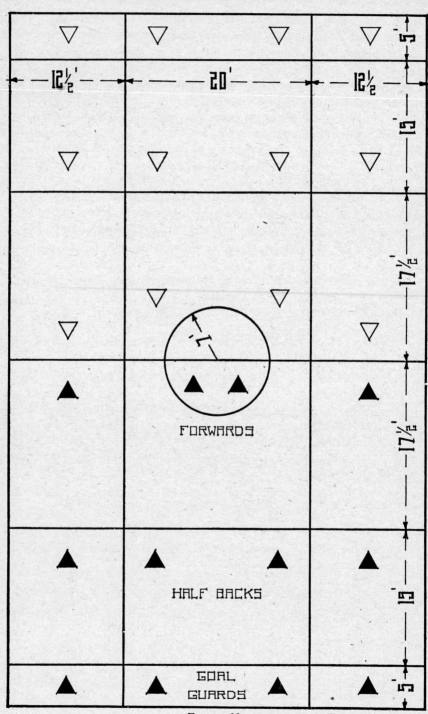

FIGURE 66.

passing with the foot, and attempt to get it over the opponents' goal. The forwards may not play back of the twenty-foot line on their own side.

The halfbacks may follow the forwards to the twenty-foot line on the opposite territory. The goal guards are not permitted to leave the goal area.

All players must remain in their own lanes extending lengthwise of the field.

Rotation of Players.—When a point has been made the forwards take the places of the goalkeepers; the goalkeepers take the places of the halfbacks, and the halfbacks take the places of the forwards. Play then begins again with a kick-off made by the side against whom the score was made.

If the play continues longer than three or four minutes without a score, the referee should blow the whistle and have the players rotate. In this case, play is resumed at the spot where the ball was when the whistle blew.

Fouls.—Fouls are called in the following cases:

1. If the players touch the ball with the hands or the forearm, except on the part of the goalkeepers, who may catch the ball with the hands.
2. If the players push, hold, shove, or block an opponent.
3. If a player oversteps the restraining lines.
4. If the ball is kicked over the heads of the goalkeepers.

Penalties.—For the first three of the above fouls, a free-kick is awarded to the opposing team. The free-kick is executed as in Soccer.

For foul number 4, a throw-in is given to the opponents and the goal does not count.

Out of Bounds.—A ball kicked over the side lines is put in play by a throw-in as in Soccer.

Scoring.—One point is scored each time the ball is forced over the opponents' goal line, except as described under foul number 4, above. No goal may be scored on a kick-off or on a free-kick.

Modified Soccer

Playground   *Late Elementary and Junior High Schools*

This modification of Soccer restricts the players to certain areas of the field, thus preventing over-exertion.

Field.—The field is 90 by 120 feet in size; it may be made larger or smaller to suit the capacity of the players. Three cross lines are drawn across the field, dividing it into four equal courts. These lines are known as center line and halfback lines. The goals are twenty-four feet wide and eight feet high. Goal areas and penalty areas are not used.

Ball.—The regulation soccer football is used.

Length of Game.—The game consists of two periods of eight minutes, with a five-minute intermission.

Teams.—Same as in Soccer.

Positions of Players.—The five forwards line up on the center line facing the opponents' territory. Once lined up they must keep their relative positions. The two outside players must remain outside; the center player must remain in the center and the two players between the center and the outside players must remain between. During play these forwards may go to the opponents' goal but may not play back of or on their own side of the center line.

The three halfbacks must confine their play to the area between their own halfback line and center line. The two fullbacks play between their own goal line and the halfback line. The goalkeeper plays in front of and immediately adjacent to the goal.

Start.—The play is started as in Soccer.

The Play.—The forwards advance the ball toward the opponents' goal. The rules of Soccer apply in respect to touching the ball, and holding, pushing, tripping, and kicking. When a foul is committed a free-kick is allowed from the point where the foul took place, with all players at least six feet away from the kicker. A free-kick is allowed when an opposing player leaves his restricting zone. When the ball goes out of bounds it is put in play as in Soccer.

Scoring.—Same as in Soccer.

Gymnasium Soccer [5]

Gymnasium   *Junior High School to College*

Gymnasium Soccer follows very closely the rules of Soccer and is played on a basketball court.

Court.—A basketball court is used, with the goals placed on the end lines equidistant from the side lines. The goals consist of two jumping standards placed nine feet apart, connected by a crossbar six feet from the floor. For younger boys, the basketball free-throw line is used for the penalty mark; for older boys and men, the section of the free-throw arc most distant from the goal is used.

Ball.—An old basketball is used, inflated just enough so that a good kick will cause it to go the length of the court.

Teams.—Six to nine players may be used on a team.

Start.—The ball is dropped between the two centers in the basketball center circle, and may be kicked as soon as it touches the floor.

Scoring.—As in Soccer.

Fouls and Penalties.—A penalty-kick is awarded for roughness, for kicking, holding, tripping, or striking an opponent, and for touching the ball with the hands by a player inside his own goal area. For touching the ball with the hands outside the player's own penalty area, the ball is

[5] Contributed by Roger Gray.

given to an opponent out of bounds. Follow-up play is allowed when a foul is committed by the defensive team in its own penalty area. Otherwise the ball is centered after a penalty-kick try or when a penalty-kick is awarded to both teams.

Out of Bounds.—The throw-in from out of bounds over the side lines is as in Soccer. The side walls of the gymnasium may be considered in bounds to make a faster game. When a ball goes over the end line, and is last touched (1) by a defending player, a corner-kick follows as in Soccer; (2) by an attacking player, the ball is awarded to the goalkeeper who puts it in play by a place-kick within six feet of the goal line, with all opponents at least fifteen feet away until the kick has been made.

If the officials cannot determine who caused the ball to go out of bounds, the ball is "centered" as at the start of the game at the point where it went out of bounds.

Other Rules.—Points not covered are as in Soccer.

Speedball

Playground   *Junior High School to Adults*

Speedball was invented by E. D. Mitchell of the University of Michigan in 1921 as a fall game to be played and enjoyed by players of average athletic ability. It is an outgrowth of the athletics-for-all movement. The game combines the skills of Soccer, Rugby Football, and Basketball. It can be enjoyed the first time or two that it is played because the average player already possesses the necessary skills.

Field.—The official field is the same as that used in Rugby Football. The fifty-yard line is called the middle line and the two forty-yard lines are the restraining lines. The ten-yard area between the goal line and the end line on which the goal posts stand is called the end zone and penalty area. Ten yards in front of each goal and midway between the side lines, a penalty mark is placed (Figure 67). The official football goals are used.

It is recommended that the size of the field be reduced for younger players and for intramural play in colleges. Two small speedball fields may be made on a football field by making them forty yards wide and running them crosswise of the field. The goal posts are then placed ten yards back from the side lines, making the field 220 feet long.

Speedball is adaptable to the fields and goal posts that are available. It can be played very satisfactorily on a soccer field, using the soccer goals.

Equipment.—An official speedball or soccer ball is used. The speedball is a round ball slightly larger than a soccer ball and slightly smaller than a basketball.

Teams.—The official size of a team is eleven players. When the game is played on a smaller field, the teams may consist of nine or seven players.

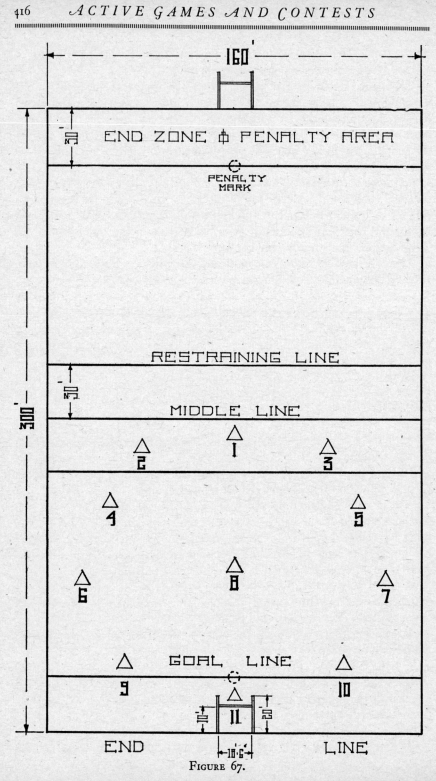

FIGURE 67.

Kick-off.—The team winning the toss has the privilege of selecting to kick-off or to receive at the goal of its choosing.

The game starts by a place-kick from the center of the field in the direction of the opponents' goal. Each team must be at its own end of the field at the time of the kick-off and no player may cross the middle line until after the kick-off. The ball must move more than its own circumference and the kicker may not play it again until it has been played by someone else.

The Play.—After the kick-off each team attempts to work the ball down the field and score. A "fly ball" (explained later) may be caught and thrown to team mates and in this respect the game resembles Basketball. A "ground ball" must be kicked or dribbled without the use of arms, and in this respect the game resembles Soccer.

The ball may be given momentum by throwing, punting, drop-kicking, and dribbling with feet or hands, under the conditions stated below.

A ball may be caught or played with the hands when it is clearly a fly ball, that is, one that has been raised into the air directly from a kick. A ball thus kicked into the air may be played with the hands until it again hits the ground. When such a fly ball is caught, the ball may be given momentum by any of the means described above.

A ground ball is one that is stationary, rolling, or bouncing. Even though in the air, as in bouncing, it is considered a ground ball unless it rises direct from a kick or comes from a pass. Ground balls may not be played by the hands or arms.

A player may dribble with his feet at will. He may use one overhead dribble without the aid of his team mates but may not score a touchdown by this method. He may bat or tip fly balls at will. He may kick a ground ball into the air and catch it himself.

A player who is standing still when a ball is caught may take one step but must get rid of the ball before the second step is finished. If running, he is allowed two steps and if at full speed, the referee decides whether or not he stops as soon as possible. Violation of these rules is called "carrying the ball." A player cannot step over the goal line to score.

A player may guard an opponent who has the ball but must play the ball and in no way hold the opponent. No obstruction may be given to an opponent who does not have the ball.

In case two opponents hold the ball, or the referee is uncertain as to which side played it last before it went out of bounds, the ball is tossed up as in Basketball.

Out-of-Bounds.—When a ball goes over the side lines, it is given to a member of the opposing team at the point where it went out. This player throws the ball in. No score may be made by the pass.

When a ball goes over the end line it is ruled as a touchback or safety.

Touchback.—When the offensive team puts the ball over the end line and it does not result in a score, it is ruled a touchback and is put in play by an opponent at the point where it crossed the line by a punt, place-kick, or pass.

Safety.—When a defensive player last touches a ball before it goes over the end line, and no score results, it is given to a member of the offensive team at the point and is put in play by a punt, place-kick, or pass.

Scoring.—Points are scored as follows:

Field goal	3 points
Touchdown	2 points
End-kick	1 point
Penalty-kick	1 point
Drop-kick	1 point

A field-goal is made when the ball is kicked or legally given impetus with the body over the goal line between the goal posts and under the crossbar.

A touchdown is scored when a player standing in the end zone catches a forward pass.

An end-kick is scored when a ground ball is kicked or legally given impetus over the goal line from within the end zone.

Following a foul, a penalty-kick is awarded. The ball is placed by the referee on the penalty mark, and the kicker attempts to kick it between the goal posts under the crossbar. Only one defensive player may attempt to guard the goal and he stands on the end line between the goal posts.

A drop-kick is scored when a ball legally caught is drop-kicked over the crossbar. The kick must be made from the field outside the defensive zone area.

Fouls.—The following are *personal fouls:* (1) kicking, tripping, charging, pushing, holding, or blocking an opponent; (2) unnecessary roughness.

The following are *technical fouls:* (1) making an illegal substitution; (2) taking more than three time-outs in a game; (3) having more than eleven men on the field; (4) delaying the game.

The following are *violations:* (1) carrying the ball; (2) touching a ground ball with the hands; (3) making two successive overhead dribbles; (4) violating the kick-off rule; (5) violating the penalty-kick restrictions; (6) violating the rules in returning an out-of-bounds ball to play; (7) violating free-kick restrictions; (8) violating the tie-ball rule; (9) kicking or kneeing a fly ball by a player unless he has caught it.

Penalties.—The penalty for a *personal foul,* committed outside the player's end zone, is a penalty-kick by the offended player. If missed, a touchback is declared. For a personal foul in a player's own end zone, the penalty is two penalty-kicks by the offended player.

The penalty for a *technical foul* committed outside the player's own penalty area is a penalty-kick by any member of the offended team. If missed, a touchback is declared. If the technical foul is committed inside the player's own penalty area, the penalty is a penalty-kick by any member of the offended team. The ball is in play as soon as kicked.

The penalty for a *violation* outside the player's own penalty area is the awarding of the ball out of bounds to a member of the offended team.

The penalty for a *violation* inside the player's own penalty area is a penalty-kick by the opponents with the opportunity of a follow-up if missed.

Penalty-Kick.—Following a personal or technical foul, the referee places the ball in the penalty mark and the kicker attempts to kick the ball through the goal posts under the crossbar. On penalty-kicks where no follow-up is allowed, only the kicker and the goal guard are concerned. When a follow-up play is allowed, the team mates of both kicker and goal-tender may not encroach upon the end zone until the ball is actually kicked.

Length of Game.—The official game consists of four periods of ten minutes each with an intermission of two minutes after the first and third quarters, and ten minutes between halves. For junior- and senior-high-school and intramural use in colleges, the periods should be five minutes long at the start of the season, and six to eight minutes long later in the season when the players are in good physical condition.

In case of a tie, one or more over-time periods of three minutes are played.

Time Out.—Time out may be taken three times by a team in the course of the game. Each additional time out is ruled as a technical foul.

Substitutes.—A player may be taken out of the game and resubstituted once during the game. A substitute must report first to the linesman, who waits until the ball is dead, then blows his whistle to allow the change.

Officials:—The game is in charge of a referee and two linesmen. The referee has general charge of the game. The linesmen are stationed on opposite sides of the field and assist the referee on out-of-bounds plays and in calling fouls.

Speedball for Women.—The maximum dimensions of the field are 100 yards by 60 yards; the recommended size for high-school players is 80 yards by 40 yards. The end zone is six yards wide instead of the ten-yard width used in the men's game, and the penalty mark is twelve yards from the goal. In other respects, the field corresponds to that used by men.

The girls' rules for speedball differ from those used by men in the following respects:

1. A drop-kick scores two points instead of one.
2. When the ball is being thrown in from out of bounds, a two-handed overhand throw is required as in Soccer, the ball being in play as soon as it hits the ground.
3. The guarding rules are as in Basketball for Women.

4. The penalty for a violation is a free-kick with the opponents at least six yards away.

5. When two players touch a ball, causing it to go out of bounds, and the referee can not determine which player touched it last, it is put in play by a throw down between two opposing players.

Indoor Speedball [6]

Gymnasium   *Junior High School to College*

This game is Speedball adapted to an indoor space of the size of a basketball court. The rules follow those of Speedball with the following exceptions:

Court.—A basketball court is used. The end lines of the court are the goal lines. The space beyond the end lines to the wall or some line (not exceeding five yards) is the end zone. The goals are placed on the goal lines equidistant from the side lines, these consisting of two jumping standards placed nine feet apart, and connected by a crossbar six feet from the floor. The basketball backboard is used for scoring drop-kicks. The penalty area is the space between the basketball free-throw line and the end lines. The penalty mark is the basketball free-throw line.

Ball.—It is important that the ball is not too lively. An old basketball or volleyball is used which is inflated so that it is quite soft—it should just travel the length of the court when given a good kick.

Teams.—A team consists of seven players.

Start.—Instead of using a kick-off, the game starts with a toss-up on the center line, similar to that used in Basketball. Following each score and at the beginning of each quarter, the same play is used.

Scoring.—Scoring is as follows: field-goal, three points; touchdown, two points; penalty-kick, one point; drop-kick, one point.

The rules for touchdowns, field-goals and penalty-kicks are as in Speedball.

A ball legally caught may be drop-kicked against the basketball backboard to score a drop-kick. The kick must be made from some point in the court in back of the penalty mark.

Free-Kick.—There is no free-kick in Indoor Speedball—instead the ball is awarded to the offended team out of bounds.

Out of Bounds.—To speed up the play it is recommended that the side walls be considered in bounds. If not, out-of-bounds balls on the side lines are thrown in as in Soccer.

The rules on the touchback are the same as in Speedball, and the rule on the safety is the same except that no score may be made until the ball has been returned at least as far as the nearest penalty mark.

[6] Contributed by Roger Gray.

Fouls and Penalties.—Fouls and penalties are the same as in Speedball except for the free-kick rule mentioned above.

Basket Speedball.—This is played as in Indoor Speedball with the exception of the method of scoring the touchdown. Instead of the ball being thrown into the end zone for a touchdown, it is thrown into the basketball goal. This scores two points. Other methods of scoring are as in Indoor Speedball.

Simball [7]

Playground   *Senior High School to College Girls*

This is a combination of Speedball and Basketball, suitable for girls. It was originated by Ralph Simpson.

Field.—Same as in Speedball.

Ball.—Same as in Speedball.

Start.—The game is started by a kick from the middle of the field.

The Play.—The ball may be taken from the ground, dribbled (using one hand only), passed, or kicked. After one dribble the ball must be passed or kicked before the same person may dribble again. Guarding is as in Basketball. In case of a tie ball, a toss-up follows as in Basketball.

Out of Bounds.—When the ball is caused to go out of bounds over the side lines, it is thrown in by an opposing player by an overhead throw with both hands. The first receiver may not catch the ball but may bat it to another who may catch it.

When the ball is caused to go over the end line (1) by the attacking team, the goalkeeper punts the ball in; (2) by the defending team, the ball is passed in by an overhead throw and must be touched by two players before it may be passed over the end line for a score.

Scoring.—As in Speedball.

Length of Game.—Four eight-minute quarters.

Other Rules.—In other respects, the rules of Speedball apply.

Tag Speedball

Playground   *Junior and Senior High Schools*

Tag Speedball is a variation of Speedball which permits running with the ball. The rules of Speedball apply with the following exceptions:

1. A player after catching a fly ball may run with it. The penalty for "progress with the ball" is therefore necessarily discontinued. No interference is permitted for the runner, and such personal contact would come under the rules as blocking and be penalized accordingly. A player who, while advancing the ball by running, is tagged by an opponent forfeits the ball to the opponent at the spot where he was tagged, and the tagging side puts the ball in play from out of bounds at the nearest boundary line.

---

[7] Contributed by Winnefred Horn Poss.

2. A touchdown may be scored by running over the goal line while carrying the ball, and by the use of the overhead dribble. Touchdowns scored these ways count two points.

Field-Handball [8]

Playground   *Junior High School to Adults*

Field-Handball is a German game of recent origin which was given international standing in 1927 by the International Amateur Athletic Federation. It was scheduled as an event in the 1936 Olympics for the first time. It is a fast and strenuous game, making severe demands upon the players.

The game is played on a field approximating that used in Soccer with minor variations around the goal and penalty areas. The ball resembles a soccer ball but is slightly smaller (twenty-four inches in circumference). Eleven players constitute a team.

The method of play resembles Soccer in form but the handling of the ball is more similar to that used in Basketball. The ball is passed or driven with the hands down the field and the use of legs below the knees is prohibited by all except the goalkeeper. Scores are made when the ball is thrown through the goals.

The ball may be thrown, struck, knocked, or caught in any way, using the arms, hands, head, body, and legs above the knee. A player is not allowed to hold the ball longer than three seconds, nor take more than three steps while holding it. He is not allowed to touch it twice in succession until after it has touched another player or object. It is permissible to throw the ball on the ground and catch it again while running or standing.

The ball may be knocked out of a player's hands with the flat of the hand but may not be taken away with both hands or the fist. It is permissible to block an opponent's way, but such tactics are forbidden as holding or stopping with the hands, hitting, pushing, and charging from the rear.

The goal area may be occupied only by the goalkeeper and he may stop the ball with any part of his body including the feet. He may kick it, however, only when it is moving toward the goal.

The penalty for most fouls is a free-throw from the spot where the foul was committed. There are corner-throw and penalty-throw rules resembling the corner-kick rules in Soccer.

The game consists of two halves of thirty minutes each with an interval of ten minutes. For women and players under fourteen years of age, the halves are twenty minutes each.

---

[8] See International Amateur Athletic Federation, *The Game of Field-Handball*. Munich: Deutsche Sportbehörde für Leichtathletik, 1928.

Fieldball

Fieldball in its original form was devised by L. R. Burnett and quickly found favor as a game for girls. It combines the best features of Soccer, Hockey, and Basketball, with chances of injury minimized.

Fieldball is not a true game of the Soccer type in that there is no handling of the ball with the feet—the manipulation of the ball resembles Basketball more than Soccer. In layout of field, make-up of teams, and methods of scoring, however, it resembles Soccer.

Field.—The maximum size of the field is 180 by 100 feet. It can be played on a smaller field if space is limited. Figure 68 shows the lining on the field.

Goal posts are placed in the middle of the end lines. The posts are ten feet apart and the crossbar eight feet above the ground. When permanent goals are not feasible temporary posts are frequently erected by the use of portable volleyball standards or jumping standards with a rope stretched between them for a crossbar. Failing here, the width of the goals may be marked on the ground with lime.

Ball.—A soccer ball is used.

Teams.—Eleven players constitute a team, five forwards, three halfbacks, two fullbacks, and a goalkeeper. The goalkeeper is not permitted to leave the goal area.

Object of the Game.—The object is to work the ball toward the opponents' goal line and get it through the goals, and at the same time to prevent the opponents from scoring.

Start.—The captain winning the toss has the option of choice of goals or throwing off. One member of the team which throws off throws the ball into the opponents' territory. No member of the team which throws off may cross the center line until the ball has crossed it. Opposing players are not permitted to block the ball within fifteen feet of the center line; breaking this rule necessitates a repetition of the throw-off.

At the beginning of the second half the ball is put in play in the same way as at the start of the game.

The Play.—The ball may be thrown, batted, bounced, or juggled in any direction. The ball may be bounced only once and juggled only once, however, before being handled by another player; a bounce may not be followed by a juggle, nor a juggle followed by a bounce.

The ball must be caught with both hands, but once caught may be retained in one hand and thrown with one hand. The ball must be thrown within three seconds; if the player has fallen to the ground, the three seconds are counted from the time when all the weight is on the feet.

In passing the ball to another player, it must be thrown, batted, or bounced; it may not be handed or rolled.

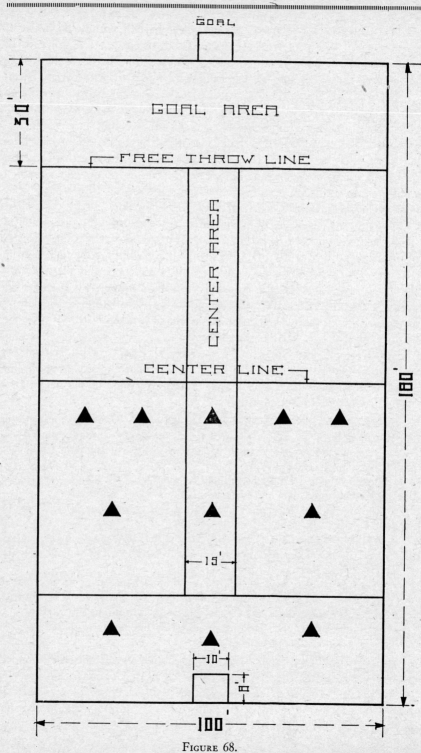

FIGURE 68.

The goalkeeper is permitted to run with the ball within the limits of the goal area. The goal areas are open to both teams.

Scoring.—One point is scored by a team each time it causes the ball to go between the opponents' goal uprights and under the crossbar. The offensive team also scores if the defensive team causes the ball to go through its own goal. If no crossbar is being used the score is made when the ball goes through the uprights within eight feet of the ground.

Out of Bounds.—When the ball goes out of bounds over the side lines it is put in play by a player of the opposing team to the one that caused it to go out. This player stands out of bounds at the point where the ball went out and throws or bounces the ball into the court. Unnecessary delay in throwing in the ball is considered delaying the game.

When the ball goes out of bounds over the end lines, the disposition of the ball depends upon which team caused it to go out. If it is the offensive team's ball out, one of the offensive team's players throws the ball in from a corner where the side line and end line meet; opposing players must remain at least fifteen feet away until the ball is thrown. If it is the defensive team's ball out, the goalkeeper throws the ball into the field from any point within the goal area, and may make a running throw provided he does not step over the free-throw line.

Center Area.—The center area is closed to all except the center forwards and center halfbacks. It is a foul for any other player to step over the line into this area, or for the center players to step over the line out of the area.

Fouls.—The following are fouls:

1. Taking more than one step while holding the ball. (One foot must remain in place while throwing unless both feet are off the ground during a jump.)

2. Juggling or bouncing the ball twice in succession or combining a bounce with a juggle in the same play.

3. Holding the ball longer than three seconds.

4. Throwing the ball while lying down.

5. Kicking the ball, handing it to another player, or touching it when held by another player.

6. Pushing, striking, interfering with the progress of a player, over guarding the ball or the player holding it, or using rough tactics. (The judgment of the referee determines these points.)

7. Center forward or center halfback stepping over the boundary lines out of the center area, or any other player stepping over the line into the center area.

8. If the goalkeeper steps outside the goal area when the ball is in play.

9. Intentionally striking, pushing, holding, or interfering with the progress of a player or otherwise using rough tactics.

Penalties.—When one of the first eight of the above fouls is committed outside the goal area the ball is given to the nearest opponent on the spot where the foul occurred for an unguarded throw with all opponents at least five yards away. When foul Number 8 is committed, the fouled side is given a free-throw from the free-throw line.

When fouls are committed inside the goal area, the penalty depends upon which team committed the foul. If the defensive team commits the foul, the offensive team is given a free-throw from any boundary of the goal area except the end line. The goal may be guarded only by the goalkeeper and fullbacks—all the other players must be outside the goal area. If the goal is not made the ball is in play.

When the foul is committed by the offensive team within the goal area the ball is given to the goalkeeper for a free-throw from any point within the goal area. All other players must be five yards away.

When two opposing players commit a foul simultaneously in the goal area, time out is called and each side is given a free-throw from the free-throw line, after which the ball is put in play as at the beginning of the game. If such a foul is committed outside the goal area the ball is tossed up between the two nearest opponents at the point where the ball is in play.

Off-Side.—At the time of the throw-off at the start of the game, if a player of the side throwing off steps over the center line ahead of the ball the throw-off is repeated from a point five yards back from the center line. The same penalty is inflicted if the throw-off fails to go at least fifteen feet into the opponents' half of the field. If these offenses are committed twice in succession the ball goes to the opponents for a throw-off.

Length of Game.—The game consists of four quarters of five minutes each with a two-minute rest after the first and third periods and a ten-minute rest after the second period.

At the beginning of the second and fourth quarters the ball is put in play at the place it was last played when the preceding quarter ended. It is given to the player who possessed it when the period ended. This player puts the ball in play by an unguarded throw; all players must be five yards away.

Officials.—The officials consist of a referee, an umpire, timer, scorer, and four linesmen.

Punch Ball

Playground   *Late Elementary to Senior High School*

This game was first introduced in the playgrounds of Youngstown, Ohio. It is similar to Soccer except that the ball is advanced by slapping, punching, or butting it with the head. Since there is no footing of the ball, it is not a true game of the Soccer type. There are few fouls and consequently the play is fast.

Field.—The game is played on a field of the size of a regulation football field (160 by 300 yards). Smaller dimensions may be used, a length of seventy-five yards being very satisfactory. No goal posts are necessary; the goal lines are the goals.

Ball.—A sport ball ten inches in diameter is used.

Teams.—From six to twenty players may play on a side. The best results are obtained by using eleven players on the small field and fifteen on the full-sized field.

Start.—The game is started by punching the ball with the fist from a point half way between the punching team's goal and the center of the field.

The Play.—The ball may be punched, slapped, or butted, but not kicked. It may be tossed in the air before being struck, but the runner must not take more than one step in so doing. No dribbling or running with the ball is permitted. The players may catch it but may not take more than one step while holding it.

Fouls and Penalties.—Kicking, dribbling, and running with the ball are fouls. The ball is given to the opposing side on the side line directly in line with the spot where the foul occurred; and is thrown in with the teams "on side."

Out of Bounds.—When the ball crosses the side line, it is thrown in by a member of the team opposite to the one that put it out.

Scoring.—One point is scored each time the ball is put over the opponents' goal line. After a goal the opposite team puts the ball in play.

Length of Game.—The game is played in four ten-minute quarters, with a one-minute rest between quarters, and ten minutes between halves.

Punch Soccer.—This game uses a soccer ball or a sport ball six inches in diameter. The play is exactly like the above except for the following two points:

1. The ball may be advanced by footing and heading as in Soccer, and also by punching and throwing.

2. The penalty for a foul is a free-kick for the opposing team at the point where the foul occurred.

Mass Soccer

Playground   *Junior High School to College*

Mass Soccer is played on a regular soccer field except that the goal lines constitute the goals, and the soccer goal posts, goal areas, and penalty areas are not used.

It is played according to Soccer rules with the following modifications to meet the needs of mass play:

1. The game is started by lining the teams up behind their goals. The ball is placed in the center of the field. The players rush for it and attempt to kick it over the opposing goal. After each goal, the ball is put in play in the same way.

2. In the case of fouls, a free-kick is awarded the opposing team at the point at which the foul occurred. Opponents must be ten yards away when the ball is kicked. Unnecessary roughness eliminates the player.

3. When the ball goes out of bounds it is thrown back in by the referee.

4. One point is scored each time the ball crosses the opponents' goal line.

5. Two periods of ten minutes each constitute a game.

Variation.—Use soccer goal posts and score one point each time the ball is kicked through the goals. Four players on each team are assigned to guard the goals; these goalkeepers may catch the ball and throw it when it comes in the area of the goal.

Two-ball Soccer

Soccer Field　　　　　　　　　　　　　　　　*Senior High School to College*

This is a sand-lot type of Soccer using two balls. All rules of Soccer are followed except that the off-side rule is ignored. If the two balls go through the same goal at the same time, two goals are scored.

Two referees should be used, one following each ball.

Hand Soccer [9]

Gymnasium　　　　　　　　　　　　　　　*Junior and Senior High Schools*

This is a gymnasium game resembling Soccer except that the ball is played chiefly with the hands.

Court.—A basketball court is used with the free-throw lines extended across the court. The section behind one of these lines is known as the goal area. The wall at the end of the gymnasium constitutes the goal, and the end lines of the court are not used. A line is drawn across the wall six feet from the floor.

Ball.—A volleyball or soccer ball is used.

Teams.—Eight to sixteen men may play on a side depending on the size of the court.

Half of the players are guards and the other half forwards. The forwards may go all over the floor while the guards must remain in the goal area nearest the goal they are protecting. One forward is selected to act as center.

Object of the Game.—The object is to hit the ball with the hand so that it will hit the opponents' wall below the six-foot line, and at the same time to prevent the opponents from scoring.

Start.—The two centers stand with their feet outside the center circle and with their hands on their knees. The forwards stand on the front line of the goal area nearest the goal they are defending. The ball is placed in the center circle. On signal the centers hit the ball and the forwards rush forward.

[9] This game is contributed by Don Harshbarger, Naperville, Illinois.

Fouls.—The following are fouls: (1) hitting the ball with the closed hand; (2) taking a full arm swing at the ball (the ball must be hit with bent arms); (3) kicking the ball (not a foul to stop ball with foot); (4) stopping the ball with two hands; (5) charging, pushing, pulling, and tripping.

Penalty for Fouls.—A free-hit from the center circle is awarded the opposing team when a foul is committed. All members of the fouling team must be touching the side lines until the whistle blows, when they rush out to prevent the goal. The forwards of the team trying for the goal may not stand on the side lines inside the goal area nearest the goal for which they are trying.

Scoring.—One point is scored each time the ball hits the opponents' wall below the six-foot mark.

Rotation of Players.—After each goal, the forwards and guards exchange places.

Length of Game.—Four three-minute periods constitute a game.

Bolo Ball

Playground, Gymnasium   *Junior and Senior High Schools*

This game was contributed by K. H. Murray and is an attempt to teach Handball skills. It is a combination of Soccer, Basketball, and Handball, but the main object is putting a ball through a goal of the Soccer type. The following is Mr. Murray's own statement of the rules.

Court.—The entire gymnasium is used as the court. A goal is formed at each end by setting up two volleyball standards seven feet apart under the basketball backstop.

Ball.—A basketball is used.

Teams.—There are six players on a team—two forwards, one center, two defense players, and one goalkeeper.

Start.—The players arrange themselves as in basketball except that the two centers stand outside the center circle. The referee bounces the ball on the floor in the center of the circle and the ball if not touched should bounce higher than either center can reach. The ball may be hit by the centers as soon as it is waist high.

After a foul the ball is put in play by the same method at the point where the foul occurred.

Advancing the Ball.—The ball is played throughout the game by using only one hand at a time. The ball may be advanced (1) by an overhead dribble (tapping the ball up off the hand) while the player runs; (2) by the basketball dribble of which only three bounces are permitted during a player's time in possession of the ball; (3) by the smash with the hands as in Handball (this is the method used most in the game at present); (4) by the scoop throw off the floor (in this method the ball is scooped off the floor and leaves the hand, and the player may or may not retain possession of the ball); (5) the ball can be advanced by any other method providing the player does not deliberately touch the ball with the body below the waist (bouncing the ball off the chest, head, or shoulders is permitted, but a foul would be committed if the ball were kicked along with the legs or trunk below the waist). Any or all of these methods may be used during a player's possession of the ball.

It is not a game of bowling the ball along the floor. The ball should be kept up in the air as much as possible.

Scoring.—A legally advanced ball passing between the goal uprights and under the backboard scores one point. The ball must have last touched the player above the waist—balls deflected off the feet or legs of a player and going through the goal do not score.

The Goalkeeper.—The goalkeeper may score a goal by throwing the ball through the opposite goal. (This opens the game up and provides a constant scoring threat. Many goalkeepers throw the ball to a position in front of the opposite goal for a forward to deflect in for a goal.) The goalkeeper may take only two steps while in possession of the ball, and may be body-checked or charged while in possession of the ball. He may use any part of his body in protecting and clearing the goal of the ball.

Penalties.—Penalties of one minute on the bench are provided for the following infractions of the rules:

1. Throwing the ball (except the goalkeeper).
2. Touching the ball with two hands at the same time (except the goalkeeper).
3. Charging or body-checking an opponent if he is not in possession of the ball at the time.
4. Body-checking or charging an opponent into the wall whether he has the ball in his possession or not.
5. Tripping or unnecessary rough play.
6. Body-checking or charging an opponent from the rear.
7. Using the arms or hand to retard the movements of opponents.
8. Running with the ball held stationary in the hand. (The ball must be advanced in the ways given. No running with the ball is allowed.)
9. Taking more than three bounces in a basketball dribble during a time in possession of the ball.
10. Kicking or deliberately touching the ball with the hips or legs.
11. Goalkeeper taking more than two steps with the ball.

Boundaries.—All walls are in bounds. Special ground rules will probably be necessary in local situations.

Substitutions.—Substitutions may be made at any time when the referee is in possession of the ball. Substitutes must report to the referee.

Length of Game.—Two twenty-minute periods constitute a game.

Push Ball

Playground, Open Field   *Junior High School to College*

The push ball is a large inflated ball five to six feet in diameter. Since these balls are very expensive the game is commonly played with the thirty-inch cage ball. The cage ball is an inflated canvas-covered ball.

Establish two lines thirty to fifty yards apart. Any number may play on a side, and the numbers are usually large. One team lines up or masses itself behind each line. The ball is placed midway between the lines. At the signal the teams rush for the ball and attempt to push it across the opposite line. The team wins which puts the ball across the opposing goal line first.

Balloon Push Ball.—This is a thrilling contest for a small space, and even though it is played with a toy balloon it is very strenuous. The balloon remains in the air a long time and the players constantly jump and stretch to reach it. The contest can be played in a space of any size from a room in a home to a gymnasium.

Divide the players into two teams and place one at each end of the gymnasium or room. Toss a toy balloon in the air in the center of the floor and at the same time give the starting signal. The teams rush forward and attempt to bat the balloon to the opposite wall. The team wins which succeeds in causing the balloon to touch the opposite wall.

Keep a few extra inflated balloons handy. When the balloon is broken, immediately toss another in the air at the spot where the accident occurred.

Scrimmage Ball

Playground   *Junior High School to College*

Field.—The game is played on a football field or similar area approximately 60 by 100 yards in size. The area may be reduced to meet the needs of young players.

Ball.—A cageball or soccer ball is used.

Teams.—Ten to twenty-five players may play on a team.

Object of the Game.—The object is to force the ball over the opponents' goal.

Start.—The teams line up at the center of the field, ten yards apart and facing each other. The end line behind each team is that team's goal. The ball is tossed in the air, and the teams rush for it. After each score, the ball is put in play in the same way.

Play.—The ball may be thrown, batted, or punched, but must not be carried or kicked. Unnecessary roughness and hitting the ball when down are fouls entitling an opposing player to an unguarded throw. Goal defenders may have one foot only behind the goal line.

Scoring.—One point is scored each time the ball is forced over the opponents' goal line.

Length of Game.—The playing period is ten minutes.

Soccer Batball

Playground, Gymnasium   *Late Elementary to Senior High School*

This game follows the general rules of Batball except that the ball may not be played with the hands. The rules of Batball should be read.

A soccer ball is used and the kicker (batter) kicks it into the field. The fielders play the ball with the feet or head. The runner is out if he is hit by a kicked ball or if a fielder dribbles the ball across the goal line before the runner reaches it.

GAMES INVOLVING SOCCER SKILLS IN OTHER CHAPTERS

Soccer Tag.   Soccer Dodgeball.
Roll Ball.   Soccer Center-Ball

SOCCER LEAD-UP CONTESTS

Many of the minor games of the Soccer type described in this chapter are valuable in developing Soccer skills for the major sport. The following contests, described in the chapters on contests, may be used to advantage for this purpose also.

Soccer Throw for Distance.   Speedball Place-kick for Distance.
Soccer Punt for Distance.   Speedball Place-kick for Accuracy.
Soccer Place-Kick for Distance   Speedball Kick and Catch.
Soccer Place-Kick for Accuracy.   Speedball Drop-kick for Distance.
Codeball Kick for Distance.   Speedball Drop-kick for Accuracy.
Kick, Bounce, and Catch.   Speedball Punt for Distance.
Foot Dribble Relay.   Overhead Dribble for Distance.
Soccer Bowling.

CHAPTER XXIII

GAMES OF THE RUGBY FOOTBALL TYPE

THE Rugby games are much more complicated than Association Football. Scores are made in several ways, and a greater variety of plays is permitted—kicking, running with the ball, and passing, all being used. This necessarily makes the rules more complex and difficult to understand. American Rugby and English Rugby differ considerably. In American Rugby there is much mass play, while the English game is much more open. The use of mass play in the American game comes about principally through the use of what is called "interference," which consists in sending a group of men ahead of the man carrying the ball to protect him from the opposing tacklers. The players ahead of the ball are "off-side," and passing to an "off-side" man is not allowed in English Rugby; therefore passing the ball forward is not permitted in the English game, while in American Rugby it is only allowed once in each play, and was not allowed at all until the season of 1906.

American Rugby

Playground   *Senior High School to Adults*

This is the game usually called College Football.

Field.—The field is 300 feet long and 160 feet wide, with an "end zone" at each end 30 feet long and as wide as the field. This makes the whole space 360 feet long. The two end zones are used especially for the forward pass, which may be legally caught in these sections, as well as on the playing field. At each end are the goals, on the middle of the end line. Each goal has two posts eighteen-and-one-half feet apart with a crossbar ten feet up. The side lines and end lines are marked with lime and similar lines are marked across the field every five yards to help the officials to measure the distances. The goal line is marked with a double line of lime to make it easily distinguishable from the yard lines, and the end zones contain diagonal markings. (See Figure 69.)

General Description of the Play.—It is the object of each team, which consists of eleven men, to defend its own goal and to carry the ball into the opponents' territory and score. A player carrying the ball may be stopped by grasping him and throwing him to the ground. This is called "tackling." No one may be tackled except the man with the ball. The ball carrier is down when any portion of his person except his hands or feet touches the ground. When the down is made the referee blows his

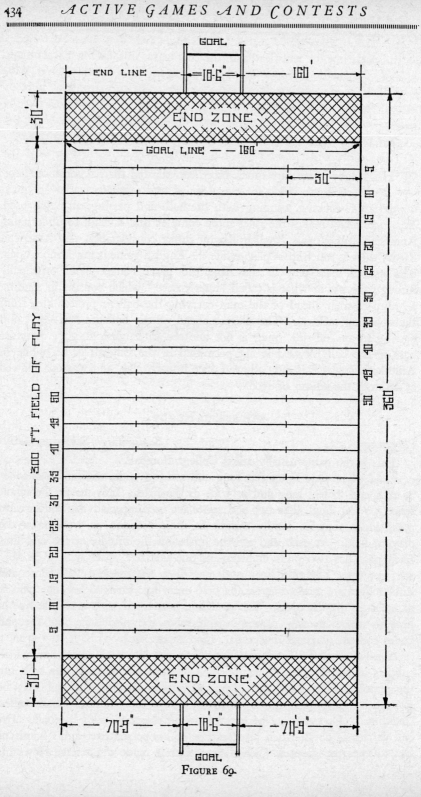

FIGURE 69.

whistle declaring the ball dead and the two teams line up for a scrimmage as later described. To prevent opponents from tackling the player with the ball, his team mates often form a group and run in front of him, or between him and his opponents. Men thus acting as protection for the man carrying the ball are said to form an "interference." Men on the side having the ball may not use their hands to keep opponents away, but may run against them with hip, shoulder, or arms held against the body. After the ball has been kicked, however, the players of the kicker's team may use their hands to ward off or push opponents who are attempting to block them. The side not in possession of the ball may use hands or arms freely to aid them in getting to the man with the ball.

Scoring.—A touchdown counts six; a score following a touchdown counts one; a goal from the field counts three; a safety counts two for the opponents. The way in which each of these scores is won will be described in the proper place in the following description of the play.

Kick-Off.—The game begins by a play known as the kick-off. Before beginning the game, the captains toss a coin and the winner may have the choice of goal, or of kicking off, or of receiving the kick-off. The loser has the choice of the remaining two options. At the start of the second half the privileges as to choice are reversed.

Upon the referee's signal the team having the ball place-kicks it from any point on its own forty-yard line or some point behind it. The kicker's side must all be in bounds and behind the ball when it is kicked. The opponents must be in bounds and behind their restraining line ten yards in advance of the ball; at least five players must remain within five yards of this line until the ball is kicked. The ball must be kicked to or beyond the opponents' restraining line to continue in play, unless it is touched by an opponent. When the ball is kicked, the kicker's team charges down the field as fast as possible to the vicinity where it strikes. A player of the opposing side attempts to catch or secure the ball and run it back as far as he can before being tackled. The referee then blows his whistle as signal for play to stop.

During the minute intermission preceding the second and fourth quarters of the game, the players change goals but do not leave the field of play. The ball is placed in the same relative position only facing the opposite direction from which it was when the preceding period ended. Otherwise the play proceeds as though no change was made, the number of downs and distance to gain being the same.

A Scrimmage.—Following the kick-off the two teams line up in a formation known as a scrimmage, shown by Figure 70.

Notice that there are seven forwards, one quarterback, two halfbacks, and one fullback. The ball is held by the center player. The captain or the quarterback calls a signal which all the men of that team understand as the call for a certain play, having agreed upon it and rehearsed it in practice beforehand; the whole team unites in an effort to carry it out successfully. Such plays usually begin by the center passing the ball to a back, and in many plays this back passes it to a third player, who runs with it, so as to advance with it toward the opponents' goal. Each team has learned a variety of plays and the quarterback uses them according to his judgment.

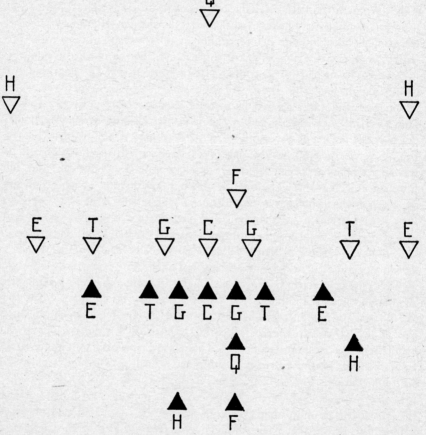

FIGURE 70.—Positions of Players: black team, side with the ball; white team, defending side. C, center; G, G, guards; T, T, tackles; E, E, ends; Q, quarterback, H, H, halfbacks; F, fullback.

A scrimmage ends when the player carrying the ball is tackled, falls so that one knee touches the ground, carries the ball over the goal line, or is forced out of bounds. A down is then declared. It is also a down if a forward pass hits the ground before being caught. Four downs are allowed in which to make the necessary ten yards. In case this distance is made before the four downs are used up, a new first down is declared.

Punting.—When a team finds itself unable to make the required ten yards in four trials, punting is the usual resort. Since even an indifferent punter can advance the ball several yards, it is better to punt on the fourth trial than to lose the ball on downs with no advance. The punter is placed well back, so as to enable him to get the ball away before an opponent can reach him; the center sends him the ball by a long pass, and it is punted down the field into the opponents' territory. The two ends run down the field after the ball so as to be ready to tackle the man who catches it before he can gain much distance in running; the other team mates must hesitate before running after the ball, as they must first obstruct opponents trying to break through the line to block the punt. If the man catching it is a good punter he may punt it back again, but this is seldom done.

On the punt play it must be remembered that players of the kicking side, who are ahead of the ball when it is kicked, are "off-side" and may not play the ball themselves until it has first been touched by an opponent.

The Forward Pass.—The forward pass consists in passing the ball toward the opponents' goal. It not only is a means of gaining ground, but is a threat which serves to keep the defense spread out so as to enhance the chances of a successful running attack. The ball is gripped with the fingers near one end and thrown end first so that it is offered the least resistance in its flight. It is possible to throw the ball a distance of forty or fifty yards. The ball may be passed forward by any player and such a forward pass may be caught by any player of the same side who was a yard behind the line of scrimmage, or was an end man on the line of scrimmage. Any opponent is eligible to catch a forward pass—this is called "intercepting a pass." After a pass has been touched by a member of the defense, and while it is still in the air, it becomes a free ball for either side. If the ball falls to the ground it counts as a down and the play starts once more from the spot of the preceding scrimmage. Such a failure is termed an "incompleted pass."

Lateral Pass.—There is another type of pass in which a runner carrying the ball may pass it to another player at any time, provided that player is behind him or on a line with him (not in front of him—this would constitute a forward pass). Such a play is called a lateral pass. Passes of this type are usually resorted to by runners making an end run or by players who have just received a forward pass, when they see that they are about to be tackled. Any number of lateral passes may be thrown in succession, and any player is eligible to receive the pass. Following a completed forward pass, if a lateral pass is attempted and fumbled, the play is considered as an incomplete forward pass. In the same situation, if the attempted lateral goes forward, making two forward passes, the ball is brought back to the point where the play started.

Fumble.—It is a fumble when a player holding the ball in play loses possession and control of it other than by passing or kicking it. Fumbles usually result from dropping the ball, having it snatched away by an opponent, or by failing to complete a backward pass.

When a fumble occurs, the players of either team may recover it. If the team which fumbled recovers the ball it may advance it. If the opposing team recovers the ball after it strikes the ground the ball is dead at the point of recovery and may not be advanced, but if the opposing team recovers it before it strikes the ground, it may be advanced.

Out of Bounds.—The ball is out of bounds when either the ball or any part of a player holding it touches the ground, an obstruction, or any person other than a player on or outside the side line or the end line.

When the ball goes out of bounds across the side lines (except in the case of a forward pass or a kick-off), or when it becomes dead within ten yards of a side line, it is put in play at a spot ten yards from that side line and on a line drawn at right angles to the side line through the point where the ball became dead.

Penalties.—In most cases fouls are penalized by loss of distance—five, fifteen, or more yards, according to the nature of the offense. Distance penalties are provided for holding, tripping, illegal use of the hands and arms in interference, and rough play; also for off-side play in scrimmage, and for fouls of a technical nature.

Some fouls include loss of the ball to the offended side without a distance penalty; a case is where a foul occurs when neither side is in possession of the ball, or when an off-side player on a punt touches the ball.

The most common fouls of all are being off-side in scrimmage, which means a five-yard penalty, and holding or illegal interference by the offensive team, which is penalized to the extent of fifteen yards.

It is important to note that, with a few exceptions, when the defensive side is penalized a first down is given the team with the ball in addition to the distance gain; however, when the offensive side is the violator, the distance penalty is made, setting the ball back, but the number of the down and the place to be reached remain the same as before.

When a penalty is inflicted on a team, the opposing team may refuse the penalty if it so desires. Such a refusal usually takes place when the defensive team commits a foul on a play in which the offensive team made more yardage than that allowed by the penalty.

Touchdown.—The game may continue by a succession of scrimmages until the ball becomes legally dead on, above, or behind one of the goal lines. This constitutes a touchdown, and also gives the successful team the privilege of a try-at-goal. To do this the ball is brought out into the field two yards from the goal and the two teams line up against each other. The team that has just scored is allowed one down to score again by any means it may choose. If successful an additional point is added to their score. Following a touchdown and the attendant try-at-goal, play is resumed by a kick-off. The side scored upon has the right to decide who shall kick. Rugby is the only game in which scores are made by merely carrying the ball over the goal line; in all other games of this type it must go through the goal. Kicking the ball over the goal line, however, does not score

Goal from the Field.—When a team finds itself in front of the opponents' goal and within kicking distance, a goal from the field is often attempted. A punt is not permitted, the rules requiring a drop-kick or place-kick. The ball in the latter case is passed far back by the center to the quarterback or other back, who holds it for the kicker. If the ball goes over the crossbar or directly over one of the goal posts, a goal is scored, and the play is resumed as in case of a touchdown.

Safety and Touchback.—A "safety" is scored when a player with the ball is downed behind his own goal line, provided the impetus came from his own team. A safety usually occurs unintentionally, as when a bad pass by the center, or a fumble by the receiver, causes the ball to roll behind a team's own goal. If, however, the ball is declared dead behind the goal line in the possession of a defending player, the force which sent it there coming from the attackers, no score is made, and the play is called a "touchback."

Following a safety, the team scored upon puts the ball in play by a free-kick anywhere on its own twenty-yard line or any point back of it. Following a touchback, the team making it puts the ball in play by a scrimmage anywhere on its own twenty-yard line.

Length of the Game.—The game consists of four periods of fifteen minutes each, or a shorter time agreed upon. In high-school competition, twelve-minute periods are used, and in junior-high-school games, eight minute periods. Fifteen minutes' rest is given between halves and one minute between quarters.

Time Out.—Time out is allowed upon request of a captain or for the purpose of completing a substitution made by the coach. Not more than two minutes are allowed each time. Each team is allowed three time-outs during a half. After the third time-out, however, a loss of five yards is inflicted for an additional time out, unless an injured player for whose benefit time is taken out is removed from the game.

Substitutions.—A player may be substituted for another, but must go onto the field when the ball is dead, and must first report to the umpire before engaging in play. He is not allowed to communicate with his fellow players until after one down has occurred.

A player taken from the game may not return in the same period or intermission in which he was withdrawn, but may return in the following period. This right, however, is not extended to a player who has been disqualified or suspended from the game. A player removed in the last period may not return at all.

Officials.—The officials of the game are a referee, an umpire, a linesman, and a field judge. The referee has general charge of the ball and is judge of its position and progress. His whistle stops the play. He calls fouls. His position is behind the team having possession of the ball.

The umpire is the judge of the conduct of the players, and has for his duty the calling of certain classes of fouls apt to occur near his position in the field. He stands behind the defensive team.

The linesman, under the direction of the referee, marks the distance gained, and has jurisdiction over the positions of the players when the ball is put in play. He also assists in watching for fouls involving personal conduct. He takes a position to the side of the play and stands his stick even with the forward point of the ball. He has assistants who stand on the side line with stakes marking the distance to be gained in the series of downs.

It is the duty of the field judge to occupy a position well back of the team not in possession of the ball and toward the side of the field opposite from the linesman, and to relieve the referee of some of his duties in this part of the field; also to keep the time and report fouls not coming to the attention of the umpire.

MINOR GAMES OF THE RUGBY TYPE

Punt Back
(*Five Steps, Drive*)

Playground   *Late Elementary to Senior High School*

A field of the size of a football field is used with only the side lines and goal lines marked. Either a rugby or soccer football may be used. Divide the players into two teams and scatter the members of each over their half of the field.

Object.—The object is to work the ball by punting into the opponents' territory and then punt it over the opponents' goal line.

Start.—The game is started by a place-kick from about the kicker's thirty-five-yard line.

The Play.—When the ball is kicked the opponents secure it and punt it back. If the ball is caught the player catching it is permitted to take five steps (sometimes played by taking three steps) from the point where he caught it, before punting it back. If it is not caught, it must be kicked back from the point where the player gets possession of it. No opponent may be within ten feet of a player when he is punting. Breaking this rule permits the kicker to take five steps.

If the ball goes out of bounds it is returned to the field even with the point where it crossed the side line and kicked from that line. No steps are taken when a ball is caught out of bounds.

When a player is close enough to the goal line, he attempts to punt the ball over it. In defending against such a kick, no player is permitted to step back over his own line.

Scoring.—One point is scored for each punt crossing the goal line. If the ball is touched by an opponent it does not count. One point is scored for the opponents if a defending player steps back over his own goal line.

Variation.—This game is played just like Punt Back except for the method of scoring. When a player thinks that he is close enough to the goal line to drop-kick the ball over it, he attempts to do so. Drop-kicks over the goal line which are not touched by the opponents score one point. Punts or place-kicks over the goal line do not score—the ball goes to the defending team and is punted back from the goal line.

Variation.—Mark out a goal area on the ground at each end of the field thirty by fifteen feet in size. These goal areas are extensions of the football field and are placed in the middle of the goal line; the center section of the goal line is used for one of the thirty-foot lines and the fifteen-foot lines extend back at right angles to it. To score, the ball must be drop-kicked so that it drops in the goal area.

Variation.—This is similar to Punt Back, except for the kicking rules. If a ball is caught by an opponent, he may kick it back by punting or any other type of kick. If it is not caught, the ball must be drop-kicked from the point where it was first touched. No steps are taken as in Punt Back when the ball is caught.

Drop-Kick Drive.—This is played like Punt Back, except that all kicks must be drop-kicks—no punting is allowed. Three points are scored each time the ball is drop-kicked over the goal posts.

Forward-Pass Drive.—This is played like Punt Back except that the ball is passed and not kicked. One point is scored each time a team succeeds in passing the ball over the opponents' goal line. The game is played on a football field or area of similar size, but when young players are competing, it is well to reduce the size of the area.

Kick-and-Pass Drive.—This is a combination of Punt Back, Drop-Kick Drive, and Forward-Pass Drive.

The ball may be advanced by punting, drop-kicking, or forward-passing as the player chooses, with the rules of Punt Back applying. When the ball is put over the goal line by these methods, scores are made as follows:

Drop-kicked goal	3 points
Forward-passed goal	2 points
Punted goal	1 point

Forward-Pass Newcomb

Forward-Pass Newcomb is described in Chapter XXV, "Games of the Basketball Type."

Newcomb over the Goal Posts is also described in the same chapter.

Kicking Field Goals

Football Field   *Junior and Senior High Schools*

The two teams scatter either side of the football goal posts. A player of one team attempts to drop-kick the ball over the goal and the opponents attempt to catch the kick. If the kick crosses the bar one point is scored; if the opponents fail to catch the kick one additional point is scored.

The teams alternate in kicking, and the members of each team rotate in kicking. All kicks must be made from a point at least fifteen yards back from the goal posts and directly in front of them. The team scoring eleven (or twenty-one) points first wins.

Running Back Kick-Offs

Football Field   *Junior and Senior High Schools*

The teams line up as for the kick-off in Football. One team kicks off and the receiving team runs the ball back until the ball carrier is tagged. The receiving team scores points depending on the area in which the runner was tagged:

Behind the ten-yard line	0 points
Ten to twenty-yard line	1 point
Twenty to thirty-yard line	2 points
Thirty to forty-yard line	3 points
Forty to fifty-yard line	5 points
Beyond fifty-yard line	10 points

Each team kicks off three times in succession and then the opposing team kicks.

Rush Ball

Gymnasium, Playground, Club   Late Elementary and Junior High Schools

This is a combative game of very low organization which is much enjoyed by boys. It is played in an area the size of the ordinary gymnasium. Stuff a burlap sack with paper and place it in the center of the area. Divide the players into two teams and place one at each end line.

At the signal both teams rush for the bag and attempt to take it to the opposite goal. The team getting it, or a major part of it, there first, wins. There are no rules except that unnecessary roughness and violent play are prohibited.

Touch Football

Football Field, Playground   *Junior High School to Adults*

Touch Football is an adaptation of Rugby Football designed for more informal play by teams that do not have the opportunity for the practice and training that Rugby Football requires.

The Touch Football rules have not been standardized yet but are gradually evolving into a standard form. Where there are conflicting practices, both points of view are mentioned in the following rules.

Field and Goals.—Same as in Rugby Football.

Ball.—Same as in Rugby Football.

Teams.—A team consists of nine players.

Length of Game.—For players of senior-high-school age and older, the game consists of four fifteen-minute periods with a three-minute rest after the first and third periods, and a five-minute rest at the half. For junior-high-school players the periods are ten minutes long. These periods may be shortened to meet conditions.

Choice of Goals.—As in Rugby Football.

Kick-off.—As in Rugby Football. The team receiving the kick-off may *not* form interference for the ball carrier; the ball may be advanced on the return by running, kicking, or passing sideward or backward.

Scrimmage.—The general rules of Rugby Football apply. The offensive team must have at least five men on the line of scrimmage. The center passes the ball back between his legs to one of the backfield men who endeavors to advance it by running, kicking, or passing forward, sideward, or backward. The backfield players may not be moving toward the line of scrimmage before the ball is snapped.

If the offensive team has not advanced the ball ten yards in four consecutive downs, the ball goes to the opponents. (Some prefer to require twenty yards instead of ten.)

Passes.—All players of the offensive team are eligible pass receivers. Any defensive player may intercept a pass. One forward pass may be attempted on each play in a series of downs, even though previous passes were incomplete. An incompleted forward pass is returned to the line of scrimmage, even though it may have been preceded by a successful lateral pass.

In case of interference with the pass receiver by a defensive player, the pass is ruled as complete. In case of interference with a defensive player during a pass, the offensive team is penalized ten yards from the previous line of scrimmage.

A forward pass may be thrown from any point behind the line of scrimmage.

If a player passes to himself, the ball is dead at the point where it was passed.

If a forward pass is incomplete and hits the ground across the goal line, it is regarded merely as an incomplete pass. (Some prefer to use the standard football rule here: after two such incomplete passes in the same series of downs, the ball goes to the opposing team on the twenty-yard line).

Dead Ball.—An incompleted sideward or backward pass is a dead ball. The same applies to a pass from center which is fumbled. In both cases, a down is charged against the offensive team.

Downed Ball.—A ball carrier is considered down and the ball dead when an opposing player touches him with two hands. (Some authorities prefer to consider the ball carrier tackled when touched with one hand.)

Out of Bounds.—As in Rugby Football.

Scoring.—A touchdown scores six points and a safety scores two points. The definition of both touchdown and safety is the same as in Rugby Football.

There is no play for point after touchdown as in Rugby Football, nor may points be scored from a field goal.

Fouls and Penalties.—The following are fouls:

1. Tackling, pushing, tripping, holding, or roughing another player. Penalty—loss of fifteen yards.

2. Off-side—rule and penalty as in Rugby Football.

3. Use of hands or leaving feet in an attempt to block an opponent. Penalty—loss of fifteen yards.

4. Intentionally delaying the game. Penalty—loss of five yards for first two offenses; loss of ball for third offense.

5. Kicking or attempting to kick a free ball. Penalty—loss of ball.

6. Substitute not reporting to referee. Penalty—loss of five yards.

Points not covered by Rules.—All points not covered by these rules are governed by the rules of Rugby Football.

High-Low Ball

Playground   *Junior and Senior High Schools*

The original form of this game was invented by James Naismith, and intended to serve as an introduction to Football. The team play is not complicated, individual skill being stressed more. It is sometimes played by girls.

Field.—A football field is used with a center circle ten feet in diameter added as in Soccer. A soccer field and soccer goals may be used if desired.

Ball.—A soccer ball is used.

Teams.—Eleven men compose a team, named as in Rugby Football.

Object.—The object is to work the ball into the opponents' territory by kicking, passing, or carrying it, and then score by carrying or passing it over the goal line, or kicking it over the goal.

Start.—The game starts by a kick-off. The winner of the toss has the choice of goal, and the loser kicks off. The ball is kicked from the center line by a place-kick and all other players must stand at least ten yards away.

Scoring.—Points are scored as follows:

A touchdown scores six points.
A drop-kick over the goal after a touchdown scores one point.
A drop-kick or punt over the goal during play scores three points.
A kick over the goal from the restraining circle (fifty yards) scores one point.
A safety scores two points.

The Play.—The ball must be played with the feet or legs when it is below the height of the hips. When above the height of the hips, the ball must be played by the hands, head, body, or arms. The ball may be caught when it is as high as the hip line; when below the level of the knee, it must be lifted with foot or knee. Having caught the ball, the player may pass or kick it or run with it. All kicks must be punts or drop-kicks except on the kick-off.

When a player runs with the ball, he may be tackled, but only above the hips and below the head. The tackle must be made with two arms. Team mates are allowed to tackle opponents in this way and clear the way for the runner.

When the player running with the ball is tackled, the referee calls a down at the point. After a down, the player tackled retains the ball for a free-kick and stands facing his own players and kicks the ball to one of them.

When a player running with the ball is tackled he may call "Held" if the referee has not blown his whistle, or if the runner is being forced backward, may call "Down," and the referee calls the ball down at the spot. Interference with a player attempting to catch a pass is not permitted, but other players may be blocked or tackled.

After a team has had four successive downs the ball is given to the opponents for a free-kick. No player of either side may be nearer than ten feet until the ball is kicked and all players must be "on side."

When a ball crosses the end line by other means than being carried over and does not result in a score, it is given to the defending team for a kick from a point five yards inside the goal line, in front of the goal posts. All players of the defending side must be behind the ball.

Touchdown.—A touchdown is scored when the ball is carried over or passed to a player over the goal line.

Goal After Touchdown.—A player of the scoring team stands on the ten-yard line with his back to the goal and facing his team mates. He kicks the ball to one of them who kicks for the goal from the point where the ball is received. The ball must be caught—if fumbled, the privilege of kicking is lost. The defending team must stay behind the goal line until the first kick is made, then may rush in to block the try for goal.

Safety.—A safety is scored by the attacking side when the defending team kicks the ball behind their own goal line, or when it is sent over the goal line by the attacking side and touches a defensive player there, or the defensive team's goal posts or crossbar.

Out of Bounds.—When the ball goes across the side lines it is returned by an end player of the team opposed to the team that put it out. This player drop-kicks or punts it into the field at right angles to the side line at the point where it went out, and may not touch it again until it has been played by another player. All other players must be ten feet away and "on side."

Fouls and Penalties.—Fouls are called when players violate the rules described above regarding playing the ball with hands and feet and tackling.

The penalty for a foul is a free-kick by the opponents at the point where the foul occurred, toward the opponents' goal. However, if the defending team commits a foul inside their own twenty-five-yard line, the ball may be kicked by a member of the attacking team toward his own team.

Length of Game.—The game consists of four ten-minute quarters with rest periods of from three to five minutes.

Beeball

Playground   *Junior and Senior High Schools*

Beeball was originated by C. W. Beeman in 1924 as a game for the autumn season combining the most interesting and recreative values of Rugby Football and Soccer. The following is Mr. Beeman's own condensation of the rules.

Ball.—The game is played with a round leather (rubber inflated) ball slightly smaller in circumference than a soccer ball, twenty-two to twenty-three inches in circumference, weight twelve to fourteen ounces.

The Field.—Maximum dimensions are the same as the football field (160 by 360 feet). The game is, however, very adaptable to smaller school-yard spaces. Five-yard lines plainly marked are a decided asset in the conduct of the game.

The Goals.—The goals consist of two posts with a crossbar on top placed in the middle of the end lines. Regulation posts are eight yards apart with the crossbar eight feet above the ground.

Players.—A regulation team is composed of nine players: four forwards, four guards, and one goal guard. The chief function of the forwards is attack; that of the goal guard and guards, defense. However, at any stage of the game a guard may become an attacking player and a forward a defensive man, and so forth.

The Game.—The game consists of two twenty-minute halves which may be shortened by mutual consent. The game begins by a kick-off from

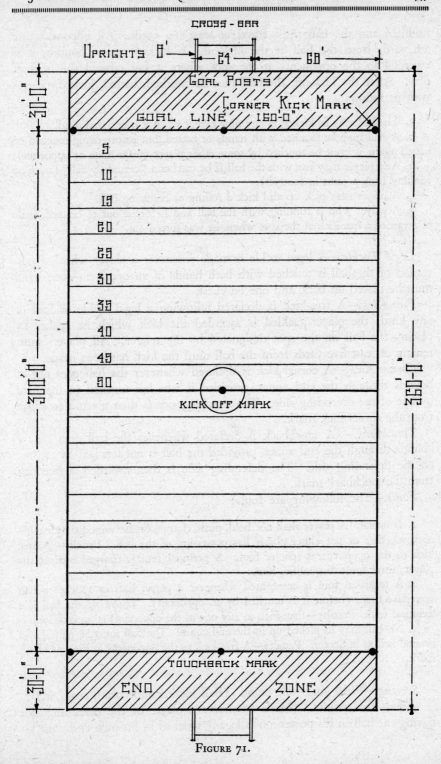

FIGURE 71.

midfield and the ball must travel at least ten yards. All opponents are ten yards from the ball at the kick-off. If kicked out of bounds, it is awarded to the opponents at the spot where it last crossed the field of play. After the kick-off, the ball may be touched, batted, kicked, or run with as follows:

1. The ball may be kicked at any time except when it is declared dead.
2. A ball may be touched with hands or batted, but before being touched or batted again, it must be touched by some other player (team mate or opponent).
3. Any player may run with the ball if he catches a "kicked fly ball" (same as running back a punt in football).
4. A player may pick up and kick a rolling or bouncing ball.
5. A player who is running with the ball and is forced out of bounds, shall be awarded a free-kick at the spot where he was forced out.

Legal Tackle.—A legal tackle is made whenever a player who has possession of the ball is touched with both hands of an opponent—one hand must be placed on back and one on chest.

Free-Kick.—A free-kick is declared following a legal tackle or foul of any kind; the player tackled is awarded the kick which he makes by placing the ball on the spot designated by the referee. All players must remain at least five yards from the ball until the kick has been made.

Corner-Kick.—A corner-kick is declared whenever the ball goes out of bounds through the end zones, provided it was last touched in the field by one of the defending side. The attacking side is then given a free-kick from the corner-kick mark.

Touchback.— A touchback is declared whenever the ball goes out of bounds through the end zones, provided the ball is not touched by anyone on the defending side. The defending side is then awarded a free-kick from the touchback mark.

Fouls.—The following are fouls:

1. Personal: A player shall not hold, push, charge, or use unnecessary roughness, whether or not either player has possession of the ball. Penalty—A free kick to the opponent at spot of foul. A personal foul is charged against the player; three fouls disqualifies him.
2. A technical foul is committed whenever a player bats or touches a ball successive times (before it is touched by an opponent). Throwing the ball is a technical foul. Penalty—Free-kick to any one of the opponents at spot of foul.
3. No ball may be picked up in the end zones. The ball must be played as a ground ball as in Soccer. Penalty—A free-kick to the opponents at the touchback mark.

Scoring.—Field goal—one point. (Ball kicked underneath crossbar.)
Safety—two points. (Made whenever a player of the defending side having the ball in his possession is legally touched in his own end zone.)

Touchdown—three points: (1) whenever any player of the attacking side after catching a "fly kicked ball" runs across his opponents' goal line; (2) whenever any player of the attacking side catches a "fly kicked ball" anywhere in the end zone. (This cannot be scored on a ball kicked in from out of bounds.)

Officials.—A referee and an umpire are in charge of the game.

Tag Speedball

This game is described in Chapter XXII, "Games of the Soccer Type."

Foot Volleyball

Playground   *Junior High School to College*

Field.—The size of the field depends on the size and ability of the players. For older boys the field is one hundred by two hundred feet. Two lines are drawn across the field parallel to the end lines, creating an area across the center of the field fifteen feet wide, known as the neutral zone. The end areas are the playing courts.

For girls and small boys, the field should be ninety-five feet long and forty feet wide.

Ball.—A soccer ball is used. For boys, the game may also be played with a rugby football.

Teams.—Seven to fourteen players constitute a team. The players scatter over their half of the court.

Service.—The ball is served from the middle of the serving side's court, by punting it so that it falls into the opposing court. One try only is allowed. Failure gives the service to the opposing team.

The Play.—The team receiving the service catches the ball and punts it back into the opposing court.

Scoring.—Only the serving team scores. It serves as long as it continues to score. It scores one point when the opposing team (1) allows

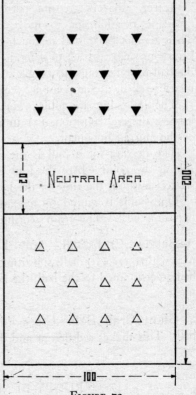

FIGURE 72.

the ball to touch the ground in their court; (2) kicks it out of bounds, or into the neutral area, or so that it falls within its own court.

Rotation of service.—Each time a team receives the ball for service the players rotate one position. This gives each player a chance to serve and to play each position.

Crab Ball

Gymnasium, Club   *Late Elementary and Junior High Schools.*

This is an excellent boys' game of low organization and is always popular among those who know it.

Establish two goal lines forty feet apart. Divide the players into two teams and have them sit on the goal lines facing each other with arms extended backward supporting the body from the floor. Place a soccer ball, sport ball, or codeball on the floor midway between the goals.

At the signal both teams move toward the ball, keeping the crab position described, and attempt to kick the ball over the opposing goal. They may kick it with one foot or drop to the buttocks and kick with both feet. Players are not permitted to stand up and run to a more favorable position, or to move in any position except that described. They are not permitted to touch the ball with the hands. Teams should keep some players back to defend the goal and send others forward to drive the ball over the opponent's goal. When the ball goes out of bounds, it is tossed back in at the point it went out by the referee.

The following are fouls: (1) touching the ball with the hands, (2) leaving the crab position, (3) unnecessary roughness in kicking, striking, or shoving an opponent.

The penalty for a foul is the awarding of a free-kick to the offended side at the point where the foul occurred. All opposing players must be six feet away at the time of the kick.

One point is scored by a team each time it kicks the ball over the opposing goal. The team scoring ten points first wins.

Balloon Crab Ball.—After the game has been played for a few minutes with the soccer ball, substitute a large toy balloon for the ball. After being accustomed to the ball, the slow-moving balloon causes much amusement.

Giant Crab Ball.—Use a thirty-inch cageball instead of the soccer ball. This makes a different and, if anything, a more interesting game.

RUGBY LEAD-UP CONTESTS

Many of the minor Rugby games described in this chapter are valuable in developing skills for the major game. The following contests, described in the chapters on contests, may also be used to advantage in developing skills in handling the rugby ball.

Circle-Passing Relay.
Catch, Throw, and Sit.
Catch, Throw, and Squat.
Ten Trips.
Pass-and-Toss Relay.
Zigzag Ball-Passing Relay.
Throwing Shuttle Relay.
Football Center-Pass Relay.
Football Center-Pass.

Forward Pass for Distance.
Forward Pass for Accuracy.
Football Center-Pass for Accuracy.
Rugby Punt for Distance.
Rugby Place-Kick for Distance.
Drop-Kick for Distance.
Football Target Punt.
Football Snatch-Ball.

CHAPTER XXIV

GAMES OF THE HOCKEY TYPE

HOCKEY has been played in Great Britain in its present form for over sixty years; as a crude game with an indefinite number of players it has been common in northern Europe for many centuries. In the earliest times it was not distinguished from football; it was played for a long time in Ireland with a small ball but with no club, and was called "Hurling."

Ice hockey in the crude form is still older, having been played by the Scandinavians from ancient times, but it is one of the latest games to have definite rules, the first set being adopted by the Canadian Hockey Association only a few years ago. Lacrosse is a running game played by the American Indians. About 1850 it was revised by the Canadians and shortly afterwards introduced into the United States. A number of colleges have taken up the game. Polo is of Asiatic origin, and was probably played by the Persians at the time of Alexander the Great. It was introduced from Tibet into China in the sixth century A. D., and was common in India for several centuries, but had entirely disappeared when that country was first occcupied by the English. Shortly after 1850 it was being played again and its modern world-wide popularity dates from that time.

Hockey and Football games differ in the size of the ball and the way of handling it. In Hockey games there is a small ball driven by a bent stick; in Football there is a large ball handled with the hands and feet only.

The principal games of the hockey type are Field Hockey, Ice Hockey, Lacrosse, and Polo. Field Hockey is played by both men and women in England, but in the United States it is played by women only, and is their major fall sport. A simpler form known as Shinney is played by small boys, using home-made sticks and a tin can or block of wood.

Field Hockey

Playground   *Senior High School to College*

Field.—The field should be a level, smooth stretch of turf, kept short and well rolled. The better the condition of the ground, the greater can be the accuracy and skill of play.

The dimensions of the regulation hockey field are 100 yards in length by no less than 50 and not more than 60 yards in width, the space being marked out with lime lines and with a flag stationed at each corner. For secondary schools the dimensions should be reduced to a length of 85 yards and a width of 45 yards.

The goals are erected in the middle of the end lines; the goal posts are twelve feet apart and the crossbar seven feet high. The field is divided as shown in Figure 73.

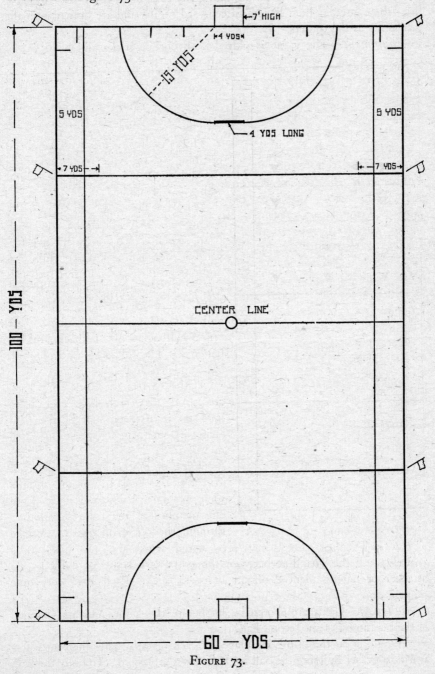

FIGURE 73.

The striking circles around the goals are laid out as follows: a twelve-foot line is drawn parallel to the goals and fifteen yards out from them; circular lines are then drawn connecting the ends of this line with the goal line—these circular lines have a fifteen-yard radius and are drawn with the goal posts as the centers.

Equipment.—The game is played with hockey sticks and ball. Sticks must not weigh more than twenty-three ounces; players on the forward line use lighter sticks, while those playing in the backfield use the heavier weight.

Heavy boots or shoes with low heels are best for the sake of protection to the ankles and feet. Metal cleats and spikes are prohibited.

Players.—The game is played by twenty-two players, eleven on each team. Each eleven consists of five forwards, three halfbacks, two fullbacks, and one goalkeeper. The five forwards are center forward, right inside forward, left inside forward, right wing, and left wing. The halfbacks are center halfback, right halfback, and left halfback. The fullbacks are right fullback and left fullback.

At the start of the game, after each goal, and after each half, each team lines up in its own half of the field facing its opponent's goal, as illustrated in Figure 74.

Object of the Game.—The object is to carry the ball by means of the stick, using passes and hits, from one member of the team to another, through the opponent's goal. A goal is scored when the ball has passed entirely over the goal line between the posts as a result of a hit by an attacker or having glanced off an attacker's stick. Each goal scores one point.

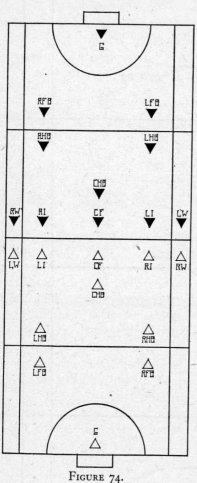

FIGURE 74.

Bully-Off.—Goals are chosen by lot before the game, and are changed at the beginning of the second half.

The game is started by one player of each team, usually the center forwards, together bullying the ball in the center of the field. To bully the ball, each player strikes first the ground on her own side of the ball and then her opponent's stick, alternately, three times, after which one of these two players must strike the ball before it is in general play. The two players who are bullying stand squarely facing the side lines while every other player must be nearer her own goal line than the ball.

For any breach of this rule, the bully shall be taken again.

The Play.—The ball may be caught (but must be released at once to fall to the ground) or stopped, but may not be picked up, carried, kicked, thrown, knocked forward or backward, except with the stick. No player may gain an advantage by the use of any part of her person except as may result from stopping the ball. No player may in any way interfere with the game unless her stick is in her hand.

Out of Bounds over the Side Lines.—When the ball passes over the side lines, it is rolled by hand along the ground (not bounced) into play from the point where it crossed the side line by one of the players of the team opposite to that of the player who last touched it. It may be rolled in any direction. No player may stand within the five yard line, but may cross it as soon as the ball leaves the hand of the roller-in. The roller-in must have both feet and stick behind the side line, and may not play the ball again until another player has played it.

Breach of the rule by the roller-in: the roll-in is taken by a player of the other team.

Breach of the rule by any other player: the roll-in is taken again.

Out of Bounds over the Goal Line.—When the ball is sent over the goal line (not between the goal posts) by a player of the attacking team or a player of the defending team who is farther from her own goal than twenty-five yards, it is brought out twenty-five yards from the point where it crossed the goal line and bullied.

If the ball glances off the stick, or is unintentionally sent behind the goal line by any player of the defending team, behind the twenty-five yard line, it is given as a corner-hit to the opposing team.

Corner-Hit.—To make a corner-hit a player of the attacking team hits the ball from a point on the side or goal line within three yards of the corner, and at the moment of such hit, all of the defending team must be behind their own goal line, and all of the attacking team must be outside the circle in the field of play.

No player may stand within five yards of the striker, and a goal may not be scored from a corner-hit, unless the ball has been stopped (not necessarily motionless) on the ground by one of the attacking team, or has touched the person or stick of one of the defending team, before the last stroke of the attacking team. The player making the corner-hit may not participate in the game again until the ball has been played by another player. In case she does, a free-hit is given the defending team from anywhere within the circle. In case of "sticks" (see fouls below) by the striker of the corner, the defending team is awarded a free-hit; a free-hit is also allowed for shooting at goal before the ball has been stopped.

Off-Side.—When a player hits or rolls in the ball, any other player of the same team is off-side under the following conditions:

1. If she is in her opponents' half of the field.
2. If she is nearer her opponents' goal line than the striker or roller-in.
3. If there are not three of her opponents nearer their own goal line than she.

An off-side player may not play the ball nor in any way interfere with any other player until the ball has been touched or hit by one of her opponents. No player may be penalized for merely standing in an off-side position; there is no breach of the rule unless a player when in such a position gains an advantage, or plays the ball, or interferes with another player.

Fouls.—In addition to the fouls resulting from the violation of the above details, there are certain prohibitions regarding the handling of the stick, such as playing with the back or rounded side of the stick, raising the stick above the shoulders in playing the ball (called "sticks"), undercutting the ball or hitting it in a dangerous way, or striking or interfering with an opponent's stick.

There are rules prohibiting handling or propelling the ball in any way other than with the stick, except for the purpose of stopping the ball.

Furthermore, there are restrictions on personally handling an opponent, such as shoving, charging, or obstructing an opponent.

Penalties for Fouls Outside the Striking Circles.—For any breach of the above rules, the penalty is a free-hit for one of the opposing team on the spot where the breach occurred.

Free-Hit.—On the occasion of a free-hit, no other player than the striker may be within five yards of the spot where the hit is made, and after taking the hit, the striker may not again touch the ball or play it until the ball has been touched or hit by another player.

Penalty for Fouls inside the Striking Circles.—When the foul is committed by the attacking team, the penalty is a free-hit for the defending team from any point inside the circle. When the foul is committed by the defending team, the penalty is a penalty-corner for the attacking team. In case of a willful breach of the rule or when a goal would probably have been scored but for the foul, a penalty-bully is given.

Penalty-Corner.—A player of the attacking team is given a hit from any point on the goal line she may choose, provided it is at a distance of not less than ten yards from the nearest goal post. All players of the defending team must be behind their own goal line; all the attacking team must be outside the striking circle in the field of play. A goal may not be scored by the attacking team unless the ball has been stopped by one of the attacking team or has touched the person or stick of a player of the defending team before the last stroke of the attacking team. A player hitting a penalty-corner hit may not again participate in the game until the ball has been played by another player.

Penalty-Bully.—The penalty-bully is played by the offender and by any other player selected by the other team, on the spot where the breach of the rule occurred. All other players must remain beyond the nearer twenty-five-yard line until the penalty-bully is completed. If during the progress of the bully the ball goes over the goal line not between the goal posts, off the stick of the offender, the penalty-bully is taken again. If the ball goes over the goal lines between the goal posts off the stick or person of the offender, a penalty goal is awarded the attackers. In all other cases as soon as the ball has passed wholly over the goal line (not between the goal posts) or outside the striking circle, the game is restarted with a bully on the center of the nearer twenty-five yard line. A breach of any rule of the penalty-bully by the offender gives the attacking team a penalty goal. A breach of the rule by the attacker selected for the bully gives the defending team a free-hit.

Scoring.—One point is scored each time the ball goes entirely through the opponent's goal off the stick of an attacker.

Length of Game.—The game consists of two thirty-minute halves. For secondary schools the length of the halves may be shortened to twenty-five, twenty, or fifteen minutes. Time out may not be taken except for accidents and then not to exceed five minutes.

Officials.—The officials consist of two umpires, two scorers, and two timekeepers. Each umpire has charge of half of the field.

Ice Hockey

Ice Skating Rink   *Senior High School to College*

Ice Hockey is a game played on skates on the ice and is a very popular winter sport in the northern states and Canada. In many respects the game follows closely the plan of Field Hockey.

Rink.—The field is similar to that used in Field Hockey, but is smaller, and is called a rink. This rink should measure not less than 160 feet long by 60 feet wide, but for the best results should be 200 feet by 85 feet. It should be surrounded by a board fence three-and-one-half to four feet high, called the banking board, although the game may be played on an open space. The purpose of the bank is to allow a rebound of the "puck." This rebound from the side is an important element in the game.

A goal is placed at each end of the rink at least ten feet and not more than fifteen feet out from the end, and is either a stationary or movable cage made of wire or net; it is four feet high and six feet wide.

A zone line is drawn sixty feet from each end line and parallel to it.

The center area is known as the center zone, and the end areas as end zones.

The layout of the rink is shown in Figure 75. The squares in front of the goals indicate the spots at which face-offs take place.

Equipment.—An official ice-hockey puck is used. It is a vulcanized black rubber disk, one inch thick and three inches in diameter.

Each player is equipped with an official ice-hockey stick.

The players wear shin guards to prevent injuries from the puck, and heavy gloves to protect their hands from blows from an opponent's stick when they are checked by an opponent.

The goaltender is padded with a stomach protector and guards which reach from the ankles to the hips.

Players.—A team is composed of six players and is made up of three forwards (a center and two wing players), two defense men, and a goal-tender.

Object of the Game.—The object is to advance the puck into the op-ponents' territory and shoot it into the opponents' goal, and at the same time to prevent the opponents from scoring.

Start.—The game is started by a play called "facing off." The players of the two teams line up as shown in Figure 75, and the referee blows his whistle and throws the puck on the ice between the sticks of the two opposing center players, who try to get possession of it. These two players, as they face the puck, must have their right sides toward their own end of the rink, and must have their sticks resting on the ice at least twelve inches apart.

The Play.—The puck is generally advanced by the player pushing it along the ice with his stick; this is called "carrying the puck." Dodging, encircling, or caroming the puck off the board are all legal methods of passing an opposing player.

All players on the team are eligible to score goals, but the greater amount of the scoring is done by the forwards, even though the defense men often rush the puck down the ice and score. In shooting for the goal, the best way to deliver the puck is a quick draw stroke accompanied by a turning of the blade of the stick so as to raise the puck off the ice and send it with a whirling motion which is difficult to stop.

Zone Play.—A player may pass the puck to any team mate in the same zone as the player at the time the puck left his stick, irrespective of their relative positions in the zone, and he may pass to any player in another zone nearer his own end of the rink.

He may pass or carry the puck from his own end zone into the center zone and any team mate who was in the same zone (end zone) at the time the puck crossed the zone line may play the puck in the center zone. If the team mate was in the center zone, he may not play it.

A player may pass or carry the puck from the center zone into the opponents' end zone provided no team mate is in the opponents' end zone.

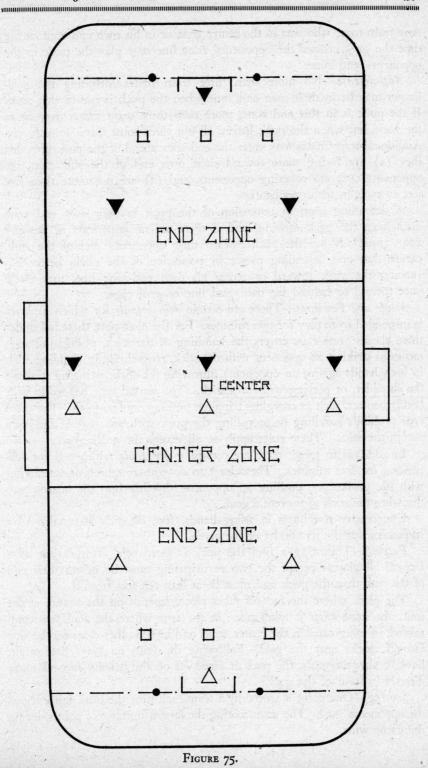

FIGURE 75.

Any team mate who was in the center zone or in his own end zone at the time the puck crossed the opponents' zone line *may* play the puck in the opponents' end zone.

Anti-defense.—No more than three team mates including the goal-keeper may be in their own end zone when the puck is not in that zone. If the puck is in this end zone, more than three team mates may be in the zone, but when the puck leaves, all but three must leave immediately. Additional team mates may enter the end zone ahead of the puck provided they (1) are facing more toward their own end of the rink than the opponents,' (2) are covering opponents, and (3) are not more than five feet away from such opponents.

A defending team in possession of the puck in their own end zone must keep the puck moving, and if there are no opponents in the end zone, must advance the puck toward their opponents' end of the rink, except that one defending player in possession of the puck, before advancing the puck toward or across his own end-zone line, may circle once toward or behind his own goal line or goal cage.

Fouls and Penalties.—There are certain *minor fouls* for which a player is suspended from play for two minutes. For the most part, these fall under three classes: one class covers the handling of the stick, prohibiting such tactics as striking an opponent with the stick, cross-checking (holding stick in both hands against an opponent), throwing the stick, swinging it above the shoulder, or playing without a stick. The second type has to do with bodily contact, such as charging, tripping, pushing, and so forth. The third type prohibits handling or propelling the puck with any part of the body except the stick. These rules apply to all except the goalkeeper.

In addition to these, there are certain *major fouls* which call for suspension for five minutes. These have to do with roughing or interfering with the goalkeeper, pushing an opponent violently into the boards, and throwing the stick to prevent a goal.

Unnecessary roughness in using hands, feet, or stick is penalized by suspension for the remainder of the game.

Face-off.—Following a foul the puck is faced off. At the time of a face-off all players except the two participating must be nearer their end of the rink than the puck and must be at least ten feet from it.

The place where the face-off takes place depends on the nature of the foul. In some cases it takes place at the spot where the foul was committed, in other cases in the center zone, and in still other cases on the side face-off marks near the goal. Following the fouls on plays that might have resulted in goals, the puck is faced off on the penalty face-off mark directly in front of the goal.

Scoring.—One point is scored by a team each time the puck fairly enters the opponents' goal. The team scoring the largest number of points during the game wins.

Substitutions.—Substitutions may be made at any time when play has been officially stopped. Suspended players may re-enter the game immediately after the expiration of their penalty.

Length of Game.—The game consists of three periods of twenty minutes with intermissions of ten minutes. If the score is a tie at the end of the third period, there is a ten-minute intermission and an overtime period of ten minutes. If the score is still tied, there is a five-minute rest and a second overtime period of ten minutes. No more than two overtime periods may be played.

Officials.—The main official is the referee who is assisted by an assistant referee. There are also two goal umpires who stand behind the goals and decide whether the puck has gone into the goals, a penalty timekeeper who keeps time for players temporarily suspended from the game by the referee, and a timekeeper and assistant timekeeper who keep the actual playing time of the game.

Lacrosse—Boys

Playground   *Senior High School to Adults*

Lacrosse differs from Hockey in the form of the club and in the way that it is used; in Lacrosse the club is something like an elongated and loosely strung tennis racket which is used with both hands. The manner of play is to catch the ball in the crosse and then to run with it or to throw it. Much skill is necessary to pick up the ball, catch it, and throw it with this implement, while the running makes it as vigorous work as any game.

Field.—The field is 120 yards long and from 70 to 85 yards wide. A center line is drawn across the middle parallel to the end lines. A circle with a ten-foot radius is drawn in the center of the field. A barrier fence around the entire field is advisable to retain the ball; it should be ten feet from the boundary line and at least five feet high.

The goals are placed midway between the side lines, eighty yards apart, with twenty yards of playing space behind them. The goals consist of two poles six feet high and six feet apart, with a rigid top crossbar, to which the net is attached. The net is of cord and is pyramid-shaped, the point being staked to the ground seven feet back from the center of the goal. An area known as the goal crease is marked out around the goal. It is eighteen by twelve feet, and the goal is placed six feet from the front and back lines, and six feet from the side lines (See Figure 76).

Equipment.—The ball is of India-rubber sponge, from seven-and-three-fourths to eight inches in circumference, and from four-and-one-half to five ounces in weight. Summer camps frequently prefer the primitive American Indian equipment for informal play and whittle the ball from white cedar or other soft wood.

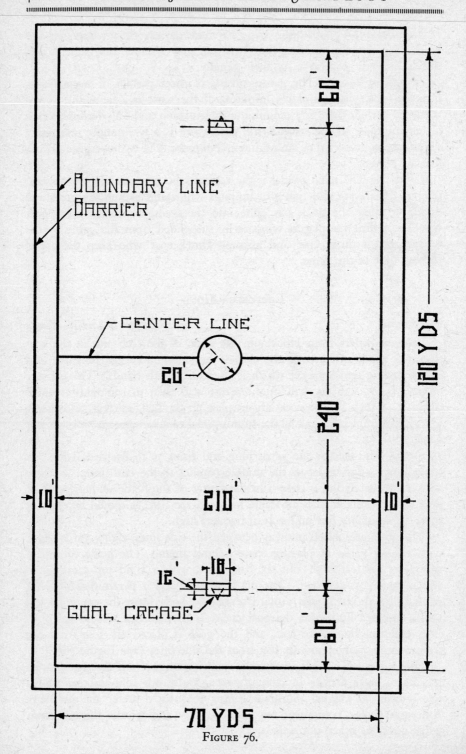

BOUNDARY LINE
BARRIER

CENTER LINE

20'

240'

210'

10'   10'

12' 18'

GOAL, CREASE

60'

60'

120 YDS

70 YDS

FIGURE 76.

The crosses may be of any length to suit the player but may not be more than a foot in width.

Teams.—Ten players constitute a team. They are designated as follows: goalkeeper, point, cover point, first and second defense, center, second and first attack, outside home, and inside home (see Figure 77).

Object of the Game.—The object is to carry or throw the ball with the crosse into the opponents' territory and cause it to enter the opponents' goal, and at the same time to prevent the opponents from scoring.

Start.—The captains toss for goals before the game. Play begins in the center of the field at the start of each quarter by a play that corresponds to the bully in hockey and to the toss-up in basketball, and which is called "facing." The two centers stand in the center circle, each having his left side toward the goal he is attacking, with their crosses touching the ground and parallel to the goal line. The ball is placed between and touching the reverse surfaces of the crosses, and resting, not on the ground, but on the reverse surfaces of the crosses. At the signal each is free to try for the possession of the ball by picking it up or driving it to a player of his own side.

The Play.—The ball is thrown from one to another by means of the crosse, and finally thrown through the goal. Running with the ball is permitted, but is not usually good play, since the ball can be passed much more rapidly than one can run.

A player on defense may stand in the way of a man running, strike an opponent's crosse with his own, or catch the ball in his crosse when it leaves that of an opponent. Each player should cover his opponent closely when any opponent has the ball, so as to prevent a good pass; he should get away from him as fast as possible when his own side gets the ball; in this respect the game is much like Basketball.

Body-check.—A player with the ball in his possession or within reach of it, may be stopped by a body-check, that is, his opponent may stop him with his body, provided the check is not made from behind, and provided the player making the check keeps both feet on the ground and does not strike his opponent below the knees. Hitting the opponent with the crosse in checking is a foul.

Entering Crease.—No member of the attacking team is permitted to enter the crease or interfere with the goalkeeper inside the crease. Doing so is a foul and a goal if scored on the play does not count.

Off-Side.—At no time shall a team have less than two men on the attack between the center line and the opponents' goal, and at no time shall a team have less than two men, not counting the goalkeeper, on the defense between the center line and the boundary behind its own goal. Violation of this rule is known as off-side play.

Out of Bounds.—When the ball goes out of bounds, the referee has the option of facing it ten feet in from where it went out, or allowing the

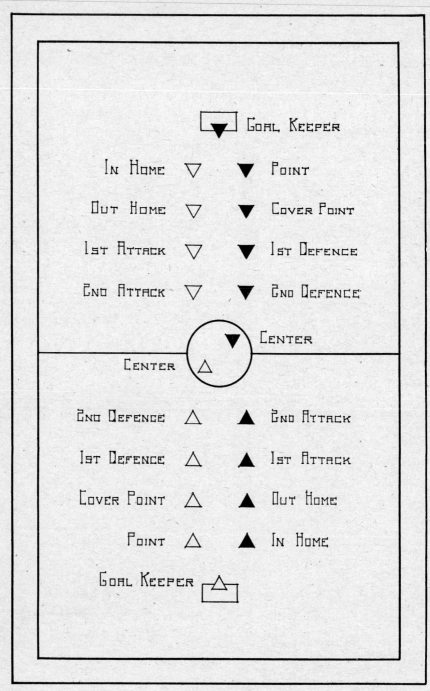

FIGURE 77.

nearest player to put it in play by a throw or run from where it went out of bounds.

Free-Throw.—A free-throw is awarded a team when it is fouled. The player fouling and the one fouled are placed at the same location they occupied immediately previous to the foul, the player fouled having the ball in his crosse. At the signal, each is allowed to play in any manner allowed by the rules of the game. A free-throw may never be made within twenty yards of the opponents' goal.

Fouls and Penalties.—There are certain fouls known as *Class A technical fouls* which are penalized by either a free-throw or suspension from the game for one minute. These have to do with such points as improper handling of the ball such as touching it with the hands, lying on it, or causing it to go out of bounds; playing without a crosse or throwing the crosse; and changing position during a time-out period.

There are other technical fouls calling for suspension for a period of one to five minutes. These are of three types: The first has to do with unnecessarily rough tactics, such as shouldering, clipping, tripping, body-checking, or forcing an opponent into the fence. The second type has to do with interfering with an opponent's play, such as holding his crosse, striking his crosse, holding him with the crosse, and running or falling in front of him to keep him from the ball. The third type deals with entering the goal crease or interfering with the goalkeeper.

A personal foul calls for suspension for the remainder of the game. Such fouls are called for deliberately striking an opponent, and for cross-checking (charging into an opponent with both hands on the crosse so that the crosse strikes him).

Substitutions.—Substitutions may be made only when play has been stopped for some other reason. A player taken from the game may return but not in the same period. When a player has been suspended for a personal foul, a substitute may be sent in for him after a period of ten minutes.

Scoring.—One point is scored each time the ball is put through the goal from the front side.

Length of Game.—The game consists of four quarters of fifteen minutes each, with a one-minute intermission after the first and third quarters, and ten minutes between the halves. Shorter periods may be agreed upon.

In the case of a tie, an overtime period of ten minutes is played after a five-minute rest. If the score is still a tie, the game is declared a tie.

Time-out may be taken for a player only in case of injury, and then not longer than two minutes.

Officials.—The officials consist of a referee, a judge of play, two umpires, and two timekeepers.

Lacrosse for Girls.—Lacrosse for girls is essentially the same as the boys' game, with certain minor restrictions and variations. Twelve players instead of ten constitute a team. In the girls' game the players have the liberty to propel the ball with the foot or leg. There are certain restrictions on bodily contact that do not apply to the boys' game. The use of arms or the crosse on an opponent's body is prohibited and the only method of detaining an opponent is body-checking. This refers to placing the body in the way of an opponent so that the opponent is merely impeded.

Box Lacrosse

Playground, Gymnasium   *Senior High School to Adults*

Box Lacrosse is similar to Lacrosse but is designed for indoor play or play on a smaller field outdoors.

Area.—When played indoors the area should be at least 60 by 160 feet. For outdoor use, the area should not be larger than 90 by 200 feet, nor smaller than 60 by 160 feet.

Each goal consists of two poles four-and-one-half feet apart and four-and-one-half feet high, joined by a rigid top piece. To these poles is attached a cone-shaped netting attached to a stake six feet back of the center of the goal. The goals are placed so that the point of the cone-shaped netting rests on the end of the rink, midway between the side lines.

The goal crease consists of a semi-circle, having a radius of nine feet from the center of a line drawn between the two goal posts. It is marked by a line two inches wide.

Equipment.—The sticks must not be more than forty-six nor less than forty-two inches in length, except for the stick used by the goalkeeper which may be of any length.

Teams.—Teams consist of seven players—goalkeeper, right defense, left defense, rover, center, right forward, and left forward.

Length of Game.—The game consists of three periods of twenty minutes each, with a ten-minute rest between periods.

Rules.—The rules follow those of Lacrosse with the following exceptions:

1. In no case may the ball be faced closer than fifteen feet from the goal crease or ten feet from the boundary line.

2. No player of the defending side may throw the ball back to the goalkeeper when in possession of the ball in front of the goal.

3. A free-throw is given to the opponents if, in the opinion of the referee, a player deliberately throws the ball out of bounds.

4. A minor penalty is two minutes, a major penalty five minutes, and a match penalty the remainder of the game except that after fifteen minutes a substitute may be used if the referee so specifies at the time of the penalty.

5. Players may be substituted at any time provided the retiring player reaches the players' bench before the change is made.

Polo

Polo is played on horseback and consequently is limited to those fortunate enough to possess several specially trained mounts.

Field.—The field is 900 feet long and 450 feet wide. The side lines are boarded to a height of eleven inches to keep the ball within bounds.

The goals are placed on the end lines midway between the side lines. The posts are placed twenty-four feet apart, are ten feet high, and made of wicker light enough so that they will break in case of a collision.

Equipment.—The ball is of light wood, usually willow, with no covering but white paint. It is three-and-one-fourth inches in diameter and weighs five-and-one-half ounces.

The mallets have cane shafts and heads of ash, set at an angle. The length varies from forty-eight to fifty-two inches.

Four ponies are usually required for each player in a game, each pony being played one or two periods.

Teams.—Four players constitute a team. The Number 1 and Number 2 players are primarily offensive players and advance the ball to the goal. Number 3 is a roving player, ready to pass the ball to the forwards, attack the goal himself, or drop back to aid in the defense. Number 4 is the back player and usually stays in the vicinity of his own goal.

Length of Game.—The game is played in eight chukkers (periods) of seven-and-one-half minutes each, with intermissions of two-and-one-half minutes. Between the fourth and fifth chukkers there is an intermission of five minutes.

At the end of a period, the timekeeper signals the end but play continues until the ball goes out of bounds, or a goal is made, or some point reached where play can be stopped without advantage to either side.

Start.—The four players of each team line up in the middle of the field, facing the side boards. The referee rides toward them, throws the ball between them, and the play is on. Play is resumed in the same way after each goal, with the teams changing goals.

The Play.—The players strike the ball with the side of the mallet attempting to drive it toward the opponents' goal and through the goal posts.

Fouls and Penalties.—The player who last hit the ball continues on its line of travel and has the right of way over a player approaching at an angle. It is a foul if the latter crosses in front of the first player or close enough to cause him to swerve or check. The penalty is a free-hit from where the foul occurred, or from the thirty, forty, or sixty-yard line, depending on the degree of danger involved and its effect upon a possible goal. In extreme cases, a goal may be awarded the offended side.

Other fouls are zigzagging in front of an approaching player, stopping on the ball, hooking with the mallet unless the ball is between two players, and dangerous riding.

Out-of-bounds.—When an attacking player drives the ball over the end line outside the goal posts, a defending player puts it in play by a free-hit from the point where it went out; in no case, however, may the hit be made closer than twelve feet from a goal post.

Should a defensive player, in an effort to prevent a goal, cause the ball to go over his own end line, a safety is called and the attacking side is given a free-hit from the sixty-yard line, the ball being placed on this line opposite the point where it went out.

Scoring.—A goal is made when the ball passes over the goal line between the goal posts. If the ball goes higher than the goal posts but between imaginary extensions of them, it is a goal. The goalkeeper waves a flag overhead when a goal is made, and waves the flag parallel with the ground when the ball goes over the end line.

MINOR GAMES OF THE HOCKEY TYPE

Hockey Keep-Ball

Playground   *Junior High School to College*

This is a hockey adaptation of Keep-Ball. Divide the players into two teams and mark the teams so that they can be easily distinguished. Each player has a hockey stick. Limit the area to prevent too much running.

The game starts by a bully in the center and thereafter each team attempts to secure the ball and pass it to its own members, preventing the other team from getting it.

Hockey Ten-Passes

Playground   *Junior High School to College*

This is a hockey adaptation of Ten-Catches and is similar to Hockey Keep-Ball. Divide the players into two teams and mark each team. Each player has a hockey stick.

The game starts with a center bully and thereafter each team attempts to secure and keep possession of the ball by passing it to team mates. The first player who gets it passes it to another and this player calls "One"; she then passes it to a third who calls "Two," and so on, attempting to run up ten consecutive passes. The other team attempts to break up the run of passes by getting possession of the ball and then passing amongst themselves for a run of ten. The team wins who first completes ten consecutive passes.

Variation.—Same as the above except that the team wins who has made the most consecutive passes when the period ends.

Hockey Snatch-Ball

Playground, Gymnasium, Club   Late Elementary to Senior High School

Divide the players into two teams and line them up forty feet apart, facing each other. Number the players of each team so that the two opponents holding the same number stand diagonally opposite each other as in Snatch-Ball (see Figure 35). Midway between the two teams place a hockey ball. Lay two field-hockey sticks on the floor, one on each side of the ball.

The leader calls a number and the two opponents holding the number run forward; each picks up a stick and, watching his chance, attempts to secure the ball and dribble it back to his position in his line. He does not score unless the ball goes through the position in the line where he is supposed to stand. When one player has secured the ball, the other may attempt to take it away from him or prevent him from returning it successfully.

The player scores one point for his team each time he returns with the ball in this way. The leader should call the numbers at random.

Variation.—Instead of returning to his own position with the ball, each player attempts to drive it through the opposing team.

Champion Hockey Snatch-Ball.—Same as the above except that all of the players except one are stationed on one line with the odd player stationed at the other line. The odd player is called the champion. He challenges a player from the line and the two run out and proceed as above. The champion exchanges places with the player if he loses.

Shinney

Playground, Yard   Elementary and Junior High Schools

Shinney is an old favorite of boys for informal play. It is essentially the same as Field Hockey, but of low organization. A field of any convenient size may be used with the side lines and end lines designated. The game may be played with a hard rubber ball or any ball not larger than a baseball; it is commonly played by boys with a tin can or block of wood. Regular hockey sticks are ideal, but boys usually make their own from a crooked stick.

The game is started by placing the ball in the center of the field between two opposing players as in Field Hockey. After the ball is in play, it is knocked down the field toward the opponents' goal. There are no off-side rules as in Hockey. It is an unwritten rule of the traditional boys' game which is played without officials, that one must "shinney on his own side," that is, one must be facing the goal toward which he is advancing the ball when he attempts to play the ball. Otherwise the offending player may be cracked on the shins by his opponent's stick.

One point is scored each time the ball crosses the opponent's goal line.

Roller Shinney.—Roller Shinney is played on roller skates and otherwise conforms to the above rules. It is a popular game of the city streets.

Ice Shinney.—See Ice Shinney in Chapter XXVII, "Winter Activities."

Charley-Horse Polo.—This is a game of low organization much loved by boys who are familiar with Shinney. It is played indoors on a basketball court and follows all the rules of shinney except that a softball or a tennis ball is used. Junior-sized hockey sticks or roller-polo sticks are used. The ends of the sticks may be wrapped with leather or string to protect the floor.

Shinney Hockey

Playground, Gymnasium   *Late Elementary to Senior High School*

This game standardizes the ever-popular game of Shinney and combines it with some of the features of Hockey.

Field.—The game may be played indoors or out. The court is 100 feet long and 50 to 75 feet wide. A basketball court may be used. Mark a section of each end line five feet long, midway between the side lines, for the goals—this is done by marking two lines five feet apart, each two feet long and at right angles to the end line.

Equipment.—Shinney sticks or light-weight field-hockey sticks and an ice-hockey puck are used. For informal play a wooden puck may be substituted.

Teams.—Five to ten players may play on a team. Seven is recommended.

The Start.—The puck is placed in mid-field. Two players, one from each team, face each other with the puck between them; all other players of their teams are behind them. They place their sticks on the ground a foot in back of the puck, raise and touch the sticks over the puck three times and then attempt to hit the puck toward their goal or to a team mate.

Object.—The object is to hit or pass the puck over the five-foot goal line and to prevent the opponents from scoring.

Fouls.—The following are fouls:

1. Failure to "shinney on your own side" as in Shinney. This means that one is not permitted to hit the puck when facing in the opposite direction from the goal over which his team is attempting to put the puck.

2. Hitting or tripping an opponent with the stick or shoving an opponent.

3. Raising or swinging the stick above the level of the hips.

4. Handling the puck with the hands, or stopping it or playing it with the feet.

Penalties.—A player on the side fouled takes the puck out of bounds at the point nearest to the spot where the foul was committed and tosses it in to a team mate. The toss may not go over five feet and no opposing player may be nearer than five feet.

Scoring.—One point is scored each time the puck legally crosses the goal line.

Length of Game.—Two methods are followed, depending on the preference of the teams: (1) the team scoring ten points first wins; (2) four five-minute quarters, with two minutes' rest between the first two and the last two, and five minutes·between the halves.

Wheelbarrow Polo

Picnics, Playground   *Junior High School to Adults*

This is a novelty feature suitable at a picnic or field day. There are eight players on each team and each team has four wheelbarrows. Four of the players ride and the other four wheel the wheelbarrows. Each rider has a house broom, or better still, a toy broom. An inflated ball such as a soccer ball or sport ball is used. The field is about sixty by eighty feet.

The two teams line up their wheelbarrows opposite each other in the center and about ten feet apart, facing the side lines. The referee rolls the ball between them and sounds his whistle; the teams turn and the game is on. The object is to hit the ball over the opposing goal.

The pusher and rider may exchange places at any time, but only the rider may play the ball and may touch it only when in the wheelbarrow.

Kiddy-Kar Polo.—Same as the above except that six players compose a team and each rides a kiddy kar and plays the ball with a toy broom.

Floor Hockey [1]

Gymnasium   *Late Elementary to Senior High School*

Floor Hockey is an indoor game designed to teach the fundamental skills of Ice Hockey without the use of ice. It is in reality a standardization of the ever-popular boys' game of Shinney.

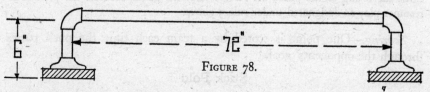

FIGURE 78.

Floor.—The full floor of the average-sized school gymnasium is used.
Goals.—The goals are frameworks made of one-inch galvanized pipe,

[1] Contributed by C. F. Gucker and G. F. Loebs, Lincoln School, Teachers' College, Columbia University.

illustrated in Figure 78. They are seventy-two inches long and six inches high, inside dimensions. The pipe is attached to a six-inch base of wood at each end. The goals can be constructed by any plumber.

Equipment.—A regulation ice-hockey puck may be used but a floor hockey practice puck is much to be preferred. It has a hole in the center and as a result is lighter and has greater resiliency.

A lighter stick than the ice-hockey stick is needed. For elementary-school players the roller-polo stick is recommended, and for upper-school players, the junior-sized hockey sticks.

Teams.—The teams are composed of six players: goalkeeper (located in front of goal), right and left guards (occupying the middle line), and center, right and left forwards (occupying the front line).

The Start.—The game is started by dropping the puck in the center of the floor between the sticks of the opposing center forwards. If preferred, either of the following methods of putting the puck in play may be used instead: (1) bullying off as in Field Hockey, (2) placing the puck on the floor with the sticks of the two opposing players firmly against it.

The Play.—The play follows the general plan of Ice Hockey. The rules should be kept as simple as possible. The following points should be noted:

1. The puck may be stopped by any part of the body, but may not be carried, held, knocked on, or kicked. The goalkeeper may kick the puck away from his goal as a defensive move.

2. No player shall raise his stick above his hips or throw it along the floor. Charging, tripping, kicking, or pushing an opponent shall not be allowed, and a player shall be ruled off the floor for such tactics.

3. No player may lie, sit, or kneel on the floor in front of his goal, nor place the full length of his stick on the floor in front of his goal.

4. For infringement of the above rules, a player shall be dropped from the game for a period of one, two, or more minutes, no substitute being allowed to take his place.

5. If the game is stopped by the referee except at the end of a period, the play shall be resumed by dropping the puck between the sticks of two opposing players at the point where it was last played.

6. In gymnasiums where obstructions such as apparatus and stall bars may cause the losing of the puck, the referee stops the game, recovers the puck, and resumes play as designated under rule 5 above.

Scoring.—One point is scored by a team each time the puck passes through the opponents' goal.

Stick Polo

Playground, Gymnasium   *Junior and Senior High Schools*

The field is the full size of the average gymnasium, or if outdoors, a rectangle about fifty feet wide and eighty feet long. Each player is provided with a stick about three feet long. Divide the players into two teams of equal size and place them on the end lines facing each other. A soccer ball is placed on the floor in the middle of the field.

At the starting signal both teams rush for the ball and attempt to knock it over the opposing goal line using the sticks only. Kicking the ball or playing it with any part of the body is prohibited. The penalty for breaking this rule is a free-hit for the opponents with opposing players at least ten feet away. When the ball goes out of bounds the referee rolls it in at the point where it went out. One point is scored each time the ball goes over the opponents' goal line. Set a time limit for the game.

Broom Hockey [2]

Playground, Gymnasium   *Late Elementary to Senior High School*

Field.—The game is played on a rectangular field, either in the gymnasium or outdoors. A basketball court may be used. A foul line is drawn ten feet from each goal line and parallel to it.

The goal is placed on each end line, midway from the side lines. The goals consist of two uprights six feet apart and connected by a crossbar three feet from the floor. Volleyball uprights and a rope for the crossbar may be used.

Equipment.—Each player carries an ordinary house broom thirty-one inches long.

A rubber inflated ball (sport ball) five inches in diameter is used. Although it is an inch over size, the six-inch codeball may be used.

Teams.—The teams consist of five players—center, right forward, left forward, guard, and goal guard. At the beginning of play the center stands at the center of the field. The two forwards stand between the center and the goal for which they are striving. The goal guard stands directly in front of the goal he is defending with the other guard some distance in front of him.

The Start.—The ball is placed in the center of the playing field. The two opposing centers stand beside it with their brooms touching the floor either side of it. At the signal they are free to strike the ball. At the beginning of each period, after each goal and after each free trial for goal, the ball is put in play in the same way.

Object.—The object is to knock the ball with the brooms through the opponent's goal.

The Play.—The ball is maneuvered about the field with the brooms. It may be played only with the broom, and all use of the body to stop or advance the ball is prohibited except on the part of the goal guard as described below.

[2] These rules follow in general those laid down in National Recreation Association, *Broom Ball League Rules* (mimeographed). By permission of the National Recreation Association.

Out of Bounds.—When the ball is knocked out of bounds, it is brought by the referee to the center of the field opposite the point where it went out and is put in play by two opposing players as at the start of the game.

Goal Guard.—The goal guard is allowed to block the ball with any part of his body, but is not allowed to catch it, hold it, kick it, or hit it with the hands. He may propel it only with his broom. He may not leave his feet except by accident. Breach of these rules is called "Unqualified action of the goal guard."

The goal guard's position is in front of the goal and, if he leaves it, he does so at his own risk. If he leaves his post entirely, he is governed by the rules applying to other players.

Fouls.—The following are fouls:

1. Holding.
2. Deliberately knocking the ball out of bounds.
3. Intentionally blocking the ball with the body (except goal guard).
4. Delaying the game.
5. Holding the ball with the hands or between the legs.
6. Unqualified action of the goal guard (as described above).
7. Unnecessary roughness.
8. Deliberately striking an opponent.

Penalties.—For any one of the first six of the above fouls, a free try for goal is awarded the team against whom the foul was committed.

For committing foul Number 7, the offender is suspended from the game for one minute and his team must play without his services or those of a substitute.

For committing foul Number 8, or for committing foul Number 7 three times, the player is suspended for the remainder of the game and a substitute sent in his place.

Free Trial for Goal.—The ball is placed in the center of the foul line (ten feet from the goal line) and a player of the team against whom the foul was committed has one attempt to hit the ball through the goal. The opposing goal guard only is permitted to attempt to stop it and he must have both heels on the floor at the time of stopping it.

After an attempt at a free trial for goal, play is resumed as at the start of the game.

Scoring.—One point is scored each time the ball is put through the goal either from play or from a free trial for goal.

Length of Game.—The game consists of four five-minute periods with a one-minute rest after the first and third periods, and a three-minute intermission after the second period.

Officials.—The game is in charge of a referee and timekeeper.

Roller-Skate Hockey

Gymnasium, Tennis Court, Skating Rink   Junior and Senior High Schools

Rink.—The size of the rink is approximately sixty by ninety feet. The goals are five feet wide and four feet high and are placed six feet from the ends of the rink, halfway between the side lines. Volleyball uprights and a rope for the crossbar may be used.

Equipment.—All players are on roller skates. The hockey sticks must not be more than three-and-one-half inches thick at any part and must be entirely of wood with tape binding permissible. The puck is of vulcanized rubber, one-inch thick and three inches in diameter.

Teams.—Six players constitute a team.

The Start.—At the start of a period and after a goal, play is started by a face at the center of the rink. In facing, the referee drops the puck between the sticks of two opponents; no player of either team may be ahead of the puck before it is dropped. Play is resumed after a cessation by a face at the point where play ceased.

Out of Bounds.—Where rinks are not equipped with side and end walls, the puck is out of play when it crosses the side or end lines. It is brought back to the rink and faced at a point ten feet in from the side line; or if it crossed the end line, on the goal line half-way between the goal and the side line.

Rules.—There is no off-side but loafing off-side is not allowed. Loafing off-side is interpreted as a player loafing near his opponents' goal when the puck is at the other end of the rink. Such players are warned once and then penalized.

The puck may not be held by the goalkeeper. He may catch it but must immediately drop it. The penalty is to face the puck ten feet in front of the goal with no other players allowed between the face and the goal.

The puck may be kicked at any time, but no goals may be scored in this manner.

Minor Fouls.—The penalty for the following fouls is suspension from the game for two minutes:

1. Catching or throwing the puck by a player other than the goalkeeper. (A foul is not called when a player uses his hands as a means of protection.)

2. Holding an opponent with the stick or the hands, tripping with stick or body, or charging into a player.

3. Loafing off-side after a warning.

4. Shooting the puck out of bounds.

5. Cross-checking (checking a player with both hands on the stick and no part of it on the floor).

6. A substitute coming on the playing area before the other player is completely off.

7. Carrying the stick above the shoulder.

8. Interfering with or impeding the progress of an opponent who does not have the puck. The last man to touch the puck is considered to be in possession of it.

Major Fouls.—The penalty for the following fouls is suspension for five minutes:

1. Tripping an opponent to prevent him from scoring
2. Charging an opponent from the rear.
3. Charging or cross-checking a goalkeeper.
4. Body-checking roughly near the fence.
5. Striking an opponent with the hand.

Match Fouls.—The penalty for any grossly unsportsmanlike conduct is expulsion from the game with a substitute allowed after five minutes.

Substitutions.—Substitutions may be made at any time but in case play has not been stopped, the player who is coming on must wait until the retiring player is completely off the rink.

At no time shall one team be compelled to play with fewer than four players. If a team which already has two players out on penalties has another penalty called, a substitute is permitted for the third offender, until one of the other penalized players is permitted to return.

Length of the Game.—A game consists of three periods of twenty minutes each. For boys fourteen or under, fifteen-minute periods are recommended. Time is taken out for every cessation of play.

In case of a tie, a five-minute overtime period is played but the game ends when the first goal is scored. If there is no score in the five minutes the game is declared a tie.

Scoring.—Each goal made scores one point. A goal is scored when the puck crosses the line between the goal uprights, provided it is not kicked or thrown.

Hand Hockey

Playground, Gymnasium *Junior and Senior High Schools*

Court.—The game is played on a basketball court or area of similar size and shape. The two end lines constitute the goals. The basketball free-throw lines are extended across the floor, forming end zones.

Ball.—A volleyball may be used but a sport ball of similar size makes a faster game.

Teams.—Teams consist of nine players—one center, five fielders, and three goalkeepers. The goalkeepers play in the end zones; the center ... yers are in the center circle at the start of the game and thereafter join ... fielders in circulating all over the floor.

... *ect of the Game.*—The object is to roll or push the ball into the opponents' territory and put it over their goal line, and at the same time to prevent the opposing team from scoring.

Start.—The ball is placed in the center circle and the two centers stand either side of it with their left side toward the opponents' goal. They place one hand on the ball. At the signal the centers try to roll or push the ball to their team mates.

The Play.—The players push or roll the ball toward the opponents' goal. The ball must be played with the hand, not kicked, and only one hand may be used. The hand must be kept open—the use of the fist is prohibited. Goalkeepers, however, may use both hands and may pick the ball up and throw it back on the floor away from the goal. They are not permitted to take more than one step with the ball or to hold it longer than three seconds.

Fouls.—The following are fouls:

1. Using two hands on the ball (except goalkeepers).
2. Kicking the ball or playing it with any part of the body except the hand or forearm.
3. Striking the ball with the closed fist.
4. Goalkeepers taking more than one step with the ball, or holding it longer than three seconds.
5. Goalkeepers stepping out of their end zone.

Penalties.—When a foul is committed a player of the opposing team is given a free bat at the ball from the spot on the floor where the foul occurred. The opposing players must be at least ten feet away.

If the foul is committed by a defending player inside his own end zone, a member of the attacking team is given a free-hit at the ball from the end zone line, with all members of the defending team behind their goal line, and all members of the attacking team behind the end zone line until the ball is struck.

Out of Bounds.—If the ball crosses the side lines of the court, it is rolled back in by a member of the team opposite the team that caused it to go out. The players may line up at right angles to the side line but may not be closer than three feet to the spot where the ball is rolled in.

Scoring.—One point is scored for a team each time the ball crosses the opponents' goal line.

Length of Game.—The game is played in two ten-minute halves.

Variation.—This is a more highly organized game of Hand Hockey. It is advanced by F. J. Moench and combines in an indoor game the fundamentals of Soccer, Basketball, Hockey, and Handball. The following is Mr. Moench's own statement of the regulations:[3]

From the New York State Physical Education Bulletin.

Size of Court.—Any ordinary basketball court. A good game for play-rooms, having four walls for use as in Handball. Height of ceiling is not essential as in Basketball.

The Ball.—A live, inflated rubber ball slightly smaller than a volley-ball is preferred for gymnasiums having out-of-bounds space. A smaller ball may be used where there are no boundary lines. Sport balls are recommended.

Number of Players.—Six to ten (seven recommended) constitute a team for junior high schools, depending on the size of the court.

Position of Players.—With seven players the positions are: center, side center, right and left attack, right and left defense, and goal guard. The goal guard is restricted to his own area; the others may move about the floor as long as three men, including the goal guard, are behind the center line. The play of the center is both offensive and defensive. The attack men are responsible for getting the ball into scoring position, playing the sides and ends of the court. The right and left defense men and the goal guard constitute the defensive unit of the team.

Goals and Markings.—The goals are uprights supporting a crossbar forming a cage five feet high and eight feet wide. A netting over the back is desirable. The goals should be placed ten or fifteen feet from the back walls, making play in back of the goals legal. In front of each goal is an area eight feet by three feet called the goal area. No one except the goal guard may enter the goal area without penalty. A free-throw line is placed ten feet in front of each goal. There is a center circle three feet in diameter. A center line divides the court in halves.

The Start.—The game is started by bouncing the ball between the two centers, who must stand outside the center circle. The ball must not be played until the rebound.

The Play.—The game is played by hitting the ball with one or both hands. It must not be caught by any player. The goal guard is the only one who may use the body to impede the progress of the ball. Each team tries to drive the ball into the opponents' goal. Dribbling and passing the ball by 'tting it with the hand makes up the attack. The number of drib'   nlimited.

e following rules should be noted:

ball out of bounds, an unobstructed pass, similar to a hand-
(Ball is dropped on the floor and batted into play with the

on the floor in a scrimmage, drop ball between two

l, the ball must be dropped to the floor at the foul
l batted at the goal; the guard defends the goal.

not involving a free try at goal (such as catching,
unobstructed free serve is allowed.

5. For a held ball, withhold from scrimmage and drop ball between two opponents.

Technical Fouls.—The following are technical fouls:

1. Opponents entering the goal area. *Penalty:* a free unobstructed serve by the goal guard from within the goal area.

2. Defensive man entering goal area. *Penalty:* a free try for the goal by the opponents, with protection by the goal guard; other players restricted to area outside free-try area. An honest attempt must be made to score the goal. The ball is in play if the goal is missed.

3. Off-side (when there are not three men back of the center line). *Penalty:* a free serve for the opponents from any point on the center line.

Personal Fouls.—The following are personal fouls:

1. Holding, pushing, charging, blocking out, or any unnecessary roughness. *Penalty:* (a) if committed by an opponent in his defensive half of the floor, a free try for goal shall be awarded; (b) if committed by an opponent not in his defensive half of the floor, a free pass from the spot where the foul is committed.

Scoring.—A point is scored for each goal made.

Length of Game.—The game is played in two halves or four quarters. For junior high schools, six-minute quarters are recommended; for senior high schools, eight-minute quarters.

Substitutions.—A substitution may be made at any time when the ball is declared dead. A penalty of a free try at goal shall be awarded if the player relieved fails to leave the floor immediately. The number of substitutions is unlimited.

Konano [4]

Playground, Gymnasium　　　　　*Junior High School to Adults—Girls*

Konano is a game somewhat similar to Lacrosse which has been adapted for girls from the Mesquaki tribe of Indians by Mrs. Theresa Anderson and Mr. L. E. Hutto. It was played by the Indian women whereas Lacrosse was played by the men.

Field.—A flat area thirty to forty yards wide and forty to eighty yards long is used. The recommended dimensions for girls are thirty by fifty yards. The goals are six feet wide and seven feet high, made of light wood strips. No side lines or end lines are needed, but a line is marked across the field half way between the goals. A goal area is marked at each goal, consisting of a semicircle with a twelve-foot radius, measured from a point meeting between the goal posts.

[4] These rules follow those given in American Physical Education Association, *The Athletic Handbook* (*Athletic Activities for Women and Girls*), p. 43. Copyright, 1934. By permission of American Sports Publishing Co., publishers.

Equipment.—Each player needs a stick about three-fourths of an inch thick, and forty-two inches long—ordinary wands serve the purpose.

The "konano" consists of two balls joined by a thong or strip of canvas. It can easily be made from canvas: Make two round sacks of canvas, pack them tightly with sawdust, and sew shut, thus forming a ball. These balls should be five inches in diameter. They are joined together by a flat strip of canvas one-and-one-half inches wide, and ten to twelve inches long. The entire konano is about twenty inches long.

Teams.—Ten or less players may constitute a team. With ten players, five are forwards, four are backs, and one is goal guard. The forwards and backs are not permitted to leave their half of the field during play, and the goal guard should remain near the goal.

Start.—The watcher (referee) tosses the konano high in the air between two opposing forwards, standing at center line. The two forwards attempt to secure the konano on their sticks or knock it back to a team mate. All players must be "on side" at the toss, and may not come within arm-and-stick reach of the two players at center until the konano has been touched. As soon as the konano is put in play, the forwards cross into their half of the field.

The Play.—The object is to catch the konano on the stick and throw or carry it through the goal. The players pass the konano back and forth and carry it on the stick until in position to throw for or run through the goal. If the goal is missed and the konano goes behind it, play continues as usual.

No one but the goal guard is allowed in the goal zone, except in the case of an attacking forward who has possession of the konano and gained possession of it before entering the zone.

Fouls.—The following are fouls:

1. Striking or slapping with the stick, or starting a stick movement from above the shoulders. (In carrying the konano or following through a swing, the stick may go above the shoulders.)
2. Carrying or directly hitting the konano with the hand. (If the konano slips down the stick and touches the hand, no foul is called provided it is moved out at once.
3. Forwards or backs crossing the center line from their respective territories.
4. Entering the goal zone in violation of the rule described above.

Penalties.—The penalty for a foul is a free-throw from the spot where the foul occurred, unless the foul occurred near the goal. In this case, the goal guard has the option of having the throw take place from the spot where it occurred or from a spot fifteen feet directly in front of the goal; no one may be between the thrower and the goal except the goal guard, who may stand just in front of the goal. In case of simultaneous fouls by opposing players, a toss-up follows.

Scoring.—One point is scored each time the konano passes through the goal from the front or field side.

Length of Game.—For high-school girls the game consists of four periods, five or six minutes long, with a one-minute intermission between quarters. For adults the periods may be lengthened, but should never be longer than eight minutes.

Mass Field Hockey

Playground   *Senior High School to College*

This game accommodates a large number of players, and is played in ten-minute periods. One or two periods may constitute a game. The play follows the rules of Field Hockey with the following exceptions: (1) players are eliminated for the committing of fouls; (2) after a foul the ball is put in play by a bully-off at the spot where the foul occurred between two opposing players; (3) there are no boundary lines and consequently there are no out-of-bounds plays; (4) the off-side rule is disregarded.

GAMES OF THE HOCKEY TYPE IN OTHER CHAPTERS

Ice Shinney.   Ice-Hockey Ten-Passes.
Ice-Hockey Keep-Ball.   Mounted Broom Polo.

GAMES OF THE HOCKEY TYPE IN *SOCIAL GAMES FOR RECREATION*

Box Hockey.   Parlor Polo.

HOCKEY LEAD-UP CONTESTS

Many of the minor games of the hockey type described in this chapter may be used as lead-up games in training for the major sport. The following contests, described in the chapters on contests, will be found useful in this connection also.

Hockey Drive for Accuracy.   Hockey-Driving Shuttle Relay.
Hit the Can.   Hockey Circle-Driving Relay.
Hockey Goal Golf.   Hockey-Dribbling Relay.
Hockey Golf.   Hockey-Dribbling Shuttle Relay.
Hockey Drive for Distance.   Hockey Circle-the-Post Relay.
Hockey-Dribbling Race.   Zigzag Hockey-Dribbling Relay.
Obstacle Hockey-Dribbling Race.   Obstacle Hockey Shuttle Relay.
Hockey-Dribbling Circle Race.   Circle Hockey-Dribbling Relay.
Zigzag Hockey-Driving Relay.   Polo Drive for Distance.

CHAPTER XXV

GAMES OF THE BASKETBALL TYPE

AS in all of the team games, we have here several games related to and often played as a preparation for the major game of the group. This makes it advisable to describe briefly the essential features of the major game first. For details of Basketball, the standard rule books can be consulted.

Basketball for Men

Playground, Gymnasium   *Junior High School to Adults*

Basketball is America's most popular indoor game. It was invented in 1892 by Dr. James Naismith, then a student at Springfield Y.M.C.A. College and since that time a director of physical education. His object was to secure an indoor game that would have the advantage of the various types of Football, with the dangers of Football eliminated as far as possible. The plan hit upon was to prohibit a player from carrying the ball, which in turn eliminated the necessity for tackling and interference. Instead, the ball is advanced by passing, or by dribbling, the latter name being applied when a player bounces the ball against the floor or tosses it in the air, but retains possession of it. This gives the game some of the qualities of Association Football and English Rugby, but perhaps it resembles Lacrosse most of all.

The maximum size of the court is ninety-four feet long and fifty feet wide, and the minimum size sixty feet long and thirty-five feet wide. For junior-high-school players the minimum dimensions should be used. The layout of the court is illustrated by Figure 79.

The goals are metal rings eighteen inches in diameter and are rigidly attached to a backboard so that they lie in a horizontal plane ten feet above the floor.

Five men constitute a team, consisting of two forwards, one center, and two guards. The special duty of the forwards is the throwing of goals. The guards cover the play of the forwards of the opposing team and pass the ball to their own forwards or center whenever they can get possession of it. The center has all-round duties, assisting the forwards when his own team has the ball and the guards when the opponents have possession of it.

The object of the game is to secure possession of the ball, work it down the floor, and throw it into the goal. The ball is put in play at the be-

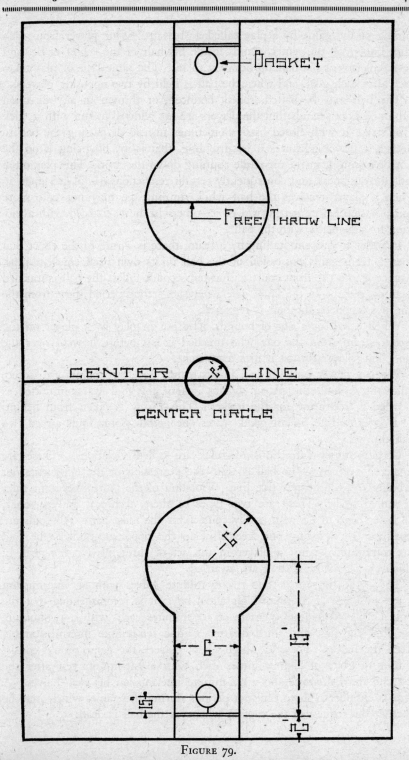

FIGURE 79.

ginning of the game by a play called a "toss-up." One player from each team, known as the center, stands inside his half of the center circle, and the referee tosses the ball up between them. The same type of play takes place after each goal, and when the ball is held by two opposing players.

The ball may be batted, rolled, bounced, or thrown in any direction with one or both hands; but the players are not allowed to run with it, kick it, or strike it with closed fists. Sometimes instead of passing the ball to another, a player advances it by dribbling, that is, by bouncing it on the floor or tossing it in the air while running down the floor. This play often leads to roughness, and consequently certain restrictions are placed upon it. When a player receives the ball while running, he may not take more than one step before getting rid of it—otherwise he is charged with a violation for advancing with the ball.

In order to prevent stalling by a team, there is a rule to the effect that when a team gains possession of the ball in its own back court, it must advance it into the front court within ten seconds unless the ball is touched by an opponent. In the latter case a new ten-second period starts from the time possession of the ball is regained.

When a ball goes out of bounds, it is put in play by a player on the opposite team from the one who touched it last before it went over the line. This player throws it to a team mate.

When a player puts the ball in his team's goal, two points are scored. Following a foul, the player against whom the foul was committed is awarded a free-throw for the basket. This throw is taken from behind the free-throw line, and if good, scores one point. Some fouls award two such throws.

Certain minor infractions of rules are called violations. These are penalized by having the ball go into the possession of the opponents out of bounds at the nearest side line. Violation of the more important rules are called fouls. There are two types of these, technical and personal; the latter have to do with bodily contact for the most part. All fouls are penalized by awarding one free-throw to the opponents, unless the foul was committed against a player in the act of throwing for the goal, in which case, two free-throws are awarded.

The game consists of two twenty-minute halves with an intermission of ten minutes. For junior-high-school boys, it is recommended that the game be played in four quarters of six minutes each, with a two-minute rest after the first and third quarters and a ten-minute intermission between the halves. For senior-high-school players, the game should consist of four quarters of eight minutes each with a one-minute rest after the first and third quarters and a ten-minute intermission between halves. A team is entitled to three time-out periods during the game, which may be taken at the request of the captain whenever the ball is dead.

Basketball for Women

Playground, Gymnasium   *Senior High School to Adults*

Basketball for women developed out of the men's game and was first played at Smith College. The game resembles closely the men's game but has several important changes designed to cut down running, make the game less strenuous, and prevent roughness and personal contact. The details of the rules can be obtained from the standard rule books.

Two types of courts are used depending on the space available—the two-division and the three-division court. The official size of the three-division court is ninety feet long by forty-five feet wide for college players, and seventy feet long by thirty-five feet wide for high schools. If the court is seventy feet or more in length, it is divided into three equal divisions by cross lines parallel to the end lines, as shown in Figure 80. If the court is less than seventy feet long, it is divided into two equal parts by one division line. These division lines are twelve inches wide. The trend at the present is toward the two-court game, regardless of the size of the court.

The teams consist of not less than six nor more than nine players. The six-player team is standard. In the three-division game of six players, each team consists of two centers, two guards, and two forwards. In the two division game of six players, each team consists of three forwards and three guards, any one of the forwards being designated to serve as center. The players are not permitted to leave their divisions during play. Centers and guards in the three-division court may not throw for the basket, nor may guards in the two-division court.

The game may be started either by a toss-up as in the boy's game, or by a center-throw, the teams agreeing on which method they prefer. In the center-throw method, the referee hands or throws the ball to the center entitled to it and blows the whistle as soon as she is certain that the center holds the ball. Each quarter starts with a play at center unless a foul has been committed during the intermission.

The ball may be either thrown or bounced from player to player, but may not be rolled, kicked, hit with the fist, or handed to another player. In catching the ball, two hands are necessary to secure it, but when caught it may be retained with one hand only and thrown with one hand. In addition to bouncing and throwing the ball to another player, a player may bounce the ball once and catch it again herself, called dribbling. A player may also juggle the ball once, that is, toss it in the air and catch it again herself. A bounce cannot follow a juggle, and vice versa.

In not allowing the ball to be rolled on the floor, to be handed to a team mate, or to be bounced against the floor more than once, the girls' rules place restrictions on advancing the ball. There is no dribble in the sense that boys use it. Another limitation that is not included in boys' rules is

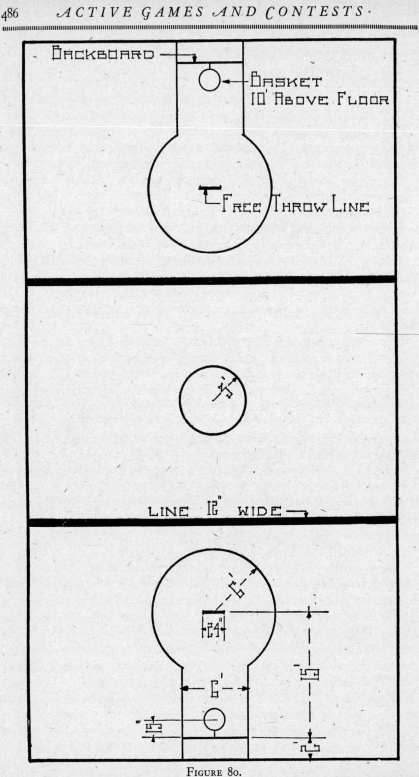

FIGURE 80.

that the player must throw the ball within three seconds after receiving it. There are also special restrictions to prevent struggling for the ball, such as not permitting a player to place a hand on the ball when an opponent holds it.

The violations and fouls are similar to those in the boys' game except that the above restrictions are labeled either as violations or fouls and penalized accordingly. Following a foul, the free-throw must be made by one of the players playing forward at the time the foul was made.

The length of the game is the same as for senior-high-school boys.

MINOR GAMES OF THE BASKETBALL TYPE

Bucketball

Yard, Playground, Picnic   *Elementary School*

This is an informal variation of Basketball, particularly suited to the back yard. A basketball is preferable but any ball may be used. Two buckets are placed on the ground for the goals. No player is allowed to run while holding the ball and the general rules of Basketball apply. Two points are scored each time the ball is put in the bucket and remains there. If the bucket upsets no points are scored.

Hobble Bucketball.—This game is suited for use as a stunt or novelty and is enjoyed for its humorous element by both players and spectators. Two buckets are placed on the ground for goals, open side up. Each player has his ankles tied together with a belt or rope and consequently must jump or hobble. The game follows the general plan of Basketball. Two points are scored each time a team puts the ball in the bucket from scrimmage. If the bucket tips over, no goal is made.

Keep-Ball
(Keep-Away)

Playground, Gymnasium   *Late Elementary to Senior High School*

This old game, frequently called "Pig" by the boys, has long been a favorite of boys of all ages for informal play. It may be used to excellent advantage as a foundation for Basketball.

Divide the group into two teams and mark them so that the teams can be clearly distinguished. If played out of doors, place restrictions on the area so as to prevent too much running. Give one team a basketball or softball. The object is to pass the ball among members of one's own team and prevent the other team from getting it. No player is allowed to hold the ball longer than five seconds, and the regular rules of Basketball apply in respect to advancing with the ball, guarding, and passing the ball. A violation of these rules gives the ball to the opponents. There is no method of scoring and consequently no winner is determined.

The type of pass to be used may be designated, such as bounce passes, push passes, one-arm passes, and so forth.

Nine-Court Keep-Ball.—The game is essentially the same as Keep-Ball, except that it is played on a court marked as in Nine-Court Basketball (page 506). The players are not permitted to step out of their respective courts. This places restrictions on running and guards against overexertion.

Three-Court Keep-Ball.—Same as the above except the three-court floor is used.

Ten-Catches

Playground, Gymnasium   *Late Elementary to Senior High School*

This game is very similar to Keep-Ball, but is a better game in that there is more of an objective in the game and a chance to win.

Divide the group into two teams and mark them so that the teams can be easily distinguished. Give one team a basketball or softball. At the signal the members of this team begin to pass the ball among themselves, attempting to pass it successfully ten times in succession. The other team attempts to get the ball. Each time a team makes a successful pass the player catching it calls the number of the catch; that is, after the first catch, "One" is called, after the second "Two," and so forth. When the ball touches the floor or is caught by opponents, all previous counts are wiped out. The team running the count up to ten wins, and a new game is started.

Basketball Passing.—This game is played on a basketball court or area of similar size. Five to twelve players may play on a team. The game is started by a toss up between two opposing players at center. After the toss, each team attempts to secure the ball and pass it among its own players, trying to make as many consecutive passes as possible. Each team calls out the number of the pass each time a player catches the ball. The team wins which in the course of the play made the greatest number of consecutive passes—the total number of passes is not counted, merely the consecutive passes each time the ball is in the possession of a team.

When the ball is touched by an opponent the ball is considered as leaving the possession of the team and the count starts over. The rules of Basketball apply to the handling of the ball. A pass is considered as completed if a team mate catches it.

Score-Ball.—Appoint one scorer for each team. The game is the same as Basketball Passing except that the total successful passes made by each team are counted. The team making one-hundred passes first wins.

Nine-Court Ten-Catches.—Same as Ten-Catches except that the players are restricted to the areas of the court used in Nine-Court Basketball (page 506).

Guard-Ball

Playground, Gymnasium   *Late Elementary and Junior High Schools*

Draw two parallel lines on the floor ten feet apart. The length of the lines depends on the number of players on a team. Allow three feet for each player. A basketball is used. Divide the players into two teams; place one team between the lines and the other team outside the lines, one-half of it on each side.

The object is for the players on the team outside the lines to pass the ball back and forth between the players in the center. The center players block the ball as in guarding in Basketball. A ball thrown above the height of the players' heads does not count. One point is scored each time the ball is passed through the center team. The game consists of four three-minute periods; after each period, the teams change positions on the floor. Bounce passes may or may not be permitted.

Boundary-Ball.—Establish two goal lines sixty feet apart and draw a center line midway between them, dividing the court into two equal courts. Divide the players into two groups and scatter them in opposing courts, facing each other. Give each team a volleyball, soccer ball, or basketball.

Each player of a team attempts to throw the ball so that it will cross the opposing goal line *on the bounce* or roll across, and at the same time, to defend their own goal. Balls crossing on the fly do not count. Players may move freely in their own court but may not cross the center line. Kicking the ball is prohibited. One point is scored each time the ball crosses the opposing goal legally.

Center Miss Ball

Playground, Gymnasium   *Late Elementary and Junior High Schools*

Arrange the players in a circle with one man in the center. Two basketballs are needed. One ball is given to the center man and the other to a player standing on the circumference of the circle. At the signal the man on the circumference passes the ball to the center man and at the same time the center man passes his ball to the next standing man on the circumference, and so on until the center man is made to miss. The player who makes the center man miss or fumble the ball exchanges places with him. The passes to the center man must be accurate and on the chest level. When skill is developed the type of pass may be specified, such as push pass, one-arm pass, cross-chest pass, and so forth.

King-Ball

Playground, Gymnasium   *Late Elementary and Junior High Schools*

Designate a playing area about thirty feet square. Divide the players into four groups and line each group on one side of the square. The corner players are "kings." A ball is given to one of the players and then is passed to someone on one of the other sides—the ball may not be thrown to anyone on the player's own side. A player fumbling the ball or making a throw that cannot be caught must recover the ball. While he is doing so the players on his team move one place to the right, and the player recovering the ball takes the vacant place at the extreme left. Each player seeks to secure and hold the king's position at the right of the line.

Pin-Guard
(*Indian-Club Guard*)

Playground, Gymnasium   *Late Elementary and Junior High Schools*

The players are standing in a twenty-foot circle. An Indian club stands in the center with a three-foot circle drawn around it. The one who is "it" guards the club, but must not step inside the circle in so doing. The players in the circle have a basketball which they throw at the club. Any player knocking down the club or causing the one who is "it" to knock it down may be "it." If the one who is "it" can get the ball he may throw it beyond the circle, thus giving himself a rest. The player who remains "it" the longest time wins.

Team Pin-Guard.—Divide the players into two teams and arrange them in separate circles, each thirty feet in diameter. Set up an Indian Club in the center of each circle. Place one player from each team in the center of the opposing team's circle (Figure 81). Give the players of each

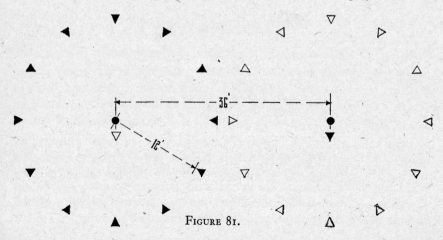

FIGURE 81.

team two soccer balls or basketballs. They throw the balls at the pin attempting to knock it down, while the guards defend the club with their hands, legs, and body. Players may run for the ball but must return to the circle to throw. The team that knocks the club down first scores one point, and the play in both circles stops. The guards return to their teams and two new guards are appointed. The team scoring the most points wins.

Circle Pole Ball [1]

Playground, Gymnasium   *Junior and Senior High Schools*

Court.—Draw two circles on the floor, one inside the other, and mark a line across the center, as illustrated in Figure 64, page 407. In the exact center place a volleyball standard or other pole which stands twelve or fifteen feet high.

Ball.—A basketball is used.

Teams.—Teams may consist of from seven to eighteen players, but nine or eleven is recommended as the size. Each team is divided into two parts, basemen and guards. The basemen stand in the space between the two circles in their half of the court. The guards stand in front of the opposing basemen in the half of the circle opposite that occupied by their own basemen. One guard from each team is designated to guard the pole and stands near the pole on the half of the circle occupied by his own team's guards.

Start.—Each of the two centers or pole guards steps across the center line and faces his own guards. The referee tosses the ball up between them as in Basketball. After the toss-up the centers return immediately to their own guarding territory.

The Play.—The guards attempt to gain possession of the ball and then to throw it to one of their basemen, who in turn attempts to hit the pole with it. Whenever the basemen are playing the ball, the opposing guards attempt to guard, following the rules of Basketball. Play continues until the pole is hit.

Violations and Penalties.—The violations include all the violations and fouls of Basketball. The penalty is the giving of the ball to an opposing guard.

Out of Bounds.—The ball is given to an opposing guard.

Bottle-Ball

Playground, Gymnasium   *Late Elementary School*

Mark out an area twenty-five feet by fifty feet and draw a center line across it dividing it into two twenty-five foot courts. In the middle of each rear line place a row of six Indian clubs, or similarly shaped objects.

[1] This game follows the description given in *Content Committee Report,* Marjorie Hillas, Chairman.

Divide the group into two teams and place one team in each court. Give one of the teams a basketball.

Team A throws the ball attempting to knock down Team B's pins. Team B attempts to defend its pins and when it secures the ball, to knock down Team A's pins. Pins knocked down are left down. The team wins which first knocks down all of the opponents' pins.

Newcomb

Playground, Gymnasium   *Late Elementary and Junior High Schools*

Newcomb is a game which cultivates the ability to throw and catch, to move quickly about the floor, and to judge where the ball will fall. It is a good preparation both for Basketball and Volleyball.

Court.—The court is twenty-five by fifty feet in size, larger or smaller if conditions demand. A net is stretched across the center seven feet from the floor, dividing the court into two courts twenty-five feet square. A rope may be used instead of the net.

Ball.—A volleyball or basketball may be used.

Teams.—Divide the group into two equal teams—teams of eight to fourteen players may be used to advantage.

Object.—The object is to throw the ball over the net and to catch it when it is thrown back.

Start.—The ball is assigned to one team to start the game. At the beginning of the second half the other team starts the play. The game is started by one player throwing the ball over the net.

The Play.—The ball is caught and thrown back over the net. Any player is eligible to catch it. It may not be relayed but must be thrown for the opposite court by the person who catches it. Play continues until a point is scored, and then recommences when the team which lost the point throws the ball over the net again. If a player touches the ball he is responsible for catching it and cannot claim that it was going out.

Scoring.—One point is scored each time the ball drops to the floor in the opponents' court and each time the opponents make one of the following fouls:

1. Hitting the net or rope with the ball.
2. Throwing the ball under the net or rope.
3. Relaying the ball or having two players touch it in succession.
4. Throwing the ball outside the opponents' court, provided it is not touched by a member of the opposing team.

Length of Game.—The game is played in two ten-minute periods.

Variation.—Score as in Volleyball. Only the serving side scores and it continues to serve until it loses. The service throw in this case is from behind the rear line and fifteen points constitute a game.

Volley Newcomb.—This game is played as in Newcomb except for the service, which is as in Volleyball.

Fence-Ball.—This is Newcomb played across a fence. There are no boundary lines. The ball is thrown rapidly back and forth in an effort to confuse the opponents as to where the ball is to be thrown. The rules of Newcomb apply.

Forward-Pass Newcomb.—Lay out a rectangular court fifteen yards wide and forty-five yards long. Across the center mark two parallel lines establishing a neutral zone ten yards wide. The two teams scatter over the opposite ends of the court.

One team passes a rugby football into the opponents' court, endeavoring to cause it to hit the ground in the court without being caught. The opponents endeavor to catch it. One point is scored each time the ball hits the ground in the opponents' court. Fifteen points constitute a game.

Newcomb Over the Goal Posts.[2]—Place the two teams on opposite sides of the rugby-football goal posts and give one team a rugby football. No boundary lines are needed. The object is to pass the football between the goal posts and over the crossbar so that the opposing team cannot catch it. The ball is passed back and forth until one team fails to catch it, or fails to throw it over the crossbar. The rules of Newcomb apply with one exception: the ball may be passed once to a team mate before it is thrown over the crossbar. This rule is necessary because a pass is frequently caught at a spot so far to one side of the goal posts that a successful pass through the goal posts is very difficult. Score as in Newcomb.

Ground-Ball.—An area approximately seventy-five feet long by twenty-five feet wide is divided by cross lines into three equal courts twenty-five feet square. The middle zone is neutral territory. Divide the group into two teams of equal size and scatter each over one of the end courts. Give one team a basketball or volleyball.

The object is to catch the ball and throw it back over the neutral territory into the opponent's court. A team scores one point each time the opposing team allows the ball to touch the ground in their court, or throws it out of bounds, or throws it in to the neutral territory. The team scoring fifteen points first wins.

Curtain-Ball

Playground, Gymnasium   *Late Elementary and Junior High Schools*

This game calls for a wall or solid fence through which the players cannot see. It should be at least eight feet high and preferably higher.

[2] Contributed by J. H. McCulloch.

In the gymnasium a curtain may be used. Place the teams either side of the fence or curtain and give one team a basketball or volleyball. No court lines are needed.

The object is to catch the ball and throw it back over the curtain. One point is scored each time the opposing team allows the ball to touch the ground on their side of the curtain or fails to throw it over the curtain.

If the curtain is such that the teams cannot detect what the other team is doing, much interest is developed because of the uncertainty as to where the ball will appear. The team scoring ten points first wins.

Newcomb-Over-the-Tent.—This is a game similar to Curtain-Ball which boys and girls frequently use of their own initiative. The ball is thrown over a tent or cabin in camp or small building any place. The rules of Curtain-Ball apply.

Cabinet-Ball

Playground, Gymnasium   *Adults*

This game was originated by Herbert Hoover and was first played by him and his cabinet on the White House lawn while he was President.

Court.—A volleyball court is used with the net placed eight feet from the ground. A service line is drawn fifteen feet from the net on each side.

Equipment.—The ball is a small medicine ball twelve inches in diameter and weighing six pounds.

Teams.—For match games there are nine players on a team. The game can be played with any number of players on a team.

Rules.—The game follows the rules of Volleyball with the following exceptions:

1. In serving, the ball is thrown with one hand from the service line. It must be assisted by one player and then clear the net.

2. In receiving, the ball is caught with one or both hands, using the body as much as necessary. It must be put in play immediately by a throw back over the net or a pass to a team mate. Holding the ball longer than five seconds, walking with it, or stepping over the boundary lines with it are fouls:

3. The ball must be thrown in a rising direction. Throwing downward or spiking is a foul. The ball may be passed to a team mate once, but must then be thrown over the net.

Circle Stride-Ball

(*Plug the Hole, Arch Ball*)

Playground, Gymnasium, Club   Late Elementary to Senior High School

Arrange the players in a circle, legs at stride, facing center. The circle should be just large enough so that the feet of the players touch those on either side when the legs are spread widely. "It" is in the center with a basketball. He attempts to throw it between the legs of the players. The players must keep their hands on their knees until the ball leaves "it's" hands and then they may use their hands to block the ball. When the ball goes through a player's legs, that player is "it," recovers the ball, and returns it to the circle. Considerable feinting on the part of "it" is frequently necessary to maneuver the ball so as to get it through the legs.

A football may be used instead of a basketball; its uncertain bouncing adds interest.

Partner Circle Stride-Ball.—Have "it" stand inside the circle and a partner outside. When "it" puts the ball between a player's legs, that player and "it" exchange places. The partner then attempts to throw the ball through the players' legs from outside the circle. When he succeeds the player through whose legs the ball passed exchanges places with him.

Soccer Circle Stride-Ball.—See Soccer Circle Stride-Ball in Chapter XXII, "Games of the Soccer Football Type."

Team Circle Stride-Ball.—Divide the players into two teams and arrange each, with the exception of one player, in a separate circle. The circles should be just large enough so that the feet of the players, standing at a wide straddle, just touch those of the players on either side. The odd player of each team is "it" and takes his position in the center of the opposing circle. Give each "it" a basketball. At the signal both "its" try to throw the ball between the legs of the players as in Circle Stride-Ball. When one "it" succeeds he scores one point for his team; play in both circles stops, the "its" return to their circles, and two new "its" are chosen. The team scoring ten points first wins.

Endball

Playground, Gymnasium   *Late Elementary and Junior High Schools*

Endball gives practice in throwing accurately, in catching while opponents stand near to guard, in guarding, and in staying in one's own territory. It is a good foundation for Basketball.

Court.—The court is fifty feet long and thirty feet wide, larger or smaller to meet conditions. Four to six feet from each end line draw a line parallel to the end line as in Figure 82. The areas thus created are known as the bases. Draw a center line dividing the court into two equal parts.

Ball.—A basketball is commonly used, but the game may be varied by using a volleyball, softball, or sport ball.

Teams.—A team of twelve to fifteen players is the size best suited for this game. Two-thirds of the players on a team are guards and occupy one court; the other one-third are basemen and occupy the opposite base. (See Figure 82.)

Object of the Game.—The object is for the guards to throw the ball over the heads of the opposing guards so that their basemen may catch the ball.

Rotation of Players.—The players should be numbered and should

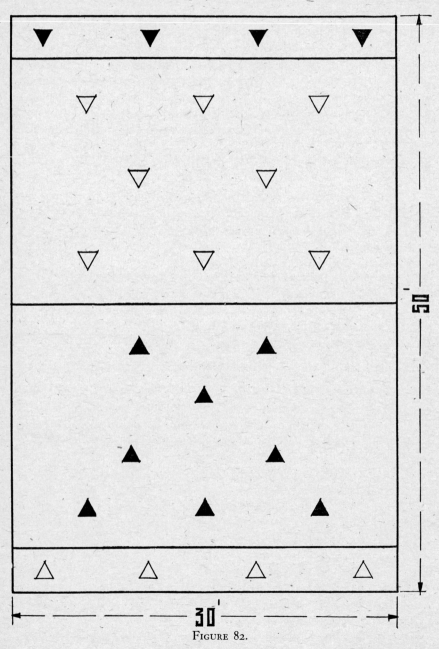

FIGURE 82.

rotate one position each time their team scores. This gives all players a chance to be basemen.

Start.—The game is started by a toss up between two opposing guards on the center line.

The Play.—Guards attempt to secure the ball and throw it so that the opposing guards cannot block it and their own baseman may catch it without stepping over the baselines. The basemen after catching it throw it back to their guards but the throw back does not score. A guard may not run with the ball, nor hold it longer than three seconds, but the guards may pass it among themselves before throwing to the basemen. Play is continuous and does not stop when a score is made.

If the ball goes out of bounds the nearest guard gets it and throws it to one of his fellow guards and the game proceeds. If it goes over the end line, the nearest baseman gets it and returns to position with it.

Fouls.—The following are fouls:

1. Stepping over the division lines.
2. Taking more than one step while holding the ball.
3. Holding the ball longer than three seconds.

Scoring.—One point is scored each time the basemen catch the ball legally on the fly, and each time the opponents commit a foul.

Length of Game.—The game is played in two ten-minute halves. The teams change sides at the end of each half.

Cornerball

Playground, Gymnasium   *Late Elementary and Junior High Schools*

Court.—The court is thirty feet wide and fifty feet long, larger or smaller to meet conditions. It is divided into two courts of equal size by a center line. In each corner a box six or eight feet square is marked out. (See Figure 83.)

Ball.—A basketball is commonly used, but a volleyball, sport ball, or softball may be substituted.

Teams.—Eight to fifteen players may play on a team. Each team occupies one court and sends two of its players to occupy the corner boxes at the opposite end of the area.

Object of the Game.—The object is for the guards to throw the ball to the corner men who attempt to catch it.

Rotation of Players.—Number the players and have those of the scoring team rotate one number after each goal is made. This gives all players a chance to be corner men.

Start.—The game is started by a toss up on the center line between two of the guards.

The Play.—The guards secure the ball and throw it so that their corner men may catch it. They may move about freely but may not run with the ball nor hold it longer than three seconds. They are not permitted to step over the division lines or the corner-box lines. When the ball goes out of bounds, the nearest guard gets it and throws it to one of his fellow guards who puts it in play immediately.

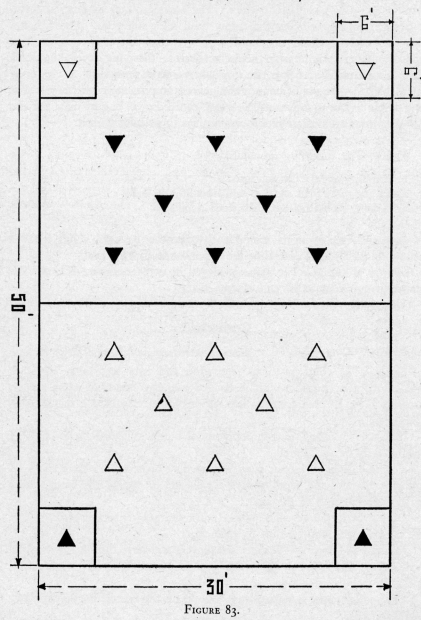

FIGURE 83.

Fouls.—The following are fouls:

1. Taking more than one step while holding the ball.
2. Holding the ball longer than three seconds.
3. Stepping over the division lines.

Scoring.—One point is scored each time a corner man catches the ball on the fly, and each time the opposing team commits a foul.

Length of Game.—The game consists of two ten-minute periods. If preferred, the game may last until one team scores fifteen points.

Lane Cornerball.[3]—The court is fifty to ninety feet long and thirty to sixty feet wide. An eight-foot square is marked in each corner as in Cornerball. Down the center of the floor a lane runs the entire length, this lane being eight to sixteen feet wide. The center line is placed as in Cornerball, extending from the side lines to the center lane but does not extend across the center lane.

The general procedure is as in Cornerball, the chief difference being that the players of both teams may go any place in the center lane. Except when in the center lane they must not cross the center line. The throws to the corner men may be made either from the center lane or the back court.

The ball is put in play by a toss as in Basketball. The rules of Basketball apply to handling the ball, running with the ball, and guarding. The penalty for a foul is the giving of the ball to the opponents out of bounds at the nearest point.

The game consists of two four-minute periods.

Captainball, Number 1
(*Centerball*)

Playground, Gymnasium   *Late Elementary and Junior High Schools*

This is the original game of Captainball and was originated by Dr. E. A. Poos of Cincinnati, Ohio, in 1896 under the name of Centerball.

Field.—The field is thirty by sixty feet. Mark the center of the field, measure one foot to each side of same and draw lines across the field, leaving two equal fields with an intervening neutral space of twenty-four inches. In each front corner put a circle twenty-four inches from the neutral space (Figure 84). Mark the middle rear circle touching the middle of each rear boundary line. The rear corner circles are marked twenty-four inches from the boundary line. The center circle is so placed in the middle of each field that the distance from the center of it to the center of the two front circles and the middle rear circle is the same. The diameter of all circles is four feet.

[3] Contributed by Marianna Packer.

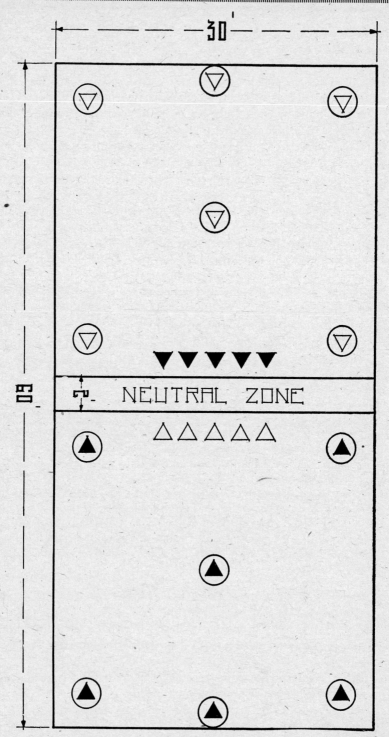

FIGURE 84.

Ball.—A basketball is used.

Players.—Eleven players constitute a team. The player occupying the center circle is called the center. The center and circle players take their respective positions in one field, while the guards of the same team line up in the other field in such a way that the two front guards take the outer positions, near the circles they are guarding, center guard the middle position, and the rear guards midway between the two. (Figure 84.)

Object.—The object of the game is: (1) for the guards to get possession of the ball and throw it to one of the circles of their side; (2) for the circles, after gaining possession, to either throw it to the center, thereby gaining one point, or pass it to the next circle, and so forth, until the ball has made a complete circuit of all the circles, thereby scoring three points.

The Start.—At the beginning of the game and after each score the referee tosses up the ball between two opposing guards. The referee should aim to throw the ball in such a way that it will descend as close to the center of the neutral space as possible.

Out of Bounds.—A ball going out of bounds on either side is given to a guard on that side.

Fouls and Penalties.—The following are fouls:

1. Direct interference: stepping into a circle to prevent a throw to the circle, or a throw from one circle to another. Penalty: the ball is awarded to the offended player. If this be the center or the last circle in a complete circuit, the points are allowed.

2. Indirect interference: stepping into a circle without in any way interfering with a play is not considered direct interference. In order to discourage stepping into the center circle a free-throw is given the center to one of the circles, and for three such offenses one point is allowed.

3. Holding of arms over the space within a circle is not allowed and a free-throw is awarded the offended side.

4. Stepping out of the circles to interfere with the play of the guards is not allowed and a free-throw is allowed the offended side.

It is the duty of the guards to keep the ball from reaching their opponents; therefore, if a ball is already resting in the hands of a circle player and is struck by a guard and knocked from his hands, the decision should be in favor of the circle or center player.

Free-Throw.—A free-throw is one in which the opponents must step aside and in no way interfere with the thrower.

Scoring.—One point is scored by a throw from a circle to the center player. Three points are scored if the ball makes the complete circuit of all circles.

Length of Game.—The game consists of two halves twelve-and-one-half minutes long, with a ten-minute intermission.

Changing Fields.—After the first half the teams change fields.

Officials.—One referee, timers and scorers are in charge of the game.

Variation.—Score two points each time the ball is thrown to the player in the center circle and one point each time the ball is passed to one of the other circle players in making the circuit of the outer circles.

Captainball, Number 2.—There are many varieties of Captainball, the differences resting largely in the arrangement of the circles on the floor and the location of the captain. The following version makes a satisfactory and interesting game. The exact arrangement of the circles in this game does not make much difference so long as the captain is located in the circle farthest from the center line.

Field.—An area approximately thirty by sixty feet is needed. Draw a center line dividing the area into two equal halves. Mark enough circles on the floor to accommodate the players, as shown in Figure 85. These circles are four feet in diameter. The circles are best arranged so that they form a larger circle, but if the number of players is small they may be arranged in a triangle as in Figure 86. For gymnasiums where painted circles are not practical, mats or pieces of linoleum may be laid on the floor and removed after the game.

Ball.—A basketball is used.

Teams.—Six to twenty players may play on a side. Divide each team into two halves; place one half of them in the circles and the other half in the opposite court to act as guards. At the beginning of the second half of the game the sides change and the basemen become guards and the guards become basemen.

Object of the Game.—The object is to throw the ball to the captain and prevent the opposing team from doing likewise.

Start.—The game begins with a toss up between two guards at the *center line.*

The Play.—The guards try to secure the ball and pass it to one of their basemen. The basemen try to throw the ball to the captain, passing it back and forth among themselves as much as necessary in finding the opportunity. The ball may not be passed directly to the captain by the guards. The guards guard the basemen and try to prevent the opponents from scoring.

Fouls.—The following are fouls:

1. Baseman stepping outside the circle with more than one foot.
2. Guards stepping over the center line or into a circle.
3. Guards touching and keeping a hand on the ball when held by a baseman.
4. Holding the ball longer than three seconds.
5. Taking more than one step while holding the ball.
6. Bouncing the ball more than once before passing it.

Penalties.—Following a foul the ball is given to the opponent of the player committing the foul for a free and unguarded throw to the captain.

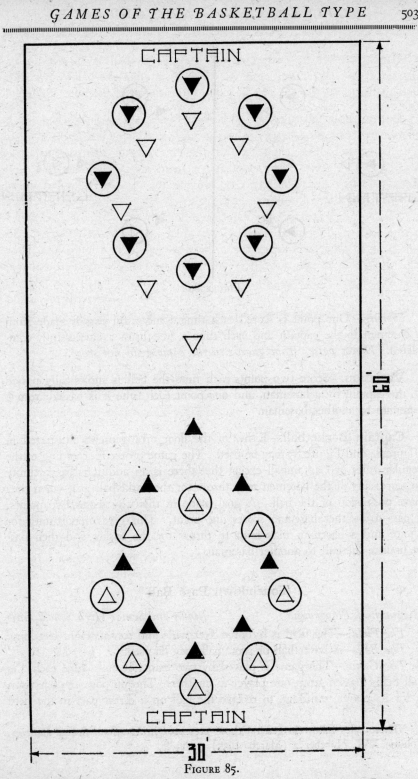

FIGURE 85.

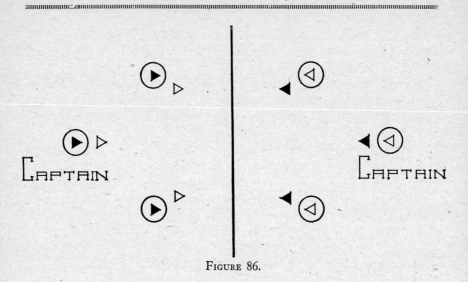

FIGURE 86.

Scoring.—One point is scored each time a successful pass is made from a baseman to the captain and each time a free-throw is successfully completed. *Direct passes from guards to the captain do not score.*

Variation.—Score two points each time the ball is successfully passed to the captain by a baseman, and one point each time it is passed from a baseman to another baseman.

Captain Basketball.—Either of the floor arrangements illustrated in Figure 84 and Figure 85 may be used. The game proceeds according to the regular rules of Captainball except that there is an additional opportunity to score: any of the basemen may throw for the basketball goal when they have possession of the ball. A goal made in this way scores two points; a pass to another baseman scores one point. This gives opportunity for choice and a baseman may feint to throw for the basket and then pass or bounce the ball to another baseman.

Touchdown Pass Ball [4]

Gymnasium, Playground   *Junior and Senior High School Girls*

The Field.—The field is forty-five feet wide and seventy-eight feet long.
The Ball.—A basketball or sport ball may be used.
The Game.—The game is played by two teams of eight girls each, the ball being passed from one player to another. The purpose of each team is for its player, standing, to receive the ball on a direct pass in the field

---

[4] These rules follow in general those presented in *Maryland School Bulletin*, Volume XVI, Number 2 (March, 1935), p. 13 ff.

of play and touch it down at any point behind the opponents' end line.
The opponents try to prevent the other team from securing possession of
the ball or from scoring.

Start.—The game starts by a toss-up at center as in Basketball, between
two opposing players who may not again play the ball until it hits the
ground or is played by another player. After each score the ball is put in
play at center. All players must be "on side" at toss-up.

Out of Bounds.—If a ball goes out of bounds, it is given to an opponent
of the player who touched it last at the point nearest where it went out.
On end lines, the ball is always awarded to the defending team.

Violations.—The ball is given to the nearest opponent of the player
committing the foul, who by a free pass (no player being within a radius
of five feet) puts the ball into play. The following are violations:

1. Carrying the ball.
2. Dribbling the ball.
3. Rolling the ball.
4. Kicking the ball.
5. Overguarding player.

Fouls.—One point is awarded a team fouled, and the ball is put into
play as in a violation.

a. Batting or pulling ball out of opponent's grasp.
b. Charging, shoving, tripping, or holding opponent.

Scoring.—A pass touched down behind end line counts two points.
A touchdown cannot be scored from a free pass.

Time.—The game consists of two five-minute halves with a two-minute
rest between them.

Officials.—The game is in charge of a referee who may appoint a timekeeper, a scorer, or linesmen.

Other rules.—Girls' basketball rules govern unspecified points.

Drive-Ball.—This is a game similar to the above which is acceptable
for players in the late elementary school. It is played on an area of the size
of a basketball court, which has a space of at least six feet wide between
each end line and the end wall. The game follows the procedure of
Touchdown Pass Ball except that scoring is accomplished by throwing the
ball so that it falls from the fly and hits the ground beyond the end lines.
Whenever a ball is touched by an opponent, it becomes the property of the
opponent at the point where it was touched. When it is put in play from
this spot, all opponents must be at least five feet away. A goal scores
one point.

Pin Basketball

Playground, Gymnasium   *Junior High School*

This game may be used when basketball goals are not available.

Court.—A basketball court or area of similar size and shape is needed, laid out as in Nine-court Basketball. A circle three feet in diameter is drawn inside each middle end court, with the edge of the circle touching the end line midway between the side lines. In each of these two circles place an Indian club. The Indian clubs should be attached to blocks of wood six inches square, to give them greater stability. The basketball goals are not used.

Ball.—A regulation basketball is used.

Rules.—The play is governed by all the rules of Nine-court Basketball, with the following exceptions:

1. Goals are scored by knocking down the Indian clubs with the ball. The ball must hit the club before it hits the floor. A field goal scores two points.

2. Free-throws are made from the free-throw line and the ball is thrown (not rolled) at the pin. Goals from free-throws score one.

3. Players may not step in the circles. (Penalty: a free-throw.)

Post Ball.[5]—This game is similar to the above except that a player, instead of the Indian club, occupies the circle. It is played on a two-court field of the size and shape of a basketball court, with a three-foot circle on each end line as in Pin Basketball. Half of each team are forwards and half are guards; the guards of one team play against the forwards of the other, and neither guards nor forwards may leave their half of the floor by stepping over the center line. Each team stations one of its forwards in its circle at the end of the court, this player being known as the "post."

The object is for the forwards to throw the ball so that their "post" can catch it. One point is scored for each ball caught. The "post" may not step outside of the circle and guards may not step inside. If play becomes too vigorous, another restraining circle, six feet in diameter, may be drawn about each post circle to keep guards farther away.

Nine-Court Basketball

Playground, Gymnasium   *Junior and Senior High Schools*

Nine-Court Basketball is probably the best and most satisfactory of the girls' basketball games. For general recreational use it is to be preferred to Three-Court Basketball, especially for young girl players and for girls of all ages under conditions where adequate medical examination and supervision of players is not possible. It offers all of the appeal and fascination of Basketball with a minimum of danger. It may be played by mixed groups.

Court.—The game is played on a regular basketball court with lines

[5] Contributed by D. K. Brace.

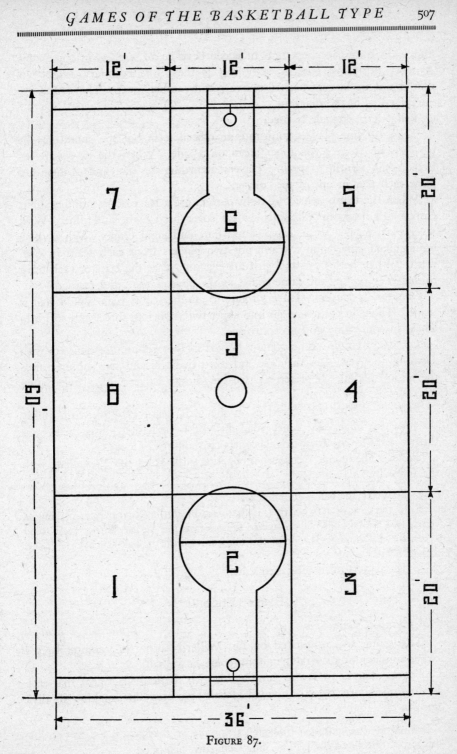

FIGURE 87.

drawn dividing the court into nine courts of equal size, as in Figure 87. A court thirty-five feet by sixty feet is ideal for secondary schools; it should not be larger than forty-five feet by ninety feet. The courts are numbered as in the diagram.

Ball.—A basketball is used.

Teams.—Nine players constitute an official team but the game may be played with from seven to eighteen on a side. When the teams are selected, pair up the opposing players according to size and ability and place each pair in one of the courts.

When the teams consist of eight players each, leave court number eight empty and have the jumping centers cover both eight and nine. With seven players on a team, leave courts four and eight empty. When there are eighteen players on a team, put two players from each team in each court. When both boys and girls are playing, place the boys of each team so that they occupy the same courts as the boys of the other team.

Rotation of players.—Players rotate to another court each time a goal is made. Those in court one go into court two, two into three, and so forth. Those in court nine go into court one.

Length of Game.—The game is played in four six-minute quarters with a two-minute rest after the first and third quarters and five minutes after the second period. If preferred, two ten-minute halves with a five-minute intermission may be used.

Scoring.—Points are scored as in the girls' game of Basketball. Only the forwards in the end courts may throw for the basket. Free-throws are thrown only by the forwards in courts two and six.

Rules.—The game is governed by the girls' rules for Basketball with the following exceptions:

1. Bouncing the ball is prohibited.
2. In the case of a free-throw, if there are more than two players playing in courts two and six, all players except the one making the free-throw must stand across the division line in one of the side courts until the ball touches the basket or backboard.
3. The players rotate after each score.

Basket Endball [6]

Playground, Gymnasium   *Junior High Schools*

This game was originated by Dr. Willard Zorn. It accommodates a larger number of players than three-court basketball.

Court.—The court is the same as for girls' Basketball, except that each of the three courts is again divided in half by a cross line, making six divisions in all (Figure 88).

[6] From W. Zorn "Basket Endball," *Mind and Body,* December, 1924. By permission of Mind and Body Publishing Company, publishers.

Ball.—A basketball is used.

Teams.—Nine to twenty-one players may play on a team. Each team is divided into three groups—guards, centers, and forwards—and arranged as in Figure 88.

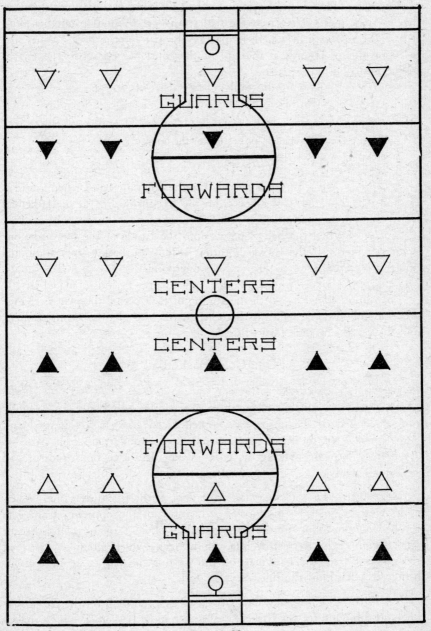

FIGURE 88.

Object of the Game.—The object is to pass the ball to the forwards and then to throw it into the basket.

Start.—The ball is tossed up between two opposing centers in the center circle.

The Play.—Players must remain in their divisions and may not step over the division lines. They pass the ball from one division to another until it reaches the forwards where it may be thrown for the goal. When the ball goes out of bounds at the end of the court, it belongs to the guards in the end division.

Fouls.—The following are fouls:

1. Carrying the ball.
2. Dribbling or bouncing the ball.
3. Playing the ball when in possession of the opposing team.
4. Stepping over the division lines.

Penalties.—A free-throw is awarded to the opposing team when a foul is committed. The throw is taken from the free-throw line as in Basketball by any one of the forwards.

Scoring.—When the ball is passed into the hands of the forwards, one point is scored. If the forwards throw it into the basket, two additional points are scored. A free-throw scores one point.

Length of Game.—The game is played in three periods of equal length.

Rotation of Players.—At the beginning of each period the players change zones as follows: the forwards become guards, the guards become centers, and the centers become forwards.

One-Goal Basketball

Playground, Gymnasium   *Late Elementary to Adults*

This game is suitable when there are not enough players for regulation Basketball or when space is limited. Only one basket is used and both teams shoot for it. There are no out-of-bound rules. The score is credited to the team making the goal. With these exceptions, the rules of Basketball apply.

Variation.—Draw a line across the floor at the free-throw line. When a throw for a goal is missed and a member of the opposing team gets the ball on the follow-up, he must pass it back to a member of his team who is behind the free-throw line. If the team which attempted the goal recovers the ball, the ball may be thrown for the basket again without being passed behind the line.

Variation.—The game starts by one player standing on the free-throw line and throwing for the basket, as after a foul in Basketball. If he makes the goal, one point is scored. He continues to throw until he fails, when he fails, all scramble for the ball and attempt to make a field goal, which counts two points. When the field goal is made, the player making it must be the next player to throw from the free-throw line. Twenty-one points is a game and two games out of three a match. The last point in the game must be made by a field goal.[7]

Dual Basketball

Playground, Gymnasium   *Junior and Senior High Schools*

This game follows all the rules of Basketball except that two balls are used. At the start and after each goal, both balls are tossed up at center at the same time.

Four-Goal Basketball [8]

Gymnasium   *Junior High School to College*

If there are four basketball goals in the gymnasium, assign two adjacent goals to one team and the other two to the other team. If there are six goals available, assign three to each team. The entire gymnasium is the court. Any number of players may be used on a team. One ball is used and the procedure is as in Basketball, except that the players of each team may throw for any one of their team's goals.

This makes a particularly interesting game. If a player is attempting to play for one goal and finds himself guarded, he may turn suddenly and play for one of the other goals.

Cage Basketball [9]

Gymnasium   *Senior High School to College*

This is a fascinating game played on a basketball court with a thirty-inch cageball. It follows the general plan of Basketball. The object is to cause the ball to hit the backboard of the basketball goal. Each goal score in this way counts two points. The game is started by the two centers standing in the center circle, holding up the ball at arm's length over head. At the whistle, they attempt to bat or throw it. In case the players pile up on the ball, holding it to the floor, play is stopped and the ball is put in play in the same way as at center.

Variation.—Play as above but use all the basketball backboards in the gymnasium, following the procedure described in Four-Court Basketball.

[7] The idea for this variation was taken from N. P. Neilson and W. Van Hagen, *Physical Education for Elementary Schools,* p. 193. Copyright, 1930. By permission of A. S. Barnes and Company, publishers.

[8] Contributed by J. H. McCulloch.

[9] Contributed by J. H. McCulloch.

One O'Gang [10]

Playground, Gymnasium   *Junior High School*

This game is played with the use of but one basket and not more than five or six participants. One boy is chosen "it" and he competes as guard against the remaining players. The object of the game is to keep the ball away from "it," using any form of legal basketball advancement. When the ball is in a position to be shot for a basket, the player may shoot. If he makes the basket he is credited with two points. If he misses he must exchange places with "it." Also, if the ball while being passed is intercepted by "it," the last person to handle the ball must change places with him. Each player keeps his individual score. All baskets made count for the man who shot them. As soon as a player has made a score of ten the game may finish.

Variation.—Take off two points from the score of the player taking a shot and missing it. This puts a premium on careful shooting.

GAMES OF THE BASKETBALL TYPE IN OTHER CHAPTERS

Water Basketball   Water Endball
Water Keep-Ball   Ice Basketball
Water Ten-Catches   Mounted Basketball

BASKETBALL LEAD-UP CONTESTS

Many of the minor games of the basketball type described in this chapter may be used as lead-up games in developing skills for the major sport. The following contests, described in the chapters on contests, may also be used for this purpose.

Catch, Throw, and Sit   Basketball Toss-Up
Catch, Throw, and Squat   Team Basketball Shooting
Ten Trips   Zigzag Ball-Passing Relay
Corner Spry   Throwing Shuttle Relay
Basketball Throw and Catch   Overtake Relay
Running and Catching   Six-Hole Basketball
Basketball Throw for Distance   Basketball Pass-and-Shoot Relay
Basketball Accuracy Pass   Basketball Dribble Relay
Basketball Foul Shoot   Basketball Run-and-Shoot Relay
Basketball Goal Shooting   Dodgeball
Basketball Twenty-one   Dodgeball—Team Form
Basketball Twenty-one—Team Form Three-Team Dodgeball
Five, Three, and One   Progressive Dodgeball
Basketball Golf   Field Dodgeball.

[10] Contributed by R. J. Schnitman.

PART V

WATER, WINTER, AND MOUNTED ACTIVITIES

CHAPTER XXVI

WATER ACTIVITIES

STANDARD SWIMMING CONTESTS

Swimming Meets

SWIMMING meets may be conducted either in swimming pools or open water. The regulations governing the events are the same in either case.

The minimum size for pools in which championship meets are to be held should be sixty feet in length and twenty feet in width. The tendency in constructing pools is toward a width of 60 feet and lengths from 75 to 150 feet. The minimum depth at the shallow end is three feet and at the deep end seven feet. Where high-board diving is expected, this depth should be increased to at least ten feet.

The lanes are marked by ten-inch lines, placed seven feet apart. More satisfactory still for races are the rope markers, buoyed up by wooden floats.

For swimming races, the take-off should be flat and not more than eighteen inches above the water level.

Events.—The official program and order of events for a high-school meet are as follows:

1. 200-Yard Relay (75-foot pools).
   160-Yard Relay (60-foot pools).
2. 100-Yard Breast Stroke.
3. 50-Yard Free Style (75-foot pools).
   40-Yard Free Style (60-foot pools).
4. 220-Yard Free Style (75-foot pools).
   200-Yard Free Style (60-foot pools).
5. 100-Yard Back Stroke.
6. 100-Yard Free Style.
7. Fancy Diving.
8. 150-Yard Medley Relay (75-foot pools).
   180-Yard Medley Relay (60-foot pools).

(Three swimmers on each team, each to swim one-third the distance; first, back stroke; breast stroke; third, free-style.)

Officials.—The following officials are needed: referee, clerk of course, scorer, finish judges, judges of fancy diving, timers, starter, announcer, and an inspector of turns and lanes. The duties of these officials are suggested by their names.

Scoring.—In dual meets, the scoring is 5 points for first place, 3 points for second, and 1 point for third. The free-style relay race scores 8 points for first and 4 points for second, while the medley relay race scores 6 points for first and 3 points for second.

In championship meets, the points are awarded 5 points for first, 4 points for second, 3 points for third, 2 points for fourth, and 1 point for fifth place. In the relay races, 8 points are given for first place, 6 points for second, 4 points for third, and 2 points for fourth.

Swimming Races

Swimming Pool, Open Water   *Late Elementary School to Adults*

At the start, the contestants should be behind their starting stations until the signal "Get on your marks" when they step to the starting mark and assume any starting position, provided that they hold a steady balance for an appreciable length of time. When the starter is assured the swimmers are steady, he starts the race with the signal "Go" or by sounding a pistol.

In all swimming races, the contestant is considered to have finished when any part of his person touches the finishing line. In the relay race, each contestant must have touched his finish line before his successor starts.

The Crawl—Free-Style.—The most common stroke used in competition and recreational swimming is the crawl or free-style. The general position of the body is prone (face down). The leg action is a relaxed thrash from the hips with a leg sweep not quite as much as when walking. The arms are carried forward about as in climbing a ladder except that the hand is slid forward and pulled downward and backward in the water. Breathing is accomplished close to the water by turning the head and face, taking the air in quickly through the mouth, and exhaling under water. The leg-kick, arm action, and breathing are coordinated into a smoothly working whole.

The Breast Stroke.—Various forms of breast stroke may be used. All call for simultaneous and symmetrical action of the arms and also of the legs. The legs are drawn up under the body and thrust forcibly backward in a frog kick. This is followed by a pull of the arms. The head is lifted by this pull sufficiently so that you can take a quick breath close to the water.

Recently the "flying-fish" style of breast stroke has been legalized in competition. In this stroke, the arms are carried forward above the water as though the alternate action of the arms in the free-style was synchronized to a simultaneous action.

The Back Stroke.—The back stroke is practically the inverted crawl. There is, however, no need to turn the face when breathing, and the arms are not only carried forward in front of the body but also exert their propelling force by a shallow pull slightly back of the shoulder line.

MINOR SWIMMING AND DIVING CONTESTS BETWEEN INDIVIDUALS

Novel Swimming-Stroke Races

Swimming Beach, Pool, Camp   *Late Elementary School to Adults*

Races may be conducted by any one of the following novel methods of propelling:

Finning.—The swimmer lies on his back, feet together and hands by his sides. The hands move up and down at the wrist, applying pressure in the movement toward the feet and relaxing the hand in the movement toward the head. The motion of the body is toward the head.

Sculling.—The position is the same as in Finning except that the hands move in and out in a "figure-of-eight" motion.

Overhead Sculling.—The swimmer lies on his back, feet together, arms overhead. He performs the sculling movement with the hands as described above. The body moves in the direction of the head.

Flutter Finning.—This is the same as Finning except that a flutter kick is added.

Bicycle Pedaling.—The swimmer lies on his back with hands on hips. He makes progress in the direction of his feet by moving the feet in bicycle-pedaling motion.

Crabbing.—Lying on his stomach, the swimmer moves in the direction of his feet by applying a reverse breast-stroke motion. The legs execute a frog kick but no pressure is applied.

Spinning Swim.—This is a combination of a front and back crawl. The swimmer makes one stroke on his face, rolls over, and makes the next on his back. The flutter kick goes on throughout.

Log Roll.—The body, arms, and legs are stretched straight out in a line. The swimmer rolls in the water.

Handicap-Position Races

Swimming Beach, Pool, Camp   *Late Elementary School to Adults*

Races may be conducted with the swimmers holding one of the following positions:

1. One arm out of the water and held in the air throughout. The swimmer uses only a side stroke.

2. Both arms out of the water, swimming on the back.

3. One leg held vertically out of the water, swimming on the back.

Frog Race

Swimming Beach, Pool, Camp   *Late Elementary School to Adults*

The swimmers lie on their backs with their hands on their hips and swim, using the frog kick only.

Steamboat Race.—The contestants lie on their stomachs with arms and head in coasting position and swim using the legs only. The feet perform the crawl kick. Distances of twenty to forty feet are sufficient.

Ball-Between-Knees Race

Swimming Beach, Pool, Camp   *Late Elementary School to Adults*

Each contestant races while carrying a water-polo ball or sport ball between his knees. If he loses it, he must return and replace it before making further progress.

Dog Race

Swimming Beach, Pool, Camp   *Elementary School*

This is a race particularly interesting to small children. The contestants line up at the dock or end of the pool, standing on the bottom. At the signal they bark three times, touch the dock or end of pool, and then swim with the dog paddle to the finish. The player finishing first wins.

Umbrella Race

Swimming Beach, Pool, Camp   *Late Elementary School to Adults*

Each swimmer races carrying an open umbrella. If the cloth top of the umbrella touches the water, the racer is disqualified. Distances of 75 to 100 feet are sufficient.

Japanese parasols add much to the color of the event.

Water Flag-Race.—This event is conducted like the Umbrella Race except that the contestants carry flags.

Fan Race.—Each swimmer carries a fan. They race on their backs fanning themselves with the fans held in one hand. The fan must not touch the water. Distances of 60 to 100 feet may be used.

Newspaper Race.—The swimmers race on their backs reading a newspaper held in their hands. The newspaper may be folded once but no more, and must not touch the water. Distances of 60 to 100 feet may be used.

Swimming Candle Race

Swimming Beach, Pool, Camp   *Late Elementary School to Adults*

The players line up fifty feet from the dock or a float. At the signal they swim to the dock, light a candle, and return to the starting line with the lighted candle. The player finishing first with the candle lighted wins.

Japanese-Lantern Race.—Each contestant carries a Japanese lantern containing a lighted candle. The player wins who finishes first with the candle lighted.

Table-Waiter Race

Swimming Beach, Pool, Camp   *Late Elementary School to Adults*

Each contestant is given a tin or paper plate with a stone on it. The contestant wins who finishes first with the stone still on the plate. A distance of twenty to forty yards is sufficient.

A large cork may be used on the plate instead of the stone. If the cork falls off the swimmer is permitted to stop and replace it.

Spoon-and-Egg Race.—The players race carrying an egg or potato in a spoon held by their teeth. The distance is fifty feet.

Banana-Eating Race

Swimming Beach, Pool, Camp
  Late Elementary School to Adults
The contestants stand in water chest deep each holding a banana. At the signal they peel the banana, duck under water, and eat it. The player wins who first comes up with the banana eaten. They may come up for air as often as they choose, but must eat the banana while under water. No chewing or swallowing is permitted when they come up for air.

Straw-Hat Race

Swimming Beach, Pool, Camp   *Late Elementary School to Adults*

The swimmers line up on the dock or end of the pool, each wearing a farmer's straw hat. At the signal they jump in the water feet first and completely submerge themselves. They then come up, recover their hats which are now floating on the water, and swim to the end of the pool or finishing line.

A player is disqualified if he fails to submerge himself completely or if he jams the hat on his head so that it fails to come off as he hits the water.

Water Balloon-Pushing Race

Swimming Beach, Pool, Camp   *Elementary School to Adults*

The contestants line up behind the starting line each holding an inflated toy balloon. At the signal they swim to the finish line pushing the balloon before them with their head or face. The distance is twenty-five yards.

With balloons of varied colors this is a colorful event.

Eggshell Race

Swimming Beach, Pool, Camp   *Late Elementary School to Adults*

Prick holes in the ends of eggs and blow out the contents, sealing the ends with tape or wax. The contestants race blowing the eggs. A player is disqualified if he touches his egg or propels it by splashing water on it or raising waves to carry it. A distance of forty to sixty feet is sufficient.

Ping-Pong Ball Race.—Same as the above except that a ping-pong ball is used.

Water Spearing-the-Ring

Swimming Pool   *Late Elementary School to Adults*

Suspend ten curtain rings at intervals from a rope stretched lengthwise of the pool. The rings should hang three feet above the water. The contestants take turns in swimming the length of the pool and back carrying a slender bamboo pole ten feet long and attempting to spear the rings. As soon as the end of the pole enters the ring the swimmers are permitted to withdraw it. They must not stop their forward motion except to withdraw the pole from a ring. Each ring speared scores one point.

Log-Obstacle Race

Swimming Beach, Camp   *Late Elementary School to Adults*

At the turning line float a log in the water. The racers race to the log, dive under it, turn and crawl over it, and return to the starting line. The player finishing first wins.

If several logs are available place them at intervals and the players dive *under* one, *over* the next, and so on.

Disrobing Race

Swimming Beach, Pool, Camp   *Late Elementary to Senior High School*

The contestants line up on the shore or dock, wearing bathing suits over which are worn shirt, trousers, and shoes. At the signal they swim to a float, climb on, undress, put clothes in a pile, leave them, and swim back to the shore. The one finishing first wins.

For a more spectacular event, they may also wear hats, gloves, and carry an open umbrella. This event is often conducted by having the contestants wear pajamas over their bathing suits.

If a raft is not available, a row of canoes or skiffs may be tied together and anchored.

Threading the Needle Under Water

Swimming Beach, Pool, Camp   *Late Elementary School to Adults*

Give each player a large darning needle and a piece of coarse thread. At the signal they duck under and thread the needle. The one wins who comes up first with the needle threaded.

Head-Carry Race

Swimming Beach, Pool, Camp   *Junior High School to Adults*

The swimmers pair up according to approximate weight. The contestants line up in the water facing and touching the dock or edge of the pool. At the signal one of the players steps behind the other and holds him with the life-saving hold known as the head carry. That is, he covers the ears with the palms of his hands and swims only with his legs. The patient lies on his back with his arms folded and feet crossed. The rescuer swims to a line fifty to seventy-five feet distant and then the players change places and the patient swims back carrying the rescuer.

Cork Retrieve

Swimming Beach, Pool, Camp   *Elementary to Senior High School*

This is one of the most popular of the swimming contests. Line up the players on the dock or side of the pool and draw a circle in front of each. Scatter two or three dozen corks or small blocks of wood on the water thirty or forty feet out from the players. At the signal each player dives in and brings back the corks, one at a time, and places them in his circle. The player wins who secures the most corks.

Team Form.—Line the teams up, one at each end of the dock or pool, and mark one circle for each team. The team gathering the most corks wins.

Weight Retrieve

Swimming Beach, Pool, Camp   *Elementary to Senior High School*

This is similar to Cork Retrieve except that objects are sunk in the water and the players dive for them. Teaspoons, tin plates, tops of tin cans, or other shining objects may be used.

At the signal the players all dive in and bring the objects to the edge of the pool or dock and place them in their individual circles. Only one object may be recovered at a time. The individual recovering the most wins.

Team Weight-Retrieve.—Divide the group into two teams and scatter the shiny objects on the bottom as described above. The first player of one team dives in and recovers as many objects as possible. The objects are counted for the individual's score and replaced. The first player of the second team then does likewise. Continue until all have tried. Total the score of the individuals on each team and the team with the highest score wins.

Sunken Treasure

Swimming Pool　　　　　　　*Elementary to Senior High School*

Scatter a large number of pennies on the bottom of the pool. At the signal all dive and scramble for the pennies. Each player may bring up as many as he can get on one dive or may dive as often as he chooses. The one securing the most pennies wins and each may keep all he gets.

Swimming Attention

Swimming Beach, Camp　　　*Late Elementary to Senior High School*

The excellent contest, Attention, may be used just as well in the water as on land. Divide the players into two teams and line the teams up in the water ten feet apart and facing each other. The water should be about chest deep. Number the players so that opposing players holding the same number stand opposite each other. Establish turning lines ten feet from each end of the lines of players by stretching a rope or driving a pole in the bottom. The two ends of the swimming pool serve admirably.

The leader calls a number—for example, "Five." The two Number Five's swim to one turning line or pole, then to the other, and then back to position (see Figure 23, page 153). The player scores one point who stands erect in his position first. Eleven points is the game. The leader should call the numbers at random.

Before the contest starts, the leader should make clear to the players the turning line to which they are to swim first.

Inner-Tube Race

Swimming Beach, Pool, Camp　　　*Elementary and Junior High Schools*

This event is always popular with small children. Secure large inner tubes from discarded truck tires and replace the straight valve stems with curved valve stems. The tire should be placed in the water so that the curved stem extends down—it is thus out of the way. The contestants sit in the tubes and paddle with their hands.

Life-saving buoys, although less satisfactory, may be substituted for the tubes.

Tub Race.—The paddlers sit in tubs and paddle with their hands. The tubs will have to be big and the paddlers small in order to stay afloat.

Water Follow-the-Leader

Swimming Beach, Pool, Camp   Late Elementary to Senior High School

This is a popular event and with a good leader at the front is good practice in swimming and diving. The players stand in file behind the leader and do everything he does. The leader should make much use of the spring board. Do not continue the event too long.

O'Grady in the Water

Swimming Beach, Pool, Camp   Late Elementary to Senior High School

The players stand in water chest deep. The leader also stands in the water, so stationed that all can see him. The leader gives commands, some prefaced by "O'Grady says," others not. The players must execute those prefaced by "O'Grady says" and stand motionless on the others. Those moving at the wrong time or executing the command incorrectly have one point scored against them. Those with three points must pay a forfeit.

Such commands as the following may be used: duck your head, float, tread water, surface dive, touch bottom, flutter kick, frog kick, duck and stick your feet out, and so forth.

Kick Fighting

Swimming Beach, Pool, Camp   Late Elementary to Senior High School

Place a long pole about five inches in diameter or a plank in the water. Divide the players into two teams and line them up one on each side of the pole, with hands on the edge of it. At the signal they all begin to kick and attempt to force the opposing team back. The team that first forces the other ten feet back wins.

The contest may be varied by having *Flutter vs. Frog Kick-Fights, Flutter vs. Scissors Kick-Fights, Frog vs. Scissors Kick-Fights*, and so forth.

Walking on Bottom

Swimming Beach, Camp   Junior and Senior High Schools

The contestants line up in water a little over waist deep. At the signal they race by walking on the bottom to the finish line not over sixty feet distant.

Water Horse-and-Rider Race.—Same as the above except that the contestants race in pairs, one riding sitting on the back of the other.

Greased-Pole Crawl

Summer Camp, Swimming Beach   *Late Elementary to Senior High School*

Fasten a smooth pole to the dock so that it extends out about fifteen feet over the water. Place the pole parallel to the shore so that the spectators can get a good view of it. Grease the pole well with axle grease, and place a colored rag on the end of it.

The players take turns in crawling out on the pole, attempting to reach and secure the rag before slipping into the water. The rag should represent a prize that the winner is awarded afterward. If two or more should reach the rag, they crawl again to determine the winner.

Throwing the Life Buoy

Swimming Beach, Camp   *Junior and Senior High Schools*

Three six-inch blocks of wood are anchored so that they float in a row parallel to the dock and thirty feet from it, the distance between the blocks being two-and-one-half feet. The center block represents a drowning man's head, and the side blocks his hands. A seventeen-inch life buoy with rope attached is used.

Each contestant is given three throws all to be completed within one minute of time. If he rings any one of the blocks on the first throw he scores five points, on the second, three points, and on the third, two points. The points are added for his score.

Dive for Accuracy

Swimming Beach, Pool, Camp   *Late Elementary School to Adults*

Secure a large inner tube from a discarded truck tire and replace the straight valve stem with a curved stem. Place the inner tube on the water under the high-diving board with the stem extending downward. Each contestant is given three dives and scores one point each time he dives through the tube.

Hoop Dive.—For an exhibition stunt cover a large hoop with colored crepe paper and hold it in the air by ropes under the high-diving board. The diver dives through the paper.

Dive for Height

Swimming Beach, Pool, Camp   *Junior High School to Adults*

Two assistants hold a rope above the diving plank over which the divers dive. The rope is moved up gradually as in the High Jump and the contestant wins who clears the rope when all others have failed. This event may be conducted for both the running and standing dives. If a diver fails to clear the rope, the assistants should release the rope as soon as the diver touches it.

Dive for Distance

Swimming Beach, Pool, Camp   *Junior High School to Adults*

Two assistants hold a rope in front of the diving plank over which the divers dive. The rope is moved farther out after each dive and the contestant wins who clears it when all others have failed. If the diver fails to clear the rope, the assistants should release the rope as soon as the diver touches it.

Novelty Dives

Swimming Beach, Pool, Camp   *Junior High School to Adults*

Hand-Stand Dive.—The diver places his hands on the end of the diving board and throws his body up to the hand-stand position. He holds it for a moment, then releases his grip and enters the water head first. The arms are thrown overhead after the grip on the board is released.

Head-Stand Dive.—The diver places his hands and head on the diving board as near the end as possible and throws the body up into a head stand. In leaving the plank he does a turn over and enters the water feet first with the arms extended overhead.

Cart-Wheel Dive.—The diver stands back from the end of the diving board a sufficient distance and executes a cart wheel, striking the hand near the end of the plank. He enters the water feet first with arms extended over head.

Military Dive.—The diver stands at the rear of the diving board and marches to the end with a brisk marching step. At the end he brings both feet to attention, then jumps and hits the plank hard, and enters the water feet first, with body rigid and with the hand at military salute.

Seal Dive.—The diver lies on his stomach at the rear of the diving board and progresses to the end of the board by the seal waddle—he walks on his hands pulling his body forward with legs extended straight out behind and dragging. On reaching the end, the diver assumes the lever position: he places his hands on the end of the plank, places his elbows at the sides of his waist, and holding the weight of the body on the elbows, lifts the legs and arches the back. He holds this position a moment, then releases his grip and enters the water head first with arms extended overhead.

Frog Dive.—The diver squats frog fashion on the rear end of the diving board and hops forward, bringing his knees up outside of his arms on each hop. On reaching the end of the board he hops high in the air and enters the water head first with knees and elbows bent sharply out.

Back-Somersault Dive.—The diver stands near the end of the board with his back toward the end. He executes a back somersault and enters the water feet first.

Tandem Side-Dive.—Two divers stand facing each other at right angles to the end of the board, with hands joined overhead. They execute a side dive together.

This dive may also be performed with the divers standing back to back.

Tandem Face-to-Face Dive.—The first diver stands at the end of the plank with his back toward the end. The second diver stands facing him and as close to him as possible. They join hands overhead. The first diver does a back dive and the second diver a front dive.

Tandem Back-to-Back Dive.—Two divers stand back to back at the end of the board with hands joined overhead. The first diver does a front dive and the second a back dive.

Comedy Dives

Swimming Pool, Beach, Camp   *Junior High School to Adults*

The diving events of a swimming meet offer an excellent setting for clown events. The following are among the more successful of the possibilities.

Dying Duck.—A diver capable of doing a good swan dive stands on the high-diving board, and another performer stands below on the side of the pool or float, holding a pistol containing a loud blank cartridge. The diver does a swan dive to the best of his ability, and when he is at the highest point, the performer below shoots the pistol at him. The diver relaxes, turns over, and falls into the water as if dead.

Buckingham-Palace Fountain.—The diver takes the high-diving board with his mouth full of water. He runs to the end of the board, hits it hard, and jumps into the air. As soon as he leaves the board, he assumes the position of a statue, one arm up and forward, the other back, and one leg in advance of the other. He holds this position, squirting water from his mouth as he falls into the water feet first.

Champion High Diver.—This event should be conducted after a good diver has performed a dive in which he attained good height from the high-diving board. This diver and the comedy diver go out on the board together. The comedy diver draws a mark in the air to indicate the height the diver attained. The diver objects, erases the "mark" and draws a higher one. This is repeated until the height is agreed upon. Then the comedy diver prepares to excel the height. He runs out on the board, hits the end, but as he does so flexes his knees, and instead of going up in the air, he does not rebound from the board at all, but topples over the end into the water.

Learning to Dive.—Following the diving exhibition, announce that the champion diver will demonstrate how easy it is to learn to dive by teaching a beginner who has never attempted to dive before. The beginner and the diver go out on the high-diving board. The beginner gets dizzy from the height and retreats. This goes on until, after a demonstration by the diver, he goes out on the end and jumps on the board a time or two. Encouraged he jumps again, loses his balance, falls, but grabs the plank with his hands and hangs under it. He hangs there kicking and hollering, and the question is how to get him down.

Bouncing the Board.—The situation is as in Learning to Dive—the champion diver is teaching a beginner to dive. The beginner stands on the end of the high-diving board and begins to jump up and down. He jumps higher and higher and can't seem to stop the board. He yells for instructions, but suddenly his feet fly out, and he comes down in sitting position on the plank and remains there, with hands on his hips and surprised look on his face. He gets up and limps off the plank, rubbing his hip.

Quadruple Somersault.—After a good diver has performed the triple somersault dive or the double somersault, the clown diver announces that that is nothing and he will do the quadruple somersault. He does three somersaults going down the board and one in the air.

Indiana Slip.—After the good divers have done some nice swan dives, the Indiana Slip is announced. The clown diver runs out, jumps on the board about four feet from the end, and dives over the end, barely missing it.

Clowning

Water meets and water play days may be made more colorful and entertaining by using clowns who mingle with the crowd and later join the divers on the diving board.

President LaDuke of the University of Paris.—Make up an individual to represent the President of the University of Paris—cutaway coat, high collar, and so forth. After the diving events the director of the meet, standing on the high-diving board, announces that the occasion is highly

528 ACTIVE GAMES AND CONTESTS

honored by the presence of President LaDuke, who, while he is not a swimmer himself, had done much to promote swimming throughout Europe; he will address the spectators. The President walks out on the high-diving board, and begins to speak in French. He gestures with increasing animation, steps as he speaks, and comes dangerously near to the sides of the plank. Suddenly he loses his balance, falls, catches hold of the plank with his hands and hangs in the air. The question is how to get him down without his falling into the water, cut-away coat and all. Two men rush out on the diving plank and attempt to rescue him. After much "business" one of the men accidentally steps on the President's fingers—the President yells and withdraws his hand, shaking his hurt fingers. In the excitement the man then steps on the fingers of the President's other hand, and down the President goes into the pool.

Hiram and Mirandy.—A farmer and his wife dressed to go to the city—the farmer wears an old-fashioned cut-away coat, brown derby, whiskers, chews a stalk of hay, carries a suitcase and a lighted lantern. He walks out on the dock or diving board arguing with Mirandy and walks off the end, falling awkwardly into the water. Mirandy jumps in to save him.

Professor Dooty.—A professor in Prince Albert coat and silk hat, carrying an umbrella and open book, walks the dock reading Latin. He absentmindedly walks off the end of the diving plank and falls in awkwardly, still reading the book.

Sugar Papa.—A doty old man dressed in the height of youthful fashion, accompanied by a girl of about twenty. The old man talks in a cracked voice and attempts to act as sprightly as possible. He backs out on the diving board, looking at the girl and waving his fingers to her, and jumps up a time or two with both feet, kicking himself with his heels as he does so, then misses the plank and falls in calling for help.

Grandpa.—An old man hobbles with a cane and the other hand on his hip. He talks to himself going out on the diving board, sidesteps off the board, and goes in with a loud yell.

The Visiting Canoe.—In the course of the swimming events a canoe appears containing a young man in sport clothes and a beautifully dressed young woman. The canoe glides slowly around the swimmers and finally floats into the line of the next race. The director of the meet asks the occupants to withdraw the canoe—he speaks loudly so as to focus attention on the canoe. The man starts to turn the canoe and upsets it tossing the lady, clothes and all, into the water. She screams and flounders around. The life savers rush to her assistance, take her to the dock, and perform artificial respiration. A boy may be dressed up as the girl.

MINOR SWIMMING AND DIVING CONTESTS BETWEEN GROUPS

Tandem and File Swimming Events

Swimming Beach, Pool, Camp   *Junior High School to Adults*

In the tandem swims two players swim attached together. These events may also be used with several players joined together in file.

Crocodile Swimming Race.—The position is on the stomach. One player is behind the other and the rear player places his hands on the hips of the player in front.

Tandem Crawl.—The front swimmer locks his legs around the waist of the back swimmer. Both do the crawl stroke with the second player keeping time with the first. The second player does the flutter kick.

Tandem Back Crawl.—Same as the above except that the swimmers are on their backs.

Tandem Breast Stroke.—The position is as in the Tandem Crawl and the swimmers swim with the breast stroke.

Tandem Back Stroke.—The position is as in the Tandem Back Crawl and the swimmers swim with the single back stroke.

Twin Swimming Race.—Two swimmers race as a team with inside arms locked.

Three-Legged Swimming Race.—Two swimmers race as a team with inside legs tied together.

Water Tug-of-War

Swimming Beach, Camp   *Junior and Senior High Schools*

These events are conducted just as in the land Tug-of-War events with the players standing in water about waist deep.

With good swimmers competing, this event may be conducted in deep water. To the rope attach loops of heavy canvas to serve as shoulder loops. Tie a handkerchief to mark the middle of the rope and stretch a rope under the handkerchief at right angles to the tug-of-war rope. The contestants adjust the shoulder loops and at the signal swim toward their own goal.

Water Touch

Swimming Beach, Pool, Camp   *Late Elementary to Senior High School*

Touch is a superior contest either on land or in the water. Divide the players into two teams and stand them facing each other about six feet apart in water about waist deep. The leader names some object and all players of both teams swim and touch the object, then return to position. The team scores one point which has all of its players in line first. The team scoring eleven first wins.

Such objects may be called as wood, rock, shore, bottom, side of pool, paint, dock, grass, boat, buoy, rope. Objects may be placed on the dock, shore, or side of pool, such as sweaters, leather balls, shoes, and shoes with rubber soles. These objects may be named, but it is better to call leather, rubber, cloth, and so on.

Lost Penny

Swimming Beach, Pool, Camp   Late Elementary to Senior High School

Divide the players into two teams and place them in file on the dock or edge of the tank. Throw a penny or other small object not easily seen in the water. The first player of one team dives and if he brings up the penny he scores one point for his team. Replace the penny and the first player of the second team repeats. Continue until all have tried. The team with the highest score wins. Each player is allowed only one dive.

Variation.—Have one player from each team dive at the same time. The one who brings up the penny scores one point for his team.

Straight Water Relay

Swimming Beach, Pool, Camp   Late Elementary School to Adults

Divide the group into teams of from six to ten players, and arrange them in parallel files. The files may stand either on the end of the pool or dock, or in the water. At the signal the first player swims to the turning line, returns, and touches off the second player who repeats. In touching off the next swimmer, he should be tagged on the foot, if standing on the dock or end of the pool, otherwise on the hand. Continue until all have swum. The team finishing first wins.

Swimming Tunnel Relay

Swimming Beach, Pool, Camp   Late Elementary School to Adults

Secure two large cans the size of small barrels of the type which oil is shipped in, and have a mechanic cut out the bottoms. Sink these midway between the starting and turning lines.

Line the two teams in parallel files at the starting line. At the signal the first player of each team swims to the can, dives, swims through it, continues across the turning line, turns and swims through the can again, then touches off the second player who repeats. Continue until all have swum. The team finishing first wins.

Between-the-Legs Relay

Swimming Beach, Pool, Camp   *Late Elementary School to Adults*

Arrange the teams in parallel files in shallow water. All players spread their legs widely. At the signal the last player of each team dives under the legs of the others and swims between the legs to the front. He may come up for air at any time, and then dive again. He then takes his position at the head of the line and spreads his legs. As soon as he appears above the surface at the head of the line the player who is now at the rear dives and repeats. Continue until all have swum. The team finishing first wins.

Disrobing Relay

Swimming Beach, Pool, Camp   *Late Elementary to Senior High School*

The teams consist of two swimmers. The first is dressed in a bathing suit with pajamas or shirt and pants over it. He may also wear a hat and carry an umbrella. At the signal he swims to the other end of the pool or to a float, takes off the clothing, leaves it in a pile and returns, touching off the second player. This player swims to the clothing, puts it on, and returns.

Water Leap-Frog Relay

Swimming Beach, Pool, Camp   *Late Elementary to Senior High School*

Divide the group into two teams and line them up in parallel files with the head men of the files in shallow water and the rear in deep water treading. At the signal the rear man in each team places his hands on the shoulders of the man in front, pushes him under water and leaps over him with legs spread. Continue in this fashion until the original head of the file is back at the head. The team finishing first wins.

Surf-Board Relay

Swimming Beach, Pool, Camp   *Late Elementary School to Adults*

Arrange the teams in parallel files. Give the first player in each team a surf board. At the signal the player mounts the surf board and swims on it to the turning line and back, giving the board to the second player who repeats. Continue until all have swum. The team finishing first wins. The turning line should not be over fifty feet distant.

Water Circle-Passing Relay

Swimming Beach, Camp   *Late Elementary to Senior High School*

Divide the group into two teams and arrange each team in a circle, standing in water about chest deep. Appoint a captain for each team. Give each captain a tin plate, stone, or other object which will sink. At the signal each captain tosses the object to the player to his right and it is thus passed around the circle. If a player drops it he must dive after it. The team wins that first completes the circuit of the circle three times.

Variation.—Use water-polo balls instead of heavy objects.

Other Novelty Relays

Swimming Beach, Pool, Camp   *Late Elementary School to Adults*

The following relays are described earlier in this chapter as individual races under a title corresponding to the title of the relay. The application of these races to the relay plan can be easily made by the reader. The relays are conducted like the Straight Water Relay (page 530).

Umbrella Relay	Fan Relay
Water Flag-Relay	Water Balloon-Pushing Relay
Japanese-Lantern Relay	Water Spearing-the-Ring
Table-Waiter Relay	Log-Obstacle Relay
Banana-Eating Relay	Head-Carry Relay
Straw-Hat Relay	Inner-Tube Relay

Many of the minor land relays described in the section on "Contests between Groups" are easily adaptable to the water.

WATER GAMES

Water Polo

Swimming Pool, Open Water   *Junior High School to Adults*

Playing Area.—The maximum dimensions for water polo are thirty yards and the minimum length nineteen yards. Areas are designated by lines two yards and four yards from the goal lines.

The goals consist of two uprights and a crossbar. They are placed one foot out at the middle of the end lines. The open space is ten feet wide, the crossbar three feet from the surface of the water.

Teams.—Seven players constitute a team. Substitutions may be made at half time or whenever a goal is scored.

Start.—Players arrange themselves in line with their respective goals. When captains are ready, the signal to go is given and the ball is released at the center of the playing area.

Scoring.—The ball may be carried or thrown through the goal. A point is scored when the entire ball has crossed the goal line between the uprights and below the crossbar.

Time of Play.—The game is fourteen minutes long, divided into two halves of seven minutes each. The teams change goals at the half.

Fouls.—The following are fouls:

1. Starting before the whistle, or assisting another player at the start, or pushing off from any support; holding on to the rails or any support.

2. Touching the ball with both hands at the same time, or holding the ball under water when tackled, or striking the ball with the clenched fist, or touching the ball before it has touched the water when the referee throws it.

3. Walking or standing on the bottom for any purpose except for resting; jumping or pushing off from the bottom or sides to play the ball or an opponent.

4. Impeding, interfering with, or swimming on the back or legs of a player unless he has the ball; holding or pushing off from an opponent; splashing water in the face of an opponent, or kicking it at him.

5. While making a free-throw, throwing or dribbling the ball directly at the goalkeeper or at a team mate within two yards of the goal.

6. Goalkeeper going more than four yards away from his goal line.

Free-Throw.—Following a foul, the free-throw is awarded the offended team at the spot where the foul occurred.

Waterball [1]

Swimming Pool   *Junior High School to Adults*

This is a game after the type of Water Polo, but which has a minimum of rules and may be enjoyed by all regardless of swimming ability.

Playing Area.—The entire pool is used.

Ball.—A water-polo ball.

Teams.—Seven men compose a team.

Start.—The teams line up behind their respective goals and the ball is tossed in at the center of the pool. The teams change goals after each score.

The Play.—The ball may be advanced in any manner—throwing, batting, kicking, swimming. The players may leave the water but may touch the ball only when in the water, that is, when some part of the body is under the surface of the water. There are no fouls except unnecessary roughness, which means disqualification.

Out of Bounds.—The ball is out of bounds when it goes out of the pool and does not immediately return, or when it is touched by a player out of the water.

Scoring.—A goal is scored when the ball is placed *in the trough* at either end of the pool while the referee counts to ten. The count is made by saying "One and two and three (etc.)."

[1] Contributed by Pat Dawson.

Length of Game.—The game consists of two halves of ten minutes with a two-minute intermission.

Substitutions.—Substitutions may be made only at the half, unless a team is short of players.

Water Push-Ball

Swimming Beach, Camp   *Junior and Senior High Schools*

This is a mass contest which always is much enjoyed. Divide the players into two teams and line them up at goals thirty to fifty yards apart. Place a thirty-inch cage ball on the water between them. At the signal they swim for the ball and try to push or bat it over the opposing goal. Ducking and roughness are prohibited.

A water-polo ball, although less satisfactory, may be used.

Water Push-Balloon.—After Water Push-Ball has been played for a few minutes with a cage ball or water-polo ball, substitute a large toy balloon for the ball. The slow floating balloon changes the nature of the game and creates a humorous situation.

Water Pillow Fighting

Swimming Beach, Camp   *Junior and Senior High Schools*

Pillow Fighting on the water is practically the same as the game on land. Whether on land or lake it is an ever-popular camp game.

Cut a straight smooth pole five inches in diameter and twenty feet long. Build two substantial tripods of saplings and place them in the water to hold the pole. The height of the pole above the water should be such that a boy of average height, when hanging from it with his legs, will miss the water with the top of his head by about six inches.

Water-proofed canoeing pillows are ideal for ordinary play, but for tournament play with hard hitting boys competing, ordinary bed pillows should be used.

The rules are exactly as in land Pillow Fighting. When a player loses his balance and hangs under the pole he is not defeated and continues to fight from this position or attempts to crawl back up. There is no rule against placing the free hand on the pole.

Canoe Tilting

Swimming Beach, Camp   *Junior and Senior High Schools*

The ancient game of Tilting when adapted to the water, makes probably the most popular of all canoeing games. The game should be played in water not over chest deep.

Equipment.—Two heavy bamboo poles six to seven feet long are needed —the use of longer poles is a common mistake which makes good tilting technique difficult and often impossible. On the end of each pole place a rubber suction cup such as plumbers sell as a bathroom accessory. These suction cups may be attached in a moment and are soft enough not to hurt the contestants; they make an ideal and quickly prepared pole.

Land tilting poles described under Tilting (page 295) may be used by covering the padded ends with oilcloth.

Two canoes are needed, each carrying a tilter and one paddler to handle the canoe for him.

Position of Tilters.—There are three methods which may be used in standing in the canoe while tilting:

1. The tilter may stand on the front seat.
2. He may stand on the gunwales at the front seat.
3. He may stand on a platform placed on the gunwales over the bow seat, this platform being about two feet square.

Standing on the gunwales is not to be recommended—the position is so uncertain that it makes good tilting impossible. Either of the other methods are satisfactory.

Object of the Game.—The object is to dislodge the opposing tilter by pushing or punching him with the pole.

The Paddler.—The paddler's only function is to handle the canoe and keep the tilter in position to tilt effectively against the opponent. The paddler may not touch the opposing canoe or its occupants. In approaching the opponent's canoe, the paddler keeps the opposing canoe on his port side.

Fouls.—It is a foul if:

1. The tilter strikes his opponent above the neck or below the knees with intent to dislodge him (punches directly at these parts).
2. The tilter strikes his opponent's canoe with his pole with intent to dislodge him (punches directly at the canoe).
3. The tilter seizes his opponent's pole. (He may ward off the opponent's pole with his hand but it is a foul to close the hand on it.)
4. The paddler touches the opponents or their canoe with hand or paddle.
5. The paddler paddles his canoe forcefully into the opponent's canoe with apparent intent to dislodge the tilter.
6. The tilter touches his own canoe with his hands.

Falls.—A tilter wins the fall under the following conditions:

1. When his opponent falls from his position, either into his canoe or the water, provided he himself is still in position. One foot slipping to the floor of the canoe is regarded as a fall.
2. When his opponent drops his spear.
3. When his opponent or his opponent's paddler commits one of the first five fouls listed above.
4. When his opponent commits foul Number 6 three times.

Match.—A match consists of the best two out of three falls.

Battle-Royal on Raft

Swimming Beach, Camp   *Junior and Senior High Schools*

This is one of the most interesting and best-loved water events, both for participants and spectators. A crew of life savers should surround the raft, of course.

A number of players stand on the raft, or if played on the dock, a line should be drawn about twelve feet from the end to mark the playing area. At the signal each tries to throw the others off the dock. The one remaining on when all others are in the water is the champion.

This event may be played by allowing players to climb back on the dock if they can. If this method is used, play for three minutes, and all who are on the dock at that time are winners.

Simple Water-Tag Games

Swimming Beach, Pool, Camp   *Elementary to Senior High School*

Many of the land-tag games may be adapted to use in the water. These games are described in detail in the chapter on Tag Games. The more commonly used types of water tag follow.

Simple Water Tag.—In the simple form of water tag, one player is "it" and chases the rest of the swimmers. When a swimmer is tagged he becomes "it."

Tag Games using Safety Objects.—In the water-tag games in which safety is achieved by touching some object or spot, the following objects may be used: wood, rope, buoys, dock, side of pool, a rock held off the bottom in hand, and so forth.

Tag Games using Safety Positions.—In the games in which safety is achieved by assuming some position or performing some movement, the following may be used; *head held under water, one foot out of water, touching bottom with one hand, holding one foot with one hand,* and so forth.

Tag games, excellent from the standpoint of developing ability in the water, are *Tread Tag,* in which a player is safe while treading water, and *Float Tag* in which he is safe while floating motionless.

Tag Games which Limit Tagging to Certain Parts of the Body. —Games of this type may be played by allowing "it" to tag players only on the head or on the foot.

Handicap Tag Games.—The player who is tagged may be handicapped by causing him to keep the hand or leg on which he was tagged out of the water. He continues to swim but must keep the arm or leg in this position. All tagging must of course be done on arms or legs.

Water Poison

Swimming Beach, Pool, Camp   Late Elementary and Junior High Schools

This game may be played in shallow water by children or in deep water by good swimmers. The players join hands in a circle around some floating object (poison) which is anchored. At the signal all try to pull the others into the poison and avoid touching it themselves. All who touch it are eliminated. If two players break their grip, both are eliminated. The player wins who remains in when all others have been eliminated.

Cross the Pool
(*Water Pom-Pom-Pull-Away*)

Swimming Beach, Pool, Camp   Late Elementary to Senior High School

The players line up on one side of the pool or stream provided it is not more than thirty feet wide. In open water, establish two boundary lines twenty feet apart and line up the players behind one line. "It" stands in the center and calls, "Cross the pool," whereupon all the swimmers swim to the other side while "it" tries to tag them. All who are tagged join "it" and help catch the others on the next command. The player wins who is the last to be caught.

Duck in the Pool

Swimming Pool   Late Elementary to Senior High School

Select a player to be "it" and place him in the center of the pool. The other players line up on the side. "It" calls "Duck in the pool" and all dive in and swim under water to the opposite side. "It" must duck under and attempt to tag them under water. All tagged join "it" and assist in tagging. The last player to survive wins.

Water Fish-Net
(*Fisherman*)

Swimming Beach, Pool, Camp   Late Elementary to Senior High School

Select one player to act as Fisherman and station him in the center of the pool. Line up the other players (Fish) on one side of the pool. If in open water, establish two goals about thirty feet apart and line the players behind one goal.

The Fisherman gives the signal and the Fish all swim to the opposite goal while the Fisherman attempts to tag them. All who are tagged join the Fisherman as taggers. When there are three taggers they join hands forming a "fish net." Only the end players of the fish net may tag and as additional Fish are tagged they take the end positions. As the net becomes lengthened the center players try to circle the Fish and hold them until the ends can reach them and tag them. The Fish may swim through or dive under the net. The last Fish caught becomes the Fisherman for the next game.

Log

Swimming Beach, Pool, Camp   Late Elementary and Junior High Schools

The players line up on either end of the pool, or if in open water behind goal lines, about sixty feet apart. Select one player to act as the log. He floats on his back midway between the goals. The other players swim around the log. Without warning the log suddenly rolls over and gives chase. The players try to reach the goals without being tagged. Those tagged become logs and float in the center with the first log. The last one caught is the log for the next game.

Water Black-and-White

Swimming Beach, Pool, Camp   Late Elementary to Senior High School

This is a water adaptation of Black-and-White (page 266). Divide the players into two teams and line them facing each other with a lane six feet wide between them. Name one team "Black" and the other "White." Throw into the water between the teams a slab of wood painted white on one side and black on the other. If it comes up black, the Blacks chase the Whites to their goal and all who are tagged join the Blacks. If it comes up white, the Whites chase the Blacks. The goals should be about thirty feet behind the teams. The team wins that has the most players when the game is stopped.

Water Crows-and-Cranes.—This is a water adaptation of Crows-and-Cranes (page 267). Divide the players into two teams and arrange them in lines facing each other with a six-foot lane between them. Name one team "Crows" and the other "Cranes." The leader calls either "Cr-r-r-r-ows" or "Cr-r-r-anes" and the team named chases the other to their goal; all who are tagged join the tagging team. The leader should trail the first part of the word a long time and occasionally add confusion by finishing with "Crackers" or "Crawfish." The goals should be about thirty feet behind the teams.

Water Dodgeball

Swimming Beach, Camp   Late Elementary to Senior High School

This is played exactly like the land game of Dodgeball. A water-polo ball or sport ball is used and the game is played in water waist deep.

Water Keep-Ball

Swimming Beach, Pool, Camp   Late Elementary to Senior High School

The players divide into two teams and scatter over the swimming area. A cork ball, water-polo ball, sport ball, or codeball may be used. The game is started by tossing the ball up between two opponents as in Basketball. Each team tries to keep the ball in its own possession by passing it among themselves. When one team has it the opposing team tries to get it and to keep it. The game is strenuous and all ducking and rough play should be carefully watched for and eliminated.

Water Ten-Catches.—This is similar to Water Keep-Ball except that the players of each team attempt to pass the ball among themselves ten times in succession. When a player gets it, he passes it to a team mate who catches it and calls "One"; this player then passes it to another who catches it and calls "Two," and so on until ten is reached. The opposing team attempts to break up the run of catches by securing the ball and passing it among its own players. When a team loses possession of the ball, or allows it to fall to the water, it forfeits all points scored, and when it regains possession of it, must start counting with one again. The team scoring ten first wins.

Water Numbers-Change

Swimming Beach, Pool, Camp   Late Elementary to Senior High School

Arrange the players in a circle in water about chest deep and have them number off. One player is "it" and is in the center of the circle. "It" calls two numbers and the holders of these numbers exchange places. "It" tries to get one of these places and if he succeeds the player left without a place is "it."

Water Knights

Swimming Beach, Camp   Junior and Senior High Schools

In water waist deep, the players pair off according to approximate weight and one partner, acting as rider, mounts the back of the other. At the signal all try to pull or push the other riders off. The pair wins that stands when all the others are down.

Variation.—Use as a dual contest. When a pair wins, another pair challenges them.

Water Spud

Swimming Beach, Camp   Junior and Senior High Schools

This is played exactly like the land game of Spud (page 255). A cork water ball or soft rubber ball is used. When "it" calls "Stop" all players stop in their tracks and stand erect. No one is permitted to duck. The game is played in water waist deep.

Water Circle-Ball

Swimming Beach, Pool, Camp   Late Elementary and Junior High Schools

The players stand in a circle with "it" in the center. The players pass a water-polo ball, sport ball, or codeball, across and around the circle while "it" attempts to touch the ball. If he succeeds the player who touched the ball last becomes "it."

Variation.—The ball must be passed around the circle rather than across it. It must be tossed each time, not handed. "It" may order the ball passed in the opposite direction whenever he chooses.

Water Endball

Swimming Beach, Pool, Camp   Late Elementary to Senior High School

Mark out a swimming area not larger than forty by sixty feet. For average swimmers, the water should not be over chest deep. Divide the court into four sections by stretching ropes across parallel to the end lines at intervals of fifteen feet. Four players from one team occupy the one end section and four from the other team occupy the other end. These are the captains. The remaining players of each team occupy the center section farthest from their respective captains. A water-polo ball, sport ball, or codeball is used.

The center players try to throw the ball over the heads of their opponents to their captains. The opposing players act as guards. One point is scored each time a captain catches the ball. It must be caught from the air, not picked up off the water.

Water Baseball

Swimming Beach, Camp   Late Elementary to Senior High School

A cork water ball or a softball is used. The bases are foot-square boards anchored in shallow water with the outfield in deeper water. The baselines should be twenty-seven feet long. The ball is batted with a bat as in Baseball. The rules of Playgroundball apply.

Water Baseball is often played with a six-inch rubber ball which is batted with the hand.

Water Baseball in Pools.—Assuming that the pool is approximately twenty by sixty feet in size, place home base on the floor above the deep end, midway between the side lines. Second base is similarly placed at the shallow end. First and third bases are placed on the sides of the pool, twenty feet from the deep end. All bases consist of a towel three feet long laid over the side of the pool. The towel and not the side of the pool under it is the base. Fifteen feet from the deep end a foul line is designated, running parallel to the deep end.

Ball.—A water-polo ball is used.

Teams.—Teams consist of nine players—catcher, three basemen, two shortstops, and three fielders.

Batter.—The batter stands at home base (or on the end of the diving board), tosses the ball in the air and bats it with his hand.

Base Swimmer.—Having hit the ball, the swimmer swims to first base and places his hand on the base (towel). He may swim under water to avoid being hit. He is not permitted to leave his base after the ball has been returned to the end of the pool for the batter until the batter has batted it. To do so is an out.

The Batter Is Out.—The batter is out:

1. When a fly ball is caught.
2. When a batted ball hits the ceiling, or falls outside the tank.
3. When he makes two strikes. (A foul on the second strike counts as a strike.)

The Base Swimmer Is Out.—The base swimmer is out:

1. When hit by a thrown ball between bases.
2. When tagged by a player with the ball between bases.
3. When first base is touched by a player holding the ball before the swimmer reaches it.
4. When he leaves a base after the ball has been returned to the end of the pool for the batter and before the batter has batted it.

Hanging on Side of Pool.—This is not allowed except where water is deeper than four-and-one-half feet. If the violator of this rule interferes with a base swimmer or the ball, the swimmer is given an extra base.

Length of Game.—The game consists of five innings.

Other Rules.—In all respects not covered by these rules the rules of Playgroundball apply.[2]

Water Batball

Swimming Beach, Pool, Camp   Late Elementary to Senior High School

Two teams of eight or ten players may play. Scatter one team (A) in the pool, facing the shallow end. Above the shallow end, line up the other team (B). One player of Team B bats a water-polo ball or sport ball with his hand toward Team A and immediately swims to the end of the pool which he touches and then returns. Team A attempts to secure the ball and hit the swimmer with it. The swimmer may dive or swim under water to avoid being hit. If the swimmer is hit he is out; if not he scores one point for his team. Three outs retires the side and the teams change positions.

[2] These rules follow those submitted by Robert Lindwall.

The fielding players are not permitted to swim with the ball, nor to hold it more than five seconds. They should pass it to team mates who are in position to hit the swimmer.

The swimmer is safe while touching the end of the tank but may not remain there longer than ten seconds.

Water Volleyball

Swimming Beach, Camp   *Junior High School to Adults*

The game is best played in water about chest deep but may be played in deeper water if the players' swimming ability permits. A rope may be used for a net and is stretched five feet above the water, or lower if the players' ability demands. Mark the four corners of the court by driving piles in the bottom and stretch ropes with wooden beads for the side lines. Two officials stand at corners diagonally opposite each other to watch the lines.

A water-polo ball or sport ball is used and the game is played as in regular Volleyball.

Water Skim Ball [3]

Swimming Pool   *Late Elementary to Senior High School*

This game was originated by Nathan H. Kaufman. It is played in the shallow end of the pool and uses the width of the pool.

Two goals are needed. These may be solid wood or a frame, measuring two feet high and four feet long. Place at water level, one on each side of the tank at a point fifteen feet from the shallow end of the pool. Five feet out from each goal a zone line is drawn parallel to the side walls. A water-polo ball is used. From four to ten may play on a team.

The teams line up at their side of the pool with one hand on the wall. The leader throws the ball between them to start the game.

The object is to skim or bounce the ball on the water so that it will strike or go through the goal after bouncing on the water once. The ball must be thrown with one hand and must be handled by more than two players before a goal can be made. One player of each team acts as goalkeeper and is the only player who may be inside the zone line. The goalkeeper must return the ball to the playing area within ten seconds or forfeit it to the other side. The goalkeeper cannot score when he swims out of the goal zone. If a ball, after skimming the water hits an opponent and then hits the goal, it does not score. A player holding the ball may be ducked until he releases it, but no other ducking is permitted.

The following are fouls:

1. Holding on to the wall while holding the ball.
2. Stopping the ball while holding on to the wall.

[3] Contributed by Nathan H. Kaufman.

3. Rough play.
4. Ducking a player who does not have the ball.

The penalty for a foul is an unguarded throw for the goal from a point midway between the goals. It must skim the water and hit or go through the goal to count.

Goals from play count two points. Goals after fouls score one point. The game consists of two five-minute halves.

Punch Bowl [4]

Swimming Beach, Pool, Camp　　　　*Junior and Senior High Schools*

This game was originated by Dr. A. D. Browne.

A heavy wire is stretched down the middle of the tank and about nine feet above the surface, running the length of the pool. Suspended from the cable on a sliding brass ring is a punch bag attached with a seven-foot rope and a snap buckle. The snap enables the coach to remove the bag when a clear pool is desired, but when attached the bag hangs a foot above the surface. The playing group is divided into two teams, each of which remains on its side of the wire. The team batting the bag to their end of the pool scores a goal.

Water Basketball

Swimming Beach, Pool, Camp　　　　*Junior and Senior High Schools*

Place a wash tub or bushel basket on each end of the swimming pool or on standards in open water, elevated so that the top of the basket is four feet above the water. If played in a tank the sides of the tank mark the out-of-bounds lines; if played in open water, ropes may outline the court but the game is more commonly and satisfactorily played with no out-of-bound rules. The water should not be over chest deep unless good swimmers are playing. A water-polo ball or sport ball is used and the procedure and scoring are as in Basketball, except that it is permissible for players to carry the ball by swimming with it. The rules of Basketball regarding personal contact apply.

Watermelon Scramble

Swimming Beach, Camp, Picnic　　*Late Elementary to Senior High School*

Place a watermelon well greased on the lake bottom in water about chest deep. Line the players up on the shore. At the signal they dash for the melon and each tries to get possession of it and get it ashore. This

[4] From American National Red Cross, *Water Games* (mimeographed), p. 2. By permission of American National Red Cross, publishers.

is a free-for-all scramble and the player holding the melon when he steps on shore keeps it.

Live-Duck Scramble

Swimming Beach, Camp, Picnic   *Junior and Senior High Schools*

This is a thrilling scramble using a live duck. The players divide into two groups and line up about a hundred feet apart at right angles to the shore. A live duck is released midway between them. At the signal the players scramble for it. The player wins who gets possession of the duck. The duck is well able to protect himself in the water and will give the players a lively chase. Once a player secures the duck the event stops immediately.

Variation.—Use as a dual contest. Two players only compete for possession of the duck. In this case it may be necessary to clip the wings of the duck.

CANOE CONTESTS

Standard Canoe Races

Swimming Beach, Camp   *Junior High School to Adults*

In canoe races the canoes are lined up on a starting line and ordered into an exact line by the starting official. The procedure is in general like the conduct of running races. At least ten feet should be allowed between the canoes at the starting line. Distances of 100 yards, 220 yards, 440 yards, and 880 yards are commonly used.

The following events may be used:

1. One man in canoe, single blade.
2. Tandem, single blade.
3. Four men in canoe, single blade.
4. One man, double blade.
5. Tandem, double blade.
6. Four men in canoe, double blade.

Figure-of-Eight Paddle

Swimming Beach, Camp   *Junior High School to Adults*

Place three markers in a row in the water ten yards apart, the first being ten yards from the starting line. Four such rows of markers should be established, permitting the contestants to compete in heats of four. The markers may be made of boards one foot square and anchored—flags stuck in them make them more conspicuous.

Each contestant paddles to the left of the first marker, to the right of the second, the left of the third, and then turns around and returns, passing to the left of the third, to the right of the second, and to the left of the first. Each canoe thus cuts a figure-of-eight course. The canoe finishing first wins.

Reversing Race

Swimming Beach, Camp   *Junior High School to Adults*

The canoes line up at a starting line, facing *away* from goal. Two paddlers comprise the crew. At the start, they turn their canoes around, paddle to the finish line, turn again, and return to starting line to end the race.

This event is sometimes conducted by prohibiting back-stroking or side-stroking on the turns. The paddlers thus have to paddle in a wide semi-circle to get the canvas turned around.

Medley Canoe-Race

Swimming Beach, Camp   *Junior and Senior High Schools*

This race consists of a fifty-yard dash, a fifty-yard swim, and a fifty-yard paddle. The canoes are staked in a row fifty yards from the shore. Each man is assigned a canoe before the race starts. The starting line is fifty yards from the shore—the contestants run to the water, swim to their assigned canoes, climb in, free the boats from their stakes, and paddle to the shore.

All-Overboard Race

Swimming Beach, Camp   *Junior and Senior High Schools*

The distance is one-hundred yards. When the canoes are part way down the stretch a signal (gun shot) is given and all the paddlers jump in the water, completely submerging themselves, keeping their canoes up-right, climb back in, and continue to the finish. Crews of two should be used.

Paddle and Tow

Swimming Beach, Camp   *Junior and Senior High Schools*

The canoes are lined up at the shore, one man to a canoe. Each paddles to a marked line about 220 yards from the shore, capsizes the canoe, and swims back to the shore with it in capsized position.

Paddle and Portage

Swimming Beach, Camp   *Senior High School to Adults*

The paddlers paddle over a given course to the shore, beach the canoe, pick it up and portage it to a point twenty-five yards in shore, turn around and portage it back, put it in the water, and paddle back to the starting line. This event calls for strong contestants—with players of average strength two paddlers should occupy each canoe. Crews of one man should not be attempted unless the paddlers are experienced in one-man portaging.

Tail-End Race

Swimming Beach, Camp   *Junior High School to Adults*

This is one of the most interesting of the novelty canoe races, particularly to the spectators. There is one paddler to a canoe. Each contestant sits on the rear seat of his canoe, *facing backward, with his feet in the small space between the rear seat of the canoe and the end.* He thus faces the stern of the canoe, the bow extending high into the air behind him. At the signal, the contestants attempt to paddle the canoes, stern first, to the finish line. The spectacle of the canoes standing well-nigh on end, and the difficulties encountered by the paddlers in steering, make this a great fun-maker.

Pie-Pan Paddling

Swimming Beach, Camp   *Late Elementary to Senior High School*

Pie pans used as paddles will make the canoes literally fly through the water. The centipede-like appearance of the arms working in unison,  together with the speed obtained, makes the event appeal strongly to the spectators. Crews of four to six paddlers in each canoe should be used. They kneel on the bottom, each man armed with two pie pans, one in each hand. With a little team work between the crew members and someone calling strokes, the canoes can be shot forward with remarkable speed. This race is great fun.

Hand Paddling

Swimming Beach, Camp   *Late Elementary to Senior High School*

No paddles are allowed in this race—the contestants kneel in the bottom of the canoe and paddle with their hands. No sticks may be carried in the hands and no appliances strapped to arms. The canoe can be navigated in this way faster than one might think. Crews of two to six may be used. Each canoe should carry a paddle, stowed in the bottom.

Standing Canoe Race

Swimming Beach, Camp   *Junior and Senior High Schools*

For those who have never tried paddling in a standing position, it is better to begin by standing on the bottom of the canoe just in front of the rear seat. The real stunt, however, is paddling from the gunwales.

If a crew of one man is navigating each canoe, he should stand on the gunwales at the rear thwart; later when he becomes more proficient he may move back as far as the rear seat. Feet must be entirely on the gunwales and not touching the thwarts or seats.

Tandem Standing Canoe Race.—The most sport in this stunt is to be found in tandem gunwales paddling. Standing paddling is not so tipsy as it appears, and two on a team get along quite well together. Either single or double paddles may be used.

Four-Man Standing Canoe Race.—Same as the Tandem Standing Canoe Race except that four contestants stand on the gunwales of each canoe.

Plank-Paddling Race

Swimming Beach, Camp　　　　　*Junior and Senior High Schools*

This novel idea furnishes much sport. Place a two-inch plank ten or twelve feet long across the canoe at the rear thwart. Two paddlers sit, one on each end of the plank, and paddle the canoe with paddles. The race is conducted as any other canoe race.

Variation.—A contestant lies on his stomach on each end of the plank and paddles with his hands.

Variation.—The contestants stand, one on each end of the plank and paddle with paddles.

Bobbing
(*Pumping*)

Swimming Beach, Camp　　　　*Junior High School to Adults*

Bobbing, sometimes called pumping, is one of the great sports of canoeing. Stand on the gunwales just in front of the rear seat. Bend

the knees and crouch a little, then suddenly straighten them and throw the body erect; this forces the stern down and up and sends the canoe forward. Start by bending and rising slowly until the canoe gets under way, then increase both speed and energy until top effort is reached. Better results are obtained the farther back on the gunwales one stands, but troubles with balancing are thus increased also. As skill is developed, it is well to practice farther and farther back.

Steering the canoe in bobbing is difficult and requires practice. It is accomplished by shifting the weight of the body to one foot or the other, thus throwing the bow of the canoe in the direction desired. Balancing is greatly facilitated if the player carries a canoe paddle held with both hands, one hand near each end. The paddle must not touch the water. Wind and waves bother so much that they destroy the sport in bobbing, but it is great stuff in quiet water.

In races, a distance of 50 to 100 yards may be used.

Tandem Bobbing.—The two partners stand, each on one gunwale, as far astern as convenient, holding inside hands, the outside hands being free to assist in balancing. Bob up and down in unison.

This requires perfect team work, but two good partners soon get the knack of working together. At best, however, there will be many upsets. The stunt is regarded as difficult and the racing distance should be short.

Canoe Tug-of-War

Swimming Beach, Camp   *Junior and Senior High Schools*

In this stunt two canoes are tied together and the paddlers paddle against each other. Allow four or five feet of rope between the sterns of the two canoes. Tie a handkerchief to the rope midway between the canoes. Drive a pole in the bottom of the lake and arrange the canoes so that the handkerchief is opposite the pole. The winning team will make progress slowly and the one that first pulls the other five feet is awarded the event.

Cats-on-the-Tow-Line

Swimming Beach, Camp   *Late Elementary to Senior High School*

This is a canoeing adaptation of the dual combat, Cats-on-the Fence. Place a ten-foot piece of two-by-four-inch material across the middle of two canoes, resting the ends on the gunwales. Two paddlers are in each canoe to steady it. The contestants walk out on the board and stand toe to toe, with the toe of the back foot touching the heel of the front and with left hands behind the back. With the right hand, they try to slap each other into the water, being permitted to strike the opponent only on his right arm. Somebody challenges the winner.

Canoe Filling

Swimming Beach, Camp   *Junior and Senior High Schools*

This interesting stunt is a contest between the crews of two canoes, each crew consisting of two boys, one of whom is equipped with a paddle and the other with a water pail. Each pail is attached to the middle of its canoe with a six-foot rope, so that it can be retrieved if dropped. The idea is to fill the other canoe with water. The pail man stands on the bottom of the canoe, dips water from the lake, and throws it in his opponent's canoe. The paddler may not touch his opponents or their canoe, and may not dip or splash water at them. No bailing of one's own canoe is permitted. The contest is won by the crew that remains afloat in their canoe when the other canoe is down, either from sinking or upsetting. The event should be staged in water waist deep.

Walking Gunwales

Swimming Beach, Camp   *Junior and Senior High Schools*

This stunt consists of standing with one foot on each gunwale at the stern and walking forward with short steps to the bow, then backing up to the stern. Experienced players are often able to hop around at the bow and walk back.

Another variation of this stunt is to hop forward with little hops instead of walking.

Torpedo Race

Swimming Beach, Camp   *Junior and Senior High Schools*

Invert the canoe above the water and lay it carefully on the water bottom side up so that as much air remains inside as possible. The player ducks his head under and comes up inside the canoe, seizes a thwart, and swims with the feet. Steering is difficult since the navigators cannot see their course, and the air soon gets bad, consequently the distance should be short.

Head-Stands

Swimming Beach, Camp   *Junior High School to Adults*

Head-stands are best done on the bow seat. With head on the seat and hands on the gunwales ten or twelve inches back from the seat, throw the legs up into the head-stand position. It may be easier to learn the stunt by starting with the feet on the gunwales instead of the bottom. Hand-stands on the gunwales are occasionally done also, but they are difficult and require strong arms and shoulders.

Double head-stands, with one of the partners on each seat, is a spectacular but difficult stunt. Perfect coordination and team work are required.

Gondolier Race

Summer Beach, Camp   *Junior and Senior High Schools*

This is an event for a row boat rather than a canoe. There is one contestant in a boat. He stands in the stern and paddles with one oar.

LOG-ROLLING CONTESTS

This delightful sport of the lumber camps has received all too little attention in camping and recreational circles in the past. It is a woodsy, colorful activity which fits into the summer-camp setting in an ideal way.

The Log.—A log fifteen to twenty-four inches in diameter and twelve to fifteen feet long is needed. Most soft woods are usable, white cedar and white pine being excellent. Hemlock sinks too far in the water. For beginners it is better to leave the bark on because it slows up the log—a stripped log is very fast. For convenience in keeping a permanent log in position in open water put a turnbuckle on one end and anchor the log by a long rope. It should be anchored in water about waist deep. Mark the middle of the log by tying a rope or painting a stripe around it.

Heavy-soled shoes equipped with calks on the soles and heels are needed. Calks can be obtained from hardware stores and a cobbler will apply them. Two or three large pairs of shoes in camp will fill the needs of the contestants. Only two players can ride the log at one time and the shoes can be passed around.

A balancing pole is also needed. A lumber jack's peavey may be used, but a slender sapling of white cedar or other light wood, twelve to fifteen feet long and three inches thick at the big end is much better. Strip the bark off it. It is held by the small end with the big end resting in the water a foot or so beneath the surface. The pole is somewhat flexible and can be whipped up and down. A heavy bamboo pole is also usable.

Rolling.—For those who have never been on the log before, it will take a few periods to get used to the action of a log in the water. Have someone hold the log at one end while the roller mounts it. Attempt nothing more than to stand erect on the floating log until this can be done easily and with confidence. Hold one end of the balancing pole with the other end out to the side and floating in the water.

To roll the log, face to one side and start running on it slowly. The log spins very freely and gains momentum rapidly. One must run fast to keep up with it and not slip off. Run high in the air, keeping the feet up and away from the log as much as possible. Stay on the front or up-coming side of the log—to attempt to ride it on the back or down-going side means a certain upset.

To slow up the log or stop it, one of two methods may be used: (1) jump with both feet on the up-coming side, driving the calks into the log; repeat a time or two until the log is stopped or moving with the desired speed; (2) when facing in one direction and rolling the log, jump in the air, turn around, and start running in the opposite direction; this stops the log and reverses the roll.

Log-Rolling Contest

Summer Camp, Swimming Beach   *Junior High School to Adults*

Two contestants toss for the ends of the log. They mount the log, one on each end, each holding a balancing pole. On the signal they begin to roll the log and continue until one goes off. The following are fouls and lose the match for the offender: (1) crossing the center mark on the log onto the opponent's end of the log; (2) touching the opponent with body or pole. The contestant winning two out of three rolls wins the event.

There are several maneuvers used to confuse one's opponent. When the log is stationary, to start it rolling suddenly and rapidly often upsets him. When it is running rapidly, to stop it suddenly makes it difficult for the opponent to retain his balance. When the log is rolling in one direction, to turn suddenly and reverse the direction of the roll often brings victory. One must keep his eyes fixed on the feet of his opponent and be alert to anticipate his moves.

Log-Rolling for Distance

Summer Camp, Swimming Beach   *Senior High School to Adults*

Place the log against the dock or other stationary object, or drive a pole in the bottom of the lake for a starting mark. The contestant mounts the log and rolls it as far as possible before falling off. The distance is measured and the other contestants compete in turn. The one rolling the greatest distance wins.

Of course, this contest is not usable for expert log rollers because they could roll it for hours. For average contestants who roll the log occasionally for sport, however, the contest is very acceptable and challenging.

Log-Riding Squat Contest

Summer Camp, Swimming Beach   *Senior High School to Adults*

The contestant mounts the floating log, facing the long way, and drives in his calks firmly. He then drops to a full squat with his buttocks touching his heels, then rises to a standing position again. His arms may be in any position to assist in balancing except that they must not touch the log. He continues until he falls in or is forced to stop.

The contestants compete in turns and the one wins who completes the greatest number of squats.

Stump Riding

Summer Camp, Swimming Beach   *Senior High School to Adults*

This is a difficult contest for expert log riders. From a soft-wood log twenty to twenty-four inches in diameter, saw off a section about thirty inches long. It should be a few inches longer than it is wide. It is not spun sideways in the water as in log rolling, but rather, end over end. The rider stands on the side, facing the end of the stump. He tips the front end up, reaches over the end with one foot, pulls the end toward him, and as it turns steps to the other side. In this way it is kept going end over end.

The contestants compete in turns and the one wins who succeeds in stepping over the end the greatest number of times without going in the water.

Mount the Barrel.—In place of a stump of similar proportion, a barrel may be used in this event. The contestants take turns in attempting to mount the barrel and stay on it in any position. The one staying on the longest wins.

Log-Ball Riding

Summer Camp, Swimming Beach   *Senior High School to Adults*

This is a difficult contest and is suitable only for experienced log rollers. From a log twenty-four to thirty inches in diameter, saw off a section as long as the diameter of the log. With an axe, turn it into a round ball and smooth it up. Place the ball in the water. The rider mounts it by stepping off the dock onto it. It is rolled in the same way as a log is spun.

The contestants compete in turns and the one wins who can roll it the greatest distance without falling off. The distance is measured from the dock at the point where the contestant mounted the ball.

Log-Riding Rope Skipping

Summer Camp, Swimming Beach   *Senior High School to Adults*

This is a contest for experienced log riders. One contestant mounts the log, holding a skipping rope. Facing the long way of the log, he attempts to skip the rope. He continues skipping until he falls off. To skip the rope successfully the log must be kept stationary and consequently the rider faces the long way of the log and not sideways. The other contestants compete in turn, and the one wins who skips the rope the greatest number of times.

Log-Riding Hand-Spring

Summer Camp, Swimming Beach   *Senior High School to Adults*

This is a contest for very expert log riders. One contestant mounts the log, places his hands on it, and turns a hand-spring, driving his calks in the log as his feet come down and regaining his balance. He continues hand-springing until he goes off the log. The other contestants compete in turn and the one completing the most hand-springs wins.

Log-Riding Push-Up

Summer Camp, Swimming Beach   *Senior High School to Adults*

The contestant mounts the floating log, faces the long way, and drives the calks at the tips of his toes firmly into the log. He then bends forward, places his hands on the log, and gradually works himself down to a prone position. He places his chin on the log and must not touch the latter with any other part of his body except his hands and feet. In this position he pushes up, straightening his arms, then goes down until his chin touches. The body must be kept rigid throughout. He continues to push up until he falls off the log or becomes tired.

The contestants compete in turns and the one wins who completes the greatest number of push-ups.

Sitting on the Log

Swimming Beach, Summer Camp   *Junior and Senior High Schools*

One player sits on each end of the log by straddling it. At the signal each tries to put the other off by rolling the log. The one remaining on the longest wins.

CHAPTER XXVII

WINTER ACTIVITIES

THE winter activities, involving as they do games and contests with snow and ice, could well be scattered throughout the various chapters of this book, classified according to the nature of the event. With the needs in mind of the practical leader who may seek winter activities, however, it was thought advisable to group these events in one chapter, dealing exclusively with winter activities.

ICE-SKATING CONTESTS

This section presents a number of novelty events on ice skates which may be conducted either on open ice or in ice-skating rinks.

Straight Skating Races

Open Ice, Skating Rink   *Late Elementary School to Adults*

Skating races are conducted in general according to the same regulations which govern foot racing. The customary distances for the various ages are as follows:

11 years and under .... 110 to 220 yards
12 and 13 years .... 110 to 220 yards
14 and 15 years .... 220 to 440 yards
16 and 17 years .... 220 to 880 yards
18 years and over .... 220 yards to one mile

Circular courses add interest in that they require skill in turning, but on outdoor skating areas they must be laid out anew each season, and consequently accurate distances are difficult to achieve. Approximate distances, however, are satisfactory for recreational events. The turns are marked by movable blocks of wood with flags inserted in them.

Flag Skate-Race.—Much color may be added to skating races by having the skaters carry colored flags.

Backward Skating Races.—The contestants line up with their backs to the starting line and skate backward to the finish line. For all except experts, distances of 110 to 440 yards are far enough.

Skateless Skating

Open Ice, Skating Rink   *Elementary to Junior High School*

The course is from twenty-five to fifty yards over ice. The players line up at the starting line without skates. At the signal they "skate" with the soles of their shoes. The player finishing first wins.

One-Skate Race

Open Ice, Skating Rink   *Late Elementary to Senior High School*

This is a great fun-maker. The contestants wear one skate only. The distance is one-hundred yards. The racers proceed by skating with one foot, and running with the other, or any way they can get there. The one finishing first wins.

Three-Legged Skate Race

Open Ice, Skating Rink   *Junior and Senior High Schools*

The players are in pairs with their inside legs tied together at the ankle and above the knee. They wear skates on their outside feet, and push with the inside feet. The distance is one-hundred yards, and the pair finishing first wins.

Tandem Skating Race

Open Ice, Skating Rink   *Elementary School to Adults*

The contestants race in pairs. The two skaters stand side by side, each taking the other's right hand in his right hand, and the other's left hand in his left hand. Thus joined they skate to the finish line 220 yards distant. The pair finishing first wins.

Variation.—The two players stand one behind the other. The back skater places his hands on the hips of the one in front.

Candle Skate-Race

Open Ice, Skating Rink   *Junior High School to Adults*

Each skater is given a candle and a box of matches. At the signal each lights his candle and skates to the finish line one-hundred yards distant. If the candle goes out, he must stop promptly and relight it. The one wins who finishes first with the candle lighted.

Tandem Candle Skate-Race.—Skating as in the Tandem Skating Race—Variation (page 555), the girl carries the candle and the boy the matches. If the candle goes out, the boy lights it.

Skating Potato-Race

Open Ice, Skating Rink   *Junior High School to Adults*

Skating potato races are conducted according to the same rules as the potato races on land. See Potato Race (page 11).

Skate-Jump for Distance

Open Ice, Skating Rink   *Junior High School to Adults*

A jumping line is established and the contestants in turn skate up to it and jump. Each is given three jumps and is credited with his best distance. The distance is measured to the nearest point where the jumper's skates or any part of his body touches the ice.

Obstacle Skating Race

Open Ice, Skating Rink   *Junior and Senior High Schools*

The course is 125 yards and four obstacles are placed, one every 25 yards. The following obstacles are recommended:

1. A tennis net which the skaters must crawl under.
2. A row of tables which must be climbed over.
3. A hurdle not over six inches high which must be jumped.
4. A row of barrels with tops and bottoms removed through which the skaters must dive.

There will be many upsets, and more fun than competition, but that helps to make the event popular.

Variation.—With expert skaters an obstacle race may be run by placing barrels sidewise along the course. The first obstacle is one barrel, the second, two barrels side by side, the third, three barrels, and the fourth, four barrels. The skaters must jump these barrels. This event should never be staged for young or inexperienced skaters.

Ice-Hockey Contests

Open Ice, Skating Rink   *Junior High School to College*

The contests built upon ice-hockey skills are the same as those used in connection with field-hockey skills, except of course that the contestants are on skates and use ice-hockey sticks and pucks. The following field-hockey events may be used in connection with Ice Hockey also:

Hockey Drive for Accuracy	Hockey-Dribbling Race
Hockey Drive for Distance	Obstacle Hockey-Dribbling
Hit the Can	Circle Hockey-Dribbling

Skate and Sled Races

The following contests are described under Sled Contests later in this chapter:

Skate-and-Sled Race.   Skating Alaskan-Serum Race.
Skate-and-Sled Centipede-Race.   Broom-Sled Race.
Skating Husky-Team Race.   Chair-Sled Race.

Other Skating Contests

The following contests already described as land events, may be used to excellent advantage on ice skates:

File Race.   Chariot Race.
Quartet Race.   Attention.
Centipede Race.   Touch.
                 Rail-Riding Race.

SLED CONTESTS

This section presents the coasting events, and the events in which sleds are pulled on foot and on skates.

Coast for Distance

Winter Playground, Camp, Club   Elementary and Junior High Schools

Establish a starting line at the top of a hill. The contestants take a running start carrying the sled, land on their stomachs on the sled, and coast for distance. Each is credited with the distance at which the front of his sled rests when the sled stops moving. All sleds must strike the ground in back of the starting line. The player wins who coasts the farthest.

Push and Coast

Winter Playground, Camp, Club   Elementary and Junior High Schools

Establish a starting line at the top of a hill. One boy sits on the sled and his partner stands behind him; they may be as far behind the starting line as they choose. The standing boy pushes his partner to the starting line, and then steps on the sled behind him, holding on to his shoulders. If the standing boy falls off, the couple is eliminated. The sled wins that travels the farthest. The distance is marked at the front of the sled when it comes to rest.

Sled Swimming Race

Winter Playground, Camp, Club   Elementary to Senior High School

The contestants lie on their stomachs on the sleds at the starting line. The course is thirty yards over level ground or ice. At the signal they propel themselves by pushing with the hands and feet on the ground. The player finishing first wins.

Sled-Pulling Race

Winter Playground, Camp, Club   Elementary and Junior High Schools

One player lies on his stomach on the sled, and the other pulls. On reaching the turning line fifty yards distant, they exchange places, and the former rider pulls the other back to the starting line to finish.

Skate-and-Sled Race

Winter Playground, Camp, Club   Elementary and Junior High Schools

The players compete in pairs, both wearing skates. One sits on the sled and the other pulls. They race to the turning line 220 yards distant, where they change places and the rider becomes the skater as they race back to finish at the starting line. The pair finishing first wins.

Variation.—There are two skaters pulling the sled and one rider. They race to the turning line, swing around, and race back to the starting line.

Sled Centipede-Race

Winter Camp, Playground, Club   Late Elementary to Senior High School

The teams consist of eight players—seven runners and one rider. A sled is needed for each team. The seven runners stand in file, each holding the belt of the man in front of him. The last man has the sled rope looped around his waist. The rider sits or lies on the sled.

At the signal they race to the turning line one-hundred yards distant, swing around, and return to the starting line. The team finishing first with all players intact wins.

Skate-and-Sled Centipede-Race.—The players are on skates and the course is over ice. Otherwise the event is the same as the above.

Husky-Team Race

Winter Camp, Playground, Club   Junior and Senior High Schools

The teams consist of eight players, seven of whom are huskies and one the driver. A thirty-foot rope is attached to a sled and the huskies scatter along it. The rider sits on the sled.

At the signal the teams race over level ground to the finish line which is 220 yards distant.

Variation.—Mark a turning line parallel to the starting line and one-hundred feet from it. The teams race across the turning line, swing around, and race back to the starting line. This adds interest because of the danger of upsets in turning.

Knot-Tying Husky-Team Race.—This combines knot tying with the race described above. Each husky has a four-foot length of rope, and stands in line beside the sled. At the signal each ties the end of his rope to that of the husky to his right, and the rider ties the end of the long rope thus made to the sled. The rider then immediately mounts the sled, and the race described above is on.

Skating Husky-Team Race.—The event is run just like the above except that the huskies are on skates, and the course is over ice.

Alaskan-Serum Race

Winter Camp, Playground, Club　　　　*Junior and Senior High Schools*

The serum must be rushed to the remote Alaskan village suffering from the disastrous epidemic. There are four intervening villages at which the huskies are to be changed. Teams consist of eight huskies and one rider. Two huskies are placed at the starting village, two at the second village, two at the third, and two at the fourth. The distance between the villages is 220 yards.

The rider sits on the sled, and the two huskies pull. At the signal they race to the second village where the huskies are relieved by the two stationed there. The huskies are thus replaced at each village. The team wins that first reaches the stricken village.

This relay may be conducted in shuttle fashion if desired.

Skating Alaskan-Serum Race.—The course is over ice and the huskies are on skates. Otherwise the event is the same as the above.

Broom-Sled Race

Winter Playground, Camp, Club　　　*Elementary to Senior High School*

A house broom is used for a sled. One player sits on it, and another holds the handle and pulls. The course is fifty yards over smooth snow. The pair finishing first wins.

Variation.—Run the event on the ice with the contestants wearing skates.

Chair-Sled Race

Winter Playground, Camp, Club　　*Late Elementary to Senior High School*

One player sits on an ordinary straight-back chair and his partner pushes by holding the back of the chair. The standing player wears skates. The distance is fifty yards over ice. The pair finishing first wins.

The event also works well with the standing player running instead of skating.

Dog-Derby Races

Winter Playground   *Junior High School to Adults*

In the dog derby, dogs are attached to sleds and the runners race them. The course must be roped off to keep spectators back. Races may be held with one and two dogs pulling, but with inexperienced contestants, it is well to hold singles only. The event should be publicized for several weeks beforehand to allow time to train the dogs.

The contestants are allowed sixty feet of running beside the sled at the start, but thereafter must be on the sled the entire distance.

The entries should be classified according to age, such as those under twelve years, those under fifteen years, and those sixteen and over.

The dogs also should be classified, such as (1) those under fifty pounds, (2) shepherds, (3) collies, (4) huskies, (5) free-for-all.

SKI AND SNOWSHOE RACES

The following events on skis and snowshoes are equally popular among both novices and experts. A high level of ability is not necessary to enjoy these contests.

Ski-Running Race

Winter Playground, Camp, Club   *Junior High School to Adults*

Lay out a fifty-yard straightaway on a level, smooth, snow surface. The players on skis line up at the starting line and the race is conducted as in a running race. Progress is made by walking or running.

Ski-Running and Turning Race.—Establish a starting line, and fifty yards distant a turning line. The contestants run on skis across the turning line, turn, and race back to the starting line. The one finishing first wins.

Uphill Ski Race

Winter Playground, Camp, and Club   *Junior High School to Adults*

Lay out a course which is uphill all the way, preferably steeper in some places than in others. For those of average ability and for immature contestants, the distance should not be over a quarter of a mile. Establish a starting line at the bottom of the hill and place the contestants on it, scattered so that each has ample room. At the signal they climb the hill using either the *step climb* or the *herring-bone*. If desired, one of these methods of climbing may be specified and required.

Step climbing consists of standing with the skis at right angles to the slope and stepping up sideways; this method is slow. In the *herring-bone*, the contestant faces the slope and proceeds straight up with the skis turned out at an angle to prevent him from slipping back. The legs are spread well apart, with the feet turned well out and the weight carried well forward. The weight is applied to the inside edge of the ski.

Cross-Country Ski Race

Winter Playground, Camp, Club   *Senior High School to Adults*

Lay out a course over rolling country, uphill and down. Distances of one-half mile to three miles may be used depending on the skill and maturity of the contestants. Mark the course as in the Cross-Country Race. The contestants make progress on the skis by any method that the lay of the land requires. The individual finishing first wins. If teams are competing, winners are selected as in the Cross-Country Race.

Skijorning Race

Winter Playground, Camp, and Club   *Junior High School to Adults*

In this event one contestant is mounted on skis and is drawn with a rope by two contestants on foot. Distances of 100 to 440 yards may be used.

Barrel-Stave Ski Races

Winter Playground, Camp, and Club   Elementary to Junior High School

Recreational organizations frequently find that boys manifest much interest in barrel-stave ski racing. The boys make their own skis. A barrel stave is used with a toe strap of leather or tin. The events described for regular skis may be used.

Snowshoe Dash

Winter Playground, Camp, and Club   *Junior High School to Adults*

Dashes on snowshoes are conducted as in foot racing. Distances of 50 and 100 yards are used. The surface should be as level as possible.

Cross-Country Snowshoe Race

Winter Playground, Camp, and Club   *Senior High School to Adults*

Lay out a course over rolling, uneven country. Distances of one-half mile to three miles may be used, depending on the skill and maturity of the players. The course is marked as in the Cross-Country Race. The individual finishing first wins. If teams are competing, the winners are selected as in the Cross-Country Race.

CONTESTS WITH SNOW

The following contests involve the use of snow. For the most part they are of the type popular among children.

Snowball-Throw for Distance

Winter Camp, Playground, Club   *Junior and Senior High Schools*

Each contestant is given three throws from behind the throwing line, and the one who throws a snowball the farthest wins. Each is credited with his longest throw.

Team Variation.—Teams of four or eight players compete. The first member of a team throws one snowball from the throwing line; the second player throws one snowball from the spot where the first's snowball hit the ground, and so on. The team throwing the greatest aggregate distance wins.

Snowball-Throw for Accuracy

Winter Camp, Playground, Club   *Elementary to Senior High School*

Mark a three-foot target on the side of a building. Each contestant is given ten throws, one each turn, from a throwing line sixty feet distant. One point is scored each time the target is hit.

This is a favorite of boys for informal play. When used in this way, a tree makes as good a target as any.

Snow Tug-of-War

Winter Playground   *Elementary to Senior High School*

Make a snow wall about four feet high and burrow a hole through it just large enough to run the tug-of-war rope through. The two teams take hold of the rope on opposite sides of the wall and pull, attempting to pull the other team through the wall or cause them to let go of the rope so that it can be pulled through.

Snowball Tenpins

Winter Playground, Yard   *Late Elementary to Junior High School*

Set up ten sticks of wood two feet long in the usual triangular arrangement of bowling pins. From a line thirty feet distant, the first player throws two snowballs at the pins and is credited with one point for each pin knocked over. The pins are then reset and the next player throws. Ten frames or turns constitute a game and the player with the highest score wins.

Pelting the Pipe

Winter Playground, Yard   *Elementary and Junior High Schools*

Make a large snow man and put a pipe in his mouth. Make a pelting line about twenty feet on each side of the snow man and station one team behind each line. Allow a few minutes for the teams to make a large supply of snowballs.

At the signal the players attempt to knock the pipe out of the snow-man's mouth. The team that first knocks the pipe out wins.

Snowball Twenty-one

Winter Playground, Yard   *Elementary and Junior High Schools*

Make a large snow man with arms outstretched, holding a barrel hoop parallel to the ground. The players line up about twenty feet distant and attempt to toss snowballs through the hoop. Each goal scores one point and the player wins that scores twenty-one (or eleven) points first.

Snowball-Rolling Contest

Winter Camp, Playground, Club   *Elementary and Junior High Schools*

Each contestant prepares a snowball one foot in diameter before the contest starts. At the signal each rolls his ball for five minutes, when the stopping signal is given and all balls must remain at the spot until measured. The balls are measured through the greatest diameter and the largest wins.

Snow-Snakes

Open Ice, Smooth Snow   *Late Elementary to Senior High School*

This is an American Indian contest played upon this continent long before the white man came. The snakes are smooth sticks of wood which are thrown over the ice or smooth snow for distance. As used by the Indians, the sticks varied from four to ten feet in length, but a length of four to six feet is all that amateur players can hope to handle. The Indians also used a bone slider in the same way they used the snow-snakes, these sliders being made of bone or horn and equipped with two feathers.

To make a snow-snake, secure a straight two-inch stick of hard wood, preferably hickory or black ash, remove the bark, and whittle the entire shaft except one end down to less than an inch in diameter; the end is rounded into an egg-shaped ball. This ball must extend up, however, so that the bottom of the shaft is perfectly flat and smooth. As in all things handled by the Indians, the snakes were carved and highly decorated, the design being that of a snake, and the round ball carved to represent the snake's head.

Hold the small end of the snake in one hand with the forefinger on the end, and the thumb and other fingers on either side of the shaft. Hurl over the ice or smooth snow. The snake going the farthest wins.

When teams played, the individual throwing the farthest scored one point for his team and one additional point was scored for each stick thrown by the winning team that went farther than any of those thrown by the opponents.[1]

Variation.—Bancroft suggests the following method of playing the contest.

Each player should have five sticks of heavy wood two feet long, and as smooth as possible. He cuts one notch on one snake, two notches on the second, and so on. Establish a throwing line on the ice. Each player selects one snake and all throw them over the ice. The stick going the farthest scores the number of notches on it. The sticks are recovered and placed in a separate pile. Each player then selects and throws one of the remaining snakes. The player wins who has the highest score when all five snakes have been thrown.

Snow-Modeling Contest

Playground, Yard   *Elementary School to Adults*

Winter brings a type of craftsmanship peculiarly its own—that of modeling in snow. The crude snow man which brings joy in childhood years is in itself a type of snow modeling, but is only a feeble indication of the possibilities in the production of projects of fine artistic merit.

Animals, varying in size from kittens to elephants, may be fashioned from snow, and will challenge the imaginations of children and call forth the best of their artistic ability. The cooperation of an artist to model a piece or two as a demonstration is all that is needed to awaken interest. Some cities conduct city-wide snow-modeling contests each year for juniors and seniors, professionals and amateurs.

Assuming that we are to start with a small animal such as a dog or cat, build a foundation of snow about two feet square and soak it with water so that it will freeze. Insert four sticks for the legs into the foundation. Wet some snow to cover the legs, moulding roughly as you go. Having completed the legs, wind some stove wire around the top of all four legs and lay a few short sticks across the wire to support the snow for the body.

Now fill a bucket or tub with snow and pour enough water in it to make it mushy. With this snow, build the body, adding to it gradually until the form takes on the right proportions. Then insert a short stick at an angle on which to build the head and another stick for the founda-

---

[1] See J. H. Bancroft, *Games for the Playground, Home, School and Gymnasium*, p. 182. New York: The Macmillan Co., 1927. Also J. H. Salomon, *The Book of Indian Crafts and Indian Lore*, p. 279 ff. New York: Harper and Brothers, Inc., 1928.

For a discussion of the use of snow-snakes by various Indian tribes, see W. H. Holmes, *Twenty-fourth Annual Report of the Bureau of Ethnology to the Secretary of the Smithsonian Institution*, 1902-1903, p. 399 ff. Washington: Government Printing Office, 1907.

tion for the tail. When the animal is thus roughly shaped, we are ready to begin the careful modeling with fingers, stick, and spoon. When all is complete, sprinkle water gently over it and let it freeze.

To color the animal, dissolve in water some ordinary paint powder of the color desired, obtainable at paint stores, and paint the model with it.

A committee of judges should be appointed to pick the winning models. The contestants should be classified according to age, such as juniors, intermediates, and seniors, and according to experience, such as professionals and amateurs.

ICE GAMES

There are certain games that are played only on ice skates. There are also many group games of the playground and gymnasium type that are equally enjoyable on ice skates. The following games indicate the possibilities in the use of ice-skating games.

Ice Hockey

See Ice Hockey in Chapter XXIV, "Games of the Hockey Type."

Curling

Ice   *Senior High School to Adults*

Curling is an ice sport closely resembling quoits in general plan. A section of ice forty-two yards long and ten yards wide should be cleared for the rink. Two holes, called tees, are cut in the ice, but not through it—these correspond to the stakes. They are thirty-eight yards apart. To aid in measuring, two circles are drawn around each tee, with radii of seven feet and four feet. A line is drawn across the middle of each tee, called the sweeping score, and another seven yards in front of each tee, called the hog score. A middle line is drawn midway between the tees. Four yards behind the middle of each tee an eighteen-inch line is marked, called the foot score.

Each player needs two "stones" which are spherical balls of granite weighing thirty-three to forty or more pounds. They are finely polished on the under side and equipped with a handle on top. Each player also has a "besom" or broom with which to sweep the ice.

Teams consist of four players headed by a captain called the "skip" who is in absolute charge of his team's play.

Standing behind one tee, the first player slides his stone toward the other tee. The players of the two teams throw alternately until all eight have thrown their stones.

At the conclusion of the round, the stones of one team that are found to be nearest to the tee score as shots. The game is twenty-one shots.

A unique feature of Curling is found in the sweeping of the ice to aid the running stones. Since one member of the team is the skip or captain and another is throwing, there are two players free to act as sweepers. When the stone has passed the middle line, if the skip feels that it needs help to reach the tee, he gives the order to sweep and the two sweepers sweep the ice ahead of the stone to give it a clear passage. Good sweeping may cause a stone to turn into the tee when otherwise it might come to rest far behind it. Once the stone has passed the sweeping line, which is drawn through the tee, the other team may sweep the ice ahead of it. All sweeping is done under absolute orders from the skip.

Ice Shuffleboard

Open Ice, Skating Rink   *Juniors to Adults*

Paint or scratch five concentric circles on the ice, the inner one with a six-inch radius, and each of the other circles six inches from the next smaller. Number the circles from the inside out, 5, 4, 3, 2, and 1. Mark a line twenty-five feet away. Use regular shuffleboard disks and cues (see Shuffleboard).

Two teams of two players each play. Each team has six disks. The players shoot in rotation, attempting to slide the disks with the cues so that they will come to rest in the circles. When all the twelve disks have been shoved, each team's points are added, the smaller subtracted from the larger, and the difference credited as the score to the team making the most points. Disks resting on the line score in the higher circle.

Variation.—The circle which scores three points in the above game is marked as "5 off." Disks resting in this circle cause five points to be subtracted from the score.

Ice Shinney

Open Ice, Skating Rink   *Late Elementary and Junior High Schools*

The old favorite, Shinney (page 469), is as popular on ice skates as on land. The description of the game has already been given in detail.

Ice-Hockey Keep-Ball

Open Ice, Skating Rink   *Junior and Senior High Schools*

Divide the players into two teams and mark each conspicuously. Each player has a hockey stick. The game is started by a bully between two players and thereafter each team tries to secure the puck and pass it to team mates, preventing the other team from getting it.

Ice-Hockey Ten-Passes.—This is essentially the same as Ice-Hockey Keep-Ball, except that each team attempts to make ten consecutive passes before the other team secures the puck. When one player gets the puck he passes it to a team mate and the team mate calls "One." He then passes to another who calls "Two," and so on. The opposing team attempts to secure the puck, and thus break up the run of ten. The team wins that first makes ten consecutive passes.

Crack the Whip

Open Ice   *Elementary to Senior High School*

The players on skates join hands forming a line. The player at the left end is the snapper, and the player at the right end the cracker.

The snapper skates forward with the others following with joined hands. The line goes faster and faster, then suddenly the snapper cracks the whip by turning and skating back in the opposite direction with the rest of the line following. The object is to snap the cracker off the end of the whip. If the cracker parts hands with the line, he becomes the snapper, and the next to the last player becomes the cracker. If the cracker is not snapped off, he stays in that position until he is snapped off.

Baseball on Skates

Open Ice   *Late Elementary to Senior High School*

Baseball on Skates is played with a softball with all the rules of Playgroundball applying. Marks on the ice are used for bases.

Ice Basketball

Open Ice, Skating Rink   *Junior and Senior High Schools*

Lay out a basketball court on the ice and place an empty barrel at each end for the basket. The players are on skates. The play and scoring are as in Basketball.

Other Ice Games

The following games already described are particularly interesting when played on skates:

Various Tag Games.	Black-and-White.
Pom-Pom-Pull-Away.	Crows-and-Cranes.
Stingo.	Shinney Hockey.

SNOW GAMES

These are games played with snow which are perenially popular among children.

Tilting on Skis

Winter Playground, Camp, Club   *Junior and Senior High Schools*

Regular tilting poles as described under Tilting are used. The two contestants stand on skis and tilt, following all the rules of tilting on tubs or stools. When any part of the tilter's body touches the snow he is considered down; otherwise winners are selected as in Tilting.

Fox and Geese

Winter Playground, Camp, Yard   *Elementary and Junior High Schools*

For this old favorite of the winter days, tramp down in the snow

the design shown in Figure 89. Select a fox and station him at the hub of the wheel. The geese scatter along the rivers (trodden paths of the wheel). The game is played as in ordinary tag except that the runners cannot leave the rivers. A goose who is tagged by the fox becomes the fox, and tagging back immediately is permitted. The intersections of the spokes with the outer circle constitute safety zones—the geese cannot be tagged while standing on them.

FIGURE 89.

Variation. — The intersection of the cross lines is known as the goose shed. The outer circle is known as the goose ring, and the inner circle as the fox ring. The object of the geese is to reach the goose shed without being caught. The geese roam about the rivers at will and risk capture only on the cross lines between the fox ring and the goose shed.

The more noise a goose makes in dashing for the goose shed the greater the honor of the achievement.

Should the game continue too long without a goose being captured, the farmer (leader) begins to cluck, calling the geese to the goose shed immediately, for since it is now night the fox may roam at will around the rivers and capture a goose any place.

A goose who is tagged immediately becomes the fox.

Variation.—Tramp down a single circle as in Figure 90. The game is played as before except that there are no safety zones.

Snow Dodgeball

Playground, Camp, Club
     Late Elementary and Junior High Schools

Snow Dodgeball differs from Dodgeball as played in the gymnasium in that the throwing is done by the team inside the circle rather than the circle team.

FIGURE 90.

Mark out a circle in the snow about thirty feet across, larger or smaller to meet the players' ability. Divide the players into two teams and have one team form a circle standing just inside the circle in the snow; the other team scatters in the center of the circle.

The center players throw snowballs at the circle players, and each player hit below the head joins the center team. The last player remaining in the circle wins, and the teams reverse positions for the next game.

The circle players are not permitted to step back of the circle in the snow. Those who do, join the center team.

Variation.—Arrange all the players except one in a circle as above. The odd player stands in the center and throws snowballs at the circle players. All who are hit join the odd player in throwing at the others.

Variation.—See Three-Team Dodgeball.

Snowball Duck-on-the-Rock

Winter Playground, Camp, Club   *Elementary and Junior High Schools*

Duck-on-the-Rock is never more enjoyable than when played with snowballs. It follows all the rules of Duck-on-the-Rock (page 254). Roll a large snowball for the center and "it" places his duck (an ordinary snowball) on it. Each player makes himself a solid snowball with which to knock off the duck.

Arctic Flag-Fight

Winter Playground, Camp   *Late Elementary to Senior High School*

Build two large mounds of snow about thirty yards apart and place a flag on the top of each. Divide the players into two teams and allow a period for each to make a large supply of snowballs and pile them behind its mound.

At the signal the players attempt to secure the other team's flag and at the same time to defend their own. Some players go out in attack and others stay back for defense. The players use snowballs to fight their way to the flag and to fight off the attackers. The side wins that secures the other's flag first.

Snow-Fort Siege

Winter Playground, Camp   *Late Elementary and Junior High Schools*

Make a snow fort sufficient in size to hold one-third of the players. It should be six feet high and have holes in the walls through which snowballs may be thrown. The inside should contain steps in which the defenders may stand. The walls must be made thicker at the bottom than at the top, and the holes must be well enforced to prevent the attackers from breaking through.

One-third of the players are in the fort as defenders and the remaining players are outside as attackers. Both sides should be well supplied with snowballs before the fight starts. Any player hit by a snowball is considered dead and must withdraw. The attackers win if they succeed in getting possession of the fort within fifteen minutes of fighting; otherwise the defenders win.

Variation.—Eliminate the rule to the effect that a player hit by a snowball is killed. The attackers win if they enter the fort before an agreed upon number of snowballs is exhausted.

Storming the Snow Wall

Winter Playground, Camp   *Late Elementary and Junior High Schools*

Build a snow wall five feet high and ten to fifteen feet long, depending on the number of players. The wall should be wide and solid enough to allow players to crawl over it. Divide the group into attackers and defenders, with twice as many attackers as defenders. Each group makes an agreed upon number of snowballs before the fight starts, the attackers being entitled to twice as many as the defenders. The defenders take their position behind the wall, and the attackers some distance in front of it.

The attackers try to drive the defenders from the wall. If they succeed before the supply of snowballs is exhausted, they win; otherwise the defenders win.

Snowball Pom-Pom-Pull-Away

Winter Playground, Camp, Yard   *Late Elementary to Senior High School*

Establish two goals about sixty feet apart. Select a player to serve as "it" and place him midway between the goals. The players line up behind one goal. "It" calls "Pom-pom-pull-away, come away or I'll fetch you away." The players then run across to the other goal, and "it" tries to tag them by hitting them below the shoulders with snowballs. All who are hit join "it" in hitting the rest.

Variations.—See the several variations listed under Pom-Pom-Pull-Away.

Snowball Tag

Winter Playground, Yard   *Late Elementary and Junior High Schools*

This is played as in ordinary tag except that "it" tags a player by hitting him with a snowball. Hits above the shoulders do not count.

Variations.—The most of the tag games described in Chapter XVIII may be adapted to use in the snow with the tagging done by hitting with snowballs.

Siberian Man-Hunt

Winter Woods   *Late Elementary and Junior High Schools*

This is an ever-popular game among boys in the winter when snow is abundant.

Select one player to act as fugitive and send him out to find a hiding place and conceal himself. He, of course, leaves tracks in the snow, and consequently should be careful to circle, back track, and use all possible devices to throw his pursuers off the trail. After ten minutes the pursuers take up the hunt, following the tracks. When they discover the fugitive, a snowball battle follows and all who are hit must drop dead. The fugitive, however, must be hit three times to be considered killed. The fugitive must stay out one-half hour, and if he then returns to the starting point without being killed, he wins.

Relievo in the Snow

Winter Playground, Camp, Club   Late Elementary to Senior High School

The ever-popular game of Relievo is particularly interesting when played in the snow. The rules for the snow game are the same as those already given.

CHAPTER XXVIII

HORSEBACK-RIDING ACTIVITIES

RIDING games and contests are essential to a successful riding program in any summer camp or riding club. While riding in itself is a challenging and intriguing activity and does not need artificial stimulation, yet too much formal instruction and formal riding is as defeating there as in the program of any other sport or physical activity.

Riding games develop good horsemanship and riding confidence. They present constantly changing situations to which the rider must adjust himself quickly. They stimulate practice and striving for perfection. But more important than any of these they bring joy and enhance the love of the sport itself. They should be part of the regular riding activities, once riders have passed beyond the elementary stage.

HORSEBACK-RIDING CONTESTS

Here are a number of simple contests on horseback which are suitable for summer camps and riding clubs. The horseback-riding games are treated later in the chapter.

Mounted Potato-Race

Summer Camp, Riding Club   *Junior High School to Adults*

Five or more potatoes are placed in each lane twenty yards apart, the first potato being twenty yards from the starting line. A corrugated box is placed in each lane at the starting line. Each rider holds a stick three-and-one-half feet long with a nail inserted in the end.

At the signal each rider rides down his lane to the first potato, spears it without dismounting, returns, and puts it in the box without dismounting. He then returns and secures the second potato, and so on. The one wins who has all of his potatoes in the box first.

Variation.—The arrangements are the same as in the above race except that the spears are not used. Each contestant rides to his first potato, dismounts and picks up the potato, mounts and rides back to the box and drops the potato in it. He then secures the other potatoes in the same way. He does not dismount to put the potatoes in the box, unless of course his aim is bad and the potato does not go in the box, in which case he must put it in before securing the remaining potatoes.

Variation.—Instead of using potatoes, use blocks of wood six inches square and two inches thick, into which a broomstick three-and-one-half feet long has been inserted. A circle three feet in diameter is used at the starting line instead of the corrugated box. The blocks are placed in the same position as the potatoes with the handles extending up. The riders pick up the blocks by the handle without dismounting.

Doughnut Spearing

Summer Camp, Riding Club   *Junior High School to Adults*

While specially prepared doughnuts with a hole two-and-one-half inches in diameter may be used, it is better to use rope rings or small wooden embroidery hoops. Suspend from six to ten of these rings by string from crossbars nailed to poles placed twenty yards apart. The rings should hang seven or eight feet from the ground.

The riders take turns in competing. The first contestant, holding a slender bamboo pole ten feet long, trots or canters past the rings and attempts to spear them with the pole. He is not permitted to hesitate at the rings nor to walk the horse. The one spearing the most rings wins.

Mounted Zigzag Race

Summer Camp, Riding Club   *Junior High School to Adults*

The riders take turns, competing against time. Place five or more poles in the ground in a row, twenty yards apart, the first pole being twenty yards from the starting line.

The rider zigzags between the poles, to the left of the first, to the right of the second, and so forth. On reaching the last pole he circles it and rides straight back to the starting line. The one making the best time wins.

Mounted Obstacle-Race

Summer Camp, Riding Club   *Junior High School to Adults*

Twenty yards from the starting line a pole is placed in the ground; twenty yards farther a second pole is placed, and twenty yards beyond this a jump one foot high is erected.

The contestants take turns, competing against time. The rider rides to the left of the first pole, to the right of the second, rides to the jump and dismounts, leads the horse over it, mounts and rides back to the starting line. The one making the best time wins.

Mounted Chair-Race

Summer Camp, Riding Club   *Junior High School to Adults*

Mark out two lines on the ground one-hundred yards apart. Line up the riders on one line. Place a folding chair on the line in front of each rider and another chair on the other line directly opposite each rider. Midway between the lines place three chairs.

At the signal the riders ride to the opposite line, dismount and sit on the chair, mount and ride back to the starting line and dismount and sit on the chair, then ride to the center and dismount and sit on one of the chairs. Since there are only three chairs in the center, the three players securing them win first, second, and third places.

One-Horse Relay

Summer Camp, Riding Club   *Junior High School to Adults*

This is an ideal contest when horses are scarce and there are many contestants. Teams of from four to six riders are assigned to one horse. The teams are arranged as in the Shuttle Relay, the distance between the lines being two-hundred yards. Riders Number 1, 3, and 5 are behind one line and Number 2, 4, and 6 behind the other line.

Rider Number 1 mounts the horse at the starting line and at the signal rides to Number 2. Number 1 dismounts and Number 2 mounts and rides to Number 3, and so on. The team finishing first wins.

Mounted Shuttle Relay.—When there are enough horses for all, this race may be used instead of the above. Arrange the mounted riders as in the Shuttle Relay, the distance between the lines being two-hundred yards. Rider Number 1 rides to Number 2, who rides back to Number 3, and so forth. The team finishing first wins.

Equipment-Removing Relay

Summer Camp, Riding Club   *Junior High School to Adults*

This is another contest ideal for situations where the number of horses available are fewer than the riders.

One horse is assigned to each team of four riders. The riders are stationed as in the Shuttle Relay, Number 1 and 3 of each team behind one line, and Number 2 and 4 behind the opposite line. The distance between the lines is two-hundred yards.

Rider Number 1 of each team mounts the fully equipped horse and at the signal rides to Number 2 and dismounts. Number 2 takes off one stirrup and rides back to Number 3 who removes the other stirrup and rides to Number 4. Number 4 removes the saddle and rides back to the starting line. The team finishing first wins.

Saddling Race

Summer Camp, Riding Club   *Junior High School to Adults*

Tie or picket the horses in a row and place the saddles and bridles in a row opposite the horses on a line 75 to 100 yards distant. Each contestant is assigned a horse by number or name, and stands beside his saddle and bridle.

At the signal each contestant picks up his saddle and bridle, runs to his horse, saddles and bridles him, mounts, and rides to the starting line. The one finishing first with equipment properly put on wins.

If it meets the ability of the contestants better, the saddles and bridles may be placed beside the horses. The contestants line up at the starting line, run to the horses, and pick up the equipment.

Pony-Express Race

Summer Camp, Riding Club   *Junior High School to Adults*

The Pony Express is less practical than some of the other riding races in that it requires four horses for one rider. Unless mounts are plentiful and the entries few, about the only way it can be conducted is on the time basis or in heats.

Arrange the four saddled horses in shuttle fashion, two behind one line and the other two behind the other line. The distance between the lines is two-hundred yards. At the signal the rider mounts horse Number 1 and rides to the opposite line, dismounts, and mounts Number 2. He then rides to the starting line and changes to Number 3, and so on. The player making the best time wins.

Variation.—When older boys or men are competing the race may be conducted by having only horse Number 1 saddled and bridled. At each change the rider must change the saddle and bridle to the new mount.

Mounted Old-Clothes Race

Summer Camp, Riding Club   *Junior High School to Adults*

This is a colorful and humorous event. Conceal five or six boxes of old clothes at different points around the grounds—neckties in one, old hats in another, coats or shirts in a third, and so forth.

Give the riders each an envelope with instructions as to the approximate location of the first box. The riders ride to the box and put on one of the articles of clothing. They then hunt for the instruction sheet concealed nearby telling the location of the second station. They proceed to it and put on the clothing, and so on. Having put on the clothing at each station they ride to the starting point, and the one finishing first with all clothing on wins.

Mounted Touch

Summer Camp, Riding Club   *Junior High School to Adults*

Divide the riders into two teams and line them up facing each other about five yards apart. The leader calls some object to be touched and all the riders ride and touch the object, then ride back into line. The team scores one point that first lines up in the original position. The team wins that scores ten points first.

Such objects as the following may be named: tree, leaves, fence, rock, metal, water, wood, barn, rail, white-oak tree, sumac bush, and so forth. Nothing worn by a player nor any equipment on the mounts may be touched. That is, if metal is called, the riders could not score by touching a stirrup.

The game is excellent training in drilling riders to bring their horses into a straight line.

Mounted Attention

Summer Camp, Riding Club   *Junior High School to Adults*

Divide the riders into two teams and line them facing each other about fifteen feet apart. Number the players on each team so that the two players holding the same number stand opposite each other. About twenty yards beyond each end of the teams, draw a line on the ground.

The leader calls a number—"Three," for example. The two Number 3's ride across one line, turn, and ride across the other line, then back into position. The rider returning first and bringing his horse into position scores one point. The team scoring ten points first wins.

Mounted Little-Treasures

Summer Camp, Riding Club   *Junior and Senior High Schools*

Hide ten slips of paper at different points around the grounds, carefully concealed with but one corner showing. Assemble the mounted riders and announce that the first slip is hidden "within twenty feet of the watering trough." All ride to the trough and hunt until the slip is located. Then announce the location of the second slip, and so on.

When all slips are found the winners turn them in and collect their prizes. Each slip contains the name of a different make of candy bar or chewing gum.

Mounted Treasure-Hunt

Summer Camp, Riding Club   *Junior High School to Adults*

Riding treasure hunts are no different than the unmounted treasure hunts, except that the distances are longer and most of the instruction cards are tacked to trees so that they can be read without dismounting. Occasionally, however, the riders should be caused to dismount to read the directions.

It is well to use many instruction sheets with short distances between them in order to prevent the contest from resulting in a straight-away race. The racing angle can be easily eliminated by careful arrangement of the in-

structions. Rests are easily secured by hiding some of the instruction
sheets. The directions should be so worded as to require careful reading,
and cause the rider who scans them too hastily to be thrown off the trail in
false directions.

Mounted Paper-Chase

Summer Camp, Riding Club   *Junior High School to Adults*

A rider goes out through the woods and across country with a bag of
chopped-up paper and leaves a trail of paper along the route. He makes
many blind trails and leaves occasional skips in the trail, as illustrated in
Figure 91.

If the group is small all start at once, but if it is large, it is better to

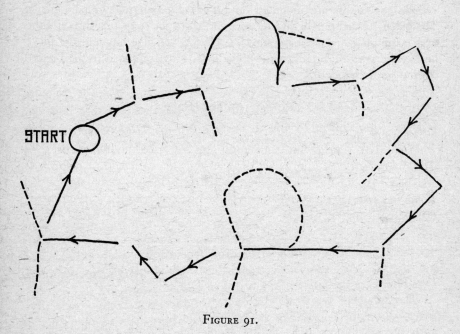

FIGURE 91.

start them in groups of three or four at five-minute intervals and keep
the time of the squads. The rider wins who first returns to the starting
point, or who reaches it in the best time.

Mounted Map-Race

Summer Camp, Riding Club   *Senior High School to Adults*

This is a long cross-country riding contest which calls for good riding
and careful organization.

Each rider is given a map of the country marking the location of the
first station. Pairs of riders start out at five-minute intervals, or longer if

thought advisable. They ride to the first station, check in to the official there, and get a map showing the location of the second station. The distance between the stations is one to two miles. From four to six stations may be used. The pair wins which completes the ride in the shortest time.

An official must be located at each station. When a pair of riders check in at a station with horses in distress, the riders are penalized by being caused to remain two minutes. If horses are still unfit to continue, two minutes longer is required, and if unfit at the end of four minutes the pair is disqualified.

Polo Drive for Distance

Summer Camp, Riding Club   *Senior High School to Adults*

The contestants are mounted on horseback, each with a polo mallet. The ball is placed on the hitting line and each player in turn hits it either with a running or stationary start. Each is given five hits and the player hitting the greatest distance wins. The measuring is done as in the Baseball Throw for Distance.

Polo Dribbling Race

Summer Camp, Riding Club   *Senior High School to Adults*

Establish a starting line and a turning line one-hundred yards apart. The mounted riders line up on the starting line, each with a polo mallet and ball. At the signal they ride to the turning line dribbling the ball along the ground as they go. Reaching the turning line, they turn and dribble back to the starting line. The rider finishing first wins.

Polo Drive for Accuracy

Polo Field   *Senior High School to Adults*

The mounted players take turns in driving a polo ball with a polo mallet through the polo goal from the sixty-yard line, or forty or twenty-yard line, depending on the skill of the players. Each is given five (or ten) attempts and scores one point for each successful drive. The one with the highest score wins.

HORSEBACK-RIDING GAMES

The foregoing section described the horseback-riding contests. In this section are the riding games.

Polo

See Polo in Chapter XXIV, "Games of the Hockey Type."

Broom Polo

Summer Camp, Riding Club   *Senior High School to Adults*

The field is about 100 yards by 75 yards. The mounted players each hold an old house broom. A codeball, sport ball, or soccer ball is used. Four to six players may play on a team.

The procedure is as in Polo and the rules of Polo should be read.

Donkey Baseball

See Donkey Baseball in Chapter XX, "Games of the Baseball Type."

Mounted Musical-Chairs

Summer Camp, Riding Club   *Junior High School to Adults*

This is a popular event at riding clubs and camps, and is even used in the rodeos. Music of some sort is needed—harmonica, accordion, banjo, victrola, or any instrument that happens to be available. Arrange a circle of chairs, one less than the number of riders. The music is in the center of the circle.

As the music plays the riders ride at trot around the circle, and when the music stops, all dismount, and holding the horse by the reins, attempt to find a seat. The one who fails is eliminated. One chair is removed and the game is repeated. The one wins who remains in when all others are eliminated.

With a large group two chairs may be removed each time.

Mounted Hat-Boxing

Summer Camp, Riding Club   *Junior High School to Adults*

Two mounted riders compete at one time, each wearing a farmer's straw hat. The hat must be put on lightly and not jammed down over the ears. They ride around each other, darting in and out, in an effort to knock off the opponent's hat with the hand. Players are not permitted to touch their own hats.

Someone challenges the winner, and the event continues until a champion is determined.

Mounted Hare-and-Hounds

Summer Camp, Riding Club   *Junior High School to Adults*

This event calls for more experienced riders than most of the games in this chapter, and an area providing good going. Select one rider to act as the hare and attach a tail of some sort to him, extending out so that it can be easily grasped. The remaining riders are the hounds. Limit the area for the game.

The hare starts out under cover, and when he breaks from the cover all give chase and attempt to secure the tail. The one getting it wins.

Mounted Push-Ball

Summer Camp, Riding Club   *Junior High School to Adults*

This event should be played in the riding paddock. The ideal ball is the big push ball, but since they are rare and expensive, the thirty-inch canvas cage ball may be used instead. The horses will shy away from the ball on the start, but a few days in contact with it will train them so that the game will become very successful.

Place the ball in the middle of the paddock with one team at each end. At the signal the players ride toward the ball and attempt to force it to the opposing goal. The ball is pushed with the front feet of the horses. One point is scored by a team each time the ball crosses the opposing goal.

Mounted Flag-Raid

Summer Camp, Riding Club   *Junior and Senior High Schools*

This game is best played in an enclosure such as the riding paddock. Stick a pole with a flag in the ground at each end of the paddock, and place one team at each end. At the signal the players ride out with the object of securing the opponent's flag and defending their own. Some players ride out in attack, and others stay back to form a defense. The team wins that first secures the enemies' flag.

Mounted Basketball [1]

Summer Camp, Riding Club   *Junior and Senior High Schools*

Basketball on horseback is a very interesting game providing the horses are equipped with stock or western saddles—the game is not possible with saddles of other types. It is excellent as a means of developing confidence in the saddle. Girls are particularly fond of it.

Two standard basketball goals and backboards are erected ninety to one-hundred feet apart, and the side and end lines of the court are marked out. A basketball is used. Five players constitute a team. The referee is not mounted.

The game is started with a toss-up between the two mounted centers, who stand their horses side by side so that their right sides are toward each other. The play follows the general plan of Basketball except that the players may carry the ball at will. If the ball is dropped the referee secures

[1] Contributed by Frank H. Cheley.

and gives it to the player who touched it last, or, if he cannot determine this, tosses it up between the two nearest opponents. Rough and dangerous riding is a foul. The rules of Basketball apply whenever possible.

Mounted Tag

Summer Camp, Riding Club   *Junior and Senior High Schools*

This event is most successful in an enclosure such as the riding paddock. Select one player as "it" and the game proceeds as in ordinary tag. When "it" tags a player, that player becomes "it."

Mounted Wood-Tag.—A player is safe from being tagged when touching the wooden rail at the side of the paddock.

Mounted Pom-Pom-Pull-Away

Summer Camp, Riding Club   *Junior and Senior High Schools*

This game should be played in the riding paddock. The riders line up at one end, with "it" in the center. "It" calls, "Pom-pom-pull-away, come away or I'll fetch you away," and the riders ride to the other end of the paddock. As they do so "it" attempts to tag them, and all who are tagged become "it" and assist "it" in tagging the rest. The last player to be tagged wins.

Mounted Hide-and-Seek

Summer Camp, Riding Club   *Junior and Senior High Schools*

This game calls for woods and brush which provide hiding places. Establish a base about twenty feet square around which the riders gather. Select one to serve as "it" and send him out to hide. After about three minutes the rest yell "Coming" and ride out in search. When a rider sees "it" he calls "Rider" and all dash back to the base, including "it." The last one back is "it" for the next game.

GYMKHANA EVENTS

An occasional gymkhana or riding meet does much to liven up the riding program of a summer camp or club. Such meets serve to stimulate good riding and practice for perfection, as well as being much enjoyed by riders and spectators.

These little meets are not to be confused with horse shows, where riders display their form in riding and jumping and demonstrate the qualities of their mounts. There is a distinct place for the latter type of event, particularly near the end of the camp or club season, but the little meets under discussion feature novel games and contests and are participated in just for the joy of the game.

Gymkhana Program

Selections may be made from the following events for the gymkhana program:

Mounted Potato-Race.

Doughnut Spearing.

Mounted Zigzag Race.

Mounted Obstacle-Race.

Mounted Chair-Race.

Mounted Shuttle Relay.

One-Horse Relay.

Equipment-Removing Relay.

Saddling Race.

Pony-Express Race.

Mounted Old-Clothes Race.

Polo Drive for Distance.

Polo Dribbling Race.

Broom Polo.

Mounted Musical-Chairs.

Mounted Hat-Boxing.

Mounted Push-Ball.

Mounted Flag-Raid.

BIBLIOGRAPHY

ANGELL, E. D., *Real Games for Real Kids*. Chicago: A. G. McClurg and Company, 1923.

ANDERSEN, L., *Athletic Program for Elementary Schools*. New York: A. S. Barnes and Company, 1927.

ANDERSEN, L., and MCKINLEY, F., *An Outline of Physical Education for the First and Second Grades*. New York: A. S. Barnes and Company, 1930.

BANCROFT, J. H., *Games for the Playground, Home, School, and Gymnasium*. New York: Macmillan Company, 1919.

BANCROFT, J. H. and PULVERMACHER, W. D., *Handbook of Athletic Games*. New York: Macmillan Company, 1916.

BICKLEY, G., *Handbook of Athletics for Coaches and Players*. New York: A. S. Barnes and Company, 1929.

BOWERS, E., *Recreation for Girls and Women*. New York: A. S. Barnes and Company, 1924

Boy Scouts of America, *The Rally Book*. New York: Boy Scouts of America, 1929.

CAMP, W. C. (editor), *Book of Sports and Games*. New York: T. Y. Crowell Company, 1923.

COOKE, D. M., Selby, H. J., and Douglas, A. C., *Games Coaching for Schools and Colleges*. London: Sir Isaac Pitman and Sons, Ltd., 1932.

CROMIE, W. J., *Group Contests for the Playground and School*. New York: Macmillan Company, 1920.

DRAPER, G. O., *Games for Church, Home, and Gymnasium*. New York: Association Press, 1927.

ELMORE, E. W., *A Practical Handbook of Games*. New York: Macmillan Company, 1922.

FEDDERSEN, M. H., *Deck Sports*. Boston: Hale, Cushman and Flint, Inc., 1933.

FORBUSH, W. B. and ALLEN, H. R., *Book of Games*. Philadelphia: John C. Winston Company, 1927.

FRYMIR, A. W., and HILLAS, M., *Team Sports for Women*. New York: A. S. Barnes and Company, 1935.

Gilcraft's Book of Games. London: C. Arthur Pearson, Ltd., 1928.

Girl Scouts, Inc., *Girl Scout Game Book*. New York: Girl Scouts, Inc.

HEBBERT, E. N., *Recreational Games*. New York: G. P. Putnam's Sons, 1929.

HEDGES, S. G., *Games for Small Lawns*. Philadelphia: J. B. Lippincott Company, 1933.

HEDGES, S. G., *Indoor and Community Games*. Philadelphia: J. B. Lippincott Company, 1932.

HILLAS, M., and KNIGHTON, M., *An Athletic Program for High School and College Women*. New York: A. S. Barnes and Company, 1929.

LaPorte, W. R., *A Handbook of Games and Programs.* New York: The Abingdon Press, 1922.

LaSalle, D., *Play Activities for Elementary Grades.* New York: A. S. Barnes and Company, 1926.

Lawson, A. H., *Homemade Games.* Philadelphia: J. B. Lippincott and Company, 1934.

Lindwall, R., *Intramural Activities.* Manitowoc, Wisconsin. Published by the author.

Lonsdale Library of Sports, Games and Pastimes. Philadelphia: J. B. Lippincott and Company.

Maroney, E. W., *Physical Education Teaching Manual.* Chicago: Lyons and Carnahan, 1928.

Mason, B. S., and Mitchell, E. D., *Social Games for Recreation.* New York: A. S. Barnes and Company, 1935.

Menke, F. G. (editor), *All-Sports Record Book.* New York: All-Sports Record Book, Inc., published annually.

Miller, C. M., *Kitecraft and Kite Tournaments.* Peoria, Illinois: The Manual Arts Press, 1915.

Mitchell, E. D., *Intramural Athletics.* New York: A. S. Barnes and Company, 1925.

Mitchell, E. D., and Mason, B. S., *The Theory of Play.* New York: A. S. Barnes and Company, 1934.

National Recreation Association, *Athletic Badge Tests for Boys and Girls.* Washington: Bureau of Education, Department of Interior, 1923.

National Recreation Association, *88 Successful Play Activities.* New York: National Recreation Association, 1933.

National Recreation Association: *Recreative Activities.* New York: A. S. Barnes and Company, 1925.

Neilson, N. P., and VanHagen, W., *Physical Education for Elementary Schools.* New York: A. S. Barnes and Company, 1930.

Pearl, N. H., and Brown, H. E., *Health by Stunts.* New York: Macmillan Company, 1922.

Post, J. H., and Shirley, M. J., *Selected Recreational Sports for Girls and Women.* New York: A. S. Barnes and Company, 1933.

Ripley, G. S., *Games for Boys.* New York: Henry Holt and Company, 1920.

Robertson, L., *Modern Athletics.* New York: Charles Scribner's Sons, 1932.

Rodgers, M., *A Handbook of Stunts.* New York: Macmillan Company, 1928.

Spalding's Athletic Library. (Rulebooks and manuals for all major sports.) New York: American Sports Publishing Company.

Seton, E. T., *The Birch Bark Roll of Woodcraft.* New York: A. S. Barnes and Company, 1931.

Smith, C. F., *Games and Game Leadership.* New York: Dodd, Mead and Company, 1932.

Smith, C. F., *Games and Recreational Methods.* New York: Dodd, Mead and Company, 1924.

Smith, H. N., and Coops, H. L., *Play Days.* New York: A. S. Barnes and Company, 1928.

Staley, S. C., *Individual and Mass Athletics.* New York: A. S. Barnes and Company, 1925.

STALEY, S. C., *Games, Contests and Relays*. New York: A. S. Barnes and Company, 1924.

State Manuals. (Most states publish manuals of physical education which may be obtained through the State Departments of Education.)

State University of Iowa, Department of Physical Education for Women, *Games for Junior and Senior High Schools*. Iowa City: State University of Iowa.

STOWE, E., *Boys' Games Among North American Indians*. New York: E. P. Dutton and Company, Inc., 1924.

University of Michigan, Department of Physical Education for Women, *Physical Education Activities for High School Girls*. Philadelphia: Lea and Febiger, 1928.

WEGENER, A. B., *Play Games*. New York: Abingdon Press, 1930.

Women's Athletic Section, American Physical Education Association, *The Athletic Handbook*. New York: American Sports Publishing Company, 1934.

INDEX